HOME
FRONTS

Also by Michael S. Foley

Confronting the War Machine: Draft Resistance during the Vietnam War (2003)

Dear Dr. Spock: Letters about the Vietnam War to America's Favorite Baby Doctor (2005)

HOME
A Wartime
FRONTS
America Reader

Edited by Michael S. Foley
and Brendan P. O'Malley

THE NEW PRESS

NEW YORK
LONDON

Requests for permission to reproduce selections from this book should be
mailed to: Permissions Department, The New Press, 38 Greene Street,
New York, NY 10013.

Published in the United States by The New Press, New York, 2008
Distributed by W. W. Norton & Company, Inc., New York

ISBN 978-1-59558-014-6 (pb)
CIP data is available

The New Press was established in 1990 as a not-for-profit alternative to
the large, commercial publishing houses currently dominating the book
publishing industry. The New Press operates in the public interest rather
than for private gain, and is committed to publishing, in innovative ways,
works of educational, cultural, and community value that are often deemed
insufficiently profitable.

www.thenewpress.com

Composition by Westchester Book Group

Printed in Canada

2 4 6 8 10 9 7 5 3 1

In memory of François Ngolet

And for Emily and Kevin O'Malley

Contents

CHAPTER THREE
The Great War, Part II: Social Consequences

CHAPTER FOUR
World War II, Part I: Mobilization and the Early War

In the summer of 2004, Magnet America sold, on average, 100,000 "Support Our Troops" yellow ribbon car magnets per week. Although that sales figure dropped to about 1,000 per week by August 2007, the magnets remained a familiar wartime symbol on American streets and highways. (*Photograph of "Yellow Ribbon" by FadderUri used under Creative Commons Attribution-Noncommercial-No Derivative Works 2.0 Generic*)

Acknowledgments

This project started as a glimmer of an idea tossed around with a lot of other ideas over drinks at the Lucky Strike in SoHo. Two friends of ours, John McMillian and Tim McCarthy, had just published a documentary history on American radicalism with The New Press, and as we celebrated their achievement, their editor, Marc Favreau, listened to an earnest but vague pitch for a wartime America reader. Without Marc's encouragement and patience, this book would still be that glimmer of an idea, floating by somewhere in the stratosphere. It has been a pleasure to work with Marc and everyone at The New Press, including champion editorial assistant, Jason Ng, and meticulous production editor Debbie Masi.

The College of Staten Island's Women's Studies Program and SEEK Program funded two student research assistants, Jess King and Gerard Forte, who saved us more hours than we could hope to count. A sabbatical from the City University of New York finally gave Foley enough time to finish his half of this project and work on others, even while the institution continued to exact its pound of flesh from O'Malley.

We are the beneficiaries of the generous guidance of many people who directed us to documents or helped us find the authors/creators of some of the sources in this volume: Phil Napoli, Ian Lekus, John McMillian, Jeremy Varon, Mark Rudd, Leni Wildflower, Frida Berrigan, Matt Daloisio, David McReynolds, Ian Marvy, Doug Marvy, Scott Bennett, Penny Von Eschen, Dave Rick, Brad Simpson, Julia Rodriguez, Lorena Oropeza, Jorge Mariscal, Paul Buhle, Jim O'Brien, Michael Wreszin, Judith Pasternak, and Michael Ferber. Andrew Huebner, in particular, offered suggestions on nearly every chapter and fielded frequent email queries graciously and with enthusiasm. We got valuable feedback on possible cover images from Joshua Brown, Jeremy Varon, Frida Berrigan, Matt Daloisio, Kathy Dale, Angela Kao, and Dave Rick. O'Malley thanks advisor David Nasaw for sound advice about historical writing that he hopes he followed here. Foley thanks David Lichtenstein for nothing in particular (but for everything, too). A huge thanks, as well, to everyone who gave us permission to reprint their work, especially those who did not charge us (or charged us a humane fee) for the privilege.

Finally, our families sustain us through everything. Foley continues to draw inspiration from Emma who, at age ten, seems to understand better than some American politicians the evils of offshore gulags, raining bombs on civilians, and the suspension of civil liberties. O'Malley thanks parents Kevin and Emily and sister Jessica for their constant encouragement and support. Our wives, Kathryn Dale and Angela Kao, especially, deserve more thanks than we could hope to give for putting up with our wacky, sleep-deprived selves, the fun sacrificed so we could work on this book, and all the sundry kvetching we have done over the last year. Maybe they have been commiserating about this project with each other, but if so, they have not let it slip to us, to whom their support seems unwavering.

Introduction

The people of the United States have spent much of the last century living in war's long shadow. From the Spanish War to the present—indeed, for only thirty of the last hundred years—have Americans lived in peacetime; and even periods of relative peace have featured U.S. forces discharging their weapons. The wartime experience, therefore, has done much to shape American history in the last hundred years, and, as a result, the lives Americans lead today have in no small way been influenced by their nation being at war.

Traditionally, that history—the history of American wars—has been a subject of endless fascination for the public. Few subjects produce and sell more books than, say, the Civil War, World War II, or the Vietnam War. For a long time, though, the history writing on America's years in combat tended to focus on the conflicts themselves: the bold political choices of presidents, the strategic brilliance of generals and commanders, and the intrigue of spies and saboteurs. Good stuff, all, and the grist not only for Hollywood movies but for textbooks and politicians' speeches. Invoking the heroism and sacrifice of warriors, past and present, has always been a favorite rhetorical tactic of film makers and vote-seekers. More recently, it has worked splendidly in promotional spots for PBS and the History Channel, too.

Lost in all of this attention on the battlefields and seats of power were the equally fascinating experiences of the ordinary folk on the wartime home front. Very few such stories made it into history books until the 1970s, when, thanks to shifts in the practice of researching and writing history (deriving primarily from the surge of grassroots social movement activity in the 1960s), a great many historians became more interested in the warp and weft of daily life in American communities and neighborhoods than in the halls of Congress or the White House. Of course, how American citizens on the home front experience life during wartime is shaped by decisions in the halls of power; likewise, what happens in the halls of power during wartime is often shaped with an eye on the American people. The sum of these wartime experiences, from Main Street to 1600 Pennsylvania Avenue, is what captivates us now.

Those changes in the practice of history, therefore, have been enormously important in focusing our attention on that give-and-take between government and the people. Owing to the kind of history that has been written in the last forty years, we may look back now and see more clearly the tension between patriotism and protest, assent and dissent. Moreover, we can see things about a past war today that were difficult to understand at the time. We now understand the migration of African Americans from the rural South to the urban North that began during World War I as the start of the Great Migration that helped to shift political power in the United States and became a precondition to the end of segregation. Likewise, the famous image of Rosie the Riveter from World War II reminds us of women working in large numbers in war industries—well known to anyone who remembers those years—but today we also understand Rosie the Riveter as a symbol of hope for women's equality, a popular image among feminists in the 1960s, 1970s, and beyond. The African American migration during World War I and the surge of women in the work force during World War II were not laid out and planned by the White House. They just happened, out of necessity, and out of opportunity. That is another lesson of living in the shadow of war: it brings the unpredictable, the unknown, and sometimes on a large scale.

As this book goes to press, the United States has been at war for nearly seven years—America's new longest war—and the president vows that the country may be at war indefinitely. Following ten years of relative peace, many Americans found themselves bewildered and divided over the Bush administration's unending operations in Afghanistan and the quicksand war in Iraq; that sense of the unpredictable, the unknown, as a lurking shadow in American life is no mere illusion. Anxiety over what the enemy may do—or what the administration may do—produces ulcers not only in citizens' stomachs but in their sense of themselves as Americans. In competition with natural patriotic tendencies—so cynically elicited by certain politicians and pundits—Americans have recently expressed a wide array of concerns about the long-term effects of these wars not only on the nation's global role but also on American society. In short, America at constant war is an unfamiliar—and often uncomfortable—experience for a great many citizens.

Home Fronts presents a documentary history of wartime America in an effort to help readers understand the range of historical effects of war on American life. By highlighting original sources that show the social, cultural, political, economic, and legal impact of wars on American society from 1898 to 2007, the book offers a historical grounding for understanding the changes brought to contemporary America by the current political climate of endless war. Although each war's home front differed in circumstance, some wartime phenomena seem timeless. The sad truth is that, across more than a century, when the United States has gone to war, history has often repeated itself on the home front.

To take an obvious example, government-cultivated wartime hysteria—with its attendant targeting of certain ethnic groups—has punctuated nearly every combat war's home front experience since 1898. President McKinley and his expansionist supporters often referred to the Spanish as "butchers" of the Cuban people; the Wilson administration, both before and after American entry into World War I, described the Kaiser as a "beast" and the Germans as "barbarous" and "Huns"; likewise, in World War II, editorial cartoonists—with no protest from official Washington—demonized both the Germans and the Japanese as animals, a phenomenon continued in Korea and Vietnam, when slurs against Asians—mixed with hyperbole over the communist threat to American national security—dominated public discourse; and beginning in the late twentieth century, Arabs and Muslims were labeled not only "enemies of freedom," but "savages" and "barbarians."

Similarly, as we have recently seen the Justice Department under both John Ashcroft and Alberto Gonzales effectively profile certain immigrant groups for arguably unconstitutional scrutiny, we can point to earlier examples of government repression of German Americans in World Wars I and II; of Japanese American internment during World War II; and of targeting Jewish "reds" during the Cold War. And as an extension of this government-sanctioned repression, an unquestioning media has often contributed to a climate of vigilantism that extends from lynchings of German Americans during World War I to attacks on Arab Americans and Muslims in the years after September 11, 2001. Pick a label: in the early twentieth century, Americans feared "anarchists", in the middle of the century, they feared "communists", and today they fear "terrorists." As some of the documents in this reader show, this thread of fear has often sewn into the broader American psyche a willingness to grant the executive branch wide latitude in pursuing global strategy and, most germane, support for that strategy at home.

Just as most Americans have yielded to executive authority, however, others have dissented. One important goal of this book is to demonstrate that antiwar protest did not originate, as so many Americans seem to think, with the Vietnam War. Indeed, from the Spanish War to the Bush Wars in Iraq, dissent has been a central force in the national discourse on American war policies and has almost always been met by government repression and citizen attacks on dissenters. Consider William Jennings Bryan in 1898; Emma Goldman, Eugene Debs, and the Wobblies in 1917; David Dellinger and the War Resisters League in the 1940s; Dorothy Day in the 1950s; draft resisters in 1967; Voices in the Wilderness in the 1990s; and Cindy Sheehan in 2005. In part, this book calls on voices like these to demystify the notion of dissent during wartime—to make clear that the cries of "rallying around the flag" could mean both support for, and opposition to, a particular war.

Home Fronts also documents the economic, social, and cultural ramifications that arise both independently and frequently as an extension of the political climate during wartime. We have included documents, for example, showing the opening and closing of labor opportunities for women and African Americans during the two world wars. In fact, the operation of business—defense contractors—constitutes a common theme through many of the book's chapters, demonstrating that the Halliburtons of today have historical parallels dating to the nineteenth century and resulting in President Eisenhower's 1961 naming of the military-industrial complex of which they are a part.

Finally, *Home Fronts* includes a variety of cultural reflections of life during wartime. Songs, poems, editorial cartoons, radio plays, television, and film have been used throughout the twentieth century both in support of and in opposition to American wars. Just as recently penned songs such as Public Enemy's "MKLVFKWR" and Sleater-Kinney's "Combat Rock" have competed for American hearts and minds with the likes of Toby Keith's "Courtesy of the Red, White, and Blue (the Angry American)" and Lee Greenwood's "God Bless the USA," the famous World War I ballad "I Didn't Raise My Boy to Be a Soldier" was answered by George M. Cohan's "Over There"; and Phil Ochs's "Draft Dodger Rag" was challenged by Merle Haggard's "Okie from Muskogee" and Terry Nelson and C Company's "The Battle Hymn of Lt. Calley," the latter of which sympathetically argues that the officer who presided over the My Lai massacre had, in fact, been raised to be a soldier.

George Santayana's maxim that "those who cannot remember the past are condemned to repeat it" remains one of the overused tropes in popular history, suffering from trivialization in an era when even well-educated national leaders seem so ready to repeat the mistakes of past wars. At a time when the American future seems poised to be defined by war, our task here is a daunting one, yet we hope the documents in this collection help readers better understand wartime America through the years and, by extension, in their own time. Thomas Jefferson long ago wrote that "an informed citizenry is the only true repository of the public will." If that is true—and we believe it is—then citizen knowledge and understanding of home fronts in past wars can, perhaps, be equated with a certain kind of power. And if that power can somehow provide a bulwark against history repeating itself—against quagmire wars, wartime hysteria, and hyper-patriotism— maybe Santayana's words of wisdom can be redeemed.

CHAPTER ONE

The War with Spain, 1898

1. *New York World,* "The War Must Be Ended"

(1897)

By the mid-1890s, Cuban insurrectionists, fueled by desire for both independence and racial equality, had been fighting Spanish colonial authorities intermittently for roughly thirty years. A new outbreak of hostilities in 1895 captured the imagination of the public in the United States. Fierce guerrilla fighting by the insurgents and ferocious suppression by the Spanish under General Valeriano Weyler led to the commission of atrocities by both sides. Locked in a fierce circulation battle, Joseph Pulitzer's *New York World* and William Randolph Hearst's *New York Journal* (acquired in 1895) competed to disseminate the most sensational accounts of Spanish atrocities against Cuban rebels and of the detention of American citizens by Spanish authorities in and around Cuba. These accounts emphasized Spanish cruelty toward Cubans and the sexualized humiliation of American women, who supposedly were strip-searched on vessels boarded by Spanish forces. According to the newspapers, the Cuban population was suffering horrifically as a result of the war. Whether this "yellow journalism" helped to whip up public feelings for the war or merely confirmed sentiments that already existed is a matter of historical debate. In either case, some evidence exists suggesting that public opinion ultimately did play a role in eventually convincing the McKinley administration to act. The following editorial ran in the *New York World* on February 13, 1897, more than a year before the United States entered the conflict in April 1898.

SOURCE: *New York World,* February 13, 1897.

How long are the Spaniards to drench Cuba with the blood and tears of her people? How long is the peasantry of Spain to be drafted away to Cuba to die miserably in a hopeless war, that Spanish nobles and Spanish officers may get medals and honors?

How long shall old men and women and children be murdered by the score, the innocent victims of Spanish rage against the patriot armies they cannot conquer?

3

How long shall the sound of rifles in Castle Morro at sunrise proclaim that bound and helpless prisoners of war have been murdered in cold blood?

How long shall Cuban women be the victims of Spanish outrages and lie sobbing and bruised in loathsome prisons?

How long shall women passengers on vessels flying the American flag be unlawfully seized and stripped and searched by brutal, jeering Spanish officers, in violation of the laws of nations and of the honor of the United States?

How long shall American citizens, arbitrarily arrested while on peaceful and legitimate errands, be immured in foul Spanish prisons without trial?

How long shall the navy of the United States be used as the sea police of barbarous Spain?

How long shall the United States sit idle and indifferent within sound and hearing of rapine and murder? How long?

2. *Pittsburg Post,* "What Emma Goldman Thinks of Patriotism"

(1898)

One of the foremost radical political activists of the late nineteenth and early twentieth century, anarchist Emma Goldman (1869–1940) was born in a Jewish ghetto in Kaunas, a city in Lithuania, then a province of the Russian empire (the city was called Kovno by the Russians). Goldman immigrated to the United States in 1885, settling in Rochester, New York, where she found employment as a factory worker. By marrying fellow Russian immigrant Jacob Kershner, she obtained American citizenship in 1887. Goldman was already well versed in radical Russian revolutionary politics, and the widespread simmering class resentment that followed the Haymarket bombings in Chicago in 1886 and the execution of four anarchists for the crime in 1887 evidently consolidated her political commitments. By 1889, she had ended her marriage to Kershner and made her way to New York City. There she befriended a circle of anarchists, including her soon-to-be lover Alexander Berkman, who would later attempt to assassinate industrialist Henry Clay Frick in revenge for the killing of steelworkers by Pinkerton detectives hired by Frick during the Homestead strike. By 1890, Goldman embarked on a series of lecture tours, honing her skills as one of the foremost radical speakers of her era.

A little more than a month before the outbreak of the war with Spain, with much public sentiment apparently in favor of intervention, Goldman set out to link this wave of patriotism to blood lust and the preservation of capitalist inequity in a speech delivered to a gathering in Pittsburgh on February 25, 1898. She invoked an 1897 incident in Lattimer, Pennsylvania, during which a sheriff and his deputies shot and killed several striking workers without incurring any legal consequences as an example of this brand of "patriotism." Goldman speculated that a war abroad might trigger a revolutionary uprising at home due to the country's increasingly volatile class dynamics.

SOURCE: Candace Falk et al., eds., *Emma Goldman: A Documentary History of the American Years,* vol. 1: *Made for America, 1890–1901* (Berkeley: University of California Press, 2003), 327–28.

Emma Goldman, anarchist, agitated in Odd Fellows' hall, South Eighteenth and Sarah streets, last night. It was the opening of a series of meetings which she contemplates holding in this vicinity during the next few weeks. She was brought here by the agitation committee of Western Pennsylvania, working under the direction of the International Workingmen's Association. Her subject last night was "Patriotism," and a large crowd was present to hear the fiery utterances as they fell, laden with molten metal, from the speaker's lips. Judging from the infrequency of any demonstration, however, the great majority of those present were there through curiosity more than sympathy with the cause which Miss Goldman represents.

"Patriotism," Miss Goldman thinks, is a word the meaning of which the vast majority of the people of the United States takes in entirely the contrary sense. "To be a patriot," she said, "one must wade ankle-deep in the blood of his fellow men. He must kill, slay, destroy in every conceivable manner and form, else he is not living up to the sacred meaning of that sacred word. The sheriff and deputies who ruthlessly shot down the miners at Hazleton were patriots in the strictest American sense. And as such, you may rest assured, they will be acquitted of the crime.

"In Chicago, some years ago, someone threw a bomb into a crowd around the Haymarket. For this supposed crime the lives of five men paid the forfeit. And yet who knows who threw that bomb? Was it ever clearly proved? No, but the voice of capital cried aloud for the blood of the accused, and in this country the voice of capital is always heeded. The tragedy in Hazleton is not hidden by any cloaks of mystery. Men among those deputies have been heard to say, 'I killed five of them, and could have killed nine,' making no secret of the crime, and yet he will go unpunished, for the voice and influence and wealth of the mine owners is whispering insidiously into the ears of justice that these men who did the shooting did so in preservation of the law, and in so doing acted solely as patriots, and should be protected rather than condemned for a crime so brutal.

"What constitutes a good citizen in this beloved free country of America? I can tell you. If a man has the ability to rob his neighbor under the guise of a legitimate speculation. If by slipping stealthily up behind him and inserting the knife into his back he robs him of his life under the pretext that the crime was committed to preserve the integrity of the Nation, men in office, and, alas, even many of you here to-night, place a crown of laurel and roses on his brow, and he is at once crowned a public-spirited citizen and a patriot of the first water. Is it so with the man whose daily existence and the lives of his family depends on a crust? Hardly. Let him but purloin one loaf from the bakery of his neighbor and a cell yawns before him.

"There is talk of a war between America and Spain. I am not allied with either country, but I tell you it is unsafe, even dangerous, for America to war with any nation. Her own governmental props need bolstering; they totter and are likely to fall at any moment, and it is my candid belief that if war would ensue an uprising of thousands upon whom the country is now depending for support would follow."

At the conclusion Miss Goldman was asked how she expected to bring about the reforms in the labor question which she agitates. She replied that there was only one way in which it could be done: that was by a popular uprising of the people. A revolution such as that of more than a century ago was surely fomenting, and in time, a short time at that, the clouds were bound to break. That, she said, is the only solution, and that was a day to which she is confidently looking forward.

3. William McKinley, "Declaration of War"

(1898)

President William McKinley (1841–1901) appeared before Congress on April 11, 1898, to ask for its authorization for U.S. forces to intervene in the civil war in Cuba. McKinley justified military action on several different levels: out of humanitarian concern for the Cubans themselves; for the protection of the lives, property, and business interests of American citizens in Cuba; and for the protection of maritime commerce in an area in such close proximity to American shores. Before the American intervention, the conflict's momentum was moving decidedly in favor of the Cuban insurgents; independence for the long-embattled island looked increasingly likely by early 1898. In McKinley's whole speech (and in the excerpt presented here), there is no mention of Cuban independence, plans for a future provisional government in Cuba, or sympathy for the Cuba Libre resistance fighters. The language McKinley uses about the sinking of the battleship *Maine* is also worth noting: he does not blame Spain directly for the tragedy, but rather uses the incident as evidence that Spain is incapable of providing safe harbor for ships in Cuban ports. McKinley may have employed a purposeful vagueness so as not to commit to any specific course of action and leave all possibilities open; he does his best to present the proposed intervention as one by a neutral arbiter. Early twenty-first-century readers of this speech may be cynical about McKinley's intentions, but the great majority of commentators at the time, initially including even the diehard anti-imperialist William Jennings Bryan, seemed to accept the humanitarian motivations claimed by the president.

SOURCE: James D. Richardson, ed., *Messages and Papers of the Presidents,* vol. 10 (Washington, D.C.: Government Printing Office, 1899), 139–50.

To the Congress of the United States:

... The present revolution is but the successor of other similar insurrections which have occurred in Cuba against the dominion of Spain, extending over a period of nearly half a century, each of which during its progress has subjected the United States to great effort and expense in enforcing its neutrality laws, caused enormous losses to American trade and commerce, caused irritation, annoyance, and disturbance among our citizens, and, by the exercise of cruel, barbarous, and uncivilized practices of warfare, shocked the sensibilities and offended the human sympathies of our people. . . .

Our trade has suffered, the capital invested by our citizens in Cuba has been largely lost, and the temper and forbearance of our people have been so sorely tried as to beget a perilous unrest among our own citizens, which has inevitably found its expression from time to time in the National Legislature, so that issues wholly external to our own body politic engross attention and stand in the way of that close devotion to domestic advancement that becomes a selfcontained commonwealth whose primal maxim has been the avoidance of all foreign entanglements.

All this must needs awaken, and has, indeed, aroused, the utmost concern on the part of this Government, as well during my predecessor's term as in my own. . . . The overtures of this Government [to the Spanish government] . . . were met by assurances that home rule in an advanced phase would be forthwith offered to Cuba, without waiting for the war to end, and that more humane methods should thenceforth prevail in the conduct of hostilities.

* * *

The war in Cuba is of such a nature that, short of subjugation or extermination, a final military victory for either side seems impracticable. The alternative lies in the physical exhaustion of the one or the other party, or perhaps of both. . . . The prospect of such a protraction and conclusion of the present strife is a contingency hardly to be contemplated with equanimity by the civilized world, and least of all by the United States, affected and injured as we are, deeply and intimately, by its very existence. . . .

The spirit of all our acts hitherto has been an earnest, unselfish desire for peace and prosperity in Cuba, untarnished by differences between us and Spain and unstained by the blood of American citizens. The forcible intervention of the United States as a neutral to stop the war . . . is justifiable on rational grounds . . . [which] may be briefly summarized as follows:

First. In the cause of humanity and to put an end to the barbarities, bloodshed, starvation, and horrible miseries now existing there, and which the parties to the conflict are either unable or unwilling to stop or mitigate. It is no answer to say this is all in another country, belonging to another nation, and is therefore none of our business. It is specially our duty, for it is right at our door.

Second. We owe it to our citizens in Cuba to afford them that protection and indemnity for life and property which no government there can or will afford, and to that end to terminate the conditions that deprive them of legal protection.

Third. The right to intervene may be justified by the very serious injury to the commerce, trade, and business of our people and by the wanton destruction of property and devastation of the island.

Fourth, and which is of the utmost importance. The present condition of affairs in Cuba is a constant menace to our peace and entails upon this Government an enormous expense. With such a conflict waged for years in an island so near us and with which our people have such trade and business relations; when the lives and liberty of our citizens are in constant danger and their property destroyed and themselves ruined; where our trading vessels are liable to seizure and are seized at our very door by war ships of a foreign nation; the expeditions of filibustering that we are powerless to prevent altogether, and the irritating questions and entanglements thus arising—all these and others that I need not mention, with the resulting strained relations, are a constant menace to our peace and compel us to keep on a semi-war footing with a nation with which we are at peace.

These elements of danger and disorder already pointed out have been strikingly illustrated by a tragic event which has deeply and justly moved the American people. I have already transmitted to Congress the report of the naval court of inquiry on the destruction of the battleship *Maine* in the harbor of Havana during the night of the 15th of February. The destruction of that noble vessel has filled the national heart with inexpressible horror.

*   *   *

The naval court of inquiry, which, it is needless to say, commands the unqualified confidence of the Government, was unanimous in its conclusion that the destruction of the *Maine* was caused by an exterior explosion—that of a submarine mine. It did not assume to place the responsibility. That remains to be fixed. In any event, the destruction of the *Maine*, by whatever exterior cause, is a patent and impressive proof of a state of things in Cuba that is intolerable. That condition is thus shown to be such that the Spanish Government can not assure safety and security to a vessel of the American Navy in the harbor of Havana on a mission of peace, and rightfully there. . . .

The long trial has proved that the object for which Spain has waged the war can not be attained. The fire of insurrection may flame or may smolder with varying seasons, but it has not been and it is plain that it can not be extinguished by present methods. The only hope of relief and repose from a condition which can no longer be endured is the enforced pacification of Cuba. In the name of humanity, in the name of civilization, in behalf of endangered American interests which give us the right and the duty to speak and to act, the war in Cuba must stop.

In view of these facts and of these considerations I ask the Congress to authorize and empower the President to take measures to secure a full and final termination of hostilities between the Government of Spain and the people of Cuba, and to secure in the island the establishment of a stable government, capable of maintaining order and observing its international obligations, insuring peace and tranquility and the security of its citizens as well as our own, and to use the military and naval forces of the United States as may be necessary for these purposes. . . .

4. Charles Denby, "Shall We Keep the Philippines?"

(1898)

Lieutenant Colonel Charles H. Denby (1830–1904), a Union soldier during the Civil War who then pursued a career in diplomacy, had returned home after a thirteen-year stint as American ambassador to China just as the war with Spain was winding down in the summer of 1898. In January 1899, President McKinley chose Denby to be one of the five members of the Schurman Commission, the body sent to investigate and report back on conditions in the Philippine Islands. The group ultimately came to the consensus that the Filipinos were not yet ready for political independence. Just before being selected for this commission, Denby put forth an argument for retaining possession of the Philippines in the following article, published in the November 1898 issue of the *Forum*, a monthly periodical to which he contributed frequently. Dismissing anything as grandiose as a "manifest destiny," he viewed the retention of the Philippines as nothing more than the acquisition of a way station for commerce with the Far East. He much preferred that the United States hold on to the Philippines rather than participate in the dividing up of China into "spheres of influence" that several European powers had been undertaking at this time. His hope was for China to grow more stable, thus providing a new and sizeable market for American manufactures.

A lifelong Democrat, Denby was appointed as ambassador during Grover Cleveland's first term but was respected enough to serve through the Republican administration of Benjamin Harrison, through Cleveland's second term, and a year into McKinley's administration. His two-volume study, *China and Her People*, was published posthumously in 1905.

SOURCE: *Forum*, November 1898.

Dewey's victory has changed our attitude before the world. We took no part in international questions. We had no standing in the councils of the nations. We were a *quantité négligeable*. . . .

The position of absolute indifference to what is happening in the world is difficult of maintenance; and when it is maintained it is humiliating. . . .

We have a great commerce to take care of. We have to compete with the commercial nations of the world in far-distant markets. Commerce, not politics, is king. The manufacturer and the merchant dictate to diplomacy and control elections. The art of arts is the extension of commercial relations—in plain language, the selling of native products and manufactured goods. . . .

I am in favor of holding the Philippines because I cannot conceive of any alternative to our doing so, except the seizure of territory in China; and I prefer to hold them rather than to oppress further the helpless government and people of China. I want China to preserve her autonomy, to become great and prosperous; and I want these results, not for the interests of China but for our interests. I am not the agent or attorney of China; and, as an American, I do not look to the promotion of China's interests, or Spain's, or any other country's, but simply of our own.

The whole world sees in China a splendid market for our native products—our timber, our locomotives, our rails, our coal oil, our sheetings, our mining plants, and numberless other articles. We are closer to her than any other commercial country except Japan. There is before us a boundless future which will make the Pacific more important to us than the Atlantic. . . .

The Philippines are a foothold for us in the Far East. Their possession gives us standing and influence. It gives us also valuable trade both in exports and imports.

Should we surrender the Philippines, what will become of them? Will Spain ever conquer the insurgents, and, should she do so, will she retain the islands? To her they will be valueless; and if she sells them to any continental power she will, by that act, light the torches of war. . . .

There is, perhaps, no such thing as manifest destiny; but there is an evident fitness in the happening of events and a logical result of human action.

Dewey's victory is an epoch in the affairs of the Far East. We hold our heads higher. We are coming to our own. We are stretching out our hands for what nature meant should be ours. We are taking our proper rank among the nations of the world. We are after markets, the greatest markets now existing in the world. Along with these markets will go our beneficent institutions, and humanity will bless us.

5. William Jennings Bryan, "The Army"

(1899)

Before the 1898 war, the United States had a relatively small professional standing army of about 28,000 men known as the Regular Army. Recruited and maintained entirely by the federal government, the Regular Army had been reduced in size after the Civil War and was then stationed mostly along the Indian frontier. The 1898 war had been fought with an amalgam of Regular Army and state militia units. The "citizen-soldiers" who made up the state militias volunteered for federal service during the wave of patriotism at the beginning of the war, and for the most part were not as well trained as those in the Regular Army. Yet both types of units proved woefully unprepared for the conflict; logistical difficulties led to shortages of food, ammunition, and critical medical supplies throughout the Cuban campaign. Although U.S. forces readily defeated those of Spain, both civilian and military leadership came under severe criticism for the disorganized and incompetent way the war effort was managed. Secretary of War Russell A. Alger resigned in August 1899 as a result.

In the following opinion, published in William Randolph Hearst's *New York Journal* on New Year's Day, 1899, Bryan criticized President McKinley's endorsement of Alger's suggestion for a permanent increase in the size of the Regular Army. While seeing a small standing army as necessary, Bryan viewed its authoritarian culture as an antidemocratic force in American society. He thought that the continued reliance on citizen-soldiers of state militias in times of war provided an essential check on the government's militaristic and imperialistic ambitions. Such soldiers would be eager to return home to their civilian lives as soon as possible, unwilling to serve as an army of occupation. Many members of Congress felt as Bryan did. Not long after the following opinion was published, a compromise bill was passed. It put off the question of expanding the Regular Army while relieving the state militia volunteers still stationed in the Philippines (it also helped relieve the Regular Army, which was stretched to its breaking point). The legislation allowed the president to create twenty-five temporary volunteer regiments under direct federal control, but strictly limited them to a two-year term of service. Yet, those in favor of the expansion of the Regular Army won out soon thereafter. A few years later, Secretary of War Elihu Root, a New York corporate lawyer appointed by McKinley after Secretary Alger's resignation, presided over a massive buildup of the Regular Army and a standardization of state militias that created the National Guard system as we now know it.

SOURCE: *New York Journal,* January 1, 1899.

In his annual message sent to Congress December 5, 1898, the President makes the following recommendations in favor of a permanent increase in the standing army:

"The importance of legislation for the permanent increase of the army is therefore manifest, and the recommendation of the Secretary of War for that purpose has my unqualified approval. There can be no question that at this time, and probably for some time in the future, one hundred thousand men will be none too many to meet the necessities of the situation."

It is strange that this request for so large an increase in the permanent army should be asked of a peace-loving people just at the time when the Czar of Russia is urging the nations of the world to join in the reduction of military establishments. But, strange as it may seem, the President not only requests it, but the Republican leaders in Congress seem inclined to grant the request.

Progress in Europe; retrogression in the United States!

In the old world "the currents of destiny" seem to be running in the direction of relief to the people from military burdens. Shall they run in an opposite direction here?

During the recent campaign the people were urged to support the party in power until the "fruits of victory" could be made secure. Is the first fruit of victory to be realized in the transfer of a large body of men from the field and workshop to the camp and barracks—from the ranks of the wealth producers to the ranks of the tax consumers? Such a transfer will lessen the nation's wealth-producing power and at the same time exact a larger annual tribute from those who toil.

Any unnecessary increase in the regular army is open to several objections, among which may be mentioned the following:

First—It increases taxes, and thus does injustice to those who contribute to the support of the Government.

Second—It tends to place force above reason in the structure of our Government.

Third—It lessens the nation's dependence upon its citizen soldiery—the sheet-anchor of a republic's defense.

No one objects to the maintenance of a regular army sufficient in strength to maintain law and order in time of peace and to form the nucleus of such an army as may be required when the military establishment is placed upon a war footing; but the taxpayers are justified in entering a vigorous protest against excessive appropriations for military purposes.

It is not surprising that the protest is most vigorous from the masses, because under our system of taxation the bulk of our Federal revenues is collected from import duties and internal revenue taxes upon liquors and tobaccos, all of which bear most heavily upon the poor. Import duties are collected upon articles used by the people, and the people do not use the articles taxed in proportion to income.

For instance, a man with an income of $100,000 does not eat, nor wear, nor use a hundred times as much of articles taxed as the average man with an income of $1,000. The people with small incomes, therefore, pay, as a rule, a larger percentage of their incomes to support the Federal Government than people with large incomes. The same is true of internal revenue taxes collected upon liquors and tobaccos. Men do not use liquor and tobacco in proportion to their incomes. Thus it will be seen that our Federal taxes are, in effect, an income tax; not only an income tax, but a graded income tax, and heaviest in proportion upon the smallest incomes.

If we could supply a part of our necessary revenues from a direct income tax the burdens of a large army would be more equitably borne, but, according to the decision of the Supreme Court, the income of an individual is more sacred than the individual, because the citizen can be drafted in time of danger, while his income cannot be taxed either in peace or war.

The army is the impersonation of force. It does not deliberate, it acts; it does not decide, it executes; it does not reason, it shoots.

Militarism is the very antithesis of Democracy; they do not grow in the same soil; they do not draw their nourishment from the same source.

In an army orders come down from the commander to the soldier, and the soldier obeys; in a republic mandates issue from the sovereign people, and the public servant gives heed. If any one doubts the demoralizing results which follow the use of force, even when that force is justified by necessity, let him behold the change which has taken place in the views of many of our people during the last eight months and then estimate, if he can, the far-reaching effect which a large increase in the permanent army would have upon the thoughts, the purposes and the character of our people.

Our Government derives its just powers from the consent of the governed, and its strength from the people themselves. We cannot afford to weaken the Government's reliance upon the people by cultivating the idea that all the work of war must be done by professional soldiers. The citizen is a safer lawmaker when he may he called upon to assist in the enforcement of the laws, and legislation is more likely to be just when the Government relies largely upon volunteers, because the support is surest when the Government is so beneficent that each citizen is willing to die to preserve its blessings to posterity. The readiness with which the American people have always responded to their country's call is a guarantee as to the future.

I have suggested some of the reasons (not all, by any means) why the regular army should not be increased, unless such increase be actually necessary. I now ask whether there is any such necessity for increasing that branch of the army which is held for service in the United States. There may, from time to time, be need of small additions to man new coast fortifications; but what is there in the domestic situation to justify or excuse the demand for more soldiers?

An army of occupation for service in Cuba, Puerto Rico and the Philippines is made necessary by the conditions growing out of the war. But such an army is temporary in character, and should not be made a pretext for an increase of 200 percent in our standing army.

The President assures us, in his last message, that the only purpose our Government has in taking possession of Cuba is to assist the Cubans in establishing a stable government. When that is accomplished our troops are to be withdrawn.

The number needed in the Philippines will depend largely upon the course pursued by the Government in regard to those islands. It will require fewer soldiers and less time to give self-government to the inhabitants of the Philippines than it will to give them a military government or a "carpet-bag" government. Since our standing army was sufficient for all domestic purposes prior to the war, and since there is much uncertainty in regard to the army of occupation, it would seem the part of wisdom to separate the two branches of the service and make provision at once for the latter, leaving the friends and opponents of a large standing army to settle that question after the volunteers are mustered out.

Most of the volunteers have no taste for military life; they left peaceful pursuits and enlisted, at a great sacrifice to themselves and their relatives, because their country needed them. Now that the war is over they desire to return home, and their desire should be gratified at the earliest possible moment. They were willing to fight when fighting was necessary; they were ready to lay down their arms as soon as hostilities ceased. If an attempt be made to secure a large increase in the army at home, merely because of a temporary need for an insular army, a prolonged Congressional debate is inevitable. Is it fair to keep the volunteers in the service while this question is being disposed of?

Unless Republican leaders desire to hold the volunteers as hostages to compel Congress to consent to a large army, they ought to be willing to postpone the consideration of the Regular Army bill and accept a substitute authorizing the President to recruit an army of occupation for service outside of the United States. The soldiers can be enlisted for two or three years, and before their term expires the nation's policy will be defined and conditions so settled that provision can be made for the future with more intelligence.

In recruiting the army of occupation opportunity should be given for the re-enlistment of such volunteers as desire to continue in the service. And I may add that it will encourage re-enlistment if a company or battalion formed from a volunteer regiment is allowed to select its officers from among the members of the regiment.

The pay of enlisted men serving in the army of occupation should be considerably increased over the present rate to compensate for greater risk to health incurred in the islands.

When the time arrives for the deliberate consideration of the permanent military establishment it will be found safer and more economical to provide complete modern equipment for the State militia, together with liberal appropriations for instruction and for annual encampments, than to increase the regular army. Soldiers in the regular service are withdrawn from productive labor and must be supported the year around, while members of the State militia receive military training without abandoning civil pursuits and without becoming a pecuniary burden to either State or Nation.

To recapitulate: There is no immediate necessity for the consideration of the proposition to permanently increase the military establishment; there is immediate necessity for the relief of the volunteers.

Let the army of occupation be recruited at once; let the size of the regular army be determined after the volunteers have been released.

The people are united in the desire to muster out the volunteers; they are divided in opinion in regard to the regular army.

Let each question be decided upon its merits.

6. Carl Schurz, "The Issue of Imperialism"

(1899)

Carl Schurz (1829–1906) was a prominent newspaper editor, statesman, and general who served during the American Civil War. Born in Prussia, Schurz was deeply involved while still a student in the liberal 1848 revolutions that shook the German states and much of Europe. A political exile, he immigrated to the United States in 1852 and became active in Republican politics later that decade. During Abraham Lincoln's 1860 presidential campaign, Schurz traveled extensively to promote the candidate to German Americans. After the war, Schurz became a newspaper editor, working for such papers as the *New York Tribune* and the *Detroit Post*. In 1868, he became the first German American to be elected U.S. senator, representing Missouri from 1869 to 1875. In 1877, Schurz accepted the position of secretary of the interior in the Hayes administration, but quickly became disgusted with the corruption he witnessed. Schurz resigned from his position in 1881 and dedicated a great deal of the rest of his life to civil service reform.

Strongly anti-imperialist, Schurz felt that the new territories acquired from the war with Spain should not be annexed, largely because he thought people on the islands were racially incompatible with the American form of government. He articulates this position in the following excerpt from a speech delivered at the University of Chicago on January 4, 1899.

SOURCE: Frederic Bancroft, ed., *Speeches, Correspondence, and Political Papers of Carl Schurz*, vol. 6 (New York: G.P. Putnam & Sons, 1913), 1–8.

By inviting me to address its faculty, its students and its friends upon so distinguished an occasion, the University of Chicago has done me an honor for which I am profoundly grateful. I can prove that gratitude in no better way than by uttering with entire frankness my honest convictions on the great subject you have given me to discuss—a subject fraught with more momentous consequence than any ever submitted to the judgment of the American people since the foundation of our Constitutional Government.

It is proposed to embark this Republic in a course of imperialistic policy by permanently annexing to it certain islands taken, or partly taken, from Spain in the late war. The matter is near its decision, but not yet decided. The peace treaty made at Paris is not yet ratified by the Senate; but even if it were, the question whether those islands, although ceded by Spain, shall be permanently incorporated in the territory of the United States would still be open for final determination by Congress. As an open question, therefore, I shall discuss it.

If ever, it behooves the American people to think and act with calm deliberation, for the character and future of the Republic and the welfare of its people now living and yet to be born are in unprecedented jeopardy. To form a candid judgment of what this Republic has been, what it may become and what it ought to be, let us first recall to our minds its condition before the recent Spanish war.

Our Government was, in the words of Abraham Lincoln, the greatest American of his time and the most genuine type of true Americanism, "the Government of the people, by the people and for the people." It was the noblest ambition of all true Americans to carry this democratic government to the highest degree of perfection in justice, in probity, in assured peace, in the security of human rights, in progressive civilization; to solve the problem of popular self-government on the grandest scale, and thus to make this Republic the example and guiding-star of mankind.

We had invited the oppressed of all nations to find shelter here, and to enjoy with us the blessings of free institutions. They came by the millions. Some were not as welcome as others, but, under the assimilating force of American life in our temperate climate, which stimulates the working energies, nurses the spirit of orderly freedom and thus favors the growth of democracies, they became good Americans, most in the first generation, all in the following generations. And so with all the blood-crossings caused by the motley immigration, we became a substantially homogeneous people, united by common political beliefs and ideals, by common interests, laws and aspirations—in one word, a nation. Indeed, we were not without our difficulties and embarrassments, but only one of them, the race antagonism between the negroes and the whites, especially where the negroes live in mass, presents a problem which so far has baffled all efforts at practical solution in harmony with the spirit of our free institutions, and thus threatens complications of a grave character.

We gloried in the marvelous growth of our population, wealth, power and civilization, and in the incalculable richness of the resources of our country capable of harboring three times our present population, and of immeasurable further material development. Our commerce with the world abroad, although we had no colonies, and but a small navy, spread with unprecedented rapidity, capturing one foreign market after another, not only for the products of our farms, but also for many of those of our manufacturing industries, with prospects of indefinite extension.

Peace reigned within our borders, and there was not the faintest shadow of a danger of foreign attack. Our voice, whenever we chose to speak in the councils of nations, was listened to with respect, even the mightiest sea Power on occasion yielding to us a deference far beyond its habit in its intercourse with others. We were considered ultimately invincible, if not invulnerable, in our continental stronghold. It was our boast, not that we possessed great and costly armies and navies, but that we did not need any. This exceptional blessing was our pride as it was the envy of the world. We looked down with pitying sympathy on other nations which submissively groaned under the burden of constantly increasing armaments, and we praised our good fortune for having saved us from so wretched a fate.

Such was our condition, such our beliefs and ideals, such our ambition and our pride, but a short year ago. Had the famous peace message of the Czar of Russia, with its protest against growing militarism and its plea for disarmament, reached us then, it would have been hailed with enthusiasm by every American as a triumph of our example. We might have claimed only that to our Republic, and not to the Russian monarch, belonged the place of leadership in so great an onward step in the progress of civilization.

Then came the Spanish war. A few vigorous blows laid the feeble enemy helpless at our feet. The whole scene seemed to have suddenly changed. According to the solemn proclamation of our Government, the war had been undertaken solely for the liberation of Cuba, as a war of humanity and not of conquest. But our easy victories had put conquest within our reach, and when our arms occupied foreign territory, a loud demand arose, that, pledge or no pledge to the contrary, the conquests should be kept, even the Philippines on the other side of the globe, and that as to Cuba herself, independence would be only a provisional formality. Why not? was the cry. Has not the career of the Republic almost from its very beginning been one of territorial expansion? Has it not acquired Louisiana, Florida, Texas, the vast countries that came to us through the Mexican war and Alaska, and has it not digested them well? Were not those acquisitions much larger than those now in contemplation? If the Republic could digest the old, why not the new? What is the difference?

Only look with an unclouded eye, and you will soon discover differences enough warning you to beware. There are five of decisive importance.

(1.) All the former acquisitions were on this continent and, excepting Alaska, contiguous to our borders.

(2.) They were situated, not in the tropical, but in the temperate zone, where democratic institutions thrive, and where our people could migrate in mass.

(3.) They were but very thinly peopled—in fact, without any population that would have been in the way of new settlements.

(4.) They could be organized as territories in the usual manner, with the expectation that they would presently come into the Union as self-governing States with populations substantially homogeneous to our own.

(5.) They did not require a material increase of our Army and Navy, either for their subjection to our rule or for their defense against any probable foreign attack provoked by their being in our possession.

Acquisitions of that nature we might, since the slavery trouble has been al-
layed, make indefinitely without in any dangerous degree imperiling our great
experiment of democratic institutions on the grandest scale; without putting the
peace of the Republic in jeopardy, and without depriving us of the inestimable
privilege of comparatively unarmed security on a compact continent which may,
indeed, by an enterprising enemy, be scratched on its edges, but is, with a people
like ours, virtually impregnable. Even of our far-away Alaska it can be said that,
although at present a possession of doubtful value, it is at least mainly on this
continent, and may at some future time, when the inhabitants of the British possessions happily wish to unite with us, be within our uninterrupted boundaries.

Compare now with our old acquisitions as to all these important points those
at present in view.

They are not continental, not contiguous to our present domain, but beyond
seas, the Philippines many thousand miles distant from our coast. They are all situated in the tropics, where people of the Northern races, such as Anglo-Saxons,
or generally speaking, people of Germanic blood, have never migrated in mass to
stay; and they are more or less densely populated, parts of them as densely as
Massachusetts—their populations consisting almost exclusively of races to whom
the tropical climate is congenial—Spanish creoles mixed with negroes in the
West Indies, and Malays, Tagals, Filipinos, Chinese, Japanese, Negritos and various more or less barbarous tribes in the Philippines.

When the question is asked whether we may hope to adapt those countries
and populations to our system of government, the advocates of annexation answer cheerily, that when they belong to us, we shall soon "Americanize" them.
This may mean that Americans in sufficiently large numbers will migrate there to
determine the character of those populations so as to assimilate them to our own.

This is a delusion of the first magnitude. We shall, indeed, be able, if we go
honestly about it, to accomplish several salutary things in those countries. But
one thing we cannot do. We cannot strip the tropical climate of those qualities
which have at all times deterred men of the Northern races, to which we belong,
from migrating to those countries in mass, to make their homes there, as they
have migrated and are still migrating to countries in the temperate zone. This is
not a mere theory, but a fact of universal experience.

It is true, you will find in the towns of tropical regions a sprinkling of persons
of Anglo-Saxon or of other Northern origin—merchants, railroad builders, speculators, professional men and mechanics; also here and there an agriculturist.
But their number is small, and most of them expect to go home again as soon as
their moneymaking purpose is more or less accomplished.

Thus we observe now that business men with plenty of means are casting
their eyes upon our "new possessions" to establish mercantile-houses there, or
manufactories to be worked with native labor, and moneyed syndicates and "improvement companies" to exploit the resources of those countries, and speculators and promoters to take advantage of what may turn up—the franchise
grabber, as reported, is already there—many having perfectly legitimate ends in
view, others ends not so legitimate and all expecting to be more or less favored

by the power of our Government; in short, the capitalist is thinking of going there, or sending his agents, his enterprises in most cases to be directed from these more congenial shores. But you will find that laboring men of the Northern races, as they have never done so before, so they will not now go there in mass to do the work of the country, agricultural or industrial, and to found there permanent homes; and this not merely because the rate of wages in such countries is, owing to native competition, usually low, but because they cannot thrive there under the climatic conditions.

But it is the working-masses, those laboring in agriculture and the industries, that everywhere form the bulk of the population; and these are the true constituency of democratic government. And as the Northern races cannot do the work of the tropical zone, they cannot furnish such a constituency. It is an incontestable and very significant fact that the British, the best colonizers in history, have, indeed, established in tropical regions governments, and rather absolute ones, but they have never succeeded in establishing there democratic commonwealths of the Anglo-Saxon type, like those in America or Australia.

The scheme of Americanizing our "new possessions" in that sense is therefore absolutely hopeless. The immutable forces of nature are against it. Whatever we may do for their improvement, the people of the Spanish Antilles will remain in overwhelming numerical predominance—Spanish creoles and negroes, and the people of the Philippines, Filipinos, Malays, Tagals and so on—some of them quite clever in their way, but the vast majority utterly alien to us, not only in origin and language, but in habits, traditions, ways of thinking, principles, ambitions—in short, in most things that are of the greatest importance in human intercourse and especially in political coöperation. And under the influences of their tropical climate they would prove incapable of becoming assimilated to the Anglo-Saxon. They would, therefore, remain in the population of this Republic a hopelessly heterogeneous element—in some respects much more hopeless than the colored people now living among us. . . .

7. "Platform of the American Anti-Imperialist League"

(1899)

A group of elite New Englanders founded the American Anti-Imperialist League in June 1898 during the debate over the annexation of the Philippines. Its members viewed annexation as a violation of the principles of self-determination embodied by the Declaration of Independence and the Constitution. The organization rapidly expanded into a national network that claimed some of the most prominent figures of the day as members, including social reformer Jane Addams, journalist Ambrose Bierce, industrialist Andrew Carnegie, writer Samuel Clemens (Mark Twain), former president Grover Cleveland, philosopher John Dewey, psychologist William James, and statesman and journalist Carl Schurz. Members of the League were particularly horrified by the war against the Filipino resisters led by former U.S. ally Emiliano Aguinaldo (1867–1964) that had begun in February 1899. Aguinaldo had declared Philippine independence on June 12, 1898, but this declaration was not recognized by the United States or Spain. The 1898 Treaty of Paris, signed in December, officially brought the conflict between the United States and Spain to a close, and stipulated that the United States would pay $20 million to Spain for the purchase the Philippines. As the following document makes clear, the League members felt the United States had merely switched places with Spain as the oppressor and tormentor of the Filipino people.

SOURCE: Frederic Bancroft, ed., *Speeches, Correspondence, and Political Papers of Carl Schurz*, vol. 6 (New York: G.P. Putnam & Sons, 1913), 77–79 fn.

Platform of the Anti-Imperialist League October 1899

We hold that the policy known as imperialism is hostile to liberty and tends toward militarism, an evil from which it has been our glory to be free. We regret that it has become necessary in the land of Washington and Lincoln to reaffirm that all men, of whatever race or color, are entitled to life, liberty, and the pursuit of happiness. We maintain that governments derive their just powers from the consent of the governed. We insist that the subjugation of any people is "criminal aggression" and open disloyalty to the distinctive principles of our Government.

We earnestly condemn the policy of the present National Administration in the Philippines. It seeks to extinguish the spirit of 1776 in those islands. We deplore the sacrifice of our soldiers and sailors, whose bravery deserves admiration even in an unjust war. We denounce the slaughter of the Filipinos as a needless horror. We protest against the extension of American sovereignty by Spanish methods.

We demand the immediate cessation of the war against liberty, begun by Spain and continued by us. We urge that Congress be promptly convened to announce to the Filipinos our purpose to concede to them the independence for which they have so long fought and which of right is theirs.

The United States have always protested against the doctrine of international law which permits the subjugation of the weak by the strong. A self-governing state cannot accept sovereignty over an unwilling people. The United States cannot act upon the ancient heresy that might makes right.

Imperialists assume that with the destruction of self-government in the Philippines by American hands, all opposition here will cease. This is a grievous error. Much as we abhor the war of "criminal aggression" in the Philippines, greatly as we regret that the blood of the Filipinos is on American hands, we more deeply resent the betrayal of American institutions at home. The real firing line is not in the suburbs of Manila. The foe is of our own household. The attempt of 1861 was to divide the country. That of 1899 is to destroy its fundamental principles and noblest ideals.

Whether the ruthless slaughter of the Filipinos shall end next month or next year is but an incident in a contest that must go on until the Declaration of Independence and the Constitution of the United States are rescued from the hands of their betrayers. Those who dispute about standards of value while the Republic is undermined will be listened to as little as there who would wrangle about the small economies of the household while the house is on fire. The training of a great people for a century, the aspiration for liberty of a vast immigration are forces that will hurl aside those who in the delirium of conquest seek to destroy the character of our institutions.

We deny that the obligation of all citizens to support their Government in times of grave National peril applies to the present situation. If an Administration may with impunity ignore the issues upon which it was chosen, deliberately create a condition of war anywhere on the face of the globe, debauch the civil service for spoils to promote the adventure, organize a truth suppressing censorship and demand of all citizens a suspension of judgment and their unanimous support while it chooses to continue the fighting, representative government itself is imperiled.

*   *   *

We propose to contribute to the defeat of any person or party that stands for the forcible subjugation of any people. We shall oppose for reelection all who in the White House or in Congress betray American liberty in pursuit of un-American gains. We still hope that both of our great political parties will support and defend the Declaration of Independence in the closing campaign of the century.

We hold, with Abraham Lincoln, that "no man is good enough to govern another man without that other's consent. When the white man governs himself, that is self-government, but when he governs himself and also governs another man, that is more than self-government that is despotism." "Our reliance is in the love of liberty which God has planted in us. Our defense is in the spirit which prizes liberty as the heritage of all men in all lands. Those who deny freedom to others deserve it not for themselves, and under a just God cannot long retain it."

8. I.D. Barnett et al., "Open Letter to President McKinley by Colored People of Massachusetts"

(1899)

At a mass protest meeting held on October 3, 1899, at the Charles Street Church in Boston, the activist, author, diplomat, and lawyer Archibald H. Grimké (1849–1930) read aloud the statement that follows. Grimké had been born into slavery near Charleston, South Carolina, one of three sons of an enslaved woman, Nancy Weston, and her white owner, Henry Grimké. After the Civil War, Grimké and his brothers enrolled in Lincoln University in Pennsylvania, one of the earliest schools founded for the education of African Americans. Around this time, the Grimké brothers also made contact with their famous aunts, Sarah Grimké and Angelina Grimké Weld, white slaveholding southern women who broke with their past and rose to fame as prominent abolitionists. Archibald Grimké enrolled at Harvard Law School in 1872, becoming one of that institution's first African American students. After attaining his law degree, he edited a Boston Republican newspaper, *The Hub*, aimed at a black audience. Becoming disillusioned with the Republican Party's increasing disinterest in African Americans, Grimké broke with it in 1886 and started to gravitate more toward Democratic politics. In 1894, President Cleveland appointed him consul to Santo Domingo, where he was astounded by the lack of attention paid to his skin color. Grimké returned to the United States in 1898 and embarked on a career of campaigning for African American rights.

The following letter brings to light the hypocrisy of the McKinley administration, which employed rhetoric of humanitarian concern for Cubans being oppressed by the Spanish while at the same time ignoring the plight of black U.S. citizens suffering under Jim Crow discrimination and terror at home. Other prominent signatories to the letter included the tireless antilynching crusader and suffragist Ida D. Wells-Barnett (1862–1931), as well as the prominent black politician and lawyer Edwin G. Walker, widely believed to be the son of abolitionist David Walker, author of the famed *Appeal to the Colored Citizens of the World* (1829).

SOURCE: I.D. Barnett et al., "Open Letter to President McKinley by Colored People of Massachusetts" (n.p., n.d.), 2–4, 10–12.

Sir:—We, colored people of Massachusetts in mass meeting assembled to consider our oppressions and the state of the country relative to the same, have resolved to address ourselves to you in an open letter, notwithstanding your extraordinary, your incomprehensible silence on the subject of our wrongs in your annual and other messages to Congress, as in your public utterances to the country at large. We address ourselves to you, sir, not as suppliants, but as of right, as American citizens, whose servant you are, and to whom you are bound to listen, and for whom you are equally bound to speak, and upon occasion to act, as for any other body of your fellow-countrymen in like circumstances. We ask nothing for ourselves at your hands, as chief magistrate of the republic, to which all American citizens are not entitled. We ask for the enjoyment of life, liberty and the pursuit of happiness equally with other men. We ask for the free and full exercise of all the rights of American freemen, guaranteed to us by the Constitution and laws of the Union, which you were solemnly sworn to obey and execute. We ask you for what belongs to us by the high sanction of Constitution and law, and the Democratic genius of our institutions and civilization. These rights are everywhere throughout the South denied to us, violently wrested from us by mobs, by lawless legislatures, and nullifying conventions, combinations, and conspiracies, openly, defiantly, under your eyes, in your constructive and actual presence. And we demand, which is a part of our rights, protection, security in our life, our liberty, and in the pursuit of our individual and social happiness under a government, which we are bound to defend in war, and which is equally bound to furnish us in peace protection, at home and abroad.

We have suffered, sir,—God knows how much we have suffered!—since your accession to office, at the hands of a country professing to be Christian, but which is not Christian, from the hate and violence of a people claiming to be civilized, but who are not civilized, and you have seen our sufferings, witnessed from your high place our awful wrongs and miseries, and yet you have at no time and on no occasion opened your lips in our behalf. Why? we ask. Is it because we are black and weak and despised? Are you silent because without any fault of our own we were enslaved and held for more than two centuries in cruel bondage by your forefathers? Is it because we bear the marks of those sad generations of Anglo-Saxon brutality and wickedness, that you do not speak? Is it our fault that our involuntary servitude produced in us widespread ignorance poverty and degradation? Are we to be damned and destroyed by the whites because we have only grown the seeds which they planted? Are we to be damned by bitter laws and destroyed by the mad violence of mobs because we are what white men made us? And is there no help in the federal arm for us, or even one word of audible pity, protest and remonstrance in your own breast, Mr. President, or in that of a single member of your Cabinet? Black indeed we are, sir, but we are also men and American citizens. . . .

Had, eighteen months ago, the Cuban revolution to throw off the yoke of Spain, or the attempt of Spain to subdue the Cuban rebellion, any federal aspect? We believe that you and the Congress of the United States thought that they had, and therefore used, finally, the armed force of the nation to expel Spain from that island. Why? Was it because "the people of the Island of Cuba are, and of right ought to be free and independent?" You and the Congress said as much, and may we fervently pray, sir, in passing, that the freedom and independence of that brave people shall not much longer be denied them by our government? But to resume, there was another consideration which, in your judgment, gave to the Cuban question a federal aspect, which provoked at last the armed interposition of our government in the affairs of that island, and this was "the chronic condition of disturbance in Cuba so injurious and menacing to our interests and tranquility, as well as shocking to our sentiments of humanity." Wherefore you presently fulfilled "a duty to humanity by ending a situation, the indefinite prolongation of which had become insufferable."

Mr. President, had that "chronic condition of disturbance in Cuba so injurious and menacing to our interest and tranquility as well as shocking to our sentiments of humanity," which you wished to terminate and did terminate, a federal aspect, while that not less "chronic condition of disturbance" in the South, which is a thousand times more "injurious and menacing to our interests and tranquility," as well as far more "shocking to our sentiments of humanity," or ought to be, none whatever? Is it better to be Cuban revolutionists fighting for Cuban independence than American citizens striving to do their simple duty at home? Or is it better only in case those American citizens doing their simple duty at home happen to be negroes residing in the Southern States?

Are crying national transgressions and injustices more "injurious and menacing" to the Republic, as well as "shocking to its sentiments of humanity," when committed by a foreign state, in foreign territory, against a foreign people, than when they are committed by a portion of our own people at home? There were those of our citizens who did not think that the Cuban question possessed any federal aspect, while there were others who thought otherwise; and these, having the will and power eventually found a way to suppress a menacing danger to the country and a wrong against humanity at the same time. Where there is a will among constitutional lawyers and rulers, Mr. President, there is ever a way; but where there is no will, there is no way. Shall it be said that the federal government, with arms of Briareus, reaching to the utmost limits of the habitable globe for the protection of its citizens, for the liberation of alien islanders and the subjugation of others, is powerless to guarantee to certain of its citizens at home their inalienable right to life, liberty and the pursuit of happiness, because those citizens happen to be negroes residing in the Southern section of our country? Do the colored people of the United States deserve equal consideration with the Cuban people at the hands of your administration, and shall they, though late, receive it?

9. "Unsigned Letter to the Editor of the *New York Age*"

(1900)

Many people in the African American community took great pride in the service of black soldiers in Cuba and the Philippines, viewing this group as strengthening black claims to citizenship rights. How could a nation deny basic human freedoms to citizens willing to fight and die for their country? News from black soldiers on the front proved very popular with readers at home, so editors of local African American newspapers (which were virtually all weeklies) printed many such letters that the papers received themselves and culled them from other papers as well. Many letters detailed the achievement and bravery of black troops, but others—like the one below—reflected deeply ambivalent feelings about the African American position both in the white-dominated military and in American society. While traveling to Florida, black soldiers had been harassed by whites. And while waiting to ship out in Tampa, conflicts between black soldiers and whites broke out almost daily, the worst being a bloody race riot that left twenty-seven blacks and three whites severely wounded, according to newspaper reports. Black soldiers' ambivalence about their mission seemed especially intense in the Philippines, where they arrived in the summer of 1899 to help put down the Filipino "insurrection" against U.S. forces that started earlier that year. They could not fail to draw parallels between the white soldiers' persecution of Filipinos and the Jim Crow treatment that they received back home. As this anonymous letter writer notes, white soldiers often referred to both American blacks and Filipinos interchangeably as "niggers," thus fostering a sympathetic bond between the supposed adversaries. Many observers noted that black soldiers got along better with Filipinos than white troops, some even taking Filipina brides.

SOURCE: *New York Age* letter reprinted in the *Wisconsin Weekly Advocate* (Milwaukee), May 17, 1900; from Willard B. Gatewood, Jr., *"Smoked Yankees" and the Struggle for Empire: Letters from Negro Soldiers, 1898–1902* (Urbana: University of Illinois Press, 1971), 279–81.

Editor, *New York Age*

I have mingled freely with the natives and have had talks with American colored men here in business and who have lived here for years, in order to learn of them the cause of their (Filipino) dissatisfaction and the reason for this insurrection, and I must confess they have a just grievance. All this never would have occurred if the army of occupation would have treated them as people. The Spaniards, even if their laws were hard, were polite and treated them with some consideration; but the Americans, as soon as they saw that the native troops were desirous of sharing in the glories as well as the hardships of the hard-won battles with the Americans, began to apply home treatment for colored peoples: cursed them as damned niggers, steal [from] and ravish them, rob them on the street of their small change, take from the fruit vendors whatever suited their fancy, and kick the poor unfortunate if he complained, desecrate their church property, and after fighting began, looted everything in sight, burning, robbing the graves.

This may seem a little tall—but I have seen with my own eyes carcasses lying bare in the boiling sun, the results of raids on receptacles for the dead in search of diamonds. The [white] troops, thinking we would be proud to emulate their conduct, have made bold of telling their exploits to us. One fellow, member of the 13th Minnesota, told me how some fellows he knew had cut off a native woman's arm in order to get a fine inlaid bracelet. On upbraiding some fellows one morning, whom I met while out for a walk (I think they belong to a Nebraska or Minnesota regiment, and they were stationed on the Malabon road) for the conduct of the American troops toward the natives and especially as to raiding, etc., the reply was: "Do you think we could stay over here and fight these damn niggers without making it pay all it's worth? The government only pays us $13 per month: that's starvation wages. White men can't stand it." Meaning they could not live on such small pay. In saying this they never dreamed that Negro soldiers would never countenance such conduct. They talked with impunity of "niggers" to our soldiers, never once thinking that they were talking to home "niggers" and should they be brought to remember that at home this is the same vile epithet they hurl at us, they beg pardon and make some effeminate excuse about what the Filipino is called.

I want to say right here that if it were not for the sake of the 10,000,000 black people in the United States, God alone knows on which side of the subject I would be. And for the sake of the black men who carry arms and pioneer for them as their representatives, ask them to not forget the present administration at the next election. Party be damned! We don't want these islands, not in the way we are to get them, and for Heaven's sake, put the [Democratic] party in power that pledged itself against this highway robbery. Expansion is too clean a name for it.

[Unsigned]

10. William Jennings Bryan, "The Paralyzing Influence of Imperialism"

(1900)

After his tough loss in the presidential race against McKinley in 1896, Bryan was up for nomination again in 1900. He faced virtually no opposition within the Democratic Party after the naval hero of the 1898 war, Admiral George Dewey (1837–1917), dropped out of the race in May after a series of public relations mishaps. Most eastern Democrats, like Tammany Hall boss Richard Croker, would have greatly preferred someone else, but no other candidate materialized. Many observers felt that Bryan had less of a chance of victory than in 1896, since the McKinley campaign, run by the brilliant strategist and fundraiser Marcus A. Hanna (1837–1904), had exponentially more funds at its disposal. While not softening his position against the gold standard, Bryan chose to emphasize anti-imperialism in his campaign, thinking that the issue had a broader appeal. He delivered the speech excerpted below at the nominating convention in Kansas City in July, and its enthusiastic reception briefly brightened his fortunes, rallying many key supporters behind him, including some prominent financiers and the influential Anti-Imperialist League. Yet, as Bryan later toured throughout the Midwest and several big cities, he found less and less popular enthusiasm for his anti-imperialist message, and started to emphasize his antitrust position more. The future president Harry S. Truman (1884–1972) worked at the St. Louis convention as a page.

SOURCE: *Official Proceedings of the Democratic National Convention Held in Kansas City, Mo., July 4th, 5th & 6th, 1900* (Chicago: McLellan Printing Co.), 205–27.

If it is right for the United States to hold the Philippine Islands permanently and imitate European empires in the government of colonies, the Republican Party ought to state its position and defend it, but it must expect the subject races to protest against such a policy and to resist to the extent of their ability.

The Filipinos do not need any encouragement from Americans now living. Our whole history has been an encouragement, not only to the Filipinos but to

31

all who are denied a voice in their own government. If the Republicans are prepared to censure all who have used language calculated to make the Filipinos hate foreign domination, let them condemn the speech of Patrick Henry. When he uttered that passionate appeal, "Give me liberty or give me death," he expressed a sentiment which still echoes in the hearts of men.

Let them censure Jefferson; of all the statesmen of history none have used words so offensive to those who would hold their fellows in political bondage. Let them censure Washington, who declared that the colonists must choose between liberty and slavery. Or, if the statute of limitations has run against the sins of Henry and Jefferson and Washington, let them censure Lincoln, whose Gettysburg speech will be quoted in defense of popular government when the present advocates of force and conquest are forgotten.

Someone has said that a truth once spoken can never be recalled. It goes on and on, and no one can set a limit to its ever widening influence. But if it were possible to obliterate every word written or spoken in defense of the principles set forth in the Declaration of Independence, a war of conquest would still leave its legacy of perpetual hatred, for it was God Himself who placed in every human heart the love of liberty. He never made a race of people so low in the scale of civilization or intelligence that it would welcome a foreign master.

Those who would have this nation enter upon a career of empire must consider not only the effect of imperialism on the Filipinos but they must also calculate its effects upon our own nation. We cannot repudiate the principle of self-government in the Philippines without weakening that principle here.

Lincoln said that the safety of this nation was not in its fleets, its armies, its forts, but in the spirit which prizes liberty as the heritage of all men, in all lands, everywhere, and he warned his countrymen that they could not destroy this spirit without planting the seeds of despotism at their own doors.

Even now we are beginning to see the paralyzing influence of imperialism. Heretofore this nation has been prompt to express its sympathy with those who were fighting for civil liberty. While our sphere of activity has been limited to the Western Hemisphere, our sympathies have not been bounded by the seas. We have felt it due to ourselves and to the world, as well as to those who were struggling for the right to govern themselves, to proclaim the interest which our people have, from the date of their own independence, felt in every contest between human rights and arbitrary power. . . .

A colonial policy means that we shall send to the Philippine Islands a few traders, a few taskmasters, and a few officeholders, and an army large enough to support the authority of a small fraction of the people while they rule the natives.

If we have an imperial policy we must have a great standing army as its natural and necessary complement. The spirit which will justify the forcible annexation of the Philippine Islands will justify the seizure of other islands and the domination of other people, and with wars of conquest we can expect a certain, if not rapid, growth of our military establishment.

That a large permanent increase in our regular army is intended by Republican leaders is not a matter of conjecture but a matter of fact. In his message of Dec. 5, 1898, the President asked for authority to increase the standing army to 100,000. In 1896 the army contained about 25,000. Within two years the President asked for four times that many, and a Republican House of Representatives complied with the request after the Spanish treaty had been signed, and when no country was at war with the United States.

If such an army is demanded when an imperial policy is contemplated but not openly avowed, what may be expected if the people encourage the Republican Party by endorsing its policy at the polls?

A large standing army is not only a pecuniary burden to the people and, if accompanied by compulsory service, a constant source of irritation but it is even a menace to a republican form of government. The army is the personification of force, and militarism will inevitably change the ideals of the people and turn the thoughts of our young men from the arts of peace to the science of war. The government which relies for its defense upon its citizens is more likely to be just than one which has at call a large body of professional soldiers.

A small standing army and a well-equipped and well-disciplined state militia are sufficient at ordinary times, and in an emergency the nation should in the future as in the past place its dependence upon the volunteers who come from all occupations at their country's call and return to productive labor when their services are no longer required—men who fight when the country needs fighters and work when the country needs workers. . . .

The Republican platform promises that some measure of self-government is to be given the Filipinos by law; but even this pledge is not fulfilled. Nearly sixteen months elapsed after the ratification of the treaty before the adjournment of Congress last June and yet no law was passed dealing with the Philippine situation. The will of the President has been the only law in the Philippine Islands wherever the American authority extends.

Why does the Republican Party hesitate to legislate upon the Philippine question? Because a law would disclose the radical departure from history and precedent contemplated by those who control the Republican Party. The storm of protest which greeted the Puerto Rican bill was an indication of what may be expected when the American people are brought face to face with legislation upon this subject.

If the Puerto Ricans, who welcomed annexation, are to be denied the guarantees of our Constitution, what is to be the lot of the Filipinos, who resisted our authority? If secret influences could compel a disregard of our plain duty toward friendly people living near our shores, what treatment will those same influences provide for unfriendly people 7,000 miles away? If, in this country where the people have a right to vote, Republican leaders dare not take the side of the people against the great monopolies which have grown up within the last few years, how can they be trusted to protect the Filipinos from the corporations which are waiting to exploit the islands?

Is the sunlight of full citizenship to be enjoyed by the people of the United States and the twilight of semi-citizenship endured by the people of Puerto Rico, while the thick darkness of perpetual vassalage covers the Philippines? The Puerto Rico tariff law asserts the doctrine that the operation of the Constitution is confined to the forty-five states.

The Democratic Party disputes this doctrine and denounces it as repugnant to both the letter and spirit of our organic law. There is no place in our system of government for the deposit of arbitrary and irresistible power. That the leaders of a great party should claim for any President or Congress the right to treat millions of people as mere "possessions" and deal with them unrestrained by the Constitution or the Bill of Rights shows how far we have already departed from the ancient landmarks and indicates what may be expected if this nation deliberately enters upon a career of empire.

The territorial form of government is temporary and preparatory, and the chief security a citizen of a territory has is found in the fact that he enjoys the same constitutional guarantees and is subject to the same general laws as the citizen of a state. Take away this security and his rights will be violated and his interests sacrificed at the demand of those who have political influence. This is the evil of the colonial system, no matter by what nation it is applied.

What is our title to the Philippine Islands? Do we hold them by treaty or by conquest? Did we buy them or did we take them? Did we purchase the people? If not, how did we secure title to them? Were they thrown in with the land? Will the Republicans say that inanimate earth has value but that when that earth is molded by the Divine Hand and stamped with the likeness of the Creator it becomes a fixture and passes with the soil? If governments derive their just powers from the consent of the governed, it is impossible to secure title to people, either by force or by purchase.

We could extinguish Spain's title by treaty, but if we hold title we must hold it by some method consistent with our ideas of government. When we made allies of the Filipinos and armed them to fight against Spain, we disputed Spain's title. If we buy Spain's title, we are not innocent purchasers. There can be no doubt that we accepted and utilized the services of the Filipinos and that when we did so we had full knowledge that they were fighting for their own independence; and I submit that history furnishes no example of turpitude baser than ours if we now substitute our yoke for the Spanish yoke . . .

Some argue that American rule in the Philippine Islands will result in the better education of the Filipinos. Be not deceived. If we expect to maintain a colonial policy, we shall not find it to our advantage to educate the people. The educated Filipinos are now in revolt against us, and the most ignorant ones have made the least resistance to our domination. If we are to govern them without their consent and give them no voice in determining the taxes which they must pay, we dare not educate them lest they learn to read the Declaration of Independence and the Constitution of the United States and mock us for our inconsistency.

11. Erving Winslow,
"The Anti-Imperialist Position"

(1900)

Erving Winslow (1839–1922), a prominent Boston commissions merchant, society figure, and man of letters, served as the national secretary of the Anti-Imperialist League from its inception. As the platform of the American Anti-Imperialist League made clear, Winslow and his fellow League members were vehemently opposed to territorial expansion on moral and ideological grounds. In the following excerpts from an essay published in the popular magazine *North American Review,* Winslow carefully catalogs an array of reasons why he feels that "imperial aggression" will "sow the seeds" of the republic's destruction. He shows the contradictions involved in the American republic holding territory outside of the jurisdiction of the Constitution, and then the shrewd businessman provides a list of reasons why he believes that colonial possessions make poor financial sense.

The League's endorsement of William Jennings Bryan, the anti-imperialist Democratic nominee for president in the 1900 election, was quite controversial since Bryan offended many members who favored the retention of a gold standard (Bryan had spoken passionately for its abolishment). In this document, Winslow tacitly approves of Bryan, but some "Gold Democrats" went so far as to try to convince former president Grover Cleveland to run as a third-party candidate to provide another anti-imperialist alternative to Bryan.

SOURCE: *North American Review,* 171 (October 1900), 460–68.

. . . The momentous character of the imperial aggression transcends the issues of the Civil War, or those of any imaginable question that could be presented to a Republic. Its aim is more deadly than to rend the Republic in twain. We believe that it is to sap the sources of its life and to sow the seeds of its destruction. Its most bigoted adherent cannot minimize the fact that the addition of tropical and unassimilable peoples, in permanent colonial relations, to our Republic is the most tremendous departure conceivable from our traditions and principles and practice. No mere phrases ringing changes upon "expansion," "world power" and "destiny," can disguise the right and duty of each citizen to ponder, and decide for himself, propositions so serious and so pregnant that the attempt which has been made to forestall his judgment concerning them is in itself the grossest act of Imperialism.

The few words which follow are to treat of the historical, the legal or constitutional, the commercial-financial and the ethical aspects of the paramount question, the wrong side of which is represented by William McKinley, and the right by William Jennings Bryan. . . .

. . . The Constitutional aspect of the imperial aggression has been discussed by many writers and speakers according to their points of view. It seems hardly necessary to controvert the extreme assertions which have been made, that the sanction of a treaty with a foreign nation can supersede the sanctions of a Constitution. The right of the Congress to dispose of territory, which has been availed of in similar cases, obviously makes it possible to transfer such sovereignty as has been acquired in the Philippine Islands to their inhabitants. The authority to retain them as territory and to govern them permanently outside of the Constitution, will doubtless be sought from the Supreme Court, as the recognition of an existing political fact. Hitherto, the march of the Constitution, as the progress of the interpretations of that instrument has been called where doubts existed, has been enlightened by the principles of the Declaration of Independence. John Marshall, who has been justly characterized as the guide, the light and the defender of the Constitution, won his imperishable fame by the diligence with which he sought the attainment of those objects for which it is declared to have been instituted. While Marshall might not have adopted the strict construction in the Dred Scott case maintained by Judge Taney and his associates, because it involved the extension of human slavery contrary to the spirit of the instrument and of the Declaration of Independence, it can hardly be doubted that now, since this construction involves, under the changed conditions, the extension of liberty, Marshall would have to-day maintained that very construction. The survivors of those who then opposed it may now support that construction with absolute consistency. If the Supreme Court is still inspired by the spirit of its great leaders, its illumination, from the Declaration of Independence and the traditions of the Government, will enlighten its counsels so that the contentions of the present Administration will be defeated, and those arrogated powers which have been exerted with such fatal results will be overthrown. Then Puerto Rico must have statehood or it must be alienated, and the Philippines must have statehood or they must be alienated.

It is a part of the Constitutional or legal aspect of the matter, that no embarrassment need be feared from possible complications involved in such a protectorate as has been suggested for the Philippines, or which might be implied by an enfranchised Puerto Rico. Who can doubt that the nations of the world would accept, at the suggestion of the United States, the neutralization of these countries, as in the case of Belgium and Switzerland?

Finally, it should be noted that the Administration has never even suggested the obvious and legal method by way of amendment to the Constitution for so vast an extension of the powers of the Government, but that it has endeavored to foist upon the people a party measure, which transcends in importance any change of which its authors could have dreamed.

There are several aspects in which the commercial or financial results of tropical colonial expansion may be regarded, all equally fatal to the specious arguments which have been exploited by the friends of the Administration.

(1.) The consideration of the balance between the cost of subjugation, now called "policing" vassal states, and any possible profit therefrom, is one of the most interesting of these. The expenses incurred on account of the Philippines are at the rate of about $200,000,000 per annum. There is no immediate prospect of any considerable reduction in this pretty little bill. The total sum of the exports and imports of the archipelago has not exceeded $30,000,000 a year. Let the Imperialist indicate any possible source of increase in the consuming or producing power of the islands which can overcome the frightful debit.

(2.) It is impossible to believe, after the uprising against the "scuttle" policy of the Administration in the matter of the Puerto Rican tariff, that the tyrannical policy could be maintained of imposing duties to prevent colonial productions from competing with our own industries. Thus the sugar growing of tropical dependencies, promoted by our own capital, will ruin the sugar industry of the United States. The tobacco trade will, by similar means, be largely transferred to these favorable regions. Labor will be brought to the level of the standard of Asiatic living. For, even though sovereignty did not imply freedom of movement on the part of the subject peoples, the indentured labor system, a form of slavery, which English emissaries are endeavoring to induce the United States to graft upon our colonial system after the example of Great Britain, would probably sooner or later be adopted by the Imperialists.

(3.) The ultimate result of the extension of our Eastern policy to China is easily foreseen. A development of commercial opportunity in that densely populated country, to which we are pointed with such enthusiasm, means what? Not a market but a menace—the opportunity to export some tools and machinery to create Chinese industries which may soon supply the markets of the world. As Richtofen says: "The slumbering factors of an immense industrial production all exist here." There are already five large cotton mills in Shanghai. Wages average about ten cents a day, and the ready adaptiveness of the labor is indicated by the fact that productive capacity has increased twenty-five per cent in one year. Not prosperity but ruin and disaster are the auguries of expansion.

The ethical side of a condition which has followed avoidable war need only, it might be supposed, be calmly contemplated to arouse the conscience of the whole nation in vehement opposition. In Cuba, a population on the verge of revolution; a broken and bitter subject race in Puerto Rico; in the Philippines, a defiant and persistent enemy. Corruption in the Administration, horrible licensed vice in Manila, the outrages of an irregular contest beyond even the cruel laws of war and the chartered savagery of barbarous allies, the treatment of Catholic Christians as heathens, the desecration of churches, rapine, ravishing and murder; in what a horrible propaganda of wickedness the United States has been engaged for months, which are now gathering up their dread account into years. This explains the censorship which keeps the truth from America. While all these horrors are going on, because they do not come within reach of the senses, the defenders of the Administration rely upon the comfort and prosperity which are as yet superficially apparent in domestic affairs to dull the ears and steel the hearts of the American people. It is the old Imperial idea that nothing matters while there is a plenty of bread and circuses. It is impossible that we should long remain thus callous; but, even should we otherwise do so, there is reason to expect that the inflation of a vastly expanded currency is about to collapse, and that wages, which have not now the purchasing power of four years ago, will be reduced or cut off, and that bad times will arouse the people to the wrong which is being done at home and abroad.

As for the bogie which the Republican party is trying to manufacture out of the corpse embalmed in the Democratic Platform it may be said that, if it has any living menace, the mind which could place the Silver Issue in the same plane with or above the issue of Imperialism would have sacrificed the Union in the war between the States, rather than have risked the depression of the currency.

President McKinley, as Governor Boutwell has eloquently said, was given "an opportunity for the enrollment of his name with that of the Czar of Russia, who emancipated millions of hereditary serfs; with the name of Lincoln, a name that can never die; with the name of the Emperor of Brazil, who struck the shackles from the last slave on the American continent. President McKinley could have said to the inhabitants of Puerto Rico and the Philippines: "We have acquired the title of Spain, such as it is; but your title, by possession, is the better title. We are prepared to surrender the Spanish title to you. The yoke of Imperialism is broken. Organize free governments and prepare to found free states, and thus to create happy and prosperous commonwealths. . . ."

12. William McKinley, "Second Inaugural Address"

(1901)

President McKinley soundly defeated William Jennings Bryan in the November 1900 presidential election, obtaining 292 electoral votes to Bryan's 155. The popular vote was a little bit closer, with McKinley garnering 51.1 percent of the total votes compared to Bryan's 45.5 percent. Bryan's idea to make imperialism the centerpiece of the election backfired as many Americans seemed to lose interest in the issue. The following excerpt from McKinley's 1901 inaugural speech justified the presence of American troops in both Cuba and the Philippines as necessary for the safety of the peoples of those islands. "We are not making war on the people of the Philippine Islands," McKinley claimed, but, rather, fighting a portion of the people who chose to make war on the United States. According to McKinley, the Filipinos would be given self-government "as fast as they were ready for it," with the U.S. government obviously determining how and when that readiness was attained.

SOURCE: *Inaugural Addresses of the Presidents of the United States: From George Washington 1789 to George Bush 1989* (Washington, D.C.: Government Printing Office, 1989).

. . . We face at this moment a most important question that of the future relations of the United States and Cuba. With our near neighbors we must remain close friends. The declaration of the purposes of this Government in the resolution of April 20, 1898, must be made good. Ever since the evacuation of the island by the army of Spain, the Executive, with all practicable speed, has been assisting its people in the successive steps necessary to the establishment of a free and independent government prepared to assume and perform the obligations of international law which now rest upon the United States under the treaty of Paris. The convention elected by the people to frame a constitution is approaching the completion of its labors. The transfer of American control to the new government is of such great importance, involving an obligation resulting from our intervention and the treaty of peace, that I am glad to be advised by the recent act of Congress of the policy which the legislative branch of the Government deems essential to the best interests of Cuba and the United States. The principles which led to our intervention require that the fundamental law upon which the new government rests should be adapted to secure a government capable of performing the duties and discharging the functions of a separate nation, of observing its international obligations of protecting life and property, insuring order, safety, and liberty, and conforming to the established and historical policy of the United States in its relation to Cuba.

The peace which we are pledged to leave to the Cuban people must carry with it the guaranties of permanence. We became sponsors for the pacification of the island, and we remain accountable to the Cubans, no less than to our own country and people, for the reconstruction of Cuba as a free commonwealth on abiding foundations of right, justice, liberty, and assured order. Our enfranchisement of the people will not be completed until free Cuba shall "be a reality, not a name; a perfect entity, not a hasty experiment bearing within itself the elements of failure."

While the treaty of peace with Spain was ratified on the 6th of February, 1899, and ratifications were exchanged nearly two years ago, the Congress has indicated no form of government for the Philippine Islands. It has, however, provided an army to enable the Executive to suppress insurrection, restore peace, give security to the inhabitants, and establish the authority of the United States throughout the archipelago. It has authorized the organization of native troops as auxiliary to the regular force. It has been advised from time to time of the acts of the military and naval officers in the islands, of my action in appointing civil commissions, of the instructions with which they were charged, of their duties and powers, of their recommendations, and of their several acts under executive commission, together with the very complete general information they have submitted. These reports fully set forth the conditions, past and present, in the islands, and the instructions clearly show the principles which will guide the Executive until the Congress shall, as it is required to do by the treaty, determine "the civil rights and political status of the native inhabitants." The Congress having added the sanction of its authority to the powers already possessed and exercised by the Executive under the Constitution, thereby leaving with the Executive the responsibility for the government of the Philippines, I shall continue the efforts already begun until order shall be restored throughout the islands, and as fast as conditions permit will establish local governments, in the formation of which the full co-operation of the people has been already invited, and when established will encourage the people to administer them. The settled purpose, long ago proclaimed, to afford the inhabitants of the islands self-government as fast as they were ready for it will be pursued with earnestness and fidelity. Already something has been accomplished in this direction. The Government's representatives, civil and military, are doing faithful and noble work in their mission of emancipation and merit the approval and support of their countrymen. The most liberal terms of amnesty have already been communicated to the insurgents, and the way is still open for those who have raised their arms against the Government for honorable submission to its authority. Our countrymen should not be deceived. We are not waging war against the inhabitants of the Philippine Islands. A portion of them are making war against the United States. By far the greater part of the inhabitants recognize American sovereignty and welcome it as a guaranty of order and of security for life, property, liberty, freedom of conscience, and the pursuit of happiness. To them full protection will be given. They shall not be abandoned. We will not leave the destiny of the loyal millions the islands to the disloyal thousands who are in rebellion against the United States. Order under civil institutions will come as soon as those who now break the peace shall keep it. Force will not be needed or used when those who make war against us shall make it no more. May it end without further bloodshed, and there be ushered in the reign of peace to be made permanent by a government of liberty under law!

13. George Ade, "Hike," from *The Sultan of Sulu*

(1902)

Popular Chicago newspaper columnist and humorist George Ade (1866–1944) paired with composer Alfred Wathall to create the musical *The Sultan of Sulu* in 1902. Ade had become a national literary celebrity for his collection published in 1899, *Fables in Slang,* which gently lampooned the lives of everyday Americans. *The Sultan of Sulu* functioned both as a vehicle for feminine spectacle and as a satire of the American occupation of the Philippines. It was one of the few musicals originating in Chicago that managed to move to Broadway and become a hit. Ade borrowed the basic framework of the London-originated hit musical, *Florodora,* which also took place on a Philippine isle, and gave his story a more political edge, much in the spirit of Ade's literary and anti-imperialist idol, Mark Twain. The first performance took place on March 11, 1902, at the Studebaker Theatre in Chicago, and the first performance on Broadway took place on December 29, 1902.

In the song "Hike," excerpted below, Ade savages much of the altruistic rhetoric about the American presence in the archipelago: a unit of American soldiers, having recently landed on the remote Philippine island of Sulu, sing about "educating" and "taming" their "brother who is brown" while firing bullets at him. As Ade knew, the bloody Filipino uprising against American forces that began in 1899 was no laughing matter, with horrific atrocities committed on both sides. Even within the framework of this lighthearted musical farce, Ade throws into question who is truly the arbiter of "civilization" in the Philippines.

SOURCE: George Ade, *The Sultan of Sulu: An Original Satire in Two Acts* (New York: R.H. Russell, 1903), 11–12.

> We haven't the appearance, goodness knows,
> Of plain commercial men;
> From a hasty glance, you might suppose

We are fractious now and then.
But though we come in warlike guise
   And battle-front arrayed,
It's all a business enterprise;
   We're seeking foreign trade.

REFRAIN

We're as mild as any turtle-dove
   When we see the foe a-coming,
Our thoughts are set on human love
   When we hear the bullets humming.
We teach the native population
   What the golden rule is like,
And we scatter public education
   On ev'ry blasted hike!

We want to assimilate, if we can,
   Our brother who is brown,
We love our dusky fellow-man
   And we hate to hunt him down.
So, when we perforate his frame,
   We want him to be good.
We shoot at him to make him tame,
   If he but understood.

CHAPTER
TWO

The Great War, Part I: Politics, Protest, and the Law

14. Emma Goldman, "Preparedness, the Road to Universal Slaughter"

(1915)

The widespread public sentiment for keeping the United States out of the war in Europe began to falter somewhat after the sinking of the British passenger liner *Lusitania* by a German submarine in May 1915, even though the imperial German government agreed to scale down such attacks. A total of 1,198 people were killed, including 128 Americans. The catchword "preparedness" was on the tip of the tongues of all who clamored for a military buildup, including former president Theodore Roosevelt. The following excerpt is from an essay by radical activist Emma Goldman, published in the monthly anarchist journal that she edited, *Mother Earth*. Goldman argues that a military buildup would benefit only the privileged classes, and equates the rising demand for "preparedness" with autocratic Prussian militarism. In Goldman's eyes, President Woodrow Wilson, under the guise of a calm and collected college professor, was ultimately as willing "to serve the big interests" as the blustering elitist Roosevelt. At this time, Goldman was persecuted by the government more for her lecturing on birth control than for her radical politics. The authorities would become more concerned with her political message after the U.S. entry into the war, and especially after the Bolshevik Revolution.

SOURCE: *Mother Earth* 10, no. 10 (December 1915).

. . . America is essentially the melting pot. No national unit composing it is in a position to boast of superior race purity, particular historic mission, or higher culture. Yet the jingoes and war speculators are filling the air with the sentimental slogan of hypocritical nationalism, "America for Americans," "America first, last, and all the time." This cry has caught the popular fancy from one end of the country to another. In order to maintain America, military preparedness must be engaged in at once. A billion dollars of the people's sweat and blood is to be expended for dreadnaughts and submarines for the army and the navy, all to protect this precious America.

The pathos of it all is that the America which is to be protected by a huge military force is not the America of the people, but that of the privileged class; the class which robs and exploits the masses, and controls their lives from the cradle to the grave. No less pathetic is it that so few people realize that preparedness never leads to peace, but that it is indeed the road to universal slaughter.

With the cunning methods used by the scheming diplomats and military cliques of Germany to saddle the masses with Prussian militarism, the American military ring with its Roosevelts, its Garrisons, its Daniels, and lastly its Wilsons, are moving the very heavens to place the militaristic heel upon the necks of the American people, and, if successful, will hurl America into the storm of blood and tears now devastating the countries of Europe.

Forty years ago Germany proclaimed the slogan: "Germany above everything. Germany for the Germans, first, last and always. We want peace; therefore we must prepare for war. Only a well armed and thoroughly prepared nation can maintain peace, can command respect, can be sure of its national integrity." And Germany continued to prepare, thereby forcing the other nations to do the same. The terrible European war is only the culminating fruition of the hydra-headed gospel, military preparedness.

Since the war began, miles of paper and oceans of ink have been used to prove the barbarity, the cruelty, the oppression of Prussian militarism. Conservatives and radicals alike are giving their support to the Allies for no other reason than to help crush that militarism, in the presence of which, they say, there can be no peace or progress in Europe. But though America grows fat on the manufacture of munitions and war loans to the Allies to help crush Prussians the same cry is now being raised in America which, if carried into national action, would build up and American militarism far more terrible than German or Prussian militarism could ever be, and that because nowhere in the world has capitalism become so brazen in its greed and nowhere is the state so ready to kneel at the feet of capital.

Like a plague, the mad spirit is sweeping the country, infesting the clearest heads and staunchest hearts with the deathly germ of militarism. National security leagues, with cannon as their emblem of protection, naval leagues with women in their lead have sprung up all over the country, women who boast of representing the gentler sex, women who in pain and danger bring forth life and yet are ready to dedicate it to the Moloch War. Americanization societies with well known liberals as members, they who but yesterday decried the patriotic clap-trap of to-day, are now lending themselves to befog the minds of the people and to help build up the same destructive institutions in America which they are directly and indirectly helping to pull down in Germany—militarism, the destroyer of youth, the raper of women, the annihilator of the best in the race, the very mower of life.

Even Woodrow Wilson, who not so long ago indulged in the phrase "A nation too proud to fight," who in the beginning of the war ordered prayers for peace, who in his proclamations spoke of the necessity of watchful waiting, even he has been whipped into line. He has now joined his worthy colleagues in the jingo movement, echoing their clamor for preparedness and their howl of "America for Americans." The difference between Wilson and Roosevelt is this: Roosevelt, a born bully, uses the club; Wilson, the historian, the college professor, wears the smooth polished university mask, but underneath it he, like Roosevelt, has but one aim, to serve the big interests, to add to those who are growing phenominally rich by the manufacture of military supplies. . . .

15. Alfred Bryan and Al Piantadosi, "I Didn't Raise My Boy to Be a Soldier"

(1915)

The Canadian-born lyricist Alfred Bryan (1871–1958) teamed up with composer Al Piantadosi (both were regulars among the group of Manhattan-based songwriters, composers, and music publishers collectively known as "Tin Pan Alley") to produce this controversial 1915 antiwar song that was banned in England and France. Bryan had achieved previous success with such hit songs as "Peg o' My Heart" and "Come, Josephine, in My Flying Machine." The popularity of "I Didn't Raise My Boy to Be a Soldier" in the United States reflected the sentiments of many Americans who wished to remain uninvolved with the European conflict. People across the political spectrum, from ardent capitalists like Andrew Carnegie to dedicated socialists like Eugene V. Debs, opposed U.S. entry into the war. Other people's antiwar sentiments were grounded in ethnicity: many German Americans felt a strong aversion to going to war with their homeland, while some Irish Americans felt reluctant about spilling blood to aid their British oppressors. Theodore Roosevelt, former president and passionate advocate of military "preparedness," was so irked by the song that in a July 1915 speech in San Francisco he proclaimed, "A mother who is not willing to raise her boy to be a soldier is not worthy of citizenship." In 1916, songwriter Frank Hudson responded to Bryan's song by publishing the pro-intervention "I Tried to Raise My Boy to Be a Hero." By the time the United States entered the conflict in 1917, most popular songs rallied behind the war effort.

SOURCE: Leo Feist, New York, 1915.

> Ten million soldiers to the war have gone,
> Who may never return again.
> Ten million mothers' hearts must break,
> For the ones who died in vain.
> Head bowed down in sorrow in her lonely years,
> I heard a mother murmur thro' her tears:

Chorus:
I didn't raise my boy to be a soldier,
I brought him up to be my pride and joy,
Who dares to put a musket on his shoulder,
To shoot some other mother's darling boy?
Let nations arbitrate their future troubles,
It's time to lay the sword and gun away,
There'd be no war today,
If mothers all would say,
I didn't raise my boy to be a soldier.

(Chorus)
What victory can cheer a mother's heart,
When she looks at her blighted home?
What victory can bring her back,
All she cared to call her own?
Let each mother answer in the year to be,
Remember that my boy belongs to me!

(Chorus)

16. Will Dixon and Albert Von Tilzer, "Don't Take My Darling Boy Away"

(1915)

Like "I Didn't Raise My Boy to Be a Solder," the following song became tremendously popular in the period before the U.S. entry in the war, and also embodied antiwar sentiment in the figure of a mother. This march was written by lyricist Will Dixon and legendary Tin Pan Alley composer Albert Von Tilzer (1878–1956), who also wrote the music for "Take Me Out to the Ballgame," among other memorable tunes. The melodramatic lyrics imagine a mother who has already lost her husband and three other sons to war, and now a captain comes knocking on her door to take her only surviving son. Before 1917, the idea of conscription was a hugely controversial one—the sole major political figure advocating it was Theodore Roosevelt—but opposition to it disintegrated rapidly after war was declared in April 1917, and draft legislation passed both houses in Congress by May 1917. The imagined scenario thus was not yet possible in the United States when the song was written, but it was unquestionably being debated.

SOURCE: Broadway Music Co., New York, 1915.

A mother was kneeling to pray
For loved ones at war far away
And there by her side, her one joy and pride,
knelt down with her that day

Then came a knock on the door
Your boy is commanded to war
"No Captain please, here on my knees,
I plead for one I adore"

Don't take my darling boy away from me,
Don't send him off to war
You took his father and brothers three,
Now you've come back for more

Who are the heroes that fight your war
Mothers who have no say
But my duty's done so for god's sake leave one!
And don't take my darling boy away.

Tenting tonight, Tenting tonight
Tenting on the old campground

You took his father and brothers three,
Now you've come back for more

Tenting tonight, Tenting tonight
Tenting on the old campground

But my duty's done so for god's sake leave one!
And don't take my darling boy away.

A hero is now laid to rest, A hero and one of the best
He fought with each son, The battles he'd won,
And the battles that proved a test

Though she never went to the war,
She was a hero by far, they gave a gun
But who gave a son,
M. O. T. H. E. R.

Don't take my darling boy away from me,
Don't send him off to war
You took his father and brothers three,
Now you've come back for more

Who are the heroes that fight your war
Mothers who have no say
But my duty's done so for god's sake leave one!
And don't take my darling boy away.

Tenting tonight, Tenting tonight
Tenting on the old campground

You took his father and brothers three,
Now you've come back for more

Tenting tonight, Tenting tonight
Tenting on the old campground

But my duty's done so for god's sake leave one!
And don't take my darling boy away.

17. George M. Cohan, "Over There"

(1917)

The Irish American entertainer, actor, playwright, composer, lyricist, producer, and director George M. Cohan (1878–1942) claims to have come up with the idea for this perhaps most famous of all prowar songs while on a train between his home in New Rochelle and New York City, just as the United States declared war on Germany in April 1917. He based the music on a three-note bugle call. A veteran vaudeville performer, Cohan enjoyed major commercial success with his 1904 show, *Little Johnnie Jones,* which featured his songs "Give My Regards to Broadway" and "Yankee Doodle Boy." He was also known for another patriotic staple, "You're a Grand Old Flag," which Cohan claimed that he wrote in 1906 after an encounter with a Civil War veteran who had preserved a flag flown during the Battle of Gettysburg. "Over There" became a nationwide hit, capturing the general enthusiasm many Americans felt for the war effort in its initial months.

SOURCE: William Jerome Publishing, New York, 1917.

> Johnnie, get your gun,
> Get your gun, get your gun,
> Take it on the run,
> On the run, on the run.
> Hear them calling, you and me,
> Every son of liberty.
> Hurry right away,
> No delay, go today,
> Make your daddy glad
> To have had such a lad.
> Tell your sweetheart not to pine,
> To be proud her boy's in line.
> (chorus sung twice)

Johnnie, get your gun,
Get your gun, get your gun,
Johnnie show the Hun
Who's a son of a gun.
Hoist the flag and let her fly,
Yankee Doodle do or die.
Pack your little kit,
Show your grit, do your bit.
Yankee to the ranks,
From the towns and the tanks.
Make your mother proud of you,
And the old Red, White and Blue.
(chorus sung twice)

Chorus
Over there, over there,
Send the word, send the word over there -
That the Yanks are coming,
The Yanks are coming,
The drums rum-tumming
Ev'rywhere.
So prepare, say a pray'r,
Send the word, send the word to beware.
We'll be over, we're coming over,
And we won't come back till it's over
Over there.

18. Samuel Gompers, "American Labor's Position in Peace or War"

(1917)

The trade unionist Samuel Gompers (1850–1924) served as president of the American Federation of Labor (AFL) from its inception in 1886 to his death, with the exception of one year (1895). When outbreak of war appeared imminent in spring 1917, the AFL represented 2.4 million mostly white skilled laborers; its leadership had little interest in reaching out beyond this constituency. Compared to the radical International Workers of the World (IWW) or other unions with socialist tendencies, the AFL was politically moderate, associated primarily with the Democratic Party. The central tenet of the AFL was that collective bargaining could serve as the basis for an industrial democracy. While Gompers himself had pacifist tendencies, he was not opposed to the war effort— as he indicates in the following official statement of the AFL—as long as wage laborers were treated equitably in the wartime reorganization of the economy. A pragmatist, Gompers saw that workers were already benefiting from the improved economy as the supposedly neutral United States increasingly supplied war materials for the Allies. His public stance favoring "preparedness" before the war earned him an appointment as an advisor on the Council for National Defense in October 1916. Gompers thought the war would provide an opportunity for the AFL to expand its influence over the labor movement at the expense of the socialists, especially when the latter's antiwar position proved so unpopular. This strategy worked, as the AFL's membership greatly expanded over the course of the war. In this March 1917 statement, Gompers outlines the AFL's stance toward the likely entrance of the United States into the war in Europe.

SOURCE: Peter J. Albert and Grace Palladino, eds., *The Samuel Gompers Papers*, vol. 10: *The American Federation of Labor and the Great War, 1917–18* (Urbana: University of Illinois Press, 2007), 39–44.

. . . We speak for millions of Americans. We are not a sect. We are not a party. We represent the organizations held together by the pressure of our common needs. We represent the part of the nation closest to the fundamentals of life.

Those we represent wield the nation's tools and grapple with the forces that are brought under control in our material civilization. The power and use of industrial tools is greater than the tools of war and will in time supersede agencies of destruction.

A world war is on. The time has not yet come when war has been abolished.

Whether we approve it or not, we must recognize that war is a situation with which we must reckon. The present European war, involving as it does the majority of civilized nations and affecting the industry and commerce of the whole world, threatens at any moment to draw all countries, including our own, into the conflict. Our immediate problem, then, is to bring to bear upon war conditions instructive forethought, vision, principles of human welfare and conservation that should direct our course in every eventuality of life. The way to avert war is to establish constructive agencies for justice in times of peace and thus control for peace situations and forces that might otherwise result in war. The methods of modern warfare, its new tactics, its vast organization, both military and industrial, present problems vastly different from those of previous wars. But the nation's problems afford an opportunity for the establishment of new freedom and wider opportunities for all the people. Modern warfare includes contests between workshops, factories, the land, financial and transportation resources of the countries involved; and necessarily applies to the relations between employers and employes, and as our own country now faces an impending peril, it is fitting that the masses of the people of the United States should take counsel and determine what course they shall pursue should a crisis arise necessitating the protection of our Republic and defense of the ideals for which it stands.

In the struggle between the forces of democracy and special privilege, for just and historic reasons the masses of the people necessarily represent the ideals and the institutions of democracy. There is in organized society one potential organization whose purpose is to further these ideals and institutions—the organized labor movement.

In no previous war has the organized labor movement taken a directing part.

Labor has now reached an understanding of its rights, of its power and resources, of its value and contributions to society, and must make definite constructive proposals.

It is timely that we frankly present experiences and conditions which in former times have prevented nations from benefiting by the voluntary, wholehearted cooperation of wage-earners in war time, and then make suggestions how these hindrances to our national strength and vigor can be removed.

War has never put a stop to the necessity for struggle to establish and maintain industrial rights. Wage-earners in war times must, as has been said, keep one eye on the exploiters at home and the other upon the enemy threatening the national government. Such exploitation made it impossible for a warring nation to mobilize effectively its full strength for outward defense.

We maintain that it is the fundamental step in preparedness for the nation to set its own house in order and to establish at home justice in relations between men. Previous wars, for whatever purpose waged, developed new opportunities for exploiting wage-earners. Not only was there failure to recognize the necessity for protecting rights of workers that they might give that whole-hearted service to the country that can come only when every citizen enjoys rights, freedom and opportunity, but under guise of national necessity, Labor was stripped of its means of defense against enemies at home and was robbed of the advantages, the protections, the guarantees of justice that had been achieved after ages of struggle. For these reasons workers have felt that no matter what the result of war, as wage-earners they generally lost.

In previous times Labor had no representatives in the councils authorized to deal with the conduct of war. The rights, interests and welfare of workers were autocratically sacrificed for the slogan of "national safety."

The European war has demonstrated the dependence of the governments upon the cooperation of the masses of the people. Since the masses perform indispensable service, it follows that they should have a voice in determining the conditions upon which they give service.

The workers of America make known their beliefs, their demands and their purposes through a voluntary agency which they have established—the organized labor movement. This agency is not only the representative of those who directly constitute it, but it is the representative of all those persons who have common problems and purposes but who have not yet organized for their achievement.

Whether in peace or in war the organized labor movement seeks to make all else subordinate to human welfare and human opportunity. The labor movement stands as the defender of this principle and undertakes to protect the wealth-producers against the exorbitant greed of special interests, against profiteering, against exploitation, against the detestable methods of irresponsible greed, against the inhumanity and crime of heartless corporations and employers.

Labor demands the right in war times to be the recognized defender of wage-earners against the same forces which in former wars have made national necessity an excuse for more ruthless methods.

As the representatives of the wage-earners we assert that conditions of work and pay in government employment and in all occupations should conform to principles of human welfare and justice.

A nation can not make an effective defense against an outside danger if groups of citizens are asked to take part in a war though smarting with a sense of keen injustice inflicted by the government they are expected to and will defend.

The cornerstone of national defense is justice in fundamental relations of life—economic justice.

The one agency which accomplishes this for the workers is the organized labor movement. The greatest step that can be made for national defense is not to bind and throttle the organized labor movement but to afford its greatest scope and opportunity for voluntary effective cooperation in spirit and in action.

During the long period in which it has been establishing itself, the labor movement has become a dynamic force in organizing the human side of industry and commerce. It is a great social factor, which must be recognized in all plans which affect wage-earners.

Whether planning for peace or war the government must recognize the organized labor movement as the agency through which it must cooperate with wage-earners.

Industrial justice is the right of those living within our country. With this right there is associated obligation. In war time obligation takes the form of service in defense of the Republic against enemies.

We recognize that this service may be either military or industrial, both equally essential for national defense. We hold this to be incontrovertible that the government which demands that men and women give their labor power, their bodies or their lives to its service should also demand the service, in the interest of these human beings, of all wealth and the products of human toil—property.

We hold that if workers may be asked in time of national peril or emergency to give more exhausting service than the principles of human welfare warrant, that service should be asked only when accompanied by increased guarantees and safeguards, and when the profits which the employer shall secure from the industry in which they are engaged have been limited to fixed percentages.

We declare that such determination of profits should be based on cost of processes actually needed for product.

Workers have no delusions regarding the policy which property owners and exploiting employers pursue in peace or in war, and they also recognize that wrapped up with the safety of this Republic are ideals of democracy, a heritage which the masses of the people received from our forefathers, who fought that liberty might live in this country—a heritage that is to be maintained and handed down to each generation with undiminished power and usefulness.

The labor movement recognizes the value of freedom and it knows that freedom and rights can be maintained only by those willing to assert their claims and to defend their rights. The American labor movement has always opposed unnecessary conflicts and all wars for aggrandizement, exploitation and enslavement, and yet it has done its part in the world's revolutions, in the struggles to establish greater freedom, democratic institutions and ideals of human justice.

Our labor movement distrusts and protests against militarism, because it knows that militarism represents privilege and is the tool of special interests, exploiters and despots. But while it opposes militarism, it holds that it is the duty of a nation to defend itself against injustice and invasion.

The menace of militarism arises through isolating the defensive functions of the state from civic activities and from creating military agencies out of touch with masses of the people. Isolation is subversive to democracy—it harbors and nurtures the germs of arbitrary power.

The labor movement demands that a clear differentiation be made against military service for the nation and police duty, and that military service should be carefully distinguished from service in industrial disputes.

We hold that industrial service shall be deemed equally meritorious as military service. Organization for industrial and commercial service is upon a different basis from military service—the civic ideals still dominate. This should be recognized in mobilizing for this purpose. The same voluntary institutions that organized industrial, commercial and transportation workers in times of peace will best take care of the same problems in time of war.

It is fundamental, therefore, that the government cooperate with the American organized labor movement for this purpose. Service in government factories and private establishments, in transportation agencies, all should conform to trade union standards.

The guarantees of human conservation should be recognized in war as well as in peace. Wherever changes in the organization of industry are necessary upon a war basis, they should be made in accord with plans agreed upon by representatives of the government and those engaged and employed in the industry. We recognize that in war, in certain employments requiring high skill, it is necessary to retain in industrial service the workers specially fitted therefor. In any eventuality when women may be employed, we insist that equal pay for equal work shall prevail without regard to sex.

Finally, in order to safeguard all the interests of the wage-earners organized labor should have representation on all agencies determining and administering policies for national defense. It is particularly important that organized labor should have representatives on all boards authorized to control publicity during war times. The workers have suffered much injustice in war times by limitations upon their right to speak freely and to secure publicity for their just grievances.

Organized labor has earned the right to make these demands. It is the agency that, in all countries, stands for human rights and is the defender of the welfare and interests of the masses of the people. It is an agency that has international recognition which is not seeking to rob, exploit or corrupt foreign governments but instead seeks to maintain human rights and interests the world over, nor does it have to dispel suspicion nor prove its motives either at home or abroad.

The present war discloses the struggle between the institutions of democracy and those of autocracy. As a nation we should profit from the experiences of other nations. Democracy can not be established by patches upon an autocratic system. The foundations of civilized intercourse between individuals must be organized upon principles of democracy and scientific principles of human welfare. Then a national structure can be perfected in harmony with humanitarian idealism—a structure that will stand the tests of the necessities of peace or war.

We, the officers of the National and International Trade Unions of America in national conference assembled in the capital of our nation, hereby pledge ourselves in peace or in war, in stress or in storm, to stand unreservedly by the standards of liberty and the safety and preservation of the institutions and ideals of our Republic.

In this solemn hour of our nation's life, it is our earnest hope that our Republic may be safeguarded in its unswerving desire for peace; that our people may be spared the horrors and the burdens of war; that they may have the opportunity to cultivate and develop the arts of peace, human brotherhood and a higher civilization.

But, despite all our endeavors and hopes, should our country be drawn into the maelstrom of the European conflict, we, with these ideals of liberty and justice herein declared, as the indispensable basis for national policies, offer our services to our country in every field of activity to defend, safeguard and preserve the Republic of the United States of America against its enemies whomsoever they may be, and we call upon our fellow workers and fellow citizens in the holy name of Labor, Justice, Freedom and Humanity to devotedly and patriotically give like service.

19. Woodrow Wilson, "Speech to Congress Recommending a Declaration of War"

(1917)

In the summer of 1915, President Woodrow Wilson still stood against a military buildup that many interventionists advocated, but he began to change his stance later in that year. He viewed German submarine warfare as morally outrageous, and demanded that it be restrained after the sinking of the British passenger ship *Lusitania,* which killed 128 Americans in May 1915. The German imperial government did comply for a while. But by early 1916, the United States began arming merchant ships to protect themselves against submarines, and the German Navy announced that it would sink these armed vessels without warning. Despite his increasing receptivity to war preparation, Wilson positioned himself as less likely to lead the country into war than the Republican candidate, Charles Evans Hughes, during the 1916 presidential election, embracing the slogan "He kept us out of war." When the German military command decided to pursue unrestricted submarine warfare in January 1917 to try to break the military stalemate, it provided Wilson with the moral weight he needed to push the United States into the conflict. In March, three American ships were attacked by German U-boats. Additionally, the first phase of the Russian Revolution took place that month, overthrowing the tsarist autocracy in favor of a republic. For Wilson, the downfall of the tsarist government removed a significant obstacle; he had been reluctant to enter the war to fight alongside such a backward and tyrannical regime.

The following excerpts are from a speech Wilson delivered before a joint session of Congress on April 2, 1917, advising a declaration of war. For Wilson, the barbarity of submarine warfare was a challenge not just to the United States, but "to all mankind." A formal declaration of war was approved by Congress on April 6 (see document 20).

SOURCE: Sixty-fifth Congress, 1st session, Senate Document No. 5.

I have called the Congress into extraordinary session because there are serious, very serious, choices of policy to be made, and made immediately, which it was neither right nor constitutionally permissible that I should assume the responsibility of making.

On the third of February last I officially laid before you the extraordinary announcement of the Imperial German Government that on and after the first day of February it was its purpose to put aside all restraints of law or of humanity and use its submarines to sink every vessel that sought to approach either the ports of Great Britain and Ireland or the western coasts of Europe or any of the ports controlled by the enemies of Germany within the Mediterranean.

That had seemed to be the object of the German submarine warfare earlier in the war, but since April of last year the Imperial Government had somewhat restrained the commanders of its undersea craft in conformity with its promise then given to us that passenger boats should not be sunk and that due warning would be given to all other vessels which its submarines might seek to destroy, when no resistance was offered or escape attempted, and care taken that their crews were given at least a fair chance to save their lives in their open boats.

The precautions taken were meagre and haphazard enough, as was proved in distressing instance after instance in the progress of the cruel and unmanly business, but a certain degree of restraint was observed. The new policy has swept every restriction aside. Vessels of every kind, whatever their flag, their character, their cargo, their destination, their errand, have been ruthlessly sent to the bottom without warning and without thought of help or mercy for those on board, the vessels of friendly neutrals along with those of belligerents.

Even hospital ships and ships carrying relief to the sorely bereaved and stricken people of Belgium, though the latter were provided with safe conduct through the proscribed areas by the German Government itself and were distinguished by unmistakable marks of identity, have been sunk with the same reckless lack of compassion or of principle.

I was for a little while unable to believe that such things would in fact be done by any government that had hitherto subscribed to the humane practices of civilized nations. International law had its origin in the attempt to set up some law which would be respected and observed upon the seas, where no nation had right of dominion and where lay the free highways of the world.

This minimum of right the German Government has swept aside under the plea of retaliation and necessity and because it had no weapons which it could use at sea except these which it is impossible to employ as it is employing them without throwing to the winds all scruples of humanity or of respect for the understandings that were supposed to underlie the intercourse of the world.

I am not now thinking of the loss of property involved, immense and serious as that is, but only of the wanton and wholesale destruction of the lives of noncombatants, men, women, and children, engaged in pursuits which have always, even in the darkest periods of modern history, been deemed innocent and legitimate. Property can be paid for; the lives of peaceful and innocent people cannot be. The present German submarine warfare against commerce is a warfare against mankind.

It is a war against all nations. American ships have been sunk, American lives taken, in ways which it has stirred us very deeply to learn of, but the ships and people of other neutral and friendly nations have been sunk and overwhelmed in the waters in the same way. There has been no discrimination.

The challenge is to all mankind. Each nation must decide for itself how it will meet it. The choice we make for ourselves must be made with a moderation of counsel and a temperateness for judgment befitting our character and our motives as a nation. We must put excited feeling away. Our motive will not be revenge or the victorious assertion of the physical might of the nation, but only the vindication of right, of human right, of which we are only a single champion.

When I addressed the Congress on the twenty-sixth of February last I thought that it would suffice to assert our neutral rights with arms, our right to use the seas against unlawful interference, our right to keep our people safe against unlawful violence.

But armed neutrality, it now appears, is impracticable. Because submarines are in effect outlaws when used as the German submarines have been used against merchant shipping, it is impossible to defend ships against their attacks as the law of nations has assumed that merchantmen would defend themselves against privateers or cruisers, visible craft giving chase upon the open sea. It is common prudence in such circumstances, grim necessity indeed, to endeavour to destroy them before they have shown their own intention.

They must be dealt with upon sight, if dealt with at all. The German Government denies the right of neutrals to use arms at all within the areas of the sea which it has proscribed, even in the defence of rights which no modern publicist has ever before questioned their right to defend.

The intimation is conveyed that the armed guards which we have placed on our merchant ships will be treated as beyond the pale of law and subject to be dealt with as pirates would be. Armed neutrality is ineffectual enough at best; in such circumstances and in the face of such pretensions it is worse than ineffectual: it is likely only to produce what it was meant to prevent; it is practically certain to draw us into the war without either the rights or the effectiveness of belligerents.

There is one choice we cannot make, we are incapable of making: we will not choose the path of submission and suffer the most sacred rights of our Nation and our people to be ignored or violated. The wrongs against which we now array ourselves are no common wrongs; they cut to the very roots of human life.

With a profound sense of the solemn and even tragical character of the step I am taking and of the grave responsibilities which it involves, but in unhesitating obedience to what I deem my constitutional duty, I advise that the Congress declare the recent course of the Imperial German Government to be in fact nothing less than war against the government and people of the United States; that it formally accept the status of belligerent which has thus been thrust upon it; and that it take immediate steps not only to put the country in a more thorough state of defence but also to exert all its power and employ all its resources to bring the Government of the German Empire to terms and end the war. . . .

Neutrality is no longer feasible or desirable where the peace of the world is involved and the freedom of its people, and the menace to that peace and freedom lies in the existence of autocratic governments backed by organized force which is controlled wholly by their will, not by the will of their people.

We have seen the last of neutrality in such circumstances. We are at the beginning of an age in which it will be insisted that the same standards of conduct and of responsibility for wrong done shall be observed among nations and their governments that are observed among the individual citizens of civilized states.

We have no quarrel with the German people. We have no feeling towards them but one of sympathy and friendship. It was not upon their impulse that their government acted in entering this war. It was not with their previous knowledge or approval.

It was a war determined upon as wars used to be determined upon in the old, unhappy days when peoples were nowhere consulted by their rules and wars were provoked and waged in the interest of dynasties or of little groups of ambitious men who were accustomed to use their fellow men as pawns and tools.

We are accepting this challenge of hostile purpose because we know that in such a Government, following such methods, we can never have a friend; and that in the presence of its organized power, always lying in wait to accomplish we know not what purpose, there can be no assured security for the democratic Governments of the world.

We are now about to accept gauge of battle with this natural foe to liberty and shall, if necessary, spend the whole force of the nation to check and nullify its pretensions and its power. We are glad, now that we see the facts with no veil of false pretense about them, to fight thus for the ultimate peace of the world and for the liberation of its peoples, the German peoples included: for the rights of nations great and small and the privilege of men everywhere to choose their way of life and of obedience.

The world must be made safe for democracy. Its peace must be planted upon the tested foundations of political liberty. We have no selfish ends to serve. We desire no conquest, no dominion. We seek no indemnities for ourselves, no material compensation for the sacrifices we shall freely make. We are but one of the champions of the rights of mankind. We shall be satisfied when those rights have been made as secure as the faith and the freedom of nations can make them.

Just because we fight without rancour and without selfish object, seeking nothing for ourselves but what we shall wish to share with all free peoples, we shall, I feel confident, conduct our operations as belligerents without passion and ourselves observe with proud punctilio the principles of right and of fair play we profess to be fighting for. . . .

20. "Formal U.S. Declaration of War with Germany"

(1917)

Four days after Woodrow Wilson made his speech recommending war with Germany (see document 19), Congress passed a formal declaration of war. The vote approving it was 82–6 in the Senate and 373–50 in the House. A spike in enlistments ensued in the weeks that followed, yet the number of volunteers was nowhere near enough to prevent President Wilson from instituting conscription.

SOURCE: Charles F. Horne, ed., *Source Records of the Great War,* vol. 5 (New York: National Alumni, 1923).

Joint Resolution Declaring That a State of War Exists Between the Imperial German Government and the Government and the People of the United States and Making Provision to Prosecute the Same.

Whereas the Imperial German Government has committed repeated acts of war against the Government and the people of the United States of America; Therefore be it Resolved by the Senate and the House of Representatives of the United States of America in Congress Assembled, that the state of war between the United States and the Imperial German Government which has thus been thrust upon the United States is hereby formally declared; and that the President be, and he is hereby, authorized and directed to employ the entire naval and military forces of the United States and the resources of the Government to carry on war against the Imperial German Government; and to bring the conflict to a successful termination all of the resources of the country are hereby pledged by the Congress of the United States.

CHAMP CLARK
Speaker of the House of Representatives

THOS. R. MARSHALL
Vice President of the United States and President of the Senate
Approved, April 6, 1917

21. "War Proclamation and Program Adopted at National Convention, Socialist Party"

(1917)

The Socialist Party of America (SPA) reached the height of its strength between 1910 and 1912. At this time, many socialist candidates were elected to positions in municipal governments and state legislatures. The party found recent Jewish, German, and Scandinavian immigrants especially receptive to its message. In the 1912 presidential election, voters cast almost a million ballots for the party's candidate, Eugene V. Debs (1855–1926), giving him roughly 6 percent of the popular vote. A founder and leader of the American Railroad Union (ARU), Debs became a socialist while jailed for the ARU's role in the Pullman strike in 1894. Charges that the union had interfered with the delivery of the mail led to Debs's imprisonment. Debs ran for president as the candidate of the Social Democratic Party in 1900. In 1901, this party merged with the wing of another socialist party to form the Socialist Party of America; Debs would run as its presidential candidate in 1904, 1908, and 1912. After 1912, internal disputes contributed to a decline in the party's membership. At the heart of the dissension was the right wing's desire to focus on electoral strategies for gaining more power, while the left wing demanded more direct revolutionary action.

Despite its waning influence, the SPA still provided an influential antiwar voice. When war broke out in Europe, it argued forcefully for the United States to stay out of what it deemed a capitalist and imperialist conflict. As American entry into the war seemed imminent in early 1917, the party's leadership planned an emergency convention to clarify its position in case the United States did intervene. A total of 193 SPA delegates from across the nation assembled in St. Louis on April 7, one day after the formal declaration of war. Several party leaders worried that the convention would not condemn the war strongly enough, but their fears were soon abated. The staunch antiwar document excerpted here was approved by a substantial majority. Yet the party's highly critical stance did not prove popular, alienating a significant portion of the rank and file and exacerbating the decline in membership. In several locations, mobs vandalized Socialist Party headquarters after this proclamation was released.

SOURCE: New York Senate, Joint Legislative Committee Investigating Seditious Activities, Part I: "Revolutionary and Subversive Movements Abroad and at Home," *Revolutionary Radicalism*, vol. 1 (Albany, N.Y., 1920), 613–18.

. . . The 6,000,000 men of all countries and races who have been ruthlessly slain in the first thirty months of this war, the millions of others who have been crippled and maimed, the vast treasures of wealth that have been destroyed, the untold misery and sufferings of Europe, have not been sacrifices exacted in a struggle for principles or ideals, but wanton offerings upon the altar of private profit.

The forces of capitalism which have led to the war in Europe are even more hideously transparent in the war recently provoked by the ruling class of this country.

When Belgium was invaded, the government enjoined upon the people of this country the duty of remaining neutral, thus clearly demonstrating that the "dictates of humanity," and the fate of small nations and of democratic institutions were matters that did not concern it. But when our enormous war traffic was seriously threatened, our government calls upon us to rally to the "defense of democracy and civilization."

Our entrance into the European War was instigated by the predatory capitalists in the United States who boast of the enormous profit of $7,000,000,000 from the manufacture and sale of munitions and war supplies and from the exportation of American food stuffs and other necessaries. They are also deeply interested in the continuance of war and the success of the Allied arms through their huge loans to the governments of the Allied powers and through other commercial ties. It is the same interests which strive for imperialistic domination of the Western Hemisphere.

The war of the United States against Germany cannot be justified even on the plea that it is a war in defense of American rights or American "honor." Ruthless as the unrestricted submarine war policy of the German government was and is, it is not an invasion of the rights of the American people, as such, but only an interference with the opportunity of certain groups of American capitalists to coin cold profits out of the blood and sufferings of our fellow men in the warring countries of Europe.

It is not a war against the militarist regime of the Central Powers. Militarism can never be abolished by militarism.

It is not a war to advance the cause of democracy in Europe. Democracy can never be imposed upon any country by a foreign power by force of arms.

It is cant and hypocrisy to say that the war is not directed against the German people, but against the Imperial Government of Germany. If we send an armed force to the battlefields of Europe, its cannon will mow down the masses of the German people and not the Imperial German Government.

Our entrance into the European conflict at this time will serve only to multiply the horrors of the war, to increase the toll of death and destruction and to prolong the fiendish slaughter. It will bring death, suffering and destitution to the people of the United States and particularly to the working class. It will give the powers of reaction in this country the pretext for an attempt to throttle our rights and to crush our democratic institutions, and to fasten upon this country a permanent militarism.

The working class of the United States has no quarrel with the working class of Germany or of any other country. The people of the United States have no quarrel with the people of Germany or any other country. The American people did not want and do not want this war. They have not been consulted about the war and have had no part in declaring war. They have been plunged into this war by the trickery and treachery of the ruling class of the country through its representatives in the National Administration and National Congress, its demagogic agitators, its subsidized press, and other servile instruments of public expression.

We brand the declaration of war by our government as a crime against the people of the United States and against the nations of the world.

In all modern history there has been no war more unjustifiable than the war in which we are about to engage.

No greater dishonor has ever been forced upon a people than that which the capitalist class is forcing upon this nation against its will.

In harmony with these principles, the Socialist Party emphatically rejects the proposal that in time of war the workers should suspend their struggle for better conditions. On the contrary, the acute situation created by war calls for an even more vigorous prosecution of the class struggle, and we recommend to the workers and pledge ourselves to the following course of action:

1. Continuous, active, and public opposition to the war through demonstrations, mass petitions, and all other means within our power.
2. Unyielding opposition to all proposed legislation for military or industrial conscription. Should such conscription be forced upon the people we pledge ourselves to continuous efforts for the repeal of such laws and to the support of all mass movements in opposition to conscription. We pledge ourselves to oppose with all our strength any attempt to raise money for payment of war expense by taxing the necessaries of life or issuing bonds which will put the burden upon future generations. We demand that the capitalist class, which is responsible for the war, pay its cost. Let those who kindled the fire, furnish the fuel.
3. Vigorous resistance to all reactionary measures, such as censorship of press and mails, restriction of the rights of free speech, assemblage, and organization, or compulsory arbitration and limitation of the right to strike.
4. Consistent propaganda against military training and militaristic teaching in the public schools.
5. Extension of the campaign of education among the workers to organize them into strong, class-conscious, and closely unified political and industrial organizations, to enable them by concerted and harmonious mass action to shorten this war and to establish lasting peace.
6. Widespread educational propaganda to enlighten the masses as to the true

relation between capitalism and war, and to rouse and organize them for action, not only against present war evils, but for the prevention of future wars and for the destruction of the causes of war.

7. To protect the masses of the American people from the pressing danger of starvation which the war in Europe has brought upon them, and which the entry of the United States has already accentuated, we demand—

   (a) The restriction of food exports so long as the present shortage continues, the fixing of maximum prices and whatever measures may be necessary to prevent the food speculators from holding back the supplies now in their hands;

   (b) The socialization and democratic management of the great industries concerned with the production, transportation, storage, and the marketing of food and other necessaries of life;

   (c) The socialization and democratic management of all land and other natural resources now held out of use for monopolistic or speculative profit.

These measures are presented as means of protecting the workers against the evil results of the present war. The danger of recurrence of war will exist as long as the capitalist system of industry remains in existence. The end of wars will come with the establishment of socialized industry and industrial democracy the world over. The Socialist Party calls upon all the workers to join it in its struggle to reach this goal, and thus bring into the world a new society in which peace, fraternity, and human brotherhood will be the dominant ideals.

22. Woodrow Wilson, "Proclamation Establishing Conscription"

(1917)

While the Regular Army had increased from approximately 28,000 at the start of the war with Spain to 110,000 in April 1917, it was apparent from the stunning casualty figures in Europe thus far that a much larger American force was needed to push the balance decisively in favor of the Allies. In the weeks immediately following Wilson's declaration of war, only 32,000 men volunteered, a far from adequate number in the view of strategists. Politicians had discussed a draft before the war, but the idea met with overwhelming opposition in Congress. Many politicians feared the outbreak of civil disturbances if conscription were imposed, as was the case with the 1863 Draft Riots in New York City during the Civil War. Progressive Democrats argued that a draft was antidemocratic, while socialists condemned it as capitalist oppression. But significant opposition to conscription in Congress quickly disintegrated after the declaration of war in April; what became known as the Selective Service Act was passed on May 18, 1917.

The following document is President Wilson's official public proclamation announcing conscription on May 28. The legislation had been drafted by Brigadier General Hugh Johnson; it required all males between the ages of twenty-one and thirty to register at local polling stations for potential military service. It created a bureaucracy, the Selective Service System, to administer this process. The legislation also prohibited individuals from hiring a replacement if drafted. This practice, allowed in the Civil War draft, generated class antagonisms that were a contributing factor in the 1863 riots. In 1917, registration went off uneventfully, although not flawlessly. Almost 24 million men registered, while between 2 million and 3 million never did. Twelve percent of those drafted (338,000) failed to report when they were called for training or quickly deserted soon thereafter. Those who refused to fight because their religion forbade it could apply for noncombatant positions, but those who were pacifists on nonreligious grounds were not given this option. Several hundred people ultimately were imprisoned for refusing to fight.

SOURCE: Charles F. Horne, ed., *Source Records of the Great War*, vol. 5 (New York: National Alumni, 1923).

Whereas, Congress has enacted and the President has on the 18th day of May, one thousand nine hundred and seventeen, approved a law, which contains the following provisions:

Section 5

That all male persons between the ages of 21 and 30, both inclusive, shall be subject to registration in accordance with regulations to be prescribed by the President:

And upon proclamation by the President or other public notice given by him or by his direction stating the time and place of such registration it shall be the duty of all persons of the designated ages, except officers and enlisted men of the regular army, the navy, and the National Guard and Naval Militia while in the service of the United States, to present themselves for and submit to registration under the provisions of this act:

And every such person shall be deemed to have notice of the requirements of this act upon the publication of said proclamation or other notice as aforesaid, given by the President or by his direction:

And any person who shall wilfully fail or refuse to present himself for registration or to submit thereto as herein provided shall be guilty of a misdemeanour and shall, upon conviction in the District Court of the United States having jurisdiction thereof, be punished by imprisonment for not more than one year, and shall thereupon be duly registered; provided that in the call of the docket precedence shall be given, in courts trying the same, to the trial of criminal proceedings under this act; provided, further, that persons shall be subject to registration as herein provided who shall have attained their twenty-first birthday and who shall not have attained their thirty-first birthday on or before the day set or the registration; and all persons so registered shall be and remain subject to draft into the forces hereby authorized unless excepted or excused therefrom as in this act provided; provided, further, that in the case of temporary absence from actual place of legal residence of any person liable to registration as provided herein, such registration may be made by mail under regulations to be prescribed by the President.

Section 6

That the President is hereby authorized to utilize the service of any or all departments and any or all officers or agents of the United States and of the several States, Territories, and the District of Columbia and subdivisions thereof in the execution of this act, and all officers and agents of the United States and of the several States, Territories, and subdivisions thereof, and of the District of Columbia; and all persons designated or appointed under regulations prescribed by the President, whether such appointments are made by the President himself or by the Governor or other officer of any State or Territory to perform any duty in the execution of this act, are hereby required to perform such duty as the President shall order or direct, and all such officers and agents and persons so designated or appointed shall hereby have full authority for all acts done by them in the execution of this act by the direction of the President.

Correspondence in the execution of this act may be carried in penalty envelopes, bearing the frank of the War Department.

Any person charged, as herein provided, with the duty of carrying into effect any of the provisions of this act or the regulations made or directions given thereunder who shall fail or neglect to perform such duty, and any person charged with such duty or having and exercising any authority under said act, regulations, or directions, who shall knowingly make or be a party to the making of any false or incorrect registration, physical examination, exemption, enlistment, enrolment, or muster, and any person who shall make or be a party to the making of any false statement or certificate as to the fitness or liability of himself or any other person for service under the provisions of this act, or regulations made by the President thereunder, or otherwise evades or aids another to evade the requirements of this act or of said regulations, or who, in any manner, shall fail or neglect fully to perform any duty required of him in the execution of this act, shall, if not subject to military law, be guilty of a misdemeanour, and upon conviction in the District Court of the United States having jurisdiction thereof be punished by imprisonment for not more than one year, or, if subject to military law, shall be tried by court-martial and suffer such punishment as a court-martial may direct.

Now, Therefore, I, Woodrow Wilson, President of the United States, do call upon the Governor of each of the several States and Territories, the Board of Commissioners of the District of Columbia, and all officers and agents of the several States and Territories, of the District of Columbia, and of the counties and municipalities therein, to perform certain duties in the execution of the foregoing law, which duties will be communicated to them directly in regulations of even date herewith.

And I do further proclaim and give notice to all persons subject to registration in the several States and in the District of Columbia, in accordance with the above law, that the time and place of such registration shall be between 7 a.m. and 7 p.m. on the fifth day of June, 1917, at the registration place in the precinct wherein they have their permanent homes.

Those who shall have attained their twenty-first birthday and who shall not have attained their thirty-first birthday on or before the day here named are required to register, excepting only officers and enlisted men of the regular army, the navy, the Marine Corps, and the National Guard and Navy Militia, while in the service of the United States, and officers in the Officers' Reserve Corps and enlisted men in the Enlisted Reserve Corps while in active service.

In the Territories of Alaska, Hawaii, and Porto Rico a day for registration will be named in a later proclamation.

And I do charge those who through sickness shall be unable to present themselves for registration that they apply on or before the day of registration to the County Clerk of the county where they may be for instructions as to how they may be registered by agent.

Those who expect to be absent on the day named from the counties in which they have their permanent homes may register by mail, but their mailed registration cards must reach the places in which they have their permanent homes by the day named herein. They should apply as soon as practicable to the County Clerk of the county wherein they may be for instructions as to how they may accomplish their registration by mail.

In case such persons as, through sickness or absence, may be unable to present themselves personally for registration shall be sojourning in cities of over 30,000 population, they shall apply to the City Clerk of the city wherein they may be sojourning rather than to the Clerk of the county. The Clerks of counties and of cities of over 30,000 population in which numerous applications from the sick and from non-residents are expected are authorized to establish such agencies and to employ and deputize such clerical force as may be necessary to accommodate these applications.

The power against which we are arrayed has sought to impose its will upon the world by force. To this end it has increased armament until it has changed the face of war. In the sense in which we have been wont to think of armies, there are no armies in this struggle, there are entire nations armed.

Thus, the men who remain to till the soil and man the factories are no less a part of the army that is in France than the men beneath the battle flags. It must be so with us. It is not an army that we must shape and train for war; it is a nation.

To this end our people must draw close in one compact front against a common foe. But this cannot be if each man pursues a private purpose. All must pursue one purpose.

The nation needs all men; but it needs each man not in the field that will most pleasure him, but in the endeavour that will best serve the common good. Thus, though a sharpshooter pleases to operate a trip-hammer for the forging of great guns and an expert machinist desires to march with the flag, the nation is being served only when the sharpshooter marches and the machinist remains at his levers.

The whole nation must be a team, in which each man shall play the part for which he is best fitted. To this end, Congress has provided that the nation shall be organized for war by selection; that each man shall be classified for service in the place to which it shall best serve the general good to call him.

The significance of this cannot be overstated. It is a new thing in our history and a landmark in our progress. It is a new manner of accepting and vitalizing our duty to give ourselves with thoughtful devotion to the common purpose of us all.

It is in no sense a conscription of the unwilling; it is, rather, selection from a nation which has volunteered in mass. It is no more a choosing of those who shall march with the colours than it is a selection of those who shall serve an equally necessary and devoted purpose in the industries that lie behind the battle line.

The day here named is the time upon which all shall present themselves for assignment to their tasks. It is for that reason destined to be remembered as one of the most conspicuous moments in our history. It is nothing less than the day upon which the manhood of the country shall step forward in one solid rank in defence of the ideals to which this nation is consecrated.

It is important to those ideals no less than to the pride of this generation in manifesting its devotion to them, that there be no gaps in the ranks.

It is essential that the day be approached in thoughtful apprehension of its significance, and that we accord to it the honour and the meaning that it deserves. Our industrial need prescribes that it be not made a technical holiday, but the stern sacrifice that is before us urges that it be carried in all our hearts as a great day of patriotic devotion and obligation, when the duty shall lie upon every man, whether he is himself to be registered or not, to see to it that the name of every male person of the designated ages is written on these lists of honour.

In witness whereof, I have hereunto set my hand and caused the seal of the United States to be affixed.

Done at the City of Washington this 28th day of May in the year of our Lord one thousand nine hundred and seventeen, and of the Independence of the United States of America the one hundred and forty-first.

By the President

23. Emma Goldman, "No-Conscription League Manifesto"

(1917)

Emma Goldman's monthly journal, *Mother Earth,* was banned by the federal government for its antiwar stance in 1917. But Goldman was not intimidated, and refused to cease her antiwar activities. In May of that year, Goldman and her partner, Alexander Berkman, created the No-Conscription League in response to the passage of the Selective Service Act. On June 4, they launched their campaign to discourage compliance with the legislation's requirement that all men between twenty-one and thirty years of age register for the draft, and also sought to educate people about applying for conscientious objector status. On June 15, in a warrantless raid on their Manhattan offices, Goldman and Berkman were arrested on charges of interfering with the draft. During the subsequent trial, Goldman invoked her First Amendment rights and pointed to the irony of the government suppressing free speech at home while supposedly fighting for democracy in Europe. Both were eventually convicted and sentenced to two years of imprisonment with the possibility of deportation after the terms were served. On February 6, 1918, following an unsuccessful appeal, Goldman began serving her term at the Missouri State Penitentiary.

SOURCE: Records of the Department of War and Military Intelligence Division, Record Group 165, National Archives, Washington D.C.

No Conscription!

CONSCRIPTION has now become a fact in this country. It took England fully 18 months after she engaged in the war to impose compulsory military service on her people. It was left for "free" America to pass a conscription bill six weeks after she declared war against Germany.

What becomes of the patriotic boast of America to have entered the European

76

war in behalf of the principle of democracy? But that is not all. Every country in Europe has recognized the right of conscientious objectors of men who refuse to engage in war on the ground that they are opposed to taking life. Yet this democratic country makes no such provision for those who will not commit murder at the behest of the war profiteers. Thus the "land of the free and the home of the brave" is ready to coerce free men into the military yoke.

No one to whom the fundamental principle of liberty and justice is more than an idle phrase, can help realize that the patriotic claptrap now shouted by press, pulpit and the authorities, betrays a desperate effort of the ruling class in this country to throw sand in the eyes of the masses and to blind them to the real issue confronting them. That issue is the Prussianizing of America so as to destroy whatever few liberties the people have achieved through an incessant struggle of many years.

Already all labor protective laws have been abrogated, which means that while husbands, fathers and sons are butchered on the battlefield, the women and children will be exploited in our industrial bastiles to the heart's content of the American patriots for gain and power.

Freedom of speech, of press and assembly is about to be thrown upon the dungheap of political guarantees. But crime of all crimes, the flower of the country is to be forced into murder whether or not they believe in war or in the efficacy of saving democracy in Europe by the destruction of democracy at home.

Liberty of conscience is the most fundamental of all human rights, the pivot of all progress. No man may be deprived of it without losing every vestige of freedom of thought and action. In these days when every principle and conception of democracy and individual liberty is being cast overboard under the pretext of democratizing Germany, it behooves every liberty-loving man and woman to insist on his or her right of individual choice in the ordering of his life and actions.

The NO-CONSCRIPTION LEAGUE has been formed for the purpose of encouraging conscientious objectors to affirm their liberty of conscience and to make their objection to human slaughter effective by refusing to participate in the killing of their fellow men. The NO-CONSCRIPTION LEAGUE is to be the voice of protest against the coercion of conscientious objectors to participate in the war. Our platform may be summarized as follows:

We oppose conscription because we are internationalists, antimilitarists, and opposed to all wars waged by capitalistic governments.

We will fight for what we choose to fight for; we will never fight simply because we are ordered to fight.

We believe that the militarization of America is an evil that far outweighs, in its antisocial and anti-libertarian effects, any good that may come from America's participation in the war.

We will resist conscription by every means in our power, and we will sustain those who, for similar reasons, refuse to be conscripted.

We are not unmindful of the difficulties in our way. But we have resolved to go ahead and spare no effort to make the voice of protest a moral force in the life of this country. The initial efforts of the conscientious objectors in England were fraught with many hardships and danger, but finally the government of Great Britain was forced to give heed to the steadily increasing volume of public protest against the coercion of conscientious objectors. So we, too, in America, will doubtless meet the full severity of the government and the condemnation of the war-mad jingoes, but we are nevertheless determined to go ahead. We feel confident in arousing thousands of people who are conscientious objectors to the murder of their fellowmen and to whom a principle represents the most vital thing in life.

Resist conscription. Organize meetings. Join our League. Send us money. Help us to give assistance to those who come in conflict with the government. Help us to publish literature against militarism and against conscription.

NO-CONSCRIPTION LEAGUE
20 East 125th St., New York.

24. Roger Nash Baldwin, "Statement of Conscientious Objection"

(1917)

An exemplary product of the Progressive Era, Roger Nash Baldwin (1884–1984) was a Harvard-trained sociologist and social worker who came to national prominence while teaching at Washington University and working with juvenile delinquents in St. Louis. Baldwin found himself in New York during the lead-up to the U.S. entry into the war, and as a dedicated pacifist, he became involved with the founding of the American Union Against Militarism (AUAM). To protect the rights of conscientious objectors and other war dissidents, the AUAM set up the Civil Liberties Bureau (CLB) in July 1917 under Baldwin's direction. The CLB broke away from the AUAM in October, renaming itself the National Civil Liberties Bureau. It was this organization that changed its name to the American Civil Liberties Union (ACLU) in 1920, with Baldwin serving as its first executive director. Standing by his beliefs, Baldwin refused to register for the 1917 draft, and submitted the following "Statement of Conscientious Objection" to explain his reasons for disobeying the law. His defiance resulted in a celebrated trial; ultimately Baldwin was convicted of evading the draft and spent one year in prison.

SOURCE: Norman Thomas, *The Conscientious Objector in America* (New York: B.W. Heubsch, 1923), 23–28.

The compelling motive for refusing to comply with the draft act is my uncompromising opposition to the principle of conscription of life by the state for any purpose whatever, in time of war or peace. I not only refuse to obey the present conscription law, but I would in future refuse to obey any similar statute which attempts to direct my choice of service and ideals. I regard the principle of conscription of life as a flat contradiction of all our cherished ideals of individual freedom, democratic liberty, and Christian teaching.

I am the more opposed to the present act, because it is for the purpose of conducting war. I am opposed to this and all other wars. I do not believe in the use of physical force as a method of achieving any end, however good. . . .

I am not complaining for myself or others. I am merely advising the court that I understand full well the penalty of my heresy, and am prepared to pay it. The conflict with conscription is irreconcilable. Even the liberalism of the President and Secretary of War in dealing with objectors leads those of us who are "absolutists" to a punishment longer and severer than that of desperate criminals.

But I believe most of us are prepared even to die for our faith, just as our brothers in France are dying for theirs. To them we are comrades in spirit—we understand one another's motives, though our methods are wide apart. We both share deeply the common experience of living up to the truth as we see it, whatever the price.

Though at the moment I am of a tiny minority, I feel myself just one protest in a great revolt surging up from among the people—the struggle of the masses against the rule of the world by the few—profoundly intensified by the war. It is a struggle against the political state itself, against exploitation, militarism, imperialism, authority in all forms. . . .

Having arrived at the state of mind in which those views mean the dearest things in life to me, I cannot consistently, with self-respect, do other than I have, namely, to deliberately violate an act which seems to me to be a denial of everything which ideally and in practice I hold sacred.

25. Jane Addams, "Personal Reactions during War"

(1917)

Social reformer and feminist Jane Addams (1860–1935) is perhaps best known as a founder of Hull-House, one of the first settlement houses in the United States, in Chicago in 1889. This institution offered night classes for adults, an art gallery, kindergarten classes, and many other amenities for the slum dwellers who lived around it. For her efforts in using "applied sociology" to address chronic urban poverty, Addams became an internationally respected figure with access to top politicians (including President Wilson) and a close connection to the esteemed Department of Sociology at the University of Chicago. However, as the following memoir passage makes clear, Addams felt that mainstream American society increasingly marginalized her over the course of the war because of her work in the women's peace movement. Addams helped found the Women's Peace Party in January 1915, and then traveled to the International Women's Congress for Peace and Freedom held at The Hague from April 28 to 30 that same year. Upon her return, a remark Addams made was misconstrued by some as belittling the manhood of soldiers fighting in Europe, thereby causing a firestorm in the American press. Addams writes candidly here about the alienation she began to feel as a result of this incident. Her work in the women's peace movement was later widely recognized when she was awarded the Nobel Peace Prize in 1931, becoming the first American woman to attain this honor.

SOURCE: Jane Addams, *Peace and Bread in Time of War* (Boston: G.K. Hall, 1960), 132–51.

. . . My temperament and habit had always kept me rather in the middle of the road; in politics as well as in social reform I had been for "the best possible." But now I was pushed far toward the left on the subject of the war and I became gradually convinced that in order to make the position of the pacifist clear it was perhaps necessary that at least a small number of us should be forced into an unequivocal position. If I sometimes regretted having gone to the Woman's

Congress at The Hague in 1915, or having written a book on *Newer Ideals of Peace* in 1911 which had made my position so conspicuously clear, certainly far oftener I was devoutly grateful that I had used such unmistakable means of expression before the time came when any spoken or written word in the interests of Peace was forbidden.

It was on my return from The Hague Congress in July, 1915, that I had my first experience of the determination on the part of the press to make pacifist activity or propaganda so absurd that it would be absolutely without influence and its authors so discredited that nothing they might say or do would be regarded as worthy of attention. I had been accustomed to newspaper men for many years and had come to regard them as a good natured fraternity, sometimes ignorant of the subject on which they asked an interview, but usually quite ready to report faithfully albeit somewhat sensationally. Hull-House had several times been the subject of sustained and inspired newspaper attacks, one, the indirect result of an exposure of the inefficient sanitary service in the Chicago Health Department had lasted for many months; I had of course known what it was to serve unpopular causes and throughout a period of campaigning for the Progressive Party I had naturally encountered the "opposition press" in various parts of the country, but this concerted and deliberate attempt at misrepresentation on the part of newspapers of all shades of opinion was quite new in my experience. After the United States entered the war, the press throughout the country systematically undertook to misrepresent and malign pacifists as a recognized part of propaganda and as a patriotic duty. We came to regard this misrepresentation as part of the war technique and in fact an inevitable consequence of war itself, but we were slow in the very beginning to recognize the situation, and I found my first experience which came long before the United States entered the war rather overwhelming.

Upon our return from the Woman's International Congress at The Hague in 1915, our local organization in New York City with others, notably a group of enthusiastic college men, had arranged a large public meeting in Carnegie Hall. Dr. Anna Howard Shaw presided and the United States delegates made a public report of our impressions in "war stricken Europe" and of the moral resources in the various countries we visited that might possibly be brought to bear against a continuation of the war. We had been much impressed with the fact that it was an old man's war, that the various forms of doubt and opposition to war had no method of public expression and that many of the soldiers themselves were far from enthusiastic in regard to actual fighting as a method of settling international difficulties. War was to many of them much more anachronistic than to the elderly statesmen who were primarily responsible for the soldiers' presence in the trenches.

It was the latter statement which was my undoing, for in illustration of it I said that in practically every country we had visited, we had heard a certain type of young soldier say that it had been difficult for him to make the bayonet charge (enter into actual hand to hand fighting) unless he had been stimulated; that the English soldiers had been given rum before such a charge, the Germans

ether and that the French were said to use absinthe. To those who heard the address it was quite clear that it was not because the young men flinched at the risk
of death but because they had to be inflamed to do the brutal work of the bayonet, such as disembowelling, and were obliged to overcome all the inhibitions of
civilization.

Dr. Hamilton and I had notes for each of these statements with the dates and
names of the men who had made them, and it did not occur to me that the
information was new or startling. I was, however, reported to have said that no
soldier could go into a bayonet charge until he was made half drunk, and this in
turn was immediately commented upon, notably in a scathing letter written to
the *New York Times* by Richard Harding Davis,* as a most choice specimen of a
woman's sentimental nonsense. Mr. Davis himself had recently returned from
Europe and at once became the defender of the heroic soldiers who were being
traduced and belittled. He lent the weight of his name and his very able pen to
the cause, but it really needed neither, for the misstatement was repeated, usually with scathing comment, from one end of the country to the other.

I was conscious, of course, that the story had struck athwart the popular and
long-cherished conception of the nobility and heroism of the soldier as such, and
it seemed to me at the time that there was no possibility of making any explanation, at least until the sensation should have somewhat subsided. I might have
repeated my more sober statements with the explanation that whomsoever the
pacifist held responsible for war, it was certainly not the young soldiers themselves who were, in a sense, its most touching victims, "the heroic youth of the
world whom a common ideal tragically pitted against each other." Youth's response to the appeal made to their self-sacrifice, to their patriotism, to their sense
of duty, to their high-hearted hopes for the future, could only stir one's admiration, and we should have been dull indeed had we failed to be moved by this
most moving spectacle in the world. That they had so responded to the higher appeals only confirms Ruskin's statement that "we admire the soldier not because
he goes forth to slay but to be slain." The fact that many of them were obliged to
make a great effort to bear themselves gallantly in the final tests of "war's brutal-
ities" had nothing whatever to do with their courage and sense of devotion. All
this, of course, we had realized during our months in Europe.

After the meeting in Carnegie Hall and after an interview with President
Wilson in Washington, I returned to Chicago to a public meeting arranged in the
Auditorium; I was met at the train by a committee of aldermen appointed as a
result of a resolution in the City Council. There was an indefinite feeling that the
meeting at The Hague might turn out to be of significance, and that in such an
event its chairman should have been honored by her fellow citizens. But the bayonet story had preceded me and every one was filled with great uneasiness. To
be sure, a few war correspondents had come to my rescue—writing of the over-
powering smell of ether preceding certain German attacks; the fact that English
soldiers knew when a bayonet charge was about to be ordered because rations of

*a famous war correspondent, *ed.*

rum were distributed along the trenches. Some people began to suspect that the
story, exaggerated and grotesque as it had become, indicated not cowardice but
merely an added sensitiveness which the modern soldier was obliged to overcome. Among the many letters on the subject which filled my mail for weeks,
the bitter and abusive were from civilians or from the old men to whom war experiences had become a reminiscence, the larger number and the most understanding ones came from soldiers in active service.

Only once did I try a public explanation. After an address in Chautauqua,
New York, in which I had not mentioned bayonets, I tried to remake my original
statement to a young man of the associated press only to find it once more so
garbled that I gave up in despair, quite unmoved by the young man's letter of
apology which followed hard upon the published report of his interview.

I will confess that the mass psychology of the situation interested me even
then and continued to do so until I fell ill with a serious attack of pleuro-
pneumonia, which was the beginning of three years of semi-invalidism. During
weeks of feverish discomfort I experienced a bald sense of social opprobrium and
wide-spread misunderstanding which brought me very near to self pity, perhaps
the lowest pit into which human nature can sink. Indeed the pacifist in war
time, with his precious cause in the keeping of those who control the sources of
publicity and consider it a patriotic duty to make all types of peace propaganda
obnoxious, constantly faces two dangers. Strangely enough he finds it possible
to travel from the mire of self pity straight to the barren hills of self-righteousness
and to hate himself equally in both places.

From the very beginning of the great war, as the members of our group gradually became defined from the rest of the community, each one felt increasingly
the sense of isolation which rapidly developed after the United States entered the
war into that destroying effect of "aloneness," if I may so describe the opposite
of mass consciousness. We never ceased to miss the unquestioning comradeship
experienced by our fellow citizens during the war, nor to feel curiously outside
the enchantment given to any human emotion when it is shared by millions of
others. The force of the majority was so overwhelming that it seemed not only
impossible to hold one's own against it, but at moments absolutely unnatural,
and one secretly yearned to participate in "the folly of all mankind." Our modern democratic teaching has brought us to regard popular impulses as possessing
in their general tendency a valuable capacity for evolutionary development. In
the hours of doubt and self-distrust the question again and again arises, has the
individual or a very small group, the right to stand out against millions of his fellow countrymen? Is there not a great value in mass judgment and in instinctive
mass enthusiasm, and even if one were right a thousand times over in conviction, was he not absolutely wrong in abstaining from this communion with his
fellows? The misunderstanding on the part of old friends and associates and the
charge of lack of patriotism was far easier to bear than those dark periods of
faint-heartedness. We gradually ceased to state our position as we became convinced that it served no practical purpose and, worse than that, often found that
the immediate result was provocative.

We could not, however, lose the conviction that as all other forms of growth begin with a variation from the mass, so the moral changes in human affairs may also begin with a differing group or individual, sometimes with the one who at best is designated as a crank and a freak and in sterner moments is imprisoned as an atheist or a traitor. Just when the differing individual becomes the centro-egotist, the insane man, who must be thrown out by society for its own protection, it is impossible to state. The pacifist was constantly brought sharply up against a genuine human trait with its biological basis, a trait founded upon the instinct to dislike, to distrust and finally to destroy the individual who differs from the mass in time of danger. Regarding this trait as the basis of self-preservation it becomes perfectly natural for the mass to call such an individual a traitor and to insist that if he is not for the nation he is against it. To this an estimated nine million people can bear witness who have been burned as witches and heretics, not by mobs, for of the people who have been "lynched" no record has been kept, but by order of ecclesiastical and civil courts.

There were moments when the pacifist yielded to the suggestion that keeping himself out of war, refusing to take part in its enthusiasms, was but pure quietism, an acute failure to adjust himself to the moral world. Certainly nothing was clearer than that the individual will was helpless and irrelevant. We were constantly told by our friends that to stand aside from the war mood of the country was to surrender all possibility of future influence, that we were committing intellectual suicide, and would never again be trusted as responsible people or judicious advisers. Who were we to differ with able statesmen, with men of sensitive conscience who also absolutely abhorred war, but were convinced that this war for the preservation of democracy would make all future wars impossible, that the priceless values of civilization which were at stake could at this moment be saved only by war? But these very dogmatic statements spurred one to alarm. Was not war in the interest of democracy for the salvation of civilization a contradiction of terms, whoever said it or however often it was repeated? . . .

26. "Espionage Act"

(1917)

Passed by the U.S. Congress on June 15, 1917, after nine weeks of intense debate, the Espionage Act proved to be one of the most controversial pieces of legislation in American history. While the bulk of the law essentially updated and superseded older espionage laws, its text had several provisions that were without precedent, overreaching the powers of even the long-expired Sedition Act of 1798. As the following text demonstrates, the act made it a crime to convey false reports about the war, promote the success of enemies of the United States, attempt to cause insubordination within the U.S. military, and obstruct recruitment or enlistment. Sending materials that fit these criteria through the mail was also made illegal; radical magazines like the *Masses* and *American Socialist* were thus banned by the postmaster. Violators of the Espionage Act could be fined up to $10,000 and serve up to twenty years in jail as well. Congress had eliminated some of the most restrictive proposed provisions before passing the bill, including one allowing press censorship that President Wilson thought vital to the war effort. Nonetheless, the vague wording of much of the law did give the government a great deal of leeway in interpreting how it should be enforced. Furthermore, the Sedition Act of 1918 (see the next document) amended the Espionage Act, expanding its scope to forbid any language criticizing the government, the Constitution, or the armed forces of the United States during wartime.

SOURCE: Espionage Act of 1917, 40 Stat. 217.

Be It Enacted by the Senate and House of Representatives of the United States of America in Congress Assembled

Title I
ESPIONAGE
Section 1

That:

(a) whoever, for the purpose of obtaining information respecting the national defence with intent or reason to believe that the information to be obtained is to be used to the injury of the United States, or to the advantage of any foreign nation, goes upon, enters, flies over, or otherwise obtains information, concerning any vessel, aircraft, work of defence, navy yard, naval station, submarine base, coaling station, fort, battery, torpedo station, dockyard, canal, railroad, arsenal, camp, factory, mine, telegraph, telephone, wireless, or signal station, building, office, or other place connected with the national defence, owned or constructed, or in progress of construction by the United States or under the control or the United States, or of any of its officers or agents, or within the exclusive jurisdiction of the United States, or any place in which any vessel, aircraft, arms, munitions, or other materials or instruments for use in time of war are being made, prepared, repaired. or stored, under any contract or agreement with the United States, or with any person on behalf of the United States, or otherwise on behalf of the United States, or any prohibited place within the meaning of section six of this title; or

(b) whoever for the purpose aforesaid, and with like intent or reason to believe, copies, takes, makes, or obtains, or attempts, or induces or aids another to copy, take, make, or obtain, any sketch, photograph, photographic negative, blue print, plan, map, model, instrument, appliance, document, writing or note of anything connected with the national defence; or

(c) whoever, for the purpose aforesaid, receives or obtains or agrees or attempts or induces or aids another to receive or obtain from any other person, or from any source whatever, any document, writing, code book, signal book, sketch, photograph, photographic negative, blue print, plan, map, model, instrument, appliance, or note, of anything connected with the national defence, knowing or having reason to believe, at the time he receives or obtains, or agrees or attempts or induces or aids another to receive or obtain it, that it has been or will be obtained, taken, made or disposed of by any person contrary to the provisions of this title; or

(d) whoever, lawfully or unlawfully having possession of, access to, control over, or being entrusted with any document, writing, code book, signal book, sketch, photograph, photographic negative, blue print, plan, map, model, instrument, appliance, or note relating to the national defence, wilfully communicates or transmits or attempts to communicate or transmit the same and fails to deliver it on demand to the officer or employee of the United States entitled to receive it; or

(e) whoever, being entrusted with or having lawful possession or control of any document, writing, code book, signal book, sketch, photograph, photographic negative, blue print, plan, map, model, note, or information, relating to the national defence, through gross negligence permits the same to be removed from its proper place of custody or delivered to anyone in violation of his trust, or to be list, stolen, abstracted, or destroyed, shall be punished by a fine of not more than $10,000, or by imprisonment for not more than two years, or both.

Section 2

Whoever, with intent or reason to believe that it is to be used to the injury or the United States or to the advantage of a foreign nation, communicated, delivers, or transmits, or attempts to, or aids, or induces another to, communicate, deliver or transmit, to any foreign government, or to any faction or party or military or naval force within a foreign country, whether recognized or unrecognized by the United States, or to any representative, officer, agent, employee, subject, or citizen thereof, either directly or indirectly and document, writing, code book, signal book, sketch, photograph, photographic negative, blue print, plan, map, model, note, instrument, appliance, or information relating to the national defence, shall be punished by imprisonment for not more than twenty years: Provided, That whoever shall violate the provisions of subsection:

(a) of this section in time of war shall be punished by death or by imprisonment for not more than thirty years; and

(b) whoever, in time of war, with intent that the same shall be communicated to the enemy, shall collect, record, publish or communicate, or attempt to elicit any information with respect to the movement, numbers, description, condition, or disposition of any of the armed forces, ships, aircraft, or war materials of the United States, or with respect to the plans or conduct, or supposed plans or conduct of any naval of military operations, or with respect to any works or measures undertaken for or connected with, or intended for the fortification of any place, or any other information relating to the public defence, which might be useful to the enemy, shall be punished by death or by imprisonment for not more than thirty years.

Section 3

Whoever, when the United States is at war, shall wilfully make or convey false reports or false statements with intent to interfere with the operation or success of the military or naval forces of the United States or to promote the success of its enemies and whoever when the United States is at war, shall wilfully cause or attempt to cause insubordination, disloyalty, mutiny, refusal of duty, in the military or naval forces of the United States, or shall wilfully obstruct the recruiting or enlistment service of the United States, to the injury of the service or of the United States, shall be punished by a fine of not more than $10,000 or imprisonment for not more than twenty years, or both.

Section 4

If two or more persons conspire to violate the provisions of section two or three of this title, and one or more of such persons does any act to effect the object of the conspiracy, each of the parties to such conspiracy shall be punished as in said sections provided in the case of the doing of the act the accomplishment of which is the object of such conspiracy. Except as above provided conspiracies to commit offences under this title shall be punished as provided by section thirty-seven of the Act to codify, revise, and amend the penal laws of the United States approved March fourth, nineteen hundred and nine.

Section 5

Whoever harbours or conceals any person who he knows, or has reasonable grounds to believe or suspect, has committed, or is about to commit, an offence under this title shall be punished by a fine of not more than $10,000 or by imprisonment for not more than two years, or both.

Section 6

The President in time of war or in case of national emergency may by proclamation designate any place other than those set forth in subsection:

(a) of section one hereof in which anything for the use of the Army or Navy is being prepared or constructed or stored as a prohibited place for the purpose of this title: Provided, That he shall determine that information with respect thereto would be prejudicial to the national defence.

Section 7

Nothing contained in this title shall be deemed to limit the jurisdiction of the general courts-martial, military commissions, or naval courts-martial under sections thirteen hundred and forty-two, thirteen hundred and forty-three, and sixteen hundred and twenty-four of the Revised Statutes as amended.

Section 8

The provisions of this title shall extend to all Territories, possessions, and places subject to the jurisdiction of the United States whether or not contiguous thereto, and offences under this title, when committed upon the high seas or elsewhere within the admiralty and maritime jurisdiction of the United States and outside the territorial limits thereof shall be punishable hereunder.

Section 9

The Act entitles "An Act to prevent the disclosure of national defence secrets," approved March third, nineteen hundred and eleven, is hereby repealed.

27. "Sedition Act"

(1918)

In the spring of 1918, the Department of Justice sought to put more teeth into the Espionage Act. U.S. Attorney General Thomas Watt Gregory argued that, in the view of some loyal citizens of the United States, the law as it stood was not strong enough, so much so that some were taking the matter into their own hands. Gregory pointed to the lynching of a supposedly disloyal German American in Collinsville, Illinois. The victim, Robert Prager, was a coal miner who had recently attended a socialist meeting. A mob hanged him from a tree a little after midnight on April 5, claiming he had made remarks disloyal to the United States. (Ironically, Prager had complied with the draft registration of 1917.) As a result of Gregory's initiative, an amendment was proposed to the Espionage Act, replacing the third section of the older law with considerably more restrictive language. In effect, the amendment made it illegal to criticize or show disrespect for the government of the United States, its Constitution, its armed forces, its flag, and even the uniforms of its military personnel. Although a few senators protested that calm and rational consideration of such grave measures was virtually impossible in the feverish environment of the time (recent events in Russia looked particularly menacing to many Americans), the amendment was approved by the Senate by a margin of 48 to 26 and by the House by a 293 to 1 vote. It was signed into law on May 16. Ultimately, only a small number of cases were prosecuted under the Sedition Act since it was enacted quite late in the war. Most of its provisions were repealed by 1921.

SOURCE: The Sedition Act of 1918, 40 Stat. 553.

Be it enacted, That section three of the Act . . . approved June 15, 1917, be . . . amended so as to read as follows:

"SEC. 3. Whoever, when the United States is at war, shall wilfully make or convey false reports or false statements with intent to interfere with the operation or success of the military or naval forces of the United States, or to promote the success of its enemies, or shall wilfully make or convey false reports, or false statements, or say or do anything except by way of bona fide and not disloyal advice to an investor . . . with intent to obstruct the sale by the United States of bonds . . . or the making of loans by or to the United States, or whoever, when the United States is at war, shall wilfully cause . . . or incite . . . insubordination, disloyalty, mutiny, or refusal of duty, in the military or naval forces of the United States, or shall wilfully obstruct . . . the recruiting or enlistment service of the United States, and whoever, when the United States is at war, shall wilfully utter, print, write, or publish any disloyal, profane, scurrilous, or abusive language about the form of government of the United States, or the Constitution of the United States, or the military or naval forces of the United States, or the flag . . . or the uniform of the Army or Navy of the United States, or any language intended to bring the form of government . . . or the Constitution . . . or the military or naval forces . . . or the flag . . . of the United States into contempt, scorn, contumely, or disrepute . . . or shall wilfully display the flag of any foreign enemy, or shall wilfully . . . urge, incite, or advocate any curtailment of production in this country of any thing or things . . . necessary or essential to the prosecution of the war . . . and whoever shall wilfully advocate, teach, defend, or suggest the doing of any of the acts or things in this section enumerated and whoever shall by word or act support or favour the cause of any country with which the United States is at war or by word or act oppose the cause of the United States therein, shall be punished by a fine of not more than $10,000 or imprisonment for not more than twenty years, or both. . . ."

28. Eugene V. Debs, "The Canton, Ohio Speech"

(1918)

On June 16, 1918, socialist leader Eugene V. Debs gave a speech to about 1,200 people attending a socialist convention in Canton, Ohio. Debs spoke in a small park just a short distance from a jailhouse where three socialist war dissidents with whom he had visited earlier that day were imprisoned. His remarks were recorded by government stenographers, and this evidence was later used to try Debs for violating the terms of the Espionage Act on grounds that the speech obstructed recruitment and enlistment of men into the armed forces. In the excerpts that follow, Debs praises the sacrifice of the three dissidents (cognizant that he was most likely about to follow in their steps), lauds the Bolshevik Revolution in Russia as a sign of socialism's ascendancy, and levels the charge that the "Wall Street gentry" always declares war but leaves the fighting to working people.

SOURCE: Eugene V. Debs, *The Writings and Speeches of Eugene V. Debs* (New York: Hermitage Press, 1948), 417–33.

COMRADES, friends and fellow-workers, for this very cordial greeting, this very hearty reception, I thank you all with the fullest appreciation of your interest in and your devotion to the cause for which I am to speak to you this afternoon. (Applause.)

To speak for labor; to plead the cause of the men and women and children who toil; to serve the working class, has always been to me a high privilege; (Applause) a duty of love.

I have just returned from a visit over yonder (pointing to the workhouse), where three of our most loyal comrades [who were imprisoned for opposing the war] are paying the penalty for their devotion to the cause of the working class. (Applause.) They have come to realize, as many of us have, that it is extremely dangerous to exercise the constitutional right of free speech in a country fighting to make democracy safe in the world. (Applause.)

I realize that, in speaking to you this afternoon, there are certain limitations placed upon the right of free speech. I must be exceedingly careful, prudent, as to what I say, and even more careful and prudent as to how I say it. (Laughter.) I may not be able to say all I think; (Laughter and applause) but I am not going to say anything that I do not think. (Applause.) I would rather a thousand times be a free soul in jail than to be a sycophant and coward in the streets. (Applause and shouts.) They may put those boys in jail—and some of the rest of us in jail—but they can not put the Socialist movement in jail. (Applause and shouts.) Those prison bars separate their bodies from ours, but their souls are here this afternoon. (Applause and cheers.) They are simply paying the penalty, that all men have paid in all the ages of history, for standing erect, and for seeking to pave the way to better conditions for mankind. (Applause.) . . .

Socialism is a growing idea; an expanding philosophy. It is spreading over the entire face of the earth. It is as vain to resist it as it would be to arrest the sunrise on the morrow. It is coming, coming, coming all along the line. Can you not see it? If not, I advise you to consult an oculist. There is certainly something the matter with your vision. It is the mightiest movement in the history of mankind. What a privilege to serve it! I have regretted a thousand times that I can do so little for the movement that has done so much for me. (Applause.) The little that I am, the little that I am hoping to be, I owe to the Socialist movement. (Applause.) It has given me my ideas and ideals; my principles and convictions, and I would not exchange one of them for all of Rockefeller's blood-stained dollars. (Cheers.) It has taught me how to serve—a lesson to me of priceless value. It has taught me the ecstasy in the handclasp of a comrade. It has enabled me to hold high communion with you, and made it possible for me to take my place side by side with you in the great struggle for the better day; to multiply myself over and over again; to thrill with a fresh-born manhood; to feel life truly worth while; to open new avenues of vision; to spread out glorious vistas; to know that I am kin to all that throbs; to be class-conscious, and to realize that, regardless of nationality, race, creed, color or sex, every man, every woman who toils, who renders useful service, every member of the working class without an exception, is my comrade, my brother and sister—and that to serve them and their cause is the highest duty of my life. (Great applause.) . . .

Yes, my comrades, my heart is attuned to yours. Aye, all our hearts now throb as one great heart responsive to the battle-cry of the social revolution. Here, in this alert and inspiring assemblage (Applause) our hearts are with the Bolsheviki of Russia. (Deafening and prolonged applause.) Those heroic men and women, those unconquerable comrades have by their incomparable valor and sacrifice added fresh lustre to the fame of the international movement. . . . The very first act of the triumphant Russian revolution was to proclaim a state of peace with all mankind, coupled with a fervent moral appeal, not to kings, not to emperors, rulers or diplomats but to *the people* of all nations. . . . When the Bolsheviki came into power and went through the archives they found and exposed the secret treaties—the treaties that were made between the Czar and the French Government, the British Government and the Italian Government, proposing, after the victory was achieved, to dismember the German Empire and destroy the Central

Powers. These treaties have never been denied nor repudiated. Very little has been said about them in the American press. I have a copy of these treaties, showing that the purpose of the Allies is exactly the purpose of the Central Powers, and that is the conquest and spoliation of the weaker nations that has always been the purpose of war.

Wars throughout history have been waged for conquest and plunder. In the Middle Ages when the feudal lords, who inhabited the castles whose towers may still be seen along the Rhine, concluded to enlarge their domains, to increase their power, their prestige and their wealth, they declared war upon one another. But they themselves did not go to war any more than the modern feudal lords, the barons of Wall Street go to war. (Applause.) The feudal barons of the Middle Ages, the economic predecessors of the capitalists of our day, declared all wars. And their miserable serfs fought all the battles. The poor, ignorant serfs had been taught to revere their masters; to believe that when their masters declared war upon one another, it was their patriotic duty to fall upon one another and to cut one another's throats for the profit and glory of the lords and barons who held them in contempt. And that is war in a nutshell. The master class has always declared the wars; the subject class has always fought the battles. The master class has had all to gain and nothing to lose, while the subject class has had nothing to gain and all to lose—especially their lives. (Applause.) . . .

And here let me emphasize the fact—and it cannot be repeated too often—that the working class who fight all the battles, the working class who make the supreme sacrifices, the working class who freely shed their blood and furnish the corpses, has never yet had a voice in either declaring war or making peace. It is the ruling class that invariably does both. They alone declare war and they alone make peace.

> Yours not to reason why;
> Yours but to do and die.

That is their motto and we object on the part of the awakening workers of this nation. . . .

What a compliment it is to the Socialist movement to be persecuted for the sake of the truth! The truth alone will make the people free. (Applause.) And for this reason the truth must not be permitted to reach the people. The truth has always been dangerous to the rule of the rogue, the exploiter, the robber. So the truth must be ruthlessly suppressed. That is why they are trying to destroy the Socialist movement; and every time they strike a blow they add a thousand new voices to the hosts proclaiming that Socialism is the hope of humanity and has come to emancipate the people from their final form of servitude. (Applause.) . . .

The capitalist system affects to have great regard and reward for intellect, and the capitalists give themselves full credit for having superior brains. When we have ventured to say that the time would come when the working class would rule they have bluntly answered "Never! it requires brains to rule." The workers of course have none. And they certainly try hard to prove it by proudly supporting the political parties of their masters under whose administration they are kept in poverty and servitude. . . .

These are the gentry who are today wrapped up in the American flag, who shout their claim from the housetops that they are the only patriots, and who have their magnifying glasses in hand, scanning the country for evidence of disloyalty, eager to apply the brand of treason to the men who dare to even whisper their opposition to Junker rule in the United States. No wonder Sam Johnson declared that "patriotism is the last refuge of the scoundrel." He must have had this Wall Street gentry in mind, or at least their prototypes, for in every age it has been the tyrant, the oppressor and the exploiter who has wrapped himself in the cloak of patriotism, or religion, or both to deceive and overawe the people. (Applause.) . . .

They are continually talking about your patriotic duty. It is not *their* but *your* patriotic duty that they are concerned about. There is a decided difference. Their patriotic duty never takes them to the firing line or chucks them into the trenches. . . .

29. Eugene V. Debs, "Address to the Jury"

(1918)

Eugene Debs's trial for violating the Espionage Act culminated in September 1918. He made the following remarks to the jury before hearing his verdict, powerfully rooting his dissent in American history. Observing that "the minority are usually right," he noted that some segment of the population has usually condemned the wars in which the United States has engaged without being thrown into jail. He asks why the northern Democrats who condemned the Civil War in 1864 were not prosecuted for disloyalty like the antiwar socialists in his own day, and puts forth the irony that the Socialist Party seemed to be almost alone in defending the Constitution. Convicted of the crime, Debs immediately appealed his case, which was argued before the Supreme Court on January 27 and 28, 1919. His defense was that his right to make the speech was protected by the First Amendment to the Constitution. The decision, unanimously against Debs, was handed down on March 10. Justice Oliver Wendell Holmes Jr. (1841–1935) wrote the majority opinion, noting that the case was very similar to the recently decided *Schenck v. United States* (see next document) and therefore did not merit close attention. The court thus upheld the Espionage Act and Debs's sentence of ten years, and he entered prison on April 13.

From his cell in an Atlanta federal prison, Debs ran for president in 1920, receiving well over 900,000 votes. Republican president Warren G. Harding released Debs and several other "prisoners of conscience" on Christmas Day, 1921. Debs died at age seventy on October 20, 1926.

SOURCE: Eugene V. Debs, *The Writings and Speeches of Eugene V. Debs* (New York: Hermitage Press, 1948), 434.

May it please the court, and gentlemen of the jury:

When great changes occur in history, when great principles are involved as a rule the majority are wrong. The minority are usually right. In every age there have been a few heroic souls who have been in advance of their time, who have been misunderstood, maligned, persecuted, sometimes put to death. Long after their martyrdom monuments were erected to them and garlands woven for their graves.

This has been the tragic history of the race. In the ancient world Socrates sought to teach some new truths to the people, and they made him drink the fatal hemlock. This has been true all along the track of the ages. The men and women who have been in advance, who have had new ideas, new ideals, who have had the courage to attack the established order of things, have all had to pay the same penalty.

A century and a half ago when the American colonists were still foreign subjects; when there were a few men who had faith in the common people and their destiny, and believed that they could rule themselves without a king; in that day to question the divine right of the king to rule was treason. If you will read Bancroft or any other American historian, you will find that a great majority of the colonists were loyal to the king and actually believed that he had a divine right to rule over them. . . . But there were a few men in that day who said, "We don't need a king; we can govern ourselves." And they began an agitation that has immortalized them in history.

Washington, Jefferson, Franklin, Paine and their compeers were the rebels of their day. When they began to chafe under the rule of a foreign king and to sow the seed of resistance among the colonists they were opposed by the people and denounced by the press. . . . But they had the moral courage to be true to their convictions, to stand erect and defy all the forces of reaction and detraction; and that is why their names shine in history, and why the great respectable majority of their day sleep in forgotten graves.

At a later time there began another mighty agitation in this country. It was directed against an institution that was deemed eminently respectable in its time— the age-old, cruel and infamous institution of chattel slavery. . . . All the organized forces of society and all the powers of government upheld and defended chattel slavery in that day. And again the few advanced thinkers, crusaders and martyrs appeared. One of the first was Elijah Lovejoy who was murdered in cold blood at Alton, Illinois, in 1837 because he was opposed to chattel slavery—just as I am opposed to wage slavery. Today as you go up or down the Mississippi River and look up at the green hills at Alton, you see a magnificent white shaft erected there in memory of the man who was true to himself and his convictions of right and duty even unto death.

It was my good fortune to personally know Wendell Phillips. I heard the story of his cruel and cowardly persecution from his own eloquent lips just a little while before they were silenced in death.

William Lloyd Garrison, Wendell Phillips, Elizabeth Cady Stanton, Susan B. Anthony, Gerrit Smith, Thaddeus Stevens and other leaders of the abolition movement who were regarded as public enemies and treated accordingly, were true to their faith and stood their ground. They are all in history. You are now teaching your children to revere their memories, while all of their detractors are in oblivion.

Chattel slavery has disappeared. But we are not yet free. We are engaged to-day in another mighty agitation. It is as wide as the world. It means the rise of the toiling masses who are gradually becoming conscious of their interests, their power, and their mission as a class; who are organizing industrially and politically and who are slowly but surely developing the economic and political power that is to set them free. These awakening workers are still in a minority, but they have learned how to work together to achieve their freedom, and how to be patient and abide their time.

From the beginning of the war to this day I have never by word or act been guilty of the charges embraced in this indictment. If I have criticized. If I have condemned, it is because I believed it to be my duty, and that it was my right to do so under the laws of the land. I have had ample precedents for my attitude. This country has been engaged in a number of wars and every one of them has been condemned by some of the people, among them some of the most eminent men of their time. The war of the American Revolution was violently opposed. The Tory press representing the "upper classes" denounced its leaders as criminals and outlaws.

The war of 1812 was opposed and condemned by some of the most influential citizens; the Mexican war was vehemently opposed and bitterly denounced, even after the war had been declared and was in progress, by Abraham Lincoln, Charles Sumner, Daniel Webster, Henry Clay and many other well-known and influential citizens. These men denounced the President, they condemned his administration while the war was being waged, and they charged in substance that the war was a crime against humanity. They were not indicted; they were not charged with treason nor tried for crime. They are honored today by all of their countrymen.

The Civil War between the states met with violent resistance and passionate condemnation. In the year 1864 the Democratic Party met in national convention at Chicago and passed a resolution condemning the war as a failure. What would you say if the Socialist Party were to meet in convention today and condemn the present war as a failure? You charge us with being disloyalists and traitors. Were the Democrats of 1864 disloyalists and traitors because they condemned the war as a failure?

And if so, why were they not indicted and prosecuted accordingly? I believe in the Constitution. Isn't it strange that we Socialists stand almost alone today in upholding and defending the Constitution of the United States? The revolutionary fathers who had been oppressed under king rule understood that free speech, a free press and the right of free assemblage by the people were fundamental principles in democratic government. The very first amendment to the Constitution reads:

"Congress shall make no law respecting an establishment of religion, or prohibiting the free exercise thereof; or abridging the freedom of speech, or of the press; or the right of the people peaceably to assemble, and to petition the government for a redress of grievances."

That is perfectly plain English. It can be understood by a child. I believe the revolutionary fathers meant just what is here stated—that Congress shall make no law abridging the freedom of speech or of the press, or of the right of the people to peaceably assemble, and to petition the government for a redress of their grievances.

That is the right I exercised at Canton on the sixteenth day of last June; and for the exercise of that right, I now have to answer to this indictment. I believe in the right of free speech, in war as well as in peace. I would not, under any circumstances suppress free speech. It is far more dangerous to attempt to gag the people than to allow them to speak freely what is in their hearts.

I have told you that I am no lawyer, but it seems to me that I know enough to know that if Congress enacts any law that conflicts with this provision in the Constitution, that law is void. If the Espionage Law finally stands, then the Constitution of the United States is dead. If that law is not the negation of every fundamental principle established by the Constitution, then certainly I am unable to read or to understand the English language. . . .

Now, gentlemen of the jury, I am not going to detain you too long. . . . I cannot take back a word I have said. I cannot repudiate a sentence I have uttered. I stand before you guilty of having made this speech. . . . I do not know, I cannot tell, what your verdict may be; nor does it matter much, so far as I am concerned.

Gentlemen, I am the smallest part of this trial. I have lived long enough to realize my own personal insignificance in relation to a great issue that involves the welfare of the whole people. What you may choose to do to me will be of small consequence after all. I am not on trial here. There is an infinitely greater issue that is being tried today in this court, though you may not be conscious of it. American institutions are on trial here before a court of American citizens. The future will render the final verdict.

And now, your honor, permit me to return my thanks for your patient consideration. And to you, gentlemen of the jury, for the kindness with which you have listened to me.

I am prepared for your verdict.

30. *Schenck v. United States*

(1919)

This famed case involved the prosecution of Charles Schenck, general secretary of the Socialist Party in Philadelphia, and Elizabeth Baer, its recording secretary. Schenck and Baer were charged with circulating a leaflet to men who had been called for military service that strongly encouraged them to resist the draft. The pamphlet, entitled "Assert Your Rights!," posed the question, "Would you let cunning politicians and a mercenary capitalist press wrongly and untruthfully mould your thoughts?" It then declares conscription unconstitutional because it violates the Thirteenth Amendment's prohibition against involuntary servitude unless someone is convicted of a crime. The leaflet thus asserts that "a conscript is little better than a convict."

The case was argued before the Supreme Court on January 9 and 10, 1919, and decided on March 3, with a unanimous decision against Schenck. Justice Oliver Wendell Holmes Jr. wrote the majority opinion, which is excerpted here. In it, Holmes argued that the First Amendment does not protect speech that provokes insubordination during wartime, and in doing so formulated his famed "clear and present danger" standard. He stated that if the nation had not been at war, the defendants' right to disseminate this leaflet most likely would have been protected. He constructed his analogy of a false cry of "Fire!" in a crowded theater not being protected by the First Amendment because it creates a "clear and present danger" of panic. Later in 1919, Holmes surprised observers by dissenting in a somewhat similar case, *Abrams v. United States*, noting that the five convicted pamphleteers were expressing their opinions and not posing a threat to the war effort.

SOURCE: U.S. Supreme Court, *Schenck v. U.S.*, 249 U.S. 47 (1919).

. . . The document in question, upon its first printed side, recited the first section of the Thirteenth Amendment, said that the idea embodied in it was violated by the Conscription Act, and that a conscript is little better than a convict. In impassioned language, it intimated that conscription was despotism in its worst form, and a monstrous wrong against humanity in the interest of Wall Street's chosen few. It said "Do not submit to intimidation," but in form, at least, confined itself to peaceful measures such as a petition for the repeal of the act. The other and later printed side of the sheet was headed "Assert Your Rights." It stated reasons for alleging that anyone violated the Constitution when he refused to recognize "your right to assert your opposition to the draft," and went on "If you do not assert and support your rights, you are helping to deny or disparage rights which it is the solemn duty of all citizens and residents of the United States to retain." It described the arguments on the other side as coming from cunning politicians and a mercenary capitalist press, and even silent consent to the conscription law as helping to support an infamous conspiracy. It denied the power to send our citizens away to foreign shores to shoot up the people of other lands, and added that words could not express the condemnation such cold-blooded ruthlessness deserves, &c., &c., winding up, "You must do your share to maintain, support and uphold the rights of the people of this country." Of course, the document would not have been sent unless it had been intended to have some effect, and we do not see what effect it could be expected to have upon persons subject to the draft except to influence them to obstruct the carrying of it out. The defendants do not deny that the jury might find against them on this point.

But it is said, suppose that that was the tendency of this circular, it is protected by the First Amendment to the Constitution. Two of the strongest expressions are said to be quoted respectively from well known public men. It well may be that the prohibition of laws abridging the freedom of speech is not confined to previous restraints, although to prevent them may have been the main purpose, as intimated in *Patterson v. Colorado,* 205 U.S. 454, 462. We admit that, in many places and in ordinary times, the defendants, in saying all that was said in the circular, would have been within their constitutional rights. But the character of every act depends upon the circumstances in which it is done. *Aikens v. Wisconsin,* 195 U.S. 194, 205, 206. The most stringent protection of free speech would not protect a man in falsely shouting fire in a theatre and causing a panic. It does not even protect a man from an injunction against uttering words that may have all the effect of force. *Gompers v. Bucks Stove & Range Co.,* 221 U.S. 418, 439. The question in every case is whether the words used are used in such circumstances and are of such a nature as to create a clear and present danger that they will bring about the substantive evils that Congress has a right to prevent. It is a question of proximity and degree. When a nation is at war, many things that might be said in time of peace are such a hindrance to its effort that their utterance will not be endured so long as men fight, and that no Court could regard them as protected by any constitutional right. It seems to be admitted that, if an actual obstruction of the recruiting service were proved, liability for words that produced that effect might be enforced. The statute of 1917, in § 4, punishes conspiracies to obstruct as well as actual obstruction. If the act (speaking, or circulating a paper), its tendency and the intent with which it is done are the same, we perceive no ground for saying that success alone warrants making the act a crime. *Goldman v. United States, 245 U.S. 474, 477.* Indeed that case might be said to dispose of the present contention if the precedent covers all media concludendi. But as the right to free speech was not referred to specially, we have thought fit to add a few words.

It was not argued that a conspiracy to obstruct the draft was not within the words of the Act of 1917. The words are "obstruct the recruiting or enlistment service," and it might be suggested that they refer only to making it hard to get volunteers. Recruiting heretofore usually having been accomplished by getting volunteers the word is apt to call up that method only in our minds. But recruiting is gaining fresh supplies for the forces, as well by draft as otherwise. It is put as an alternative to enlistment or voluntary enrollment in this act. . . .

CHAPTER THREE

The Great War, Part II: Social Consequences

31. *New York Times*, "Urge Unity for the War: Suffrage Leaders Demand 'Whole-Hearted Allegiance' to the Country"

(1917)

The National American Woman Suffrage Association (NAWSA) formed in 1890 when two older suffrage groups combined. NAWSA's strategy for attaining the vote for women was to pursue suffrage at the state level, eventually forcing the federal government to pass an amendment to the Constitution. Oregon was the first state to grant suffrage, California followed in 1911, and four other western states joined them in 1912. Throughout this period, NAWSA was the most nationally prominent and mainstream suffrage group, growing from a membership of 13,000 in 1893 to over 2 million in 1917. Before the war, former NAWSA president Carrie Chapman Catt (1859–1947) focused her organizing efforts on a campaign to make New York the first eastern state to grant women's suffrage. Her first campaign led to a referendum that failed in 1915, but in 1917 the war afforded new opportunities. Suffragists successfully linked the idea of women's national service during the war to their right to vote. A new referendum was introduced in 1917, and a last-minute decision by the Democratic Tammany Hall political machine not to oppose it proved critical. The referendum carried New York City by roughly 100,000 votes; these in turn broke the virtual tie vote in the rest of the state. New York State's passage pushed national political momentum in favor of a constitutional amendment.

During the war, Catt once again served as president of NAWSA, guiding the organization through this critical phase of the suffrage campaign. She was also appointed to the Woman's Division of the Council for National Defense, and from that platform was able to urge Congress to submit the Nineteenth Amendment in June 1919; it was passed and signed into law on August 26, 1920. In the statement summed up in the following *New York Times* piece, Catt urged suffragists to rally behind the war effort and to be critical of divisive protest tactics of dissenters and more radical feminists. Many historians credit Catt's strategic moderation with the eventual passage of the Nineteenth Amendment.

SOURCE: *New York Times*, October 6, 1917, p. 4.

The official board of the National American Woman Suffrage Association, Mrs. Carrie Chapman Catt, President, at a meeting at the headquarters, 171 Madison Avenue, yesterday adopted a resolution urging whole-hearted allegiance to the country, with no pseudo patriotism to insure the success of the war. The resolution assailed as un-American "those discriminations and injustices that set class against class, race against race, sex against sex, and furnish opportunity for insidious alien propaganda that trades upon them to the internal disturbance of our country; maintains that all Americans, men or women, white or black, in the trenches or in the home and the factory, who are giving their lives to uphold the ideals of democracy shall share equally in the privileges and protection of democracy; and deplores all lawlessness based on race or sex or class prejudice."

It also asked for a broad stand for American democracy "that knows no bias on the ground of race, color, creed, or sex."

32. "Petition from the Women Voters Anti-Suffrage Party of New York to the United States Senate"

(1917)

By 1916, pro-suffrage groups rallied behind a constitutional amendment as the best way to bring about the vote for women. With the outbreak of the war, suffragists successfully made a rhetorical linkage between their service to the war effort and their right to vote. Yet, not all women were in favor of gaining this right, as the text of the following anti-suffrage petition makes clear, especially in the "hour of peril" that the country faced. The suffrage movement is here portrayed as a waste of energies that could otherwise be devoted to the war effort. The anti-suffragists who signed this particular petition listed their affiliations with organizations like the Red Cross and the National League for Women's Service to bolster this point.

SOURCE: Records of the U.S. Senate, Record Group 46, National Archives, Washington, D.C.

Whereas, This country is now engaged in the greatest war in history, and

Whereas, The advocates of the Federal Amendment, though urging it as a war measure, announce, through their president, Mrs. Catt, that its passage "means a simultaneous campaign in 48 States. It demands organization in every precinct; activity, agitation, education in every corner. Nothing less than this nation-wide, vigilant, unceasing campaign will win ratification," therefore be it

Resolved, That our country in this hour of peril should be spared the harassing of its public men and the distracting of its people from work for the war, and further

Resolved, That the United States Senate be respectfully urged to pass no measure involving such a radical change in our government while the attention of the patriotic portion of the American people is concentrated on the all important task of winning the war, and during the absence of over a million men abroad.

33. Woodrow Wilson, "Appeal for Woman Suffrage"

(1918)

By September 1918, President Wilson had at last strongly come down in favor of granting women the right to vote. In this address to Senate, Wilson sees the vote as cementing the "partnership" men had made with women in conducting the war effort. The proposal for a constitutional amendment was submitted to Congress in June 1919 and finally signed into law in August 1920, culminating the women's suffrage struggle that had lasted over seventy years (see introduction to document 31).

SOURCE: Woodrow Wilson, *Address of the President of the United States Delivered in the Senate of the United States, September 30, 1918* (Washington, D.C.: Government Printing Office, 1918).

I regard the concurrence of the Senate in the constitutional amendment proposing the extension of the suffrage to women as vitally essential to the successful prosecution of the great war of humanity in which we are engaged. I have come to urge upon you the considerations which have led me to that conclusion. It is not only my privilege, it is also my duty to apprise you of every circumstance and element involved in this momentous struggle which seems to me to affect its very processes and its outcome. It is my duty to win the war and to ask you to remove every obstacle that stands in the way of winning it. . . .

We have made partners of the women in this war; shall we admit them only to a partnership of suffering and sacrifice and toil and not to a partnership of privilege and right? This war could not have been fought, either by the other nations engaged or by America, if it had not been for the services of the women,—services rendered in every sphere,—not merely in the fields of effort in which we have been accustomed to see them work, but wherever men have worked and upon the very skirts and edges of the battle itself. . . .

The women of America are too noble and too intelligent and too devoted to be slackers whether you give or withhold this thing that is mere justice; but I know the magic it will work in their thoughts and spirits if you give it them. I propose it as I would propose to admit soldiers to the suffrage, the men fighting in the field for our liberties and the liberties of the world, were they excluded. The tasks of the women lie at the very heart of the war, and I know how much stronger that heart will beat if you do this just thing and show our women that you trust them as much as you in fact and of necessity depend upon them. . . .

I tell you plainly that this measure which I urge upon you is vital to the winning of the war and to the energies alike of preparation and of battle.

34. New York Age, "Editorial on the East St. Louis Riot"

(1917)

In May and June 1917, one of the worst episodes of racial violence in American history ripped apart the community of East St. Louis, Illinois. During the Great Migration of African Americans from the South to industrial cities in the North, East St. Louis was both a destination and a way station as blacks made their way further north to cities like Chicago. The booming wartime economy made plenty of work available in the city's meatpacking, steel, and aluminum industries. The city was experiencing considerable labor unrest at this time, including a strike at its big aluminum plant. The city became a racial tinderbox when whites working in factories worried that this influx of African American workers would depress wages. Rumors also began to spread about sexual relationships between black men and white women, and blacks were beginning to move into previously segregated neighborhoods. On May 28, a mass meeting of whites gathered to protest the continued black migration into the city. A mob that emerged from the meeting attacked blacks but did not kill anyone. Smaller outbursts of racial violence simmered throughout June, but it was in July that the city truly erupted. The triggering event came on July 1 when two white police officers were accidentally shot and killed by blacks trying to protect their neighborhood against a white mob. On July 2, white mobs gathered downtown and went on a rampage, killing and shooting blacks, and burning down black neighborhoods. The police and National Guard units called in to quell the riots for the most part stood by and watched the violence. The *Chicago Defender* estimated that at least 150 blacks were killed. As a result, roughly 6,000 blacks fled the city.

While some black newspapers, including the *Cleveland Gazette* and the *California Eagle*, encouraged blacks to arm themselves and retaliate, the following piece from the *New York Age* called for calmer heads to prevail. The environment that caused the riots was indicative of the rapid and powerful social changes unleashed by the wartime economy. Similar tensions would lead to outbursts of violence in Chicago in 1919 as many black soldiers were returning from the war and again during World War II in Detroit in 1943 (see document 51).

SOURCE: *New York Age,* July 12, 1917.

The Unruly Tongues.

An unruly tongue is frequently a source of danger and a breeder of disturbance for its possessor and those associated with him. The Negro race is afflicted with many individuals whose wagging tongues are apt to lead them into indiscreet utterances that reflect upon the whole race.

No man, or woman either, for that matter, is a friend to the race, who publicly advises a resort to violence to redress the wrongs and injustices to which members of the race are subjected in various sections of the country at the present time.

Those who advise the resort to firearms and the throwing of bombs as a means of reprisal for such outrages as the slaughter at East St. Louis are playing with fire. The indiscreet talkers will probably be the last to suffer from their empty mouthings, as those who preach violence are the last to practice it. But their bombast can only do harm.

We are insisting on the maintenance of law and order; we are claiming the protection of the law and invoking the law for the redress of those evils that confront us; we cannot therefore afford to encourage lawlessness on our behalf. We must, therefore, maintain law and order on our own part.

Let the limber tongued brethren restrain their natural, but dangerous vaporings. Let them unite in a manly insistent appeal to the proper authorities to maintain the supremacy of the law. Public sentiment is opposed to such outrages as the race has just suffered and will back up such an appeal. The unruly tongues should not be allowed to alienate public sympathy from the cause of the oppressed.

35. W.E.B. DuBois, "Close Ranks"

(1918)

This controversial editorial appeared in the July 1918 issue of the *Crisis*, the monthly journal of the National Association for the Advancement of Colored People (NAACP), a prominent civil rights organization. The journal's editor, W.E.B. DuBois (1868–1963), wrote that African Americans should put aside their "special grievances" during the course of the war and contribute wholeheartedly to the conflict, portraying it as a struggle for democracy. The editorial provoked a furor among the civil rights community, even earning an official condemnation from the Washington, D.C. branch of the NAACP. Many activists thought that under no circumstances, even in times of war, should the struggle for equal rights be abandoned. Yet DuBois felt strongly that African Americans fighting with valor abroad would be invaluable to strengthening their claims to citizenship rights once the war was over.

SOURCE: *Crisis,* July 1918, p. 1.

This is the crisis of the world. For all the long years to come men will point to the year 1918 as the great Day of Decision, the day when the world decided whether it would submit to military despotism and an endless armed peace—if peace it could be called—or whether they would put down the menace of German militarism and inaugurate the United States of the World.

We of the colored race have no ordinary interest in the outcome. That which the German power represents today spells death to the aspirations of Negroes and all darker races for equality, freedom and democracy. Let us not hesitate. Let us, while this war lasts, forget our special grievances and close our ranks shoulder to shoulder with our own white fellow citizens and the allied nations that are fighting for democracy. We make no ordinary sacrifice, but we make it gladly and willingly with our eyes lifted to the hills.

36. A. Mitchell Palmer, "The Case Against the Reds"

(1920)

A. Mitchell Palmer (1872–1936) served as U.S. attorney general under President Woodrow Wilson from March 1919 until March 1921. Before that time, he had served three terms in Congress. The Pennsylvania Quaker turned down the office of secretary of war when Wilson offered it to him due to his pacifism. In 1919, fear that communist agents were plotting to overthrow the government of the United States took hold of the public imagination. In June, a series of bomb blasts, including one that damaged Palmer's home in Washington, D.C., unnerved many people. Palmer, using the powers granted by the 1917 Espionage Act and the 1918 Sedition Act, since no peace treaty had yet been signed, conceived of an elaborate series of raids against communist and anarchist radicals. He put young J. Edgar Hoover in charge of planning them. On November 7, 1919, the anniversary of the Bolshevik Revolution, a raid was launch that rounded up numerous radicals with Russian roots, including Emma Goldman and Alexander Berkman. This group of roughly 250 people was eventually deported. A second major raid occurred on New Year's Day, 1920.

SOURCE: *Forum* 63 (February 1920), 173–85.

Like a prairie-fire, the blaze of revolution was sweeping over every American institution of law and order a year ago. It was eating its way into the homes of the American workman, its sharp tongues of revolutionary heat were licking into the altars of the churches, leaping into the belfry of the school bell, crawling into the sacred corners of American homes, seeking to replace marriage vows with libertine laws, burning up the foundations of society.

Robbery, not war, is the ideal of communism. This has been demonstrated in Russia, Germany, and in America. As a foe, the anarchist is fearless in his own life, for his creed is a fanaticism that admits no respect for any other creed. Obviously it is the creed of any criminal mind, which reasons always from motives impossible to clean thought. Crime is the degenerate factor in society.

Upon these two basic certainties, first that the "Reds" were criminal aliens, and secondly that the American Government must prevent crime, it was decided that there could be no nice distinctions drawn between the theoretical ideals of the radicals and their actual violations of our national laws. An assassin may have brilliant intellectuality, he may be able to excuse his murder or robbery with fine oratory, but any theory which excuses crime is not wanted in America. This is no place for the criminal to flourish, nor will he do so, so long as the rights of common citizenship can be exerted to prevent him. . . .

By stealing, murder and lies, Bolshevism has looted Russia not only of its material strength, but of its moral force. A small clique of outcasts from the East Side of New York has attempted this, with what success we all know. Because a disreputable alien—Leon Bronstein, the man who now calls himself Trotzky— can inaugurate a reign of terror from his throne room in the Kremlin: because this lowest of all types known to New York can sleep in the Czar's bed, while hundreds of thousands in Russia are without food or shelter, should Americans be swayed by such doctrines? . . .

My information showed that communism in this country was an organization of thousands of aliens, who were direct allies of Trotzky. Aliens of the same misshapen cast of mind and indecencies of character, and it showed that they were making the same glittering promises of lawlessness, of criminal autocracy to Americans, that they had made to the Russian peasants. How the Department of Justice discovered upwards of 60,000 of these organized agitators of the Trotzky doctrine in the United States, is the confidential information upon which the Government is now sweeping the nation clean of such alien filth. . . .

One of the chief incentives for the present activity of the Department of Justice against the "Reds" has been the hope that American citizens will, themselves, become voluntary agents for us, in a vast organization for mutual defense against the sinister agitation of men and women aliens, who appear to be either in the pay or under the spell of Trotzky and Lenine [sic] . . . .

The whole purpose of communism appears to be a mass formation of the criminals of the world to overthrow the decencies of private life, to usurp property that they have not earned, to disrupt the present order of life regardless of health, sex, or religious rights. By a literature that promises the wildest dreams of such low aspirations, that can occur to only the criminal minds, communism distorts our social law. . . .

These are the revolutionary tenets of Trotzky and the Communist Internationale. Their manifesto further embraces the various organizations in this country of men and women obsessed with discontent, having disorganized relations to American society. These include the I. W. W.'s, the most radical socialists, the misguided anarchists, the agitators who oppose the limitations of unionism, the moral perverts and the hysterical neurasthenic women who abound in communism. The phraseology of their manifesto is practically the same wording as was used by the Bolsheviks for their International Communist Congress.

. . . The Department of Justice will pursue the attack of these "Reds" upon the Government of the United States with vigilance, and no alien, advocating the overthrow of existing law and order in this country, shall escape arrest and prompt deportation.

It is my belief that while they have stirred discontent in our midst, while they have caused irritating strikes, and while they have infected our social ideas with the disease of their own minds and their unclean morals, we can get rid of them! And not until we have done so shall we have removed the menace of Bolshevism for good.

37. William Allen White, "The Red Scare Is Un-American"

(1920)

The Kansas native William Allen White (1868–1944) bought his hometown newspaper, the *Emporia Gazette*, in 1895, and edited it for the rest of his life. In 1896 White wrote an editorial titled "What's a Matter with Kansas?" that critiqued the popularity of the Populists in his home state. While he never published it himself, it somehow landed in the hands of the leaders of the national Republican organization, who reprinted it widely during that year's presidential campaign, thus garnering White a national reputation. Public sentiment seemed largely supportive of Attorney General Palmer's raids in January 1920, but White and a few other voices protested vigorously. In his paper, White also savaged the Ku Klux Klan, which was resurgent in the years following the war. He won a Pulitzer Prize in 1923 for his powerful editorial advocating free speech, "To an Anxious Friend."

SOURCE: *Emporia Gazette*, January 8, 1920.

The Attorney General seems to be seeing red. He is rounding up every manner of radical in the country; every man who hopes for a better world is in danger of deportation by the Attorney General. The whole business is un-American. There are certain rules which should govern in the treason cases.

First, it should be agreed that a man may believe what he chooses.

Second, it should be agreed that when he preaches violence he is disturbing the peace and should be put in jail. Whether he preaches violence in politics, business, or religion, whether he advocates murder and arson and pillage for gain or for political ends, he is violating the common law and should be squelched—jailed until he is willing to quit advocating force in a democracy.

Third, he should be allowed to say what he pleases so long as he advocates legal constitutional methods of procedure. Just because a man does not believe this government is good is no reason why he should be deported.

Abraham Lincoln did not believe this government was all right seventy-five

116

years ago. He advocated changes, but he advocated constitutional means, and he had a war with those who advocated force to maintain the government as it was.

Ten years ago Roosevelt advocated great changes in our American life—in our Constitution, in our social and economic life. Most of the changes he advocated have been made, but they were made in the regular legal way. He preached no force. And if a man desires to preach any doctrine under the shining sun, and to advocate the realization of his vision by lawful, orderly, constitutional means—let him alone. If he is Socialist, anarchist, or Mormon, and merely preaches his creed and does not preach violence, he can do no harm. For the folly of his doctrine will be its answer.

The deportation business is going to make martyrs of a lot of idiots whose cause is not worth it.

CHAPTER
FOUR

World War II, Part I: Mobilization and the Early War

38. Canute Frankson, "Letter from Spain from an Abraham Lincoln Brigade Soldier"

(1937)

The Spanish Civil War (1936–39) was in essence a trial run for several of the future combatant nations in World War II. War broke out when parts of the Spanish Army attempted to overthrow the government of the Second Republic. Those who supported the uprising, known as the Nationalists, tended to be conservative Catholics and rural landowners. The Republicans tended to be urban and secular, comprised of a broad coalition of liberal democrats, Communists, socialists, and anarchists. Fascist Italy under Benito Mussolini and Nazi Germany under Adolf Hitler both sent troops and weaponry to back the rebel Nationalist forces (including the German Condor Legion, the volunteer Luftwaffe unit that bombed Guernica, the horrific event memorialized in Pablo Picasso's famous painting). Republican forces received volunteers and aid from the Soviet Union and Mexico. The United States declared an embargo on aid for either side, although some American corporations sold trucks and petroleum to the Nationalists. Great Britain and France did not come to the rescue of the embattled Republic, maintaining a policy of nonintervention. Nonetheless, left-wing organizations from numerous countries sponsored volunteer units who came to fight for the Republic against fascism. These non-Spanish units were known collectively as the International Brigades.

Approximately 2,800 young volunteers served in the Abraham Lincoln Brigade, the American unit of the International Brigades. Most of the volunteers had some sort of affiliation with the Communist Party or other radical left groups, and a great many of them were from working-class backgrounds. Canute Frankson was an African American who served in the Abraham Lincoln Brigade, and in his letter, he makes a direct linkage between his fight against international fascism and fighting Jim Crow segregation back in the United States.

SOURCE: Cary Nelson and Jefferson Hendricks, eds., *Madrid 1937: Letters of the Abraham Lincoln Brigade from the Spanish Civil War* (New York: Routledge, 1996).

Albacete, Spain
July 6, 1937

My Dear Friend:

I'm sure that by this time you are still waiting for a detailed explanation of what has this international struggle to do with my being here. Since this is a war between whites who for centuries have held us in slavery, and have heaped every kind of insult and abuse upon us, segregated and jim-crowed us; why I, a Negro who have fought through these years for the rights of my people, am here in Spain today?

Because we are no longer an isolated minority group fighting hopelessly against an immense giant. Because, my dear, we have joined with, and become an active part of, a great progressive force, on whose shoulders rests the responsibility of saving human civilization from the planned destruction of a small group of degenerates gone mad in their lust for power. Because if we crush Fascism here we'll save our people in America, and in other parts of the world from the vicious persecution, wholesale imprisonment, and slaughter which the Jewish people suffered and are suffering under Hitler's Fascist heels.

All we have to do is to think of the lynching of our people. We can but look back at the pages of American history stained with the blood of Negroes; stink with the burning bodies of our people hanging from trees; bitter with the groans of our tortured loved ones from whose living bodies ears, fingers, toes have been cut for souvenirs—living bodies into which red-hot pokers have been thrust. All because of a hate created in the minds of men and women by their masters who keep us all under their heels while they suck our blood, while they live in their bed of ease by exploiting us.

But these people who howl like hungry wolves for our blood, must we hate them? Must we keep the flame which these masters kindled constantly fed? Are these men and women responsible for the programs of their masters, and the conditions which force them to such degraded depths? I think not. They are tools in the hands of unscrupulous masters. These same people are as hungry as we are. They live in dives and wear rags the same as we do. They, too, are robbed by the masters, and their faces kept down in the filth of a decayed system. They are our fellowmen. Soon, and very soon, they and we will understand. Soon, many Angelo Herndons will rise from among them, and from among us, and will lead us both against those who live by the stench of our burnt flesh. We will crush them. We will build us a new society—a society of peace and plenty. There will be no color line, no jim-crow trains, no lynching. That is why, my dear, I'm here in Spain.

Canute

39. The Almanac Singers, "'C' Is for Conscription"

(1941)

The folk group the Almanac Singers formed in New York City in 1940 to play at political rallies and union events. Its initial members were Lee Hays, Pete Seeger, and Millard Lampell. In existence for not much more than a year, the group changed personnel frequently, at times including the songwriter and radio commentator Woody Guthrie and singers Josh White and Sam Gary, the blues artist Leadbelly, and several others. The Almanacs' first album, *Songs for John Doe*, was released in May 1941, when the United States was still officially neutral in the conflict that was engulfing the globe. The songs on this album stood strongly against American entry into the war, as evidenced by "'C' is for Conscription." But when the Nazis invaded the Soviet Union on June 22, breaking the terms of the Molotov-Ribbentrop Pact of 1939, the Almanac Singers, along with many other leftists, began to make the case for American intervention, as reflected on their February 1942 album, *Dear Mr. President* (see document 44).

SOURCE: Almanac Records, New York, May 1941.

> Well, it's 'C' for Conscription
> And it's 'C' for Capitol Hill!
> Well, it's 'C' for Conscription
> And it's 'C' for Capitol Hill!
> And it's 'C' for the Congress
> That passed that goddamn bill!
> [YODEL]
>
> I'd rather be at home,
> Even sleeping in a holler log,
> I'd rather be here home,
> Even sleeping in a holler log.
> Than go to the army
> Be treated like a dirty dog!
> [YODEL]

40. Charles Lindbergh, "Address to a Mass Meeting of the America First Committee"

(1941)

The America First Committee (AFC) was organized in September 1940 to apply political pressure on President Roosevelt to keep the United States out of the war. The group's founders viewed Roosevelt's Destroyers for Bases program in 1940, his March 1941 Lend-Lease program supplying war materials to the Allies, and his economic sanctions against Japan as compromising American neutrality. The AFC capitalized on a strong noninterventionist sentiment in the Midwest, making Chicago the focal point of its organizing efforts. It claimed roughly 800,000 members at its peak, including politicians Senator Burton K. Wheeler of Montana, Senator Gerald P. Nye of North Dakota, and Socialist Party leader Norman Thomas, as well popular entertainment figures like actress Lillian Gish and animator Walt Disney. Yet its most prominent spokesperson was undoubtedly the famed aviator Charles A. Lindbergh (1902–74), most famous for making the first solo trans-Atlantic flight in 1927. Lindbergh's speech excerpted below was delivered in front of an AFC mass meeting of about 10,000 people at the Manhattan Center in New York City on April 23, 1941. Overall, the speech emphasized that the United States should prepare its own defenses rather than weaken itself in an overseas war. Many observers thought of Lindbergh as a Nazi sympathizer; this reputation was somewhat strengthened by a speech he delivered in Des Moines later in 1941, which many viewed as anti-Semitic. The efforts of the AFC were rendered moot by the Pearl Harbor attack. Lindbergh requested that the military commission he had resigned during the 1930s be restored, but President Roosevelt refused.

SOURCE: Charles A. Lindbergh, *Address, New York, April 23, 1941* (Chicago: America First Committee, 1941).

... WAR is not inevitable for this country. Such a claim is defeatism in the true sense. No one can make us fight abroad unless we ourselves are willing to do so. No one will attempt to fight us here if we arm ourselves as a great nation should be armed. Over a hundred million people in this nation are opposed to entering the war. If the principles of Democracy mean anything at all, that is reason enough for us to stay out. If we are forced into a war against the wishes of an overwhelming majority of our people, we will have proved Democracy such a failure at home that there will be little use fighting for it abroad.

THE time has come when those of us who believe in an independent American destiny must band together, and organize for strength. We have been led toward war by a minority of our people. This minority has power. It has influence. It has a loud voice. But it does not represent the American people. During the last several years, I have travelled over this country, from one end to the other. I have talked to many hundreds of men and women, and I have had letters from tens of thousands more, who feel the same way as you and I. Most of these people have no influence or power. Most of them have no means of expressing their convictions, except by their vote which has always been against this war. They are the citizens who have had to work too hard at their daily jobs to organize political meetings. Hitherto, they have relied upon their vote to express their feelings; but now they find that it is hardly remembered except in the oratory of a political campaign. These people—the majority of hard-working American citizens are with us. *They* are the true strength of our country. And they are beginning to realize, as you and I, that there are times when we must sacrifice our normal interests in life in order to insure the safety and the welfare of our nation.

SUCH a time has come. Such a crisis is here. That is why the America First Committee has been formed—to give voice to the people who have no newspaper, or news reel, or radio station at their command; to the people who must do the paying, and the fighting, and the dying, if this country enters the war.

WHETHER or not we do enter the war, rests upon the shoulders of you in this audience, upon us here on this platform, upon meetings of this kind that are being held by Americans in every section of the United States today. It depends upon the action we take, and the courage we show at this time. If you believe in an independent destiny for America, if you believe that this country should not enter the war in Europe, we ask you to join the America First Committee in its stand. We ask you to share our faith in the ability of this nation to defend itself, to develop its own civilization, and to contribute to the progress of mankind in a more constructive and intelligent way than has yet been found by the warring nations of Europe. We need your support, and we need it now. The time to act is here.

41. Franklin D. Roosevelt, "Declaration of War"

(1941)

The following address was delivered to a joint session of Congress by President Franklin D. Roosevelt (1882–1945) on December 8, 1941, one day after the Japanese attack on the U.S. naval base at Pearl Harbor on the Hawaiian island of Oahu. The speech encouraged Congress to declare war on the Japanese Empire. The attack was an attempt to deal a tremendous blow to the U.S. Pacific Fleet before Japanese imperial forces invaded the British colony of Malaya and the Dutch East Indies to gain control of the critical supplies of oil and rubber there. Japanese military leadership thought that these provocations would draw the United States into the war, thus creating the need for a preemptive strike. The attack focused on the eight battleships in the harbor, all of which were either sunk or damaged. None of the fleet's aircraft carriers were in the harbor at the time of the attack, and were thus spared. The destruction of the battleships forced the U.S. Pacific Fleet to rely more on aircraft carriers and submarines, which ultimately proved effective in stopping Japanese expansion. Over 2,400 Americans were killed in the attack, while the Japanese lost only twenty-nine planes. Roosevelt's description of December 7, 1941, as "a date which will live in infamy" remains one of the most memorable phrases in American history.

SOURCE: Records of the U.S. Senate, Record Group 46, National Archives, Washington, D.C.

Yesterday, December 7, 1941—a date which will live in infamy—the United States of America was suddenly and deliberately attacked by naval and air forces of the Empire of Japan. The United States was at peace with that nation and, at the solicitation of Japan, was still in conversation with its Government and its Emperor looking toward the maintenance of peace in the Pacific. Indeed, one hour after Japanese air squadrons had commenced bombing in Oahu, the Japanese Ambassador to the United States and his colleague delivered to the Secretary of State a formal reply to a recent American message.

While this reply stated that it seemed useless to continue the existing diplomatic negotiations, it contained no threat or hint of war or armed attack It will be recorded that the distance of Hawaii from Japan makes it obvious that the attack was deliberately planned many days or even weeks ago. During the intervening time the Japanese Government has deliberately sought to deceive the United States by false statements and expressions of hope for continued peace. The attack yesterday on the Hawaiian Islands has caused severe damage to American naval and military forces. Very many American lives have been lost. In addition American ships have been reported torpedoed on the high seas between San Francisco and Honolulu.

Yesterday the Japanese Government also launched an attack against Malaya. Last night Japanese forces attacked Hong Kong. Last night Japanese forces attacked Guam. Last night Japanese forces attacked the Philippine Islands. Last night the Japanese attacked Wake Island. This morning the Japanese attacked Midway Island. Japan has, therefore, undertaken a surprise offensive extending throughout the Pacific area. The facts of yesterday speak for themselves. The people of the United States have already formed their opinions and well understand the implications to the very life and safety of our Nation. As Commander in Chief of the Army and Navy I have directed that all measures be taken for our defense. Always will we remember the character of the onslaught against us. No matter how long it may take us to overcome this premeditated invasion, the American people, in their righteous might, will win through to absolute victory.

I believe I interpret the will of the Congress and of the people when I assert that we will not only defend ourselves to the uttermost but will make very certain that this form of treachery shall never endanger us again. Hostilities exist. There is no blinking at the fact that our people, our territory, and our interests are in grave danger. With confidence in our armed forces—with the unbounded determination of our people—we will gain the inevitable triumph—so help us God. I ask that the Congress declare that since the unprovoked and dastardly attack by Japan on Sunday, December 7, a state of war has existed between the United States and the Japanese Empire.

42. Franklin D. Roosevelt, "On Inflation and Progress of the War"

(1942)

The following excerpts are from President Roosevelt's 1942 Labor Day radio address, just one in his series of "Fireside Chats" that began during the worst days of the Great Depression. Roosevelt delivered approximately thirty of these nationally broadcasted radio talks between 1933 and 1944, each lasting about fifteen to forty-five minutes. Presented in an informal style, they were broadcast at 10:00 P.M. Eastern Time so that people on the West Coast would be home from work and people on the East Coast would not yet be asleep. In what follows, Roosevelt explained his administration's measures to control price inflation. He attempted to justify further action that he was about to take to stabilize the price of farm goods in hopes of preventing future surges or crashes, bringing them under the control of the Office of Price Administration (OPA). In this speech, he directly linked the economic stability of the domestic economy to the success of the war effort abroad.

SOURCE: Franklin D. Roosevelt Presidential Library and Museum, Hyde Park, New York.

. . . Today I sent a message to the Congress, pointing out the overwhelming urgency of the serious domestic economic crisis with which we are threatened. Some call it "inflation," which is a vague sort of term, and others call it a "rise in the cost of living," which is much more easily understood by most families.

That phrase, "the cost of living," means essentially what a dollar can buy.

From January 1, 1941, to May of this year, nearly a year and a half, the cost of living went up about 15%. And at that point last May we undertook to freeze the cost of living. But we could not do a complete job of it, because the Congressional authority at the time exempted a large part of farm products used for food and for making clothing, although several weeks before, I had asked the Congress for legislation to stabilize all farm prices.

At that time I had told the Congress that there were seven elements in our national economy, all of which had to be controlled; and that if any one essential element remained exempt, the cost of living could not be held down.

On only two of these points—both of them vital however—did I call for Congressional action. These two vital points were: First, taxation; and, second, the stabilization of all farm prices at parity.

"Parity" is a standard for the maintenance of good farm prices. It was established as our national policy way back in 1933. It means that the farmer and the city worker are on the same relative ratio with each other in purchasing power as they were during a period some thirty years before—at a time then the farmer had a satisfactory purchasing power. One hundred percent of parity, therefore, has been accepted by farmers as the fair standard for the prices they receive.

Last January, however, the Congress passed a law forbidding ceilings on farm prices below 110 percent of parity on some commodities. And on other commodities the ceiling was even higher, so that the average possible ceiling is now about 116 percent of parity for agricultural products as a whole.

This act of favoritism for one particular group in the community increased the cost of food to everybody—not only to the workers in the city or in the munitions plants, and their families, but also to the families of the farmers themselves.

Since last May, ceilings have been set on nearly all commodities, rents and services, except the exempted farm products. Installment buying, for example, has been effectually stabilized and controlled.

Wages in certain key industries have been stabilized on the basis of the present cost of living.

But it is obvious to all of us that if the cost of food continues to go up, as it is doing at present, the wage earner, particularly in the lower brackets, will have a right to an increase in his wages. I think that would be essential justice and a practical necessity.

Our experience with the control of other prices during the past few months has brought out one important fact—the rising cost of living can be controlled, providing that all elements making up the cost of living are controlled at the same time. I think that also is an essential justice and a practical necessity. We know that parity prices for farm products not now controlled will not put up the cost of living more than a very small amount; but we also know that if we must go up to an average of 116 percent of parity for food and other farm products—which is necessary at present under the Emergency Price Control Act before we can control all farm prices—the cost of living will get well out of hand. We are face to face with this danger today. Let us meet it and remove it.

I realize that it may seem out of proportion to you to be (worrying about) over-stressing these economic problems at a time like this, when we are all deeply concerned about the news from far distant fields of battle. But I give you the solemn assurance that failure to solve this problem here at home—and to solve it now—will make more difficult the winning of this war.

If the vicious spiral of inflation ever gets under way, the whole economic system will stagger. Prices and wages will go up so rapidly that the entire production program will be endangered. The cost of the war, paid by taxpayers, will jump beyond all present calculations. It will mean an uncontrollable rise in prices and in wages, which can result in raising the overall cost of living as high as another 20 percent soon. That would mean that the purchasing power of every dollar that you have in your pay envelope, or in the bank, or included in your insurance policy or your pension, would be reduced to about eighty cents worth. I need not tell you that this would have a demoralizing effect on our people, soldiers and civilians alike.

Overall stabilization of prices, and salaries, and wages and profits is necessary to the continued increasing production of planes and tanks and ships and guns.

In my Message to Congress today, I have said that this must be done quickly. If we wait for two or three or four or six months it may well be too late.

I have told the Congress that the Administration can not hold the actual cost of food and clothing down to the present level beyond October first.

Therefore, I have asked the Congress to pass legislation under which the President would be specifically authorized to stabilize the cost of living, including the price of all farm commodities. The purpose should be to hold farm prices at parity, or at levels of a recent date, whichever is higher. The purpose should also be to keep wages at a point stabilized with today's cost of living. Both must be regulated at the same time; and neither one of them can or should be regulated without the other.

At the same time that farm prices are stabilized, I will stabilize wages.

That is plain justice—and plain common sense.

And so I have asked the Congress to take this action by the first of October. We must now act with the dispatch, which the stern necessities of war require.

I have told the Congress that inaction on their part by that date will leave me with an inescapable responsibility, a responsibility to the people of this country to see to it that the war effort is no longer imperiled by the threat of economic chaos.

As I said in my Message to the Congress:

In the event that the Congress should fail to act, and act adequately, I shall accept the responsibility, and I will act.

The President has the powers, under the Constitution and under Congressional Acts, to take measures necessary to avert a disaster which would interfere with the winning of the war.

I have given the most careful and thoughtful consideration to meeting this issue without further reference to the Congress. I have determined, however, on this vital matter to consult with the Congress.

There may be those who will say that, if the situation is as grave as I have stated it to be, I should use my powers and act now. I can only say that I have approached this problem from every angle, and that I have decided that the course of conduct which I am following in this case is consistent with my sense of responsibility as President in time of war, and with my deep and unalterable devotion to the processes of democracy.

The responsibilities of the President in wartime to protect the Nation are very grave. This total war, with our fighting fronts all over the world, makes the use of the executive power far more essential than in any previous war.

If we were invaded, the people of this country would expect the President to use any and all means to repel the invader.

Now the Revolution and the War between the States were fought on our own soil, but today this war will be won or lost on other continents and in remote seas. I cannot tell what powers may have to be exercised in order to win this war.

The American people can be sure that I will use my powers with a full sense of responsibility to the Constitution and to my country. The American people can also be sure that I shall not hesitate to use every power vested in me to accomplish the defeat of our enemies in any part of the world where our own safety demands such defeat.

And when the war is won, the powers under which I act will automatically revert to the people of the United States—to the people to whom those powers belong. . . .

All of us here at home are being tested—for our fortitude, for our selfless devotion to our country and to our cause.

This is the toughest war of all time. We need not leave it to historians of the future to answer the question whether we are tough enough to meet this unprecedented challenge. We can give that answer now. The answer is "Yes."

43. "Warning and Instructions on Ration Book One"

(1942)

The Office of Price Administration was created as an agency within the Office of Emergency Management by an executive order on August 28, 1941, combining two existing agencies under one rubric. The OPA's main functions were to ration consumer goods made scarce by war and to keep inflation in check through price controls. Initially, agricultural goods were not rationed, but eventually they were brought under the OPA's control, as were items like sugar and coffee. Ration books were issued by the OPA to control individual allotments of consumer goods subject to wartime scarcity. What follows is the text of the warning and instructions printed on the first ration book issued by the OPA.

SOURCE: Government Printing Office, Washington, D.C., 1942.

Warning

1. Punishments ranging as high as Ten Years' Imprisonment or $10,000 Fine, or Both, may be imposed under United States Statutes for violations thereof arising out of infractions of Rationing Orders and Regulations.

2. This book must not be transferred. It must be held and used only by or on behalf of the person to whom it has been issued, and anyone presenting it thereby represents to the Office of Price Administration, an agency of the United States Government, that it is being so held and so used. For any misuses of this book it may be taken from the holder by the Office of Price Administration.

3. In the event either of the departure from the United States of the person to whom this book is issued, or his or her death, this book must be surrendered in accordance with the Regulations.

4. Any person finding a lost book must deliver it promptly to the nearest Ration Board.

Instructions

Your first ration book has been issued to you, originally containing 28 war ration stamps. Other books may be issued at later dates. The following instructions apply to your first book and will apply to any later books, unless otherwise ordered by the Office of Price Administration. In order to obtain a later book, the first book must be turned in. You should preserve War Rations Books with the greatest possible care.

1. From the time the Office of Price Administration may issue orders rationing certain products. After the dates indicated by such orders, these products can be purchased only through the use of War Ration Books containing valid War Ration Stamps.

2. The orders of the Office of Price Administration will designate the stamps to be used for the purchase of a particular rationed product, the period during which each of these stamps may be used, and the amounts which may be bought with each stamp.

3. Stamps become valid for use only when and as directed by the Orders of the Office of Price Administration.

4. Unless otherwise announced, the Ration Week is from Saturday midnight to the following Saturday midnight.

5. War Ration stamps may be used in any retail store in the United States.

6. War Ration Stamps may be used only by or for the person named and described in the War Ration Book.

7. Every person must see that this War Ration Book is kept in a safe place and properly used. Parents are responsible for the safekeeping and use of their children's War Ration Book.

8. When you buy any rationed product, the proper stamp must be detached in the presence of the storekeeper, his employee, or the person making the delivery on his behalf. If a stamp is torn out of the War Ration Book in any other way than above indicated, it becomes void. If a stamp is partly torn or mutilated and more than one half of it remains in the book, it is valid. Otherwise it becomes void.

9. If your War Ration Book is lost, destroyed, stolen or mutilated, you should report that fact to the local Ration Board.

10. If you enter a hospital, or other institution, and expect to be there for more than 10 days, you must turn your War Ration Book over to the person in charge. It will be returned to you upon your request when you leave.

11. When a person dies, his War Ration Book must be returned to the local Ration Board, in accordance with the regulations.

12. If you have any complaints, questions, or difficulties regarding your War Ration Book, consult your local Ration Board.

44. The Almanac Singers, "Deliver the Goods"

(1942)

By 1942, with the war against fascism under way, the Almanac Singers switched from the isolationist stance of their first album, *Songs for John Doe*, to one that fully embraced the war effort (see introduction to document 39). Their final album, *Dear Mr. President*, was filled with patriotic songs like "Round and Round Hitler's Grave" and "Deliver the Goods." Radio producer Norman Corwin heard the group and, in February 1942, had them perform on his CBS radio program, *This Is War!*, which featured an elaborate mix of music and propaganda radio plays. The Almanacs enjoyed considerable popularity after the performance, but also came under attack for the members' connections to the Communist Party. Despite the brief life of the Almanac Singers, they proved immensely influential by popularizing the protest song and by inspiring artists like Bob Dylan. Members Pete Seeger and Lee Hays would go on to found the long-lived popular folk group The Weavers.

SOURCE: Keynote Records, New York, 1942.

> It's gonna take everybody to win this war
> The butcher and the baker and the clerk in the store.
> The guys who sail the ships, and the guys who run the trains
> And the farmer raisin' wheat upon the Kansas plains.
>
> The butcher, the baker, the tinker and the tailor
> Will all work behind the soldier and the sailor.
> We're workin' in the cities, we're workin' in the woods
> And we'll all work together to deliver the goods.
>
> Now, me and my boss, we never did agree
> If a thing helped him then it didn't help me.
> But when a burglar tries to bust into your house
> You stop fighting with the landlord and throw him out.

I got a new job and I'm workin' overtime
Turning out tanks on the assembly line.
Gotta crank up the factories like the President said
Damn the torpedoes, full speed ahead.

I bet this tank will look mighty fine
Punching holes in Mr. Hitler's line.
And if Adolph wakes up after the raid
He'll find every piece of shrapnel says "U.S.A."

From New York City to Frisco Bay
We're speedin' up production every day.
And every time a wheel goes around
It carries Mr. Hitler to the burying ground.

45. "Williams Decides to Play One Season"

(1942)

In this *New York Times* piece, young baseball star Ted Williams (1918–2002) explains why he decided to play the 1942 season before enlisting in the army. He mentioned his draft classification as 3-A, which meant that Williams was not to be drafted right away since it would cause hardship to dependents. (Baseball players were paid far less than they are now, and Williams's mother relied on him financially.) The Selective Service labeled a man 1-A if he could be drafted right away, while a 2-A classification meant that the individual did some sort of work that was vital to the "national interest" and thus should receive a deferment. (Curiously, actor John Wayne, who came to embody the American fighting man in many Hollywood films made during the war, obtained a 3-A classification early in the war, and in 1944 obtained a 2-A classification when his studio appealed his reclassification to 1-A. Wayne never served.) Heckled by fans as "un-American" for taking a deferment in 1942, Williams enlisted in the Navy Reserves in May and then entered the service full-time after the baseball season was over. He spent the rest of the war training and learning how to become a fighter pilot, never seeing active duty. Yet he learned his craft well and put his skills to use during the Korean War, flying thirty-eight combat missions.

SOURCE: *New York Times,* March 6, 1942, p. 26.

Red Sox Batting Star Says He Will Enlist After Coming Baseball Campaign

MINNEAPOLIS, March 5 (AP)—Ted Williams, Boston Red Sox slugger and American League batting champion, decided today to play one more season of baseball and then enlist with Uncle Sam's forces in the war.

After conferring by telephone with Red Sox officials at the team's Spring training camp at Sarasota, Fla., Williams announced his decision and prepared to leave for the South.

Williams yesterday visited the Great Lakes, Ill., Naval Training Station, "just to look around," he said.

Later, Williams said:

"While deferred from the draft in a 3-A classification, I made certain financial commitments. I must carry through with them. Therefore, despite a strong urge to enter the service now, I have decided to play ball with the Red Sox this Summer. That will enable me to fulfill my obligations to my family and make everything right all around."

CHAPTER FIVE

World War II, Part II: A Society at War

46. Franklin D. Roosevelt, "Executive Order 9066 (Internment Order)"

(1942)

On February 19, 1942, President Roosevelt issued the following executive order, which enabled the secretary of war to prescribe military areas "from which any or all persons may be excluded." No specific ethnic group was mentioned in the order, but the meaning was clear: areas seen as militarily sensitive or susceptible to invasion were to be cleared of all people descended from enemy nationalities, even if they were American citizens. Some Germans and Italians endured arrest and internment under this order, but people of Japanese ancestry suffered the most by far. Roughly 5,000 Germans and 300 Italians were interned, compared with approximately 120,000 Japanese. Military strategists feared an invasion of the West Coast by the Japanese Empire, so a fifty-to-sixty-mile swath of coastline stretching from Washington State to California was cleared of all people of Japanese ethnicity. They were forced to their leave jobs and property behind and to move to one of ten exceedingly remote and hastily constructed internment camps. The sites were often in desert or mountain regions, and the cheaply constructed buildings barely protected the residents from the extreme climates. This complete disregard for citizenship rights was unprecedented in American history. Two prominent Washington insiders, Eleanor Roosevelt and J. Edgar Hoover, director of the Federal Bureau of Investigation (FBI), opposed the order but could not prevent the president from issuing it.

SOURCE: Executive Order No. 9066, *Federal Register,* Doc. 42-1563, February 12, 1942.

Executive Order No. 9066

The President
EXECUTIVE ORDER
AUTHORIZING THE SECRETARY OF WAR TO PRESCRIBE MILITARY AREAS
WHEREAS the successful prosecution of the war requires every possible

protection against espionage and against sabotage to national-defense material, national-defense premises, and national-defense utilities as defined in Section 4, Act of April 20, 1918, 40 Stat. 533, as amended by the Act of November 30, 1940, 54 Stat. 1220, and the Act of August 21, 1941, 55 Stat. 655 (U.S.C., Title 50, Sec. 104);

NOW, THEREFORE, by virtue of the authority vested in me as President of the United States, and Commander in Chief of the Army and Navy, I hereby authorize and direct the Secretary of War, and the Military Commanders whom he may from time to time designate, whenever he or any designated Commander deems such action necessary or desirable, to prescribe military areas in such places and of such extent as he or the appropriate Military Commander may determine, from which any or all persons may be excluded, and with respect to which, the right of any person to enter, remain in, or leave shall be subject to whatever restrictions the Secretary of War or the appropriate Military Commander may impose in his discretion. The Secretary of War is hereby authorized to provide for residents of any such area who are excluded therefrom, such transportation, food, shelter, and other accommodations as may be necessary, in the judgment of the Secretary of War or the said Military Commander, and until other arrangements are made, to accomplish the purpose of this order. The designation of military areas in any region or locality shall supersede designations of prohibited and restricted areas by the Attorney General under the Proclamations of December 7 and 8, 1941,[1] and shall supersede the responsibility and authority of the Attorney General under the said Proclamations in respect of such prohibited and restricted areas.

I hereby further authorize and direct the Secretary of War and the said Military Commanders to take such other steps as he or the appropriate Military Commander may deem advisable to enforce compliance with the restrictions applicable to each Military area hereinabove authorized to be designated, including the use of Federal troops and other Federal Agencies, with authority to accept assistance of state and local agencies.

I hereby further authorize and direct all Executive Departments, independent establishments and other Federal Agencies, to assist the Secretary of War or the said Military Commanders in carrying out this Executive Order, including the furnishing of medical aid, hospitalization, food, clothing, transportation, use of land, shelter, and other supplies, equipment, utilities, facilities, and services.

This order shall not be construed as modifying or limiting in any way the authority heretofore granted under Executive Order No. 8972,[2] dated December 12, 1941, nor shall it be construed as limiting or modifying the duty and responsibility of the Federal Bureau of Investigation, with respect to the investigation of alleged acts of sabotage or the duty and responsibility of the Attorney General and the Department of Justice under the Proclamations of December 7 and 8, 1941, prescribing regulations for the conduct and control of alien enemies, except

1. 6 F.R. 6321, 6323, 6324.
2. 6 F.R. 6420. Source: *Federal Register*, Vol. 7, No. 38, p. 1407 (Feb. 25, 1942).

as such duty and responsibility is superseded by the designation of military areas hereunder.

FRANKLIN D. ROOSEVELT
THE WHITE HOUSE,
February 19, 1942.

[No. 9066]

[F. R. Doc. 42–1563; Filed, February 21, 1942; 12:51 p.m.]

47. Korematsu v. United States (Supreme Court Opinion Upholding Internment)

(1944)

This highly controversial case was decided by the Supreme Court on December 18, 1944. Fred Korematsu (1919–2005) was an American citizen born in Oakland, California, to Japanese parents. Soon after President Roosevelt issued Executive Order 9066 in February 1942, Japanese Americans in the prescribed "military areas" (which encompassed much of the West Coast) were ordered to report to assembly centers to be processed in preparation for being sent to relocation camps. When the Korematsu family was forced to report to such a center south of San Francisco, Fred refused to go and went into hiding. He may have been reluctant to leave on account of his relationship with his Italian American girlfriend. Fred was captured on May 30, 1942, and eventually sent to the Topaz internment camp in Utah. He decided to appeal his case, taking it all the way to the Supreme Court. In a 6–3 vote, the Court affirmed the constitutionality of relocation. Excerpts from Justice Hugo Black's "Opinion of the Court" and Justice Robert H. Jackson's "Dissenting Opinion" follow.

SOURCE: 140 F.2d 289, affirmed (1944).

BLACK, J., Opinion of the Court

MR. JUSTICE BLACK delivered the opinion of the Court.

The petitioner, an American citizen of Japanese descent, was convicted in a federal district court for remaining in San Leandro, California, a "Military Area," contrary to Civilian Exclusion Order No. 34 of the Commanding General of the Western Command, U.S. Army, which directed that, after May 9, 1942, all persons of Japanese ancestry should be excluded from that area. No question was raised as to petitioner's loyalty to the United States. The Circuit Court of Appeals affirmed, and the importance of the constitutional question involved caused us to grant certiorari.

It should be noted, to begin with, that all legal restrictions which curtail the civil rights of a single racial group are immediately suspect. That is not to say that all such restrictions are unconstitutional. It is to say that courts must subject them to the most rigid scrutiny. Pressing public necessity may sometimes justify the existence of such restrictions; racial antagonism never can.

In the instant case, prosecution of the petitioner was begun by information charging violation of an Act of Congress, of March 21, 1942, 56 Stat. 173, which provides that . . . whoever shall enter, remain in, leave, or commit any act in any military area or military zone prescribed, under the authority of an Executive order of the President, by the Secretary of War, or by any military commander designated by the Secretary of War, contrary to the restrictions applicable to any such area or zone or contrary to the order of the Secretary of War or any such military commander, shall, if it appears that he knew or should have known of the existence and extent of the restrictions or order and that his act was in violation thereof, be guilty of a misdemeanor and upon conviction shall be liable to a fine of not to exceed $5,000 or to imprisonment for not more than one year, or both, for each offense.

Exclusion Order No. 34, which the petitioner knowingly and admittedly violated, was one of a number of military orders and proclamations, all of which were substantially based upon Executive Order No. 9066, 7 Fed. Reg. 1407. That order, issued after we were at war with Japan, declared that the successful prosecution of the war requires every possible protection against espionage and against sabotage to national defense material, national defense premises, and national defense utilities. . . .

One of the series of orders and proclamations, a curfew order, which, like the exclusion order here, was promulgated pursuant to Executive Order 9066, subjected all persons of Japanese ancestry in prescribed West Coast military areas to remain in their residences from 8 p.m. to 6 a.m. As is the case with the exclusion order here, that prior curfew order was designed as a "protection against espionage and against sabotage." In *Hirabayashi v. United States,* 320 U.S. 81, we sustained a conviction obtained for violation of the curfew order. The Hirabayashi conviction and this one thus rest on the same 1942 Congressional Act and the same basic executive and military orders, all of which orders were aimed at the twin dangers of espionage and sabotage.

The 1942 Act was attacked in the *Hirabayashi* case as an unconstitutional delegation of power; it was contended that the curfew order and other orders on which it rested were beyond the war powers of the Congress, the military authorities, and of the President, as Commander in Chief of the Army, and, finally, that to apply the curfew order against none but citizens of Japanese ancestry amounted to a constitutionally prohibited discrimination solely on account of race. To these questions, we gave the serious consideration which their importance justified. We upheld the curfew order as an exercise of the power of the government to take steps necessary to prevent espionage and sabotage in an area threatened by Japanese attack.

In the light of the principles we announced in the *Hirabayashi* case, we are unable to conclude that it was beyond the war power of Congress and the

Executive to exclude those of Japanese ancestry from the West Coast war area at the time they did. True, exclusion from the area in which one's home is located is a far greater deprivation than constant confinement to the home from 8 p.m. to 6 a.m. Nothing short of apprehension by the proper military authorities of the gravest imminent danger to the public safety can constitutionally justify either. But exclusion from a threatened area, no less than curfew, has a definite and close relationship to the prevention of espionage and sabotage. The military authorities, charged with the primary responsibility of defending our shores, concluded that curfew provided inadequate protection and ordered exclusion. They did so, as pointed out in our *Hirabayashi* opinion, in accordance with Congressional authority to the military to say who should, and who should not, remain in the threatened areas.

In this case, the petitioner challenges the assumptions upon which we rested our conclusions in the *Hirabayashi* case. He also urges that, by May, 1942, when Order No. 34 was promulgated, all danger of Japanese invasion of the West Coast had disappeared. After careful consideration of these contentions, we are compelled to reject them.

Here, as in the *Hirabayashi* case, *supra,* at p. 99, . . . we cannot reject as unfounded the judgment of the military authorities and of Congress that there were disloyal members of that population, whose number and strength could not be precisely and quickly ascertained. We cannot say that the war-making branches of the Government did not have ground for believing that, in a critical hour, such persons could not readily be isolated and separately dealt with, and constituted a menace to the national defense and safety which demanded that prompt and adequate measures be taken to guard against it.

Like curfew, exclusion of those of Japanese origin was deemed necessary because of the presence of an unascertained number of disloyal members of the group, most of whom we have no doubt were loyal to this country. It was because we could not reject the finding of the military authorities that it was impossible to bring about an immediate segregation of the disloyal from the loyal that we sustained the validity of the curfew order as applying to the whole group. In the instant case, temporary exclusion of the entire group was rested by the military on the same ground. The judgment that exclusion of the whole group was, for the same reason, a military imperative answers the contention that the exclusion was in the nature of group punishment based on antagonism to those of Japanese origin. That there were members of the group who retained loyalties to Japan has been confirmed by investigations made subsequent to the exclusion. Approximately five thousand American citizens of Japanese ancestry refused to swear unqualified allegiance to the United States and to renounce allegiance to the Japanese Emperor, and several thousand evacuees requested repatriation to Japan.

We uphold the exclusion order as of the time it was made and when the petitioner violated it. *Cf. Chastleton Corporation v. Sinclair,* 264 U.S. 543, 547; *Block v. Hirsh,* 256 U.S. 135, 155. In doing so, we are not unmindful of the hardships imposed by it upon a large group of American citizens. *Cf. Ex parte Kawato,* 317 U.S.

69, 73. But hardships are part of war, and war is an aggregation of hardships. All citizens alike, both in and out of uniform, feel the impact of war in greater or lesser measure. . . .

ROBERTS, J., Dissenting Opinion

MR. JUSTICE ROBERTS.

I dissent, because I think the indisputable facts exhibit a clear violation of Constitutional rights.

This is not a case of keeping people off the streets at night, as was *Hirabayashi v. United States,* 320 U.S. 81, nor a case of temporary exclusion of a citizen from an area for his own safety or that of the community, nor a case of offering him an opportunity to go temporarily out of an area where his presence might cause danger to himself or to his fellows. On the contrary, it is the case of convicting a citizen as a punishment for not submitting to imprisonment in a concentration camp, based on his ancestry, and solely because of his ancestry, without evidence or inquiry concerning his loyalty and good disposition towards the United States. If this be a correct statement of the facts disclosed by this record, and facts of which we take judicial notice, I need hardly labor the conclusion that Constitutional rights have been violated.

The Government's argument, and the opinion of the court, in my judgment, erroneously divide that which is single and indivisible, and thus make the case appear as if the petitioner violated a Military Order, sanctioned by Act of Congress, which excluded him from his home by refusing voluntarily to leave, and so knowingly and intentionally defying the order and the Act of Congress.

The petitioner, a resident of San Leandro, Alameda County, California, is a native of the United States of Japanese ancestry who, according to the uncontradicted evidence, is a loyal citizen of the nation.

A chronological recitation of events will make it plain that the petitioner's supposed offense did not, in truth, consist in his refusal voluntarily to leave the area which included his home in obedience to the order excluding him therefrom. Critical attention must be given to the dates and sequence of events.

48. A. Philip Randolph, "Call to Negro America to March on Washington"

(1941)

A. Philip Randolph (1889–1979) was a political activist, civil rights crusader, and longtime president of the first major African American trade union in the United States. Born in Crescent City, Florida, he moved to New York City in 1911 in hopes of becoming an actor, but instead attended City College and studied politics and economics. In 1917, he founded a magazine with Chandler Owen called the *Messenger* (later called *Black Worker*), which promoted labor unionism and socialism among blacks. In 1925, he helped to organize the Brotherhood of Sleeping Car Porters (BSCP), a union for employees of the Pullman Company, a major employer of African Americans. Randolph served as the BSCP's president, a position he held until 1968. In May 1941, Randolph, along with activists Bayard Rustin and A.J. Muste, planned a major march of 150,000 blacks on Washington, D.C., to apply pressure on President Roosevelt to fight employment discrimination in mobilizing defense industries and expanding government agencies. Roosevelt responded right before the march was about to take place, creating the Fair Employment Practices Committee (FEPC) by executive order. Black employment in federal agencies did significantly increase in the years after the FEPC was instituted, but the committee had little influence outside of the federal bureaucracy, exerting no control over private employers or labor unions.

SOURCE: *Black Worker* 14 (May 1941).

We call upon you to fight for jobs in National Defense. We call upon you to struggle for the integration of Negroes in the armed forces. . . .

We call upon you to demonstrate for the abolition of Jim-Crowism in all Government departments and defense employment.

This is an hour of crisis. It is a crisis of democracy. It is a crisis of minority groups. It is a crisis of Negro Americans.

What is this crisis?

To American Negroes, it is the denial of jobs in Government defense projects.

It is racial discrimination in Government departments. It is widespread Jim-Crowism in the armed forces of the Nation.

While billions of the taxpayers' money are being spent for war weapons, Negro workers are finally being turned away from the gates of factories, mines and mills—being flatly told, "NOTHING DOING." Some employers refuse to give Negroes jobs when they are without "union cards," and some unions refuse Negro workers union cards when they are "without jobs."

What shall we do?

What a dilemma!

What a runaround!

What a disgrace!

What a blow below the belt!

Though dark, doubtful and discouraging, all is not lost, all is not hopeless. Though battered and bruised, we are not beaten, broken, or bewildered.

Verily, the Negroes' deepest disappointments and direst defeats, their tragic trials and outrageous oppressions in these dreadful days of destruction and disaster to democracy and freedom, and the rights of minority peoples, and the dignity and independence of the human spirit, is the Negroes' greatest opportunity to rise to the highest heights of struggle for freedom and justice in Government, in industry, in labor unions, education, social service, religion, and culture.

With faith and confidence of the Negro people in their own power for self-liberation, Negroes can break down that barriers of discrimination against employment in National Defense. Negroes can kill the deadly serpent of race hatred in the Army, Navy, Air and Marine Corps, and smash through and blast the Government, business and labor-union red tape to win the right to equal opportunity in vocational training and re-training in defense employment.

Most important and vital of all, Negroes, by the mobilization and coordination of their mass power, can cause PRESIDENT ROOSEVELT TO ISSUE AN EXECUTIVE ORDER ABOLISHING DISCRIMINATIONS IN ALL GOVERNMENT DEPARTMENT, ARMY, NAVY, AIR CORPS AND NATIONAL DEFENSE JOBS.

Of course, the task is not easy. In very truth, it is big, tremendous and difficult.

It will cost money.

It will require sacrifice.

It will tax the Negroes' courage, determination and will to struggle. But we can, must and will triumph.

The Negroes' stake in national defense is big. It consists of jobs, thousands of jobs. It may represent millions, yes hundreds of millions of dollars in wages. It consists of new industrial opportunities and hope. This is worth fighting for.

But to win our stakes, it will require an "all-out," bold and total effort and demonstration of colossal proportions.

Negroes can build a mammoth machine of mass action with a terrific and tremendous driving and striking power that can shatter and crush the evil fortress of race prejudice and hate, if they will only resolve to do so and never stop, until victory comes.

Dear fellow Negro Americans, be not dismayed by these terrible times. You possess power, great power. Our problem is to harness and hitch it up for action on the broadest, daring and most gigantic scale.

In this period of power politics, nothing counts but pressure, more pressure, and still more pressure, through the tactic and strategy of broad, organized, aggressive mass action behind the vital and important issues of the Negro. To this end, we propose that ten thousand Negroes MARCH ON WASHINGTON FOR JOBS IN NATIONAL DEFENSE AND EQUAL INTEGRATION IN THE FIGHTING FORCES OF THE UNITED STATES.

An "all-out" thundering march on Washington, ending in a monster and huge demonstration at Lincoln's Monument will shake up white America.

It will shake up official Washington.

It will give encouragement to our white friends to fight all the harder by our side, with us, for our righteous cause.

It will gain respect for the Negro people.

It will create a new sense of self-respect among Negroes.

But what of national unity?

We believe in national unity which recognizes equal opportunity of black and white citizens to jobs in national defense and the armed forces, and in all other institutions and endeavors in America. We condemn all dictatorships, Fascist, Nazi and Communist. We are loyal, patriotic Americans all.

But if American democracy will not defend its defenders; if American democracy will not protect its protectors; if American democracy will not give jobs to its toilers because of race or color; if American democracy will not insure equality of opportunity, freedom and justice to its citizens, black and white, it is a hollow mockery and belies the principles for which it is supposed to stand. . . .

Today we call on President Roosevelt, a great humanitarian and idealist, to . . . free American Negro citizens of the stigma, humiliation and insult of discrimination and Jim-Crowism in Government departments and national defense.

The Federal Government cannot with clear conscience call upon private industry and labor unions to abolish discrimination based on race and color as long as it practices discrimination itself against Negro Americans.

49. *Pittsburgh Courier*, "Double V Campaign"

(1942)

By the 1930s, the *Pittsburgh Courier* had become one of the most widely read African American newspapers, along with the *Chicago Defender*. The concept for a promotional campaign linking military victory overseas with a victorious struggle for domestic civil rights came from a letter to the editor from James G. Thompson of Wichita, Kansas, published on January 31, 1942, entitled "Should I Sacrifice to Live 'Half American?'" Running with Thompson's ideas, the editors rolled out a "Double V" insignia above the masthead designed by staff artist Wilbert L. Holloway in its February 7 edition, and on February 14 added the slogan "The Courier's Double 'V' for a Double Victory Campaign Gets Country-Wide Support." The editors filled the paper with photos of people of different races making the Double V sign with their fingers. The text of the April 11 spread introducing the two creators of the campaign follows.

SOURCE: *Pittsburgh Courier,* April 11, 1942.

These Men Developed the "Double V" Idea

EDITORS NOTE: The Pittsburgh Courier's "Double V" idea, created in the name of James G. Thompson of Wichita, Kansas, and brought to glowing light through the brilliant pen of Wilbert L. Holloway, Courier staff artist, has swept the nation like wildfire.

The letter of Mr. Thompson, which appeared first in our issue of January 31, is reprinted here, because of its over-all significance and because of his gem-like literary value.

The editors of The Pittsburgh Courier suggest that everyone who reads this letter, slip it out and place it in a conspicuous place . . . where all may see AND read!

DEAR EDITOR:

Like all true Americans, my greatest desire at this time, this crucial point of our history; is a desire for a complete victory over the forces of evil, which threaten our existence today. Behind that desire is also a desire to serve, this, my country, in the most advantageous way. Most of our leaders are suggesting that we sacrifice every other ambition to the paramount one, victory. With this I agree: but I also wonder if another victory could not be achieved at the same time. After all the things that beset the world now are basically the same things which upset the equilibrium of nations internally, states, counties, cities, homes and even the individual.

Being an American of dark complexion and some 26 years, these questions flash through my mind:

"Should I sacrifice my life to live half American?"

"Will things be better for the next generation in the peace to follow?"

"Would it be demanding too much to demand full citizenship rights in exchange for the sacrificing of my life."

"Is the kind of America I know worth defending?"

"Will America be a true and pure democracy after this war?"

"Will colored Americans suffer still the indignities that have been heaped upon them in the past?"

These and other questions need answering; I want to know, and I believe every colored American, who is thinking, wants to know.

This may be the wrong time to broach such subjects, but haven't all good things obtained by men been secured through sacrifice during just such times of strife?

I suggest that while we keep defense and victory in the forefront that we don't lose sight of our fight for true democracy at home.

The "V for Victory" sign is being displayed prominently in all so-called democratic countries which are fighting for victory over aggression, slavery and tyranny. If this V sign means that to those now engaged in this great conflict then let colored Americans adopt the double VV for a double victory—The first V for victory over our enemies from without, the second V for victory over our enemies within. For surely those who perpetrate these ugly prejudices here are seeking to destroy our democratic form of government just as surely as the Axis forces.

This should not and would not lessen our efforts to bring this conflict to a successful conclusion; but should and would make us stronger to resist these evil forces which threaten us. America could become united as never before and become truly the home of democracy.

In way of an answer to the foregoing questions in a preceding paragraph. I might say that there is no doubt that this country is worth defending: things will be different for the next generation; colored Americans will come into their own, and America will eventually become the true democracy it was designed to be. These things will become a reality in time; but not through any relaxation of the efforts to secure them.

In conclusion let me say that though these questions often permeate my mind, I love America and am willing to die for the America I know will someday become a reality.

JAMES G. THOMPSON.

50. A. Philip Randolph, "Why Should We March?"

(1942)

In this editorial, A. Philip Randolph called for continued pressure on President Roosevelt, noting that the creation of the Fair Employment Practices Committee in response to the threat of a march on Washington by African Americans had "only scratched the surface" in the struggle for job equality (see document 48). Randolph firmly argues against the old notion that blacks should close ranks during wartime and put aside their fight for civil rights until the war's successful conclusion.

SOURCE: *Survey Graphic,* November 1942.

When the defense program began and billions of the taxpayers' money were appropriated for guns, ships, tanks, and bombs, Negroes presented themselves for work only to be given the cold shoulder. North as well as South, and despite their qualifications, Negroes were denied skilled employment. Not until their wrath and indignation took the form of a proposed protest march on Washington, scheduled for July 1, 1941, did things begin to move in the form of defense jobs for Negroes. The march was postponed by the timely issuance (June 25, 1941) of the famous Executive Order No. 8802 by President Roosevelt. But this order and the President's Committee on Fair Employment Practice, established thereunder, have as yet only scratched the surface by way of eliminating discriminations on account of race or color in war industry. Both management and labor unions in too many places and in too many ways are still drawing the color line.

It is to meet this situation squarely with direct action that the March on Washington Movement launched its present program of protest mass meetings. Twenty thousand were in attendance at Madison Square Garden, June 16; 16,000 in the Coliseum in Chicago, June 26; 9,000 in the city Auditorium of St. Louis, August 14. Meetings of such magnitude were unprecedented among Negroes. . . .

By fighting for their rights now, American Negroes are helping to make America a moral and spiritual arsenal of democracy. Their fight against the poll tax, against lynch law, segregation, and Jim Crow, their fight for economic, political, and social equality, thus becomes part of the global war for freedom.

51. Walter White, "What Caused the Detroit Riots?"

(1943)

Detroit, often referred to as the "Arsenal of Democracy" during World War II, erupted into racial violence in June 1943. Earlier that month, 25,000 workers at the Packard plant, which produced engines for bombers and PT boats, struck to protest the promotion of three black workers, having been whipped into a frenzy by a small core of racist agitators. Overcrowding in black neighborhoods and the relegation of blacks to the most menial positions in war plants added to the volatile racial situation. To protest unfair conditions, some blacks had started a "bumping campaign," during which they walked into whites on the street to make them aware of the situation. On June 20, blacks and whites engaged in a few fights in the city park on Belle Isle, and in the tense environment of the time, this minor incitement was enough to set off a major wave of racial violence. The thirty-six hours of rioting that ensued left thirty-four people dead, twenty-four of them black. Walter White (1893–1955), who served as the executive director of the NAACP from 1929 to 1955, provides his perspective on the causes for the explosion of racial violence in the city that was so crucial to the war effort.

SOURCE: Walter White, *What Caused the Detroit Riots?* (New York: NAACP, 1943).

In 1916 there were 8,000 Negroes in Detroit's population of 536,650. In 1925 the number of Negroes in Detroit had been multiplied by ten to a total of 85,000. In 1940, the total had jumped to 149,119. In June 1943, between 190,000 and 200,000 lived in the Motor City . . . The overwhelming majority—between 40,000 and 50,000—of the approximately 50,000 Negroes who went to Detroit in this three year period moved there during the fifteen months prior to the race riot of June 1943. According to Governor Harry S. Kelly, of Michigan, a total of 345,000 persons moved into Detroit during the same fifteen month period. There was comparatively little out-migration as industry called for more and more workers in one of the tightest labor markets in the United States. The War Manpower Commission failed almost completely to enforce its edict that no in migration be permitted into any industrial area until all available local labor was utilized. Thus a huge reservoir of Negro labor existed in Detroit, crowded into highly congested slum areas. But they did have housing of a sort and this labor was already in Detroit . . .

Politically minded public officials have winked at the activities of agencies like the Klan, the Black Legion, the National Workers League, the followers of Father Coughlin and other similar groups. During the 30s especially where there was keen competition for jobs because of the depression, Southern whites sought and secured jobs on the police force of Detroit and in the courts. There was a period of years when cold-blooded killings of Negroes by policemen were a constant source of bitterness among Negroes. Eventually protest by such organizations as the Detroit branch of the NAACP and other Negro and inter-racial groups led to a diminution and . . . a practical cessation of such killings. But a residue of distrust of the police remained. When the riot of June 1943 broke forth, this suspicion of police by Negroes was more than justified . . . .

The willful inefficiency of the Detroit police in its handling of the riot is one of the most disgraceful episodes in American history. When the riot broke out on Sunday night, June 20, following a dispute between a white and Negro motorist on the Belle Isle Bridge, an efficient police force armed with night sticks and fire hoses could have broken up the rioting . . . and broken the back of the insurrection, had the police been determined to do so. Instead, the police did little or nothing . . . .

The anti-Negro motivation of the Detroit police department is further illustrated by these facts and figures. It has already been pointed out that the Negro population of Detroit at the time of the riot was 200,000 or less, out of a total population of more than 2,000,000. The inevitable riot was the product of anti-Negro forces which had been allowed to operate without check or hindrance by the police over a period of many years. But 29 of 35 persons who died during the riot were Negroes. An overwhelming majority of the more than 600 injured were Negroes. Of the 1,832 persons arrested for rioting, more than 85 percent were Negroes. And this in the face of the indisputable fact that the aggressors over a period of years were not Negroes but whites.

52. Dr. Leslie Hohman, "Can Women in War Industry Be Good Mothers?"

(1942)

Dr. Leslie B. Hohman (b. 1891) was a renowned psychiatrist who specialized in child development and issues of sexuality. He rose to prominence as both a clinical practitioner and a popular writer on these topics. Hohman published a popular "commonsense" child-rearing advice book, *As the Twig Is Bent*, in 1939 and also contributed frequently to venues like *Ladies' Home Journal* (from which this piece is taken). He taught at Johns Hopkins Medical School during the war years and then moved to Duke University in 1946 to take a position as professor of neuropsychiatry; he remained at Duke until 1979. As the war economy heated up, absorbing many women workers into industries that traditionally employed only men, much popular hand-wringing ensued about the effect this new situation might have on children. In this piece, Hohman describes a visit to the home of Fred and Mary Berckman in Hartford, Connecticut, to investigate how Mary's working outside of the home in a war production plant affected her children.

SOURCE: *Ladies' Home Journal,* October 1942.

The task of working women who are mothers, too, involves unquestionable difficulties which we must face squarely. Yet it gives women and their husbands a chance to prove dramatically and quickly where their deepest interests are.

If I had had any doubts on the question, my trip to the Hartford home of Fred and Mary Berckman would have converted me. Their whole household teems with evidence that their children are to them the most important consideration in the world. Their unflagging interest is the solid foundation for the first of the specific rules to be drawn from their highly successful experience.

The first rule is that mothers who are working must deliberately and determinedly plan to spend ample time with their children. To Mary this is not in the least burdensome. She delights in helping with the lessons of all her merry brood—second-grader son Junie, and the daughters Eileen, Fredrica and the eldest, Catherine, in the fifth grade. Mary sings with them, laughs with them, tells them stories in her fine Irish brogue of County Mayo, where she was born and lived until she came to America nineteen years ago.

"We make things interesting in this house," Mary said—an excellent boost for girls and boys along the road to happiness and security.

With all her fondness for her children, Mary could not accomplish so much time with them if both she and Fred had not organized their days carefully with that very purpose in mind. Her early shift at the Colt arms plant brings her home in the afternoons about the time the children arrive from school. She mixes them a malted milk, does preliminary work on dinner, then lies down for an hour until the children call out that their father is home from work. Fred is there at noon, too, from the Royal Typewriter plant just across the street, to help the youngsters prepare the lunch that has been arranged by Mary before she left for work.

Not much is to be gained by a detailed study of the exact schedule Fred and Mary use. Each working mother will have to arrange a schedule according to her individual working hours and her individual problems. We can be sure in advance that those who haven't the will to succeed will seek excuses for not doing so well as Fred and Mary—such as, "Neither my husband nor I can come home at noon." We can be equally sure that those who sincerely try will find some way to make certain that their children are well cared for while they are at work.

One mother I know who has an important executive position and commutes every working day to her desk rises much earlier every morning than she otherwise would have to, so that she can have breakfast and a long chat with her daughter. In the evenings, also, she always manages to spend some time with the child. They talk gaily of topics which interest the little girl. Their companionship is far closer than that of most daughters with mothers who haven't any outside work to do.

A writing assistant on a daily radio program who has few unfilled hours at home during the week still arranges to find brief and happy intervals for her young son every day. The main feature of her admirable plan comes every Sunday. The entire day is her son's. Any reasonable suggestion he makes on how they shall spend his day, she follows merrily. They have grand fun. The scheme often means that she and her husband decline weekend invitations, but they hold to their plan and enjoy themselves more than they would on the missed parties. The result is that the son is held to his parents by the strongest possible bonds of wholesome affection.

The general attitude of mothers—and fathers too—is a more powerful influence than the actual number of hours they spend with their children. Couples who want to act childless and who find association with their children irksome and dull, do not fool their children by staying home and snapping at them. Fewer hours and more companionship would be much better.

A child's sense of security is fostered psychologically by stability in his environment. Despite all protestations of love at odd moments, young children in a harum-scarum household are likely to develop unstable emotional habits and a feeling of insecurity.

I am convinced that jobs for mothers outside the home generally help to create the stability of environment that is so essential. The gain usually more than offsets the loss of the hours in which the mother has to be away. Besides the scheduling of household routine imposed by regular employment, there is the added advantage for children that the inefficient mothers whose home management is hit-or-miss and disturbingly unreliable will learn to be more efficient by working where efficiency is required.

The skill and willingness in housework which Fred acquired when he took it over completely while his heart would not permit more strenuous exertion, makes him an ideal partner for a working wife. This suggests still another flat rule:

If children are to be reared successfully in families with employed mothers who haven't enough money for nursemaids and servants, it is absolutely necessary for husbands to help their wives with home duties and with the children's training.

Many unemployed wives would say offhand that their husbands could never learn. They probably would be pleasantly surprised. An outside job for a wife usually seems to cause a striking improvement in the husband's domesticity. Every husband of a working wife to whom I have mentioned the problem assured me that he felt obligated to help. "I never did before my wife got a job," several said. "After all, why should I when I had done my part and she had nothing else to do?" Not taking the husbands' statements of their own virtues as final, I made extensive inquiries among employed wives I knew. With hardly any exceptions, they cited their husbands for extraordinary household accomplishments.

Even when father knuckles down to do his share, there will be plenty of chores left for children in homes where both parents have outside jobs and abundant assistance cannot be hired. That is a great good fortune for the children. If we had enough working mothers, there would be a reinstatement of work training and early feeling for useful accomplishment. Too many young boys and girls are missing this valuable training.

Watching the Berckman children, I thought how much more fortunate they were than the ten-year-old son of an idle, prosperous mother who recently sought my advice because she saw, at last, that something was going wrong with him. Something had been going wrong since infancy. His mother and nursemaid and later his whole family waited on him hand and foot. An important part of my prescription was that useful chores be found for him. The family is having a hard time following the prescription after its long habit of spoiling the boy.

The troubles of mothers who have jobs will be greatly lessened if they and their husbands enforce good training while they are at home. Mary and Fred established a cornerstone by affectionate discipline from infancy, not shying from occasional punishment when it was necessary to stop the development of traits that would handicap their children.

Merely the presence of a mother in the house will not make children behave—as harried neighbors can testify. Mothers cannot incessantly watch children old enough to go out and play, and it would be harmful to the children's self-reliance if they could. The best guaranty is the trained-in reliability and independence that enable Mary to say confidently: "My children never have done anything I told them not to do. I can trust them completely."

War or no war, outside work should never be undertaken by mothers until adequate care and training of their young children are assured. The arrangements frequently are hard to make, but rarely impossible. Where there is money enough, a qualified woman can be paid to come in and take charge. In most neighborhoods where money is not too plentiful, some woman who has proved her skill with her own children will be glad to augment the family income a little by taking care of one or two more for eight or nine hours a day.

No story of the problems and difficulties that working mothers meet could give a complete picture without prominent mention of the intangible gain that is nearly always overlooked. With few exceptions, women are made more interesting to their girls and boys by an outside job. Mary Berckman is a shining example. She is in brisk step with the world of today. She has sorted out her values under the test of stern realities. She has no time to be bored, no time for gossip. She always has time for companionship. It is not surprising that she, with Fred's excellent help, fills her children's lives with happiness.

53. "The Women's Bureau's Assessment of Women's Progress in the Work Place"

(1944)

The Women's Bureau of the U.S. Department of Labor was originally organized during World War I to monitor women's working conditions and to develop the first U.S. standards for the employment of women workers. During wartime, it worked closely with trade unions and middle-class women's groups and gathered statistics about women in the workforce. The following excerpts from its 1944 report dissect the problem of women not being put on the same seniority track as men in war plants. The bureau still exists.

SOURCE: Special Bulletin No. 18 of the Women's Bureau (Washington, D.C.: Government Printing Office, March 1944).

In the past the opportunity given women workers to learn and to exercise skills has been narrower in range than men's has been. In consequence, very large numbers of women were little thought of in connection with other types of work, and so they continued to be given little opportunity to develop additional skills. The war situation has changed that considerably. With shortages of men workers, women have been employed in a greater variety of occupations than before. . . .

Unfortunately, there are many cases where women still have been given far too little chance to be upgraded to their highest skills. In 1943, the National Industrial Conference Board analyzed reports from some 130 plants, chiefly in heavier metal industries, plants that had employed relatively few women or none. In nearly 60 percent of these plants there were no plans for advancing women from the top production jobs they held at the time of reporting to more highly skilled jobs. Moreover, numerous instances are reported of the placement of women in jobs that are not in the usual line for the job progression; in such blind-alley jobs neither proficiency nor length of service can bring these women beyond a limited early stage of work. If this situation continues, it will be a great disadvantage to women after the war, and in fact government agencies are finding promotional discrimination against them as one of the major reasons why women quit jobs in war plants. . . .

Plant seniority practices under the clauses of many union agreements give women workers very inadequate protection. For example, some agreements definitely provide that women's occupation of jobs formerly held by men shall be for the duration only. Some agreements give women employed at time of signing the agreement full seniority rights with men, but for women employed after that time set up a list for women separate from that for men. Some agreements provide for the seniority of women as "separate and distinct from the seniority of men." Agreements fixing seniority by department only may affect women and men quite differently. Other agreements are so vaguely worded as to permit interpretations that are of disadvantage to women.

54. *New York Times*, "WPB Bars 'Zoot Suit' Made in Any Material"

(1942)

The "Zoot Suit Riots" were a series of confrontations among young men of the Mexican American community in Los Angeles, white servicemen who were stationed in the city, and the police. These skirmishes took place from roughly the summer of 1942 into the summer of 1943. Mexican American men who wore zoot suits, garments with extra-long jackets and baggy pants, were often targeted by white sailors and soldiers for harassment and beating. Retaliatory violence frequently ensued. The murder of one zoot suit–wearing "pachuco" in August 1942 near a lake popularly known as the "Sleepy Lagoon" led to a sensational trial of seventeen youths. The Mexican American community was outraged that so many young men were being "railroaded," and many progressive entertainers, among them Orson Welles, Rita Hayworth, and Nat King Cole, protested publicly on the boys' behalf. All seventeen were released by 1944. As the following *New York Times* piece announces, the War Production Board banned the production of zoot suits, since government officials viewed them as wasteful in a time of scarcity.

SOURCE: *New York Times*, September 12, 1942, p. 8.

WASHINGTON, Sept. 11—Disappearance of the "zoot suit" for the duration of the war was assured here today with an order from the War Production Board prohibiting the manufacture of the garments out of any material. The "zoot suit" includes an over-length coat and baggy trousers, and it has been made of wool.

When a WPB order last week banned the use of wool in manufacture of the suits, many producers planned to turn to rayon, cotton or other fabrics.

"We have no desire to restrict styles or types of garments so long as there is no waste of fabrics," Frank Walton, deputy chief of WPB's textile, clothing and leather branch, said. "But the demand on looms of production of cloth is at an all-time peak. We can avoid serious shortages of essential cloth for the needs of our armed forces, our Allies and our civilians, only if we eliminate waste wherever possible. In a war we cannot afford the luxury of wasteful garments."

55. Timothy G. Turner, "Significance of Zoot-Suit Gangsters"

(1943)

Los Angeles Times editorialist Timothy G. Turner here attempts to provide a white liberal perspective on the causes of the outbreak of "zoot suit" violence in Los Angeles (see introduction to document 54). Curiously, the piece does not mention the violence of white servicemen against zoot suiters. Turner claims some expertise on the matter due to his previous experience as a war correspondent covering the Mexican Revolution.

SOURCE: *Los Angeles Times*, January 14, 1943, p. A4.

It is high time to inquire dispassionately into the recent outbreaks of Mexican-American gangsterism in Los Angeles, which resulted in the conviction of 17 youths on various charges Tuesday. There has been much nonsense about it, and some sad mistakes made.

The police have committed the stupidity, common to police in all cities, of making wholesale arrests when anything gets out of hand. To throw probably innocent youths in jail makes more criminals than it cures, and it is likely to arouse sympathy which is applied to the guilty as well as the innocent.

On the other hand the mush-headed sentimentalists are busy with their talk of "naughty boys" who should not be punished too severely. The fact that these young men wear silly looking zoot suits and that most of them are in their teens does not change the facts. It is hardly a boy's prank to invade peaceful social gatherings and knife people to death, or to pick up people off the street, drag them into automobiles, beat them and then throw them into the street bleeding and groaning.

Then the Communists as usual are making trouble and confusing issues. They say that the gangsterism is inspired by Axis agents. This is absurd.

Of course, enemy propagandists may take advantage of it after the fact.

The reasons for zoot-suit gangsterism are complex. This writer, who has had a lifetime of association with Mexicans, can testify that they generally are a kindly, polite and goodhearted people. The gains of the revolution were mostly to the good, but there is no denying that some classes of Mexicans lost much of their fine culture and the restraining influences of the Catholic religion. Many of these boys come from homes of recent immigrants of the worst kind, and our lavish relief system has not helped matters. It is the fault of our culture, however, that they have been exposed to an idealization of gangsterism which has existed since the days of prohibition, the evil effects of which are not yet over. These young men thus represent the worst of both races, and the shame of it should be mutual.

Primary Reason

But those reasons do not include the principal one. It lies in the social problem of first generation Americans and there is nothing new about it. Gangsters in eastern cities in recent years have been mostly young men raised in this country, sons of recent Italian and Jewish immigrants. Some 40 or 50 years ago they were Irish, though then the gangster was called a tough. In all these cases the thing is the same as we find in Los Angeles today. The gangsterism is inspired by a love of lawless adventure; seldom at first is it for purposes of robbery. Gangs fight gangs and anybody who comes in their way. It is a youthful return to complete savagery. It is the breeding ground of future criminals in the fullest sense.

According to best opinion, it is due to a feeling of separation from the rest of society due to prejudices against the recent immigrants and their children. The youth feels he is no part of the community and starts war on it. He is in the academic phrase socially maladjusted.

When this first generation problem is removed or passes, the gangsterism disappears. On our own East Side we had a similar problem years ago with children of the Russian Molokons colony. There is now none.

The Mexican problem confronting this city today is compounded by color prejudice. Most of these young Mexicans have much Indian blood. There is a definite caste system against them. It is not like that against the Negro. Like Orientals they can go into restaurants and theaters. But a young Mexican-American finds the economic bars up against him. He or she cannot get a job in stores or offices, even as a waiter or waitress in restaurants. The Mexican, however, can be a bus boy. This is being changed by the man power shortage, and we are beginning to see Mexican faces where we never saw them before. This only serves to emphasize the barrier. Mexicans have been barred from many factories engaged in war work, causing much bitterness. The Mexican, generally speaking, is left to hard labor or the most menial work. We have graduated a whole generation of young Mexicans out of high school, educated sons and daughters of Mexican laborers into a middle class which for them does not exist. If we study a city like El Paso, which is half Mexican and half Anglo-Saxon American, we find young Mexicans as a rule are capable of almost any kind of work in shop or office and are socially most charming people and politically good citizens. In El

Paso for various reasons they got a break they never have had in Los Angeles or San Antonio.

Something to Do

The writer has no solution to offer for these disturbances. But he suggests that the first thing to do is to punish the young men found guilty by fair trial of these atrocities, but to avoid anything savoring of persecution of the innocent. In other words, the authorities should be just.

Above all we should not close our eyes to it. It is true, but it is not enough, to say that these young gangsters are an insignificant percentage of the large and generally lawful Mexican population. They represent a symptom of a more serious disorder, our own minority problem in the Southwest. We should not be hypocrites and protest against minority problems abroad when we cannot solve our own at home.

CHAPTER

SIX

World War II, Part III: Ethical Dilemmas

56. Richard B. Gregg, "Pacifist Program in Time of War, Threatened War, or Fascism"

(1939)

How could a pacifist uphold his or her moral opposition to war and fascism at the same time? With the outbreak of war in Europe in 1939, this question loomed large to those who adhered to the pacifist philosophy. Richard B. Gregg (1885–1974), an eminent American social philosopher and friend of Mohandas K. Gandhi, addressed this issue in the pamphlet excerpted below. In the 1920s, Gregg traveled to India to study Gandhi's tactics of nonviolent resistance and befriended the leader. Gregg's 1934 book, *The Power of Non-Violence,* proved enormously influential among later civil rights leaders like Bayard Rustin and Martin Luther King Jr.; the 1960 revision of this book would have a foreword by King.

SOURCE: *Pendle Hill Pamphlet,* no. 5 (Wallingford, Pa.: Pendle Hill, 1939).

Program for the Pacifist

Pledge Not to Fight or Help War
Before war comes, absolute pacifists of eighteen years or over, men and women, ought first of all to sign a written pledge not to support or take part in any war, and file that pledge with some appropriate organization.

Such a pledge is more than a public gesture of refusal to do something on moral grounds. It is an affirmation that the human will is free, that a man can resist the slavery and dictatorship inherent in war. It is a step toward the renunciation of all domination, a step in support of a deeper freedom and democracy. Furthermore, such a written statement objectifies purpose, gets it outside. One can look at it and realize more fully and clearly its implications, relationships, and probable effects. Filing the pledge with a pacifist organization commits the signer to new relationships and new efforts, brings into play his sense of consistency, of honor, and of pride, starts new consistent friendships and gains strength from them. Modern war is so highly mechanized that more energy is needed for making and repairing machines than for fighting. Industrial conscription will be needed almost more than military conscription; women can do many industrial and farm jobs; so women as well as men will probably be conscripted. For all these reasons, women as well as men should sign such pledges.

Those who oppose such pledging of individuals perhaps forget that the governments of the United States, Great Britain, France, Germany, Japan, and many other countries took such a public pledge in the Briand-Kellogg Pact of Paris. That Pact states that "The High Contracting Parties solemnly declare in the names of their respective peoples that they condemn recourse to war for the solution of international controversies, and renounce it as an instrument of national policy in their relations with one another. The High Contracting Parties agree that the settlement or solution of all disputes or conflicts of whatever nature or of whatever origin they may be, which may arise among them, shall never be sought except by pacific means."

Each government that signed that Pact asked by implication all of its citizens to uphold it in so doing; that is, asked each citizen also to refuse to go to war. This is especially true in the United States where treaties of the Federal Government with other nations are considered a part of the law of the nation. And since each government that signed that Pact maintains courts to uphold and enforce the sanctity of contracts and of solemn public oaths, no government can with moral consistency demand that any one of its pacifist citizens who has given a public pledge renouncing war, should break that pledge. If you say that such a pledge is contrary to public policy and therefore invalid, I would say that by the Pact of Paris the governments explicitly stated what their public policy would be in this matter. . . .

. . . If the government offers to the conscientious objector the chance to do ambulance work, nursing, or hospital work, may he or she accept it as legitimate alternative, non-combatant service? I believe not. Granted the compassionate motive for it, yet the compassion is being used by the government to make the wounded fit for further fighting, if possible, or at least to keep them and their families and friends loyal. Hospitals and nursing help to prolong the war. The wounded will be cared for even though the pacifists refuse such work. There will be no dearth of war-minded nurses, ambulance men, surgeons, physicians and hospital orderlies. If there were a real danger of such a shortage, it would mean that pacifism would be so widespread that there would be no danger of war.

I am assuming that the pacifist in refusing such service is not doing so out of cowardice. If he is afraid, he should either do some equally dangerous service independent of government and try to develop his courage or else join the army and fight.

If he has not chosen his own form of service to the community before war begins, and finds it necessary suddenly to choose an alternative service, let him insist on a job not subject to governmental control and orders, and serving civilians. Inasmuch as most civilians will be doing war work directly or indirectly, and war is now totalitarian, it may prove almost impossible to do any form of work which will not be warped and used by the government for war ends. But service to civilians can be done before war and after war, and therefore cannot be so completely bent to war uses as service to the fighting forces. Let him try to serve the community or society rather than the national state, for it is to the former that we owe most of our social and cultural heritage. Always there is work at housing, road making, farming, forestry, building flood control dams, civilian hospital work, subsistence gardens, drainage of swampy ground, racial reconciliation, promotion of friendship between people of different religions, helping the unemployed and very poor of every race or religious persuasion within reach, helping civil prisoners or orphans, helping refugees, interned enemy aliens and prisoners of war, educational and recreational work, and care of children, provided such jobs are wholly under civilian direction. If the government will not permit the pacifist to work free from its orders, then he is a candidate for jail.

Work with the Y. M. C. A., Y. W. C. A., Boy or Girl Scouts, Salvation Army, or any similar organization, if it is under military command, would be taboo for the pacifist. Nor would chaplaincy in the army or navy be right. But relief work under strictly civilian or pacifist church direction in or outside the war zone, or in neutral zones, may be regarded as consistent.

Refuse to Demonstrate with Communists or Fascists

In an industrial struggle should pacifists demonstrate together with Communists? Most Communists, being intelligent people, do not want to use violence, but they believe, quite rightly, that it is pretty sure to be used by the employer group and by the State in any big struggle, and Communists are willing in that event to use it in self-defense. Also their general attitude toward employers and financiers as a class and often toward them as individuals is not only one of distrust but ranges through contempt, anger, fear, hatred, and desire for revenge. Witness the adjectives of Communist leaders and the cartoons of Communist artists. Under severe stress such feelings inevitably find expression in physical violence. So if the police attack a crowd of demonstrators containing both pacifists and Communists, the latter are almost sure to fight back, and in the melée it is not easy to distinguish between pacifists and Communists. So the public will condemn the pacifists as severely as the Communists—indeed more so since their pacifism will seem to be mere hypocrisy. For these reasons I doubt whether, in justice to their beliefs and the desire to win converts, pacifists can afford to take part in public demonstrations with Communists. Since Fascists are committed to violence from the beginning, the same refusal applies to them. This is no "holier than thou" attitude, but a deep-seated conviction of the importance of method. And it involves a further conviction that no "popular front," no civil liberties, and no thorough democracy can nowadays be successful or enduring except on the basis of non-violence. Because modern violence is totalitarian, to it as a near-absolute one must oppose another near-absolute, pacifism without compromise.

Behave Wisely If Imprisoned

On one further matter pacifists will want to be prepared. I refer to their conduct in prison, if they go there. What I suggest here is based chiefly on the advice of Gandhi to his followers.

Pacifists in jail are political prisoners, not ordinary criminals. They have courted imprisonment to prove the strength of their convictions, to testify to the truth as they see it, to try to win public opinion, and to try to persuade the government by their voluntary suffering. They are not trying at present to do away with jails.

Legal punishment is based, at least in theory, not on a desire for cruel revenge, but implies that the prisoner has a personality capable of change and growth, and therefore worthy of respect. A political prisoner has not, like the ordinary criminal, disobeyed the law for selfish reasons, but for the sake of ethical principles. Therefore he deserves more respect than an ordinary criminal. Certainly the pacifist has an unusual degree of respect for personality. But public hysteria in wartime is often cruel, and some prison superintendents and guards fail to act up to the highest standards of their occupation.

Pacifists in jail should work hard at the tasks set them, provided those tasks are regular prison work and not for military use. They should obey prison rules and regular discipline; should not object to inconveniences or mere hardships; should wear without objection prison clothing provided it is not military uniform; should not ask for or accept special privileges. They should be courteous and conform to all self-respecting, non-military gestures, modes of address or other signs of respect toward prison officials. They should be open and aboveboard, and not deceitful. They should not ask for any unnecessary conveniences.

But they are entitled to refuse to obey orders clearly intended to humiliate them or to insult or violate their beliefs, taking without protest any lawful punishment for their disobedience. They must use common sense and not be touchy or filled with false pride. If past history is repeated, there will probably be attempts by some prison officials to provide work which would get the conscientious objectors into an inconsistent position, thus undermining their resistance. If this happens, the conscientious objectors will be wise to refuse to do such work. Some of the prisons may be hastily arranged concentration camps without rules or facilities for work. In such case the prisoners can perhaps help the authorities develop kinds of work consistent with their position and good for the morale of all concerned, jailers as well as prisoners. Pacifist prisoners may protest against cruel treatment, against filth and insanitation of all kinds, or spoiled food. Any protests should be addressed at proper times to the duly constituted authorities. If, after adequate time has been allowed for consideration by the authorities, no answer or an utterly unsatisfactory answer is returned, the prisoners may refuse to work, taking as cheerfully as possible the legal penalties for such refusal. They should not resort to hunger strike unless the matter is of the gravest importance. It is usually countered by forcible feeding. Hunger strike is a two-edged weapon very dangerous to use—I mean morally dangerous—except on very rare occasions and by very clear-thinking, experienced persons who have a long record of orderly, responsible, well-balanced, and markedly un-selfish conduct.

Perhaps the three hardest things about prison life are loneliness, weakening of initiative, and a temptation to resentment. To offset the first the prisoner will be wise to read as much as the prison permits, and when that is not possible, to develop as many ways of enriching and cultivating his inner life as possible. In this way he will also develop a field for initiative. If sooner or later he can get permission to have paper, pen and ink, he will find that recording his thoughts and then pondering on them will help him to solve many problems and develop a well-integrated personal philosophy that will give him poise and serenity. Or he may write stories, essays or poetry. The prisoner will find it a great help to set aside a regular time each day for silent meditation, even though it be very brief. If he is religious, he will use prayer as well as meditation, but meditation is ad-visable in all cases. It is not an escape from reality, but a way of making contact with underlying reality, principles and truths. It will enrich his inner world, do away with inner conflicts, and provide a field for initiative, spontaneity and free-dom. Thus he may keep himself from being stunted and crippled by his punish-ment.

If prison officials are cruel, he can try to remember that it is probably due to frustrations, indignities, humiliations, or cruelties that they themselves suffered, perhaps when they were young, or perhaps to war hysteria. So it is a symptom of the evils of our civilization, and not all their personal fault.

In some situations it will be very difficult to decide what is the wisest way to act in prison. Many situations cannot be foreseen. The foregoing considerations will perhaps serve as a general guide. It will be helpful if pacifists, in advance of going to prison, can read accounts of the experiences of former conscientious objectors. . . .

It should be remembered that we are all partly responsible for our corporate failures to live up to our ideals of democracy, justice, equality, and freedom. We are all involved in economic and political mistakes. The changes in our economy are so rapid as to come close to breakdown. The need for economic security de-mands swift action to prevent starvation and suffering on a scale too great to be endured. It may be that all of us, pacifists included, may have to yield up tem-porarily large amounts of liberty of action and speech in order that the largest possible numbers of people may live. In so doing we would be paying part of the price for our own and our predecessors' failures and mistakes. Such yielding would not be mere cringing to an arbitrary and wholly personal tyrant. Yet per-sonal and bureaucratic tyranny creeps in soon. To resist that tyranny non-violently and to suffer punishment voluntarily for our resistance will be another part of the price we must pay for past errors. And the toil of building non-violent and better forms and modes of human association will be yet another part of the price we must pay. But we can have joy and deep satisfaction in such work.

Some may say that the foregoing proposals are an abandonment of the method which Gandhi advocates and has used so successfully against the impe-rial dictatorship he opposes. But if they will study his writings and the record of his activities more carefully, they will find that most of his time and energy have been spent in constructive organization and propaganda for reforms among his own people. The time he has devoted to direct, open struggle against the Government in campaigns of non-coöperation or civil disobedience has been relatively small. Even during the times of open struggle, his criticisms of the Government have been impersonal. He has not imputed evil motives to any individuals in the Government, but has always spoken of them as friends or as people he would like to be friendly with. He has clearly indicated that silence combined with constructive work is often the wisest policy.

57. Donald Benedict, "Why We Refused to Register"

(1941)

Eight students at the Union Theological Seminary in New York City were arrested and jailed on November 14, 1940, for refusing to register for the draft, making national headlines. Donald Benedict (b. 1917) was one of these students. Historians have paid less attention to the conscientious objectors of World War II than to those of the Great War largely because the Burke-Wadsworth Bill of 1940, which set up the conscription system, provided considerably more alternatives to military service for conscientious objectors than its equivalent in the earlier war in the form of the Civilian Public Service camps. Yet, even with nonmilitary options available, many conscientious objectors still felt that registering for the draft presented a morally unacceptable level of complicity with the state apparatus of war. While serving his second term in prison, Benedict had a change of heart and decided to enlist in the army in 1945. In the following excerpt, Benedict elaborates his initial position.

SOURCE: "Excerpts from the Joint Statement of Donald Benedict, Joseph J. Bevilacqua, Meredith Dallas, David Dellinger, George M. Houser, William M. Lovell, Howard E. Spragg and Richard J. Wichlei," *Why We Refused to Register,* published jointly by the Fellowship of Reconciliation, Keep America Out of the War Congress, National Council for Prevention of War, Youth Committee Against War, Young People's Socialist League, and War Resisters League (New York, 1941[?]).

It is impossible for us to think of the conscription law without at the same time thinking of the whole war system, because it is clear to us that conscription is definitely a part of the institution of war. . . .

To us, the war system is an evil part of our social order, and we declare that we cannot cooperate with it in any way. War is an evil because it is in violation of the Way of Love as seen in God through Christ. It is a concentration and accentuation of all the evils of our society. War consists of mass murder, deliberate starvation, vandalism, and similar evils. Physical destruction and moral disintegration are the inevitable result. The war method perpetuates and compounds the evils it purports to overcome. It is impossible, as history reveals, to overcome evil with evil. The last World War is a notorious case of the failure of the war system, and there is no evidence to believe that this war will be any different. It is our positive proclamation as followers of Jesus Christ that we must overcome evil with good. We seek in our daily living to reconcile that separation of man from man and man from God which produces war.

We have also been led to our conclusion on the conscription law in the light of its totalitarian nature. It is a totalitarian move when our government insists that the manpower of the nation take a year of military training. It is a totalitarian move for the President of the nation to be able to conscript industry to produce certain materials which are deemed necessary for national defense without considering the actual physical needs of the people. We believe, therefore, that by opposing the Selective Service law, we will be striking at the heart of totalitarianism as well as war. . . .

We feel a deep bond of unity with those who decide to register as conscientious objectors, but our own decision must be different for the following reasons:

If we register under the act, even as conscientious objectors, we are becoming part of the act. The fact that we as conscientious objectors may gain personal exemption from the most crassly un-Christian requirements of the act does not compensate for the fact that we are complying with it and accepting its protection. If a policeman (or a group of vigilantes) stops us on the street, our possession of the government's card shows that we are "all right"—we have complied with the act for the militarization of America. If that does not hurt our Christian consciences, what will? If we try to rationalize on the theory that we must go along with the act in order to fight the fascism and militarism of which it is a part, it seems to us that we are doing that very thing which all pacifist Christians abhor: we are consciously employing bad means on the theory that to do so will contribute to a good end. . . .

In similar vein, it is urged that great concessions have been won for religious pacifists and that we endanger these by our refusal to accept them. Fascism, as it gradually supplanted democracy in Germany, was aided by the decision of Christians and leftists to accept a partial fascism rather than to endanger those democratic concessions which still remained. It is not alone for our own exemption from fighting that we work—it is for freedom of the American people from fascism and militarism.

Partial exemption of conscientious objectors has come about partly through the work of influential pacifists and partly through the open-mindedness of certain non-pacifists. But it has also been granted because of the fear of the government that, without such a provision, public opposition to war would be too great to handle. In particular, it seems to us that one of the reasons the government has granted exemption to ministers and theological students is to gain a religious sanction for its diabolical war. Where actual support could not be gained, it hoped to soothe their consciences so that they could provide no real opposition.

We do not contend that the American people maliciously choose the vicious instrument of war. In a very perplexing situation, they lack the imagination, the religious faith, and the precedents to respond in a different manner. This makes it all the more urgent to build in this country and throughout the world a group trained in the techniques of non-violent opposition to the encroachments of militarism and fascism. Until we build such a movement, it will be impossible to stall the war machine at home. When we do build such a movement, we will have forged the only weapon which can ever give effective answer to foreign invasion. Thus in learning to fight American Hitlerism we will show an increasing group of war-disillusioned Americans how to resist foreign Hitlers as well.

For these reasons we hereby register our refusal to comply in any way with the Selective Training and Service Act. We do not expect to stem the war forces today; but we are helping to build the movement that will conquer in the future.

58. David Dellinger, "Statement on Entering Prison"

(1943)

David Dellinger (1915–2004), like Donald Benedict, was among the eight students at the Union Theological Seminary who refused to register for the draft (see introduction to document 57). Dellinger's career as a political activist and advocate of nonviolence extended from the 1930s through his death in 2004. He graduated from Yale University with honors in economics in 1936. He had been arrested for protesting during a campaign to unionize workers at Yale, and also became a pacifist while still an undergraduate. He won a fellowship to study at Oxford University and took time off to drive an ambulance during the Spanish Civil War. Returning from Europe, he enrolled in the Union Theological Seminary. Although eligible for deferment, he refused to register for the draft and was arrested. He was tried and sentenced to a year in prison in Danbury, Connecticut, where he refused to recognize the segregated eating arrangements. After the war, he founded a magazine called *Direct Action* with fellow pacifists Dorothy Day and A.J. Muste and criticized the decision to use atomic weapons in the first editorial. Dellinger would become the elder statesman of the nonviolent protest movement against the Vietnam War in the 1960s. What follows is an excerpt from a statement he made as he was about to begin his prison term for refusing to register for the draft.

SOURCE: David Dellinger, *Revolutionary Non-Violence: Essays by Dave Dellinger* (New York: Bobbs-Merrill, 1970), 7–11.

I. I believe that all war is evil and useless. Even a so-called war of defense is evil in that it consists of lies, hatred, self-righteousness, and the most destructive methods of violence that man can invent. These things corrupt even the most idealistic supporters of the war. They harm even the most innocent children of "enemy" countries.

Even a war fought with the highest idealism is useless in that it can produce no good result that could not be secured better in other ways. Just as it would be stupid to plant weeds and to try to harvest vegetables, so it would be stupid to encourage the lies, conscription and murder of war, and to hope to produce democracy, freedom, and brotherhood. War is a Trojan horse from which emerge at home the enemies that destroy us.

The fact that some people sincerely believe that war will help us cannot persuade me to cooperate in their mistake. Instead it makes it all the more important to do everything possible to help free them from their error and to show them a substitute for war.

II. I believe that when anyone supports war he violates the life and teachings of Jesus.

III. I believe that the so-called United Nations and each individual resident of them bear a tremendous responsibility for this present war.

A. The rest of the world has been driven to desperation by the economic cruelty of the United States, with its Big Business Empire, and of England with her Colonial Empire. We produced the economic, social, and psychological conditions that made war inevitable. Russia, for all her social reforms, is a bloody dictatorship that has followed a policy of selfish nationalism for years. As part of this policy she has subsidized political parties, all over the world, that have poisoned the left wing movement with dishonesty, opportunism, and violence.

B. So far as Germany and Italy are concerned, British and American politicians and industrialists supported the rise of Hitler and Mussolini. One reason they did this was to make private profits out of various business deals. A second reason was that Hitler and Mussolini were destroying the labor and socialist movements of Europe, which had the power to introduce economic and social democracy to oppressed peoples everywhere. If you find this hard to believe, let me remind you that the United States government is following a similar policy today. Of course they cannot support the two individuals, Hitler and Mussolini, but they are supporting totalitarian forces in every country—Giraud, Peyroutan, Franco, Prince Otto Hapsburg, the Junkers of Germany, the land owners and business interests of Italy, the dictators of Latin America, etc. At the same time they are opposing the democratic forces of Europe—and their representatives in this country.

Even after the early honeymoon with Hitler and Mussolini, when these men began to emerge as dangerous Frankensteins, the United States and England were still ready to sell the democratic freedoms of Spain, Austria, Czechoslovakia, etc., down the river. They resisted every suggestion that we offer the hungry people of Europe the economic and social equality that would have uprooted both fascism and war.

C. So far as Asia is concerned, we introduced modern violence and robbery to the Japanese, by our rape of the orient. Later we were partners of Japan in her invasion of China. American oil, steel, and munitions were sold at huge profits for that purpose. President Roosevelt, the State Department, and politicians all conspired in this. *Every one of them is as guilty of murder as are the Japanese whom they accuse.*

We began to boycott Japan only when it began to threaten our damnable mastery of the orient, and when we needed an incident to strengthen the propaganda by which we were trying to sell the war to our own peace-loving people.

Churchill himself has admitted in Parliament that President Roosevelt committed us to war against Japan in August 1941, four months before Pearl Harbor. Shortly afterward we started issuing ultimatums and threats for *the sole purpose* of carrying out this promise—that we would wage war against Japan before the year was out.

We also began a policy of limited naval warfare. Naval officers have admitted that *before Pearl Harbor*, they were sent on secret expeditions with orders to shoot Japanese ships and aircraft—on sight and without warning. See Jeannette Rankin's speech in the House of Representatives on December 8, 1942. The same policy was pursued in the Atlantic. Rather brazen proof of this terrible policy of our government has just been given by the Navy Department in General Order No. 190, whereby the Navy, Marine Corps, and Coast Guard personnel have been ordered to wear a bronze letter A on their American defense medal service ribbon "to commemorate service on ships operating in actual or potential belligerent contact with Axis forces in the Atlantic Ocean prior to December 7, 1941."

How many Japanese ships were sunk in this way, we do not know. Nor do we know how many peace-loving Japanese reluctantly accepted the war because of our treachery. But the governments of the United States and Japan each exploited the treachery of the other, forcing war upon its own people.

D. We also went to war to avoid facing up to the failures of our selfishly organized private-ownership, private-profit system.

At home we have a system whereby the mines, factories, and other means of production are owned and operated—not for the good of all but for the private profit of a few. *Such organized selfishness will not work.* It produced years of mass unemployment, depression and unrest. But even the misery of millions did not persuade the privileged classes to give up their stranglehold on God's material gifts and to embrace the total democracy and brotherhood that alone will work. Instead, after seven desperate years of bread lines and boondoggling, they turned to the manufacture of armaments. Roosevelt himself, in an interview recorded in the *New York Times*, pointed to Nazi Germany and said that she had lots of armaments plants and no unemployment.

At the same time they played up war scares and international hatreds as an excuse for making bombs instead of bread, and as a scapegoat on which to blame the sufferings of the people.

After a time "national defense" was an insufficient excuse for slavery and injustice. The people were restless. Our privileged classes had to choose: brotherhood or war. The Axis threatened the financial and business empire of certain private interests. War offered an excellent smoke-screen for profiteering, for feeling important, and for suppressing American freedom, with all its dangers to economic selfishness. Finally, the brutality of the Axis presented the idealistic mask without which neither the people nor most of their masters would have been able to face the terrible choice they made.

Very few people actually chose war. They chose selfishness and the result was war. Each of us, individually and nationally, must choose: total love or total war.

Most people are afraid to choose total love and brotherhood. It is too new, too daring. It seems to require too many sacrifices. For the privileged classes who control the normal instruments for manufacturing public opinion and making public decisions, it means abandoning certain traditional privileges which bring no real happiness—so long as they are private privileges—but which possess a superficial glitter and attractiveness. For all of us it means abandoning our pride, our self-centeredness, and whatever special privileges we have or hope to have some day.

The selfishness of all of us underlies the dishonesty of our Roosevelts and Tojos, the brutality of our Hitlers and Churchills. . . .

59. Ralph A. Bard, "Memorandum on Use of the S-1 Bomb"

(1945)

Ralph A. Bard (1884–1975) served as assistant secretary of the navy from 1941 to 1944 and as under secretary of the navy from 1944 to 1945. A respected Chicago financier before the war, he also served on the secret eight-man Interim Committee that was formed to advise President Truman about the use of the atomic bomb (referred to as the "S-1 bomb"). On June 1, 1945, the committee handed down a unanimous decision recommending that the bomb be used on a civilian target in Japan without any warning, and reconfirmed this recommendation in a meeting on June 21. Yet Bard began to have second thoughts, thinking that using the bomb without any preliminary warning might jeopardize the United States' status as a "great humanitarian nation." On June 27, 1945, in the following memo to Secretary of War Henry L. Stimson, Bard proposed trying to contact the Japanese to offer them a chance to surrender before the bomb was dropped. Bard may have met with President Truman in early July to discuss the memo, but that meeting obviously did not change the president's mind.

SOURCE: "Interim Committee, International Control," Records of the Chief of Engineers, Manhattan Engineer District, Harrison-Bundy File, folder 77, Record Group 77, National Archives.

Ever since I have been in touch with this program I have had a feeling that before the bomb is actually used against Japan that Japan should have some preliminary warning for say two or three days in advance of use. The position of the United States as a great humanitarian nation and the fair play attitude of our people generally is responsible in the main for this feeling.

During recent weeks I have also had the feeling very definitely that the Japanese government may be searching for some opportunity which they could use as a medium of surrender. Following the three-power conference emissaries from this country could contact representatives from Japan somewhere on the China Coast and make representations with regard to Russia's position and at the same time give them some information regarding the proposed use of atomic power, together with whatever assurances the President might care to make with regard to the Emperor of Japan and the treatment of the Japanese nation following unconditional surrender. It seems quite possible to me that this presents the opportunity which the Japanese are looking for.

I don't see that we have anything particular to lose in following such a program. The states are so tremendous that it is my opinion very real consideration should be given to some plan of this kind. I do not believe under present circumstances existing that there is anyone in this country whose evaluation of the chances of the success of such a program is worth a great deal. The only way to find out is to try it out.

60. American Institute for Public Opinion, "On Treatment of the Japanese Emperor"

(1945)

By June 29, 1945, the advances of American forces across the Pacific made the defeat of Japan look inevitable. On that day, President Truman approved the plans of the joint chiefs of staff to invade Japan with a force of 5 million, mostly composed of American troops. Roughly a third of those surveyed on that day favored the execution of emperor; it would be interesting to know if the same feelings persisted after the atomic bombs fell more than a month later. Many experts did feel that lenient treatment of the emperor could lead to the survival of the culture of militarism that had driven the Japanese Empire's war effort.

SOURCE: *Public Opinion Quarterly* 9, no. 2 (Summer 1945), 246.

What Do You Think We Should Do with the Japanese Emperor after the War?

June 29, 1945—AIPO: American Institute for Public Opinion

Execute him	33%
Let court decide his fate	17
Keep him in prison the rest of his life	11
Exile him	9
Nothing (he's only figurehead for warlords)	4
Use him as a puppet to run Japan	3
Miscellaneous/no opinion	23

61. Scientists at the Chicago Metallurgical Laboratory, "Petition to the President of the United States"

(1945)

This petition, dated July 17, 1945, was signed by the sixty-nine scientists who worked at the Chicago Metallurgical Laboratory, just one of the critical facilities of the Manhattan Project that were scattered across the United States. (Ironically, there were no metallurgists working at this laboratory.) Under the direction of Enrico Fermi, scientists at the lab developed an "atomic pile" in racquetball courts underneath the stands of the University of Chicago's athletic stadium, Alonzo Stagg Field. In essence, they created the world's first nuclear reactor, although that term was not used until 1952. In the petition that follows, the scientists urge President Truman to exercise restraint in the use of atomic weapons, giving the Japanese Empire a chance to surrender before such a weapon would be employed. They felt strongly that using the weapon without warning would compromise the moral authority of the United States.

SOURCE: Dennis Merrill, ed., *Documentary History of the Truman Presidency*, vol. 1 (Bethesda, Md.: University Publications of America, 1995).

Discoveries of which the people of the United States are not aware may affect the welfare of this nation in the near future. The liberation of atomic power which has been achieved places atomic bombs in the hands of the Army. It places in your hands, as Commander-in-Chief, the fateful decision whether or not to sanction the use of such bombs in the present phase of the war against Japan.

We, the undersigned scientists, have been working in the field of atomic power. Until recently we have had to fear that the United States might be attacked by atomic bombs during this war and that her only defense might lie in a counterattack by the same means. Today, with the defeat of Germany, this danger is averted and we feel impelled to say what follows:

The war has to be brought speedily to a successful conclusion and attacks by atomic bombs may very well be an effective method of warfare. We feel, however, that such attacks on Japan could not be justified, at least not unless the terms which will be imposed after the war on Japan were made public in detail and Japan were given an opportunity to surrender.

If such public announcement gave assurance to the Japanese the they could look forward to a life devoted to peaceful pursuits in their homeland and if Japan still refused to surrender our nation might then, in certain circumstances, find itself forced to resort to the use of atomic bombs. Such a step, however, ought not to be made at any time without seriously considering the moral responsibilities which are involved.

The development of atomic power will provide the nations with new means of destruction. The atomic bombs at our disposal represent only the first step in this direction, and there is almost no limit to the destructive power which will become available in the course of their future development. Thus a nation which sets the precedent of using these newly liberated forces of nature for purposes of destruction may have to bear the responsibility of opening the door to an era of devastation on an unimaginable scale.

If after this war a situation is allowed to develop in the world which permits rival powers to be in uncontrolled possession of these new means of destruction, the cities of the United States as well as the cities of other nations will be in continuous danger of sudden annihilation. All the resources of the United States, moral and material, may have to be mobilized to prevent the advent of such a world situation. Its prevention is at present the solemn responsibility of the United States–singled out by virtue of her lead in the field of atomic power.

The added material strength which this lead gives to the United States brings with it the obligation of restraint and if we were to violate this obligation our moral position would be weakened in the eyes of the world and in our own eyes. It would then be more difficult for us to live up to our responsibility of bringing the unloosened forces of destruction under control.

In view of the foregoing, we, the undersigned, respectfully petition, first, that you exercise your power as Commander-in-Chief, to rule that the United States shall not resort to the use of atomic bombs in this war unless the terms which will be imposed upon Japan have been made public in detail and Japan knowing these terms has refused to surrender; second, that in such an event the question whether or not to use atomic bombs be decided by you in the light of the considerations presented in this petition as well as all the other moral responsibilities which are involved.

62. Henry L. Stimson, "Prepared Statement for the Public Regarding the Use of the Atomic Bomb"

(1945)

On July 31, 1945, Secretary of War Henry L. Stimson (1867–1950) sent the following revised statement that he had prepared for the president to read to the public after the dropping of the first atomic bomb on Japan. Stimson was a Republican lawyer and statesman renowned for his extraordinary organizational abilities. He had served as secretary of war under President William Howard Taft, governor-general of the Philippines under President Calvin Coolidge, and secretary of state under President Herbert Hoover. In 1940 President Roosevelt appointed Stimson secretary of war, and he skillfully presided over the massive prewar mobilization of American forces. Stimson was a key decision maker in both the program to develop the atomic bomb and the deliberations about whether or not to use it. He was highly respected by Presidents Roosevelt and Truman, and both usually followed his advice. This version of the statement was virtually the same as the one Truman read after the Hiroshima bombing on August 6, 1945 (the paragraph starting with "But the greatest marvel . . ." was excised from the official announcement).

SOURCE: President's Secretary's File, Truman Papers, Independence, Mo., July 31, 1945.

July 31, 1945

Dear Mr. President:

Attached are two copies of the revised statement which has been prepared for release by you as soon as the new weapon is used. This is the statement about which I cabled you last night.

The reason for the haste is that I was informed only yesterday that, weather permitting, it is likely that the weapon will be used as early as August 1st, Pacific Ocean Time, which as you know is a good many hours ahead of Washington time.

This message and inclosure are being brought to you by Lt. R. G. Ame-

son, whom Secretary Byrnes will recognize as the Secretary of the Interim
Committee, appointed with your approval, to study various features of the
development and use of the atomic bomb.

Faithfully yours,
Secretary of War.

Draft of 30 July 1945

_____ hours ago an American airplane dropped one bomb on _____ and destroyed it usefulness to the enemy. That bomb has more power than 20,000 tons
of T.N.T. It has more than two thousand times the blast power of the British
"Grand Slam" which is the largest bomb ever yet used in the history of warfare.

The Japanese began the war from the air at Pearl Harbor. They have been re-
paid many fold. And the end is not yet. With this bomb we have now added
a new and revolutionary increase in destruction to supplement the growing
power of our armed forces. In their present form these bombs are now in production and even more powerful forms are in development.

It is an atomic bomb. It is a harnessing of the basic power of the universe. The
force from which the sun draws its power has been loosed against those who
brought war to the Far East.

Before 1939, it was the accepted belief of scientists that it was theoretically
possible to release atomic energy. But no one knew any practical method of doing it. By 1942, however, we knew that the Germans were working feverishly to
find a way to add atomic energy to the other engines of war with which they
hoped to enslave the world. But they failed. We may be grateful to Providence
that the Germans got the V-1's and the V-2's late and in limited quantities and
even more grateful that they did not get the atomic bomb at all.

The battle of the laboratories held fateful risks for us as well as the battles of
the air, land and sea, and we have now won the battle of the laboratories as we
have won the other battles.

Beginning in 1940, before Pearl Harbor, scientific knowledge useful in war
was pooled between the United States and Great Britain, and many priceless
helps to our victories have come from that arrangement. Under that general policy the research on the atomic bomb was begun. With American and British scientists working together we entered the race of discovery against the Germans.

The United States had available the large number of scientists of distinction
in the many needed areas of knowledge. It had the tremendous industrial and
financial resources necessary for the project and they could be devoted to it
without undue impairment of other vital war work. In the United States the laboratory work and the production plants, on which a substantial start had already
been made, would be out of reach of enemy bombing, while at that time Britain
was exposed to constant air attack and was still threatened with the possibility of
invasion. For these reasons Prime Minister Churchill and President Roosevelt
agreed that it was wise to carry on the project here. We now have two great plants
and many lesser works devoted to the production of atomic power. Employment
during peak construction numbered 125,000 and over 65,000 individuals are

even now engaged in operating the plants. Many have worked there for two and a half years. Few know what they have been producing. They see great quantities of material going in and they see nothing coming out of these plants, for the physical size of the explosive charge is exceedingly small. We have spent two billion dollars on the greatest scientific gamble in history—and won.

But the greatest marvel is not the size of the enterprise, its secrecy, nor its cost, but the achievement of scientific brains in putting together infinitely complex pieces of knowledge held by many men in different fields of science into a workable plan. And hardly less marvellous has been the capacity of industry to design, and of labor to operate, the machines and methods to do things never done before so that the brain child of many minds came forth in physical shape and performed as it was supposed to do. Both science and industry worked under the direction of the United States Army, which achieved a unique success in managing so diverse a problem in the advancement of knowledge in an amazingly short time. It is doubtful if such another combination could be got together in the world. What has been done is the greatest achievement of organized science in history. It was done under high pressure and without failure.

We are now prepared to obliterate more rapidly and completely every productive enterprise the Japanese have above ground in any city. We shall destroy their docks, their factories, and their communications. Let there be no mistake; we shall completely destroy Japan's power to make war.

It was to spare the Japanese people from utter destruction that the ultimatum of July 26 was issued at Potsdam. Their leaders promptly rejected that ultimatum. If they do not now accept our terms they may expect a rain of ruin from the air, the like of which has never been seen on this earth. Behind this air attack will follow sea and land forces in such numbers and power as they have not yet seen and with the fighting skill of which they are already well aware.

The Secretary of War, who has kept in personal touch with all phases of the project, will immediately make public a statement giving further details.

His statement will give facts concerning the sites at Oak Ridge near Knoxville, Tennessee, and at Richland near Pasco, Washington, and an installation near Santa Fe, New Mexico. Although the workers at the sites have been making materials to be used in producing the greatest destructive force in history they have not themselves been in danger beyond that of many other occupations, for the utmost care has been taken of their safety. A scientific report of the project will be made public tomorrow.

The fact that we can release atomic energy ushers in a new era in man's understanding of nature's forces. Atomic energy may in the future supplement the power that now comes from coal, oil, and falling water, but at present it cannot be produced on a basis to compete with them commercially. Before that comes there must be a long period of intensive research.

It has never been the habit of the scientists of this country or the policy of this Government to withhold from the world scientific knowledge. Normally, therefore, everything about the work with atomic energy would be made public.

But under present circumstances it is not intended to divulge the technical

processes of production or all the military applications, pending further examination of possible methods of protecting us and the rest of the world from the
danger of sudden destruction.

I shall recommend that the Congress of the United States consider promptly
the establishment of an appropriate commission to control the production and
use of atomic power within the United States. I shall give further consideration
and make further recommendations to the Congress as to how atomic power
can become a powerful and forceful influence towards the maintenance of
world peace.

63. Senator Richard B. Russell, "Cable from Russell to Truman and Response from Truman (Favoring the Use of the Bomb)"

(1945)

Richard B. Russell (1897–1971), a Democrat from Georgia, served in the U.S. Senate from 1933 until his death. Before that, he served as governor of Georgia from 1931 to 1933. The following correspondence between President Truman and Russell—an initial telegram from Russell dated August 7 and a follow-up letter in response from Truman dated August 9—reflects Russell's unqualified support of Truman's decision to drop the bomb on Hiroshima and continue the war effort, and Truman's need to refer to the Japanese as somehow less than human in order to justify his decision.

SOURCE: President's Secretary's File, Truman Papers, Independence, Mo., August 9, 1945.

August 9, 1945

WU80 LG GOVT
WINDER GA AUG 7 427P THE PRESIDENT
(PERSONAL DELIVERY) THE WHITE HOUSE

PERMIT ME TO RESPECTFULLY SUGGEST THAT WE CEASE OUR EFFORTS TO CAJOLE JAPAN INTO SURRENDERING IN ACCORDANCE WITH THE POTSDAM DECLARATION. LET US CARRY THE WAR TO THEM UNTIL THEY BEG US TO ACCEPT THE UNCONDITIONAL SURRENDER. THE FOUL ATTACK ON PEARL HARBOR BROUGHT US INTO WAR AND I AM UNABLE TO SEE ANY VALID REASON WHY WE SHOULD BE SO MUCH MORE CONSIDERATE AND LENIENT IN DEALING WITH JAPAN THAN WITH GERMANY. I EARNESTLY INSIST JAPAN SHOULD BE DEALT WITH AS HARSHLY AS GERMANY AND THAT SHE SHOULD NOT BE THE BENEFICIARY OF A SOFT PEACE. THE VAST MAJORITY OF THE AMERICAN PEOPLE, INCLUDING MANY SOUND THINKERS WHO HAVE INTIMATE KNOWLEDGE OF THE ORIENT, DO NOT AGREE WITH MR. GREW IN HIS ATTITUDE THAT THERE IS ANY THING SACROSANCT

ABOUT HIROHITO. HE SHOULD GO. WE HAVE NO OBLIGATION TO SHINTO-
ISM. THE CONTEMPTUOUS ANSWER OF THE JAPS TO THE POTSDAM ULTI-
MATUM JUSTIFIES A REVISION OF THAT DOCUMENT AND STERNER PEACE
TERMS.

IF WE DO NOT HAVE AVAILABLE A SUFFICIENT NUMBER OF ATOMIC
BOMBS WITH WHICH TO FINISH THE JOB IMMEDIATELY, LET US CARRY ON
WITH TNT AND FIRE BOMBS UNTIL WE CAN PRODUCE THEM.

I ALSO HOPE THAT YOU WILL ISSUE ORDERS FORBIDDING THE OFFI-
CERS IN COMMAND OF OUR AIR FORCES FROM WARNING JAP CITIES
THAT THEY WILL BE ATTACKED. THESE GENERALS DO NOT FLY OVER
JAPAN AND THIS SHOWMANSHIP CAN ONLY RESULT IN THE UNNECESSARY
LOSS OF MANY FINE BOYS IN OUR AIR FORCE AS WELL AS OUR HELPLESS
PRISONERS IN THE HANDS OF THE JAPANESE, INCLUDING THE SURVIVORS
OF THE MARCH OF DEATH ON BATAAN WHO ARE CERTAIN TO BE
BROUGHT INTO THE CITIES THAT HAVE BEEN WARNED.

THIS WAS A TOTAL WAR AS LONG AS OUR ENEMIES HELD ALL OF THE
CARDS. WHY SHOULD WE CHANGE THE RULES NOW, AFTER THE BLOOD,
TREASURE AND ENTERPRISE OF THE AMERICAN PEOPLE HAVE GIVEN US
THE UPPER HAND. OUR PEOPLE HAVE NOT FORGOTTEN THAT THE JAPANESE
STRUCK US THE FIRST BLOW IN THIS WAR WITHOUT THE SLIGHTEST
WARNING. THEY BELIEVE THAT WE SHOULD CONTINUE TO STRIKE THE
JAPANESE UNTIL THEY ARE BROUGHT GROVELING TO THEIR KNEES. WE
SHOULD CEASE OUR APPEALS TO JAPAN TO SUE FOR PEACE. THE NEXT
PLEA FOR PEACE SHOULD COME FROM AN UTTERLY DESTROYED TOKYO.
WELCOME BACK HOME. WITH ASSURANCES OF ESTEEM

RICHARD B. RUSSELL, US SENATOR.

Dear Dick:

I read your telegram of August seventh with a lot of interest.

I know that Japan is a terribly cruel and uncivilized nation in warfare
but I can't bring myself to believe that, because they are beasts, we should
ourselves act in the same manner.

For myself, I certainly regret the necessity of wiping out whole populations because of the "pigheadedness" of the leaders of a nation and for
your information, I am not going to do it unless it is absolutely necessary.
It is my opinion that after the Russians enter into war the Japanese will
very shortly fold up.

My object is to save as many American lives as possible but I also have a
humane feeling for the women and children in Japan.

Sincerely yours,
Harry S. Truman

64. Samuel McCrea Cavert, "Cable to President Truman (August 9) and Letter of Response (August 11)"

(1945)

Reverend Samuel McCrea Cavert (1888–1976) was a prominent Presbyterian minister and leader in the American Protestant ecumenical movement, an effort to bring the varied Protestant denominations more closely together. This movement was best embodied by the Federal Council of the Churches of Christ in America, founded in 1905; Cavert was its long-standing general secretary up through World War II. Cavert and many members of his organization were appalled by the devastation wrought by the bomb dropped on Hiroshima on August 6, viewing it as entirely antithetical to Christian morality. Cavert pleaded with the president to allow more time for the Japanese to respond to the ultimatum for total surrender that the United States issued before using an atomic weapon again, but a bomb was dropped on Nagasaki that same day. Truman's terse reply justifies the inhumanity of the bombings by claiming that the Japanese were inhuman themselves, no better than "beasts."

SOURCE: President's Secretary's File, Truman Papers, Independence, Mo., August 11, 1945.

Cable from Samuel McCrea Cavert to President Truman, August 9, 1945

WE71 114 2 EXTRA

WUX NEWYORK NY AUG 9 1945 1046A

HONORABLE HARRY S TRUMAN, PRESIDENT OF THE UNITED STATES
THE WHITE HOUSE

MANY CHRISTIANS DEEPLY DISTURBED OVER USE OF ATOMIC BOMBS AGAINST JAPANESE CITIES BECAUSE OF THEIR NECESSARILY INDISCRIMINATE DESTRUCTIVE EFFORTS AND BECAUSE THEIR USE SETS EXTREMELY DANGEROUS PRECEDENT FOR FUTURE OF MANKIND. BISHOP OXNAM,

PRESIDENT OF THE COUNCIL, AND JOHN FOSTER DULES, CHAIRMAN OF ITS COMMISSION ON A JUST AND DURABLE PEACE ARE PREPARING STATEMENT FOR PROBABLE RELEASE TOMORROW URGING THAT ATOMIC BOMBS BE REGARDED AS TRUST FOR HUMANITY AND THAT JAPANESE NATION BE GIVEN GENUINE OPPORTUNITY AND TIME TO VERIFY FACTS ABOUT NEW BOMB AND TO ACCEPT SURRENDER TERMS. RESPECTFULLY URGE THAT AMPLE OPPORTUNITY BE GIVEN JAPAN TO RECONSIDER ULTI-MATUM BEFORE ANY FURTHER DEVASTATION BY ATOMIC BOMB IS VIS-ITED UPON HER PEOPLE.

FEDERAL COUNCIL OF THE CHURCHES OF CHRIST IN AMERICA

SAMUEL MCCREA CAVERT GENERAL SECRETARY.

Letter from President Truman to Samuel McCrea Cavert August 11, 1945

August 11, 1945

My dear Mr. Cavert:

I appreciated very much your telegram of August ninth.

Nobody is more disturbed over the use of Atomic bombs than I am but I was greatly disturbed over the unwarranted attack by the Japanese on Pearl Harbor and their murder of our prisoners of war. The only language they seem to understand is the one we have been using to bombard them.

When you have to deal with a beast you have to treat him as a beast. It is most regrettable but nevertheless true.

Sincerely yours,

HARRY S. TRUMAN

65. J. Robert Oppenheimer, "Letter to the Secretary of War (Advice on Future Atomic Development)"

(1945)

J. Robert Oppenheimer (1904–67) is perhaps best known for serving as the director of the Manhattan Project, the program that developed the atomic bombs that were dropped on Hiroshima and Nagasaki. A brilliant theoretical physicist, before the war Oppenheimer was an enormously productive and popular professor at the University of California, Berkeley. While at Berkeley, he learned to read Sanskrit, and he later said while lecturing that during the detonation of the first atomic bomb at Los Alamos, he had thought of a quote from the sacred Hindu text, the *Bhagavad Gita:* "If the radiance of a thousand suns were to burst at once into the sky, that would be like the splendor of the mighty one." After the detonation of the Hiroshima and Nagasaki bombs, Oppenheimer was asked by the Interim Committee (see introduction to document 59) to lead a panel of scientists to advise on the future development of atomic weaponry. The conclusions of that panel are summed up in the following letter, dated August 17, 1945. The panel admitted that the continued development of more effective atomic weapons was a natural course for defense policy to take, but did not see that course as necessarily guaranteeing future security.

After the war, Oppenheimer became the chairman of the General Advisory Committee of the newly created Atomic Energy Committee. During the early 1950s, Oppenheimer's outspoken criticism of the McCarthy anticommunist hearings led to a successful effort by politicians to have him stripped of his security clearance. Oppenheimer continued a fruitful academic career. He occupied the same chair at the Institute for Advanced Study in Princeton, New Jersey, formerly held by Albert Einstein.

SOURCE: J. Robert Oppenheimer, *Letters and Recollections* (Cambridge, Mass.: Harvard University Press, 1980).

August 17, 1945

Dear Mr. Secretary:

The Interim Committee has asked us to report in some detail on the scope and program of future work in the field of atomic energy. One important phase of this work is the development of weapons; and since this is the problem which has dominated our war time activities, it is natural that in this field our ideas should be most definite and clear, and that we should be most confident of answering adequately the questions put to us by the coinmittee. In examining these questions we have, however, come on certain quite general conclusions, whose implications for national policy would seem to be both more immediate and more profound than those of the detailed technical recommendations to be submitted. We, therefore, think it appropriate to present them to you at this time.

1. We are convinced that weapons quantitatively and qualitatively far more effective than now available will result from further work on these problems. This conviction is motivated not alone by analogy with past developments, but by specific projects to improve and multiply the existing weapons, and by the quite favorable technical prospects of the realization of the super bomb.

2. We have been unable to devise or propose effective military countermeasures for atomic weapons. Although we realize that future work may reveal possibilities at present obscure to us, it is our firm opinion that no military countermeasures will be found which will be adequately effective in preventing the delivery of atomic weapons.

The detailed technical report in preparation will document these conclusions, but hardly alter them.

3. We are not only unable to outline a program that would assure to this nation for the next decades hegemony in the field of atomic weapons; we are equally unable to insure that such hegemony, if achieved, could protect us from the most terrible destruction.

4. The development, in the years to come, of more effective atomic weapons, would appear to be a most natural element in any national policy of maintaining our military forces at great strength; nevertheless we have grave doubts that this further development can contribute essentially or permanently to the prevention of war. We believe that the safety of this nation—as opposed to its ability to inflict damage on an enemy power—cannot lie wholly or even primarily in its scientific or technical prowess. It can be based only on making future wars impossible. It is our unanimous and urgent recommendation to you that, despite the present incomplete exploitation of technical possibilities in this field, all steps be taken, all necessary international arrangements be made, to this one end.

5. We should be most happy to have you bring these views to the attention of other members of the Government, or of the American people, should you wish to do so.

Very sincerely,
J. R. Oppenheimer

For the Panel

CHAPTER SEVEN

The Cold War, Part I: Anticommunism and Civil Liberties

66. Harry S. Truman, "Executive Order 9835"

(1947)

The establishment of the Federal Employee Loyalty Program reflected the Truman administration's commitment to contain Soviet communism at home as well as abroad. Harry S. Truman (1884–1972) grew up in Independence, Missouri, and served as a captain in the 129th Field Artillery in France during the Great War. After the war, he gradually became more active in Missouri Democratic Party politics. He won election to the United States Senate in 1934. In 1944, Franklin D. Roosevelt chose Truman as his running mate in his successful campaign for reelection, and when Roosevelt died in April 1945, Truman assumed the presidency. The end of World War II and the start of the Cold War dominated Truman's early years in the White House. In March 1947, just nine days after the president announced the Truman Doctrine—a pledge to "support free peoples who are resisting attempted subjugation by armed minorities or by outside pressures"—he issued Executive Order 9835.

Against the backdrop of intensifying concerns that Soviet spies and sympathizers had penetrated the federal government, Truman's loyalty program seemed a reasonable response, complete with provisions for hearings and appeals. In practice, however, those accused of disloyalty could not confront their accusers or see evidence regarded as secret. Within five years, loyalty boards dismissed approximately 1,200 federal employees; another 6,000 federal employees chose resignation over the humiliation of being investigated. No formal charges of espionage or treason were filed in any of these cases. Some have seen this document as opening the door to the abuses of the House Un-American Activities Committee and McCarthyism.

SOURCE: Executive Order 9835, Prescribing Procedures for the Administration of an Emloyee's Loyalty Program in the Executive Branch of the Government, 12 *Federal Register*, 1935.

Part I—Investigation of Applicants

1. There shall be a loyalty investigation of every person entering the civilian employment of any department or agency of the executive branch of the Federal Government.

   a. Investigations of persons entering the competitive service shall be conducted by the Civil Service Commission, except in such cases as are covered by a special agreement between the Commission and any given department or agency.

   b. Investigations of persons other than those entering the competitive service shall be conducted by the employing department or agency. Departments and agencies without investigative organizations shall utilize the investigative facilities of the Civil Service Commission.

2. The investigations of persons entering the employ of the executive branch may be conducted after any such person enters upon actual employment therein, but in any such case the appointment of such person shall be conditioned upon a favorable determination with respect to his loyalty. . . .

3. An investigation shall be made of all applicants at all available pertinent sources of information and shall include reference to:

   a. Federal Bureau of Investigation files.

   b. Civil Service Commission files.

   c. Military and naval intelligence files.

   d. The files of any other appropriate government investigative or intelligence agency.

   e. House Committee on Un-American Activities files.

   f. Local law-enforcement files at the place of residence and employment of the applicant, including municipal, county, and State law-enforcement files.

   g. Schools and colleges attended by applicant.

   h. Former employers of applicant.

   i. References given by applicant.

   j. Any other appropriate source.

4. Whenever derogatory information with respect to loyalty of an applicant is revealed a full field investigation shall be conducted. A full field investigation shall also be conducted of those applicants, or of applicants for particular positions, as may be designated by the head of the employing department or agency, such designations to be based on the determination by any such head of the best interests of national security. . . .

Part II—Investigation of Employees

   a. An officer or employee who is charged with being disloyal shall have a right to an administrative hearing before a loyalty board in the employing department or agency. He may appear before such board personally, accompanied by counsel or representative of his own choosing, and present evidence on his own behalf, through witnesses or by affidavit.

b. The officer or employee shall be served with a written notice of such hearing in sufficient time, and shall be informed therein of the nature of the charges against him in sufficient detail, so that he will be enabled to prepare his defense. The charges shall be stated as specifically and completely as, in the discretion of the employing department or agency, security considerations permit. . . .

3. A recommendation of removal by a loyalty board shall be subject to appeal by the officer or employee affected, prior to his removal, to the head of the employing department or agency or to such person or persons as may be designated by such head, under such regulations as may be prescribed by him, and the decision of the department or agency concerned shall be subject to appeal to the Civil Service Commission's Loyalty Review Board, hereinafter provided for, for an advisory recommendation. . . .

Part III—Responsibilities of Civil Service Commission

1. There shall be established in the Civil Service Commission a Loyalty Review Board of not less than three impartial persons, the members of which shall be officers or employees of the Commission. . . .

3. The Loyalty Review Board shall currently be furnished by the Department of Justice the name of each foreign or domestic organization, association, movement, group or combination of persons which the Attorney General, after appropriate investigation and determination, designates as totalitarian, fascist, communist or subversive, or as having adopted a policy of advocating or approving the commission of acts of force or violence to deny others their rights under the Constitution of the United States, or as seeking to alter the form of government of the United States by unconstitutional means.

a. The Loyalty Review Board shall disseminate such information to all departments and agencies.

Part IV—Security Measures in Investigations

1. At the request of the head of any department or agency of the executive branch an investigative agency shall make available to such head, personally, all investigative material and information collected by the investigative agency concerning any employee or prospective employee of the requesting department or agency, or shall make such material and information available to any officer or officers designated by such head and approved by the investigative agency.

2. Notwithstanding the foregoing requirement, however, the investigative agency may refuse to disclose the names of confidential informants, provided it furnishes sufficient information about such informants on the basis of which the requesting department or agency can make an adequate evaluation of the information furnished by them and provided it advises the requesting department or agency in writing that it is essential to the protection of the

informants or to the investigation of other cases that the identity of the informants not be revealed. Investigative agencies shall not use this discretion to decline to reveal sources of information where such action is not essential.

3. Each department and agency of the executive branch should develop and maintain, for the collection and analysis of information relating to the loyalty of its employees and prospective employees, a staff specially trained in security techniques, and an effective security control system for protecting such information generally and for protecting confidential sources of such information particularly.

Part V—Standards

1. The standard for the refusal of employment or the removal from employment in an executive department or agency on grounds relating to loyalty shall be that, on all the evidence, reasonable grounds exist for belief that the person involved is disloyal to the Government of the United States.

2. Activities and associations of an applicant or employee which may be considered in connection with the determination of disloyalty may include one or more of the following:

   a. Sabotage, espionage, or attempts or preparations therefor, or knowingly associating with spies or saboteurs;

   b. Treason or sedition or advocacy thereof;

   c. Advocacy of revolution or force or violence to alter the constitutional form of government of the United States;

   d. Intentional, unauthorized disclosure to any person, under circumstances which may indicate disloyalty to the United States, of documents or information of a confidential or nonpublic character obtained by the person making the disclosure as a result of his employment by the Government of the United States;

   e. Performing or attempting to perform his duties, or otherwise acting so as to serve the interests of another government in preference to the interests of the United States;

   f. Membership in, affiliation with or sympathetic association with any foreign or domestic organization, association, movement, group or combination of persons, designated by the Attorney General as totalitarian, fascist, communist, or subversive, or as having adopted a policy of advocating or approving the commission of acts of force or violence to deny other persons their rights under the Constitution of the United States, or as seeking to alter the form of government of the United States by unconstitutional means.

Part VI—Miscellaneous

1. Each department and agency of the executive branch, to the extent that it has not already done so, shall submit to the Federal Bureau of Investigation of the

Department of Justice, either directly or through the Civil Service Commission, the names (and such other necessary identifying material as the Federal Bureau of Investigation may require) of all of its incumbent employees.

a. The Federal Bureau of Investigation shall check such names against its records of persons concerning whom there is substantial evidence of being within the purview of paragraph 2 of Part V hereof, and shall notify each department and agency of such information.

b. Upon receipt of the above-mentioned information from the Federal Bureau of Investigation, each department and agency shall make, or cause to be made by the Civil Service Commission, such investigation of those employees as the head of the department or agency shall deem advisable. . . .

67. J. Edgar Hoover, "Testimony, House Committee on Un-American Activities"

(1947)

In a rare appearance before a congressional committee, FBI director J. Edgar Hoover reported on the alleged threat posed by communists within the United States and identified the areas of American life that communists had most successfully infiltrated. Hoover (1895–1972) was born in Washington, D.C., and earned his law degree at George Washington University. As assistant to Attorney General A. Mitchell Palmer, he participated in the crackdowns on radicals known as the Palmer Raids. In 1924, Hoover was named director of the FBI, a post he held for nearly fifty years. By 1947, Hoover was regarded as the nation's leading authority on communism, the Communist Party, and the "diabolic machinations of sinister figures engaged in un-American activities." He found an eager audience in the House Committee on Un-American Activities (HUAC), which had been created in 1938 to investigate fascist sympathizers in the United States. Not only did Hoover target the Communist Party of the USA (CPUSA) for abolition, but he urged Congress and the American people to root out communists in the film industry, labor unions, and the government itself—to quarantine them "so they can do no harm."

SOURCE: J. Edgar Hoover, Testimony, House Committee on Un-American Activities, *Hearings on H.R. 1884 and H.R. 2122*, 80th Congress, 1st Session, March 26, 1947.

The Communist movement in the United States began to manifest itself in 1919. Since then it has changed its name and its party line whenever expedient and tactical. But always it comes back to fundamentals and bills itself as the party of Marxism-Leninism. As such, it stands for the destruction of our American form of government; it stands for the destruction of American democracy; it stands for the destruction of free enterprise; and it stands for the creation of a "Soviet of the United States" and ultimate world revolution.

The historic mission: The preamble of the latest constitution of the Communist Party of the United States, filled with Marxian "double talk," proclaims that the party "educates the working class, in the course of its day-to-day struggles, for its historic mission, the establishment of socialism."

The phrase "historic mission" has a sinister meaning. To the uninformed person it bespeaks tradition, but to the Communist, using his own words, it is "achieving the dictatorship of the proletariat"; "to throw off the yoke of imperialism and establish the proletarian dictatorship"; "to raise these revolutionary forces to the surface and hurl them like a devastating avalanche upon the united forces of bourgeois reaction, frenzied at the presentment of their rapidly approaching doom."

In recent years, the Communists have been very cautious about using such phrases as "force and violence"; nevertheless, it is the subject of much discussion in their schools and in party caucus where they readily admit that the only way in which they can defeat the present ruling class is by world revolution.

The Communist, once he is fully trained and indoctrinated, realizes that he can create his order in the United States only by "bloody revolution."

Their chief textbook, *The History of the Communist Party of the Soviet Union,* is used as a basis for planning their revolution. Their tactics require that to be successful they must have:

1. The will and sympathy of the people.
2. Military aid and assistance.
3. Plenty of guns and ammunition.
4. A program for extermination of the police as they are the most important enemy and are termed "trained Fascists."
5. Seizure of all communications, buses, railroads, radio stations, and other forms of communications and transportation.

They evade the question of force and violence publicly. They hold that when Marxists speak of force and violence they will not be responsible—that force and violence will be the responsibility of their enemies. They adopt the novel premise that they do not advocate force and violence publicly but that when their class resists to defend themselves then they are thus accused of using force and violence. A lot of double talk. . . .

One thing is certain. The American progress which all good citizens seek, such as old-age security, houses for veterans, child assistance, and a host of others is being adopted as window dressing by the Communists to conceal their true aims and entrap gullible followers. . . .

The numerical strength of the party's enrolled membership is insignificant. But it is well known that there are many actual members who because of their position are not carried on party rolls. . . .

What is important is the claim of the Communists themselves that for every party member there are 10 others ready, willing, and able to do the party's work. Herein lies the greatest menace of communism. For these are the people who infiltrate and corrupt various spheres of American life. So rather than the size of the Communist Party, the way to weigh its true importance is by testing its influence, its ability to infiltrate.

The size of the party is relatively unimportant because of the enthusiasm and iron-clad discipline under which they operate. In this connection, it might be of interest to observe that in 1917 when the Communists overthrew the Russian Government there was one Communist for every 2,277 persons in Russia. In the United States today there is one Communist for every 1,814 persons in the country.

One who accepts the aims, principles, and program of the party, who attends meetings, who reads the party press and literature, who pays dues, and who is active on behalf of the party "shall be considered a member." The open, avowed Communist who carries a card and pays dues is no different from a security standpoint than the person who does the party's work but pays no dues, carries no card, and is not on the party rolls. In fact, the latter is a greater menace because of his opportunity to work in stealth.

Identifying undercover Communists, fellow travelers, and sympathizers: The burden of proof is placed upon those who consistently follow the ever-changing, twisting party line. Fellow travelers and sympathizers can deny party membership, but they can never escape the undeniable fact that they have played into the Communist hands thus furthering the Communist cause by playing the role of innocent, gullible, or willful allies.

Propaganda activities: The Communists have developed one of the greatest propaganda machines the world has ever known. . . .

The Communist propaganda technique is designed to promote emotional response with the hope that the victim will be attracted by what he is told the Communist way of life holds in store for him. The objective, of course, is to develop discontent and hasten the day when the Communists can gather sufficient support and following to overthrow the American way of life.

Communist propaganda is always slanted in the hope that the Communist may be alined [sic] with liberal progressive causes. The honest liberal and progressive should be alert to this, and I believe the Communists' most effective foes can be the real liberals and progressives who understand their devious machinations.

The deceptiveness of the Communist "double talk" fulfills the useful propaganda technique of confusion. . . .

. . . The use of the term "democracy" by the Communists, we have learned to our sorrow, does not have the meaning to them that it does to us. To them it means communism and totalitarianism and our understanding of the term is regarded by them as imperialistic and Fascist. . . .

Motion pictures: The American Communists launched a furtive attack on Hollywood in 1935 by the issuance of a directive calling for a concentration in Hollywood. The orders called for action on two fronts. (1) An effort to infiltrate the labor unions; (2) infiltrate the so-called intellectual and creative fields. . . .

. . . The entire industry faces serious embarrassment because it could become a springboard for Communist activities. Communist activity in Hollywood is effective and is furthered by Communists and sympathizers using the prestige of prominent persons to serve, often unwittingly, the Communist cause.

The party is content and highly pleased if it is possible to have inserted in a picture a line, a scene, a sequence, conveying the Communist lesson, and more particularly, if they can keep out anti-Communist lessons.

Infiltration: The Communist tactic of infiltrating labor unions stems from the earliest teachings of Marx, which have been reiterated by party spokesmen down through the years. They resort to all means to gain their point and often succeed in penetrating and literally taking over labor unions before the rank and file of members are aware of what has occurred. . . .

I am convinced that the great masses of union men and women are patriotic American citizens interested chiefly in security for their families and themselves. They have no use for the American Communists but in those instances where Communists have taken control of unions, it has been because too many union men and women have been outwitted, outmaneuvered, and outwaited by Communists.

The Communists have never relied on numerical strength to dominate a labor organization. Through infiltration tactics they have in too many instances captured positions of authority. Communists have boasted that with 5 percent of the membership the Communists with their military, superior organizational ability and discipline could control the union. . . .

If more union members took a more active role and asserted themselves it would become increasingly difficult for Communists to gain control. Patriotic union members can easily spot sympathizers and party members in conventions and union meetings because invariably the latter strive to establish the party line instead of serving the best interests of the union and the country. . . .

Government: The recent Canadian spy trials revealed the necessity of alertness in keeping Communists and sympathizers out of Government services. . . .

Since July 1, 1941, the FBI has investigated 6,193 cases under the Hatch Act, which forbids membership upon the part of any Government employee in any organization advocating the overthrow of the government of the United States. . . .

One hundred and one Federal employees were discharged as a result of our investigation, 21 resigned during the investigation, and in 75 cases administrative action was taken by the departments. A total of 1,906 individuals are no longer employed by the Government while 122 cases are presently pending consideration in various Government agencies.

The FBI does not make recommendations; it merely reports facts, and it is up to the interested Government department to make a decision. Almost invariably, of course, subjects of investigations deny affiliation with subversive groups, often despite strong evidence to the contrary. . . .

Mass and front organizations: . . .

. . . Literally hundreds of groups and organizations have either been infiltrated or organized primarily to accomplish the purposes of promoting the interests of the Soviet Union in the United States, the promotion of Soviet war and peace aims, the exploitation of Negroes in the United States, work among foreign-language groups, and to secure a favorable viewpoint toward the Communists in domestic, political, social, and economic issues.

The first requisite for front organizations is an idealistic sounding title.

Hundreds of such organizations have come into being and have gone out of existence when their true purposes have become known or exposed while others with high-sounding names are continually springing up. . . .

The Communist Party of the United States is a fifth column if there ever was one. It is far better organized than were the Nazis in occupied countries prior to their capitulation.

They are seeking to weaken America just as they did in their era of obstruction when they were alined [sic] with the Nazis. Their goal is the overthrow of our Government.

There is no doubt as to where a real Communist's loyalty rests. Their allegiance is to Russia, not the United States. . . .

. . . What can we do? And what should be our course of action? The best antidote to communism is vigorous, intelligent, old-fashioned Americanism with eternal vigilance. I do not favor any course of action which would give the Communists cause to portray and pity themselves as martyrs. I do favor unrelenting prosecution wherever they are found to be violating our country's laws.

As Americans, our most effective defense is a workable democracy that guarantees and preserves our cherished freedoms.

I would have no fears if more Americans possessed the zeal, the fervor, the persistence, and the industry to learn about this menace of Red fascism. I do fear for the liberal and progressive who has been hoodwinked and duped into joining hands with the Communists. I confess to a real apprehension so long as Communists are able to secure ministers of the gospel to promote their evil work and espouse a cause that is alien to the religion of Christ and Judaism. I do fear so long as school boards and parents tolerate conditions whereby Communists and fellow travelers, under the guise of academic freedom, can teach our youth a way of life that eventually will destroy the sanctity of the home, that undermine[s] faith in God, that causes them to scorn respect for constituted authority and sabotage our revered Constitution.

I do fear so long as American labor groups are infiltrated, dominated, or saturated with the virus of communism. I do fear the palliation and weasel-worded gestures against communism indulged in by some of our labor leaders who should know better but who have become pawns in the hands of sinister but astute manipulations for the Communist cause.

I fear for ignorance on the part of all our people who may take the poisonous pills of Communist propaganda. . . .

The Communists have been, still are, and always will be a menace to freedom, to democratic ideals, to the worship of God, and to America's way of life.

I feel that once public opinion is thoroughly aroused as it is today, the fight against communism is well on its way. Victory will be assured once Communists are identified and exposed, because the public will take the first step of quarantining them so they can do no harm. Communism, in reality, is not a political party. It is a way of life—an evil and malignant way of life. It reveals a condition akin to disease that spreads like an epidemic and like an epidemic a quarantine is necessary to keep it from infecting the Nation.

68. Ronald Reagan, "Testimony, House Committee on Un-American Activities"

(1947)

When HUAC, based on J. Edgar Hoover's analysis, launched an investigation of Hollywood's alleged communist infestation, it began by calling several "friendly witnesses," including the president of the Screen Actors' Guild (SAG), Ronald Reagan (1911–2004). The event marked the start of a political transformation for Reagan from New Deal Democrat to conservative Republican. Reagan grew up poor in Dixon, Illinois, the son of an alcoholic shoe salesman. After college and several years as a radio sports announcer, Reagan passed a Hollywood screen test and, in 1937, began acting in Warner Brothers films. During World War II, Reagan served in the First Motion Picture Division of the Army Air Force and made a number of training and propaganda films. After the war, he joined the SAG board, and in 1947 became the union's president. By then, both he and his wife, actress Jane Wyman, had been enlisted by the FBI as informants, naming SAG members they suspected of being communists. In this testimony before HUAC, Reagan made clear his dislike of the communists he saw infiltrating Hollywood, but he expressed concern that the government might compromise its democratic principles in hunting communists. In the years that followed, though, Reagan grew more hard-line in supporting the blacklist of supposed communists in the film industry.

SOURCE: *Hearings Regarding the Communist Infiltration of the Motion Picture Industry*, 80th Congress, 1st Session, October 23–24, 1947.

Testimony of Ronald Reagan . . .

Mr. Stripling: As a member of the board of directors, as president of the Screen Actors Guild, and as an active member, have you at any time observed or noted within the organization a clique of either Communists or Fascists who were attempting to exert influence or pressure on the guild?

Mr. Reagan: Well, sir, my testimony must be very similar to that of Mr. (George) Murphy and Mr. (Robert) Montgomery. There has been a small group within the Screen Actors Guild which has consistently opposed the policy of the guild board and officers of the guild, as evidenced by the vote on various issues. That small clique referred to has been suspected of more or less following the tactics that we associate with the Communist Party.

Mr. Stripling: Would you refer to them as a disruptive influence within the guild?

Mr. Reagan: I would say that at times they have attempted to be a disruptive influence.

Mr. Stripling: You have no knowledge yourself as to whether or not any of them are members of the Communist Party?

Mr. Reagan: No, sir; I have no investigative force, or anything, and I do not know.

Mr. Stripling: Has it ever been reported to you that certain members of the guild were Communists?

Mr. Reagan: Yes, sir; I have heard different discussions and some of them tagged as Communists. . . .

Mr. Stripling: Would you say that this clique has attempted to dominate the guild?

Mr. Reagan: Well, sir, by attempting to put their own particular views on various issues, I guess in regard to that you would have to say that our side was attempting to dominate, too, because we were fighting just as hard to put over our views, in which we sincerely believed, and I think, we were proven correct by the figures—Mr. Murphy gave the figures—and those figures were always approximately the same, an average of 90 percent or better of the Screen Actors Guild voted in favor of those matters now guild policy.

Mr. Stripling: Mr. Reagan, there has been testimony to the effect here that numerous Communist-front organizations have been set up in Hollywood. Have you ever been solicited to join any of those organizations or any organization which you considered to be a Communist-front organization?

Mr. Reagan: Well, sir, I have received literature from an organization called the Committee for a Far-Eastern Democratic Policy. I don't know whether it is Communist or not. I only know that I didn't like their views and as a result I didn't want to have anything to do with them.

Mr. Stripling: Were you ever solicited to sponsor the Joint Anti-Fascist Refugee Committee?

Mr. Reagan: No, sir; I was never solicited to do that, but I found myself misled into being a sponsor on another occasion for a function that was held under the auspices of the Joint Anti-Fascist Refugee Committee.

Mr. Stripling: Did you knowingly give your name as a sponsor?

Mr. Reagan: Not knowingly. Could I explain what that occasion was?

Mr. Stripling: Yes sir.

Mr. Reagan: I was called several weeks ago. There happened at the time in Hollywood to be a financial drive on to raise money to build a badly needed hospital in a certain section of town, called the All Nations Hospital. I think the purpose of the building is so obvious by the title that it has the support of most of the people of Hollywood—or, of Los Angeles, I should say. Certainly of most of the doctors, because it is very badly needed.

Some time ago I was called to the telephone. A woman introduced herself by name. Knowing that I didn't know her I didn't make any particular note of her name and I couldn't give it now. She told me that there would be a recital held at which Paul Robeson would sing and she said that all the money for the tickets would go to the hospital and asked if she could use my name as one of the sponsors. I hesitated for a moment because I don't think that Mr. Robeson's and my political views coincide at all and then I thought I was being a little stupid because, I thought, here is an occasion where Mr. Robeson is perhaps appearing as an artist and certainly the object, raising money, is above any political consideration, it is a hospital supported by everyone. I have contributed money myself. So I felt a little bit as if I had been stuffy for a minute and I said, certainly, you can use my name.

I left town for a couple of weeks and when I returned I was handed a newspaper story that said that this recital was held at the Shrine Auditorium in Los Angeles under the auspices of the Joint Anti-Fascist Refugee Committee. The principal speaker was Emil Lustig, Robert Burman took up a collection, and the remnants of the Abraham Lincoln Brigade were paraded to the platform. I did not in the newspaper story see one word about the hospital. I called the newspaper and said I am not accustomed to writing to editors, but would like to explain my position, and he laughed and said, "You needn't bother, you are about the fiftieth person that has called with the same idea, including most of the legitimate doctors who had also been listed as sponsors of that affair."

Mr. Stripling: Would you say from your observation that that is typical of the tactics or strategy of the Communists, to solicit and use the names of prominent people to either raise money or gain support?

Mr. Reagan: I think it is in keeping with their tactics; yes, sir.

Mr. Stripling: Do you think there is anything democratic about those tactics?

Mr. Reagan: I do not, sir. . . .

Mr. Stripling: Mr. Reagan, what is your feeling about what steps should be taken to rid the motion-picture industry of any Communist influences, if they are there?

Mr. Reagan: Well, sir . . . 99 percent of us are pretty well aware of what is going on, and I think within the bounds of our democratic rights, and never once stepping over the rights given us by democracy, we have done a pretty good job in our business of keeping those people's activities curtailed. After all, we must recognize them at present as a political party. On that basis we have exposed their lies when we came across them, we have opposed their propaganda, and I can

certainly testify that in the case of the Screen Actors Guild we have been eminently successful in preventing them from, with their usual tactics, trying to run
a majority of an organization with a well organized minority.

So that fundamentally I would say in opposing those people that the best
thing to do is to make democracy work. In the Screen Actors Guild we make it
work by insuring everyone a vote and by keeping everyone informed. I believe
that, as Thomas Jefferson put it, if all the American people know all of the facts
they will never make a mistake.

Whether the party should be outlawed, I agree with the gentlemen that preceded me that that is a matter for the Government to decide. As a citizen I would
hesitate, or not like, to see any political party outlawed on the basis of its political ideology. We have spent 170 years in this country on the basis that democracy is strong enough to stand up and fight against the inroads of any ideology.
However, if it is proven that an organization is an agent of a power, a foreign
power, or in any way not a legitimate political party, and I think the Government is capable of proving that, if the proof is there, then that is another
matter. . . .

I happen to be very proud of the industry in which I work; I happen to be
very proud of the way in which we conducted the fight. I do not believe the
Communists have ever at any time been able to use the motion-picture screen as
a sounding board for their philosophy or ideology. . . .

The Chairman: There is one thing that you said that interested me very much. That
was the quotation from Jefferson. That is just why this committee was created by
the House of Representatives, to acquaint the American people with the facts.
Once the American people are acquainted with the facts there is no question but
what the American people will do a job, the kind of a job that they want done;
that is, to make America just as pure as we can possibly make it.

We want to thank you very much for coming here today.

Mr. Reagan: Sir, if I might, in regard to that, say that what I was trying to express,
and didn't do very well, was also this other fear. I detest, I abhor their philosophy, but I detest more than that their tactics, which are those of the fifth column,
and are dishonest, but at the same time I never as a citizen want to see our country become urged, by either fear or resentment of this group, that we ever compromise with any of our democratic principles through that fear or resentment.
I still think that democracy can do it.

69. Ring Lardner Jr., "Testimony, House Committee on Un-American Activities"

(1947)

A week after hearing from "friendly witnesses," HUAC called a group of writers and directors who challenged the authority of the committee's investigation of their political affiliations. Nine of the ten witnesses—soon dubbed the Hollywood Ten—were screenwriters and members of the Screen Writers Guild, including Ring Lardner Jr. (1915–2000). The son of the famous baseball writer, Lardner was born in Chicago and grew up on Long Island. Following graduation from Phillips Andover Academy, he was accepted at Princeton and, in his sophomore year, traveled to the Soviet Union, where he enrolled at the Anglo-American Institute at the University of Moscow. He joined the Communist Party in Hollywood not long after starting his career as a screenwriter under David O. Selznick. In 1941, he won an Academy Award for writing *Woman of the Year*. Serving on the board of the Screen Writers Guild, which supported the striking Disney workers in 1941, Lardner was an outspoken proponent of the progressive Conference of Studio Unions, an organization distrusted by the likes of Reagan and Walt Disney.

Lardner and the other members of the Hollywood Ten asserted that the First Amendment to the U.S. Constitution protected their right to belong to any organization, and refused to answer questions about their affiliation with the Communist Party or other groups. They were held in contempt of Congress, blacklisted by the Hollywood studios, and sent to prison. Lardner served nine months of a twelve-month sentence in the federal prison in Danbury, Connecticut, where he once again encountered HUAC chairman J. Parnell Thomas, himself an inmate after being convicted of payroll fraud. In 1970, after twenty years on the blacklist that forced him to often write under a pseudonym, Lardner won his second Academy Award under his own name for writing the screenplay for *M*A*S*H*.

SOURCE: *Hearings Regarding the Communist Infiltration of the Motion Picture Industry*, 80th Congress, 1st Session, October 27–30, 1947.

Stripling: Mr. Lardner, are you a member of the Screen Writers Guild?

Lardner: Mr. Stripling, I want to be cooperative about this, but there are certain limits to my cooperation. I don't want to help you divide or smash this particular guild, or to infiltrate the motion-picture business in any way for the purpose which seems to me to be to try to control that business, to control what the American people can see and hear in their motion-picture theaters.

Chairman: Now, Mr. Lardner, don't do like the others, if I were you, or you will never read your statement. I would suggest—

Lardner: Mr. Chairman, let me—

Chairman: You will be responsive to the question. . . .

The question is: Are you a member of the Screen Writers Guild? . . .

[Lardner spars with Thomas about whether he will be able to read his prepared statement.]

Chairman: That is a very simple question. You can answer that "yes" or "no." You don't have to go into a long harangue or speech. If you want to make a speech you know where you can go out there.

Lardner: Well, I am not very good in haranguing, and I won't try it, but it seems to me that if you can make me answer this question, tomorrow you could ask somebody whether he believed in spiritualism.

Chairman: Oh, no; there is no chance of our asking anyone whether they believe in spiritualism, and you know it. That is just plain silly.

Lardner: You might—

Chairman: Now, you haven't learned your lines very well.

Lardner: Well—

Chairman: I want to know whether you can answer the question "yes" or "no."

Lardner: If you did, for instance, ask somebody about that you might ask him—

Chairman: Well, now, never mind what we might ask him. We are asking you now, Are you a member of the Screen Writers Guild?

Lardner: But—

Chairman: You are an American—

Lardner: But that is a question—

Chairman: And Americans should not be afraid to answer that.

Lardner: Yes; but I am also concerned as an American with the question of whether this committee has the right to ask me—

Chairman: Well, we have got the right and until you prove that we haven't got the right then you have to answer that question.

Lardner: As I said, if you ask somebody, say, about spiritualism—

Chairman: You are a witness, aren't you? Aren't you a witness?

Lardner: Mr. Chairman—

Chairman: Aren't you a witness here?

Lardner: Yes; I am.

Chairman: All right, then, a congressional committee is asking you: Are you a member of the Screen Writers Guild? Now you answer it "yes" or "no."

Lardner: Well, I am saying that in order to answer that—

Chairman: All right, put the next question. Go to the $64 question.

Lardner: I haven't—

Chairman: Go to the next question.

Stripling: Mr. Lardner, are you now or have you ever been a member of the Communist Party?

Lardner: Well, I would like to answer that question, too.

Stripling: Mr. Lardner, the charge has been made before this committee that the Screen Writers Guild which, according to the record, you are a member of, whether you admit it or not, has a number of individuals in it who are members of the Communist Party. This committee is seeking to determine the extent of Communist infiltration in the Screen Writers Guild and in other guilds within the motion-picture industry.

Lardner: Yes.

Stripling: And certainly the question of whether or not you are a member of the Communist Party is very pertinent. Now, are you a member or have you ever been a member of the Communist Party?

Lardner: It seems to me you are trying to discredit the Screen Writers Guild through me and the motion-picture industry through the Screen Writers Guild and our whole practice of freedom of expression.

Stripling: If you and others are members of the Communist Party you are the ones who are discrediting the Screen Writers Guild.

Lardner: I am trying to answer the question by stating first what I feel about the purpose of the question which, as I say, is to discredit the whole motion-picture industry.

Chairman: You won't say anything first. You are refusing to answer this question.

Lardner: I am saying my understanding is as an American resident—

Chairman: Never mind your understanding. There is a question: Are you or have you ever been a member of the Communist Party?

Lardner: I could answer exactly the way you want, Mr. Chairman—

Chairman: No—

Lardner [continuing]: But I think that is a—

Chairman: It is not a question of our wanting you to answer that. It is a very simple question. Anybody would be proud to answer it—any real American would be proud to answer the question, "Are you or have you ever been a member of the Communist Party?"—any real American.

Lardner: It depends on the circumstances. I could answer it, but if I did I would hate myself in the morning.

Chairman: Leave the witness chair.

Lardner: It was a question that would—

Chairman: Leave the witness chair.

Lardner: Because it is a question—

Chairman [pounding gavel]: Leave the witness chair.

Lardner: I think I am leaving by force.

Chairman: Sergeant, take the witness away.

[Applause.]

70. Howard Fast, "The Peekskill Riots"

(1949)

Beyond government efforts to contain communism at home, grassroots anti-communism took a variety of forms, primarily in personal and local displays of patriotism. At times, however, super-patriots behaved like the anti-German vigilantes of World War I. Here, novelist Howard Fast (1914–2003) recounts his experience on the receiving end of one of the most notorious incidents of Cold War vigilantism. Fast grew up in New York City and made a name for himself as a young writer of historical novels set primarily during the era of the American Revolution. He was also, by 1943, a member of the Communist Party. On August 27, 1949, a group of leftist artists including Fast and folk singer Pete Seeger planned to host a concert featuring Paul Robeson to benefit the Civil Rights Congress. While on a tour in Europe not long before this—including a performance in the Soviet Union—Robeson had commented that he did not believe that American blacks would go to war against the Soviets "on behalf of those who have oppressed us for generations." Thanks to the violence described by Fast, the concert never got started. A rescheduled performance, held on September 4, brought more than 20,000 people to Peekskill; after the concert ended, however, hundreds of anticommunist vigilantes again struck, pelting the departing concertgoers' automobiles with rocks. Dozens had to be hospitalized. The next year, the State Department stripped Robeson of his passport.

SOURCE: Howard Fast, *Being Red: A Memoir* (Boston: Houghton Mifflin, 1990), 228–39.

A boy running. I watched him as he came in sight around the bend of the road, running frantically, and then we crowded around him and he told us that there was trouble and would some of us come—because the trouble looked bad; and he was frightened too.

We started back with him. There were twenty-five or thirty of us, I suppose; you don't count at a moment like that, although I did count later. There were men and boys, almost all the men and boys. I thought that this would be no more than foul names and fouler insults. So we ran on up to the entrance, and as we appeared, they poured onto us from the road, at least a hundred of them with billies and brass knuckles and rocks and clenched fists, and American Legion caps, and suddenly my disbelief was washed away in a wild melee. Such fights don't last long; there were three or four minutes of this, and because the road was narrow and embanked, we were able to beat them back, but the mass of them filled the entranceway, and behind them were hundreds more, and up and down the road, still more.

I said that we beat them back and held the road for the moment, panting, hot with sweat and dust, bleeding only a little now; but they would have come at us again had not three deputy sheriffs appeared. They hefted their holstered guns, and they turned and spread their arms benignly at the mob. "Now, boys," they said, "now take it easy, because we can do this just as well legal, and it always pays to do it legal."

"Give us five minutes and we'll murder the white niggers," the boys answered.

"Just take it easy—just take it slow and easy, boys, because it don't pay to have trouble when you don't have to have no trouble."

And then the three deputy sheriffs turned to us and wanted to know what we were doing there making all this kind of trouble.

I kept glancing at my watch. It was ten minutes after seven then. The interruption helped us to survive. Not that the deputies intended that; but it was a beginning and there was no precedent for this kind of thing in Westchester County in New York State, and the three sheriffs with the polished gold-plated badges were uncertain as how to play their own role. For that reason they held back the "boys" and asked us why we were provoking them.

I became the spokesman then, and a good many of the things I did afterward were the result of this—chiefly because I was older than most of our handful and because the merchant seamen and the trade unionists nodded for me to talk. Anyway, I had agreed to be chairman and it seemed that this was the kind of concert we would have, not with Paul Robeson and Pete Seeger singing their lovely tunes of America, but with a special music that had played its melody out in Germany and Italy. So I said that we were not looking for any trouble, but were here to hold a concert, and why didn't they clear the road so that our people could come in and listen to the concert in peace?

"You give me a pain in the ass with that kind of talk," said one of the deputies delicately. "Just cut out the trouble. We don't want no trouble and we don't want no troublemakers."

I explained it again. I explained to them carefully that we were not making trouble, that we had not lured these innocent patriots to attack us, and that all we desired was for them to clear the road so that people could come to the concert.

"How the hell can we clear the road? Just look up there," they told me.

"Tell them to get out and they'll get out," I said.

"Don't tell me what to tell them!"

"Look, mister," I said, "we hold you responsible for whatever happens here."

"Up your ass," said the guardian of the law.

"We'll talk to the boys," another said.

And then they talked to the boys, and we had five minutes. I didn't listen to what they said to the boys. I was beginning to realize that they had no intention of doing anything about them, and when I looked up at the road and saw the roadblocks and the solid mass of men, I began to realize that not only was it extremely unlikely that anyone else on our side would get in, but quite unlikely that any of us already here would get out. Just as the sheriffs turned back to talk to the mob, a man came walking through. This man was in his middle twenties. He was tall; he wore a beard, a beret, and loose, brightly colored slacks. I asked him who he was and what he was doing here. "I'm a music lover," he said.

No self-respecting writer dares to invent such things; but they happen. "Can you fight, Music Lover?" I asked him.

"I can't and I won't." There was indignation and disgust in his voice.

"But you can and you will," I pointed out. "Otherwise, go back up there. This time they'll tear you to pieces."

Later that evening, I spoke to the music lover again. I never learned his name; he will always be Music Lover to me, but when I spoke to him again he had lost his beret, his slacks were torn, and there was blood all over him—and a wild glint in his eyes.

The men and boys had clustered around me in the little respite. "We're in a very bad place," I told them, "but we'll keep our heads and in a little while some real cops will come and put an end to all this insanity. Meanwhile, we have to keep the mob here where the road is narrow and high, and it's a good place to defend in any case. We keep them here because there's a lot of kids and women down below. That's our whole tactic. Agreed?"

They agreed.

"All right. Just two things. Let me do the talking and let me decide when there's a quick decision, because there won't be time to talk it over."

They agreed again, and our time was running out. A compression of incident and event began. First I told the girls to run back down the road, get all the women and children onto the platform, keep them there for the time being, and send every able-bodied man and boy up to us. Then I asked for a volunteer.

"I want someone to crawl through those bushes, reach the road, find a telephone, and call the troopers—call *The New York Times* and *The Daily Worker*, call Albany and get through to the governor—I want someone who can do that."

I got him. I don't know what I can say about him, except that he had great inventiveness and lots of guts. We pooled our nickels and gave them to him. He was small and bright-eyed, and I have never seen him since that night. Three times he went back and forth and he did what he was supposed to do.

Now the remaining men from below appeared and I counted what we had. All told, including myself, there were forty-two men and boys. I divided them into seven groups of six, three lines of two groups each—in other words, three lines of twelve—formed across the road where the embankment began, each line anchored on a wooden fence, our flanks protected by the ditch and the water below. The seventh group was held in reserve in our rear.

I looked at my watch again. It was seven-thirty. The three deputy sheriffs had disappeared. The mob was rolling toward us for the second attack. This was, in a way, the worst of that night. For one thing, it was still daylight; later, when night fell, our own sense of organization helped us much more, but this was daylight and they poured down the road and into us, swinging broken fenceposts, billies, bottles, and wielding knives. Their leaders had been drinking from pocket flasks and bottles right up to the moment of the attack, and now as they beat and clawed at our line, they poured out a torrent of obscene words and slogans. "We'll finish Hitler's job! Fuck you white niggers! Give us Robeson! We'll string that big nigger up!" and more and more of the same.

I'm not certain how long that second fight lasted. It seemed forever, yet it couldn't have been more than a few minutes. In that time, the sun sank below the hills to the west of us, and the shadow of twilight came. We concentrated on holding our lines. The first line took the brunt of the fighting, the brunt of the rocks and the clubs. The second line linked arms, as did the third, forming a human wall to the mob. In that fight, four of our first line were badly injured. When they went down, we pulled them back, and men in the second line moved into their places. Here were forty-two men and boys who had never seen each other before, and they were fighting like a well-oiled machine, and the full weight of the screaming madmen did not panic them or cause them to break. By sheer weight, we were forced back foot by foot, but they never broke the line. And then they pulled back. For the moment, they had enough. They drew off, leaving about twenty feet between the front of their mob and our line of defense.

On our part, we were hurt, but not so badly that every man couldn't stand on his feet. We linked arms and waited. As it darkened, change came into the ranks of the mob, a sense of organization. Three men appeared as their leaders, one a dapper, slim, well-dressed middle-aged man who was subsequently identified as a prosperous Peekskill real estate broker. A fourth man joined them, and a heated discussion in whispers started. At the same time, cars up the road were swinging around so that their headlights covered us. Though the police and state troopers were remarkably, conspicuously absent, the press were on the scene. Newspaper photographers were everywhere, taking picture after picture, and reporters crouched in the headlights, taking notes of all that went on. In particular, my attention was drawn to three quiet, well-dressed, good-looking men who stood just to one side at the entrance; two of them had notebooks in which they wrote methodically and steadily. When I first saw them I decided that they were newspapermen and dismissed them from my mind. But I saw them again and again, and later talked to them, as you will see. Subsequently, I discovered they were agents of the Department of Justice. Whether they were assigned to a left-wing concert or to an attempted mass murder, I don't know. They were polite, aloof, neutral, and at one point decently helpful. They were always neutral—even though what they saw was attempted murder, a strangely brutal terrible attempt.

The four men in front of the mob broke off their discussion now, and one of them, a good-looking man of thirty or so, came toward us. He wore a white shirt, sleeves rolled up; his hands were in his pockets; he walked to our line and in a not unfriendly manner said, "Who's running this?"

"I'll talk to you," I said.

He told me he was a railroad worker, a Peekskill resident, and had been drawn into this because he belonged to the local Legion post. He underlined the fact that he liked commies no better than the next man, but that this kind of thing turned his stomach. "I'm on the wrong side," he said. "What I want to know is this—will you call it off if we do?"

I told him that we had never called it on, and that if he could get them to empty the road, we'd leave. He said he'd try. He went back and resumed his whispered argument with the three leaders of the mob, and now behind us our truck appeared. That did it. The mob saw it coming and they attacked again. I had not fought this way in twenty years, not since my days in the slums where I was raised, not since the gang fights of a kid in the New York streets; but now it was for our lives, for all that the cameras were flashing and the newspapermen taking it down blow by blow, so you could read in your morning papers how a few reds in Westchester County were lynched.

It was night now, and now for the first time I understood our situation completely and could guess what the odds were that we would all die in this way, so uselessly and stupidly.

And the FBI men watched calmly and took notes.

I looked at my watch—still less than two hours since I had kissed my little daughter.

And then we were fighting again, and then we beat them off again. Their courage was so small that when we turned and came at them, cursing them and telling them that we'd kill a few of them, they fell back until some thirty feet of the embanked road were clear in front of us. But three of us had been hurt very badly, and we helped them into the truck, where they could lie down. We had no bandages except handkerchiefs and shirts, which we used to stop bleeding. And at that moment, something very curious happened. As they came at us again, we began to sing, "Just like a tree that's standing by the water, we shall not be moved." It stopped them cold. They saw a line of bloody, ragged men, standing with their arms locked, standing calmly and singing in a kind of inspired chorus, and they stopped. They couldn't understand us.

They didn't want to touch us now, or they couldn't, so they turned to the rocks. First a rock here and there, then more, and then there was the heavy music as they beat a tattoo against the metal side of the truck. The man on my left was struck in the temple and collapsed without a sound. You didn't have to look; when you heard the fleshy thud, the sound of bone and skin breaking, you knew that someone was hit and that there was one fewer to stand on his feet and face the mob. First I counted how many of us were hit, and then I stopped counting and dropped back to the truck and put my head together with one of the seamen.

"Five minutes more of this," he said, "and we'll be finished." I suggested that we use the truck as a moving shield while the driver took it down to the hollow in low gear. Suddenly, the motor roared.

"All right, let's go!"

There were about twenty of us still on our feet. We dashed around the truck as it lurched forward, and then because the driver had forgotten to switch on his lights, he drove off the road, missed it completely, and sent his truck lurching and careening across the meadow into the night.

Now we ran down into the hollow, and we held together as we ran. As we swung around the curve of the road below, I saw the amphitheater for the first time since I had driven down there earlier in the evening: the platform with the women and children on it and huddled close, the two thousand chairs standing empty, the table of songbooks and pamphlets—and all of it bright as day in the brilliant glare of floodlights. These lit the whole of the meadow, and as we swung around at the bottom, we saw the mob of screaming, swearing patriots, chanting their new war cry, "Kill a commie for Christ," and their lust to kill the "white niggers," break over the hillside and pour down into the light.

For just a moment we stood there, trying to catch our breath, and then we drove into them because there was nothing else to do. At this point, we were half crazy, as full of hate as they were, and so violent was our fury and our own screams that they broke and ran. They turned at forty or fifty yards, formed a wide circle, and stared at us and swore at us with every filthy word they could remember. We, on the other hand, climbed onto the platform and made a line in front of the women and kids. Here, at least, we could use our feet to kick. The children, half frozen with terror, watched all this. The women began to sing the "Star-Spangled Banner," urging the children, most of them in tears, to join in. A few of the braver hoodlums ran at the platform. We beat them back.

And then the lights went out. Someone had cut the line from the generator, and now the mob, in utter frustration at finding a handful of "commies" so hard to kill, seemed to go absolutely crazy. They attacked the chairs. We couldn't see them, but through the darkness we heard them raging among the folding chairs, throwing them around, splintering and splashing them. It was not only senseless, it was sick—horrible and pathological. Then one of them lit a fire, about thirty or forty yards from the platform. A chair went on the fire, and then another and another, and then a whole pile of the chairs, which belonged not to us but to a Peekskill businessman from whom we had rented them. Then they discovered our table of books and pamphlets, and then, to properly crown the evening, they reenacted the Nuremberg book burning, which had become a world symbol of fascism. Standing there, arms linked, we watched the Nuremberg memory come alive again. The fire roared up and the defenders of the "American way of life" seized piles of our books and danced around the blaze, flinging the books into the fire as they danced. Suddenly, up in the direction of the road, an army flare arched into the sky, made a balloon of bright light, hung there, and then swept slowly and gracefully to earth. I looked at my watch. It was a quarter to ten.

Silence, broken only by the half-hysterical sobbing of women and the whimpering cries of little children. It was not easy to sit there in the dark. We had to be firm and sometimes harsh with them, but we had decided that no one would leave the platform until some civil or military force from the outside came through to us.

And then we saw a pair of headlights. Slowly, searchingly, the car drove down into the hollow and toward us, stopping only a few feet away. Three men got out. They walked toward us, leaving the headlights of the car on to light their way. A few feet from me they stopped, nodded at me, and stood quietly for a moment. I recognized them now; they were the well-dressed men with the notebooks who had watched the fighting on the road up above and taken notes as they watched, the FBI.

"You did all right," one of them said suddenly.

"You did a damn good piece of work up there," from another. "It was damn fine discipline all the way through."

"What in hell do you want?" I demanded. I was in no mood to be polite to anyone now.

"We thought we might help you out. You got some badly hurt people, so if you want us to, we'll take them to the hospital."

"Go to hell!" I said, and then one of our men was plucking my sleeve and pulled me back and whispered that he knew them, that they were FBI and that I could trust them.

"Why?"

"Because right now they got no stake in this either way. Didn't you see them before? They're neutral. This is just a big experiment to them and they're neutral. Some of the kids are bleeding badly and I think one of them has a fractured skull. If they say they'll take them to the hospital, they will."

I asked him how he knew who they were, and he replied that he had been working in Westchester County long enough to know. "Anyway, the kids are hurt. We'll take a chance." We selected the three worst hurt. They got into the car, and the FBI men drove off. We were again in the quiet darkness.

The fire burned down. In the dark, we waited the minutes through, one after another, and then suddenly the silence in the hollow erupted into noise and action.

First an ambulance, which came roaring down into the hollow, siren wide open and red headlights throwing a ghostly glare. Then car after car of troopers and Westchester County police. All in a moment, there were a dozen cars in the meadow in front of us and the place was swarming with troopers and police.

One more chapter in that night of horror had to be played through, and it began with an officer of the troopers who stalked up to us and demanded, "Who in hell is running this show?" I told him that he could talk to me.

"Look," I said to him, "we've had a rough time here."

"You'll have a rougher time if you don't god damn well do as we say. Who are you anyway?"

I told him I was the chairman of the concert that never happened. He then told me to keep everyone where they were, and that if anyone tried to get away, there'd be trouble. I said that we had little children here, as he could see, and he replied that I was looking for trouble. I told him I had enough trouble.

In a way, that was the hardest part of the evening, not so much waiting in front of a dozen state troopers, their legs spread, fingering their guns and clubs— but being there after I learned what was behind all this tough talk. They let me walk around, and one of the Westchester police was willing to talk. Briefly, he told me that one of the mob, William Secor his name, had been knifed and had been taken to the hospital, and the rumor had just come through that he had died. If Secor was dead, every one of us who had held the road against the attack would face a murder charge. That was why we were being kept here this way— so that they could get a report from the hospital and if necessary pull us in on a murder rap.

(There was no knife among our men. Later, it was proved that Secor had been knifed by one of his mates in the drunken frenzy of their attack.)

Cars were coming back and forth now. The hollow was alive with action and with blue uniforms and with gray uniforms, and the fine jackbooted palace guards of Thomas E. Dewey were strutting all over the place, showing their slim waists and handsome profiles, and there was a conference taking place too among the big brass of the little army which had descended upon us.

The local Westchester cop, the one with a core of something human left inside of him—a small-town cop from a small town nearby—nodded at me and I went over to him and he whispered that it was all right now. Secor was not going to die, and in fact he only had a small cut in his belly and they didn't know who cut him.

I went back and spread the news around, and we began to smile a little. There was a sudden change in the attitude of the state troopers; they became courteous, kind, obedient, cheerful, just as the book says they are, those fine gray guardians of the law and the people of the sovereign State of New York, and the big brass of them came over to me and put his hand on my shoulder, nice and warm and friendly, and said, "Look, Fast, what we want now is to get your people out of here, and we're going to get them out so that not a hair on anyone's head is harmed, and I guess you've had a tough night of it, but it's over now and you can just stop worrying. Now I want you to separate them into groups according to the town or place or resort they came from and my troopers will drive them home in our own cars."

It was past midnight when I reached home, put my car in the garage, and went into the house. . . .

A few days later, the concert was again attempted. This time, the arrangements were more carefully designed. Several thousand members of the Fur and Leather Workers' Union, the Teachers' Union, and District 65, a large local union, formed a ring, shoulder to shoulder, around the Hollow Brook Country Club picnic grounds, where the second Peekskill concert was held. Even though there was almost no time to prepare, over five thousand people came to the concert, and here Paul Robeson did sing. But before the second concert, I took Juliette and the children back to New York. I had had enough of the peaceful suburbs.

Like the first concert, the second concert ended in disaster. Discovering that we had planned carefully, that we had surrounded the picnic grounds with almost three thousand men, standing beside one another within arm's reach, the well-organized gang of hoodlums changed their plans accordingly. The road that led to the picnic grounds was almost a narrow country lane. All along this road, groups gathered piles of rock and waited. Farther along where the road was crossed by highway bridges, they gathered tons of rocks and waited. Then, when the concert was finished, each car leaving the grounds ran a gauntlet of rocks. Car after car was smashed, windows shattered, cuts, bruises, skull fractures, splinters of glass embedded in eyes—all of this inflicted on the drivers and passengers to such an extent that every hospital in the vicinity was turned into an emergency trauma facility.

I doubt that Peekskill is much remembered, even by those who call themselves revisionists in the historical sense and who try to include in our history hundreds of happenings like the incidents at Peekskill, artfully omitted by the scholarly establishment. That was a strange year, 1949.

71. Chief Justice Fred M. Vinson and Justice Hugo Black, *Dennis et al. v. United States*

(1951)

In 1949, the Truman administration targeted the Communist Party directly, indicting, trying, and convicting eleven of its leaders under the Smith Act, a 1940 law that made it illegal to advocate—or belong to an organization that advocated—the overthrow of the United States government. In the two opinions here, Chief Justice Fred Vinson (1890–1953) and Justice Hugo L. Black (1886–1971) differ in their interpretation of the constitutionality of the Smith Act. Vinson was born and raised in Kentucky, where he attended law school, practiced law, and was elected to the U.S. Congress. In 1938, President Roosevelt appointed Vinson to the United States Court of Appeals for the District of Columbia Circuit, and Vinson later served in a number of wartime administrative posts. In 1946, President Truman nominated Vinson to be Chief Justice of the Supreme Court, and the Senate quickly confirmed him. Hugo Black followed a similar track, but in his home state of Alabama. A former prosecutor and World War I veteran, Black was elected to the U.S. Senate in 1927. In 1937, President Roosevelt named him to the Supreme Court.

In the Supreme Court's upholding of the convictions in the *Dennis* case, the precedent in *Schenck* v. *U.S.*—with its "clear and present danger" standard for restricting free speech—loomed large (see Chapter 2). Vinson, who wrote for the majority, accepted that the Communist Party leaders were part of "a highly organized conspiracy" who could at any moment turn from advocacy to action. Black, however, saw no threat in their mere speech—oral or written—that justified suspension of the First Amendment's protection of free speech. The Court's ruling effectively outlawed the Communist Party; the eleven defendants were sentenced to five years in prison and fined $10,000 each.

SOURCE: *Dennis et al. v United States*, 341 U.S. 494, 71 S. Ct. 857, 95 L. Ed. 1137 (1951).

Chief Justice Fred Vinson

Majority Opinion in *Dennis et al. v. United States*
June 4, 1951

II

The obvious purpose of the statute is to protect existing Government, not from change by peaceable, lawful, and constitutional means, but from change by violence, revolution, and terrorism. That it is within the *power* of the Congress to protect the Government of the United States from armed rebellion is a proposition which requires little discussion. Whatever theoretical merit there may be to the argument that there is a "right" to rebellion against dictatorial governments is without force where the existing structure of the government provides for peaceful and orderly change. We reject any principle of governmental helplessness in the face of preparation for revolution, which principle, carried to its logical conclusion, must lead to anarchy. No one could conceive that it is not within the power of Congress to prohibit acts intended to overthrow the Government by force and violence. The question with which we are concerned here is not whether Congress has such *power*, but whether the *means* which it has employed conflict with the First and Fifth Amendments to the Constitution.

One of the bases for the contention that the means which Congress has employed are invalid takes the form of an attack on the face of the statute [the Smith Act] on the grounds that by its terms it prohibits academic discussion of the merits of Marxism-Leninism, that it stifles ideas and is contrary to all concepts of a free speech and a free press. . . .

The very language of the Smith Act negates the interpretation which petitioners would have us impose on that Act. It is directed at advocacy, not discussion. . . . Congress did not intend to eradicate the free discussion of political theories, to destroy the traditional rights of Americans to discuss and evaluate ideas without fear of governmental sanction. Rather Congress was concerned with the very kind of activity in which the evidence showed these petitioners engaged.

III

But although the statute is not directed at the hypothetical cases which petitioners have conjured, its application in this case has resulted in convictions for the teaching and advocacy of the overthrow of the Government by force and violence, which, even though coupled with the intent to accomplish that overthrow, contains an element of speech. For this reason, we must pay special heed to the demands of the First Amendment marking out the boundaries of speech. . . .

. . . Speech is not an absolute, above and beyond control by the legislature when its judgment, subject to review here, is that certain kinds of speech are so undesirable as to warrant criminal sanction. . . . To those who would paralyze our Government in the face of impending threat by encasing it in a semantic straitjacket we must reply that all concepts are relative.

In this case we are squarely presented with the application of the "clear and present danger" test, and must decide what that phrase imports. We first note that many of the cases in which this Court has reversed convictions by use of this or similar tests have been based on the fact that the interest which the State was attempting to protect was itself too insubstantial to warrant restriction of speech. . . .

. . . Overthrow of the Government by force and violence is certainly a substantial enough interest for the Government to limit speech. Indeed, this is the ultimate value of any society, for if a society cannot protect its very structure from armed internal attack, it must follow that no subordinate value can be protected. If, then, this interest may be protected, the literal problem which is presented is what has been meant by the use of the phrase "clear and present danger" of the utterances bringing about the evil within the power of Congress to punish.

Obviously, the words cannot mean that before the Government may act, it must wait until the *putsch* is about to be executed, the plans have been laid and the signal is awaited. If Government is aware that a group aiming at its overthrow is attempting to indoctrinate its members and to commit them to a course whereby they will strike when the leaders feel the circumstances permit, action by the Government is required. The argument that there is no need for Government to concern itself, for Government is strong, it possesses ample powers to put down a rebellion, it may defeat the revolution with ease needs no answer. For that is not the question. Certainly an attempt to overthrow the Government by force, even though doomed from the outset because of inadequate numbers or power of the revolutionists, is a sufficient evil for Congress to prevent. The damage which such attempts create both physically and politically to a nation makes it impossible to measure the validity in terms of the probability of success, or the immediacy of a successful attempt. In the instant case the trial judge charged the jury that they could not convict unless they found that petitioners intended to overthrow the Government "as speedily as circumstances would permit." This does not mean, and could not properly mean, that they would not strike until there was certainty of success. What was meant was that the revolutionists would strike when they thought the time was ripe. We must therefore reject the contention that success or probability of success is the criterion. . . .

Chief Judge Learned Hand, writing for the majority below, interpreted the phrase as follows: "In each case [courts] must ask whether the gravity of the 'evil,' discounted by its improbability, justifies such invasion of free speech as is necessary to avoid the danger." . . . We adopt this statement of the rule. . . .

Likewise, we are in accord with the court below, which affirmed the trial court's finding that the requisite danger existed. The mere fact that from the period 1945 to 1948 petitioners' activities did not result in an attempt to overthrow the Government by force and violence is of course no answer to the fact that there was a group that was ready to make the attempt. The formation by petitioners of such a highly organized conspiracy, with rigidly disciplined members subject to call when the leaders, these petitioners, felt that the time had come for action, coupled with the inflammable nature of world conditions, similar uprisings in other countries, and the touch-and-go nature of our relations with countries with whom petitioners were in the very least ideologically attuned, convince us that their convictions were justified on this score. And this analysis disposes of the contention that a conspiracy to advocate, as distinguished from the advocacy itself, cannot be constitutionally restrained, because it comprises only the preparation. It is the existence of the conspiracy which creates the danger. . . . If the ingredients of the reaction are present, we cannot bind the Government to wait until the catalyst is added. . . .

Justice Hugo Black

Dissenting Opinion in *Dennis et al. v. United States*
June 4, 1951

. . . At the outset I want to emphasize what the crime involved in this case is, and what it is not. These petitioners were not charged with an attempt to overthrow the Government. They were not charged with overt acts of any kind designed to overthrow the Government. They were not even charged with saying anything or writing anything designed to overthrow the Government. The charge was that they agreed to assemble and to talk and publish certain ideas at a later date: The indictment is that they conspired to organize the Communist Party and to use speech or newspapers and other publications in the future to teach and advocate the forcible overthrow of the Government. No matter how it is worded, this is a virulent form of prior censorship of speech and press, which I believe the First Amendment forbids. . . .

But let us assume, contrary to all constitutional ideas of fair criminal procedure, that petitioners although not indicted for the crime of actual advocacy, may be punished for it. Even on this radical assumption, the other opinions in this case show that the only way to affirm these convictions is to repudiate directly or indirectly the established "clear and present danger" rule. This the Court does in a way which greatly restricts the protections afforded by the First Amendment. The opinions for affirmance indicate that the chief reason for jettisoning the rule is the expressed fear that advocacy of Communist doctrine endangers the safety of the Republic. Undoubtedly, a governmental policy of unfettered communication of ideas does entail dangers. To the Founders of this Nation, however, the benefits derived from free expression were worth the risk. . . .

So long as this Court exercises the power of judicial review of legislation, I cannot agree that the First Amendment permits us to sustain laws suppressing freedom of speech and press on the basis of Congress' or our own notions of mere "reasonableness." Such a doctrine waters down the First Amendment so that it amounts to little more than an admonition to Congress. The Amendment as so construed is not likely to protect any but those "safe" or orthodox views which rarely need its protection. . . .

Public opinion being what it now is, few will protest the conviction of these Communist petitioners. There is hope, however, that in calmer times, when present pressures, passions, and fears subside, this or some later Court will restore the First Amendment liberties to the high preferred place where they belong in a free society.

72. Senator Joseph R. McCarthy, "Speech, Wheeling, West Virginia"

(1950)

Although the Truman administration had introduced the Federal Employee Loyalty Program in 1947, forcing thousands from their jobs, Senator Joseph McCarthy (1909–57) saw a political opportunity in hammering the president and especially the State Department for harboring communists. McCarthy hailed from Grand Chute, Wisconsin. Before being elected to the Senate in 1946, he had served as a state circuit court judge and in the Marine Corps as a lieutenant during World War II. His apocryphal tales of his exploits as "Tail Gunner Joe"—he lied, claming that he had flown dozens of combat missions and received the Purple Heart—helped him win his Senate seat. At the time of the Wheeling speech, McCarthy was planning his reelection campaign and soon found that baseless accusations of communists in the government made good news copy. For the next four years, he hammered away at the Truman and Eisenhower administrations for not doing enough to remove communists from the government. Although he never once produced solid evidence of a single subversive in government, he attacked or ignored his critics.

SOURCE: *Congressional Record*, Senate, 81st Congress, 2nd Session, February 20, 1950.

Six years ago, at the time of the first conference to map out the peace—Dumbarton Oaks[1]—there was within the Soviet orbit 180,000,000 people. Lined up on the antitotalitarian side there were in the world at that time roughly 1,625,000,000 people. Today, only six years later, there are 800,000,000 people under the absolute domination of Soviet Russia—an increase of over 400 percent. On our side, the figure has shrunk to around 500,000,000. In other words, in less

---

[1]Dumbarton Oaks, an estate in Washington, D.C., was the scene of a 1944 conference at which the United States, Great Britain, China, and the Soviet Union agreed to create the United Nations.

than six years the odds have changed from nine to one in our favor to eight to five against us. This indicates the swiftness of the tempo of Communist victories and American defeats in the cold war. As one of our outstanding historical figures once said, "When a great democracy is destroyed, it will not be because of enemies from without, but rather because of enemies from within."

The truth of this statement is becoming terrifyingly clear as we see this country each day losing on every front.

At war's end we were physically the strongest nation on earth and, at least potentially, the most powerful intellectually and morally. Ours could have been the honor of being a beacon in the desert of destruction, a shining living proof that civilization was not yet ready to destroy itself. Unfortunately, we have failed miserably and tragically to arise to the opportunity.

The reason why we find ourselves in a position of impotency is not because our only powerful potential enemy has sent men to invade our shores, but rather because of the traitorous actions of those who have been treated so well by this Nation. It has not been the less fortunate or members of minority groups who have been selling this Nation out, but rather those who have had all the benefits that the wealthiest nation on earth has had to offer—the finest homes, the finest college education, and the finest jobs in Government we can give.

This is glaringly true in the State Department. There the bright young men who are born with silver spoons in their mouths are the ones who have been worst. . . .

. . . In my opinion the State Department, which is one of the most important government departments, is thoroughly infested with Communists.

I have in my hand fifty-seven cases of individuals who would appear to be either card carrying members or certainly loyal to the Communist Party, but who nevertheless are still helping to shape our foreign policy.

One thing to remember in discussing the Communists in our Government is that we are not dealing with spies who get thirty pieces of silver to steal the blueprints of a new weapon. We are dealing with a far more sinister type of activity because it permits the enemy to guide and shape our policy. . . .

This brings us down to the case of one Alger Hiss who is important not as an individual any more, but rather because he is so representative of a group in the State Department. It is unnecessary to go over the sordid events showing how he sold out the Nation which had given him so much. Those are rather fresh in all of our minds.

However, it should be remembered that the facts in regard to his connection with this international Communist spy ring were made known to the then Under Secretary of State Berle three days after Hitler and Stalin signed the Russo-German alliance pact. . . .

Under Secretary Berle promptly contacted Dean Acheson and received word in return that Acheson (and I quote) "could vouch for Hiss absolutely"—at which time the matter was dropped. . . .

Again in 1943, the FBI had occasion to investigate the facts surrounding Hiss' contacts with the Russian spy ring. But even after that FBI report was submitted, nothing was done.

Then late in 1948—on August 5—when the Un-American Activities Committee called Alger Hiss to give an accounting, President Truman at once issued a Presidential directive ordering all Government agencies to refuse to turn over any information whatsoever in regard to the Communist activities of any Government employee to a congressional committee. . . .

If time permitted, it might be well to go into detail about the fact that Hiss was Roosevelt's chief adviser at Yalta when Roosevelt was admittedly in ill health and tired physically and mentally . . . and when, according to the Secretary of State, Hiss and Gromyko[2] drafted the report on the conference . . .

Of the results of this conference, Arthur Bliss Lane of the State Department had this to say: "As I glanced over the document, I could not believe my eyes. To me, almost every line spoke of a surrender to Stalin."

As you hear this story of high treason, I know that you are saying to yourself, "Well, why doesn't the Congress do something about it?" Actually, ladies and gentlemen, one of the important reasons for the graft, the corruption, the dishonesty, the disloyalty, the treason in high Government positions—one of the most important reasons why this continues is a lack of moral uprising on the part of the 140,000,000 American people. . . .

As you know, very recently the Secretary of State proclaimed his loyalty to a man guilty of what has always been considered as the most abominable of all crimes—of being a traitor to the people who gave him a position of great trust. The Secretary of State in attempting to justify his continued devotion to the man who sold out the Christian world to the atheistic world, referred to Christ's Sermon on the Mount as a justification and reason therefor, and the reaction of the American people to this would have made the heart of Abraham Lincoln happy.

When this pompous diplomat in striped pants, with a phony British accent, proclaimed to the American people that Christ on the Mount endorsed communism, high treason, and betrayal of a sacred trust, the blasphemy was so great that it awakened the dormant indignation of the American people.

He has lighted the spark which is resulting in a moral uprising and will end only when the whole sorry mess of twisted, warped thinkers are swept from the national scene so that we may have a new birth of national honesty and decency in Government.

---

[2]Andrei Gromyko was a Soviet diplomat and longtime foreign minister.

73. United States House of Representatives, "Debate on Homosexuals as Security Risks in Government"

(1950)

In the months following Joseph McCarthy's first speech claiming the pervasive presence of communists working for the government, some members of Congress began to call for expanded authority for the FBI and the Loyalty Boards to investigate employees who, if not disloyal, were nonetheless "security risks." As the discussion between Representatives Arthur Miller (R-Neb) and Cliff Clevenger (R-Ohio) demonstrates, homosexuals, in particular, came under increased scrutiny. Arthur Lewis Miller (1892–1967), a physician by training, was first elected as a Republican to Congress in 1942. Cliff Clevenger (1885–1960) came to Congress in 1939 from Bryan, Ohio, where he had managed a chain of department stores. In the discussion that follows, Clevenger, especially, dismisses the notion that federal employees should be fired only for "overt acts" of disloyalty; in his view, anything embarrassing in an employee's private life could be used to blackmail them into breaching national security. In time, such thinking prompted President Eisenhower, in his first months in office, to supersede Executive Order 9835 with Executive Order 10450, which called for the retention of federal employees only when "clearly consistent with the interests of national security."

SOURCE: *Congressional Record*, Vol. 94, Part 4, 81st Congress, 2nd Session, March 29–April 24, 1950.

On the Floor of the House of Representatives:

Mr. Miller of Nebraska. . . . Recently the spotlight of publicity has been focused not only upon the State Department but upon the Department of Commerce because of homosexuals being employed in these and other departments of Government. Recently Mr. Peurifoy, of the State Department, said he had allowed 91 individuals in the State Department to resign because they were homosexuals. Now they are like birds of a feather, they flock together. Where did they go?

You must know what a homosexual is. It is amazing that in the Capital City of

Washington we are plagued with such a large group of those individuals. Washington attracts many lovely folks. The sex crimes in the city are many.

In the Eightieth Congress I was the author of the sex pervert bill that passed this Congress and is now a law in the District of Columbia. It can confine some of these people in St. Elizabeths Hospital for treatment. They are the sex perverts. Some of them are more to be pitied than condemned, because in many it is a pathological condition, very much like the kleptomaniac who must go out and steal, he has that urge; or like the pyromaniac, who goes to bed and wakes up in the middle of the night with an urge to go out and set a fire. He does that. Some of these homosexuals are in that class. Remember there were 91 of them dismissed in the State Department. That is a small percentage of those employed in Government. We learned 2 years ago that there were around 4,000 homosexuals in the District. The Police Department the other day said there were between five and six thousand in Washington who are active and that 75 percent were in Government employment. There are places in Washington where they gather for the purpose of sex orgies, where they worship at the cesspool and flesh pots of iniquity. . . . Some of those people have been in the State Department, and I understand some of them are now in the other departments. The 91 who were permitted to resign have gone some place, and, like birds of a feather, they flock together. . . .

So I offer this amendment, and when the time comes for voting upon it, I hope that no one will object. I sometimes wonder how many of these homosexuals have had a part in shaping our foreign policy. How many have been in sensitive positions and subject to blackmail. It is a known fact that homosexuality goes back to the Orientals, long before the time of Confucius; that the Russians are strong believers in homosexuality, and that those same people are able to get into the State Department and get somebody in their embrace, and once they are in their embrace, fearing blackmail, will make them go to any extent. Perhaps if all the facts were known these same homosexuals have been used by the Communists.

I realize that there is some physical danger to anyone exposing all of the details and nastiness of homosexuality, because some of these people are dangerous. They will go to any limit. These homosexuals have strong emotions. They are not to be trusted and when blackmail threatens they are a dangerous group.

The Army at one time gave these individuals a dishonorable discharge and later changed the type of discharge. They are not knowingly kept in Army service. They should not be employed in Government. I trust both sides of the aisle will support the amendment. . . .

Mr. Clevenger. I will say to the gentleman, I brought that question up a year ago, as to whether the other departments would be altered so that they might not hire these—we can name them—these homosexuals. . . .

I am going to address myself now to conditions we have discovered in the Department of Commerce. When I asked the security officer if he would flag them, he said he would. I told him I was very much afraid he could not, because of an Executive order which was issued restricting the information being given on these people.

The air is full of stories. The press is full of stories. I am not passing on that.

In discussing the constitutionality of the so-called loyalty program, John Edgar Hoover, Director of the FBI, had occasion to cite a decision of the circuit court of appeals rendered on August 11, 1949, involving the Joint Anti-Fascist Committee. A portion of that decision is worthy of repetition here:

> Contrary to the contentions of the committee, nothing in the Hatch Act or the loyalty program deprives the committee or its members of any property rights. Freedom of speech and assembly is denied no one. Freedom of though and belief is not impaired. Anyone is free to join the committee and give it his support and encouragement. Everyone has the constitutional right to do these things, but no one has a constitutional right to be a Government employee.

For emphasis permit me to repeat the last phrase, "but no one has a constitutional right to be a Government employee."

It seems to me that the crux of our entire security program lies in that phrase. It is indeed a privilege and certainly not a right to work for the Government and it is time we cleared the air on the misconceptions of a good many well-intentioned people who have been misled by the propaganda of the Communist and the fellow traveler into the belief that the burden of "proof of qualification" lies on the employer in this case, the Government, rather than on the employee. Nothing could be further from the truth. The Government has the right, nay the obligation, to set up standards for performance of duty not only for prospective employees but for those already on the rolls. This sacred obligation to the tax-payer implies the summary removal of any employee who does not measure up to these standards, the avails and crocodile tears of the fuzzy-minded to the contrary notwithstanding. It is tragically true that our present administration has been sadly lacking in the courage or capacity necessary to carry out these obligations but this does not excuse, or in no way alter or mitigate these obligations.

We have heard a great deal in recent weeks concerning the security risks within the Department of State and I would like to say that while I am not familiar with the charges being bandied about I think the basic issue has been somewhat obscured in the unfortunate partisanship that has developed in this inquiry that is of prime importance to every American, Republican or Democrat.

The sob sisters and thumb-sucking liberals are crying for proof of disloyalty in the form of overt acts, on any security risks who are being removed from the Government rolls, but shed no tears for the lives lost as a result of the activities of the Hiss', Coplon's, and the Wadleigh's, all of whom would or did pass the loyalty standards with flying colors.

I wish the American people would keep in mind the fact that a security risk does not have to be a member of the Communist Party or even of a Communist-

front organization. It is not only conceivable but highly probable that many security risks are loyal Americans; however, there is something in their background
that represents a potential possibility that they might succumb to conflicting
emotions to the detriment of the national security. Perhaps they have relatives
behind the iron curtain and thus would be subject to pressure. Perhaps they are
addicted to an overindulgence in alcohol or maybe they are just plain garrulous.
The most flagrant example is the homosexual who is subject to the most effective
blackmail. It is an established fact that Russia makes a practice of keeping a list of
sex perverts in enemy countries and the core of Hitler's espionage was based on
the intimidation of these unfortunate people.

Despite this fact however, the Under Secretary of State recently testified that
91 sex perverts had been located and fired from the Department of State. For
this the Department must be commended. But have they gone far enough?
Newspaper accounts quote Senate testimony indicating there are 400 more in
the State Department and 4,000 in Government. Where are they? Who hired
them? Do we have a cell of these perverts hiding around Government? Why are
they not ferreted out and dismissed? Does the Department of State have access
to information in the files of the Washington Police Department? Are we to assume that the State Department has a monopoly on this problem? What are the
other Departments of Government doing about this?

For years we had a public prejudice against mentioning in public such loath
some diseases as gonorrhea and cancer. In effecting cures for these maladies the
medical people recognized the first step was in public education. These matters
were brought before the public and frankly discussed and it was not until then
that progress was really made, It is time to bring this homosexual problem into
the open and recognize the problem for what it is.

The Commerce Department hearings are somewhat enlightening in regard to
the entire security problem . . .

Here we find that the Commerce Department has not located any homosexuals in their organization. Are we to believe that in the face of the testimony of
the District of Columbia police that 75 percent of the 4,000 perverts in the District of Columbia are employed by the Government, that the Department of
Commerce has none?

What is wrong with this loyalty program that does not uncover these matters,
and when it does, adopts an attitude of looking for proof of disloyalty in the form
of overt acts rather than elements of security risk? Is it not possible for the Government to refuse employment on the grounds of lack of qualifications where
risk is apparent? This is not necessarily an indictment or conviction; it is merely
the exercise of caution for the common welfare.

74. Senator Margaret Chase Smith, "Declaration of Conscience"

(1950)

Senator Margaret Chase Smith's "Declaration of Conscience," issued five months after Joseph McCarthy delivered his Wheeling, West Virginia, speech, marked the first serious challenge to McCarthy's slash-and-burn anticommunism. A native of Skowhegan, Maine, Smith (1897–1995) was the first woman elected to both houses of Congress. Beginning in 1942, when she succeeded her deceased husband, Clyde Smith, in the House, she served three terms in Congress, and was in her second year in the Senate when she decided to take on McCarthy. It was a lonely position to take at the time, and only six other Republican senators joined her. In fact, Smith's "Declaration of Conscience" does not mention McCarthy by name, but she did not need to. It was obvious to everyone, including McCarthy (who mocked her and the others as "Snow White and the Six Dwarfs"), that she regarded him and his demagoguery as a threat to her party and her country. By the time the Senate finally voted to censure McCarthy in December 1954, Smith had become nationally known for her principled stand.

SOURCE: Printed with Statement of Seven Senators, *Congressional Record,* Senate, 82nd Congress, 1st Session, June 1, 1950.

Mr. President, I would like to speak briefly and simply about a serious national condition. It is a national feeling of fear and frustration that could result in national suicide and the end of everything that we Americans hold dear. It is a condition that comes from the lack of effective leadership in either the legislative branch or the executive branch of our Government.

That leadership is so lacking that serious and responsible proposals are being made that national advisory commissions be appointed to provide such critically needed leadership.

I speak as briefly as possible because too much harm has already been done with irresponsible words of bitterness and selfish political opportunism. I speak as simply as possible because the issue is too great to be obscured by eloquence. I speak simply and briefly in the hope that my words will be taken to heart.

I speak as a Republican. I speak as a woman. I speak as a United States Senator. I speak as an American.

The United States Senate has long enjoyed worldwide respect as the greatest deliberative body in the world.

But recently that deliberative character has too often been debased to the level of a forum of hate and character assassination sheltered by the shield of congressional immunity.

It is ironical that we Senators can debate in the Senate directly or indirectly, by any form of words impute to any American, who is not a Senator, any conduct or motive unworthy or unbecoming an American—and without that non-Senator American having any legal redress against it—yet if we say the same thing in the Senate about our colleagues we can be stopped on the grounds of being out of order.

It is strange that we can verbally attack anyone else without restraint and with full protection and yet we hold ourselves above the same type of criticism here on the Senate floor. Surely the United States Senate is big enough to take self-criticism and self-appraisal. Surely we should be able to take the same kind of character attacks that we "dish out" to outsiders.

I think that it is high time for the United States Senate and its Members to do some soul searching—for us to weigh our consciences—on the manner in which we are performing our duty to the people of America; on the manner in which we are using or abusing our individual powers and privileges.

I think that it is high time that we remembered that we have sworn to uphold and defend the Constitution. I think that it is high time that we remembered that the Constitution, as amended, speaks not only of the freedom of speech, but also of trial by jury instead of trial by accusation.

Whether it be a criminal prosecution in court or a character prosecution in the Senate, there is little practical distinction when the life of a person has been ruined.

Those of us who shout the loudest about Americanism in making character assassinations are all too frequently those who, by our own words and acts, ignore some of the basic principles of Americanism—

The right to criticize;

The right to hold unpopular beliefs;

The right to protest;

The right of independent thought.

The exercise of these rights should not cost one single American citizen his reputation or his right to a livelihood nor should he be in danger of losing his reputation or livelihood merely because he happens to know someone who holds unpopular beliefs. Who of us doesn't? Otherwise none of us could call our souls our own. Otherwise thought control would have set in.

The American people are sick and tired of being afraid to speak their minds lest they be politically smeared as "Communists" or "Fascists" by their opponents. Freedom of speech is not what it used to be in America. It has been so abused by some that it is not exercised by others.

The American people are sick and tired of seeing innocent people smeared and guilty people whitewashed. But there have been enough proved cases, such as the Amerasia case, the Hiss case, the Coplon case, the Gold case, to cause Nation-wide distrust and strong suspicion that there may be something to the unproved, sensational accusations.

As a Republican, I say to my colleagues on this side of the aisle that the Republican Party faces a challenge today that is not unlike the challenge that it faced back in Lincoln's day. The Republican Party so successfully met that challenge that it emerged from the Civil War as the champion of a united nation—in addition to being a party that unrelentingly fought loose spending and loose programs.

Today our country is being psychologically divided by the confusion and the suspicions that are bred in the United States Senate to spread like cancerous tentacles of "know nothing, suspect everything" attitudes. Today we have a Democratic administration that has developed a mania for loose spending and loose programs. History is repeating itself—and the Republican Party again has the opportunity to emerge as the champion of unity and prudence.

The record of the present Democratic administration has provided us with sufficient campaign issues without the necessity of resorting to political smears. America is rapidly losing its position as leader of the world simply because the Democratic administration has pitifully failed to provide effective leadership. . . .

The Democratic administration has greatly lost the confidence of the American people by its complacency to the threat of communism here at home and the leak of vital secrets to Russia through key officials of the Democratic administration. There are enough proved cases to make this point without diluting our criticism with unproved charges.

Surely these are sufficient reasons to make it clear to the American people that it is time for a change and that a Republican victory is necessary to the security of this country. Surely it is clear that this nation will continue to suffer as long as it is governed by the present ineffective Democratic administration.

Yet to displace it with a Republican regime embracing a philosophy that lacks political integrity or intellectual honesty would prove equally disastrous to this Nation. The Nation sorely needs a Republican victory. But I don't want to see the Republican Party ride to political victory on the four horsemen of calumny—fear, ignorance, bigotry and smear.

I doubt if the Republican Party could—simply because I don't believe the American people will uphold any political party that puts political exploitation above national interest. Surely we Republicans aren't that desperate for victory.

I don't want to see the Republican Party win that way. While it might be a fleeting victory for the Republican Party, it would be a more lasting defeat for the American people. Surely it would ultimately be suicide for the Republican Party and the two-party system that has protected our American liberties from the dictatorship of a one-party system.

As members of the minority party, we do not have the primary authority to formulate the policy of our Government. But we do have the responsibility of rendering constructive criticism, of clarifying issues, of allaying fears by acting as responsible citizens.

As a woman, I wonder how the mothers, wives, sisters, and daughters feel about the way in which members of their families have been politically mangled in Senate debate—and I use the word "debate" advisedly.

As a United States Senator, I am not proud of the way in which the Senate has been made a publicity platform for irresponsible sensationalism. I am not proud of the reckless abandon in which unproved charges have been hurled from this side of the aisle. I am not proud of the obviously staged, undignified countercharges that have been attempted in retaliation from the other side of the aisle.

I don't like the way the Senate has been made a rendezvous for vilification, for selfish political gain at the sacrifice of individual reputations and national unity. I am not proud of the way we smear outsiders from the floor of the Senate and hide behind the cloak of congressional immunity and still place ourselves beyond criticism on the floor of the Senate.

As an American, I am shocked at the way Republicans and Democrats alike are playing directly into the Communist design of "confuse, divide and conquer." As an American, I don't want a Democratic administration "whitewash" or "cover-up" any more than I want a Republican smear or witch hunt.

As an American, I condemn a Republican "Fascist" just as much as I condemn a Democrat "Communist." I condemn a Democrat "Fascist" just as much as I condemn a Republican "Communist." They are equally dangerous to you and me and to our country. As an American, I want to see our Nation recapture the strength and unity it once had when we fought the enemy instead of ourselves.

It is with these thoughts I have drafted what I call a Declaration of Conscience. I am gratified that Senator Tobey, Senator Aiken, Senator Morse, Senator Ives, Senator Thye and Senator Hendrickson, have concurred in that declaration and have authorized me to announce their concurrence.

Statement of Seven Republican Senators

1. We are Republicans. But we are Americans first. It is as Americans that we express our concern with the growing confusion that threatens the security and stability of our country. Democrats and Republicans alike have contributed to that confusion.

2. The Democratic administration has initially created the confusion by its lack of effective leadership, by its contradictory grave warnings and optimistic assurances, by its complacency to the threat of communism here at home, by its oversensitiveness to rightful criticism, by its petty bitterness against its critics.

3. Certain elements of the Republican Party have materially added to this confusion in the hopes of riding the Republican party to victory through the selfish

political exploitation of fear, bigotry, ignorance, and intolerance. There are enough mistakes of the Democrats for Republicans to criticize constructively without resorting to political smears.

4. To this extent, Democrats and Republicans alike have unwittingly, but undeniably, played directly into the Communist design of "confuse, divide and conquer."

5. It is high time that we stopped thinking politically as Republicans and Democrats about elections and started thinking patriotically as Americans about national security based on individual freedom. It is high time that we all stopped being tools and victims of totalitarian techniques—techniques that, if continued here unchecked, will surely end what we have come to cherish as the American way of life.

75. Judge Irving R. Kaufman, *Julius and Ethel Rosenberg v. The United States of America*

(1951)

Judge Irving Kaufman's death sentence in the case of Julius and Ethel Rosenberg capped the most sensational trial of the Cold War. In February 1950, only months after the Soviet Union successfully detonated its first atomic bomb, British intelligence arrested Manhattan Project physicist Klaus Fuchs. In time, Fuchs led American investigators to Los Alamos machinist David Greenglass, and to Greenglass's sister and brother-in-law, Ethel and Julius Rosenberg. They were arrested in the summer of 1950, against the backdrop of the exploding Korean War and Joseph McCarthy's harangues that the Truman administration was not sufficiently vigilant in hunting communists. Greenglass struck a deal with the government to save his own life by agreeing to testify that Julius Rosenberg had acted as prime architect of the spy ring and passed atomic secrets, with the help of Ethel (who allegedly typed letters for him), to the KGB. The government knew that Ethel was not a spy, but indicted her as a way to pressure Julius to come clean. Although the only evidence against Ethel came from her brother's testimony, the jury found both Rosenbergs guilty.

Irving Kaufman (1910–92) grew up in the Bronx, New York, and graduated from Fordham University and Fordham Law School. President Truman appointed Kaufman to the federal bench in 1949. In the first line of Kaufman's sentencing statement in the Rosenberg case, he noted that he had "refrained from asking the Government" for a recommended sentence, but FBI files released in the 1970s revealed that the judge had, in fact, held a number of private conversations about the sentence with the prosecution. The government believed, even at that late date, that a death sentence might still prompt confessions. The Rosenbergs went to their deaths by electrocution on June 19, 1953, still insisting on their innocence. They remain the only American citizens executed in the United States for espionage. Classified documents released in 1995, and corroborated by Soviet records, definitively proved Julius Rosenberg's guilt. Ethel Rosenberg, it seems, was innocent.

SOURCE: Transcript, *Julius and Ethel Rosenberg v. The United States of America*, Supreme Court of the United States, October Term, 1951, pp. 1612–16.

Sentencing of Julius and Ethel Rosenberg
April 5, 1951

Because of the seriousness of this case and the lack of precedence, I have refrained from asking the Government for a recommendation. The responsibility is so great that I believe that the Court alone should assume this responsibility. . . .

The issue of punishment in this case is presented in a unique framework of history. It is so difficult to make people realize that this country is engaged in a life and death struggle with a completely different system. This struggle is not only manifested externally between these two forces but this case indicates quite clearly that it also involves the employment by the enemy of secret as well as overt outspoken forces among our own people. All of our democratic institutions are, therefore, directly involved in this great conflict. I believe that never at any time in our history were we ever confronted to the same degree that we are today with such a challenge to our very existence. The atom bomb was unknown when the espionage statute was drafted. I emphasize this because we must realize that we are dealing with a missile of destruction which can wipe out millions of Americans.

The competitive advantage held by the United States in super-weapons has put a premium on the services of a new school of spies—the homegrown variety that places allegiance to a foreign power before loyalty to the United States. The punishment to be meted out in this case must therefore serve the maximum interest for the preservation of our society against these traitors in our midst.

It is ironic that the very country which these defendants betrayed and sought to destroy placed every safeguard around them for obtaining a fair and impartial trial, a trial which consumed three weeks in this court. I recall the defendant Julius Rosenberg testifying that our American system of jurisprudence met with his approval and was preferred over Russian justice. Even the defendants realize—by this admission—that this type of trial would not have been afforded to them in Russia. Certainly, to a Russian national accused of a conspiracy to destroy Russia not one day would have been consumed in a trial. It is to America's credit that it took the pains and exerted the effort which it did in the trial of these defendants. Yet, they made a choice of devoting themselves to the Russian ideology of denial of God, denial of the sanctity of the individual, and aggression against free men everywhere instead of serving the cause of liberty and freedom.

I consider your crime worse than murder. Plain deliberate contemplated murder is dwarfed in magnitude by comparison with the crime you have committed. In committing the act of murder, the criminal kills only his victim. The immediate family is brought to grief and when justice is meted out the chapter is closed. But in your case, I believe your conduct in putting into the hands of the Russians the A-bomb years before our best scientists predicted Russia would perfect the bomb has already caused, in my opinion, the Communist aggression in Korea, with the resultant casualties exceeding 50,000 and who knows but that millions more of innocent people may pay the price of your treason. Indeed, by your betrayal you undoubtedly have altered the course of history to the disadvantage of our country. No one can say that we do not live in a constant state of tension. We have evidence of your treachery all around us every day—for the civilian defense activities throughout the nation are aimed at preparing us for an atom bomb attack.

Nor can it be said in mitigation of the offense that the power which set the conspiracy in motion and profited from it was not openly hostile to the United States at the time of the conspiracy. If this was your excuse the error of your ways in setting yourselves above our properly constituted authorities and the decision of those authorities not to share the information with Russia must now be obvious.

The evidence indicated quite clearly that Julius Rosenberg was the prime mover in this conspiracy. However, let no mistake be made about the role which his wife, Ethel Rosenberg, played in this conspiracy. Instead of deterring him from pursuing his ignoble cause, she encouraged and assisted the cause. She was a mature woman—almost three years older than her husband and almost seven years older than her younger brother. She was a full-fledged partner in this crime.

Indeed the defendants Julius and Ethel Rosenberg placed their devotion to their cause above their own personal safety and were conscious that they were sacrificing their own children, should their misdeeds be detected—all of which did not deter them from pursuing their course. Love for their cause dominated their lives—it was even greater than their love for their children.

What I am about to say is not easy for me. I have deliberated for hours, days and nights. I have carefully weighed the evidence. Every nerve, every fiber of my body has been taxed. I am just as human as are the people who have given me the power to impose sentence. I am convinced beyond any doubt of your guilt. I have searched the records—I have searched my conscience—to find some reason for mercy—for it is only human to be merciful and it is natural to try to spare lives. I am convinced, however, that I would violate the solemn and sacred trust that the people of this land have placed in my hands were I to show leniency to the defendants Rosenberg.

It is not in my power, Julius and Ethel Rosenberg, to forgive you. Only the Lord can find mercy for what you have done.

The sentence of the Court upon Julius and Ethel Rosenberg is, for the crime for which you have been convicted, you are hereby sentenced to the punishment of death, and it is ordered upon some day within the week beginning with Monday, May 21st, you shall be executed according to law.

76. Loyalty Investigation

(1954)

With Executive Order 10450, issued by President Eisenhower in April 1953, the hiring and retention of all federal employees became "subject to an investigation." The type of initial investigation depended on the nature of the position; jobs that afforded access to vital information required a "full field investigation," but many other jobs did not. On the other hand, the order said, if information came to light that the employment of an individual "may not be clearly consistent with the interests of national security"—regardless of the position—a full field investigation would be required. In addition to seeking information on overtly disloyal acts or deliberate misrepresentations of fact, investigators were instructed to look for "any criminal, infamous, dishonest, immoral, or notoriously disgraceful conduct, habitual use of intoxicants to excess, drug addiction, sexual perversion." Membership in or association with any organization "which seeks to overthrow" the U.S. government still stood as reason for dismissal. As the record of the loyalty investigation below makes clear, however, even employees with no access to national security information could lose their jobs for membership in a union, for signing a petition, or because of the books on their shelves.

SOURCE: Adam Yarmolinsky, ed., *Case Studies in Personnel Security* (Washington, D.C.: Bureau of National Affairs, 1955), 142–52.

CASE NO. 107
(Executive Order 10450)

In late February, 1954, the employee was working in a clerical capacity as a substitute Postal employee. He performed no supervisory duties. His tasks were routine in nature.

One year prior to the initiation of proceedings, the employee had resigned from his position as an executive officer of a local union whose parent union had been expelled from the CIO in 1949 as Communist dominated. The employee had served as an officer for one year prior to the expulsion, had helped to lead his local out of the expelled parent and back into the CIO and had thereafter remained in an executive capacity until his resignation in 1953. He resigned from that position upon being appointed a substitute clerk with the United States Post Office in early 1953.

Preliminary Notice

In the last week of February, 1954, the employee received notice, by mail, that he was under investigation by the Regional Office of the United States Civil Service Commission. This notice contained the following allegations:

> "The investigation has disclosed information that in November, 1941, you signed a petition that the Communist Party be placed on the ballot in the . . . Municipal Elections.
>
> "In addition, it has been reported that you have been a member of Lodge . . . , International Workers Order, and that you have had a close and continuing association with officers of the Socialist Workers Party. Both of these organizations fall within the purview of Executive Order 10450.
>
> "In your application for your present position, you denied that you had ever been a member of any organization which advocated the overthrow of our form of government or seeks to alter our form of government by unconstitutional means. You also failed to admit in your application that you had been employed by the National Advisory Committee for Aeronautics and the . . . Navy Yard in 1943, and that you were discharged from the latter position."

Prior to his reception of the foregoing notice, the employee had never been the subject of previous loyalty or security proceedings, nor had he been aware that he was the subject of an investigation by the Civil Service Commission.

Employee's Response

In the first week of March, 1954, without benefit of counsel, the employee responded, in writing, to the above charges. In the employee's letter of response, he expressed his confidence that his anti-Communist record would be established upon a full investigation. Thereafter, he answered the charges set forth above by a denial that he had ever been knowingly associated with persons engaged in subversive activities or associations, and denied membership in any organizations. In addition, he answered the charge that he had signed a Communist petition by explaining that the petition had been circulated about thirteen years prior to the date of the charge, and that, in his opinion, his signature thereon did not reflect—nor had it been intended to reflect—support of the

Communist Party. He stated, further, in this connection, that he would not sign such a petition today.

The employee explained his failure to mention the two past employment relationships by stating that, in each case, the employment had been brief in duration, and that he had resigned, on his own initiative, due to his dissatisfaction with each job. He added, that with respect to the Navy Yard, his eyesight did not permit him to do the welding that that job required.

Thereafter, in his letter of reply, the employee set forth his role as a leader of anti-Communist forces in the labor organization to which he had belonged, and his success in this role.

Charges

Within a week of the employee's submission of his letter and without a hearing or consultation, he received a letter from the Postmaster of the city in which he was employed which advised him that he was, that day, suspended without pay, for security reasons.

In the latter part of March, 1954, the Office of the Postmaster General advised the employee more specifically of the security reasons upon which his suspension was based. These reasons were as follows:

"1. In October, 1947, your name and that of your wife, . . . , appeared on a membership list of Lodge . . . , Jewish Peoples Fraternal Order, International Workers Order.

"2. In February, 1944, you associated with . . . and . . . , known members of the Socialist Workers Party* in . . . ; that you continued your association in October, 1947, when they were members of the Executive Committee and Secretary-Treasurer, respectively, of the Socialist Workers Party, and that such association continued to exist in January, 1949.

"3. In January, 1948, your name appeared on a general mailing list of the Spanish Refugee Appeal of the Joint Anti-Fascist Refugee Committee.*

"4. The name of your wife, . . . , has appeared on a mailing list of the . . . Chapter of the National Council of American Soviet Friendship.*

"5. Your wife, . . . , was a member of the . . . Club of the Young Communist League.*

"6. In 1950, Communist literature was observed in the book shelves and Communist art was seen on the walls of your residence in . . .

"7. Your signature appeared on a Communist Party* nominating petition in the November, 1941, Municipal Elections in . . .

"8. You falsely replied 'No' on your Standard Form 60, 'Application for Federal Employment,' in answer to question 16, which is as follows: 'Are you now,

---

*An organization cited by the Attorney General as coming within the purview of Executive Order 10450.

or have you ever been, a member of the Communist Party, USA, or any Communist or Fascist organization?'

Employee's Further Response

Thereafter, the employee retained counsel and exercised his right to answer the charges above set forth. His answer denied the first charges categorically. The employee answered charge No. 6 by stating that he had pictures on his walls, but did not know whether they could be considered as Communist art, and that he had read literature, in English, by Russian authors, but could not say that this had been Communist literature. He expressed his willingness to disclose "all the types of books on my bookshelves." With respect to charge No. 7, the employee repeated his earlier explanation that he had signed the Communist nominating petition in 1941, and that, to the best of his recollection, the petition bore a statement to the effect that signers thereof were not members of the Communist Party. With respect to charge No. 8, he stated that he had never been a member of the Communist Party or a member of any Communist or Fascist organization.

Hearing

The employee had a hearing four months later, in July, 1954. The members of the Board were three (3) civilian employees of military installations. None of them were attorneys. The Post Office establishment was represented by an Inspector, who administered the oath to the employee and his witnesses, but did not otherwise participate in the proceedings. There was no attorney-advisor to the Board. There was no testimony by witnesses hostile to the employee, nor was any evidence introduced against him.

The following summary of the hearing, which lasted three hours, is based upon the transcript of the proceedings furnished to the investigator of this case, by counsel for the employee. . . . Before the employee testified, he submitted a nine page autobiography to the Hearing Board.

The autobiography set forth in some detail the employee's activities as an officer of his local union, and discussed particularly his role therein as an anti-Communist, and his opposition to the pro-Communist policies of the National Organization with which his local was affiliated. The autobiography recited that when his National Union was expelled from the C.I.O., he and his supporters successfully won a struggle within his local and as a direct result thereof, caused the said local to disaffiliate from the expelled parent, and affiliate with a new organization established within the C.I.O. The employee's autobiography recited that the aforesaid struggle directly involved the question of Communist domination of the local's parent union, that the victory of the employee and his supporters represented a victory over Communist adherents in the local, and that the employee was the frequent target of threats and slander by the pro-Communist faction of his local.

The employee's autobiography recited further that while he was serving in an executive capacity in the local union, that local, despite the fact that it had a pro-Communist faction, adhered strictly to the non-Communist policies of the C.I.O., although the said policies were in conflict with the policies of the local's parent union.

The employee's autobiography closed with the facts adverted to above concerning the employee's resignation from his executive position with the Union, because of the demands on his time made by his temporary employment by the Post Office.

Following the submission to the members of the Board of the autobiography, counsel for the employee offered it in evidence, and thereafter offered in evidence fourteen (14) letters written on behalf of the employee by various union officials, friends and neighbors. . . .

The employee then testified concerning the charges that had been filed against him. The employee stated that he had no knowledge as to whether his name, or his wife's name had appeared on a membership list of a subversive organization. With respect to the charge that he had associated with known members of the Socialist Workers Party in early 1944, and that this association had continued to 1947, the employee testified that his relationship with the couple had been limited to a casual acquaintanceship with the wife, while the employee was a college student and that he had never had any close association with them. He testified that he had only met the husband on the street once, and that he had not seen the wife more than five times in the thirteen years prior to the hearing date.

With respect to the third charge against the employee, (that his name had been on a general mailing list of the Spanish Refugee Appeal of the Joint Anti-Fascist Refugee Committee), the employee reiterated his denial of any knowledge concerning it, and his counsel reminded the Board that no Attorney General's list existed in January, 1948—the date contained in the charge. The employee testified, further, that he had no recollection of ever having received any mail from the organization involved.

With respect to the fourth charge, (that his wife's name was on a mailing list of a chapter of the National Council of American Soviet Friendship), he testified that he had no knowledge that his wife's name had appeared on a mailing list of the organization involved; that his wife had never given him cause to believe that she was interested in the said organization, and that he had no recollection of ever having seen any mail in their house from said organization. Counsel for the employee reminded the Board that there was no date given in this charge, and suggested that the charge was therefore extremely difficult to answer.

With respect to charge No. 5 against the employee, (that his wife had been a member of the Young Communist League), the Chairman of the Hearing Board advised the employee that the date involved was March, 1944. The employee testified that he and his wife were married in February, 1944, and that the charge was ridiculous. He testified, further, that he had no independent recollection that his wife was ever a member of the said organization. In addition, the employee testified that he had never lived in the neighborhood in which the organization was alleged to have existed, and that he had never heard of said organization. (It should be noted that the neighborhood in question is approximately eight miles from any one of the neighborhoods in which the employee in his autobiography recited that he and his wife had lived since their marriage.)

The Chairman then read charge No. 6 in which it was alleged that Communist literature was observed in the employee's bookshelves at home and Communist art was seen on the walls of his residence in 1950. Immediately following his reading of the charge, the Chairman stated that:

> "The Board is at a loss just to what Communist literature they are referring to."

Counsel for the employee then questioned him concerning his courses in college, and the books which he was there required to read for those courses. In this connection, counsel for the employee asked whether books had been recommended as part of study courses by instructors, and whether one of these books had been *Das Kapital* by Karl Marx, and whether the employee had bought *Das Kapital*, following such a recommendation. The employee responded that certain books had been recommended by his instructors, that *Das Kapital* was one, and that he had bought the Modern Library Giant Edition of *Das Kapital*. Counsel for the employee then stated that he did not know whether *Das Kapital* was considered to be Communist literature or not, and that it had been written prior to the creation of the Communist Party. Counsel stated, finally,

> "There is no other book, on inquiring from Mr. . . . , that I can possibly conceive that would be a foundation for that accusation."

Counsel then asked the employee whether, in 1950, he had reproductions of paintings by great painters hanging on the walls of his home, and following the employee's answer in the affirmative, counsel asked him to name some of the artists whose reproductions were hanging upon the walls of the employee's home. The employee named Picasso, Matisse, Renoir and Moddigliotti [Modigliani?].

Counsel then asked the employee whether pictures by those artists were hanging in museums, including the largest museum in the city in which the employee resides, and following the employee's answer in the affirmative, counsel asked whether there was "any relationship between the art and the Communist Party". The employee responded that he had "no idea of what any relationship there might be that exists there at all."

Thereafter, in response to counsel's question, the employee testified that he had not read *Das Kapital* in its entirety, that he had been required to read "a chapter or two for classwork" and that "he had found it a little dull and tedious."

The Chairman of the Board then asked the employee the following questions:

"In your library at home, could you give me an idea of the type of literature or the books that you enjoy accumulating?"

Counsel for the employee objected that this question constituted an invasion of the employee's privacy, but concluded his statement on this point as follows:

"Ask the question, but I really think we are getting pretty far when we get into that."

The Chairman responded as follows:

"Well, I would be interested also in knowing the types of periodicals."

In answer to the Chairman's direct question concerning periodicals received by the employee, the latter testified that he received newspapers from the C.I.O. and A.F. of L., and a magazine known as "Consumer's Research", and that he did not subscribe to any other weekly or monthly publications. Immediately thereafter, the following colloquy between the Chairman and the employee followed:

"**Q.** I mean, do you get the Saturday Evening Post or Collier's or anything like that?

"**A.** No. I usually pick them up at news stands.

"**Q.** Do you get the daily newspaper?

"**A.** I get the [major daily morning newspaper] and [major daily evening newspaper] every day. The [morning paper] is delivered and I pick the [evening newspaper] up on the street.

"**Q.** And that about runs the gauntlet? I mean, that is the whole works?

"**A.** Two newspapers a day keeps me busy.

"**Q.** I mean, considering—

"**A.** That is the only periodicals and anything that comes to my home."

The Chairman read charge No. 7, in which it was alleged that the employee's signature appeared on a Communist Party nominating petition in 1941 municipal elections in the employee's home city.

The employee had answered this charge by stating that he had signed such a petition; that in 1941, the Communist Party appeared on the initial ballot; that his recollection was that on the cover page of the petition it stated that the signers were not members of the Communist Party, and that prior to 1941 and at all times thereafter, the employee had been registered as a member of one of the two major political parties, and that he had no recollection of voting for any political party other than one of the two major political parties.

The employee's response was read into the record by the Chairman immediately following his reading of charge No. 7.

Thereafter, counsel for the employee objected to the charge on the ground that the signing of a petition for a party which had a legal place on the ballot in 1941, had no relationship to present security. The Chairman then asked the employee to recall the circumstances in which his signature had been solicited in 1941. The employee responded by stating that, so far as he could recall, someone came down the street and seeing him working on the premises asked him to sign the petition, after explaining the petition to him. In response to a question by a member of the Board, the employee stated that he did not know the person who had solicited his signature, and that he had never seen or heard from him thereafter, nor had he thereafter heard from the Communist Party.

The Chairman then read the eighth charge, set forth above at page 144, in which it was alleged that the employee had falsely answered "No" to a standard form question on his application for Federal employment, which asked whether the applicant was now, or had ever been, a member of the Communist Party, U.S.A., or any Communist or Fascist organization. The Chairman then read the employee's reply in which he stated that to his knowledge he had never been a member of any such organization.

Immediately thereafter, counsel for the employee stated that the charge was libelous and that the one who made such a charge had a duty to show evidence in support thereof, commenting that the employee had received no such evidence.

A colloquy thereafter ensued between the Chairman and counsel for the employee, of which the following is a part:

> "The Chairman: . . . As far as I know, Mr. . . . is not on trial at this time, and in efforts to advise [pursuant to the security program] we are furnished only this information.
> "Counsel: I renew my request that we be given some basis upon which this charge is based.
> "The Chairman: All right, put that on the record. As I say, we have no more information available, no legal advice here, so we can't answer your question." . . .

Following the testimony of the employee, his counsel called the employee's witnesses. Thirteen witnesses, including the employee's wife, his mother, his mother-in-law, and his younger brother were then called by the employee. Their testimony related to the employee's good character, and loyalty as a citizen of the United States. Insofar as any of these witnesses evinced a knowledge of the employee's activities as a Union official, the Board heard their testimony concerning the employee's anti-Communist role while such an official. . . .

Thereafter the employee was recalled for further testimony. . . . The employee then testified at great length, and with specificity concerning his Union activity, and the history of his political beliefs and actions while a Union officer.

The transcript of the testimony discloses that the employee answered every question put to him by the Board or his counsel in detail. In addition to the testimony of the employee and his witnesses, the employee furnished fourteen letters written by friends, fellow employees, and union officials, in support of his loyalty and good character. . . . These letters set forth in some detail the role of the employee in leading the opposition to the pro-Communists in his local union, including his success in leading the said local union out of the parent union which remained Communist dominated and into the non-Communist C.I.O.

Result

In early September, 1954, and without notice as to whether the Board had reached a decision in his case, the employee received notice from the Post Office Department that the Postmaster General had ordered the employee's removal from the Postal service for the reasons set forth in the initial charging letter which he had received from the Post Office in March, 1954.

Upon the request of employee's counsel for information concerning appellate rights, he received notice, within ten days, from the Assistant Postmaster General in Washington, D.C., that the employee had—by appearing before the Hearing Board and offering evidence summarized above—exhausted all administrative rights open to him insofar as the Post Office Department was concerned.

Within a month of counsel's receipt of the letter from the Assistant Postmaster General denying further appeal to the employee, the employee received a letter from the Regional Office of the United States Civil Service Commission. This letter advised the employee that he had been rated ineligible for Civil Service appointment, and that he was barred from competing in Federal Civil Service examinations for a period of three years. It also advised the employee of a right to appeal this decision.

Appeal to the Regional Office of the Civil Service Commission

Counsel for the employee then submitted a letter of appeal on behalf of the employee in which he objected to the vagueness of the charges that had been filed against the employee by the Civil Service Commission, and in which he also reiterated the circumstances under which the employee had signed the Communist Party petition in 1941.

Within three weeks of the employee's submission of the appeal letter, his counsel received a letter from the Regional Director of the Civil Service Commission in which the employee's appeal to the Regional Director was denied, and notice of the right to appeal to the Civil Service Commission in Washington was set forth. This letter read as follows:

"Dear Mr. [_____]:

"This refers to your letter of November, 1954, appealing from the decision of this office rating Mr. . . . ineligible for the position of Substitute Clerk, and barring him from accepting positions in the Federal Civil Service and from competing in Federal Civil Service examinations for a period of three years.

"It is felt that the charges in our letter of February, 1954, to Mr. [_____] were sufficiently specific to enable him to adequately defend against them, as witnessed by his rather complete reply to the charges, and therefore we do not feel that another letter covering the same matters is necessary.

"Mr. [_____'s] denial that he has carried on a close and continuing association with officers of the Socialist Workers Party, or that he held membership in Lodge [_____] of the International Workers Order is contrary to reliable evidence in the possession of the Commission, and thus the credibility of such denials is open to serious question.

"In explaining his reasons for signing the Communist Party nominating petitions in question, Mr. [_____] alleges that he in no way indicated that he was in favor of the Communist Party, but that the Party had a legal right to be placed on the public ballot, and that he was assured by the individual or individuals who solicited his signature that he was not indicating any sympathy with the aims and purposes of the Communist Party by so signing. The question raised by the Commission in this matter was not the legality of placing the Communist Party on the ballot, or whether Mr. [_____] had a right to sign the petition, but rather whether he knew he was signing a Communist petition, with the knowledge of the aims and purposes of the Party. Since Mr. [_____] indicated that he either sought or was voluntarily given an alleged assurance that he was not indicating Communist sympathy by signing the petition, it would appear that he had knowledge of the aims and purposes of the organization, and that, with this knowledge, he affixed his signature. It is felt that such an action on his part is somewhat inconsistent with his claim that he later carried on anti-Communist activities as an official of a labor union, although there is some evidence to support this claim.

"The submission of false or misleading statements in an application for Federal employment, (the omission of important information is considered to fall within this description) is a serious offense which may be cause for rating an applicant ineligible. This is one of the important considerations in all decisions regarding general suitability for Federal employment, and thus was properly considered in Mr. [_____'s] case.

"The facts and circumstances in Mr. [_____'s] case have been carefully reviewed and considered, and due regard has been given to the statements contained in his appeal letter. However, we regret that no basis has been found to reverse or alter the previous decision in his case, and the original action of rating Mr. [_____] ineligible and imposing a three year period of debarment is hereby affirmed.

"No further consideration can be given Mr. [_____'s] case by this office. If he has new and material information or if he believes that the decision of this office is not proper on the basis of the facts presented, he may appeal to the U. S. Civil Service Commission, Washington 25, D. C. Any such furthur appeal must be submitted through this office within ten days from the receipt of this notice. The file will be forwarded promptly by this office to the Civil Service Commission, Washington 25, D. C. for final decision. Any subsequent correspondence should be with that office.

"Sincerely yours,"

Appeal to the Civil Service Commission

Eight days after the receipt of the letter quoted immediately above, counsel for the employee advised the Regional Director of the employee's desire to appeal from his decision to the United States Civil Service Commission. . . .

Result

In early February, 1955, and without prior notice, or opportunity for a hearing before the U. S. Civil Service Commission, Board of Appeals and Review, counsel for the employee received a letter affirming the decision of the Regional Director, from the Chairman of that Board. This letter read as follows:

"Dear Mr. [_____]:

"This refers to the appeal you entered in behalf of Mr. [_____] from the decision of the Commission's [_____] Regional Office which resulted in the finding that he is ineligible for Federal employment on suitability grounds.

"Federal employment is not a right of any individual. The Civil Service Act of 1883, as amended, and the rules and regulations pursuant thereto, vest in the United States Civil Service Commission the responsibility for administratively determining the qualifications and suitability of applicants for positions in the Federal Civil Service. Civil Service Rule V, Section 5.2, authorized the Commission to make appropriate investigations in its administration of the Civil Service Act and Rules and the Regulations issued thereunder. This includes investigations of the qualifications and suitability of applicants for positions in the competitive civil service. Information obtained by the Commission is received under a pledge of confidence, and the sources thereof cannot be disclosed. When unfavorable information concerning any applicant comes to the Commission's attention, he is furnished with substance of this information, either by letter or orally in a personal interview, to permit him to submit such explanation or rebuttal as he deems necessary. It then becomes necessary for the Commission to make a determination as to his personal fitness for Federal employment.

"A careful study of the facts in Mr. [_____'s] case has been completed. It has been established and he has admitted that he signed a petition in November, 1941 that the Communist Party be placed on the ballot in the [_____] municipal elections. It was also reported from a source described as reliable that his name and that of his wife appeared on the membership list of Lodge [_____] International Workers Order, and that he has had a close and continuing association with members of the Socialist [sic] Party. His name was reported as being on the general mailing list of the joint Anti-Fascist Refugee Committee and the name of his wife on the mailing list of the National Council of American Soviet Friendship. Mrs. [_____] is reported as having been at one time a member of the [_____] Club of Young Communist League.

"Mr. [_____] was an officer of Local [_____] of the [Parent Union] at the time this organization was expelled from the C.I.O. because of Communist domination. Consideration has been given to information that he was reputed to be one of the leaders of the anti-Communist group which brought Local [_____] back into the C.I.O. as the [_____] However, it is not felt that this information sufficiently outweighs his reported connections with organizations and individuals whose interests and aims are inimical to those of the United States to the extent that a finding that he is unswervingly loyal to the Government of the United States is warranted and the Commission must regard this record as disqualifying under the purposes and intent of Executive Order 10450. This Executive Order issued April, 1953, requires a positive finding that the employment of each candidate in the Federal Service would be clearly consistent with the interests of the national security.

"Accordingly, the Board has affirmed the action of the Commission's [_____] Regional Office in barring Mr. [_____] from civil service examinations or accepting appointment in the Federal civil service for three years from October, 1954.

"For the Commissioners:

"Sincerely yours,"

The employee has filed an action in the Federal Court, to contest the adverse determination in this case.

Counsel has not yet billed this employee for a fee and has not yet determined what the bill will be.

CHAPTER

EIGHT

The Cold War, Part II: Atomic Anxieties

77. Dwight MacDonald, "Why Destroy Draft Cards?"

(1947)

Although the destruction of draft cards is usually associated with the Vietnam War era, a protest in New York's Union Square on February 12, 1947, featured sixty-three men burning their draft cards. Although the wartime draft was coming to an end, Congress considered extending it—and ultimately did in 1948—and that elicited strong protest. The rally was organized by conscientious objector Bayard Rustin, and the speakers included David Dellinger and Dwight MacDonald (1906–82). A well-known New York intellectual, writer, and social critic, MacDonald grew up in the city and later graduated from Phillips Exeter Academy and Yale University. A Trotskyist in the 1920s and 1930s, MacDonald began his career as an editor at *Fortune*, but became better known for editing the *Partisan Review* and *politics*, and for his later writing in the *New York Review of Books* and the *New Yorker*. In his speech at Union Square, reprinted in *politics*, MacDonald paints a permanent peacetime draft as a step toward both American militarism and World War III. Equally important, however, is the defense of pacifism and civil disobedience, both of which became permanent fixtures in post-1945 antiwar and social justice campaigns.

SOURCE: *politics*, March–April 1947, pp. 54–55.

NOTE BY D.M.: On February 12 last, some four or five hundred *Americans either publicly destroyed their draft cards or mailed them in to President Truman. The demonstrations signalized these individuals' decision to refuse further cooperation with military conscription. (See p. 31, January issue, for a full statement of their position.) In* New York City *a meeting was held at which Bayard Rustin was chairman; speakers were: James Blish, David Dellinger, A. J. Muste, and myself; 63 persons destroyed their draft cards in the presence of reporters, cops, FBI agents and an audience of about 250. The following is what I said there.*

This demonstration has two purposes: one to take a public stand against military conscription; two to protest against the preparations of the U. S. Government for World War III. Or, in general terms: civil disobedience and pacifism.

As to the civil disobedience: we have decided to attack conscription by the simplest and most direct way possible: that is, by refusing, as individuals, to recognize the authority of the State in this matter. I cannot speak for the motives of my comrades in this action. But for myself, I say that I am willing to compromise with the State on all sorts of issues which don't conflict too oppressively with my own values and interests. I pay taxes, I submit to the postal and legal regulations, which are not very burdensome, about publishing a magazine. These commands of the State appear to me to affect my life only in minor, unimportant ways. But when the State—or rather, the individuals who speak in its name, for there is no such thing as the State—tells me that I must "defend" it against foreign enemies—that is, must be prepared to kill people who have done me no injury in defense of a social system which has done me considerable injury—then I say that I cannot go along. I deny altogether the competence—let alone the right— of any one else, whether they speak in the name of the State or not, to decide for me a question as important as this. If it be argued that I am an American citizen and so have an obligation to "defend my country," I would note that my being born on American soil was quite involuntary so far as I was concerned, and that I have not since signed any social contract. In such a serious matter as going to war, each individual must decide for himself; and this means civil disobedience to the State power that presumes to decide for one.

2.

Many people think of pacifism as simply a withdrawal from conflict, a passive refusal to go along with the warmaking State. This sort of pacifism is better than assenting to the coercion of the State, but it does not go far enough, in my opinion. *Pacifism to me is primarily a way of actively struggling against injustice and inhumanity: I want not only to keep my own ethical code but also to influence others to adopt it.* My kind of pacifism may be called "non-violent resistance," or, even better, "friendly resistance." Let me illustrate. Pacifists are often asked: what would you have advised the Jews of Europe to have done after Hitler had conquered the continent—to submit peacefully to the Nazis, to go along quietly to the gas chambers? The odd thing about this question is that those who ask it have forgotten that this is pretty much what most of the *Jews of Europe* did in reality, not because they were pacifists, for they weren't, but because they, like most people today, had become *accustomed to obeying the authority of the State:* that is, essentially, because they recognized the authority of force. Suppose the Jews had been pacifists—or rather, "friendly resisters." They would not have resisted the Nazis with guns, it is true. But they would have resisted them with every kind of civil disobedience—they would have made it difficult, and probably impossible, for the Nazis to have herded them by the millions into the death camps. They would have done this by *going underground in the big cities, ignoring the orders* of the Ger-man authorities to report at a certain time and place, *falsifying papers, establishing contacts* with anti-Nazi groups and families in the local population and *hiding* out with them, taking to the forests and hills in country districts. Techniques of *sabotage and evasion* can always be worked out, provided one has developed the will to resist and has thought about the problem. But if one thinks in terms of law and order, of being part of an established society, there is no hope: for law and order today means war and violence. So we get the paradox that those who accept force as a means to social ends are likely to act in a passive, if not pacifist, way when the force is on the side of their enemies. While those who reject force are free to resist it in an active way.

The most common argument against pacifism is: what would you do if you saw a man torturing a child? Wouldn't you use force to stop him? I don't know what I would do; I know that I would try to prevent such an act, and I rather imagine that, if non-violent methods didn't work, I should attempt violence. To this extent, I suppose I am not a complete pacifist. But those who pose this problem do so only in order to make an analogy: if you would use force to prevent the torture of a child, why wouldn't you use force to prevent, say, the Nazis from killing and torturing thousands of children? The analogy seems to me defective. If I use violence myself in a concrete limited situation such as the one just outlined, then I can know to some extent what will be the results. Even if I have to kill the man in order to prevent him from killing the child, it can still be argued that my action is a just one, since, if one or the other must die, it is better the man die. But in a war against Nazism—or Stalinism—those who suffer on *both* sides are mostly as helpless and innocent as the child. Nor can we see what the results will be—or rather we can see all too clearly. The means that must be employed are morally so repugnant as to poison the whole culture of the victor. How does it punish the Nazis for massacring helpless Jews and Poles to massacre ourselves helpless Germans in saturation bombings? But if we use the instrumentality of the State and organized warfare, the only way we can prevent massacre and atrocities is to commit them ourselves—first; and justice is done for the innocent Jews and Chinese not by executing their murderers but by ourselves killing hundreds of thousands German and Japanese innocents. This is a kind of book-keeping which I don't accept.

To return a moment to the problem of the man who tortures the child: Tolstoy once remarked that people were always bringing this hypothetical monster up to him—you see, the argument is not a new one—but that, in a long lifetime full of the most varied experiences in war and peace, he had never yet encountered this brute. On the other hand, he *had* encountered, every day at every step, innumerable real men who hurt and killed other real men in the name of some creed or social institution. He had frequently met, in the flesh, judges and government officials and businessmen and army officers who habitually used violence toward the weak, who forcibly exploited the great mass of their fellow human beings. So he concluded, reasonably enough, that the problem of what to do about some hypothetical individual brute whom he had never personally encountered was not so important as the problem of what to do about the numerous real users of violence whom he was constantly meeting face to face. And he further concluded that it was the real and widespread use of violence that he was against, its use in war and in the defense of an unjust social system, and that pacifism was the only way to counter *that* violence.

Finally, let me admit that the method we have chosen to implement our protest against military conscription is open to many practical objections. How effective it will be I don't know. But I have adopted it because it is the only action I can think of which directly expresses my opposition to conscription. A beginning must be made somewhere. We can only hope that others will think of more effective ways to arouse people against the violence and killing which have become the most prominent features of the age we live in.

DWIGHT MACDONALD

78. Hank Williams and Fred Rose, "No, No Joe"

(1950)

"No, No Joe," a novelty song performed by Hank Williams, was recorded as a wry warning to Soviet premier Joseph Stalin not to underestimate American resolve in the Cold War. Fred Rose (1897–1954), the legendary Nashville songwriter and producer, wrote the song. Rose had moved from New York to Nashville in 1942 and, with Roy Acuff, later formed Acuff-Rose Music, the first music publishing company in Nashville. He signed Hank Williams (1923–53), now generally regarded as the greatest country music artist of all time, to an MGM recording contract in 1947. By 1950, Williams had already soared to national stardom with hits such as "Move It on Over," "Lovesick Blues," and "I'm So Lonesome I Could Cry." He recorded "No, No Joe," and a series of other, more sermonlike narrations under the name Luke the Drifter (though little effort was made to disguise Williams's real identity). The song hit the airwaves in late August, two months after the outbreak of the Korean War—which most Americans blamed on Stalin—and just two weeks before General Douglas MacArthur launched his counteroffensive at Inchon.

SOURCE: "No, No Joe" (Fred Rose), originally released as "Luke the Drifter" (MGM 10806, Milene Music, 1950).

> Now look here Joe, quit acting smart
> Stop being that old brazen sort
> Don't you go sellin' this country short
> No, no Joe
>
> Just because you think you've found
> The system that we know ain't sound
> Don't you go throwin' your weight around
> No, no Joe
>
> 'Cause the Kaiser tried it and Hitler tried it
> Mussolini tried it, too

Now they're all sittin' around a fire and did you know something?
They're saving a place for you

Now Joe you ought to get it clear
You can't push folks around with fear
'Cause we don't scare easy over here
No, no Joe

What makes you do the things you do
You gettin' folks mad at you
Don't bite off more'n you can chew
No, no Joe

'Cause you want a scrap that you can't win
You don't know what you're getting in
Don't go around leading with your chin
No, No Joe

Now you got tanks, some fair size tanks
But you're acting like a clown
'Cause man we've got yanks, a mess of yanks
And you might get caught with your tanks down

Don't go throwin' out your chest
You'll pop the buttons off your vest
You're playing with a hornets' nest
No, no Joe

You know, you think you're somebody we should dread
Just because you're seein' red
You better get that foolishness out of your head
No, no Joe

And you might be itchin' for a fight
Quit braggin' about how your bear can bite
'Cause you're sitting on a keg of dynamite
No, no Joe

79. The War Resisters League, "War Can Be Stopped! A Statement on Korea"

(1950)

If the Korean War is still regarded as the "forgotten war," then the dissenters who opposed the war made up the "forgotten antiwar movement." Like Dwight MacDonald in 1947, the War Resisters League protested the Korean War as preface to World War III. At the end of World War II, the Soviets and the Americans divided Korea at the 38th parallel. The Soviets occupied the northern zone of the former Japanese colony, and the Americans occupied the southern zone. Plans for peaceful unification were never realized, as both the communist North Korean government and the conservative South Korean government claimed to be the legitimate government of the Korean people. Truman, whom critics blamed for "losing" China to communism, saw the June 1950 North Korean invasion of South Korea as yet another test of American resolve by the Soviets. The War Resisters League, founded in 1923 by Americans who had opposed the Great War (some of whom went to prison as conscientious objectors), affirms that "all war is a crime against humanity." In this pamphlet, the WRL predicts, in its description of "one more war," the later, more familiar critique of the United States as "global policeman." Equally important, it offers the peace movement's persistent call for disarmament.

SOURCE: "War Can Be Stopped! A Statement on Korea by the War Resisters League," Abraham Kaufman Papers, courtesy of Scott H. Bennett.

August, 1950

Third World War Threatened

The eruption of military hostilities in Korea on June 25, 1950 has brought the world a long step closer to the ultimate catastrophe of World War III. The cold war policies of distrust and tension, ruthless unbridled propaganda and interference with the affairs of smaller countries, which both sides have pursued in varying degrees for the past five years, have shown that they will lead only to open warfare. If these policies which are dividing the world are continued, Korea will be only the first of a series of ever more disastrous wars.

Attempts to avert World War III become daily more difficult under these circumstances. While the governments argue that they must depend finally upon violence with the ultimate hope of achieving peace, it would benefit the people of the world most if an immediate understanding were reached. This Civil War of Mankind must be stopped. Nobody will win if Russia and America in their fanaticism and blindness set the world on fire. The bombs and liquid gas and rockets will fall on all of us and will achieve no purpose whatsoever but disaster.

Major Peace Effort Needed

The Korean War revealed the belief in violence of the Communists, who did not hesitate to make a calculated attack when they thought they would win. But it also showed that the United States knew of no other way to reply than by mobilization and an intensification of the war. The United States is adding to the tinderbox by its failure to understand the struggles of the people of Asia to be relieved of all foreign domination. American foreign policy must be corrected before the Asian people will listen to us with confidence. The major question today is not who is the more guilty in Korea. Will the people of the world be traduced into supporting "one more war"? Or will they discover in time that humanity is one, whatever its differences?

In this crisis only a peace effort on a large scale can avert the spread of war. The will for peace must overcome the degree of differences which divide us. Only a proposal that is vast enough to be a real solution will capture the imaginations of people and avoid becoming just another propaganda weapon. Halfhearted peace efforts will not work.

World Disarmament Urgent

The most vital part of a peace program of large enough scope must be real disarmament, not only of atom bombs but of all weapons and of huge armies and navies. There must be an *exchange of visitors and information* between countries which would make such a plan work. This plan, if offered by either the United States or Russia would put new heart into people everywhere and dispel the present world nightmare.

The War Resisters League bases its opposition to all wars on a philosophy of fundamental human values. We are convinced that peace can be achieved only by peaceful means. The League refuses to support war and urges individuals to become members on this basis. We believe that war is an attack on the value of individual personality and the solidarity of mankind, values for which men have struggled through the centuries. We oppose all oppression and totalitarianism and we believe that those evils can be fought effectively only by non-violent methods.

The Program of the War Resisters League Includes:

Mediation of the War—

The League supports any proposal for peace if sincerely made and not intended as a part of the military strategy of either belligerent. It commends the efforts of *Nehru* to mediate the Korean war and looks to the people of India or of any other country which can rise above the conflict to maintain neutrality and serve as a common ground for both sides. It warns against misleading peace plans such as the *Stockholm Peace Pledge*, or other such plans designed as instruments of war policy.

Conscientious Objection—

Members of the League pledge themselves to withhold support from all wars, offensive or defensive, civil or international. In accordance with individual conscience, they refuse to work in war plants or to buy war bonds. None accepts combatant military duty, regardless of the consequences. Some refuse to register under conscription or to pay income taxes. The League supports all objectors, provides them with information about regulations and procedures and helps them to arrive at their own decisions. It is particularly concerned with serving the objector whose motivation is philosophical or political rather than traditionally religious and who therefore may have no other affiliation.

Non-violent Resistance to Dictatorship—

The League recommends the methods of non-violence as an alternative to violence and war in opposing dictatorship and oppression. These methods include education, negotiation, political action, noncooperation, the peaceful strike and boycott, picketing and other demonstrations. We believe that the record of *Gandhi* and his followers in India demonstrates the effectiveness of these methods. We seek to promote their study and use and to familiarize people with the fact that war is never "the only way out." The road to peace begins with the recognition that the interests of humanity come before those of country. The League encourages its members to cooperate with their fellow citizens in all activities which further world community.

The War Resisters League is an American affiliate of the War Resisters' International. The International headquarters are in England, and there are affiliated sections in 57 countries. Our object is to unite men and women who have determined to give no support to war irrespective of the reasons—political, religious, humanitarian—which have led them to take the stand.

For further information, write to:

WAR RESISTERS LEAGUE
Five Beekman Street, New York 7, N. Y.

80. New York Times, "Dismissal Angers South California"

(1951)

When American and United Nations forces, under General Douglas MacArthur's command, pushed the North Koreans almost to the Chinese border by late November 1950, more than a million Chinese troops streamed into North Korea and drove American forces back below the 38th parallel. MacArthur (1880–1964), hero of World War II and commander of occupation forces in Japan, now especially sneered at the idea of fighting a "limited war," believing Asia to be central to the Cold War. When news of the general's letter to Republican House leader Joseph Martin in which he declared that "there is no substitute for victory" reached Truman, the president relieved MacArthur of his command. For Truman, it was a question of both trying to avoid a third world war and restoring the constitutional authority of the president as commander-in-chief. The American public erupted in fury at Truman, however; more than 100,000 letters and telegrams poured into the White House and congressional offices. Meanwhile, MacArthur returned home to be celebrated as a national hero. He gave a farewell address to a joint session of Congress, and in New York as many as 7 million people turned out for a ticker-tape parade down Broadway for the deposed general. The article here seems to indicate that the notion of "no substitute for victory" resonated with much of the public.

SOURCE: *New York Times*, April 12, 1951.

Truman Hanged in Effigy at San Gabriel—Los Angeles Council Halts in Sorrow

Special to THE NEW YORK TIMES.

LOS ANGELES, Calif., April 11—Protests against President Truman's dismissal of General of the Army Douglas MacArthur flared through Southern California today and were capped in many cases by demands for impeachment of the President.

In San Gabriel the President was hanged in effigy. In the Los Angeles City Hall the City Council adjourned "In sorrowful contemplation of the political assassination" of General MacArthur. Mayor Bowron said he was greatly concerned, agitated and discouraged.

Automobiles suddenly appeared on downtown streets plastered with signs: "Oust President Truman."

Lifelong Democrats joined Republicans in the complaints.

Calls to Papers Continuous

Telephone calls to newspapers began immediately after the firing was announced. They continued all Tuesday night, all day today and on into the night again.

Thousands asked for information on how to write and wire their Representatives and Senators Knowland and Nixon. Others added they were sending additional telegrams direct to the White House.

Nine out of ten were vehemently critical of President Truman's action. Occasionally one voice in the deluge would rise to defend him.

James Roosevelt, unsuccessful candidate for Governor last November, said he hoped the debate over the President's action "will not resolve into a political dogfight."

"The President is the Commander in Chief," Mr. Roosevelt said. "If he felt any commander in the field was not carrying out the policy of the Government, just as Abraham Lincoln found in the Civil War, it was his duty to remove him.

"Nevertheless, having served under General MacArthur's command in the Pacific, I feel from a military point of view he is one of our greatest generals."

Legion Officer Shocked

Lewis K. Gough of Pasadena, national vice commander of the American Legion said: "I know that the amazing news of the removal of one of the greatest military leaders of all time will stun and shock the 4,000,000 members of the American Legion and its auxiliary.

"While serving as Commander in Chief in the Pacific General MacArthur's voice should have been heard and listened to in influencing proper global strategy. That it was not listened to is largely due to lack of requisite moral courage on the part of the United Nations.

"His unfortunate removal will jeopardize the United Nations position in the Far Eastern theater and undoubtedly will have shocking effect on our officers and troops there."

Patrick J. Cooney, lifelong Democrat and father of five sons who entered military service: "MacArthur repeatedly refused to obey his Commander in Chief and refused to follow the United Nations policy.

"This very momentous decision required great strength of character but was necessary if we are to preserve our governmental system set up by our founding fathers. History will record that President Truman was right."

Assistant Attorney General William V. O'Connor said "whenever any military commander in the field is unable to give loyal and wholehearted support to the policies formulated by the United States and the United Nations in the time of such a crisis, the President as Commander in Chief has no alternative but to relieve that commander."

81. Lowell Blanchard and the Valley Trio, "Jesus Hits Like an Atom Bomb"

(1950)

In the year following the Soviet Union's first successful detonation of an atomic weapon, Lowell Blanchard and the Valley Trio chided their fellow Americans for fearing the Bomb more than God. Lowell Blanchard (1910–68) was born in Palmer, Illinois, but made his name at WNOX in Knoxville, Tennessee. There Blanchard hosted the *Mid-Day Merry-Go-Round*, a daily live music show that showcased the best talent in country music, and broadcast from eastern Kentucky to Virginia and North Carolina. By 1950, Blanchard was an institution in Appalachia. "Jesus Hits Like an Atom Bomb" may have been a novelty song of sorts, but its message reflected the God-fearing culture of which WNOX was a part.

SOURCE: "Jesus Hits Like an Atom Bomb" (L. McCollum), originally released as Lowell Blanchard and the Valley Trio (Mercury 6260, 1950).

> Refrain: Everybody's worried 'bout the atomic bomb
> But nobody's worried 'bout the day my Lord will come
> When he'll hit, great God a-mighty, like an atom bomb
> When he comes, when he comes
>
> In nineteen-hundred and forty-five the atom bomb became alive
> In nineteen-hundred and forty-nine the USA got very wise
> It found a country had crossed the line, had an atom bomb of
>   the very same kind
> The people got worried all over the land, just like folks got in Japan
>
> So, I say everybody's worried (yeah) 'bout the atomic bomb
> But nobody's worried (no) 'bout the day my Lord will come
> When he'll hit, great God a-mighty, like an atom bomb
> When he comes, good Lord, when he comes

Refrain

Well now, God told Elijah, he would send down fire, send down
    fire from on high
He told the brother Noah by the rainbow sign, there'll be no water, but
    fire in the sky
Now don't get worried, just bear in mind, seek King Jesus and you shall find
Peace, happiness, and joy divine, with my Jesus in your mind

So, I say everybody's worried (yeah) 'bout the atomic bomb
But nobody's worried (no) 'bout the day my Lord will come
When he'll hit, great God a-mighty, like an atom bomb
When he comes, great God, when he comes

Refrain

82. Dorothy Day, A.J. Muste, Ralph DiGia, and Kent Larrabee, "Letter Opposing Civil Defense Drills"

(1955)

From 1955 to 1961, the city and state of New York held annual civil defense drills that required all citizens to seek shelter during an air raid drill. Just as schoolchildren across the country grew used to routine "duck and cover" drills (in which they practiced reacting to a nuclear blast by hiding under their desks), most Americans accepted that, in the nuclear age, practicing the run to the nearest fallout shelter made sense. In the following letter, Dorothy Day, A.J. Muste, Ralph DiGia, and Kent Larrabee offer their critique of that mind-set, and pledge to resist the law mandating their participation.

Day (1897–1980) was born in Brooklyn but grew up in Chicago. As a young woman, she worked as a journalist and as an activist for women's suffrage and peace. In 1927, she founded the Catholic Worker movement, which grew from publishing a newspaper of that name into a national network of communities ministering to the poor and promoting peace. Muste (1885–1967) was a minister in the Dutch Reformed Church before becoming a labor organizer and socialist. He was the first director of Brookwood Labor College, but he is best known for a long career as leader of several peace and social justice organizations, including the Fellowship of Reconciliation, the Peacemakers, and the Committee for Nonviolent Action. DiGia (1914–2008), who grew up in New York, went to prison as a conscientious objector during World War II. He worked in the War Resisters League office from 1945 to 2008. Kent Larrabee was the New York director of the Fellowship of Reconciliation.

SOURCE: Dorothy Day, A.J. Muste, Ralph DiGia, and Kent Larrabee to Abraham Stark (Acting Mayor), June 15, 1955, War Resisters League Papers, Series B, Box 8f, Swarthmore Peace Collection.

June 15, 1955

Abraham Stark, Acting Mayor
Office of the Mayor
New York City, New York

Dear Sir:

It is not possible for us to join in the activities proposed by the Civil Defense Authorities for June 15, 1955. In particular we cannot in good conscience conform to the instructions to "seek shelter" for a period at 2:05 to 2:13 o'clock.

This is not because we are insensitive to human suffering; and we trust that in a time of national disaster we would not only be willing but prepared to minister to the needs of any of our fellows, to whatever nationality, race or creed they might belong.

The question before our own people and also the rest of mankind is indeed how we may find "security" and "shelter" from the ravages of atomic and bilogical war. Even leading military authorities—not to mention political authorities, the atomic scientists, leading writers, both religious and secular—unanimously declare that the only way in which this can be done is by the abolition of war.

Instead of devoting money, energy and skill, however, to the ending of war, the nation spends billions of dollars and uses the vast resources of its industry and the skill of its scientists and technicians in preparation for war, in piling up the nuclear and bacteriological weapons of mass destruction. The notion that by engaging in an armaments race in such diabolical weapons we are actually engaged in preventing or putting an end to war seems to us too absurd for intelligent people to entertain.

The promotion of such public and publicized Civil Defense demonstrations as the one now taking place, whatever the intentions may be, *helps to create the illusion that the nation can thus devote its major resources to preparation for catastrophic war and at the same time shield people from its effects.* We can have no part in helping to create this illusion.

Moreover, apart from any such considerations, we do not believe that any nation has the moral or spiritual right to visit atomic and biological destruction upon any other people, at any time, or for any reason whatever. Those of us who are Christians declare this in the name of Christ; but on whatever ground, this is for all of us a profound conscientious conviction.

For these reasons, we feel bound to devote ourselves to the promotion of peace, the work of good will and mercy, the prevention of the catastrophe of atomic war. It is by such means that a world free from totalitarianism, oppression and militarism can be attained. To this end we here and now rededicate ourselves.

Very truly,
Dorothy Day, *Catholic Worker*
Ralph DiGia, *War Resisters League*
A. J. Muste, *Peacemakers.*
Kent Larrabee, F. O. R.

83. Murray Kempton, "Laughter in the Park"

(1960)

As described by Murray Kempton in the following New York Post column, the defiance of civil defense drills grew dramatically by 1960. Just as their counterparts in the civil rights movement learned the value of nonviolent direct action, peace activists protesting preparations for nuclear war persisted in their resistance. Although people like Dorothy Day had been jailed for thirty days in 1957 for defying the civil defense drill, the numbers who gathered in City Hall Park each year grew. Born in Baltimore, Murray Kempton (1917–97) was a World War II veteran and a former socialist when he took the job as labor reporter for the *New York Post* in 1949. In time, he became a columnist known for exposing political hypocrisy and praising those he found honorable. One year after this column ran, nearly 2,000 people turned out in City Hall Park to resist the civil defense drills. Police arrested forty, and the city stopped holding the drills.

SOURCE: *New York Post*, May 4, 1960.

We seem to be approaching a condition of sanity where within a year or so there'll be more people defying than complying with the Civil Defense drill.

There were some 700 persons assembled in City Hall Park yesterday afternoon each with a personal commitment to go to jail rather than comply with the drill. Six years ago, when this annual Spring Festival began, there were just 23 demonstrators. The whole thing is getting as fashionable as the Newport jazz festival, and as well beyond the powers of the local police.

The cops, having provided only three wagons, were able to *arrest only 27 persons* in all, leaving the rest to shout and sing and deride until the last horn had honked the all clear. The crowd was so thick in fact that the police had to overlook such veteran disturbers of the peace as Dorothy Day and Ammon Hennacy of the Catholic Worker and A. J. Muste of the Fellowship of Reconciliation.

* * *

When the first siren blew and nobody moved, the police stood awhile and looked wistfully upon the blossoming dogwoods in the park. It fell to Assistant Chief of the Police Auxiliary Henry George Hearn to represent affronted patriotism.

He stood up on a bench and began, "Please obey the law." There was a happy pulsation of laughter; I haven't heard that many people laugh in this sad city since LaGuardia died.

"Are you Americans or not?" Henry George Hearn went on. They laughed again. "Americans go home," someone called. Henry George Hearn waved a grandly futile hand over the 500 persons remaining.

"I place all of you under arrest not obeying the law."

He then dismounted and began passing around the fringes, stopping someone every now and then and asking, "You taking shelter or do you want to go to jail?" The invariable response was that they wanted to go to jail, and he and his slowly rousing auxiliaries began leading them to the wagons.

This went on for perhaps ten minutes, and may be said to have ended at the moment when one policeman, leading two lady demonstrators each by one arm, arrived in time to see the last wagon available for the salvation of the republic trundle off chockfull. He could do nothing thereafter but let them go.

The invulnerable majority of the demonstration was now lined up in something like order *singing* that *they shall not be moved*.

And *Norman Mailer was explaining to his cluster that politics is like sex: you got to go all the way*, and Dwight MacDonald was defending his movie reviews to another cluster of admiring but distrustful philistines.

*   *   *

When the all clear sounded, *David McReynolds, of the Socialist Party climbed a bench*—Assistant Chief Hearn did not contest his priority—and announced the obvious fact that *"The law is dead."* It is and it would be impossible to imagine a more engaging way to kill a law.

There remained, of course, the problem of disposing of the token victims. Part of the crowd went up to Criminal Court to see their representatives booked.

The *27 arrestees* got Youth Term *magistrate Edward D. Caiazzo.* Henry George Hearn swore to a mass complaint. Alan Hirshman, as counsel for the *nine women arrestees, pleaded guilty: his* clients, he said, were conforming to the highest standards of civil disobedience.

Judge Caiazzo said that in his opinion they had flouted the law knowing it, and *they were undermining our democratic process.* The laughter came again, and he said he'd clear the courtroom if it continued. Mrs. Lucia Shapiro, a defendant, pointed out that *she'd never had a chance to vote on Civil Defense,* and Miss *Anne Morrissett,* another, said that there is a tradition of defying tthe law and taking the consequences, at which the judge said pleasantly and politely that he had heard enough and would sentence Friday.

Leaving, there was a sudden recognition that, if enough people care, a deal of national nonsense can be quickly and pleasantly disposed of. It seemed a long time since anyone thought of that.

84. Albert S. Bigelow, "Why I Am Sailing into the Pacific Bomb-Test Area"

(1958)

For Americans like Albert Bigelow, the momentum of the nuclear arms race seemed almost insurmountable by the late 1950s. Between 1946 and 1962, the United States detonated nearly 300 nuclear weapons in tests in both Nevada and the Pacific. Beginning in 1952, most were hydrogen bombs, thermonuclear weapons many hundreds of times more powerful than the atomic bombs dropped on Japan in 1945. Bigelow (1906–1993), a former naval commander who became a Quaker after World War II, decided that only a dramatic direct action protest would bring attention to what he saw as the insanity of nuclear testing. In the statement that follows, Bigelow describes how he decided to sail his thirty-foot boat, *The Golden Rule*, into the Eniwetok nuclear test site in the Marshall Islands. While Bigelow and his crew sailed to Hawaii, the Atomic Energy Commission issued a new regulation banning civilians from entering the test site. Later, in Hawaii, the U.S. government secured a court injunction against Bigelow, and on two occasions, as *The Golden Rule* attempted to leave Honolulu, the authorities intercepted it. On the second occasion, police arrested Bigelow and four crew members; the court sentenced them to sixty days in jail. Later in the year, Earle and Barbara Leonard Reynolds—who had met Bigelow in Honolulu—succeeded in sailing their boat, *The Phoenix of Hiroshima*, sixty-five miles into the nuclear test site at Bikini.

SOURCE: *Liberation*, February 1958, pp. 4–6.

My friend Bill Huntington and I are planning to sail a small vessel westward into the Pacific H-bomb test area. By April we expect to reach nuclear testing grounds at Eniwetok. We will remain there as long as the tests of H-bombs continue. With us will be two other volunteers.

Why? Because it is the way I can say to my government, to the British government, and to the Kremlin: "Stop! Stop this madness before it is too late. For God's sake, turn back!"

How have I come to this conviction? Why do I feel under compulsion, under moral orders, as it were, to do this?

The answer to such questions, at least in part, has to do with my experience as a Naval officer during World War II. The day after Pearl Harbor was attacked, I was at the Navy recruiting offices. I had had a lot of experience in navigating vessels. Life in the Navy would be a glamorous change from the dull mechanism of daily civilian living. My experience assured me of success. All this adventure ahead and the prospect of becoming a hero into the bargain.

I suppose, too, that I had an enormous latent desire to conform, to go along with the rest of my fellows. I was swayed by the age-old psychology of meeting force with force. It did not really occur to me to resist the drag of the institution of war, the pattern of organized violence, which had existed for so many centuries. This psychology prevailed even though I had already reflected on the fantastic wastefulness of war—the German *Bismarck* hunting the British *Hood* and sending it to the bottom of the sea, and the British Navy hunting the *Bismarck* and scuttling it.

I volunteered, but instead of being sent to sea, I was assigned to 90 Church Street in New York and worked in project "plot" establishing the whereabouts of all combat ships in the Atlantic. In a couple of months I escaped from this assignment and was transferred to the Naval Training Station at Northwestern University.

I had not been at Northwestern very long when I sensed that because of my past experience I would be made an instructor there and still not get to sea. So I deliberately flunked an examination in navigation and before long was assigned to a submarine chaser in the Atlantic.

The Turkey Shoot

From March to October of 1943 I was in command of a submarine chaser in the Solomon Islands, during the fighting. It was during this period that more than 100 Japanese planes were shot down in one day. This was called "the Turkey Shoot." The insensitivity which decent men must develop in such situations is appalling. I remember that the corpse of a Japanese airman who had been shot down was floating bolt upright in one of the coves, a position resulting from the structure of the Japanese life belts, which were different from our Mae Wests. Each day as we passed the cove we saw this figure, his face growing blacker under the terrific sun. We laughingly called him Smiling Jack. As a matter of fact, I think I gave him that name myself and felt rather proud of my wit.

Later in World War II, I was Captain of the destroyer escort *Dale W. Peterson*—DE 337—and I was on her bridge as we came into Pearl Harbor from San Francisco when the first news arrived of the explosion of an atomic bomb over Hiroshima. Although I had no way of understanding what an atom bomb was I was absolutely awestruck, as I suppose all men were for a moment. Intuitively it was then that I realized for the first time that morally war is impossible.

I don't suppose I had the same absolute realization with my whole being, so to speak, of the immorality and "impossibility" of nuclear war until the morning of August 7, 1957. On that day, I sat with a score of friends, before dawn, in the Nevada desert just outside the entrance to the Camp Mercury testing grounds. The day before, eleven of us, in protest against the summer-long tests, had tried to enter the restricted area. We had been arrested as we stepped one after another over the boundary line, and had been carried off to a ghost town which stands at the entrance to Death Valley. There we had been given a speedy trial under the charge of trespassing under the Nevada laws. Sentencing had been suspended for a year, and later in the afternoon we had returned to Camp Mercury to continue the Prayer and Conscience Vigil along with others who had remained there during our civil disobedience action.

In the early morning of August 7 an experimental bomb was exploded. We sat with our backs to the explosion site. But when the flash came I felt again the utterly impossible horror of this whole business, the same complete realization that nuclear war must go, that I had felt twelve years before on the bridge of U. S. S. *Dale W. Peterson*, off Pearl Harbor.

I think also that deep down somewhere in me, and in all men at all times, there is a realization that the pattern of violence meeting violence makes no sense, and that war violates something central in the human heart—"that of God," as we Quakers sometimes say. . . .

Society of Friends

However, I am ahead of my story. At the close of the War, in spite of what I had felt on the bridge of that destroyer, I did not break away from my old life. For a time I was Housing Commissioner of Massachusetts. Like many other people who had been through the War, I was seeking some sort of unified life-philosophy or religion. I did a good deal of religious "window-shopping." I became impressed by the fact that in one way or another the saints, the wise men, those who seemed to me truly experienced, all pointed in one direction—toward nonviolence, truth, love, toward a way and a goal that could not be reconciled with war. . . .

I came into contact with the Quakers, the Society of Friends. My wife, Sylvia, had already joined the Society in 1948. As late as 1955 I was still fighting off joining the Society, which seemed to me to involve a great, awesome commitment. I suppose I was like the man in one of Shaw's plays who wanted to be a Christian—but not yet.

The Hiroshima Maidens

Then came the experience of having in our home for some months two of the Hiroshima maidens who had been injured and disfigured in the bombing of

August 6, 1945. Norman Cousins and other wonderful people brought them to this country for plastic surgery. There were two things about these girls that hit me very hard and forced me to see that I had no choice but to make the commitment to live, as best I could, a life of nonviolence and reconciliation. One was the fact that when they were bombed in 1945 the two girls in our home were nine and thirteen years old. What earthly thing could they have done to give some semblance of what we call justice to the ordeal inflicted upon them and hundreds like them? What possible good could come out of human action— war—which bore such fruits? Is it not utter blasphemy to think that there is anything moral or Christian about such behavior?

The other thing that struck me was that these young women found it difficult to believe that *we*, who were not members of their families, could love *them*. But *they* loved *us*; they harbored no resentment against us or other Americans. How are you going to respond to that kind of attitude? The newly-elected president of the National Council of Churches, Edwin T. Dahlberg, said in his inaugural talk that instead of "massive retaliation" the business of Christians is to practice "massive reconciliation." Well, these Hiroshima girls practiced "massive reconciliation" on us, on me, who had laughed derisively at "Smiling Jack." What response can one make to this other than to give oneself utterly to destroying the evil, war, that dealt so shamefully with them and try to live in the spirit of sensitivity and reconciliation which they displayed?

As I have said, I think there is that in all men that abhors and rejects war and knows that force and violence can bring no good thing to pass. Yet men are bound by old patterns of feeling, thought and action. The organs of public opinions are almost completely shut against us. It seems practically impossible, moreover, for the ordinary person by ordinary means to speak to, and affect the action of, his government. I have had a recent experience of this which has strengthened my conviction that it is only by such acts as sailing a boat to Eniwetok and thus "speaking" to the government right in the testing area that we can expect to be heard.

Tell It to the Policeman

I was asked by the New England office of the American Friends Service Committee to take to the White House 17,411 signatures to a petition to cancel the Pacific tests. Ten thousand signatures had previously been sent in. I realize that even a President in good health cannot see personally everyone who has a message for him. Yet the right of petition exists—in theory—and is held to be a key factor in democratic process. And the President presumably has assistants to see to it that all serious petitions are somehow brought to his attention. For matters of this kind, there is Maxwell Rabb, secretary to the cabinet.

Twenty-seven thousand is quite a few people to have signed a somewhat unusual petition. The A. F. S. C. is widely known and recognized as a highly useful agency. I am known to Maxwell Rabb with whom I worked in Republican politics in Massachusetts. I was a precinct captain for Eisenhower in the 1952 primaries. Yet a couple of days work on the part of the staff of the Friends Committee on National Legislation failed to secure even an assurance that some time on Tuesday, December 31, the day I would be in Washington, Max Rabb would see me to receive the petitions. On that day I made five calls and talked with his secretary. Each time I was assured that she would call me back within ten minutes. Each time the return call failed to come and I tried again. The last time, early in the afternoon, I held on to the telephone for ten minutes, only to be told finally that the office was about to close for the day.

Each time I telephoned, including the last, I was told I could, of course, leave the petitions with the policeman at the gate. This I refused to do. It seems terrible to me that Americans can no longer speak to or be seen by their government. Has it become their master, not their servant? Can it not listen to their humble and reasonable pleas? This experience may in one sense be a small matter but I am sure it is symptomatic—among other things—of a sort of fear on the part of officials to listen to what in their hearts they feel is right but on which they cannot act without breaking with old patterns of thought. At any rate, the experience has strengthened in me the conviction that we must, at whatever cost, find ways to make our witness and protest heard.

I Am Going Because . . .

I am going because, as Shakespeare said, "Action is eloquence." Without some such direct action, ordinary citizens lack the power any longer to be seen or heard by their government.

I am going because it is time to do *something* about peace, not just *talk* about peace.

I am going because, like all men, in my heart I know that *all* nuclear explosions are monstrous, evil, unworthy of human beings.

I am going because war is no longer a feudal jousting match; it is an unthinkable catastrophe for all men.

I am going because it is now the little children, and, most of all, the as yet unborn who are the front line troops. It is my duty to stand between them and this horrible danger.

I am going because it is cowardly and degrading for me to stand by any longer, to consent, and thus to collaborate in atrocities.

I am going because I cannot say that the end justifies the means. A Quaker, William Penn, said, "A good end cannot sanctify evil means; nor must we ever do evil that good may come of it." A Communist, Milovan Djilas, says, "As soon as means which would ensure an end are shown to be evil, the end will show itself as unrealizable."

I am going because, as Gandhi said, "God sits in the man opposite me; therefore to injure him is to injure God himself."

I am going to witness to the deep inward truth we all know, "Force can subdue, but love gains."

I am going because however mistaken, unrighteous, and unrepentant governments may seem, I still believe all men are really good at heart, and that my act will speak to them.

I am going in the hope of helping change the hearts and minds of men in government. If necessary I am willing to give my life to help change a policy of fear, force and destruction to one of trust, kindness, and help.

I am going in order to say, "Quit this waste, this arms race. Turn instead to a disarmament race. Stop competing for evil, compete for good."

I am going because I have to—if I am to call myself a human being.

When you see something horrible happening, your instinct is to do something about it. You can freeze in fearful apathy or you can even talk yourself into saying that it isn't horrible. I can't do that. I have to act. This is too horrible. We know it. Let's all act.

85. Dwight D. Eisenhower, "Farewell Speech"

(1961)

In this final speech of his presidency, Dwight Eisenhower warns of the growing influence of the military-industrial complex and its influence on the economy and public policy. Eisenhower (1890–1969) went to the U.S. Military Academy at West Point from his home in Abilene, Kansas. Upon graduation, and over the next twenty-five years, he steadily rose through the ranks of the army, ultimately becoming supreme commander of Allied Forces in Europe and a five-star general. His oversight of Operation Overlord, the Allied invasion at Normandy in June 1944, made him an international hero, a stature further enhanced as he pushed Allied forces through difficult fighting at the Battle of the Bulge and on to victory. Following the war, and after serving as army chief of staff, Eisenhower retired to accept the presidency of Columbia University. In 1952, he campaigned for the presidency of the United States, promising that he "would go to Korea" to bring an end to the war there. By the end of his presidency, despite minor embarrassments such as the U-2 affair, Eisenhower remained popular with and respected by the American public, especially with regard to foreign and military affairs. In this speech, Eisenhower eschewed the usual self-congratulatory ode with which so many presidents leave office and, instead, issued a sober warning to his fellow citizens about the potential perils of maintaining a "permanent armaments industry of vast proportions."

SOURCE: Public Papers of the Presidents, Dwight D. Eisenhower, 1961, pp. 1035–40.

January 17, 1961.

My fellow Americans:

Three days from now, after half a century in the service of our country, I shall lay down the responsibilities of office as, in traditional and solemn ceremony, the authority of the Presidency is vested in my successor.

This evening I come to you with a message of leave-taking and farewell, and to share a few final thoughts with you, my countrymen.

Like every other citizen, I wish the new President, and all who will labor with him, Godspeed. I pray that the coming years will be blessed with peace and prosperity for all.

Our people expect their President and the Congress to find essential agreement on issues of great moment, the wise resolution of which will better shape the future of the Nation.

My own relations with the Congress, which began on a remote and tenuous basis when, long ago, a member of the Senate appointed me to West Point, have since ranged to the intimate during the war and immediate post-war period, and, finally, to the mutually interdependent during these past eight years.

In this final relationship, the Congress and the Administration have, on most vital issues, cooperated well, to serve the national good rather than mere partisanship, and so have assured that the business of the Nation should go forward. So, my official relationship with the Congress ends in a feeling, on my part, of gratitude that we have been able to do so much together.

II

We now stand ten years past the midpoint of a century that has witnessed four major wars among great nations. Three of these involved our own country. Despite these holocausts America is today the strongest, the most influential and most productive nation in the world. Understandably proud of this preeminence, we yet realize that America's leadership and prestige depend, not merely upon our unmatched material progress, riches and military strength, but on how we use our power in the interests of world peace and human betterment.

III

Throughout America's adventure in free government, our basic purposes have been to keep the peace; to foster progress in human achievement, and to enhance liberty, dignity and integrity among people and among nations. To strive for less would be unworthy of a free and religious people. Any failure traceable to arrogance, or our lack of comprehension or readiness to sacrifice would inflict upon us grievous hurt both at home and abroad.

Progress toward these noble goals is persistently threatened by the conflict now engulfing the world. It commands our whole attention, absorbs our very beings. We face a hostile ideology-global in scope, atheistic in character, ruthless in purpose, and insidious in method. Unhappily the danger it poses promises to be of indefinite duration. To meet it successfully, there is called for, not so much the emotional and transitory sacrifices of crisis, but rather those which enable us to carry forward steadily, surely, and without complaint the burdens of a prolonged and complex struggle—with liberty at stake. Only thus shall we remain, despite every provocation, on our charted course toward permanent peace and human betterment.

Crises there will continue to be. In meeting them, whether foreign or domestic, great or small, there is a recurring temptation to feel that some spectacular and costly action could become the miraculous solution to all current difficulties. A huge increase in newer elements of our defense; development of unrealistic programs to cure every ill in agriculture; a dramatic expansion in basic and applied research—these and many other possibilities, each possibly promising in itself, may be suggested as the only way to the road we wish to travel.

But each proposal must be weighed in the light of a broader consideration: the need to maintain balance in and among national programs—balance between the private and the public economy, balance between cost and hoped for advantage-balance between the clearly necessary and the comfortably desirable; balance between our essential requirements as a nation and the duties imposed by the nation upon the individual; balance between action of the moment and the national welfare of the future. Good judgment seeks balance and progress; lack of it eventually finds imbalance and frustration.

The record of many decades stands as proof that our people and their government have, in the main, understood these truths and have responded to them well, in the face of stress and threat. But threats, new in kind or degree, constantly arise. I mention two only.

IV

A vital element in keeping the peace is our military establishment. Our arms must be mighty, ready for instant action, so that no potential aggressor may be tempted to risk his own destruction.

Our military organization today bears little relation to that known by any of my predecessors in peace time, or indeed by the fighting men of World War II or Korea.

Until the latest of our world conflicts, the United States had no armaments industry. American makers of plowshares could, with time and as required, make swords as well. But now we can no longer risk emergency improvisation of national defense; we have been compelled to create a permanent armaments industry of vast proportions. Added to this, three and a half million men and women are directly engaged in the defense establishment. We annually spend on military security more than the net income of all United States corporations.

This conjunction of an immense military establishment and a large arms industry is new in the American experience. The total influence—economic, political, even spiritual—is felt in every city, every state house, every office of the Federal government. We recognize the imperative need for this development. Yet we must not fail to comprehend its grave implications. Our toil, resources and livelihood are all involved; so is the very structure of our society.

In the councils of government, we must guard against the acquisition of unwarranted influence, whether sought or unsought, by the military-industrial complex. The potential for the disastrous rise of misplaced power exists and will persist.

We must never let the weight of this combination endanger our liberties or democratic processes. We should take nothing for granted only an alert and knowledgeable citizenry can compel the proper meshing of huge industrial and military machinery of defense with our peaceful methods and goals, so that security and liberty may prosper together.

Akin to, and largely responsible for the sweeping changes in our industrial-military posture, has been the technological revolution during recent decades.

In this revolution, research has become central; it also becomes more formalized, complex, and costly. A steadily increasing share is conducted for, by, or at the direction of, the Federal government.

Today, the solitary inventor, tinkering in his shop, has been over shadowed by task forces of scientists in laboratories and testing fields. In the same fashion, the free university, historically the fountainhead of free ideas and scientific discovery, has experienced a revolution in the conduct of research. Partly because of the huge costs involved, a government contract becomes virtually a substitute for intellectual curiosity. For every old blackboard there are now hundreds of new electronic computers.

The prospect of domination of the nation's scholars by Federal employment, project allocations, and the power of money is ever present and is gravely to be regarded.

Yet, in holding scientific research and discovery in respect, as we should, we must also be alert to the equal and opposite danger that public policy could itself become the captive of a scientific-technological elite.

It is the task of statesmanship to mold, to balance, and to integrate these and other forces, new and old, within the principles of our democratic system—ever aiming toward the supreme goals of our free society.

V

Another factor in maintaining balance involves the element of time. As we peer into society's future, we—you and I, and our government—must avoid the impulse to live only for today, plundering, for our own ease and convenience, the precious resources of tomorrow. We cannot mortgage the material assets of our grandchildren without risking the loss also of their political and spiritual heritage. We want democracy to survive for all generations to come, not to become the insolvent phantom of tomorrow.

VI

Down the long lane of the history yet to be written America knows that this world of ours, ever growing smaller, must avoid becoming a community of dreadful fear and hate, and be, instead, a proud confederation of mutual trust and respect.

Such a confederation must be one of equals. The weakest must come to the conference table with the same confidence as do we, protected as we are by our moral, economic, and military strength. That table, though scarred by many past frustrations, cannot be abandoned for the certain agony of the battlefield.

Disarmament, with mutual honor and confidence, is a continuing imperative. Together we must learn how to compose difference, not with arms, but with intellect and decent purpose. Because this need is so sharp and apparent I confess that I lay down my official responsibilities in this field with a definite sense of disappointment. As one who has witnessed the horror and the lingering sadness of war—as one who knows that another war could utterly destroy this civilization which has been so slowly and painfully built over thousands of years—I wish I could say tonight that a lasting peace is in sight.

Happily, I can say that war has been avoided. Steady progress toward our ultimate goal has been made. But, so much remains to be done. As a private citizen, I shall never cease to do what little I can to help the world advance along that road.

VII

So—in this my last good night to you as your President—I thank you for the many opportunities you have given me for public service in war and peace. I trust that in that service you find something's worthy; as for the rest of it, I know you will find ways to improve performance in the future.

You and I—my fellow citizens—need to be strong in our faith that all nations, under God, will reach the goal of peace with justice. May we be ever unswerving in devotion to principle, confident but humble with power, diligent in pursuit of the Nation's great goals.

To all the peoples of the world, I once more give expression to America's prayerful and continuing aspiration:

We pray that peoples of all faiths, all races, all nations, may have their great human needs satisfied; that those now denied opportunity shall come to enjoy it to the full; that all who yearn for freedom may experience its spiritual blessings; that those who have freedom will understand, also, its heavy responsibilities; that all who are insensitive to the needs of others will learn charity; that the scourges of poverty, disease and ignorance will be made to disappear from the earth, and that, in the goodness of time, all peoples will come to live together in a peace guaranteed by the binding force of mutual respect and love.

86. Bob Dylan, "Masters of War"

(1963)

On Bob Dylan's second album, he followed Dwight Eisenhower's critique of the military-industrial complex, naming those who profit from militarism "Masters of War." Born Robert Zimmerman, Dylan (1941–) grew up in Hibbing, Minnesota, and went on to become arguably the twentieth century's most important popular music songwriter. After a brief stint at the University of Minnesota, Dylan moved to New York City and visited with folk singer–songwriter Woody Guthrie, then hospitalized with Huntington's chorea. Modeling himself and his songwriting style on Guthrie, Dylan stirred the folk music scene in New York's Greenwich Village, and soon landed a Columbia Records contract. In addition to "Masters of War," his second record, *The Freewheelin' Bob Dylan*, included the classics "Blowin' in the Wind," "A Hard Rain's A-Gonna Fall," and "Don't Think Twice, It's Alright." Although Dylan turned away from overtly political songwriting a few years later, he dusted off "Masters of War" at the start of the first Iraq War when he and his band performed it on the 1991 Grammy Awards telecast.

SOURCE: Bob Dylan, *The Freewheelin' Bob Dylan* (Columbia Records CK 8786, 1963).

Come you masters of war
You that build the big guns
You that build the death planes
You that build all the bombs
You that hide behind walls
You that hide behind desks
I just don't want you to know
I can see through your masks

You that never done nothin'
But build to destroy
You play with my world

Like it's your little toy
You put a gun in my hand
And you hide from my eyes
And you turn and run farther
When the fast bullets fly

Like Judas of old
You lie and deceive
A world war can be won
You want me to believe
But I see through your eyes
And I see through your brain
Like I see through the water
That runs down my drain

You fasten all the triggers
For the others to fire
Then you set back and watch
When the death count gets higher
You hide in your mansion
As the young people's blood
Flows out of their bodies
And is buried in the mud

You've thrown the worst fear
That can ever be hurled
Fear to bring children
Into the world
For threatening my baby
Unborn and unnamed
You ain't worth the blood
That runs in your veins

How much do I know
To talk out of turn
You might say that I'm young
You might say I'm unlearned
But there's one thing I know
Though I'm younger than you
Even Jesus would never
Forgive what you do

Let me ask you one question
Is your money that good
Will it buy you forgiveness
Do you think that it could
I think you will find

When your death takes its toll
All the money you made
Will never buy back your soul

And I hope that you die
And your death'll come soon
I will follow your casket
In the pale afternoon
And I'll watch while you're lowered
Down to your deathbed
And I'll stand o'er your grave
'Til I'm sure that you're dead

87. Thomas Merton, "A Devout Meditation in Memory of Adolf Eichmann"

(1966)

In this essay, Thomas Merton uses a meditation on the 1961 trial of Nazi war criminal Adolf Eichmann to comment on the dangers of sane leaders who, in his view, are leading the world toward nuclear annihilation. Born and raised in France, Merton (1915–68) graduated from Columbia University, where he also converted to Catholicism. In 1941, he entered the Abbey of Gethsemani in Kentucky and became a Trappist monk. Merton became internationally known for his prolific writings through the 1950s and 1960s, and identified with the causes of racial equality and peace. Here, Merton follows political theorist Hannah Arendt's comment that Eichmann, during his trial, came across as the epitome of the "banality of evil." This man who had condemned so many to their horrific deaths seemed not psychotic, but utterly common. Merton, for his part, notes that in the coming war, it will not be an insane person who aims the missile and presses the button; rather, it will be sane ones "who coolly estimate how many millions of victims can be considered expendable in a nuclear war."

SOURCE: Thomas Merton, *Raids on the Unspeakable* (New York: New Directions, 1966).

ONE OF THE MOST disturbing facts that came out in the Eichmann trial was that a psychiatrist examined him and pronounced him *perfectly sane*. I do not doubt it at all, and that is precisely why I find it disturbing.

If all the Nazis had been psychotics, as some of their leaders probably were, their appalling cruelty would have been in some sense easier to understand. It is much worse to consider this calm, "well-balanced," unperturbed official conscientiously going about his desk work, his administrative job which happened to be the supervision of mass murder. He was thoughtful, orderly, unimaginative. He had a profound respect for system, for law and order. He was obedient, loyal, a faithful officer of a great state. He served his government very well.

He was not bothered much by guilt. I have not heard that he developed any psychosomatic illnesses. Apparently he slept well. He had a good appetite, or so it seems. True, when he visited Auschwitz, the Camp Commandant, Hoess, in a spirit of sly deviltry, tried to tease the big boss and scare him with some of the sights. Eichmann was disturbed, yes. He was disturbed. Even Himmler had been disturbed, and had gone weak at the knees. Perhaps, in the same way, the general manager of a big steel mill might be disturbed if an accident took place while he happened to be somewhere in the plant. But of course what happened at Auschwitz was not an accident: just the routine unpleasantness of the daily task. One must shoulder the burden of daily monotonous work for the Fatherland. Yes, one must suffer discomfort and even nausea from unpleasant sights and sounds. It all comes under the heading of duty, self-sacrifice, and obedience. Eichmann was devoted to duty, and proud of his job.

The sanity of Eichmann is disturbing. We equate sanity with a sense of justice, with humaneness, with prudence, with the capacity to love and understand other people. We rely on the sane people of the world to preserve it from barbarism, madness, destruction. And now it begins to dawn on us that it is precisely the *sane* ones who are the most dangerous.

It is the sane ones, the well-adapted ones, who can without qualms and without nausea aim the missiles and press the buttons that will initiate the great festival of destruction that they, *the sane ones,* have prepared. What makes us so sure, after all, that the danger comes from a psychotic getting into a position to fire the first shot in a nuclear war? Psychotics will be suspect. No one suspects the sane, and the sane ones will have *perfectly good reasons,* logical, well-adjusted reasons, for firing the shot. They will be obeying sane orders that have come sanely down the chain of command. And because of their sanity they will have no qualms at all. When the missiles take off, then, *it will be no mistake.*

We can no longer assume that because a man is "sane" he is therefore in his "right mind." The whole concept of sanity in a society where spiritual values have lost their meaning is itself meaningless. A man can be "sane" in the limited sense that he is not impeded by his disordered emotions from acting in a cool, orderly manner, according to the needs and dictates of the social situation in which he finds himself. He can be perfectly "adjusted." God knows, perhaps such people can be perfectly adjusted even in hell itself.

AND SO I ask myself: what is the meaning of a concept of sanity that excludes love, considers it irrelevant, and destroys our capacity to love other human beings, to respond to their needs and their sufferings, to recognize them also as persons, to apprehend their pain as one's own? Evidently this is not necessary for "sanity" at all. It is a religious notion, a spiritual notion, a Christian notion. What business have we to equate "sanity" with "Christianity?" None at all, obviously. The worst error is to imagine that a Christian must try to be "sane" like everybody else, that we belong in our kind of society. That we must be "realistic" about it. We must develop a sane Christianity: and there have been plenty of sane Christians in the past. Torture is nothing new, is it? We ought to be able to rationalize a little brainwashing, and genocide, and find a place for nuclear war, or at least for napalm bombs, in our moral theology. Certainly some of us are doing our best along those lines already. There are hopes! Even Christians can shake off their sentimental prejudices about charity, and become sane like Eichmann. They can even cling to a certain set of Christian formulas, and fit them into a Totalist Ideology. Let them talk about justice, charity, love, and the rest. These words have not stopped some sane men from acting very sanely and cleverly in the past . . .

No, Eichmann was sane. The generals and fighters on both sides, in World War II, the ones who carried out the total destruction of entire cities, these were the sane ones. Those who have invented and developed atomic bombs, thermonuclear bombs, missiles; who have planned the strategy of the next war; who have evaluated the various possibilities of using bacterial and chemical agents: these are not the crazy people, they are the *sane* people. The ones who coolly estimate how many millions of victims can be considered expendable in a nuclear war, I presume they do all right with the Rorschach ink blots too. On the other hand, you will probably find that pacifists and the ban-the-bomb people are, quite seriously, just as we read in Time, a little crazy.

I am beginning to realize that "sanity" is no longer a value or an end in itself. The "sanity" of modern man is about as useful to him as the huge bulk and muscles of the dinosaur. If he were a little less sane, a little more doubtful, a little more aware of his absurdities and contradictions, perhaps there might be a possibility of his survival. But if he is sane, too sane . . . perhaps we must say that in a society like ours the worst insanity is to be totally without anxiety, totally "sane."

88. John Hope Franklin, "America's Window to the World: Her Race Problem"

(1956)

In this address, delivered to the Catholic Interracial Council in New York, the nation's foremost black historian, John Hope Franklin places the issue of racial segregation squarely in a Cold War context. Franklin (1915–) grew up in Oklahoma and graduated from Fisk University before going on to get his Ph.D. at Harvard. In the 1950s, he taught at Howard University before Brooklyn College, in 1956, appointed him not only the first black historian to make full professor at a white institution in the United States, but also chairman of the history department. Perhaps his best-known book, *From Slavery to Freedom*, first published in 1947, has gone on to sell, in multiple editions, more than 3.5 million copies. Franklin here describes—in a way the Eisenhower and Kennedy administrations soon learned—that the continued racial injustice in the South caused people around the world to doubt American Cold War boasts of freedom and equality.

SOURCE: Reprinted in Peter B. Levy, ed., *Let Freedom Ring: A Documentary History of the Modern Civil Rights Movement* (New York: Praeger, 1992), 22–24.

There was a time when we in the United States could make a sharp distinction between those problems and policies having to do with our foreign relations and those having to do with our domestic relations. That distinction was always more apparent than real. Now it can hardly be said to exist at all. The contraction of the world that has come with the transportation and communication revolution and the worldwide drive toward political, social and economic democracy have certainly reduced any apparent distinctions between foreign and domestic problems. I believe, too, that there has been an increasing recognition on the part of the countries of the world of the ramifications and implications of the most intimate domestic problems and their inevitable involvement, under certain conditions, with the most delicate and difficult problems in foreign affairs. Thus, an American delegate to the current General Assembly to the United

Nations can argue before an Assembly Committee that when any nation violates the human-rights pledges of the Charter its violation is "a matter of concern to all of us."

This comment was in connection with the question of whether or not apartheid in South Africa was the business of the United Nations or any of its members other than the Union of South Africa. Twelve years ago, when a group of American Negroes called the attention of the United Nations to some of the more sordid aspects of the American race problem in a document called "An Appeal to the World," the effort was almost universally condemned here as a deliberate attempt to embarrass the United States by holding up to ridicule a problem that was peculiarly domestic. [Editor's note: this document was co-authored by W.E.B. DuBois.] It may be seriously doubted that the people of the United States would relish such a discussion of the American race problem any more today than they did twelve years ago. . . .

Whether we like it or not, many peoples of the world study race relations in the United States not merely because of their interests in the advancement of interracial justice but also to discover, if they can, the good faith or lack of it on the part of the United States in its relations with other countries. They are convinced that they can get a better understanding of the position of the United States on a vital matter by examining the status of race relations than by reading a lengthy and learned pronouncement. While they are not altogether correct in this conviction it is nevertheless a firm one with many peoples in other parts of the world. Thus they continue to peer through the window of race relations that gives a remarkable picture of American life to the world. . . .

These peoples are constantly asking themselves if the United States can be trusted to lead the world toward greater freedom for all and toward a greater recognition of the dignity of the individual. They are convinced that the answer is not to be found in the amount of military, financial and material aid given so generously by this country to the less fortunate. Rather the answer is to be found in the manner in which this country seeks to protect the rights of human beings in the area of equality, freedom and justice. . . .

When one calls our attention to the fact that the inability of the people of the United States to extend equality and justice to all its citizens is loosing friends for the United States throughout the world, we frequently shout that this is a Communist line. People who have cautioned this country that its relations were hurting an effective and constructive foreign policy have frequently been criticized as having fallen under some foreign un-American spell. But outrage or disgust with the criticism cannot wash it away. Nor can the sins of this country be expiated by the search, in which so many have indulged in recent years, for racial discrimination in the Soviet Union. It should be of no consolation to any American to learn that there is racial discrimination in the Soviet Union, if such exists. It would seem quite irrelevant to any discussion of America's position, anyway.

In the first place, we, not the Russians, have been proclaiming to the world for more than a century and a half that we subscribe to the doctrine of equality of all men. We have, therefore, set ourselves a goal that we have not attained and which a considerable number of Americans actively oppose. And this the entire world knows. . . .

We are extremely vulnerable not merely because we have our deficiencies but also because we do have our strengths, one of which is our willingness to let the world know what goes on here. . . .

In so many respects, then, race relations is our big window, our picture window, to the world. What would we like for those who gaze in upon us to see? We would, of course, like to have our observers see us as a people who not only subscribe to the principles of equality but who put these principles into practice in every conceivable way. We would want them to see us making no discrimination or segregation among peoples on the highly questionable grounds of race or creed. We would want them to see us extending to every person in the United States the rights and privileges to which we as a nation are committed: the right to equality of opportunity to make of oneself what one can, to security of one's person, to be free of the indignities that degrade human beings, to move freely among one's fellows, and to exercise all the responsibilities and privileges of citizenship. If they could look in on us and see these practices, they would then have more confidence in our preachments and would attach more importance and meaning to them. They would also have infinitely more confidence in our seriousness of purpose as we set up goals of equality and freedom for peoples in other parts of the world. . . .

Perhaps there are those among us who do not care what others think of us. We have all seen the shrug of the shoulder of some of our fellows when it was suggested that the esteem in which we were held abroad was low because of our inhumanity to each other. If enough of us shrug our shoulders and assume an attitude of indifference in this matter we shall speed the process of disrespect of other peoples for us and add to the lack of confidence they have in us. In less time than we can imagine we shall have lost our position as a moral leader in the world and when that is gone our military and economic leadership will have little value. If people begin to regard us as fundamentally incapable of achieving interracial justice at home, they will begin to turn their faces from us. It will then be too late to make explanations based on legalisms and the splitting of hairs. . . .

89. Pittsburgh Courier,
"'Satchmo' Tells Off Ike, U.S.!"

(1957)

This 1957 article, published in a leading African American newspaper, reflected the extent to which resistance to integration in the Jim Crow South became a Cold War embarrassment. The story reports jazz legend Louis Armstrong's reaction to Arkansas governor Orval Faubus's efforts to keep nine black children from enrolling at Little Rock's Central High School, despite the Supreme Court's 1954 *Brown v. Board of Education* ruling declaring racial segregation in schools unconstitutional. Armstrong (1901–1971) was not known for political pronouncements, but in this case, he canceled plans for a proposed goodwill tour of the Soviet Union sponsored by the State Department. He was surely the best-known jazz musician in the world at the time, and his comments caught the Eisenhower administration by surprise. Although his manager tried to downplay the incident, and although some southern radio stations threw out his records, Armstrong did not back down. In the global struggle of ideologies, the United States and the Soviet Union competed for allies among newly independent nations of Africa and Asia, and the violent acts of American racists—sometimes tolerated by the state—made for bad press for the United States. In 1956, Armstrong had gone to Ghana on an unofficial tour, and the State Department took notice of the great publicity generated by this visit from "Ambassador Satch." Little Rock ruined government hopes of harnessing Armstrong's popularity as a "jambassador." Secretary of State John Foster Dulles said Little Rock was "ruining our foreign policy."

When Eisenhower finally sent in paratroopers to disperse the angry mob in Little Rock and escort the nine students into the school, Armstrong sent a telegram to the White House: "If you decide to walk into the schools with the little colored kids, take me along, Daddy." In 1961, when Armstrong recorded "The Real Ambassadors" with Dave Brubeck, it included the line "Forget Moscow—when do we play New Orleans?"

SOURCE: *Pittsburgh Courier*, September 28, 1957.

Armstrong Blasts Bias In America

Turns Down Paid Trip To Russia!

FARGO, N.D.—Louis (Pops) Armstrong, in the rapid fire manner of the jazz classic, "Little Rock Getaway," has not only "sounded" on Uncle Same's treatment of "his people" once more, but has also blown some awfully sour notes in the direction of road manager Pierre Tallerie.

Tallerie earned the invective of "Pops" when he told reporters that Louis, who had blasted U. S. jim crow, had turned down a State Department tour was "sorry he spouted off."

Louis' reactions were such that there is a strong possibility that Mr. Tallerie may be removed from his job. Armstrong told the Courier, "As much as I'm trying to do for my people, this road man, Tallerie, whom I've respected for 20 years, although I've suspected him of being prejudiced, has worked with Negro musicians and made his money off them, has proved that he hates Negroes the first time he opened his mouth, and I don't see why Mr. (Joe) Giaser (booking agent) doesn't remove him from this band.

"He has done more harm than good. I can't see why Mr. Giaser doesn't transfer him to a white band where he belongs. Everything Tallerie said he made it up with that newspaperman without my signature."

"I wouldn't take back a thing I've said. I've had a beautiful life over 40 years in music, but I feel the downtrodden situation the same as any other Negro. My parents and family suffered through all of that old South and things are new now, and Tallerie and no prejudiced newspaper can make me change it. What I've said is me. I feel that."

After Tallerie had spoken to white reporters, Armstrong stated, "I was hot . . . and am still hot . . . over the school situation in Arkansas and the way Governor Faubus has mishandled it.

"My people . . . the Negroes . . . are not looking for anything . . . we just want a square shake. But when I see on television and read about a crowd spitting on and cursing at a little colored girl . . . I think I have a right to get sore and say something about it."

With respect to the proposed trip to Russia under State Department auspices, Louis said, "Maybe I will . . . if they do something to straighten out that Arkansas mess. After all, America is my country, too, and I've always tried to do anything I could to help it. But do you dig me when I say I still have a right to blow my top over injustice?"

LOUIS' SPURNING of the proposed trip had hit the headlines last week in Grand Forks, N. D., when Louis announced that he was going to spurn the trip to the Soviet.

Louis had then explained: "The people over there ask me what's wrong with my country. What am I supposed to say? The way they are treating my people in the South, the government can go to hell."

"Pops" had also described President Eisenhower as being "two-faced" and having "no guts." Louis asserted that the President was allowing the Governor of Arkansas to run the Federal Government.

It's getting almost so bad a colored man hasn't got any country," said Armstrong. Louis also had choice words to say about Faubus, whose action he called a "publicity stunt by the greatest of all publicity hounds."

Louis had some kind words for the South's "intelligent white people," noting, "It's the bad lower class people who make all the noise." As for Federal Judge Ronald N. Davies of Fargo, "He's the greatest man down there. I hope North Dakota has a lot more like him!"

* * *

STATE DEPARTMENT spokesmen have been singularly reticent about the Armstrong sounds.

In fact, Lincoln White merely observed, "Mr. Armstrong has made a tremendous hit wherever he has gone and we've always been pleased when he traveled abroad."

The Armstrong statements also shocked many of his critics who have long put him in the ranks of the "Uncle Tom's" because of his willingness to play before segregated audiences in the South.

90. Fair Play for Cuba Committee, "Cuba: A Declaration of Conscience by Afro-Americans"

(1961)

The Fair Play for Cuba Committee's advertisement in the April 25, 1961, *New York Post* followed by eight days the failed Bay of Pigs invasion. The committee had been formed in New York in 1960 when the Eisenhower administration, in reaction to Fidel Castro's nationalization of hundreds of millions of dollars' worth of American-owned property, moved to isolate Cuba economically by suspending all U.S. purchases of sugar from the island. Just as many African Americans found solidarity and common cause with the twenty-three African nations achieving independence from colonial rule between 1950 and 1960, many likewise saw the Cuban Revolution as throwing off the yoke of (American) imperialism. Anticipating that the Kennedy administration could yet launch an invasion of Cuba, the signers of the Declaration of Conscience—who included such luminaries as W.E.B. DuBois, Maya Angelou, and LeRoi Jones—warned that it would be a blow against civil rights in the United States.

SOURCE: Paid advertisement in the *New York Post*, April 25, 1961.

Because we have known oppression, because we have suffered more than other Americans, because we are still fighting for our own liberation from tyranny, we Afro-Americans have the right and the duty to raise our voices in protest against the forces of oppression that now seek to crush a free people linked to us by bonds of blood and a common heritage.

One-third of Cuba's people are Afro-Cubans, of the same African descent as we. Many of our own forefathers passed through Cuba on their way to the slave plantations in the United States. Those who remained on the island knew the same brutality that their brothers suffered on the mainland. After emancipation, they too knew disenfranchisement, they too became second-class citizens, peons exploited on the huge U.S.-owned landholdings.

Today, thanks to a social revolution which they helped make, Afro-Cubans are first-class citizens and are taking their rightful place in the life of their country where all racial barriers crumbled in a matter of weeks following the victory of Fidel Castro.

Now our brothers are threatened again—this time by a gang of ousted white Cuban politicians who find segregated Miami more congenial than integrated Havana. We charge that this group of mercenaries who hope to turn back the clock in Cuba are armed, trained and financed by the U.S. Central Intelligence Agency. This criminal aggression against a peaceful and progressive people must not be allowed to continue. But if it does, we are determined to do all we possibly can to hinder the success of this crime.

William Worthy, foreign correspondent for the Baltimore *Afro-American,* declared recently: "If Cuba is attacked, I and others who know the facts will denounce the attack as an evil and wicked colonial war deserving of opposition and resistance by Afro-Americans." Worthy warned that, if such an attack took place: "In this country we would see civil rights setbacks from coast to coast. Our enemies would be strengthened and emboldened."

Afro-Americans won't be fooled. The enemies of the Cubans are our enemies: the Jim Crow bosses of this land where we are still denied our rights. The Cubans are our friends. The Cubans are the enemies of our enemies.

CHAPTER

NINE

The Vietnam War, Part I: Johnson's War

91. Lyndon B. Johnson, "The Johns Hopkins Speech"

(1965)

Not long after the first American combat troops arrived in Vietnam, President Lyndon Johnson gave this speech at Johns Hopkins University. Johnson (1908–1973), without the kind of clear mandate for war given by Congress in 1917 and 1941, and without a precipitate act of enemy aggression as in Korea in 1950, found himself needing to explain in some detail the rationale for going to war in Vietnam. A Texan who came to Congress in 1938 and in time became Senate majority leader and vice president, Johnson, like his predecessors, was a fierce Cold Warrior. By 1965, most Americans accepted the continuing foreign policy aimed at containing communism around the world, but most were ignorant of Vietnam and its history. In the Johns Hopkins speech, the president misled his audience on two key points: (1) by stating that North Vietnam had "attacked the independent nation of South Vietnam," and (2) by implying that China was somehow orchestrating the North Vietnamese war on the South. Moreover, Johnson suggests that aggression must be met with force because, referencing World War II, "the central lesson of our time is that the appetite of aggression is never satisfied." In a Defense Department film, *Why Vietnam?* (1965), which relied in part on footage from the Johns Hopkins speech, that same parallel was drawn more directly, suggesting that, like Hitler and the Nazis, Ho Chi Minh would not stop with the conquest of South Vietnam. Only twenty years after V-E Day, such rhetoric resonated strongly with the American public.

SOURCE: Public Papers of the Presidents, *Lyndon B. Johnson, 1965* (Washington, D.C.: Government Printing Office, 1966), 394–98.

. . . Tonight Americans and Asians are dying for a world where each people may choose its own path to change.

This is the principle for which our ancestors fought in the valleys of Pennsylvania. It is the principle for which our sons fight in the jungles of Vietnam.

Vietnam is far from this quiet campus. We have no territory there, nor do we seek any. The war is dirty and brutal and difficult. And some 400 young men, born into an America bursting with opportunity and promise, have ended their lives on Vietnam's steaming soil.

Why must we take this painful road?

Why must this nation hazard its ease, its interest, and its power for the sake of a people so far away?

We fight because we must fight if we are to live in a world where every country can shape its own destiny. And only in such a world will our own freedom be finally secure.

This kind of a world will never be built by bombs or bullets. Yet the infirmities of man are such that force must often precede reason, and the waste of war, the works of peace.

We wish this were not so. But we must deal with the world as it is, if it is ever to be as we wish.

The world as it is in Asia is not a serene or peaceful place. The first reality is that North Vietnam has attacked the independent nation of South Vietnam. Its object is total conquest.

Of course, some of the people of South Vietnam are participating in this attack on their own government. But trained men and supplies, orders and arms, flow in a constant stream from North to South.

This support is the heartbeat of the war.

And it is a war of unparalleled brutality. Simple farmers are the targets of assassination and kidnapping. Women and children are strangled in the night because their men are loyal to their Government. Small and helpless villages are ravaged by sneak attacks. Large-scale raids are conducted on towns, and terror strikes in the heart of cities.

The confused nature of this conflict cannot mask the fact that it is the new face of an old enemy. It is an attack by one country upon another. And the object of that attack is a friend to which we are pledged.

Over this war, and all Asia, is another reality: the deepening shadow of Communist China. The rulers in Hanoi are urged on by Peking. This is a regime which has destroyed freedom in Tibet, attacked India, and been condemned by the United Nations for aggression in Korea. It is a nation which is helping the forces of violence in almost every continent. The contest in Vietnam is part of a wider pattern of aggressive purpose.

Why are these realities our concern? Why are we in South Vietnam? We are there because we have a promise to keep. Since 1954 every American President has offered support to the people of South Vietnam. We have helped to build, and we have helped to defend. Thus, over many years, we have made a national pledge to help South Vietnam defend its independence. And I intend to keep our promise.

To dishonor that pledge, to abandon this small and brave nation to its enemy, and to the terror that must follow, would be an unforgivable wrong.

We are also there to strengthen world order. Around the globe, from Berlin to Thailand, are people whose well-being rests, in part, on the belief that they can count on us if they are attacked. To leave Vietnam to its fate would shake the confidence of all these people in the value of American commitment, the value of America's word. The result would be increased unrest and instability, and even wider war.

We are also there because there are great stakes in the balance. Let no one think for a moment that retreat from Vietnam would bring an end to conflict. The battle would be renewed in one country and then another. The central lesson of our time is that the appetite of aggression is never satisfied. To withdraw from one battlefield means only to prepare for the next. We must say in Southeast Asia, as we did in Europe, in the words of the Bible: "Hitherto shalt thou come, but no further."

There are those who say that all our effort there will be futile, that China's power is such it is bound to dominate all Southeast Asia. But there is no end to that argument until all the nations of Asia are swallowed up.

There are those who wonder why we have a responsibility there. We have it for the same reason we have a responsibility for the defense of freedom in Europe. World War II was fought in both Europe and Asia, and when it ended we found ourselves with continued responsibility for the defense of freedom.

Our objective is the independence of South Vietnam, and its freedom from attack. We want nothing for ourselves, only that the people of South Vietnam be allowed to guide their own country in their own way.

We will do everything necessary to reach that objective. And we will do only what is absolutely necessary.

In recent months, attacks on South Vietnam were stepped up. Thus it became necessary to increase our response and to make attacks by air. This is not a change of purpose. It is a change in what we believe that purpose requires.

We do this in order to slow down aggression.

We do this to increase the confidence of the brave people of South Vietnam who have bravely borne this brutal battle for so many years and with so many casualties.

And we do this to convince the leaders of North Vietnam, and all who seek to share their conquest, of a very simple fact:

We will not be defeated.

We will not grow tired.

We will not withdraw, either openly or under the cloak of a meaningless agreement.

We know that air attacks alone will not accomplish all these purposes. But it is our best and prayerful judgment that they are a necessary part of the surest road to peace.

We hope that peace will come swiftly. But that is in the hands of others besides ourselves. And we must be prepared for a long, continued conflict. It will require patience as well as bravery, the will to endure as well as the will to resist.

I wish it were possible to convince others with words of what we now find it necessary to say with guns and planes: Armed hostility is futile. Our resources are equal to any challenge because we fight for values and we fight for principles, rather than territory or colonies. Our patience and determination are unending.

Once this is clear, then it should also be clear that the only path for reasonable men is the path of peaceful settlement.

Such peace demands an independent South Vietnam securely guaranteed and able to shape its own relationships to all others, free from outside interference, tied to no alliance, a military base for no other country.

These are the essentials of any final settlement.

We will never be second in the search for such a peaceful settlement in Vietnam.

There may be many ways to this kind of peace: in discussion or negotiation with the governments concerned; in large groups or in small ones; on the reaffirmation of old agreements or their strengthening with new ones.

We have stated this position over and over again fifty times and more, to friend and foe alike. And we remain ready with this purpose, for unconditional discussions.

And until that bright and necessary day of peace we will try to keep conflict from spreading. We have no desire to see thousands die in battle, Asians or Americans. We have no desire to devastate that which the people of North Vietnam have built with toil and sacrifice. We will use our power with restraint and with all the wisdom we can command. But we will use it.

This war, like most wars, is filled with terrible irony. For what do the people of North Vietnam want? They want what their neighbors also desire: food for their hunger, health for their bodies and a chance to learn, progress for their country, and an end to the bondage of material misery. And they would find all these things far more readily in peaceful association with others than in the endless course of battle.

These countries of Southeast Asia are homes for millions of impoverished people. Each day these people rise at dawn and struggle until the night to wrest existence from the soil. They are often wracked by disease, plagued by hunger, and death comes at the early age of 40.

Stability and peace do not come easily in such a land. Neither independence nor human dignity will ever be won by arms alone. It also requires the works of peace.

The American people have helped generously in times past in these works.

Now there must be a much more massive effort to improve the life of man in the conflict-torn corner of our world.

The first step is for the countries of Southeast Asia to associate themselves in a greatly expanded cooperative effort for development. We would hope that North Vietnam will take its place in the common effort just as soon as peaceful cooperation is possible.

The United Nations is already actively engaged in development in this area, and as far back as 1961 I conferred with our authorities in Vietnam in connection with their work there.

I would hope that the Secretary-General of the United Nations could use the prestige of his great office, and his deep knowledge of Asia, to initiate, as soon as possible, with the countries of the area, a plan for cooperation in increased development.

For our part I will ask the Congress to join in a billion-dollar American investment in this effort as soon as it is under way.

And I hope all other industrialized countries, including the Soviet Union, will join in this effort to replace despair with hope, and terror with progress.

The task is nothing less than to enrich the hopes and existence of more than a hundred million people. And there is much to be done.

The vast Mckong River can provide food and water and power on a scale to dwarf even our own TVA.

The wonders of modern medicine can be spread through villages where thousands die every year from lack of care. Schools can be established to train people in the skills that are needed to manage the process of development.

And these objectives, and more, are within the reach of a cooperative and determined effort.

I also intend to expand and speed up a program to make available our farm surplus to assist in feeding and clothing the needy in Asia. We should not allow people to go hungry and wear rags while our own warehouses overflow with an abundance of wheat and corn, rice and cotton.

I will very shortly name a special team of patriotic and distinguished Americans to inaugurate our participation in these programs. This team will be headed by Mr. Eugene Black, the very able former president of the World Bank.

In areas still ripped by conflict, of course, development will not be easy. Peace will be necessary for final success. But we cannot wait for peace to begin the job.

This will be a disorderly planet for a long time. In Asia, as elsewhere, the forces of the modern world are shaking old ways and uprooting ancient civilizations. There will be turbulence and struggle and even violence. Great social change, as we see in our own country, does not always come without conflict.

We must also expect that nations will on occasion be in dispute with us. It may be because we are rich, or powerful, or because we have made mistakes, or because they honestly fear our intentions. However, no nation need ever fear that we desire their land, or to impose our will, or to dictate their institutions.

But we will always oppose the effort of one nation to conquer another nation. We will do this because our own security is at stake.

But there is more to it than that. For our generation has a dream. It is a very old dream. But we have the power and now we have the opportunity to make it come true.

For centuries, nations have struggled among each other. But we dream of a world where disputes are settled by law and reason. And we will try to make it so.

For most of history men have hated and killed one another in battle. But we dream of an end to war. And we will try to make it so.

For all existence most men have lived in poverty, threatened by hunger. But we dream of a world where all are fed and charged with hope. And we will help to make it so.

The ordinary men and women of North Vietnam and South Vietnam—of China and India—of Russia and America—are brave people. They are filled with the same proportions of hate and fear, of love and hope. Most of them want the same things for themselves and their families. Most of them do not want their sons ever to die in battle, or see the homes of others destroyed. . . .

Every night before I turn out the lights to sleep, I ask myself this question: Have I done everything that I can do to unite this country? Have I done everything I can to help unite the world, to try to bring peace and hope to all the peoples of the world? Have I done enough?

Ask yourselves that question in your homes and in this hall tonight. Have we done all we could? Have we done enough?

We may well be living in the time foretold many years ago when it was said: "I call heaven and earth to record this day against you, that I have set before you life and death, blessing and cursing: therefore choose life, that both thou and thy seed may live."

This generation of the world must choose: destroy or build, kill or aid, hate or understand.

We can do all these things on a scale never dreamed of before.

We will choose life. And so doing we will prevail over the enemies within man, and over the natural enemies of all mankind.

92. Paul Potter, Speech at Antiwar Demonstration, Washington, D.C."

(1965)

Just as President Johnson escalated the ground war in Vietnam, Students for a Democratic Society (SDS) organized the first major demonstration against the war. On April 17, 1965, approximately 25,000 people went to Washington to protest. Compared to later demonstrations, this one was relatively small, but against the backdrop of the larger Cold War and with most Americans generally supporting Johnson's Vietnam policies, the SDS protest was almost shocking. SDS was founded in 1962 when sixty student organizers issued the Port Huron Statement, a critique of racism, the military-industrial complex, and the alienation created by a society governed by the massive institutions of government, corporations, and universities. It called for a "participatory democracy" in which Americans would take part in making the decisions that shaped their daily lives. At first, SDS focused most of its organizing efforts on university campuses, but in 1965, it started to take a leading role in opposing the Vietnam War. Paul Potter (1939–1984) grew up in Mahomet, Illinois and Charlotte, Michigan. As a student at Oberlin College, he became involved with the National Student Association, participated in the civil rights movement in Mississippi, and had attended the Port Huron founding of SDS. In 1965, he became SDS president and in this speech, called the peace movement to "name the system" that seizes the destiny of others in the name of freedom.

SOURCE: Paul Potter, "The Incredible War," speech at Washington antiwar march, April 17, 1965, reprinted in Massimo Teodori, ed., *The New Left: A Documentary History* (New York: Bobbs-Merrill, 1968), 246–48.

The incredible war in Vietnam has provided the razor, the terrifying sharp cutting edge that has finally severed the last vestiges of illusion that morality and democracy are the guiding principles of American foreign policy. The saccharine, self-righteous moralism that promises the Vietnamese a billion dollars of economic aid at the very moment we are delivering billions for economic and social destruction and political repression is rapidly losing what power it might ever have had to reassure us about the decency of our foreign policy. The further we explore the reality of what this country is doing and planning in Vietnam the more we are driven toward the conclusion of Senator Morse[1] that the U.S. may well be the greatest threat to peace in the world today. . . .

The President says that we are defending freedom in Vietnam. Whose freedom? Not the freedom of the Vietnamese. The first act of the first dictator (Diem) the U.S. installed in Vietnam was to systematically begin the persecution of all political opposition, non-Communist as well as Communist. . . .

The pattern of repression and destruction that we have developed and justified in the war is so thorough that it can only be called "cultural genocide." I am not simply talking about napalm or gas or crop destruction or torture hurled indiscriminantly on women and children, insurgent and neutral, upon the first suspicion of rebel activity. That in itself is horrendous and incredible beyond belief. But it is only part of a large pattern of destruction to the very fabric of the country. We have uprooted the people from the land and imprisoned them in concentration camps called "sunrise villages." Through conscription and direct political intervention and control we have broken or destroyed local customs and traditions, trampled upon those things of value which give dignity and purpose to life. . . .

Not even the President can say that this is war to defend the freedom of the Vietnamese people. Perhaps what the President means when he speaks of freedom is the freedom of the Americans.

What in fact has the war done for freedom in America? It has led to even more vigorous governmental efforts to control information, manipulate the press and pressure and persuade the public through distorted or downright dishonest documents such as the White Paper[2] on Vietnam. . . .

The President mocks freedom if he insists that the war in Vietnam is a defense of American freedom. Perhaps the only freedom that this war protects is the freedom of the warhawks in the Pentagon and the State Department to "experiment" with "counter-insurgency" and guerrilla warfare in Vietnam. Vietnam, we may say, is a "laboratory" run by a new breed of gamesmen who approach war as a kind of rational exercise in international power politics. . . .

Thus far the war in Vietnam has only dramatized the demand of ordinary people to have some opportunity to make their own lives, and of their unwillingness, even under incredible odds, to give up the struggle against external domination. We are told however that that struggle can be legitimately suppressed since it might lead to the development of a Communist system—and before that menace, all criticism is supposed to melt.

This is a critical point and there are several things that must be said here—not by way of celebration, but because I think they are the truth. First, if this country were serious about giving the people of Vietnam some alternative to a Com-

---

[1]U.S. Senator Wayne Morse of Oregon, one of only two congressional opponents of the Gulf of Tonkin Resolution in 1964 and a critic of U.S. intervention in Vietnam.

[2]An official statement of government policy.

munist social revolution, that opportunity was sacrificed in 1954 when we helped to install Diem and his repression of non-Communist movements. There is no indication that we were serious about that goal—that we were ever willing to contemplate the risks of allowing the Vietnamese to choose their own destinies. Second, those people who insist now that Vietnam can be neutralized are for the most part looking for a sugar coating to cover the bitter pill. We must accept the consequences that calling for an end of the war in Vietnam is in fact allowing for the likelihood that a Vietnam without war will be a self-styled Communist Vietnam. Third, this country must come to understand that the creation of a Communist country in the world today is not an ultimate defeat. If people are given the opportunity to choose their own lives it is likely that some of them will choose what we have called "Communist systems." . . . And yet the war that we are creating and escalating in Southeast Asia is rapidly eroding the base of independence of North Vietnam as it is forced to turn to China and the Soviet Union.

But the war goes on; the freedom to conduct that war depends on the dehumanization not only of Vietnamese people but of Americans as well; it depends on the construction of a system of premises and thinking that insulates the President and his advisers thoroughly and completely from the human consequences of the decisions they make. I do not believe that the President or Mr. Rusk or Mr. McNamara or even McGeorge Bundy are particularly evil men. If asked to throw napalm on the back of a 10-year-old child they would shrink in horror—but their decisions have led to mutilation and death of thousands and thousands of people.

What kind of system is it that allows "good" men to make those kinds of decisions? What kind of system is it that justifies the U.S. or any country seizing the destinies of the Vietnamese people and using them callously for our own purpose? What kind of system is it that disenfranchises people in the South, leaves millions upon millions of people throughout the country impoverished and excluded from the mainstream and promise of American society, that creates faceless and terrible bureaucracies and makes those the place where people spend their lives and do their work, that consistently puts material values before human values—and still persists in calling itself free and still persists in finding itself fit to police the world? . . .

We must name that system. We must name it, describe it, analyze it, understand it and change it. For it is only when that system is changed and brought under control that there can be any hope for stopping the forces that create a war in Vietnam today or a murder in the South tomorrow. . . .

If the people of this country are to end the war in Vietnam, and to change the institutions which create it, then, the people of this country must create a massive social movement—and if that can be built around the issue of Vietnam, then that is what we must do. . . .

But that means that we build a movement that works not simply in Washington but in communities and with the problems that face people throughout the society. That means that we build a movement that understands Vietnam, in all its horror, as but a symptom of a deeper malaise, that we build a movement that makes possible the implementation of the values that would have prevented Vietnam, a movement based on the integrity of man and a belief in man's capacity to determine his own life; a movement that does not exclude people because they are too poor or have been held down; a movement that has the capacity to tolerate all of the formulations of society that men may choose to strive for; a movement that will build on the new and creative forms of protest that are beginning to emerge, such as the teach-in, and extend their efforts and intensify them; a movement that will not tolerate the escalation or prolongation of this war but will, if necessary, respond to the Administration war effort with massive civil disobedience all over the country that will wrench the country into a confrontation with the issues of the war; a movement that must of necessity reach out to all those people in Vietnam or elsewhere who are struggling to find decency and control for their lives.

For in a strange way the people of Vietnam and the people on this demonstration are united in much more than a common concern that the war be ended. In both countries there are people struggling to build a movement that has the power to change their condition. The system that frustrates these movements is the same. All our lives, our destinies, our very hopes to live depend on our ability to overcome that system. . . .

93. Herblock, "There's Money Enough to Support Both of You"

(1967)

In this editorial cartoon, three-time Pulitzer Prize winner Herblock captures the concerns of many Americans who worried that the U.S. economy could not fund both the war in Vietnam and Lyndon Johnson's ambitious Great Society programs. Born Herbert Lawrence Block (1909–2001), but known professionally as Herblock, the man who would become best known as a syndicated cartoonist based at the *Washington Post* (1946–2001) grew up in Chicago and won a scholarship to the Chicago Art Institute at age twelve. Before moving to the *Post*, he worked at the *Chicago Daily News* and the Newspaper Enterprise Association, and served as a cartoonist during World War II. A legendary satirist, he skewered every president from Herbert Hoover to George W. Bush. Although Richard Nixon showed up in more Herblock cartoons than any other president, Johnson's handling of the Vietnam War won him Herblock's regular attention.

SOURCE: *Washington Post,* August 1, 1967.

**"There's Money Enough To Support Both Of You —
Now, Doesn't That Make You Feel Better?"**

A 1967 Herblock Cartoon, copyright by The Herb Block Foundation

94. James Burnham, "What Is the President Waiting For?"

(1966)

As James Burnham argues in this essay, prior to Korea, Americans understood that, in war, their government's objective was victory. But in Korea and in Vietnam, the strategy of a "limited war" was lost on many Americans. By 1966, Burnham (1905–87) was a well-known conservative political theorist and regular columnist for the *National Review*. Born in Chicago, and a graduate of Princeton and Oxford, Burnham started out as a Trotskyist and was active in the Socialist Workers Party. He abandoned communism during World War II, and around the same time he wrote *The Managerial Revolution* (1941), in which he predicted that a new managerial class would replace the capitalists and communists of the old order. As early as 1944, when he wrote an analysis of postwar Soviet aims for the Office of Strategic Services (forerunner of the CIA), Burnham predicted worldwide domination as the Soviet Union's main ambition. Instead of containment, Burnham called for "offensive-political-subversive warfare" (e.g., propaganda and covert subversion) inside the Soviet Union and its satellites in order to create domestic unrest. At times—as in this essay—he called for tactical use of nuclear weapons by the United States.

SOURCE: *National Review*, June 28, 1966, p. 612.

Defense Secretary McNamara has just announced commitment of 18,000 more troops to the Vietnam war; the total figure is expected to be close to 400,000 by the end of the year. U.S. casualties are now running above 1,000 weekly, more than 100 of them killed. Admitted U.S. plane losses to enemy action are nearing 300. Money costs are said to be at an annual rate of $18 billion and rising. As nonwars go, this is getting rather impressive.

The President's repeated explanations of why U.S. troops are fighting in Vietnam have not been notably persuasive—mostly because they are compounded of irrelevant Liberal abstractions. But he and his aides at least attempt *some* sort of explanation. As to why he continues, in a conflict that has reached this level, to impose such a multitude of restrictions on weapons, tactics and strategy, neither he nor any of his spokesmen has had anything at all to say for a long while. It is time to demand, on this crucial point, an accounting. In truth, the problem can be put in moral terms—a mode much favored in the Presidential rhetoric. By what moral right does the President order hundreds of thousands of young citizens into a distant and most alien land, under conditions that mean death or grievous injury for many thousands of them and hardship for nearly all, and at the same time forbid them to use the most effective available weapons and methods against the enemy.

Those of us who approve firm action in Southeast Asia find ourselves awkwardly placed. We hesitate to criticize the President, because we know this tends to play into the hands of the Vietniks and appeasers; and, in fact, we do wholeheartedly support the President as against the appeasers. Moreover, we realize, or should realize, that in the face of the massive international as well as domestic appeasement pressures, Lyndon Johnson has proved almost incredibly resolute. Criticism thus seems ungrateful as well as inexpedient. But as the war goes on and intensifies, continuing silence from the firm side has the relative effect of multiplying the sounds from the soft. The President's political problem must appear to him to be that of coming to terms with the appeasers—including the appeasers within his official family of making sufficient concessions to them to patch up his consensus. The hard critics he can take for granted.

Prior to the Korean War it would have been assumed that if we (or any other nation) started fighting against an enemy in the field, the objective would be to defeat the enemy force. Besides using the most suitable military, economic and political weapons, suitably employed, in direct relation to the enemy force, this meant shutting off—so far, at any rate, as feasible—the lines of support, supply and recruitment, and excluding any notion of a privileged sanctuary.

Korea and After

These rules are plain common sense. They were junked in the Korean War—in particular by the failure to use nuclear weapons or to bomb the Chinese bases and airfields beyond the Yalu. Though the Korean restrictions were vigorously defended at the time, I have read no subsequent analysis of the Korean War that considers them justified, and many that consider them to have been catastrophically mistaken. The same restrictions plus a number of others are currently imposed in the Vietnam war. To what conceivable purpose?

So far as I know, two and only two reasons have been publicly stated: first, that the war might otherwise escalate to a level involving direct Chinese intervention or general nuclear exchange; second, that the lower key gives a better chance of negotiating a satisfactory settlement with Hanoi. This second argument is ridiculous on its face, and besides has been disproven by experience. Naturally, the strongest inducement for Hanoi to come to terms would be Hanoi's knowledge that it is being badly hurt and was going to hurt much more badly. As for nuclear escalation, it is absurd to think that the Kremlin would hazard Moscow for Southeast Asia. If Peking were irrational enough to try to use one of its half-dozen nuclear bombs against a U.S. carrier or base, that would merely complete the case for wiping out China's nuclear installations. In fact, the U.S. has not had since the Korean War—which was the perfect moment, since at that time the enemy didn't even possess a nuclear arsenal—a better occasion for using nuclear weapons.

Professionals to the Rescue

A nuclear strike or two on a Vietcong concentration or in North Vietnam would be the best guarantee that Chinese troops would *not* intervene. However, Chinese mass intervention is in any case most improbable. The logistics problem would be all but insuperable. China is totally vulnerable to U.S. air attack. Her nuclear installations are at this stage more a hostage than a threat. Many military strategists would add: so much the better if China *did* come in; the Chinese challenge will have to be met some day, and it won't be easier when she has a functioning nuclear weapons system; let her at least be shown that, if she is going to expand, it will have to be in Siberia.

Our inhibited Vietnam strategy does not seem to express the President's own Texan instincts (though it may be in accord with the wheeler-dealer side of his complex nature); it is most certainly counter to the judgment of our professional military leadership. Perhaps the President ought to consider returning to our traditional command structure, under which the Commander-in-Chief sets the prime objectives of combat, and assigns to the professionals the conduct of operations.

95. Marty Robbins, "Ain't I Right?"

(1966)

In this song, country music star Marty Robbins takes on those who protested against the Vietnam War. Robbins (1925–82) came out of Glendale, Arizona, where he dropped out of high school to join the navy during World War II. He hosted a radio show and a television program in Phoenix before moving to Nashville and joining the Grand Ole Opry in 1953. Best known for his 1959 concept album, *Gunfighter Ballads and Trail Songs* (which included the hit "El Paso"), Robbins caught the Cold War wave of fascination with cowboys and the Old West. His simple telling of good versus evil stories continued with "Ain't I Right?" in 1966. For Robbins—and for many Americans—dissenters were made up of a "bearded, bathless bunch" of communist sympathizers.

SOURCE: Columbia Records 4-43651, 1966.

> You came down to this southern town last summer
> To show the folks a brand new way of life
> But all you've shown the folks around here is trouble
> And you've only added misery to their strife
> Your concern is not to help the people
> And I'll say again, though it's been often said
> Your concern is just to bring discomfort, my friend
> And your policy is just a little red
>
> Refrain: Now, ain't I right (ain't he right)
> (ain't he right)
>
> It matters not to you how people suffer
> And should they, you'd consider that a gain
> You bring a lot of trouble to the town and then you leave
> That's part of your Communistic game
> I detect a little Communism
> I can see it in the things ya do

Communism, Socialism call it what you like
There's very little difference in the two

Refrain

Your followers sometimes have been a bearded, bathless bunch
There's even been a minister or two
A priest, a nun, a rabbi and an educated man
Have listened and been taken in by you
Aw, the country's full of two-faced politicians
Who encourage you with words that go like this
Burn your draft card if you like, it's good to disagree
That's a get aquainted Communistic kiss

Refrain

One politician said it would be nice to send some blood
And help the enemy in Vietnam
That's what he says, here's what I say, let's just keep the blood
Instead let's send that politician man
Let's rid the country of the politicians,
Who coddle tramps that march out in our streets
Protesting those who wanna fight for freedom, my friend
This kind of leader makes our country weak

Refrain

Let's look and find the strong and able leaders
It's time we found just how our neighbors stand
If we're to win this war with Communism
Let's fight it here as well as Vietnam
Let's rise as one and meet our obligations
So Communistic boots will never trod
Across the fields of freedom that were given to us
With the blessing of our great almighty God
Across the fields of freedom that were given to us
With the blessing of our great almighty God

96. Martin Luther King Jr., "Beyond Vietnam: Address Delivered to the Clergy and Laymen Concerned about Vietnam"

(1967)

In this speech, delivered at Riverside Church in New York City on April 4, 1967, Martin Luther King Jr. went against the advice of many of his civil rights movement peers and declared his opposition to the Vietnam War. King (1929–68) was born in Atlanta, Georgia, attended Morehouse College, and earned a Ph.D. in theology at Boston University. He burst onto the national scene in 1955–56 as spokesman and leader of the Montgomery bus boycott. Over the next twelve years, he led numerous campaigns against segregation and came to be seen as the most prominent leader of the civil rights movement. In 1964, he was awarded the Nobel Peace Prize. Privately, King had opposed the Vietnam War for years but had hesitated to speak too passionately about it in public out of concern that it might hurt his civil rights efforts. As a result, for some in the antiwar movement, King's speech at Riverside came late. For others, it marked a momentous turning point in the movement against the war. The speech showed that King was a careful student of American-Vietnamese relations, and showed how the war undercut the cause of social justice in the United States and in Vietnam. Exactly one year later, on April 4, 1968, King was assassinated in Memphis.

SOURCE: Reprinted in *A Testament of Hope: The Essential Writings and Speeches of Martin Luther King, Jr.* (New York: Harper One, 1990), 231–44.

A Time to Break Silence

I come to this magnificent house of worship tonight because my conscience leaves me no other choice. I join with you in this meeting because I am in deepest agreement with the aims and work of the organization which has brought us together: Clergy and Laymen Concerned about Vietnam. The recent statement of your executive committee are the sentiments of my own heart and I found myself in full accord when I read its opening lines: "A time comes when silence is betrayal." That time has come for us in relation to Vietnam.

The truth of these words is beyond doubt but the mission to which they call us is a most difficult one. Even when pressed by the demands of inner truth, men do not easily assume the task of opposing their government's policy, especially in time of war. Nor does the human spirit move without great difficulty against all the apathy of conformist thought within one's own bosom and in the surrounding world. Moreover when the issues at hand seem as perplexed as they often do in the case of this dreadful conflict we are always on the verge of being mesmerized by uncertainty; but we must move on.

Some of us who have already begun to break the silence of the night have found that the calling to speak is often a vocation of agony, but we must speak. We must speak with all the humility that is appropriate to our limited vision, but we must speak. And we must rejoice as well, for surely this is the first time in our nation's history that a significant number of its religious leaders have chosen to move beyond the prophesying of smooth patriotism to the high grounds of a firm dissent based upon the mandates of conscience and the reading of history. Perhaps a new spirit is rising among us. If it is, let us trace its movement well and pray that our own inner being may be sensitive to its guidance, for we are deeply in need of a new way beyond the darkness that seems so close around us.

Over the past two years, as I have moved to break the betrayal of my own silences and to speak from the burnings of my own heart, as I have called for radical departures from the destruction of Vietnam, many persons have questioned me about the wisdom of my path. At the heart of their concerns this query has often loomed large and loud: Why are *you* speaking about war, Dr. King? Why are *you* joining the voices of dissent? Peace and civil rights don't mix, they say. Aren't you hurting the cause of your people, they ask? And when I hear them, though I often understand the source of their concern, I am nevertheless greatly saddened, for such questions mean that the inquirers have not really known me, my commitment or my calling. Indeed, their questions suggest that they do not know the world in which they live.

In the light of such tragic misunderstandings, I deem it of signal importance to try to state clearly, and I trust concisely, why I believe that the path from Dexter Avenue Baptist Church—the church in Montgomery, Alabama, where I began my pastorate—leads clearly to this sanctuary tonight.

I come to this platform tonight to make a passionate plea to my beloved nation. This speech is not addressed to Hanoi or to the National Liberation Front. It is not addressed to China or to Russia.

Nor is it an attempt to overlook the ambiguity of the total situation and the need for a collective solution to the tragedy of Vietnam. Neither is it an attempt to make North Vietnam or the National Liberation Front paragons of virtue, nor to overlook the role they can play in a successful resolution of the problem. While they both may have justifiable reason to be suspicious of the good faith of the United States, life and history give eloquent testimony to the fact that conflicts are never resolved without trustful give and take on both sides.

Tonight, however, I wish not to speak with Hanoi and the NLF, but rather to my fellow Americans who, with me, bear the greatest responsibility in ending a conflict that has exacted a heavy price on both continents.

Importance of Vietnam

Since I am a preacher by trade, I suppose it is not surprising that I have seven major reasons for bringing Vietnam into the field of my moral vision. There is at the outset a very obvious and almost facile connection between the war in Vietnam and the struggle I, and others, have been waging in America. A few years ago there was a shining moment in that struggle. It seemed as if there was a real promise of hope for the poor—both black and white—through the poverty program. There were experiments, hopes, new beginnings. Then came the buildup in Vietnam and I watched the program broken and eviscerated as if it were some idle political plaything of a society gone mad on war, and I knew that America would never invest the necessary funds or energies in rehabilitation of its poor so long as adventures like Vietnam continued to draw men and skills and money like some demonic destructive suction tube. So I was increasingly compelled to see the war as an enemy of the poor and to attack it as such.

Perhaps the more tragic recognition of reality took place when it became clear to me that the war was doing far more than devastating the hopes of the poor at home. It was sending their sons and their brothers and their husbands to fight and to die in extraordinarily high proportions relative to the rest of the population. We were taking the black young men who had been crippled by our society and sending them eight thousand miles away to guarantee liberties in Southeast Asia which they had not found in southwest Georgia and East Harlem. So we have been repeatedly faced with the cruel irony of watching Negro and white boys on TV screens as they kill and die together for a nation that has been unable to seat them together in the same schools. So we watch them in brutal solidarity burning the huts of a poor village, but we realize that they would never live on the same block in Detroit. I could not be silent in the face of such cruel manipulation of the poor.

My third reason moves to an even deeper level of awareness, for it grows out of my experience in the ghettos of the North over the last three years—especially the last three summers. As I have walked among the desperate, rejected and angry young men I have told them that Molotov cocktails and rifles would not solve their problems. I have tried to offer them my deepest compassion while maintaining my conviction that social change comes most meaningfully through nonviolent action. But they asked—and rightly so—what about Vietnam? They asked if our own nation wasn't using massive doses of violence to solve its problems, to bring about the changes it wanted. Their questions hit home, and I knew that I could never again raise my voice against the violence of the oppressed in the ghettos without having first spoken clearly to the greatst purveyor of violence in the world today—my own government. For the sake of those boys, for the sake of this government, for the sake of the hundreds of thousands trembling under our violence, I cannot be silent.

For those who ask the question, "Aren't you a civil rights leader?" and thereby mean to exclude me from the movement for peace, I have this further answer. In 1957 when a group of us formed the Southern Christian Leadership Conference, we chose as our motto: "To save the soul of America." We were convinced that we could not limit our vision to certain rights for black people, but instead affirmed the conviction that America would never be free or saved from itself unless the descendants of its slaves were loosed completely from the shackles they still wear. In a way we were agreeing with Langston Hughes, that black bard of Harlem, who had written earlier:

> O, yes,
> I say it plain,
> America never was America to me,
> And yet I swear this oath—
> America will be!

Now, it should be incandescently clear that no one who has any concern for the integrity and life of America today can ignore the present war. If America's soul becomes totally poisoned, part of the autopsy must read Vietnam. It can never be saved so long as it destroys the deepest hopes of men the world over. So it is that those of us who are yet determined that America *will* be are led down the path of protest and dissent, working for the health of our land.

As if the weight of such a commitment to the life and health of America were not enough, another burden of responsibility was placed upon me in 1964; and I cannot forget that the Nobel Prize for Peace was also a commission—a commission to work harder than I had ever worked before "the brotherhood of man." This is a calling that takes me beyond national allegiances, but even if it were not present I would yet have to live with the meaning of my commitment to the ministry of Jesus Christ. To me the relationship of this ministry to the making of peace is so obvious that I sometimes marvel at those who ask me why I am speaking against the war. Could it be that they do not know that the good news was meant for all men—for Communist and capitalist, for their children and ours, for black and for white, for revolutionary and conservative? Have they forgotten that my ministry is in obedience to the one who loved his enemies so fully that he died for them? What then can I say to the "Vietcong" or to Castro or to Mao as a faithful minister of this one? Can I threaten them with death or must I not share with them my life?

Finally, as I try to delineate for you and for myself the road that leads from Montgomery to this place I would have offered all that was most valid if I simply said that I must be true to my conviction that I share with all men the calling to be a son of the living God. Beyond the calling of race or nation or creed is this vocation of sonship and brotherhood, and because I believe that the Father is deeply concerned especially for his suffering and helpless and outcast children, I come tonight to speak for them.

This I believe to be the privilege and the burden of all of us who deem ourselves bound by allegiances and loyalties which are broader and deeper than nationalism and which go beyond our nation's self-defined goals and positions. We are called to speak for the weak, for the voiceless, for victims of our nation and for those it calls enemy, for no document from human hands can make these humans any less our brothers.

Strange Liberators

And as I ponder the madness of Vietnam and search within myself for ways to understand and respond to compassion my mind goes constantly to the people of that peninsula. I speak now not of the soldiers of each side, not of the junta in Saigon, but simply of the people who have been living under the curse of war for almost three continuous decades now. I think of them too because it is clear to me that there will be no meaningful solution there until some attempt is made to know them and hear their broken cries.

They must see Americans as strange liberators. The Vietnamese people proclaimed their own independence in 1945 after a combined French and Japanese occupation, and before the Communist revolution in China. They were led by Ho Chi Minh. Even though they quoted the American Declaration of Independence in their own document of freedom, we refused to recognize them. Instead, we decided to support France in its reconquest of her former colony.

Our government felt then that the Vietnamese people were not "ready" for independence, and we again fell victim to the deadly Western arrogance that has poisoned the international atmosphere for so long. With that tragic decision we rejected a revolutionary government seeking self-determination, and a government that had been established not by China (for whom the Vietnamese have no great love) but by clearly indigenous forces that included some Communists. For the peasants this new government meant real land reform, one of the most important needs in their lives.

For nine years following 1945 we denied the people of Vietnam the right of independence. For nine years we vigorously supported the French in their abortive effort to recolonize Vietnam.

Before the end of the war we were meeting eighty per cent of the French war costs. Even before the French were defeated at Dien Bien Phu, they began to despair of the reckless action, but we did not. We encouraged them with our huge financial and military supplies to continue the war even after they had lost the will. Soon we would be paying almost the full costs of this tragic attempt at recolonization.

After the French were defeated it looked as if independence and land reform would come again through the Geneva agreements. But instead there came the United States, determined that Ho should not unify the temporarily divided nation, and the peasants watched again as we supported one of the most vicious modern dictators—our chosen man, Premier Diem. The peasants watched and cringed as Diem ruthlessly routed out all opposition, supported their extortionist landlords and refused even to discuss reunification with the north. The peasants watched as all this was presided over by U.S. influence and then by increasing numbers of U.S. troops who came to help quell the insurgency that Diem's methods had aroused. When Diem was overthrown they may have been happy, but the long line of military dictatorships seemed to offer no real change—especially in terms of their need for land and peace.

The only change came from America as we increased our troop commitments in support of governments which were singularly corrupt, inept and without popular support. All the while the people read our leaflets and received regular promises of peace and democracy—and land reform. Now they languish under our bombs and consider us—not their fellow Vietnamese—the real enemy. They move sadly and apathetically as we herd them off the land of their fathers into concentration camps where minimal social needs are rarely met. They know they must move or be destroyed by our bombs. So they go—primarily women and children and the aged.

They watch as we poison their water, as we kill a million acres of their crops. They must weep as the bulldozers roar through their areas preparing to destroy the precious trees. They wander into the hospitals, with at least twenty casualties from American firepower for one "Vietcong"-inflicted injury. So far we may have killed a million of them—mostly children. They wander into the towns and see thousands of the children, homeless, without clothes, running in packs on the streets like animals. They see the children degraded by our soldiers as they beg for food. They see the children selling their sisters to our soldiers, soliciting for their mothers.

What do the peasants think as we ally ourselves with the landlords and as we refuse to put any action into our many words concerning land reform? What do they think as we test out our latest weapons on them, just as the Germans tested out new medicine and new tortures in the concentration camps of Europe? Where are the roots of the independent Vietnam we claim to be building? Is it among these voiceless ones?

We have destroyed their two most cherished institutions: the family and the village. We have destroyed their land and their crops. We have cooperated in the crushing of the nation's only non-Communist revolutionary political force—the unified Buddhist church. We have supported the enemies of the peasants of Saigon. We have corrupted their women and children and killed their men. What liberators!

Now there is little left to build on—save bitterness. Soon the only solid physical foundations remaining will be found at our military bases and in the concrete of the concentration camps we call fortified hamlets. The peasants may well wonder if we plan to build our new Vietnam on such grounds as these? Could we blame them for such thoughts? We must speak for them and raise the questions they cannot raise. These too are our brothers.

Perhaps the more difficult but no less necessary task is to speak for those who have been designated as our enemies. What of the National Liberation Front— that strangely anonymous group we call VC or Communists? What must they think of us in America when they realize that we permitted the repression and cruelty of Diem which helped to bring them into being as a resistance group in the south? What do they think of our condoning the violence which led to their own taking up of arms? How can they believe in our integrity when now we speak of "aggression from the north" as if there were nothing more essential to the war? How can they trust us when now we charge them with violence after the murderous reign of Diem and charge them with violence while we pour every new weapon of death into their land? Surely we must understand their feelings even if we do not condone their actions. Surely we must see that the men we supported pressed them to their violence. Surely we must see that our own computerized plans of destruction simply dwarf their greatest acts.

How do they judge us when our officials know that their membership is less than twenty-five percent Communist and yet insist on giving them the blanket name? What must they be thinking when they know that we are aware of their control of major sections of Vietnam and yet we appear ready to allow national elections in which this highly organized political parallel government will have no part? They ask how we can speak of free elections when the Saigon press is censored and controlled by the military junta. And they are surely right to wonder what kind of new government we plan to help form without them—the only party in real touch with the peasants. They question our political goals and they deny the reality of a peace settlement from which they will be excluded. Their questions are frighteningly relevant. Is our nation planning to build on political myth again and then shore it up with the power of new violence?

Here is the true meaning and value of compassion and nonviolence when it helps us to see the enemy's point of view, to hear his questions, to know his assessment of ourselves. For from his view we may indeed see the basic weaknesses of our own condition, and if we are mature, we may learn and grow and profit from the wisdom of the brothers who are called the opposition.

So, too, with Hanoi. In the north, where our bombs now pummel the land, and our mines endanger the waterways, we are met by a deep but understandable mistrust. To speak for them is to explain this lack of confidence in Western words, and especially their distrust of American intentions now. In Hanoi are the men who led the nation to independence against the Japanese and the French, the men who sought membership in the French commonwealth and were betrayed by the weakness of Paris and the willfulness of the colonial armies. It was they who led a second struggle against French domination at tremendous costs, and then were persuaded to give up the land they controlled between the thirteenth and seventeenth parallel as a temporary measure at Geneva. After 1954 they watched us conspire with Diem to prevent elections which would have surely brought Ho Chi Minh to power over a united Vietnam, and they realized they had been betrayed again.

When we ask why they do not leap to negotiate, these things must be remembered. Also it must be clear that the leaders of Hanoi considered the presence of American troops in support of the Diem regime to have been the initial military breach of the Geneva agreements concerning foreign troops, and they remind us that they did not begin to send in any large number of supplies or men until American forces had moved into the tens of thousands.

Hanoi remembers how our leaders refused to tell us the truth about the earlier North Vietnamese overtures for peace, how the president claimed that none existed when they had clearly been made. Ho Chi Minh has watched as America has spoken of peace and built up its forces, and now he has surely heard of the increasing international rumors of American plans for an invasion of the north. He knows the bombing and shelling and mining we are doing are part of traditional pre-invasion strategy. Perhaps only his sense of humor and of irony can save him when he hears the most powerful nation of the world speaking of aggression as its drops thousands of bombs on a poor weak nation more than eight thousand miles away from its shores.

At this point I should make it clear that while I have tried in these last few minutes to give a voice to the voiceless on Vietnam and to understand the arguments of those who are called enemy, I am as deeply concerned about our troops there as anything else. For it occurs to me that what we are submitting them to in Vietnam is not simply the brutalizing process that goes on in any war where armies face each other and seek to destroy. We are adding cynicism to the process of death, for they must know after a short period there that none of the things we claim to be fighting for are really involved. Before long they must know that their government has sent them into a struggle among Vietnamese, and the more sophisticated surely realize that we are on the side of the wealthy and the secure while we create a hell for the poor.

Somehow this madness must cease. We must stop now. I speak as a child of God and brother to the suffering poor of Vietnam. I speak for those whose land is being laid waste, whose homes are being destroyed, whose culture is being subverted. I speak for the poor of America who are paying the double price of smashed hopes at home and death and corruption in Vietnam. I speak as a citizen of the world, for the world as it stands aghast at the path we have taken. I speak as an American to the leaders of my own nation. The great initiative in this war is ours. The initiative to stop it must be ours.

This is the message of the great Buddhist leaders of Vietnam. Recently one of them wrote these words: *Each day the war goes on the hatred increases in the heart of the Vietnamese and in the hearts of those of humanitarian instinct. The Americans are forcing even their friends into becoming their enemies. It is curious that the Americans, who calculate so carefully on the possibilities of military victory, do not realize that in the process they are incurring deep psychological and political defeat. The image of America will never again be the image of revolution, freedom and democracy, but the image of violence and militarism.*

If we continue there will be no doubt in my mind and in the mind of the world that we have no honorable intentions in Vietnam. It will become clear that our minimal expectation is to occupy it as an American colony and men will not refrain from thinking that our maximum hope is to goad China into a war so that we may bomb her nuclear installations. If we do not stop our war against the people of Vietnam immediately the world will be left with no other alternative than to see this as some horribly clumsy and deadly game we have decided to play.

The world now demands a maturity of America that we may not be able to achieve. It demands that we admit that we have been wrong from the beginning of our adventure in Vietnam, that we have been detrimental to the life of the Vietnamese people. The situation is one in which we must be ready to turn sharply from our present ways.

In order to atone for our sins and errors in Vietnam, we should take the initiative in bringing a halt to this tragic war. I would like to suggest five concrete things that our government should do immediately to begin the long and difficult process of extricating ourselves from this nightmarish conflict:

1. *End all bombing in North and South Vietnam.*

2. *Declare a unilateral cease-fire in the hope that such action will create the atmosphere for negotiation.*

3. *Take immediate steps to prevent other battlegrounds in Southeast Asia by curtailing our military buildup in Thailand and our interference in Laos.*

4. *Realistically accept the fact that the National Liberation Front has substantial support in South Vietnam and must thereby play a role in any meaningful negotiations and in any future Vietnam government.*

5. *Set a date that we will remove all foreign troops from Vietnam in accordance with the 1954 Geneva agreement.*

Part of our ongoing commitment might well express itself in an offer to grant asylum to any Vietnamese who fears for his life under a new regime which included the Liberation Front. Then we must make what reparations we can for the damage we have done. We must provide the medical aid that is badly needed, making it available in this country if necessary.

Protesting the War

Meanwhile we in the churches and synagogues have a continuing task while we urge our government to disengage itself from a disgraceful commitment. We must continue to raise our voices if our nation persists in its perverse ways in Vietnam. We must be prepared to match actions with words by seeking out every creative means of protest possible.

As we counsel young men concerning military service we must clarify for them our nation's role in Vietnam and challenge them with the alternative of conscientious objection. I am pleased to say that this is the path now being chosen by more than seventy students at my own alma mater, Morehouse College, and I recommend it to all who find the American course in Vietnam a dishonorable and unjust one. Moreover I would encourage all ministers of draft age to give up their ministerial exemptions and seek status as conscientious objectors. These are the times for real choices and not false ones. We are at the moment when our lives must be placed on the line if our nation is to survive its own folly. Every man of humane convictions must decide on the protest that best suits his convictions, but we must all protest.

There is something seductively tempting about stopping there and sending us all off on what in some circles has become a popular crusade against the war in Vietnam. I say we must enter the struggle, but I wish to go on now to say something even more disturbing. The war in Vietnam is but a symptom of a far deeper malady within the American spirit, and if we ignore this sobering reality we will find ourselves organizing clergy-and-laymen-concerned committees for the next generation. They will be concerned about Guatemala and Peru. They will be concerned about Thailand and Cambodia. They will be concerned about Mozambique and South Africa. We will be marching for these and a dozen other names and attending rallies without end unless there is a significant and profound change in American life and policy. Such thoughts take us beyond Vietnam, but not beyond our calling as sons of the living God.

In 1957 a sensitive American official overseas said that it seemed to him that our nation was on the wrong side of a world revolution. During the past ten years we have seen emerge a pattern of suppression which now has justified the presence of U.S. military "advisors" in Venezuela. This need to maintain social stability for our investments accounts for the counter-revolutionary action of American forces in Guatemala. It tells why American helicopters are being used against guerrillas in Colombia and why American napalm and green beret forces have already been active against rebels in Peru. It is with such activity in mind that the words of the late John F. Kennedy come back to haunt us. Five years ago he said, "Those who make peaceful revolution impossible will make violent revolution inevitable."

Increasingly, by choice or by accident, this is the role our nation has taken—the role of those who make peaceful revolution impossible by refusing to give up the privileges and the pleasures that come from the immense profits of overseas investment.

I am convinced that if we are to get on the right side of the world revolution, we as a nation must undergo a radical revolution of values. We must rapidly begin the shift from a "thing-oriented" society to a "person-oriented" society. When machines and computers, profit motives and property rights are considered more important than people, the giant triplets of racism, materialism, and militarism are incapable of being conquered.

A true revolution of values will soon cause us to question the fairness and justice of many of our past and present policies. On the one hand we are called to play the good Samaritan on life's roadside; but that will be only an initial act. One day we must come to see that the whole Jericho road must be transformed so that men and women will not be constantly beaten and robbed as they make their journey on life's highway. True compassion is more than flinging a coin to a beggar; it is not haphazard and superficial. It comes to see that an edifice which produces beggars needs restructuring. A true revolution of values will soon look uneasily on the glaring contrast of poverty and wealth. With righteous indignation, it will look across the seas and see individual capitalists of the West investing huge sums of money in Asia, Africa and South America, only to take the profits out with no concern for the social betterment of the countries, and say: "This is not just." It will look at our alliance with the landed gentry of Latin America and say: "This is not just." The Western arrogance of feeling that it has everything to teach others and nothing to learn from them is not just. A true revolution of values will lay hands on the world order and say of war: "This way of settling differences is not just." This business of burning human beings with napalm, of filling our nation's homes with orphans and widows, of injecting poisonous drugs of hate into veins of peoples normally humane, of sending men home from dark and bloody battlefields physically handicapped and psychologically deranged, cannot be reconciled with wisdom, justice and love. A nation that continues year after year to spend more money on military defense than on programs of social uplift is approaching spiritual death.

America, the richest and most powerful nation in the world, can well lead the way in this revolution of values. There is nothing, except a tragic death wish, to prevent us from reordering our priorities, so that the pursuit of peace will take precedence over the pursuit of war. There is nothing to keep us from molding a recalcitrant status quo with bruised hands until we have fashioned it into a brotherhood.

This kind of positive revolution of values is our best defense against communism. War is not the answer. Communism will never be defeated by the use of atomic bombs or nuclear weapons. Let us not join those who shout war and through their misguided passions urge the United States to relinquish its participation in the United Nations. These are days which demand wise restraint and calm reasonableness. We must not call everyone a Communist or an appeaser who advocates the seating of Red China in the United Nations and who recognizes that hate and hysteria are not the final answers to the problem of these turbulent days. We must not engage in a negative anti-communism, but rather in a positive thrust for democracy, realizing that our greatest defense against communism is to take offensive action in behalf of justice. We must with positive action seek to remove those conditions of poverty insecurity and injustice which are the fertile soil in which the seed of communism grows and develops.

The People Are Important

These are revolutionary times. All over the globe men are revolting against old systems of exploitation and oppression and out of the wombs of a frail world new systems of justice and equality are being born. The shirtless and barefoot people of the land are rising up as never before. "The people who sat in darkness have seen a great light." We in the West must support these revolutions. It is a sad fact that, because of comfort, complacency, a morbid fear of communism, and our proneness to adjust to injustice, the Western nations that initiated so much of the revolutionary spirit of the modern world have now become the arch anti-revolutionaries. This has driven many to feel that only Marxism has the revolutionary spirit. Therefore, communism is a judgment against our failure to make democracy real and follow through on the revolutions that we initiated. Our only hope today lies in our ability to recapture the revolutionary spirit and go out into a sometimes hostile world declaring eternal hostility to poverty, racism, and militarism. With this powerful commitment we shall boldly challenge the status quo and unjust mores and thereby speed the day when "every valley shall be exalted, and every mountain and hill shall be made low, and the crooked shall be made straight and the rough places plain."

A genuine revolution of values means in the final analysis that our loyalties must become ecumenical rather than sectional. Every nation must now develop an overriding loyalty to mankind as a whole in order to preserve the best in their individual societies.

This call for a world-wide fellowship that lifts neighborly concern beyond one's tribe, race, class and nation is in reality a call for an all-embracing and unconditional love for all men. Ths oft misunderstood and misinterpreted concept— so readily dismissed by the Nietzsches of the world as a weak and cowardly force—has now become an absolute necessity for the survival of man. When I speak of love I am not speaking of some sentimental and weak response. I am speaking of that force which all of the great religions have seen as the supreme unifying principle of life. Love is somehow the key that unlocks the door which leads to ultimate reality. This Hindu-Moslem-Christian-Jewish-Buddhist belief about ultimate reality is beautifully summed up in the first epistle of Saint John:

> Let us love one another; for love is God and everyone that loveth is born of God and knoweth God. He that loveth not knoweth not God; for God is love. If we love one another God dwelleth in us, and his love is perfected in us.

Let us hope that this spirit will become the order of the day. We can no longer afford to worship the god of hate or bow before the altar of retaliation. The oceans of history are made turbulent by the ever-rising tides of hate. History is cluttered with the wreckage of nations and individuals that pursued this self-defeating path of hate. As Arnold Toynbee says: "Love is the ultimate force that makes for the saving choice of life and good against the damning choice of death and evil. Therefore the first hope in our inventory must be the hope that love is going to have the last word."

We are now faced with the fact that tomorrow is today. We are confronted with the fierce urgency of now. In this unfolding conundrum of life and history there is such a thing as being too late. Procrastination is still the thief of time. Life often leaves us standing bare, naked and dejected with a lost opportunity. The "tide in the affairs of men" does not remain at the flood; it ebbs. We may cry out desperately for time to pause in her passage, but time is deaf to every plea and rushes on. Over the bleached bones and jumbled residue of numerous civilizations are written the pathetic words: "Too late." There is an invisible book of life that faithfully records our vigilance or our neglect. "The moving finger writes, and having writ moves on. . . ." We still have a choice today; nonviolent coexistence or violent co-annihilation.

We must move past indecision to action. We must find new ways to speak for peace in Vietnam and justice throughout the developing world—a world that borders on our doors. If we do not act we shall surely be dragged down the long dark and shameful corridors of time reserved for those who possess power without compassion, might without morality, and strength without sight.

Now let us begin. Now let us rededicate ourselves to the long and bitter—but beautiful—struggle for a new world. This is the calling of the sons of God, and our brothers wait eagerly for our response. Shall we say the odds are too great? Shall we tell them the struggle is too hard? Will our message be that the forces of American life militate against their arrival as full men, and we send our deepest regrets? Or will there be another message, of longing, of hope, of solidarity with their yearnings, of commitment to their cause, whatever the cost? The choice is ours, and though we might prefer it otherwise we *must* choose in this crucial moment of human history.

As that noble bard of yesterday, James Russell Lowell, eloquently stated:

> *Once to every man and nation,*
> *Comes the moment to decide*
> *In the strife of truth and falsehood*
> *For the good or evil side;*
> *Some great cause God's new Messiah*
> *Offering each the gloom or blight*
> *And the choice goes by forever*
> *Twixt that darkness and that light.*
>
> *Though the cause of evil prosper*
> *Yet 'tis truth along is strong*
> *Though her portion be the scaffold*
> *And upon the throne be wrong*
> *Yet that scaffold sways the future*
> *And behind the dim unknown*
> *Standeth God within the shadow*
> *Keeping watch above his own.*

97. Selective Service System, "Channeling Memo"

(1965)

This memorandum, from a Selective Service training kit, revealed a more ambitious mission behind the use of the draft than merely mobilizing manpower in wartime. General Lewis Hershey (1893–1977) wrote the memo in 1965, though it was not revealed to the public until January 1967 when Students for a Democratic Society got hold of a copy and published excerpts in *New Left Notes*. Hershey had supervised the operation of the draft during World War II, and when the peacetime draft took effect in 1947, Hershey again presided over it. Thanks to the baby boom, the numbers of men reaching draft age in the late 1950s and the 1960s far outstripped the needs of the military; Hershey, therefore, came up with a system of deferments and exemptions that seemed to allow draft-age men to continue their studies or vocational ambitions without immediate threat of being drafted. In this memo, distributed to more than 4,000 local draft boards, Hershey made clear, however, that only certain career avenues—those he regarded as in the "national interest"—qualified for deferment. As the memo circulated, it became a powerful organizing tool for the draft resistance movement and evidence to most Americans of the draft's unfairness.

SOURCE: Channeling Memo, Resist Papers, Box 8/2, Watkenson Library, Trinity College, Hartford, Conn.

One of the major products of the Selective Service classification process is the channeling of manpower into many endeavors, occupations and activities that are in the national interest. . . .

The line dividing the primary function of armed forces manpower procurement from the process of channeling manpower into civilian support is often finely drawn. The process of channeling by not taking men from certain activities who are otherwise liable for service, or by giving deferment to qualified men in certain occupations, is actual procurement by inducement of manpower for civilian activities which are manifestly in the national interest.

While the best known purpose of Selective Service is to procure manpower for the armed forces, a variety of related processes take place outside delivery of manpower to the active armed forces. Many of these may be put under the heading of "channeling manpower." Many young men would not have pursued a higher education if there had not been a program of student deferment. Many young scientists, engineers, tool and die makers, and other possessors of scarce skills would not remain in their jobs in the defense effort if it were not for a program of occupational deferments. Even though the salary of a teacher has historically been meager, many young men remain in that job, seeking the reward of a deferment. The process of channeling manpower by deferment is entitled to much credit for the large number of graduate students in technical fields and for the fact that there is not a greater shortage of teachers, engineers and other scientists working in activities which are essential to the national interest. . . .

The System has also induced needed people to remain in these professions and in industry engaged in defense activities or in the support of national health, safety or interest. . . .

This was coupled with a growing public recognition that the complexities of future wars would diminish further the distinction between what constitutes military service in uniform and a comparable contribution to the national interest out of uniform. Wars have always been conducted in various ways, but appreciation of this fact and its relationship to preparation for war has never been so sharp in the public mind as it is now becoming. The meaning of the word "service," with its former restricted application to the armed forces, is certain to become widened much more in the future. This brings with it the ever increasing problem of how to control effectively the service of individuals who are not in the armed forces.

In the Selective Service System the term "deferment" has been used millions of times to describe the method and means used to attract to the kind of service considered to be most important, the individuals who were not compelled to do it. The club of induction has been used to drive out of areas considered to be less important to the areas of greater importance in which deferments were given, the individuals who did not or could not participate in activities which were considered essential to the defense of the Nation. The Selective Service System anticipates further evolution in this area. . . .

Registrants and their employers are encouraged and required to make available to the classifying authorities detailed evidence as to the occupations and activities in which the registrants are engaged. . . . Since occupational deferments are granted for no more than one year at a time, a process of periodically receiving current information and repeated review assures that every deferred registrant continues to contribute to the overall national good. This reminds him of the basis for his deferment. . . .

Patriotism is defined as "devotion to the welfare of one's country." It has been interpreted to mean many different things. Men have always been exhorted to do their duty. But what that duty is depends upon a variety of variables, most important being the nature of the threat to national welfare and the capacity and opportunity of the individual. Take, for example, the boy who saved the Netherlands by plugging the dike with his finger.

At the time of the American Revolution the patriot was the so-called "embattled farmer" who joined General Washington to fight the British. The concept that patriotism is best exemplified by service in uniform has always been under some degree of challenge, but never to the extent that it is today. In today's complicated warfare, when the man in uniform may be suffering far less than the civilians at home, patriotism must be interpreted far more broadly than ever before.

This is not a new thought, but it has had new emphasis since the development of nuclear and rocket warfare. Educators, scientists, engineers and their professional organizations, during the last ten years particularly, have been convincing the American public that for the mentally qualified man there is a special order of patriotism other than service in uniform—that for the man having the capacity, dedicated service as a civilian in such fields as engineering, the sciences and teaching constitute the ultimate in their expression of patriotism. A large segment of the American public has been convinced that this is true.

It is in this atmosphere that the young man registers at age 18 and pressure begins to force his choice. He does not have the inhibitions that a philosophy of universal service in uniform would engender. The door is open for him as a student if capable in a skill badly needed by his nation. He has many choices and he is prodded to make a decision.

The psychological effect of this circumstantial climate depends upon the individual, his sense of good citizenship, his love of country and its way of life. He can obtain a sense of well-being and satisfaction that he is doing as a civilian what will help his country most. This process encourages him to put forth his best effort and removes to some degree the stigma that has been attached to being out of uniform.

In the less patriotic and more selfish individual it engenders a sense of fear, uncertainty and dissatisfaction which motivates him, nevertheless, in the same direction. He complains of the uncertainty which he must endure; he would like to be able to do as he pleases; he would appreciate a certain future with no prospect of military service or civilian contribution, but he complies. . . .

Throughout his career as a student, the pressure—the threat of loss of deferment—continues. It continues with equal intensity after graduation. His local board requires periodic reports to find out what he is up to. He is impelled to pursue his skill rather than embark upon some less important enterprise and is encouraged to apply his skill in an essential activity in the national interest. The loss of deferred status is the consequence for the individual who has acquired the skill and either does not use it or uses it in a nonessential activity.

The psychology of granting wide choice under pressure to take action is the American or indirect way of achieving what is done by direction in foreign countries where choice is not permitted. Here, choice is limited but not denied, and it is fundamental that an individual generally applies himself better to something he has decided to do rather than something he has been told to do.

The effects of channeling are manifested among student physicians. They are deferred to complete their education through school and internship. This permits them to serve in the armed forces in their skills rather than in an unskilled capacity as enlisted men.

The device of pressurized guidance, or channeling, is employed on Standby Reservists of which more than 2-½ million have been referred by all services for availability determinations. The appeal to the Reservist who knows he is subject to recall to active duty unless he is determined to be unavailable is virtually identical to that extended to other registrants.

The psychological impact of being rejected for service in uniform is severe. The earlier this occurs in a young man's life, the sooner the beneficial effects of pressured motivation by the Selective Service System are lost. He is labeled unwanted. His patriotism is not desired. Once the label of "rejectee" is upon him all efforts at guidance by persuasion are futile. If he attempts to enlist at 17 or 18 and is rejected, then he receives virtually none of the impulsion the System is capable of giving him. If he makes no effort to enlist and as a result is not rejected until delivered for examination by the Selective Service System at about age 23, he has felt some of the pressure but thereafter is a free agent.

This contributed to establishment of a new classification of I-Y (registrant qualified for military service only in time of war or national emergency). That classification reminds the registrant of his ultimate qualification to serve and preserves some of the benefit of what we call channeling. Without it or any other similar method of categorizing men in degrees of acceptability, men rejected for military service would be left with the understanding that they are unfit to defend their country, even in wartime. . . .

From the individual's viewpoint, he is standing in a room which has been made uncomfortably warm. Several doors are open, but they all lead to various forms of recognized, patriotic service to the Nation. Some accept the alternatives gladly—some with reluctance. The consequence is approximately the same. . . .

Selective Service processes do not compel people by edict as in foreign systems to enter pursuits having to do with essentiality and progress. They go because they know that by going they will be deferred. . . .

Deciding what people should do, rather than letting them do something of national importance of their own choosing, introduces many problems that are at least partially avoided when indirect methods, the kind currently invoked by the Selective Service System, are used.

Delivery of manpower for induction, the process of providing a few thousand men with transportation to a reception center, is not much of an administrative or financial challenge. It is in dealing with the other millions of registrants that the System is heavily occupied, developing more effective human beings in the national interest. If there is to be any survival after disaster, it will take people, and not machines, to restore the Nation.   July, 1965

98. Phil Ochs, "Draft Dodger Rag"

(1965)

In this popular song, folk singer Phil Ochs manages to work in nearly two dozen reasons for which a draft registrant might get a deferment or exemption. Born in El Paso, Texas, Ochs (1940–76) grew up mostly in New York and Ohio. As a journalism major at Ohio State University, Ochs began mixing politics and music. By the early 1960s, Ochs was a fixture in the New York folk music scene and a frequent contributor to *Broadside*, a magazine that routinely published new songs by the likes of Pete Seeger and Bob Dylan. He performed at the Newport Folk Festival in 1963 and again in 1964, when he sang "Draft Dodger Rag." The song came off his second album, *I Ain't Marching Anymore*, which, like his first record, featured a host of topical songs inspired by the headlines. Recorded in 1965, just as draft calls spiked, "Draft Dodger Rag" sardonically takes the listener through a variety of references to physical ailments and hardship conditions, as well as being a student and working at a defense plant—all of which would have secured a deferment from the Selective Service.

SOURCE: Elektra Records, 1965, reissued on Hannibal Records, HNCD 4422, 1986.

Oh, I'm just a typical American boy from a typical American town
I believe in God and Senator Dodd and a-keepin' old Castro down
And when it came my time to serve I knew "better dead than red"
But when I got to my old draft board, buddy, this is what I said:

CHORUS
Sarge, I'm only eighteen, I got a ruptured spleen
And I always carry a purse
I got eyes like a bat, and my feet are flat, and my asthma's getting worse
Yes, think of my career, my sweetheart dear, and my poor old invalid aunt
Besides, I ain't no fool, I'm a-goin' to school
And I'm working in a de-fense plant

I've got a dislocated disc and a wracked up back
I'm allergic to flowers and bugs
And when the bombshell hits, I get epileptic fits
And I'm addicted to a thousand drugs
I got the weakness woes, I can't touch my toes
I can hardly reach my knees
And if the enemy came close to me
I'd probably start to sneeze

(Chorus)

Ooh, I hate Chou En Lai, and I hope he dies,
One thing you gotta see
That someone's gotta go over there
And that someone isn't me
So I wish you well, Sarge, give 'em Hell!
Kill me a thousand or so
And if you ever get a war without blood and gore
I'll be the first to go

(Chorus)

99. Anthony Wolff, "Draft Board No. 13, Springfield, Ohio"

(1968)

General Lewis Hershey, director of the Selective Service System, liked to boast that local draft boards were made up of "little groups of neighbors." Rather than centralizing the system of conscription in Washington, Hershey argued, having a network of local boards gave a human face to the draft. The men who served on the board would be more likely to know the registrants and their families and, therefore, more likely to make the right classification decisions. In truth, as a 1966 study showed, most draft boards were disproportionately made up of white professionals, the vast majority of whom were veterans. Moreover, as this article shows, boards had considerable latitude in interpreting the draft laws; the size of the draft pool in one's community and the makeup of the board, therefore, meant that the Selective Service sometimes applied the rules differently from place to place. Calls for reform led President Johnson to appoint a commission to investigate the draft's fairness in 1966, and criticism of the system did not abate until President Nixon introduced a lottery system at the end of 1969. This account of the operations of a Springfield, Ohio, draft board appeared in *Look* magazine, a large-format, general interest magazine much like *Life*.

SOURCE: *Look*, April 2, 1968.

After the first flush of coming of age, an 18-year-old boy may begin to sweat. In his wallet, keeping company with his driver's license as part of the thin dossier that proves he's a man, is a card from Uncle Sam that says the Government has a lien on his life. In most states, he cannot buy a drink, vote, marry without parental consent or sign a legal contract, but he knows that his Government can arrogate to its own purpose two years of his irreplaceable youth and subject it to unfamiliar indignities, perhaps to death.

For a lucky boy, in a lucky time and place, the draft is a remote threat. If the military is not hard up for men, his number may not come up for five or six years; an eternity to an 18-year-old, plenty of time to start a family, parlay a draft-proof education into a draft-free job or somehow avoid the draft's reach if he wants to.

Springfield, Ohio, U. S. A., this year is not a lucky time or place. The Vietnam war is forcing the draft to dig deep, and in Springfield, as elsewhere, it is reaching for the 19-year-olds and tightening up on deferments.

Most boys go to war when the Government calls. Some, who don't want to go, and who know that most men will never have to go, seek deferment. The willing and the unwilling, those who go and those who will never go, all are subject to their local draft board. In Springfield, that's Local Board No. 13.

A boy who is able and willing has only to wait his turn. Each month, from the Department of Defense via national and state Selective Service Headquarters, a call comes to Local Board No. 13 for a certain number of men. The board has individual file folders for each of its 25,000-odd registrants, indexed by draft classification and birthdate; it simply deals from the top of the I-A deck, oldest eligible men first, and mails out the required number of notices to report for induction. It is all as neat and impersonal as clerks and files and regulations can make it.

Jeannette Johnson, the grandmotherly clerk of Springfield Board, says with satisfaction, "We are like an obstetrician—we deliver them."

A boy who doesn't want to go may claim the board's personal attention at its brief weekly meeting, after the cut-and-dried classification work has been ratified. While a registrant waits to request a deferment, he may take whatever comfort he can from the printed credo thumbtacked on the bulletin board above the official list of delinquents: "Americanism . . . is an eagerness to defend [the country] against all enemies."

The board's patriotic orthodoxy is tempered by the law, but the law also reserves to the board the sole right to classify free men for conscription. Its decision is subject only to appeal within the draft system and protected by law from judicial review. Unqualified either by examination or election, the three men sitting around a gray-steel table at Local Board No. 13, Springfield, Ohio, are among the most powerful men in America.

Tom McKeever, 19, is one who waits to see the board. He is a conscientious objector the hard way: not by subscription to an official creed; rather, by conviction that human life is sacred. He waits, armed with fragments of Camus, Socrates and Sartre, the bibliography of his unorthodox faith.

Fred Cole, the Government Appeal Agent appointed to advise the Springfield Board and its registrants, has already warned Tom that "they're not going to have the remotest idea what you're talking about." From years of experience with the board, Cole knows that "they have a bias about CO's: they don't like them."

Tom has already heard his mother-in-law call him a Communist and a coward. He does not have to hear the members of the board discussing CO's:

Ed Lewis, the 74-year-old chairman, with 25 years on draft boards, says: "We get a few oddballs . . . like one fellow said he couldn't kill a fly, that if a little fly was flying around this room, he'd go get a cup . . . and he'd capture that fly and take it outside and let it loose. We get our smiles! He's I-A, or probably in Vietnam."

John Patterson, the board secretary, tells of a boy who "sent in he was a CO. Then he flew in here and brought another man with him who we couldn't hear. You see, you can't bring anybody else with you before the board. The law is specific: your father, mother, or your wife." (The law is specific: ". . . the local board may . . . permit any person to appear before it with or on behalf of a registrant. . . .")

Ed Lewis again: "The Government sets up so many religions, you know, that they consider as conscientious objectors, like the Brethrens, I think the Seventh Day Adventists, the Quakers. . . ." (The Government "sets up" no religions that give anyone CO status, probably because the Constitution wouldn't stand for it.) Both Mr. Lewis and Mr. Patterson have definite ideas about pacifists, whom they do not consider to be CO's. Mr. Patterson thinks "a pacifist just doesn't want to do *anything*—he's like the hippies." Mr. Lewis concludes, "There's nothing in the regulations to take care of a pacifist. We classify him I-A."

The board's interview with Tom McKeever is brief and polite. They ask him the questions on the CO form, which he has already answered in writing. Mr. Patterson, who has two years of college, cannot believe that McKeever, who has none, could have written such a "brilliant paper" without a "ghostwriter." Softly, in a monotone punctuated by the peck of typewriters from the outer office, McKeever repeats his answers substantially as he had written them. Mr. Patterson remains unconvinced of his authorship. All three—Lewis, Patterson and Harold Crabtree—are swayed by McKeever's lack of certified church affiliation. Unanimously, they classify him I-A.

██████████

100. Muhammad Ali, "Statement on Refusing Induction"

(1967)

In this statement, boxing's reigning heavyweight champion, Muhammad Ali, declared his refusal to be inducted into the U.S. Army. Ali (1942–) was born Cassius Marcellus Clay and grew up in Louisville, Kentucky. In 1960, he won the Golden Gloves heavyweight title as well as a gold medal at the Rome Olympics. In 1964, he won the world heavyweight championship when the seemingly unbeatable champion, Sonny Liston, did not answer the bell for the seventh round. In a rematch a year later, Ali knocked out Liston in the first round. Ali had been attending Nation of Islam meetings for several years, but did not declare his membership until after he had won the title. That same year, he changed his name from Cassius Clay to Muhammad Ali. Meanwhile, two weeks before he fought Liston for the first time, Ali failed the Selective Service mental examination and was classified as I-Y (not qualified for service). In 1966, however, the standards for passing the mental exam were lowered, and Ali was classified 1-A (available for military service). When Ali learned the news, he shocked most Americans by saying, "Man, I ain't got no quarrel with them Vietcong." The New York State Boxing Commission stripped Ali of his title on the day he refused induction. He did not fight again until 1970. A year later, the Supreme Court finally ruled in Ali's favor.

SOURCE: Robert Lipsyte, "Clay Refuses Army Oath; Stripped of Boxing Crown," *New York Times*, April 29, 1967.

The statement, in part, declared:

"It is in the light of my consciousness as a Muslim minister and my own personal convictions that I take my stand in rejecting the call to be inducted in the armed services. I do so with the full realization of its implications and possible consequences. I have searched my conscience and I find I cannot be true to my belief in my religion by accepting such a call.

"My decision is a private and individual one and I realize that this is a most crucial decision. In taking it I am dependent solely upon Allah as the final judge of these actions brought about by my own conscience.

"I strongly object to the fact that so many newspapers have given the American public and the world the impression that I have only two alternatives in taking this stand: either I go to jail or go to the Army. There is another alternative and that alternative is justice. If justice prevails, if my Constitutional rights are upheld, I will be forced to go neither to the Army nor jail. In the end I am confident that justice will come my way for the truth must eventually prevail.

"I am looking forward to immediately continuing my profession.

"As to the threat voiced by certain elements to 'strip' me of my title, this is merely a continuation of the same artificially induced prejudice and discrimination.

"Regardless of the difference in my outlook, I insist upon my right to pursue my livelihood in accordance with the same rights granted to other men and women who have disagreed with the policies of whatever Administration was in power at the time.

"I have the world heavyweight title not because it was 'given' to me, not because of my race or religion, but because I won it in the ring through my own boxing ability.

"Those who want to 'take' it and hold a series of auction-type bouts not only do me a disservice but actually disgrace themselves. I am certain that the sports fans and fair-minded people throughout America would never accept such a 'title-holder.' "

101. Resist, "A Call to Resist Illegitimate Authority"

(1967)

Over the summer of 1967, as activists across the country organized a draft resistance movement, a great number of academics, writers, artists, journalists, clergy, and others past draft age sought both to support the draft resisters and to commit themselves to some similar level of risk. "We are certainly in an embarrassing position to be looking to the young to make our will effective," Paul Goodman wrote. Consequently, these dissenters circulated and signed a variety of complicity statements, the best known of which was "The Call to Resist Illegitimate Authority." Written by Marcus Raskin and Arthur Waskow, both of the Institute for Policy Studies, and Robert Zevin, a Columbia University economist, it was first published in the *New York Review of Books* and the *New Republic* with 320 signatures; in time, the number of signers grew to more than 20,000. The act of signing the Call constituted a misdemeanor violation of the Selective Service Act, Section 12, which outlawed counseling registrants to violate the draft laws. The Call also became the basis for founding a new organization named Resist, which, for the duration of the war, raised money and funded draft resistance and antiwar organizations. When the government indicted Dr. Benjamin Spock, the Rev. William Sloane Coffin, Marcus Raskin, Mitchell Goodman, and Michael Ferber for conspiracy to aid and abet draft resisters in January 1968, it referred to the Call as "Overt Act #1" in furtherance of the alleged conspiracy.

SOURCE: "A Call to Resist Illegitimate Authority," undated (ca. October 1967), reprinted in Jessica Mitford, *The Trial of Dr. Spock* (New York: Knopf, 1969), 257–61.

To the young men of America,
to the whole of the American people,
and to all men of good will everywhere:

1. An ever growing number of young American men are finding that the American war in Vietnam so outrages their deepest moral and religious

sense that they cannot contribute to it in any way. We share their moral outrage.

2. We further believe that the war is unconstitutional and illegal. Congress has not declared a war as required by the Constitution. Moreover, under the Constitution, treaties signed by the President and ratified by the Senate have the same force as the Constitution itself. The Charter of the United Nations is such a treaty. The Charter specifically obligates the United States to refrain from force or the threat of force in international relations. It requires member states to exhaust every peaceful means of settling disputes and to submit disputes which cannot be settled peacefully to the Security Council. The United States has systematically violated all of these Charter provisions for thirteen years.

3. Moreover, this war violates international agreements, treaties and principles of law which the United States Government has solemnly endorsed. The combat role of the United States troops in Vietnam violates the Geneva Accords of 1954 which our government pledged to support but has since subverted. The destruction of rice, crops and livestock; the burning and bulldozing of entire villages consisting exclusively of civilian structures; the interning of civilian non-combatants in concentration camps; the summary executions of civilians in captured villages who could not produce satisfactory evidence of their loyalties or did not wish to be removed to concentration camps; the slaughter of peasants who dared to stand up in their fields and shake their fists at American helicopters;—these are all actions of the kind which the United States and the other victorious powers of World War II declared to be crimes against humanity for which individuals were to be held personally responsible even when acting under the orders of their governments and for which Germans were sentenced at Nuremberg to long prison terms and death. The prohibition of such acts as war crimes was incorporated in treaty law by the Geneva Conventions of 1949, ratified by the United States. These are commitments to other countries and to Mankind, and they would claim our allegiance even if Congress should declare war.

4. We also believe it is an unconstitutional denial of religious liberty and equal protection of the laws to withhold draft exemption from men whose religious or profound philosophical beliefs are opposed to what in the Western religious tradition have been long known as unjust wars.

5. Therefore, we believe on all these grounds that every free man has a legal right and a moral duty to exert every effort to end this war, to avoid collusion with it, and to encourage others to do the same. Young men in the armed forces or threatened with the draft face the most excruciating choices. For them various forms of resistance risk separation from their families and their country, destruction of their careers, loss of their freedom and loss of their lives. Each must choose the course of resistance dictated by his conscience and circumstances. Among those already in the armed forces some are refusing to obey specific illegal and immoral orders, some are attempting to educate their fellow servicemen on the murderous and barbarous nature of the war, some are absenting themselves without official leave. Among those not in the armed forces some are applying for status as conscientious objectors to American aggression in Vietnam,

some are refusing to be inducted. Among both groups some are resisting openly and paying a heavy penalty, some are organizing more resistance within the United States and some have sought sanctuary in other countries.

6. We believe that each of these forms of resistance against illegitimate authority is courageous and justified. Many of us believe that open resistance to the war and the draft is the course of action most likely to strengthen the moral resolve with which all of us can oppose the war and most likely to bring an end to the war.

7. We will continue to lend our support to those who undertake resistance to this war. We will raise funds to organize draft resistance unions, to supply legal defense and bail, to support families and otherwise aid resistance to the war in whatever ways may seem appropriate.

8. We firmly believe that our statement is the sort of speech that under the First Amendment must be free, and that the actions we will undertake are as legal as is the war resistance of the young men themselves. In any case, we feel that we cannot shrink from fulfilling our responsibilities to the youth whom many of us teach, to the country whose freedom we cherish, and to the ancient traditions of religion and philosophy which we strive to preserve in this generation.

9. We call upon all men of good will to join us in this confrontation with immoral authority. Especially we call upon the universities to fulfill their mission of enlightenment and religious organizations to honor their heritage of brotherhood. Now is the time to resist.

---

send to: RESIST/Room 510/166 Fifth Ave./New York, N.Y. 10010.

☐ I wish to sign "A Call to Resist Illegitimate Authority" and am willing to have my endorsement made public.

☐ I enclose a contribution of $_____ to support the work of RESIST. (Please make checks payable to RESIST)

☐ I am interested in organizing or joining a group in my community to support young men directly resisting the war.

name _____

address _____

city _____ state _____ zip _____

A Partial List of Signers

Nelson W. Aldrich, Jr.	Richard J. Barnel
Edwin B. Allaire	Inge Powell Bell
Gar Alperovitz	Rev. Philip Berrigan, S.S.J.
Emilo de Antonio	Rev. James Bevel
Richard Ashley	Norman Birnbaum
David Bakan	Robert Bly

Samuel Bowles
Harry M. Bracken
Robert McAfee Brown
Robert Brustein
Henry H. Bucher, Jr.
Alexander Calder
Louisa James Calder
Haydn Carruth
Jerome Charyn
Noam Chomsky
Allen Churchill
Rev. William Sloane Coffin
Dr. Arnold M. Cooper
Robert Coover
Frederick Crews
Alfred Crown
William Davidon
Martin Davis
Jean Davidson
R. G. Davis
Stanley Diamond
Dr. James P. Dixon
Rev. Thomas Dorney, S.J.
Douglas Dowd
George P. Elliott
Lawrence Ferlinghetti
W. H. Ferry
Eliot Friedson
Dr. J. W. Friedman
Norman D. Fruchter
Allen Ginsberg
Rabbi Robert E. Goldburg
Mitchell Goodman
Paul Goodman
Norman K. Gottwald
Robert Greenblatt
Balcomb Greene
Barbara Guest
John G. Gurley
Roger T. Hogan
William Hamilton
Chester W. Hartman
Richard O. Hathaway
Jules Henry
Nat Hentoff

Edward S. Herman
Hallock Hoffman
James G. Holland
Leo Huberman
Karl Hufbauer
Dell Hymes
Christopher Jencks
Donald Kolish
Herbert Kelman
Roy C. Kepler
Fr. David Kirk
Herbert Kohl
Gabriel Kolko
Hans Koningsberger
Ivor Kraft
Jean-Claude von Itallie
Burton Lane
Christopher Lasch
Irving Laucks
Paul Lauter
Sidney Lens
Jerome Lettvin
Denise Levertov
Jack Levine
Robert Lowell
Elliott Lieb
Walter Lowenfels
Staughton Lynd
Dwight Macdonald
Herbert Marcuse
Kenneth O. May
Arno J. Mayer
Everett Mendelsohn
Seymour Melman
Thomas Merton
Ashley Montagu
Ira Morris
Barrington Moore, Jr.
Rev. Richard Mumma
Otto Nathan
Jay Neugeboren
Jack Newfield
Dr. Martin Niemoller
Michael Novak
Conor Cruise O'Brien

Carl Oglesby
Richard Ohmann
Wayne O'Neil
Grace Paley
Victor Paschkis
Linus Pauling
Bishop James A. Pike
Richard H. Popkin
Hilary Putnam
Philip Rahv
Anatol Rapoport
Marc Raskin
Peter V. Ritner
Henry Robbins
Gordon Rogoff
Philip Roth
Muriel Rukeyser
Robert J. Rulman
Marshall Sahlins
Franz Schurman
Richard Seaver
John R. Seeley
Wilfred Sheed
Stanley K. Sheinbaum

James Shenton
Philip Siekevitz
Edgar Snow
Theodore Solotaroff
Susan Sontag
Raphael Soyer
Dr. Benjamin Spock
Charles Stein
Grover C. Stephans
Elizabeth Sutherland
John M. Swomley, Jr.
Albert Szenl-Gyorgyi
Paul Sweezy
Daniel Talbot
William Taylor
Karl V. Teeler
Harold Tovish
Tomi Ungerer
William Vickrey
Gerald Walker
Immanuel Wallerstein
Brendan Walsh
James E. Walsh
Arthur Waskow

102. Noam Chomsky, "On Resistance"

(1967)

In "On Resistance," Noam Chomsky recounts his experience in the October 21, 1967, march on the Pentagon and offers a meditation on the meaning and form(s) of resistance. The son of a Hebrew language scholar, Chomsky (1928–) was born in Philadelphia and earned his doctorate at the University of Pennsylvania. Credited with revolutionizing the study of linguistics in *Syntactic Structures* (1957), Chomsky was not widely known for his political analysis before the escalation of the Vietnam War. His essay "The Responsibility of Intellectuals," published in February 1967, changed that. In that piece, Chomsky criticized the intellectuals of the 1950s and 1960s who had been content to quietly accept the decisions of national security and foreighn policy "experts" on Vietnam. "It is the responsibility of intellectuals to speak the truth and expose lies," he wrote, and called his colleagues in academia forward to speak out against the war. A founder of Resist, Chomsky signed "The Call to Resist Illegitimate Authority" and frequently took part in demonstrations. Here he describes his participation at the Pentagon demonstration (where he was one of 683 arrested) and weighs various ways to "raise the cost of American aggression."

SOURCE: *New York Review of Books,* December 7, 1967.

Several weeks after the demonstrations in Washington, I am still trying to sort out my impressions of a week whose quality is difficult to capture or express. Perhaps some personal reflections may be useful to others who share my instinctive distaste for activism, but who find themselves edging towards an unwanted but almost inevitable crisis.

For many of the participants, the Washington demonstrations symbolized the transition "from dissent to resistance." I will return to this slogan and its meaning, but I want to make clear at the outset that I do feel it to be not only accurate with respect to the mood of the demonstrations but, properly interpreted, appropriate to the present state of protest against the war. There is an irresistible dynamics to such protest. One may begin by writing articles and giving speeches about the war, by helping in many ways to create an atmosphere of concern and outrage. A courageous few will turn to direct action, refusing to take their place alongside the "good Germans" we have all learned to despise. Some will be forced to this decision when they are called up for military service. The dissenting senators, writers, and professors will watch as young men refuse to serve in the armed forces, in a war that they detest. What then? Can those who write and speak against the war take refuge in the fact that they have not urged or encouraged draft resistance, but have merely helped to develop a climate of opinion in which any decent person will want to refuse to take part in a miserable war? It is a very thin line. Nor is it very easy to watch from a position of safety while others are forced to take a grim and painful step. The fact is that most of the one thousand draft cards and other documents turned in to the Justice Department on October 20 came from men who can escape military service but who insisted on sharing the fate of those who are less privileged. In such ways the circle of resistance widens. Quite apart from this, no one can fail to see that to the extent that he restricts his protest, to the extent that he rejects actions that are open to him, he accepts complicity in what the government does. Some will act on this realization, posing sharply a moral issue that no person of conscience can evade.

On Monday, October 16, on the Boston Common I listened as Howard Zinn explained why he felt ashamed to be an American. I watched as several hundred young men, some of them my students, made a terrible decision which no young person should have to face: to sever their connection with the Selective Service System. The week ended, the following Monday, with a quiet discussion in Cambridge in which I heard estimates, by an academic consultant to the Department of Defense, of the nuclear megatonnage that would be necessary to "take out" North Vietnam ("Some will find this shocking, but . . ."; "No civilian in the government is suggesting this, to my knowledge . . ."; "Let's not use emotional words like 'destruction'"; etc.), and listened to a leading expert on Soviet affairs who explained how the men in the Kremlin are watching very carefully to determine whether wars of national liberation can succeed—if so, they will support them all over the world. (Try pointing out to such an expert that on these assumptions, if the men in the Kremlin are rational, they will surely support dozens of such wars right now, since at a small cost they can confound the American military and tear our society to shreds—you will be told that you don't understand the Russian soul.)

The weekend of the peace demonstrations in Washington left impressions that are vivid and intense, but unclear to me in their implications. The dominant memory is of the scene itself, of tens of thousands of young people surrounding what they believe to be—I must add that I agree—the most hideous institution on this earth and demanding that it stop imposing misery and destruction. Tens of thousands of *young* people. This I find hard to comprehend. It is pitiful but true that by an overwhelming margin it is the young who are crying out in horror at what we all see happening, the young who are being beaten when they stand their ground, and the young who have to decide whether to accept jail or exile, or to fight in a hideous war. They have to face this decision alone, or almost alone. We should ask ourselves why this is so.

Why, for example, does Senator Mansfield feel "ashamed for the image they have portrayed of this country," and not feel ashamed for the image of this country portrayed by the institution these young people were confronting, an institution directed by a sane and mild and eminently reasonable man who can testify calmly before Congress that the amount of ordnance expended in Vietnam has surpassed the total expended in Germany and Italy in World War II? Why is it that Senator Mansfield can speak in ringing phrases about those who are not living up to our commitment to "a government of laws"—referring to a small group of demonstrators, not to the ninety-odd responsible men on the Senate floor who are watching, with full knowledge, as the state they serve clearly, flagrantly violates the explicit provisions of the United Nations Charter, the supreme law of the land? He knows quite well that prior to our invasion of Vietnam there was no armed attack against any state. It was Senator Mansfield, after all, who informed us that "when the sharp increase in the American military effort began in early 1965, it was estimated that only about 400 North Vietnamese soldiers were among the enemy forces in the South which totaled 140,000 at that time"; and it is the Mansfield Report from which we learn that at that time there were 34,000 American soldiers already in South Vietnam, in violation of our "solemn commitment" at Geneva in 1954.

The point should be pursued. After the first International Days of Protest in October 1965, Senator Mansfield criticized the "sense of utter irresponsibility" shown by the demonstrators. He had nothing to say then, nor has he since, about the "sense of utter irresponsibility" shown by Senator Mansfield and others who stand by quietly and vote appropriations as the cities and villages of North Vietnam are demolished, as millions of refugees in the South are driven from their homes by American bombardment. He has nothing to say about the moral standards or the respect for law of those who have permitted this tragedy.

I speak of Senator Mansfield precisely because he is not a breast-beating superpatriot who wants America to rule the world, but is rather an American intellectual in the best sense, a scholarly and reasonable man—the kind of man who is the terror of our age. Perhaps this is merely a personal reaction, but when I look at what is happening to our country, what I find most terrifying is not Curtis LeMay, with his cheerful suggestion that we bomb our "enemies" back into the Stone Age, but rather the calm disquisitions of the political scientists on just how much force will be necessary to achieve our ends, or just what form of government will be acceptable to us in Vietnam. What I find terrifying is the detachment and equanimity with which we view and discuss an unbearable tragedy. We all know that if Russia or China were guilty of what we have done in Vietnam, we would be exploding with moral indignation at these monstrous crimes.

There was, I think, a serious miscalculation in the planning of the Washington demonstrations. It was expected that the march to the Pentagon would be followed by a number of speeches, and that those who were committed to civil disobedience would then separate themselves from the crowd and go to the Pentagon, a few hundred yards away across an open field. I had decided not to take part in civil disobedience, and I do not know in detail what had been planned. As everyone must realize, it is very hard to distinguish rationalization from rationality in such matters. I felt, however, that the first large-scale acts of civil disobedience should be more specifically defined, more clearly in support of those who are refusing to serve in Vietnam, on whom the real burden of dissent must inevitably fall. While appreciating the point of view of those who wished to express their hatred of the war in a more explicit way, I was not convinced that civil disobedience at the Pentagon would be either meaningful or effective.

In any event, what actually happened was rather different from what anyone had anticipated. A few thousand people gathered for the speeches, but the mass of marchers went straight on to the Pentagon, some because they were committed to direct action, many because they were simply swept along. From the speakers' platform where I stood it was difficult to determine just what was taking place at the Pentagon. All we could see was the surging of the crowd. From secondhand reports, I understand that the marchers passed through and around the front line of troops and took up a position, which they maintained, on the steps of the Pentagon. It soon became obvious that it was wrong for the few organizers of the march and the mostly middle-aged group that had gathered near them to remain at the speakers' platform while the demonstrators themselves, most of them quite young, were at the Pentagon. (I recall seeing near the platform Robert Lowell, Dwight Macdonald, Monsignor Rice, Sidney Lens, Benjamin Spock and his wife, Dagmar Wilson, Donald Kalish.) Dave Dellinger suggested that we try to approach the Pentagon. We found a place not yet blocked by the demonstrators, and walked up to the line of troops standing a few feet from the building. Dellinger suggested that those of us who had not yet spoken at the rally talk directly to the soldiers through a small portable sound system. From this point on, my impressions are rather fragmentary. Monsignor Rice spoke, and I followed. As I was speaking, the line of soldiers advanced, moving past me—a rather odd experience. I don't recall just what I was saying. The gist was, I suppose, that we were there because we didn't want the soldiers to kill and be killed, but I do remember feeling that the way I was putting it seemed silly and irrelevant.

The advancing line of soldiers had partially scattered the small group that had come with Dellinger. Those of us who had been left behind the line of soldiers regrouped, and Dr. Spock began to speak. Almost at once, another line of soldiers emerged from somewhere, this time in a tightly massed formation, rifles in hand, and moved slowly forward. We sat down. As I mentioned earlier, I had no intention of taking part in any act of civil disobedience, until that moment. But when that grotesque organism began slowly advancing—more grotesque because its cells were recognizable human beings—it became obvious that one could not permit that thing to dictate what one was going to do. I was arrested at that point by a federal marshal, presumably for obstructing the soldiers (the technical term for this behavior is "disorderly conduct") I should add that the soldiers, so far as I could see (which was not very far), seemed rather unhappy about the whole matter, and were being about as gentle as one can be when ordered (I presume this was the order) to kick and club passive, quiet people who refuse to move. The federal marshals, predictably, were very different. They reminded me of the police officers I had seen in a Jackson, Mississippi, jail several summers ago, who had laughed when an old man showed us a bloody homemade bandage on his leg and tried to describe to us how he had been beaten by the police. In Washington, the ones who got the worst of it at the hands of the marshals were the young boys and girls, particularly boys with long hair. Nothing seemed to bring out the marshals' sadism more than the sight of a boy with long hair. Yet, although I witnessed some acts of violence by the marshals, their behavior largely seemed to range from indifference to petty nastiness. For example, we were kept in a police van for an hour or two with the doors closed and only a few air holes for ventilation—one can't be too careful with such ferocious criminal types.

In the prison dormitory and after my release I heard many stories, which I feel sure are authentic, of the courage of the young people, many of whom were quite frightened by the terrorism that began late at night after the TV cameramen and most of the press had left. They sat quietly hour after hour through the cold night; many were kicked and beaten and dragged across police lines (more "disorderly conduct"). I also heard stories, distressing ones, of provocation of the troops by the demonstrators—usually, it seems, those who were not in the front rows. Surely this was indefensible. Soldiers are unwitting instruments of terror; one does not blame or attack the club that is used to bludgeon someone to death. They are also human beings, with sensibilities to which one can perhaps appeal. There is in fact strong evidence that one soldier, perhaps three or four, refused to obey orders and was placed under arrest. The soldiers, after all, are in much the same position as the draft resisters. If they obey orders, they become brutalized by what they do; if they do not, the personal consequences are severe. It is a situation that deserves compassion, not abuse. But we should retain a sense of proportion in the matter. Everything that I saw or heard indicates that the demonstrators played only a small role in initiating the considerable violence that occurred.

The argument that resistance to the war should remain strictly nonviolent seems to me overwhelming. As a tactic, violence is absurd. No one can compete with the government in this arena, and the resort to violence, which will surely fail, will simply frighten and alienate some who can be reached, and will further encourage the ideologists and administrators of forceful repression. What is more, one hopes that participants in nonviolent resistance will themselves become human beings of a more admirable sort. No one can fail to be impressed by the personal qualities of those who have grown to maturity in the civil rights movement. Whatever else it may have accomplished, the civil rights movement has made an inestimable contribution to American society in transforming the lives and characters of those who took part in it. Perhaps a program of principled,

nonviolent resistance can do the same for many others, in the particular circumstances that we face today. It is not impossible that this may save the country
from a terrible future, from yet another generation of men who think it clever
to discuss the bombing of North Vietnam as a question of tactics and cost-
effectiveness, or who support our attempt to conquer South Vietnam, with the
human cost that they well know, blandly asserting that "our primary motivation
is self-interest—the self-interest of our own country in this shrinking world"
(Citizens Committee for Peace with Freedom, *New York Times*, October 26, 1967).

Returning to the demonstrations, I must admit that I was relieved to find people whom I had respected for years in the prison dormitory—Norman Mailer,
Jim Peck, Dave Dellinger, and a number of others. I think it was reassuring to
many of the kids who were there to be able to feel that they were not totally dis-
connected from a world that they knew and from people whom they admired. It
was moving to see that defenseless young people who had a great deal to lose
were willing to be jailed for what they believed—young instructors from state
universities, college kids who have a very bright future if they are willing to toe
the line, many others whom I could not identify.

What comes next? Obviously, that is the question on everyone's mind. The
slogan "From Dissent to Resistance" makes sense, I think, but I hope it is not
taken to imply that dissent should cease. Dissent and resistance are not alternatives but activities that should reinforce each other. There is no reason why
those who take part in tax refusal, draft resistance, and other forms of resistance
should not also speak to church groups or town forums, or become involved in
electoral politics to support peace candidates or referenda on the war. In my experience, it has often been those committed to resistance who have been most
deeply involved in such attempts at persuasion. Putting aside the matter of resistance for a moment, I think it should be emphasized that the days of "patiently
explain" are far from over. As the coffins come home and the taxes go up, many
people who were previously willing to accept government propaganda will become increasingly concerned to try to think for themselves. The reasons for their
change are unfortunate; the opportunities for educational activity are nevertheless very good.

Furthermore, the recent shift in the government's propaganda line offers
important opportunities for critical analysis of the war. There is a note of shrill
desperation in the recent defense of the American war in Vietnam. We hear
less about "bringing freedom and democracy" to the South Vietnamese and
more about the "national interest." Secretary Rusk broods about the dangers
posed to us by a billion Chinese; the Vice-President tells us that we are fighting
"militant Asian Communism" with "its headquarters in Peking" and adds that a
Vietcong victory would directly threaten the United States; Eugene Rostow argues that "it is no good building model cities if they are to be bombed in twenty
years time," and so on (all of this "a frivolous insult to the United States Navy,"
as Walter Lippmann rightly commented).

This shift in propaganda makes it much easier for critical analysis to attack the
problem of Vietnam at its core, which is in Washington and Boston, not in Saigon

and Hanoi. There is something ludicrous, after all, in the close attention that opponents of the war give to the political and social problems of Vietnam. Those who were opposed to the Japanese conquest of Manchuria a generation ago did not place emphasis on the political and social and economic problems of Manchuria, but on those of Japan. They did not engage in farcical debate over the exact degree of support for the puppet emperor, but looked to the sources of Japanese imperialism. Now opponents of the war can much more easily shift attention to the source of the aggression, to our own country, its ideology and institutions. We can ask whose "interest" is served by 100,000 casualties and 100 billion dollars expended in the attempt to subjugate a small country halfway around the world. We can point to the absurdity of the idea that we are "containing China" by destroying popular and independent forces on its borders, and to the cynicism of the claim that we are in Vietnam because "to Americans, peace and freedom are inseparable" and because "suppression of freedom" must not "go unchallenged" (the Citizens Committee again). We can ask why it is that those who make this claim do not suggest that an American expeditionary force be sent to Taiwan, to Rhodesia, to Greece, or to Mississippi, but only to Vietnam, where, they want us to believe, the master aggressor Mao Tse-tung is following a Hitlerian course in his cunning way, committing aggression without troops and announcing world conquest by insisting, through the medium of Lin Piao, that indigenous wars of national liberation can expect little from China beyond applause. We can ask why Secretary McNamara reads such statements as a new *Mein Kampf*—or why those who admit that "a Vietnamese communist regime would probably be . . . anti-Chinese" (Ithiel de Sola Pool, *Asian Survey*, August 1967) nevertheless sign statements which pretend that in Vietnam we are facing the expansionist aggressors from Peking. We can ask what factors in American ideology make it so easy for intelligent and well-informed men to say that we "insist upon nothing for South Vietnam except that it be free to chart its own future" (Citizens Committee) although they know quite well that the regime we imposed excluded all those who took part in the struggle against French colonialism, "and properly so" (Secretary Rusk, 1963); that we have since been attempting to suppress a "civil insurrection" (General Stillwell) led by the only "truly mass-based political party in South Vietnam" (Douglas Pike); that we supervised the destruction of the Buddhist opposition; that we offered the peasants a "free choice" between the Saigon government and the National Liberation Front by herding them into strategic hamlets from which NLF cadres and sympathizers were eliminated by the police (Roger Hilsman); and so on. The story is familiar. And we can emphasize what must be obvious to a person with a grain of political intelligence: that the present world problem is not "containing China" but containing the United States.

More important, we can ask the really fundamental question. Suppose that it were in the American "national interest" to pound into rubble a small nation that refuses to submit to our will. Would it then be legitimate and proper for us to act "in this national interest"? The Rusks and the Humphreys and the Citizens Committee say yes. Nothing could show more clearly how we are taking the road of the fascist aggressors of a generation ago.

We are, of course, in a domestic political environment very different from that of the citizens of Germany or Japan. Here, it takes no heroism to protest. We have many avenues open to us to drive home the lesson that there is not one law for the United States and one for the rest of mankind, that no one has appointed us judge and executioner for Vietnam or anywhere else. Many avenues of political education, on and off the campus, have been explored in the past two years. There can be no question that this effort should continue and grow to whatever limit the degree of commitment permits.

Some seem to feel that resistance will "blacken" the peace movement and make it difficult to reach potential sympathizers through more familiar channels. I don't agree with this objection, but I feel that it should not be lightly disregarded. Resisters who hope to save the people of Vietnam from destruction must select the issues they confront and the means they employ in such a way as to attract as much popular support as possible for their efforts. There is no lack of clear issues and honorable means, surely, hence no reason why one should be impelled to ugly actions on ambiguous issues. In particular, it seems to me that draft resistance, properly conducted (as it has been so far), is not only a highly principled and courageous act, but one that might receive broad support and become politically effective. It might, furthermore, succeed in raising the issues of passive complicity in the war which are now much too easily evaded. Those who face these issues may even go on to free themselves from the mind-destroying ideological pressures of American life, and to ask some serious questions about Amerca's role in the world, and the sources, in American society, for this criminal behavior.

Moreover, I feel that this objection to resistance is not properly formulated. The "peace movement" exists only in the fantasies of the paranoid right. Those who find some of the means employed or ends pursued objectionable can oppose the war in other ways. They will not be read out of a movement that does not exist; they have only themselves to blame if they do not make use of the other forms of protest that are available.

I have left to the end the most important question, the one about which I have least to say. This is the question of the forms resistance should take. We all take part in the war to a greater or lesser extent, if only by paying taxes and permitting domestic society to function smoothly. A person has to choose for himself the point at which he will simply refuse to take part any longer. Reaching that point, he will be drawn into resistance. I believe that the reasons for resistance I have already mentioned are cogent ones: they have an irreducible moral element that admits of little discussion. The issue is posed in its starkest form for the boy who faces induction, and in a form that is somewhat more complex for the boy who must decide whether to participate in a system of selective service that may pass the burden from him to others less fortunate and less privileged. It is difficult for me to see how anyone can refuse to engage himself, in some way, in the plight of these young men. There are many ways to do so: legal aid and financial support; participation in support demonstrations; draft counseling, organization of draft-resistance unions or community-based resistance organizations; assisting those who wish to escape the country; the steps proposed by the clergymen who recently announced that they are ready to share the fate of those who will be sent to prison. About this aspect of the program of resistance I have nothing to say that will not be obvious to anyone who is willing to think the matter through.

Considered as a political tactic, resistance requires careful thought, and I do not pretend to have very clear ideas about it. Much depends on how events unfold in the coming months. Westmoreland's war of attrition may simply continue with no foreseeable end, but the domestic political situation makes this unlikely. If the Republicans do not decide to throw the election again, they could have a winning strategy: they can claim that they will end the war, and remain vague about the means. Under such circumstances, it is unlikely that Johnson will permit the present military stalemate to persist. There are, then, several options. The first is American withdrawal, in whatever terms it would be couched. It might be disguised as a retreat to "enclaves," from which the troops could then be removed. It might be arranged by an international conference, or by permitting a government in Saigon that would seek peace among contending South Vietnamese and then ask us to leave. This policy might be politically feasible; the same public relations firm that invented terms like "revolutionary development" can depict withdrawal as victory. Whether there is anyone in the executive branch with the courage or imagination to urge this course, I do not know. A number of senators are proposing, in essence, that this is the course we should pursue, as are such critics of the war as Walter Lippmann and Hans Morgenthau, if I understand them correctly. A detailed and quite sensible plan for arranging withdrawal along with new, more meaningful elections in the South is outlined by Philippe Devillers in *Le Monde hebdomadaire* of October 26, 1967. Variants can easily be imagined. What is central is the decision to accept the principle of Geneva that the problems of Vietnam be settled by the Vietnamese.

A second possibility would be annihilation. No one doubts that we have the technological capacity for this, and only the sentimental doubt that we have the moral capacity as well. Bernard Fall predicted this outcome in an interview shortly before his death. "The Americans can destroy," he said, "but they cannot pacify. They may win the war, but it will be the victory of the graveyard. Vietnam will be destroyed."

A third option would be an invasion of North Vietnam. This would saddle us with two unwinnable guerrilla wars instead of one, but if the timing is right, it might be used as a device to rally the citizenry around the flag.

A fourth possibility is an attack on China. We could then abandon Vietnam and turn to a winnable war directed against Chinese industrial capacity. Such a move should win the election. No doubt this prospect also appeals to that insane rationality called "strategic thinking." If we intend to keep armies of occupation or even strong military bases on the Asian mainland, we would do well to make sure that the Chinese do not have the means to threaten them. Of course, there is the danger of a nuclear holocaust, but it is difficult to see why this should trouble those whom John McDermott calls the "crisis managers," the same men who were willing, in 1962, to accept a high probability of nuclear war to establish the principle that we, and we alone, have the right to keep missiles on the borders of a potential enemy.

There are many who regard "negotiations" as a realistic alternative, but I do not understand the logic or even the content of this proposal. If we stop bombing North Vietnam we might well enter into negotiations with Hanoi, but there would then be very little to discuss. As to South Vietnam, the only negotiable issue is the withdrawal of foreign troops; other matters can only be settled among whatever Vietnamese groups have survived the American onslaught. The call for "negotiations" seems to me not only empty, but actually a trap for those who oppose the war. If we do not agree to withdraw our troops, the negotiations will be deadlocked, the fighting will continue, American troops will be fired on and killed, the military will have a persuasive argument to escalate, to save American lives. In short, the Symington solution: we offer them peace on our terms, and if they refuse—the victory of the graveyard.

Of the realistic options, only withdrawal (however disguised) seems to me at all tolerable, and resistance, as a tactic of protest, must be designed so as to increase the likelihood that this option will be selected. Furthermore, the time in which to take such action may be very short. The logic of resorting to resistance as a tactic for ending the war is fairly clear. There is no basis for supposing that those who will make the major policy decisions are open to reason on the fundamental issues, in particular the issue of whether we, alone among the nations of the world, have the authority and the competence to determine the social and political institutions of Vietnam. What is more, there is little likelihood that the electoral process will bear on the major decisions. As I have pointed out, the issue may be settled before the next election. Even if it is not, it is hardly likely that a serious choice will be offered at the polls. And if by a miracle such a choice is offered, how seriously can we take the campaign promises of a "peace candidate" after the experience of 1964? Given the enormous dangers of escalation and its hateful character, it makes sense, in such a situation, to search for ways to raise the domestic cost of American aggression, to raise it to a point where it cannot be overlooked by those who have to calculate such costs. One must then consider in what ways it is possible to pose a serious threat. Many possibilities come to mind: a general strike, university strikes, attempts to hamper war production and supply, and so on.

Personally, I feel that disruptive acts of this sort would be justified were they likely to be effective in averting an imminent tragedy. I am skeptical, however, about their possible effectiveness. At the moment, I cannot imagine a broad base for such action, in the white community at least, outside the universities. Forcible repression would not, therefore, prove very difficult. My guess is that such actions would, furthermore, primarily involve students and younger faculty from the humanities and the theological schools, with a scattering of scientists. The professional schools, engineers, specialists in the technology of manipulation and control (much of the social sciences), would probably remain relatively uninvolved. Therefore the longrange threat, such as it is, would be to American humanistic and scientific culture. I doubt that this would seem important to those in decision-making positions. Rusk and Rostow and their accomplices in the academic world seem unaware of the serious threat that their policies already pose in these spheres. I doubt that they appreciate the extent, or the importance, of the dissipation of creative energies and the growing disaffection among young people who are sickened by the violence and deceit that they see in the exercise of American power. Further disruption in these areas might, then, seem to them a negligible cost.

Resistance is in part a moral responsibility, in part a tactic to affect government policy. In particular, with respect to support for draft resistance, I feel that it is a moral responsibility that cannot be shirked. On the other hand, as a tactic, it seems to me of doubtful effectiveness, as matters now stand. I say this with diffidence and considerable uncertainty.

Whatever happens in Vietnam, there are bound to be significant domestic repercussions. It is axiomatic that no army ever loses a war; its brave soldiers and all-knowing generals are stabbed in the back by treacherous civilians. American withdrawal is likely, then, to bring to the surface the worst features of American culture, and perhaps to lead to a serious internal repression. On the other hand, an American "victory" might well have dangerous consequences both at home and abroad. It might give added prestige to an already far too powerful executive. There is, moreover, the problem emphasized by A. J. Muste: ". . . the problem after a war is with the victor. He thinks he has just proved that war and violence pay. Who will now teach him a lesson?" For the most powerful and most aggressive nation in the world, this is indeed a danger. If we can rid ourselves of the naive belief that we are somehow different and more pure—a belief held by the British, the French, the Japanese, in their moments of imperial glory—then we will be able honestly to face the truth in this observation. One can only hope that we will face this truth before too many innocents, on all sides, suffer and die.

Finally, there are certain principles that I think must be stressed as we try to build effective opposition to this and future wars. We must not, I believe, thoughtlessly urge others to commit civil disobedience, and we must be careful not to construct situations in which young people will find themselves induced, perhaps in violation of their basic convictions, to commit civil disobedience. Resistance must be freely undertaken. I also hope, more sincerely than I know how to say, that it will create bonds of friendship and mutual trust that will support and strengthen those who are sure to suffer.

CHAPTER TEN

The Vietnam War, Part II: A Nation Divided

103. Dwight D. Eisenhower, "Let's Close Ranks on the Home Front"

(1968)

In the wake of the Tet offensive and plummeting public support for the Johnson administration's Vietnam policies, former president Dwight Eisenhower took on the antiwar movement and "armchair strategists" for undermining the war effort. Eisenhower remained a prominent elder statesman in the years after he left the White House. Both John F. Kennedy and Lyndon Johnson sought Eisenhower's counsel on military and foreign affairs, at times publicly, as a way of validating their own policies. The former president remained exceedingly popular with the American public. In this article, published in *Reader's Digest* in the wake of major antiwar protests, and especially the Tet offensive, Eisenhower, the war hero–president, measured domestic discourse on the war against the solidarity of the World War II home front, and found it discouraging. In calling on Americans to close ranks behind the war effort, he anticipates Richard Nixon's dismissal of protesters as a vocal minority and suggests that division at home helps only the enemy.

SOURCE: *Reader's Digest*, April 1968.

In a long life of service to my country, I have never encountered a situation more depressing than the present spectacle of an America deeply divided over a war—a war to which we have committed so much in treasure, in honor and in the lives of our young men. What has become of our courage? What has become of our loyalty to others? What has become of a noble concept called patriotism, which in former times of crisis has carried us through to victory and peace?

World War II

If in the desperate days of World War II we had been torn by this kind of discord, I doubt that we and our allies could have won. Looking back, I think how disheartening it would have been to those of us who commanded forces in the field if we had been called home to make speeches and hold press conferences—to shore up a wavering solidarity on the home front. Nothing of the sort happened then. But it is happening now. And how the enemies of freedom throughout the world—from Hanoi to Moscow—must be rejoicing!

In our war against the Axis powers a quarter of a century ago, we were fighting for the cause of freedom and human dignity, just as we are now. And in the long-range sense, we were also fighting for our own salvation, for a way of life we hold dear, just as we are now. In that war the American people understood this, and it was inspiring to see the single-minded way this country faced up to the job of fighting two first-rate military powers simultaneously.

We had a few slackers and draft dodgers, of course, but they were objects of scorn. We grumbled a bit about rationing and sometimes accused our draft boards of partiality, but these minor irrationalities were mostly a way of letting off steam. Essentially, we were united, and nearly everyone found some way of helping in the war effort. As a nation, we were dedicated to the job of winning completely and swiftly. And we did win—at least a year earlier than the most optimistic military timetables had forecast.

As commander of the Allied armies in Europe, I can testify that this solidarity, this upsurge of patriotism on the home front was a wonderfully encouraging thing. Neither I nor any other military leader had to lie awake nights wondering whether the folks back home would stick with us to the end. It never occurred to us that they might not. We knew that the American spirit had rallied to the cause, and this knowledge buoyed us up immeasurably—all of us, right down to the private in the ranks.

Today the reverse is true. We have "chosen up sides," as youngsters say in lining up their ball teams, and we call ourselves hawks and doves. This terminology in itself is inaccurate and ridiculous. A hawk is a bird of prey, a dove the helpless victim of predators. We are neither. We covet nobody's territory or property, want no dominion over others. On the other hand, we have always shown ourselves capable of self-defense. I trust we always shall.

Beyond Honorable Dissent

No one who believes in our democratic process can object to honorable dissent. This is part of the American credo, part of our birthright. There are those who now sincerely believe that we have no business being in Vietnam. I think they are terribly and dangerously wrong, but they have the right to state their views.

The current raucous confrontation, however, goes far beyond honorable dissent. Public men and private citizens alike take a stance and defend their positions angrily and unreasonably, often substituting emotion for logic and facts.

Not long ago, for example, a young U.S. Senator was quoted as saying that if we are fighting in Vietnam to protect ourselves, then we must concede that we are being selfishly immoral. To me this seems the height of tortured reasoning, if not worse. Certainly, we are fighting to defend ourselves and other free nations against the eventual domination of communism. In my opinion it would be grossly immoral *not* to resist a tyranny whose openly avowed purpose is to subjugate the earth—and particularly the United States of America. The Senator was indulging in sophistry, and I suspect his purpose was political rather than patriotic.

A ludicrous, and dangerous, aspect of this bitter quarrel is the large number of public men who regard themselves as military experts. One large defeatist group proclaims loudly and positively that "we can never win the Vietnam war." Others insist, contrary to the best military judgment and to clear evidence, that our air strikes "do no good" and we must cease all bombing of targets in the North. Still others want our troops to sit down in "defensive enclaves" and drop all offensive action—presumably until a tough enemy gets tired of looking at our military might and goes quietly home.

Instead of giving faith and backing to the men who are responsible for the conduct of the war, these armchair strategists snipe at every aspect of the conflict. Moreover, they never seem to lack a rostrum for their pronouncements. They are quoted endlessly and prominently in the press and on the airwaves, and of course their words give aid and comfort to the enemy and thus prolong the war.

A tactic of some dissenters—and this alarms me more than all the empty shouting—is their resort to force in open defiance of the laws of the land. They try to prevent recruiting officers from doing their job, and sometimes succeed. They try to halt the work of personnel recruiters from industries which manufacture war matériel. They lie down on the pavement in front of draft-induction centers; they jeer at the inductees and try to keep them from answering their call to service.

Some young Americans publicly burn their draft cards and state they will never go to war. The "peaceful" anti-war demonstrations frequently get out of hand and become bloodily violent. Dissenters of this type insist on their own right to free speech, but are unwilling to grant the same right to others. How often lately we have been subjected to the shocking spectacle of some distinguished speaker being smuggled in the back door of a lecture hall to avoid physical harm from the demonstrators out front!

These militant peace-at-any-price groups are a small minority, but all too often they get away with such illegal actions—and also get away with the headlines. There is no reason to tolerate this arrogant flouting of the law. It could be stopped—and should be stopped—at once. Their action is not honorable dissent. It is rebellion, and it verges on treason.

In the midst of this disgraceful public uproar, the dissenters continue to demand that we negotiate. I am a firm believer in constructive negotiation, provided both sides come to the conference table with honest and reasonable intentions. Thus far, North Vietnam has made it emphatically clear that it wants no negotiation—except on terms which would mean our complete capitulation. Listening to all the anti-war sound and fury on our home front, Hanoi obviously prefers to wait it out in the hope that public opinion in the United States will eventually compel our withdrawal. It is probable that the behavior of the dissenters themselves is making honorable negotiation impossible.

Reasons for Staying in Vietnam

Those who oppose the Vietnam war and insist on our unilateral withdrawal have said over and over that the American people have never been given a sound reason for our presence there. If they believe this, it must be because they refuse to read or listen to anything they don't like. There are reasons why it is critically important to fight the communists in Vietnam, and they have been stated often.

The first and most immediate reason—so obvious that it shouldn't have to be explained—is that we are trying to save a brave little country, to which we have given our solemn promise of protection, from being swallowed by the communist tyranny. We want the people of South Vietnam to have their chance to live in freedom and prosperity, and even in the midst of a bitter war we are already doing much to help them build up their economy.

If anyone doubts the determination of the communists to subjugate this small country and take it over by sheer savagery, let him read the accounts of the Vietcong's impersonal butchery of whole villages of innocent people. The communists' tactic of conquest by terror, their callous disregard for human life, their philosophy that the end justifies the means—no matter how barbarous and immoral the means may be—are precisely the same in Vietnam as they have used in gobbling up other countries and other free peoples of the world. Their objectives have not changed or softened over the years. The only language they understand is force, or the threat of force.

There is a larger reason for our military presence in Vietnam—and that is the urgent need to keep all Southeast Asia from falling to the communists. Some of our self-appointed military experts discount the "domino theory"—which, as applied to Southeast Asia, simply means that if we abandon South Vietnam to communism, the other countries of that area will also topple. In my opinion, the domino theory is frighteningly correct. I suggest that the peace-at-any-price advocates who scoff at this threat study the behavior of communism over the past two decades.

Here at home, this is election year, and I hope we do not permit the Vietnam war to become a divisive political issue. It is right and proper to advocate a change of leadership and to discuss the conduct of the war. But it is improper, and I think unpatriotic, to voice dissent in such a way that it encourages our enemies to believe we have lost the capacity to make a national decision and act on it. Meanwhile, I state this unequivocally: *I will not personally support any peace-at-any-price candidate who advocates capitulation and the abandonment of South Vietnam.*

As any citizen does, I deeply regret the necessity of pouring the blood of our young men and our treasure into this faraway war for freedom. But it is a necessity. This is an hour of grave national emergency. It is time that we do more thinking and less shouting; that we put our faith in our democratic processes and cease the dangerous tactic of deciding which laws we will and will not obey.

We should also ponder the previous successes and sacrifices we made in checking the advance of communism: how we helped save Western Europe through the Marshall Plan; how we checked aggression in Korea, on the free Chinese islands of Quemoy and Matsu, in Lebanon and the Dominican Republic. How we saved Formosa, and are successfully helping the South American nations resist the Cuban conspirators. These things we must continue to do, even when we stand alone—even when so-called friendly nations criticize our actions.

The Civil War

Sometimes I find comfort in going back even further in history. At one time during the Civil War, a profound spirit of defeatism developed in the North. A considerable portion of the people, discouraged and fearful, cried: Let the South go its way; we can never win this horrible war. Abraham Lincoln was reviled; draft laws were defied; hundreds were killed in resisting recruiting agents. The pressure on the government to acknowledge defeat was intense.

Lincoln, however, saw two things clearly. He knew that the successful secession of the South would fragment America and deny it its great destiny. And with a clear-sighted evaluation of the manpower and resources of both sides, he also knew that the North could win. He stood steadfast, and before long the courage and common sense of the people revived, the defeatists subsided, and the Union was saved.

It is my hope and belief that history will now repeat itself. I still have abiding faith in the good sense of the great majority of the American people. It is unthinkable that the voices of defeat should triumph in our land.

104. Daniel Berrigan, "A Meditation from Catonsville"

(1968)

On May 17, 1968, a group of nine Catholic antiwar activists entered the draft board offices in Catonsville, Maryland, removed some 400 draft files to the parking lot, and burned them with homemade napalm while awaiting their arrest. Two of the Catonsville Nine, as they became known, were Catholic priests: Philip Berrigan and his older brother, Daniel. A Jesuit with close ties to Dorothy Day and Thomas Merton, Daniel Berrigan (1921–) was born in Minnesota, grew up outside Syracuse, New York, and graduated from St. Andrews-on-Hudson Seminary. In 1966, following a four-month exile to Latin America—imposed by Joseph Cardinal Spellman as punishment for his outspoken peace activism—Berrigan assumed a chaplaincy at Cornell University. In 1967, he traveled to North Vietnam and returned with three American pilots freed by the enemy. A prolific poet, he wrote about that experience in *Night Flight to Hanoi*. In the following essay, Daniel Berrigan captures both the desperation and the hope of the so-called Catholic Left as it prepared for the Catonsville action. Later, after the October 1968 trial (which ended in convictions), Berrigan wrote a play, in verse, based on the trial transcripts, *The Trial of the Catonsville Nine*. After a brief period as a fugitive, he spent eighteen months in federal prison.

SOURCE: Reprinted in *Delivered into Resistance* (New Haven, Conn.: Advocate Press, 1969), 68–70.

Every page that deals, as this one tries to, with the news about today, finds itself fairly buried before it is born. Last week's omelette. This week is still in the egg shells. I sit here, breaking eggs to make an Easter, to feed the living as I hope, good news for bad.

Some 10 or 12 of us (the number is still uncertain) will, if all goes well (ill?) take our religious bodies during this week to a draft center in or near Baltimore. There we shall, of purpose and forethought, remove the 1-A files, sprinkle them in the public street with home-made napalm, and set them afire. For which act we shall, beyond doubt, be placed behind bars for some portion of our natural lives, in consequence of our inability to live and die content in the plagued city, to say "peace peace" when there is no peace, to keep the poor poor, the homeless, the thirsty and hungry homeless, thirsty and hungry.

Our apologies, good friends, for the fracture of good order, the burning of paper instead of children, the angering of the orderlies in the front parlor of the charnel house. We could not, so help us God, do otherwise. For we are sick at heart, our hearts give us no rest for thinking of the Land of Burning Children. And for thinking of that other Child, of whom the poet Luke speaks. The infant was taken up in the arms of an old man, whose tongue grew resonant and vatic at the touch of that beauty. And the old man spoke; this child is set for the fall and rise of many in Israel, a sign that is spoken against.

Small consolation; a child born to make trouble, and to die for it, the First Jew (not the last) to be subject of a "definitive solution." He sets up the cross and dies on it; in the Rose Garden of the executive mansion, on the D.C. Mall, in the courtyard of the Pentagon. We see the sign, we read the direction: you must bear with us, for his sake. Or if you will not, the consequences are our own.

For it will be easy, after all, to discredit us. Our record is bad; trouble makers in church and state, a priest married despite his vows, two convicted felons. We have jail records, we have been turbulent, uncharitable, we have failed in love for the brethren, have yielded to fear and despair and pride, often in our lives. Forgive us.

We are no more, when the truth is told, than ignorant beset men, jockeying against all chance, at the hour of death, for a place at the right hand of the dying one.

We act against the law at a time of the Poor People's March, at a time moreover when the government is announcing ever more massive paramilitary means to confront disorder in the cities. It is announced that a computerized center is being built in the Pentagon at a cost of some seven millions of dollars, to offer instant response to outbreaks anywhere in the land; that moreover, the government takes so serious a view of civil disorder, that federal troops, with war experience in Vietnam, will have first responsibility to quell civil disorder.

The implications of all this must strike horror in the mind of any thinking man. The war in Vietnam is more and more literally brought home to us. Its inmost meaning strikes the American ghettos; in servitude to the affluent. We must resist and protest this crime.

Finally, we stretch out our hands to our brothers throughout the world. We who are priests, to our fellow priests. All of us who act against the law, turn to the poor of the world, to the Vietnamese, to the victims, to the soldiers who kill and die, for the wrong reasons, for no reason at all, because they were so ordered—by the authorities of that public order which is in effect a massive institutionalized disorder.

We say: killing is disorder, life and gentleness and community and unselfishness is the only order we recognize. For the sake of that order, we risk our liberty, our good name. The time is past when good men can remain silent, when obedience can segregate men from public risk, when the poor can die without defense.

We ask our fellow Christians to consider in their hearts a question which has tortured us, night and day, since the war began. How many must die before our voices are heard, how many must be tortured, dislocated, starved, maddened? How long must the world's resources be raped in the service of legalized murder? When, at what point, will you say no to this war?

We have chosen to say, with the gift of our liberty, if necessary our lives: the violence stops here, the death stops here, the suppression of the truth stops here, this war stops here.

We wish also to place in question, by this act, all suppositions about normal times, about longings for an untroubled life in a somnolent church, about a neat timetable of ecclesiastical renewal which in respect to the needs of men, amounts to another form of time serving.

Redeem the times! The times are inexpressibly evil. Christians pay conscious, indeed religious tribute, to Caesar and Mars; by the approval of overkill tactics, by brinkmanship, by nuclear liturgies, by racism, by support of genocide. They embrace their society with all their heart, and abandon the cross. They pay lip service to Christ and military service to the powers of death.

And yet, and yet, the times are inexhaustibly good, solaced by the courage and hope of many. The truth rules, Christ is not forsaken. In a time of death, some men—the resisters, those who work hardily for social change, those who preach and embrace the unpalatable truth—such men overcome death, their lives are bathed in the light of the resurrection, the truth has set them free. In the jaws of death, of contumely, of good and ill report, they proclaim their love of the brethren.

We think of such men, in the world, in our nation, in the churches; and the stone in our breast is dissolved; we take heart once more.

105. Merle Haggard, "Okie from Muskogee"

(1969)

In "Okie from Muskogee," Merle Haggard expressed a growing sense of resentment toward the antiwar movement and the counterculture. Haggard (1937–) came from a family that had migrated from Oklahoma to California, and was born and raised near Bakersfield. He got into a lot of trouble as a youth, and wound up in and out of reform school, then spent almost three years in San Quentin prison for breaking and entering. When he got out, he dedicated himself to music, and by the late 1960s attracted a considerable following for his honky-tonk style on songs such as "Mama Tried." "Okie from Muskogee," like the following year's "Fightin' Side of Me," captured a sense of middle American patriotism, and predicted Richard Nixon's "silent majority." Nixon liked the song so much, in fact, that he invited Haggard to perform at the White House. By the second Iraq war, Haggard had changed his tune, playing "America First" (2006) with its line "Let's get out of Iraq and get back on track."

SOURCE: Capitol ST 384.

> We don't smoke marijuana in Muskogee;
> We don't take our trips on LSD
> **We don't burn our draft cards down on Main Street;**
> **We like livin' right, and bein' free.**
>
> I'm proud to be an Okie from Muskogee,
> A place where even squares can have a ball
> **We still wave Old Glory down at the courthouse,**
> **And white lightnin's still the biggest thrill of all**
>
> We don't make a party out of lovin';
> We like holdin' hands and pitchin' woo;
> **We don't let our hair grow long and shaggy,**
> **Like the hippies out in San Francisco do.**

And I'm proud to be an Okie from Muskogee,
A place where even squares can have a ball.
We still wave Old Glory down at the courthouse,
And white lightnin's still the biggest thrill of all.

Leather boots are still in style for manly footwear;
Beads and Roman sandals won't be seen.
Football's still the roughest thing on campus,
And the kids here still respect the college dean.

We still wave Old Glory down at the courthouse,
In Muskogee, Oklahoma, USA.

106. The Flying Burrito Brothers, "My Uncle"

(1969)

The Flying Burrito Brothers' song "My Uncle" plaintively captured the common experience of a young man contemplating immigration to Canada in lieu of being drafted and possibly sent to Vietnam. Started in 1968 by Gram Parsons and Chris Hillman, two former members of the Byrds, the Flying Burrito Brothers are often credited with being the first country-rock band. Their first album, *Gilded Palace of Sin*, came out just after Richard Nixon's inauguration as president, and included "My Uncle." Although the overwhelming majority of Americans saw the draft and its system of deferments as unfair, evading the draft was even more controversial than draft resistance or burning draft files. The exact number of men who left the country is not known, but most estimates put the figure at 60,000 or more, with most immigrating to Canada. Although Nixon arguably made the draft more equitable by eliminating most of the deferments and introducing a lottery system, it remained unpopular until it was phased out altogether in 1973.

SOURCE: The Flying Burrito Brothers, *Gilded Palace of Sin* (A&M SP 4175, 1969).

> A letter came today from the draft board
> With trembling hands I read the questionnaire
> It asked me lots of things about my mama and papa
> Now that ain't what I call exactly fair
>
> So I'm heading for the nearest foreign border
> Vancouver may be just my kind of town
> Because they don't need the kind of law and order
> That tends to keep a good man underground
>
> A sad old soldier once told me a story
> About a battlefield that he was on
> He said a man should never fight for glory
> He must know what is right and what is wrong

So I'm heading for the nearest foreign border
Vancouver may be just my kind of town
Because they don't need the kind of law and order
That tends to keep a good man underground

Now I don't know how much I owe my uncle
But I suspect it's more than I can pay
He's asking me to sign a three-year contract
I guess I'll catch the first bus out today

So I'm heading for the nearest foreign border
Vancouver may be just my kind of town
Because they don't need the kind of law and order
That tends to keep a good man underground
That tends to keep a good man underground

107. Students for a Democratic Society, "Bring the War Home"

(1969)

Only four years removed from the Paul Potter years, in which "naming the system" had been expected to bring about change, end the war, and refocus American priorities, Students for a Democratic Society began to splinter. One faction, Weatherman—named for a line in Bob Dylan's "Rainy Day Women"— "you don't have to be a weatherman to know which way the wind blows"— had assumed national leadership of SDS and advocated revolution. "Bring the War Home" was a widely distributed leaflet aimed at attracting like-minded would-be revolutionaries to Chicago for the "Days of Rage" in October. If the Catonsville action (and its attendant critique of the war and American culture) came across as militant, Weatherman went further. It named the system, too, but more stridently, and called for the establishment of "another front against imperialism right here in America." It did not take long for the authorities to react, and soon police and the FBI made a point of targeting Weather. Within a year, after a bomb-making episode accidentally killed three members, most of the leaders went underground, and continued to strike at the "system" surreptitiously.

SOURCE: *New Left Notes,* August 1, 1969.

Look at It: America, 1969

The war goes on, despite the jive double-talk about troop withdrawals and peace talks. Black people continue to be murdered by agents of the fat cats who run this country, if not in one way, then in another: by the pigs or the courts, by the boss or the welfare department.

Working people face higher taxes, inflation, speed-ups, and the sure knowledge—if it hasn't happened already—that their sons may be shipped off to Vietnam and shipped home in a box. And young people all over the country go to prisons that are called schools, are trained for jobs that don't exist or serve no one's real interest but the boss's, and, to top it all of, get told that Vietnam is the place to defend their "freedom."

None of this is very new. The cities have been falling apart, the schools have been bullshit, the jobs have been rotten and unfulfilling for a long time.

What's new is that today not quite so many people are confused, and a lot more people are angry: angry about the fact that the promises we have heard since first grade are all jive; angry that, when you get down to it, this system is nothing but the total economic and military put-down of the oppressed peoples of the world.

And more: it's a system that steals the goods, the resources, and the labor of poor and working people all over the world in order to fill the pockets and bank accounts of a tiny capitalist class. (Call it imperialism.) It's a system that divides white workers from blacks by offering whites crumbs off the table, and telling them that if they don't stay cool the blacks will move in on their jobs, their homes, and their schools. (Call it white supremacy.) It's a system that divides men from women, forcing women to be subservient to men from childhood, to be slave labor in the home and cheap labor in the factory. (Call it male supremacy.) And it's a system that has colonized whole nations within this country—the nation of black people, the nation of brown people—to enslave, oppress, and ultimately murder the people on whose backs this country was built. (Call it fascism.)

But the lies are catching up to America—and the slick rich people and their agents in the government bureaucracies, the courts, the schools, and the pig stations just can't cut it anymore.

Black and brown people know it.

Young people know it.

More and more white working people know it.

And you know it.

SDS Is Calling the Action This Year

But it will be a different action. An action not only against a single war or a "foreign policy," but against the whole imperialist system that made that war a necessity. An action not only for immediate withdrawal of all U.S. occupation troops, but in support of the heroic fight of the Vietnamese people and the National Liberation Front for freedom and independence. An action not only to bring "peace to Vietnam," but beginning to establish another front against imperialism right here in America—to "bring the war home."

We are demanding that all occupational troops get out of Vietnam and every other place they don't belong. This includes the black and brown communities, the workers' picket lines, the high schools, and the streets of Berkeley. No longer will we tolerate "law and order" backed up by soldiers in Vietnam and pigs in the communities and schools; a "law and order" that serves only the interests of those in power and tries to smash the people down whenever they rise up.

We are demanding the release of all political prisoners who have been victimized by the ever-growing attacks on the black liberation struggle and the people in general. Especially the leaders of the black liberation struggle like Huey P. Newton, Ahmed Evans, Fred Hampton, and Martin Sostre.

We are expressing total support for the National Liberation Front and the newly-formed Provisional Revolutionary Government of South Vietnam. Throughout the history of the war, the NLF has provided the political and military leadership to the people of South Vietnam. The Provisional Revolutionary Government, recently formed by the NLF and other groups, has pledged to "mobilize the South Vietnamese armed forces and people" in order to continue the struggle for independence. The PRG also has expressed solidarity with "the just struggle of the Afro-American people for their fundamental national rights," and has pledged to "actively support the national independence movements of Asia, Africa, and Latin America."

We are also expressing total support for the black liberation struggle, part of the same struggle that the Vietnamese are fighting, against the same enemy.

We are demanding independence for Puerto Rico, and an end to the colonial oppression that the Puerto Rican nation faces at the hands of U.S. imperialism.

We are demanding an end to the surtax, a tax taken from the working people of this country and used to kill working people in Vietnam and other places for fun and profit.

We are expressing solidarity with the Conspiracy 8 who led the struggle last summer in Chicago. Our action is planned to roughly coincide with the beginning of their trial.

And we are expressing support for GIs in Vietnam and throughout the world who are being made to fight the battles of the rich, like poor and working people have always been made to do. We support those GIs at Fort Hood, Fort Jackson, and many other army bases who have refused to be cannon fodder in a war against the people of Vietnam.

It's Almost Hard to Remember When the War Began

But, after years of peace marches, petitions, and the gradual realization that this war was no "mistake" at all, one critical fact remains: the war is not just happening in Vietnam.

It is happening in the jungles of Guatemala, Bolivia, Thailand, and all oppressed nations throughout the world.

And it is happening here. In black communities throughout the country. On college campuses. And in the high schools, in the shops, and on the streets.

It is a war in which there are only two sides; a war not for domination but for an end to domination, not for destruction, but for liberation and the unchaining of human freedom.

And it is a war in which we cannot "resist"; it is a war in which we must fight.

On October 11, tens of thousands of people will come to Chicago to bring the war home. Join us.

108. Richard M. Nixon, "The Silent Majority Speech"

(1969)

In the so-called Silent Majority Speech, President Richard Nixon responded to nationwide protests against the Vietnam War by unveiling his latest plan for peace and by dismissing his critics as a "vocal minority." Nixon (1913–94) grew up a Quaker in Whittier, California. He earned degrees at Whittier College and Duke University Law School before serving as a navy lieutenant during World War II. Nixon won election to Congress in 1946 and served on the House Un-American Activities Committee before being elected to the Senate in 1950. In 1952, running on the ticket with Dwight Eisenhower, Nixon was elected vice president. In 1954, when the French sought U.S. assistance as they faced defeat in Vietnam, Nixon unsuccessfully urged Eisenhower to send air support. After losing the presidential election to John F. Kennedy in 1960 and the California gubernatorial election to Pat Brown in 1962, Nixon mounted a stunning political comeback in 1968. Running on a platform that promised to restore law and order to American cities and campuses and to achieve "peace with honor" in Vietnam, Nixon defeated Vice President Hubert Humphrey for the presidency. In his first year in office, Nixon announced a plan to Vietnamize the war by gradually turning over responsibility for the ground war to the South Vietnamese military, introducing the draft lottery, and secretly expanding the air war into Cambodia.

On October 15, 1969, millions of Americans took the day off from work or school to participate in antiwar protests across the country under the umbrella of the Moratorium. With another Moratorium planned for November 15, Nixon took to the airwaves with this speech, calling on the great "silent majority" of Americans for support.

SOURCE: Richard Nixon, Address to the Nation on Vietnam, November 3, 1969, Public Papers of the President.

Good evening, my fellow Americans:

Tonight I want to talk to you on a subject of deep concern to all Americans and to many people in all parts of the world—the war in Vietnam.

I believe that one of the reasons for the deep division about Vietnam is that many Americans have lost confidence in what their Government has told them about our policy. The American people cannot and should not be asked to support a policy which involves the overriding issues of war and peace unless they know the truth about that policy.

Tonight, therefore, I would like to answer some of the questions that I know are on the minds of many of you listening to me . . .

Now, let me begin by describing the situation I found when I was inaugurated on January 20.

- The war had been going on for 4 years.
- 31,000 Americans had been killed in action.
- The training program for the South Vietnamese was behind schedule.
- 540,000 Americans were in Vietnam with no plans to reduce the number.

  - No progress had been made at the negotiations in Paris and the United States had not put forth a comprehensive peace proposal.
  - The war was causing deep division at home and criticism from many of our friends as well as our enemies abroad.

In view of these circumstances there were some who urged that I end the war at once by ordering the immediate withdrawal of all American forces.

From a political standpoint this would have been a popular and easy course to follow. After all, we became involved in the war while my predecessor was in office. I could blame the defeat which would be the result of my action on him and come out as the Peacemaker. Some put it to me quite bluntly: This was the only way to avoid allowing Johnson's war to become Nixon's war.

But I had a greater obligation than to think only of the years of my administration and of the next election. I had to think of the effect of my decision on the next generation and on the future of peace and freedom in America and in the world.

Let us all understand that the question before us is not whether some Americans are for peace and some Americans are against peace. The question at issue is not whether Johnson's war becomes Nixon's war.

The great question is: How can we win America's peace? . . .

In January I could only conclude that the precipitate withdrawal of American forces from Vietnam would be a disaster not only for South Vietnam but for the United States and for the cause of peace.

For the South Vietnamese, our precipitate withdrawal would inevitably allow the Communists to repeat the massacres which followed their takeover in the North 15 years before . . .

For the United States, this first defeat in our Nation's history would result in a collapse of confidence in American leadership, not only in Asia but throughout the world.

Three American Presidents have recognized the great stakes involved in Vietnam and understood what had to be done.

In 1963, President Kennedy, with his characteristic eloquence and clarity, said: ". . . we want to see a stable government there, carrying on a struggle to maintain its national independence.

"We believe strongly in that. We are not going to withdraw from that effort. In my opinion, for us to withdraw from that effort would mean a collapse not only of South Viet-Nam, but Southeast Asia. So we are going to stay there."

President Eisenhower and President Johnson expressed the same conclusion during their terms of office.

For the future of peace, precipitate withdrawal would thus be a disaster of immense magnitude.

- A nation cannot remain great if it betrays its allies and lets down its friends.

  - Our defeat and humiliation in South Vietnam without question would promote recklessness in the councils of those great powers who have not yet abandoned their goals of world conquest.

- This would spark violence wherever our commitments help maintain the peace-in the Middle East, in Berlin, eventually even in the Western Hemisphere.

Ultimately, this would cost more lives.

It would not bring peace; it would bring more war.

For these reasons, I rejected the recommendation that I should end the war by immediately withdrawing all of our forces. I chose instead to change American policy on both the negotiating front and battlefront . . .

We have adopted a plan which we have worked out in cooperation with the South Vietnamese for the complete withdrawal of all U.S. combat ground forces, and their replacement by South Vietnamese forces on an orderly scheduled timetable. This withdrawal will be made from strength and not from weakness. As South Vietnamese forces become stronger, the rate of American withdrawal can become greater.

I have not and do not intend to announce the timetable for our program. And there are obvious reasons for this decision which I am sure you will understand. As I have indicated on several occasions, the rate of withdrawal will depend on developments on three fronts.

One of these is the progress which can be or might be made in the Paris talks. An announcement of a fixed timetable for our withdrawal would completely remove any incentive for the enemy to negotiate an agreement. They would simply wait until our forces had withdrawn and then move in.

The other two factors on which we will base our withdrawal decisions are the level of enemy activity and the progress of the training programs of the South Vietnamese forces. And I am glad to be able to report tonight progress on both of these fronts has been greater than we anticipated when we started the program in June for withdrawal. As a result, our timetable for withdrawal is more optimistic now than when we made our first estimates in June. Now, this clearly demonstrates why it is not wise to be frozen in on a fixed timetable.

We must retain the flexibility to base each withdrawal decision on the situation as it is at that time rather than on estimates that are no longer valid.

Along with this optimistic estimate, I must—in all candor—leave one note of caution.

If the level of enemy activity significantly increases we might have to adjust our timetable accordingly. . . .

My fellow Americans, I am sure you can recognize from what I have said that we really only have two choices open to us if we want to end this war.

- I can order an immediate, precipitate withdrawal of all Americans from Vietnam without regard to the effects of that action.
- Or we can persist in our search for a just peace through a negotiated settlement if possible, or through continued implementation of our plan for Vietnamization if necessary-a plan in which we will withdraw all of our forces from Vietnam on a schedule in accordance with our program, as the South Vietnamese become strong enough to defend their own freedom.

I have chosen this second course.

It is not the easy way.

It is the right way.

It is a plan which will end the war and serve the cause of peace—not just in Vietnam but in the Pacific and in the world.

In speaking of the consequences of a precipitate withdrawal, I mentioned that our allies would lose confidence in America.

Far more dangerous, we would lose confidence in ourselves. Oh, the immediate reaction would be a sense of relief that our men were coming home. But as we saw the consequences of what we had done, inevitable remorse and divisive recrimination would scar our spirit as a people.

We have faced other crisis in our history and have become stronger by rejecting the easy way out and taking the right way in meeting our challenges. Our greatness as a nation has been our capacity to do what had to be done when we knew our course was right.

I recognize that some of my fellow citizens disagree with the plan for peace I have chosen. Honest and patriotic Americans have reached different conclusions as to how peace should be achieved.

In San Francisco a few weeks ago, I saw demonstrators carrying signs reading: "Lose in Vietnam, bring the boys home."

Well, one of the strengths of our free society is that any American has a right to reach that conclusion and to advocate that point of view. But as President of the United States, I would be untrue to my oath of office if I allowed the policy of this Nation to be dictated by the minority who hold that point of view and who try to impose it on the Nation by mounting demonstrations in the street.

For almost 200 years, the policy of this Nation has been made under our Constitution by those leaders in the Congress and the White House elected by all of the people. If a vocal minority, however fervent its cause, prevails over reason and the will of the majority, this Nation has no future as a free society.

And now I would like to address a word, if I may, to the young people of this Nation who are particularly concerned, and I understand why they are concerned, about this war.

I respect your idealism.

I share your concern for peace.

I want peace as much as you do.

There are powerful personal reasons I want to end this war. This week I will have to sign 83 letters to mothers, fathers, wives, and loved ones of men who have given their lives for America in Vietnam. It is very little satisfaction to me that this is only one-third as many letters as I signed the first week in office. There is nothing I want more than to see the day come when I do not have to write any of those letters.

- I want to end the war to save the lives of those brave young men in Vietnam.

  - But I want to end it in a way which will increase the chance that their younger brothers and their sons will not have to fight in some future Vietnam someplace in the world.
  - And I want to end the war for another reason. I want to end it so that the energy and dedication of you, our young people, now too often directed into bitter hatred against those responsible for the war, can be turned to the great challenges of peace, a better life for all Americans, a better life for all people on this earth.

I have chosen a plan for peace. I believe it will succeed.

If it does succeed, what the critics say now won't matter. If it does not succeed, anything I say then won't matter.

I know it may not be fashionable to speak of patriotism or national destiny these days. But I feel it is appropriate to do so on this occasion

Two hundred years ago this Nation was weak and poor. But even then, America was the hope of millions in the world. Today we have become the strongest and richest nation in the world. And the wheel of destiny has turned so that any hope the world has for the survival of peace and freedom will be determined by whether the American people have the moral stamina and the courage to meet the challenge of free world leadership.

Let historians not record that when America was the most powerful nation in the world we passed on the other side of the road and allowed the last hopes for peace and freedom of millions of people to be suffocated by the forces of totalitarianism.

And so tonight—to you, the great silent majority of my fellow Americans—I ask for your support.

I pledged in my campaign for the Presidency to end the war in a way that we could win the peace. I have initiated a plan of action which will enable me to keep that pledge.

The more support I can have from the American people, the sooner that pledge can be redeemed; for the more divided we are at home, the less likey, the enemy is to negotiate at Paris.

Let us be united for peace. Let us also be united against defeat. Because let us understand: North Vietnam cannot defeat or humiliate the United States. Only Americans can do that.

Fifty years ago, in this room and at this very desk, President Woodrow Wilson spoke words which caught the imagination of a war-weary world. He said: "This is the war to end war." His dream for peace after World War I was shattered on the hard realities of great power politics and Woodrow Wilson died a broken man.

Tonight I do not tell you that the war in Vietnam is the war to end wars. But I do say this: I have initiated a plan which Will end this war in a way that will bring us closer to that great goal to which Woodrow Wilson and every American President in our history has been dedicated-the goal of a just and lasting peace.

As President I hold the responsibility for choosing the best path to that goal and then leading the Nation along it.

I pledge to you tonight that I shall meet this responsibility with all of the strength and wisdom I can command in accordance with your hopes, mindful of your concerns, sustained by your prayers.

Thank you and goodnight.

109. Women Strike for Peace, "A Woman's Declaration of Liberation from Military Domination"

(1970)

In this "Declaration of Liberation from Military Domination," Women Strike for Peace (WSP) attempted to focus the debate over the Vietnam War on the domestic costs of the war. WSP formed in 1961 in protest against nuclear weapons testing by the United States and the Soviet Union. It was one of the first peace organizations to expand its focus from disarmament to protesting the Vietnam War, and over the next ten years it remained a powerful presence within the antiwar movement. Couching its protest in maternal rhetoric, WSP criticized the war for the damage it did to both American draftees and Vietnamese children. Accordingly, WSP operated a draft counseling service and arranged meetings between American and Vietnamese women. It also sent a delegation of women to Hanoi in a successful effort to facilitate communication between American prisoners of war and their families. Critics found it difficult to attack an organization composed primarily of middle-class mothers.

SOURCE: Women Strike for Peace (Washington, D.C.), broadside, March 18, 1970, reprinted in Dawn Keetley and John Pettegrew, eds., *Public Women, Public Words*, vol. 3 (Lanham, Md.: Rowman & Littlefield, 2005), 490–91.

We women will no longer tolerate the domination of our lives and the lives of our families by the war-makers in the Pentagon and their spokesmen in Congress and the White House.

In the past twenty-five years, men who live by and for war have spent one trillion dollars of our tax money on armies and weapons—and they want still more.

The slaughter in Vietnam has killed over 48,000 Americans, wounded 250,000 of our young men, and destroyed the lives and homes of millions of Vietnamese. It is brutalizing our nation and bringing shame to us all.

Despite the protests of millions, the war goes on and now engulfs Laos, Cambodia and Thailand. But the Pentagon demands still more—$73 billion this year for the military establishment, additional billions for the ABM, and more of our sons and brothers to be brought home in coffins.

This unparalleled military plunder of our resources has brought our nation into crisis. Cities decay and fester. People are denied decent homes, jobs, schools, medical care, protection from pollution, and crime. Thousands of young men who refuse to be impressed into an unjust war have been forced into exile or jailed for dissent. Millions of black and minority group Americans live in malignant neglect.

The Nixon Administration spends 70 times more of our tax money for war than for housing, 9 times more for war than for education, 5 times more for war than for health.

A great and terrible wrong is being inflicted upon our country, and we demand redress of our grievances. The continued appropriation of our tax dollars for war without the clear consent of the American people is taxation without representation. This must be stopped.

We demand the birthright that our forefathers pledged to all Americans in 1776. We women declare our liberation from military domination which deprives us and our loved ones of life, liberty and the pursuit of happiness.

We demand that the President and the Congress of the United States live up to their Constitutional obligation to promote the general welfare.

We demand an end to the war in Vietnam and Laos NOW and the withdrawal of ALL troops, supplies and bases from Southeast Asia.

We demand repeal of the Draft.

We demand that Congress vote "NO" on appropriations for the Pentagon.

We demand priority for human needs.

WE SAY NO MORE MEN—NO MORE MONEY FOR WAR!

110. Huey P. Newton, "Letter to the National Liberation Front of South Vietnam"

(1970)

In this letter, Huey Newton, the Black Panther minister of defense, writes in solidarity to the Viet Cong, the enemy of the United States. Born in Louisiana, Newton (1942–1989) grew up poor in Oakland, California. As a student at Oakland City College, he became politicized and read revolutionary texts by Che Guevara, Frantz Fanon, and Mao Tse-Tung. In 1966, he met another student at the college, Bobby Seale, and the two formed the Black Panther Party for Self-Defense, primarily as a way to confront Oakland police for their abuse of the city's black citizens. The Panthers patrolled the police, observing them in their duties, while openly carrying loaded firearms (a practice then permitted under California law). In October 1967, police pulled Newton over, and a shoot-out resulted in one police officer's death. Newton was tried and convicted of voluntary manslaughter, but a California appeals court overturned the verdict. Newton was released from prison just weeks before he wrote this letter to the National Liberation Front. The notion of revolutionary internationalism as expressed in this letter grew out of the Panthers' foundational belief that African Americans were colonial subjects living under U.S. role. To throw off the yoke of colonialism, therefore, it made sense to the Panthers to seek alliances with revolutionary anticolonialists around the world.

SOURCE: Huey P. Newton, *To Die for the People* (New York: Random House, 1970), 290–93.

August 29, 1970

In the spirit of international revolutionary solidarity the Black Panther Party hereby offers to the National Liberation Front and Provisional Revolutionary Government of South Vietnam an undetermined number of troops to assist you in your fight against American imperialism. It is appropriate for the Black Panther Party to take this action at this time in recognition of the fact that your struggle is also our struggle, for we recognize that our common enemy is the

American imperialist who is the leader of international bourgeois domination. There is not one fascist or reactionary government in the world today that could stand without the support of United States imperialism. Therefore our problem is international, and we offer these troops in recognition of the necessity for international alliances to deal with this problem.

Such alliances will advance the struggle toward the final act of dealing with American imperialism. The Black Panther Party views the United States as the "city" of the world, while we view the nations of Africa, Asia and Latin America as the "countryside" of the world. The developing countries are like the Sierra Maestra in Cuba and the United States is like Havana. We note that in Cuba the people's army set up bases in the Sierra Maestra and choked off Havana because it was dependent upon the raw materials of the countryside. After they won all the battles in this countryside the last and final act was for the people to march upon Havana.

The Black Panther Party believes that the revolutionary process will operate in a similar fashion on an international level. A small ruling circle of seventy-six major companies controls the American economy. This elite not only exploits and oppresses Black people within the United States; they are exploiting and oppressing everyone in the world because of the overdeveloped nature of capitalism. Having expanded industry within the United States until it can grow no more, and depleting the raw materials of this nation, they have run amuck abroad in their attempts to extend their economic domination. To end this oppression we must liberate the developing nation—the countryside of the world—and then our final act will be the strike against the "city." As one nation is liberated elsewhere it gives us a better chance to be free here.

The Black Panther Party recognizes that we have certain national problems confined to the continental United States, but we are also aware that while our oppressor has domestic problems these do not stop him from oppressing people all over the world. Therefore we will keep fighting and resisting within the "city" so as to cause as much turmoil as possible and aid our brothers by dividing the troops of the ruling circle.

The Black Panther Party offers these troops because *we are the vanguard party of revolutionary internationalists who give up all claim to nationalism.* We take this position because the United States has acted in a very chauvinistic manner and lost its claim to nationalism. *The United States is an empire which has raped the world to build its wealth here. Therefore the United States is not a nation.* It is a government of international capitalists and inasmuch as they have exploited the world to accumulate wealth this country belongs to the world. The Black Panther Party contends that the United States lost its right to claim nationhood when it used its nationalism as a chauvinistic base to become an empire.

On the other hand, the developing countries have every right to claim nationhood, because they have not exploited anyone. The nationalism of which they speak is simply their rightful claim to autonomy, self-determination and a liberated base from which to fight the international bourgeoisie.

The Black Panther Party supports the claim to nationhood of the developing countries and we embrace their struggle from our position as revolutionary internationalists. We cannot be nationalists when our country is not a nation but an empire. We contend that it is time to open the gates of this country and share the technological knowledge and wealth with the peoples of the world.

History has bestowed upon the Black Panther Party the obligation to take these steps and thereby advance Marxism-Leninism to an even higher level along the path to a socialist state, and then a non-state. This obligation springs both from the dialectical forces in operation at this time and our history as an oppressed Black colony. The fact that our ancestors were kidnapped and forced to come to the United States has destroyed our feeling of nationhood. Because our long cultural heritage was broken we have come to rely less on our history for guidance, and seek our guidance from the future. Everything we do is based upon functionalism and pragmatism, and because we look to the future for salvation we are in a position to become the most progressive and dynamic people on the earth, constantly in motion and progressing, rather than becoming stagnated by the bonds of the past.

Taking these things under consideration, it is no accident that the vanguard party—without chauvinism or a sense of nationhood—should be the Black Panther Party. Our struggle for liberation is based upon justice and equality for all men. Thus we are interested in the people of any territory where the crack of the oppressor's whip may be heard. We have the historical obligation to take the concept of internationalism to its final conclusion—the destruction of statehood itself. This will lead us into the era where the withering away of the state will occur and men will extend their hand in friendship throughout the world.

This is the world view of the Black Panther Party and in the spirit of revolutionary internationalism, solidarity and friendship we offer these troops to the National Liberation Front and Provisional Government of South Vietnam, and to the people of the world.

111. J. Anthony Lukas, "Meadlo's Home Town Regards Him as Blameless"

(1969)

On March 16, 1968, American soldiers of Charlie Company, 11th Brigade, Americal Division, carried out a search and destroy mission in which they massacred 504 unarmed men, women, and children in My Lai, a hamlet in the village of Song My, Vietnam. The army successfully suppressed reports of the crime for more than a year until reporter Seymour Hersh broke the story in November 1969. Within a week, national magazines such as *Life, Time,* and *Newsweek* ran coverage of the event, and the prime-time television news program *60 Minutes* featured a Mike Wallace interview with Private Paul Meadlo. This article by Pulitzer Prize–winning journalist J. Anthony Lukas covered the reaction in Meadlo's home town to revelations that came out in that interview. When Wallace asked Meadlo why he participated in the massacre, Meadlo said he was following orders. Wallace asked if he had killed babies, and Meadlo replied that he had. Wallace then said, "Obviously, the question that comes to my mind: The father of two little kids . . . how do you shoot babies?" Meadlo replied, "I don't know; it's just one of them things." The sympathy expressed for Meadlo by citizens of his home town anticipated a more general sense among many Americans that the individual soldiers were not as much to blame as the military brass.

SOURCE: *New York Times,* November 26, 1969.

NEW GOSHEN, Ind., Nov. 25—This village with the Biblical chime to its name woke up this morning as the home of the man who said he took part in the mass slaying of Vietnamese civilians.

But nowhere among its chunky church spires and white clapboard houses was anyone inclined to blame Paul David Meadlo, the veteran who admitted last night shooting 30 to 40 men, women and children in the massacre at Song My, South Vietnam, last year.

"Lots of people been in talking about it this morning," said Mrs. Josephine

Neview, a clerk at Neal's grocery. "But they certainly don't blame Paul David in any way. After all, he had his orders."

"Paul David" is the way everybody here refers to the 22-year-old coal miner's son.

"I heard them announcing something about Paul Meadlo on the TV last night," said Mrs. Neview. "For a moment I didn't know who they were talking about; then I said, oh, my God, that's Paul David."

Although Paul David lives now with his wife and two children in neighboring West Terre Haute, New Goshen was his home for the first 18 years of his life, and he still comes here often to visit his parents, sister, four uncles, and two aunts.

New Goshen's 450 residents all know the Meadlos and Paul David; when he's home, he is a familiar figure shouldering up to the bar at Hutch's Hut or warming his hands over the pot-bellied stove at Olivero's Grocery.

And he is popular here. Townspeople questioned today responded with one voice: "A very nice boy," "the nicest guy you'd ever want to meet," "easy-going, got along with everybody," "never had any trouble out of him. Wish I could say the same about some other youngsters around here."

So when newspaper and television people from New York, Chicago, and St. Louis began showing up around town this morning, the people of New Goshen stuck staunchly by their native son.

"How can you newspaper people blame Paul David?" asked Robert Hale as he planed down some garage doors behind the pool hall he and his wife run. "He was under orders. He had to do what his officer told him."

"The only thing I blame Paul David for was talking about this to everybody on television," said Dee Henry, who was helping Mr. Hale fix the garage doors. "Things like that happen in war. They always have and they always will. But only just recently have people started telling the press about it."

"It's bad enough to have to kill people without telling everybody about it," he said. "This sort of thing should be kept classified."

Mr. Henry was a professional soldier for 11 years, fought in World War II and the Korean war, and "would have been in this one too if I hadn't been wounded and discharged." He gives his occupation as "disabled veteran."

He feels Paul David is the victim of people who don't know how the Army works. "Anybody who's had any affiliation with the service knows you do what you're ordered to do—no questions asked."

Although others were not so emphatic, the same theme was echoed today in the town's tiny one-room post office, on front porches, and on street corners under gaunt, leafless maples.

"What else could he do?" asked 22-year-old Floyd Cheesman, a classmate of Paul David's at West Vigo High School. "Boy, I would have done just the same thing. I'd take my orders. If they give you an order under fire and you don't carry it out, they can court martial you."

The only sharply differing point of view expressed in town today came from

Paul David's father, a blunt ex-miner who still speaks with a trace of the Polish accent his father brought from the old country 67 years ago.

"If it had been me out there," he said, "I would have swung my rifle around and shot Calley instead—right between the God-damned eyes." Lieut. William L. Calley Jr. is the officer Paul David says ordered him to shoot the Vietnamese.

"Why did they have to take my son and do that to him?" said Mr. Meadlo's wife, Myrtle, as the tears she'd held back all morning began to flow.

Paul David came home without his right foot—blown off by a land mine the day after the Songmy massacre. His father stomps around the house on an artificial left leg—the result of a mine accident in 1961.

When Paul David first spoke to his mother from an Army hospital after the injury, he said, "Well, Mom, like father like son."

The Meadlos don't talk much about the victims of their son's gunfire in Song My. But at times they seem to be thinking of them.

Showing a visitor a picture of Paul, his wife, Mary, and his two babies, Paul Jr., 2½, and Tresa Lynn, 15 months, Mrs. Meadlo said through her tears: "When he's around his babies he'll pick 'em up and love 'em. Just love 'em."

112. C Company Featuring Terry Nelson, "The Battle Hymn of Lt. Calley"

(1971)

In this spoken-word song, C Company Featuring Terry Nelson defends Lieutenant William Calley, the one soldier convicted for participating in the My Lai massacre. Terry Nelson was the professional name of Alabama songwriter and disc jockey Terry Skinner; C Company was named for the company of soldiers responsible for the killings at My Lai. At trial, witness testimony revealed that Calley ordered his men to round up civilians, lead them into a ditch, and shoot them; according to Private Paul Meadlo, Calley used up numerous clips on his own M-16 as he fired into the ditch. Calley claimed that his captain, Ernest Medina, had ordered him to kill everyone in the village (Medina was tried separately but acquitted). At first, the court sentenced Calley to life imprisonment, but in a series of rulings, his sentence was reduced; ultimately, he served forty-two months under house arrest and was dishonorably discharged. By the time of his conviction, however, Calley experienced a tremendous outpouring of public support, primarily in the belief that he had been set up as a scapegoat. This song ultimately sold more than 1.5 million copies.

SOURCE: Plantation Records PL 73, 1971.

SPOKEN INTRO:

Once upon a time, there was a little boy who wanted to grow up to be a soldier and serve his country in whatever way he could.

He would parade around the house with a saucepan on his head for a helmet, a wooden sword in one hand, and the American flag in the other.

As he grew up, he'd put away the things of a child, but he never let go of the flag . . .

> My name is William Calley,
> I'm a soldier of this land,
> I've tried to do my duty
> And to gain the upper hand;

But they've made me out a villain,
They have stamped me with a brand,
As we go marching on . . .

I'm just another soldier
From the shores of USA,
Forgotten on a battlefield
Ten thousand miles away
While life goes on as usual
From New York to Santa Fe,
As we go marching on . . .

I've seen my buddies ambushed
On the left and on the right,
And their youthful bodies riddled
By the bullets of the night;
Where all the rules are broken
And the only law is might,
As we go marching on . . .

While we're fighting in the jungles
They were marching in the street,
While we're dying in the rice fields
They were helping our defeat.
While we're facing VC bullets
They were sounding a retreat,
As we go marching on . . .

With our sweat we took the bunkers,
With our tears we took the plain,
With our blood we took the mountain
And they gave it back again.
Still, all of us are soldiers,
We're too busy to complain,
As we go marching on . . .

SPOKEN:

When I reach my final campground
In that land beyond the sun,
And the Great Commander asks me,
"Did you fight or did you run?"
I'll stand both straight and tall,
Stripped of medals, rank, and gun,
And this is what I'll say,
"Sir, I followed all my orders,
And I did the best I could.
It's hard to judge the enemy

And hard to tell the good.
Yet, there's not a man among us
Who would not have understood.

We took the jungle village
Exactly like they said,
We responded to their rifle fire
With everything we had.
And when the smoke had cleared away
A hundred souls lay dead.

Sir, the soldier that's alive
Is the only one can fight.
There's no other way to wage a war
When the only one in sight
That you're sure is not a VC
Is you buddy on your right.

When all the wars are over
And the battle's finally won
Count me only as a soldier
Who never left his gun,
With a light to serve my country
As the only prize I've won . . ."

Glory, glory, hallelujah . . . [FADE-OUT]

113. Herbert Marcuse, "Reflections on Calley"

(1971)

In this essay, philosopher and political theorist Herbert Marcuse critiques the spontaneous outburst of popular support for Lieutenant William Calley. Born in Berlin, Marcuse (1898–1979) earned his doctorate at the University of Freiburg, where he worked under Martin Heidegger. He fled Nazi Germany in 1934 and, during World War II, aided the Allies as an intelligence analyst for the Office of Strategic Services. Beginning in 1952, Marcuse held faculty positions at a number of American universities, including Columbia, Harvard, Brandeis, and the University of California at San Diego. His best-known book, *One Dimensional Man* (1964), reached a wide college-age audience, and Marcuse consequently became a favored philosopher of the student New Left. Here, Marcuse, intellectual and witness to the Third Reich, asks readers to consider what happens when a society not only easily explains away a murderous rampage, but seems to identify with the murderer.

SOURCE: *New York Times*, May 13, 1971.

LA JOLLA, Calif.—The obscene haste with which a large part of the American people rushed to the support of a man convicted of multiple premeditated murder of men, women and children, the obscene pride with which they even identified themselves with him is one of those rare historical events which reveal a hidden truth.

Behind the television faces of the leaders, behind the tolerant politeness of the debates, behind the radiant happiness of the commercials appear the real people: men and women madly in love with death, violence and destruction.

For this massive rush was not the result of organization, management, machine politics—it was entirely spontaneous: an outburst of the unconscious, the soul. The silent majority has its hero: a convicted war criminal—convicted of killing at close range, smashing the head of a 2-year-old child; a killer in whose defense it was said that he did not feel that he was killing "humans," a killer who did not express regret for his deeds; he only obeyed orders and killed only "dinks" or "gooks" or "V.C." This majority has its hero—it has found its martyr, its Horst Wessel whose name was sung by hundreds of thousands of marching Nazis before they marched into war. "Lieutenant Calley's Battle Hymn Marches On," the record, sold 300,000 copies in three days.

How do Calley's worshipers justify their hero?

- "The act which Calley is accused of was committed in warfare and is thus subject to special consideration." Now Calley was tried and convicted, after long deliberation, by a military tribunal of his peers, of whom it may be assumed that they knew that he acted in war. In fact, he was tried and convicted under the international rules of warfare. The rules of his own army stipulate the duty of disobedience to illegal orders (a disobedience which, as the hearings showed, was actually practiced by other American soldiers at Mylai).

- "What Calley did was widespread practice." Scores of men have come forth denouncing themselves as having done the same Calley did. Now the fact that one murderer was caught and brought to trial while others were not, does not absolve the one who was brought to trial. On the contrary, the others, having voluntarily confessed, should also be tried. The man who wrote on the windshield of his automobile: "I killed in V.N. Hang me too!" may well have meant it. People madly in love with death, including their own.

- "Everyone knows there are few genuine civilians in Vietnam today." A most revealing statement, which admits that the war is waged against a whole people: genocide.

- "Society is to blame." This is perhaps the only weighty argument. It moves on several levels:

(a) If society alone is to blame, nobody is to blame. For "society" is an abstract which cannot be brought to trial. It is true that this society is (and must be) training its young citizens to kill. But this same society operates under the rule of law, and recognizes rights and duties of the individual. Thus it presupposes individual responsibility, that is to say the ability of the "normal" individual to distinguish between criminal and noncriminal behavior (Calley was declared "normal").

(b) If the argument implies that all individual members of society are to blame, it is blatantly false and only serves to protect those who are responsible.

The reason for the "paroxysm in the nation's conscience" is "simply that Calley is all of us. He is every single citizen in our graceless land," said the Very Rev. Francis B. Sayre, Jr. Blatantly false, and a great injustice to the Berrigans, to all those who have, at the risk of their liberty and even their life, openly and actively fought the genocidal war.

To be sure, in a "metaphysical" sense, everyone who partakes of this society is indeed guilty—but the Calley case is not a case study in metaphysics. Within the general framework (restrictive enough) of individual responsibility there are definite gradations which allow attribution of specific responsibility. If it is true that Calley's action was not isolated, but an all but daily occurrence in Vietnam (which would corroborate the findings of the Russel War Crime Tribunal and call for the prosecution of all cases recorded there), then responsibility would rest with the field commanders, and, in the last analysis, with the Supreme Commander of the United States armed forces. However, this would not eliminate the responsibility of the individual agents.

(c) Technical progress in developing the capacity to kill has led to "death in the abstract"; killing that does not dirty your hands and clothes, that does not burden you with the agony of the victims—invisible death, dealt by remote controls. But technical perfection does not redeem the guilt of those who violate the rules of civilized warfare.

* * *

What does this all add up to? Perhaps Governor Maddox gave it away when he exclaimed at a rally in support of Calley: "Thank God for Lieutenant Calley and thank God for people like you." Blasphemy or religious madness? The convicted war criminal an avatar of Jesus, the Christ? "He has been crucified," shouted a woman, berating the court-martial in a German accent (one wonders?!). "Calley killed 100 Communists single-handed. He should get a medal. He should be promoted to general." And a Reverend Lord (!) told a rally: "There was a crucifixion 2,000 years ago of a man named Jesus Christ. I don't think we need another crucifixion of a man named Rusty Calley."

Has the lieutenant taken our sins upon himself, will he redeem our sins? What sins? Could it be the wish to kill, kill without being punished? Has the Lieutenant become the national model for a new Super Ego, less exacting than the traditional one, which still preserved a trace of thou shalt not kill?

The old Super Ego still stuck to the memory of this prohibition even in war. The new Super Ego is up to date. It says: you can kill. No—you can waste and destroy. Calley never used the word "kill." He told a psychiatrist that the military avoided the word "kill" because it "caused a very negative emotional reaction among the men who had been taught the commandment "Thou shalt not kill." Instead, Lieutenant Calley employed the word "destroy" or the phrase "waste 'em." A pardon for Calley, who did not kill but only destroyed and wasted 'em would, according to some, be a "constructive step to restore the morale of our armed forces and the public at large."

The mad rush away from individual responsibility, the easy-going effort to vest guilt in anonymity is the desperate reaction against a guilt which threatens to become unbearable. Infantile regression: Billy cannot be punished because Maxie and Charlie and many others did the same thing; they do it daily and they are not punished. People incapable of the simplest adult logic: if Maxie and Charlie did the same thing, they are equally guilty and Billy is not innocent.

Has the sense of guilt, the guilt of a society in which massacres and killing and body counts have become part of the normal mental equipment, become so strong that it can no longer be contained by the traditional, civilized defense mechanisms (individual defense mechanisms)? Does the sense of guilt turn into its opposite: into the proud, sado-masochistic identification with the crime and the criminal?

Has the hysteria also gripped the left, the peace movement which finds in the indictment of Calley an indictment of the war? A strange indictment indeed which regards the war criminal as a scapegoat—scapegoat for anonymous, for other scapegoats? Even Telford Taylor, who spoke so eloquently at the Nuremberg trials, thinks that the sentence may have been too harsh. And Dr. Benjamin Spock thinks that it is unjust to punish one man for the brutality of war.

Compassion. But has it ever occurred to all those understanding and compassionate liberals that clemency for Calley might indeed "strengthen the morale of the army" in killing with a good conscience? Has it ever occurred to them that compassion may be due the men, women and children who are the victims of this "morale"? Once again, we are confronted with that principle of diseased justice which was pronounced at Kent State and which expresses so neatly the perversion of the sense of guilt: "not the murderer but the murdered one is guilty."

114. John Kerry, "Vietnam Veterans Against the War"

(1971)

Just weeks after the conclusion of William Calley's trial, John Kerry testified on behalf of Vietnam Veterans Against the War (VVAW) before the U.S. Senate Committee on Foreign Relations. Raised in Massachusetts, Kerry (1943–) graduated from Yale University in 1966. He then entered officer candidate school for the navy, and later served two tours in Vietnam. For action during his second tour, when he served as a lieutenant in charge of a "swift boat" in the Mekong Delta, Kerry was awarded a Silver Star, a Bronze Star, and three Purple Hearts. Not long after he returned home, he joined the VVAW, an organization started in 1967 by a handful of veterans that, by 1971, had come to represent the most respected subset of the antiwar movement. In January 1971, during the Calley trial, the VVAW held the New Winter Soldier Investigation, in which veterans came forward to describe atrocities in Vietnam. In April, more than 100,000 VVAW members took part in a major antiwar demonstration in Washington. Veterans camped out on the National Mall, in violation of a court order, and on April 23, hundreds threw their medals over a fence onto the steps of the Capitol. That same day, Kerry, the decorated veteran, and still an officer in the Navy Reserves, gave this testimony.

SOURCE: Statement by John Kerry to the Senate Committee on Foreign Relations, April 23, 1973.

I would like to talk on behalf of all those veterans and say that several months ago in Detroit we had an investigation at which over 150 honorably discharged, and many very highly decorated, veterans testified to war crimes committed in Southeast Asia. These were not isolated incidents but crimes committed on a day-to-day basis with the full awareness of officers at all levels of command.

It is impossible to describe to you exactly what did happen in Detroit—the emotions in the room and the feelings of the men who were reliving their experiences in Vietnam. They relived the absolute horror of what this country, in a sense, made them do.

They told stories that at times they had personally raped, cut off ears, cut off heads, taped wires from portable telephones to human genitals and turned up the power, cut off limbs, blown up bodies, randomly shot at civilians, razed villages in fashion reminiscent of Genghis Khan, shot cattle and dogs for fun, poisoned food stocks, and generally ravaged the countryside of South Vietnam in addition to the normal ravage of war and the normal and very particular ravaging which is done by the applied bombing power of this country.

We call this investigation the Winter Soldier Investigation. The term Winter Soldier is a play on words of Thomas Paine's in 1776 when he spoke of the Sunshine Patriots and summer time soldiers who deserted at Valley Forge because the going was rough.

We who have come here to Washington have come here because we feel we have to be winter soldiers now. We could come back to this country, we could be quiet, we could hold our silence, we could not tell what went on in Vietnam, but we feel because of what threatens this country, not the reds, but the crimes which we are committing that threaten it, that we have to speak out. . . .

In our opinion and from our experience, there is nothing in South Vietnam which could happen that realistically threatens the United States of America. And to attempt to justify the loss of one American life in Vietnam, Cambodia or Laos by linking such loss to the preservation of freedom, which those misfits supposedly abuse, is to us the height of criminal hypocrisy, and it is that kind of hyprocrisy which we feel has torn this country apart.

We found that not only was it a civil war, an effort by a people who had for years been seeking their liberation from any colonial influence whatsoever, but also we found that the Vietnamese whom we had enthusiastically molded after our own image were hard put to take up the fight against the threat we were supposedly saving them from.

We found most people didn't even know the difference between communism and democracy. They only wanted to work in rice paddies without helicopters strafing them and bombs with napalm burning their villages and tearing their country apart. They wanted everything to do with the war, particularly with this foreign presence of the United States of America, to leave them alone in peace, and they practiced the art of survival by siding with whichever military force was present at a particular time, be it Viet Cong, North Vietnamese or American.

We found also that all too often American men were dying in those rice paddies for want of support from their allies. We saw first hand how monies from American taxes were used for a corrupt dictatorial regime. We saw that many people in this country had a one-sided idea of who was kept free by our flag, and blacks provided the highest percentage of casualties. We saw Vietnam ravaged equally by American bombs and search and destroy missions, as well as by Viet Cong terrorism and yet we listened while this country tried to blame all of the havoc on the Viet Cong.

We rationalized destroying villages in order to save them. We saw America lose her sense of morality as she accepted very coolly a My Lai and refused to give up the image of American soldiers who hand out chocolate bars and chewing gum.

We learned the meaning of free fire zones, shooting anything that moves, and we watched while America placed a cheapness on the lives of Orientals.

We watched the United States falsification of body counts, in fact the glorification of body counts. We listened while month after month we were told the back of the enemy was about to break. We fought using weapons against "oriental human beings." We fought using weapons against those people which I do not believe this country would dream of using were we fighting in the European theater. We watched while men charged up hills because a general said that hill has to be taken, and after losing one platoon or two platoons they marched away to leave the hill for reoccupation by the North Vietnamese. We watched pride allow the most unimportant battles to be blown into extravaganzas, because we couldn't lose, and we couldn't retreat, and because it didn't matter how many American bodies were lost to prove that point, and so there were Hamburger Hills and Khe Sanhs and Hill 81s and Fire Base 6s, and so many others.

Now we are told that the men who fought there must watch quietly while American lives are lost so that we can exercise the incredible arrogance of Vietnamizing the Vietnamese.

Each day to facilitate the process by which the United States washes her hands of Vietnam someone has to give up his life so that the United States doesn't have to admit something that the entire world already knows, so that we can't say that we have made a mistake. Someone has to die so that President Nixon won't be, and these are his words, "the first President to lose a war."

We are asking Americans to think about that because how do you ask a man to be the last man to die in Vietnam? How do you ask a man to be the last man to die for a mistake? . . . We are here in Washington also to say that the problem of this war is not just a question of war and diplomacy. It is part and parcel of everything that we are trying as human beings to communicate to people in this country—the question of racism which is rampant in' the military, and so many other questions such as the use of weapons; the hypocrisy in our taking umbrage at the Geneva Conventions and using that as justification for a continuation of this war when we are more guilty than any other body of violations of those Geneva Conventions: in the use of free fire zones, harassment interdiction fire, search and destroy missions, the bombings, the torture of prisoners, the killing of prisoners, all accepted policy by many units in South Vietnam. That is what we are trying to say. It is part and parcel of everything.

An American Indian friend of mine who lives in the Indian Nation of Alcatraz put it to me very succinctly. He told me how as a boy on an Indian reservation he had watched television and he used to cheer the cowboys when they came in and shot the Indians, and then suddenly one day he stopped in Vietnam and he said "my God, I am doing to these people the very same thing that was done to my people," and he stopped. And that is what we are trying to say, that we think this thing has to end.

We are here to ask, and we are here to ask vehemently, where are the leaders of our country. Where is the leadership? We're here to ask where are McNamara, Rostow, Bundy, Gilpatrick, and so many others. Where are they now that we, the men they sent off to war, have returned. These are commanders who have deserted their troops. And there is no more serious crime in the laws of war. The Army says they never leave their wounded. The marines say they never leave even their dead. These men have left all the casualties and retreated behind a pious shield of public rectitude. They've left the real stuff of their reputations bleaching behind them in the sun in this country. . . .

We wish that a merciful God could wipe away our own memories of that service as easily as this administration has wiped away their memories of us. But all that they have done and all that they can do by this denial is to make more clear than ever our own determination to undertake one last mission—to search out and destroy the last vestige of this barbaric war, to pacify our own hearts, to conquer the hate and the fear that have driven this country these last ten years and more. And more. And so when thirty years from now our brothers go down the street without a leg, without an arm, or a face, and small boys ask why, we will be able to say "Vietnam" and not mean a desert, not a filthy obscene memory, but mean instead the place where America finally turned and where soldiers like us helped it in the turning.

115. Marvin Gaye, "What's Going On"

(1971)

A classic of 1970s soul, Marvin Gaye's "What's Going On" brought political themes to the Motown sound. The son of a preacher, Gaye (1939–84) grew up in Washington, D.C. He dropped out of high school. After a brief stint in the air force, Gaye started singing in local doo-wop groups and, in 1960, moved to Detroit. Signed to Motown Tamla Records in 1961, Gaye began a successful professional career known for hit songs such as "How Sweet It Is to Be Loved by You" and "I Heard It Through the Grapevine." "What's Going On," the lead single from an album of the same name, marked a departure for both Gaye and Motown. Indeed, when Berry Gordy, the Motown CEO, first heard the single, he did not want to release it. Gaye refused to record any more material until the label released the song; when Gordy relented, the song quickly soared to number two on the pop charts and number one on the R&B charts. The album that followed captured additional political and social themes and has been characterized as a concept album. In 2004, *Rolling Stone* ranked "What's Going On" number four on its list of 500 Greatest Songs of All Time.

SOURCE: Tamla T54201, 1971.

> Mother, mother
> There's too many of you crying
> Brother, brother, brother
> There's far too many of you dying
> You know we've got to find a way
> To bring some lovin' here today—ya
>
> Father, father we don't need to escalate
> You see, war is not the answer
> For only love can conquer hate
> You know we've got to find a way
> To bring some lovin' here today

Picket lines and picket signs
Don't punish me with brutality
Talk to me, so you can see
Oh, what's going on
What's going on
Yeah, what's going on
Ah what's going on

In the mean time
Right on, baby
Right on, Right on

Father, father, everybody thinks we're wrong
Oh, but who are they to judge us
Simply because our hair is long
Oh, you know we've got to find a way
To bring some understanding here today
Oh

Picket lines and picket signs
Don't punish me with brutality
Talk to me
So you can see
What's going on
Yeah, what's going on
Tell me what's going on
I'll tell you what's going on—Uh
Right on baby
Right on baby

116. Denise Levertov, "A Poem at Christmas, 1972, during the Terror-Bombing of North Vietnam"

(1975)

In this poems, award-winning poet Denise Levertov evokes the gathering madness of a home front witness to a brutal war. Born in England, Levertov (1923–97) first experienced the horrors of war when she worked as a nurse in London during World War II. She published her first book of poetry in 1946 and married the American writer, Mitchell Goodman, a year later. In 1948, they moved to the United States. During the 1960s, both Levertov and Goodman became outspoken critics of the Vietnam War (Goodman was one of the authors of the Call to Resist Illegitimate Authority and was convicted with Dr. Spock and others for conspiracy to counsel draft resistance). Levertov's poetry turned more overtly political during this period and lost her some of her following, though she attracted new fans with her new work. In 1967, she edited a book of poetry for the War Resisters League. She cofounded Writers and Artists Protest Against the War, and visited Hanoi in 1972. This poem was published in 1975, but it speaks to her observations of the war after her visit to North Vietnam and the December 1972 "Christmas bombings," the most intense of the war.

SOURCE: Denise Levertov, *The Freeing of the Dust* (New York: New Directions Publishing Corp., 1975).

> Now I have lain awake imagining murder.
> At first my pockets were loaded with rocks, with knives,
> wherever I ran windows smashed, but I was swift
> > and unseen,
>   I was saving the knives until I reached
> certain men . . .
>   Yes, Kissinger's smile faded,
> he clutched his belly, he reeled . . .
> But as the night
> wore on, what I held

hidden—under a napkin perhaps,
    I as a waitress at the inaugural dinner—
was a container of napalm:
and as I threw it in Nixon's face
and his crowd leapt back from the flames with crude
                            yells of horror,
and some came rushing to seize me:
    quick as thought I had ready
a round of those small bombs designed
to explode at the pressure of a small child's weight,
and these instantly
dealt with the feet of Nixon's friends and henchmen,
who fell in their own blood
while the foul smoke of his body-oils
blackened the hellish room . . .
It was of no interest
to imagine further. Instead,
the scene recommenced.
Each time around, fresh details,
variations of place and weapon.
All night imagining murder.
O, to kill
the killers!

It is
to this extremity

the infection of their evil

thrusts us . . .

117. Iggy and the Stooges, "Search and Destroy"

(1973)

The driving beat and blistering guitar riffs of Iggy and the Stooges' "Search and Destroy" seem to lead listeners into the chaos of battle—or perhaps a drug-induced hallucination of combat. Born James Osterberg, Iggy Pop (1947–) grew up in Ypsilanti, Michigan, and started playing music as a teenager in Ann Arbor. After a short stint at the University of Michigan, he formed the Stooges in 1967 with brothers Ron Asheton and Scott Asheton and Dave Alexander. Along with the MC5, the Stooges helped create a new Detroit rock and roll sound, later characterized as proto-punk. Iggy Pop is sometimes referred to as the godfather of punk. "Search and Destroy" is the first song on the Stooges' third album, *Raw Power*, which was recorded in London in 1972. Pop later claimed that the idea for the song came to him while he was high on heroin, reading a *Time* magazine article titled "Search and Destroy." The song takes no political stand, but reflects the extent to which terms such as "napalm," "fire fight," and "A-bomb" had entered the American vocabulary.

SOURCE: Iggy and the Stooges, *Raw Power* (Columbia Records, KC 32111, 1973).

> I'm a street walking cheetah with a heart full of napalm
> I'm a runaway son of the nuclear A-bomb
> I am a world's forgotten boy
> The one who searches and destroys
>
> Honey gotta help me please
> Somebody gotta save my soul
> Baby detonate for me
>
> Look out honey, cause I'm using technology
> Ain't got time to make no apology
> Soul radiation in the dead of night
> Love in the middle of a fire fight

Honey gotta strike me blind
Somebody gotta save my soul
Baby penetrate my mind

And I'm the world's forgotten boy
The one who's searchin', searchin' to destroy
And honey I'm the world's forgotten boy
The one who's searchin only to destroy

Forgotten boy, forgotten boy
Forgotten boy said hey forgotten boy

118. Gregg Barrios, "Chale Guerra"

(1982)

In this piece, playwright and journalist Gregg Barrios describes the aftermath of the war for a Chicano Vietnam veteran. Barrios was a playwright and journalist in San Antonio. The Vietnam War was as controversial in the Latino community as it was in the African American community, in large part because Latinos also were drafted and served in the military in disproportionate numbers. In California and elsewhere in the Southwest a sizeable antiwar movement developed and intersected with the Chicano civil rights movement. "Raza, Si! Guerra, No!" became a popular slogan at both antiwar and civil rights protests by the early 1970s. Meanwhile, the plight of returning veterans became a source of national shame in that decade as most Americans preferred not to hear any more about the war, and government services turned out to be woefully inadequate. In "Chale Guerra," Barrios plays with language: his character's name, "Carlos" or "Charlie," is also "Chale," which is Chicano slang for "fuck," and his last name is "Guerra" or "war." Fuck War.

SOURCE: First published in *Puro Rollo (A colores)* (Los Angeles: Posada, 1982).

Chale Guerra de Corpus Christi came home
with his body broken and crippled and hanging from his neck
he had an AirCom medal, a bronze star, a foreign service
medal, and a broken purple heart. What else?
Oh, a broken back, a silver plated brace,
a nervous tic, and a stainless wheel chair to race.
When he came home there was no xmas, no news,
no new year, no gas, no men in little white hats,
no love, no welcome home, no nothing.

Now Carlos Guerra sits in his tiny room and plots
now that his nerves are a bundle of rotten knots
and no job offers come his way, and no one gets
in his way, and he can't even get his rocks off

cause no young girl wants a cripple mess
to slob over her luscious *teen-age* bod.

But Charlie was young once and in his barrio
on Leopard Street he was bien pinche—"Chale
el jale" as he was known because he loved to party
back then he wanted to be a marine and prove himself
as a real macho and fight for the country that never gave
him a damn thing except a warped sense of who he was
and what he could do with himself.

Now he can't do anything for himself. Now he can't do
anything. Anything. You wanna drink of water, Chale?
You have to piss, Chale? You have to scratch your ass,
Chale! No Jane Fonda in the middle of the night to
offer him some afternoon delight. No one to make him
feel like a man of might.

So they put Carlos on the Domingo Peña Show
right between the Butter Krust Bread and Joe Bravo
commercials. And he looked like a real war hero
some kind of secret agent orange colored spy
as he told his tale live as thousands gasped
and they gave him a dozen loaves of bread and
the VA promised to find him a special hospital bed
and he went home that night got drunk and tried to fight
and in the morning they came and took him away.

And now all the vatos in the barrio talk about poor
Chale and listen to the jukebox in the PASTIME pool
hall as "Ya Volví de Vietnam" churns out loud
and hell, Chale might as well be dead but god would
have it that he spend the rest of his days a freak.
My aunt went to see him and when she returned
she could hardly speak about it. Chale Guerra.
That poor sonovabitch from el barrio de Leopard St.

bien pinche—very flaky
vatos—dudes
Ya Volví de Vietnam—I just got back from Vietnam

CHAPTER ELEVEN

The Cold War, Part III: Life after Vietnam

119. Church Committee, Final Report, "Intelligence Activities and the Rights of Americans"

(1976)

This excerpt from the introduction to the Church Committee's final report summarizes years of abuses by the FBI, CIA, National Security Agency (NSA), and other agencies during the Cold War. The American people had no idea such programs existed until 1971, when activists broke into an FBI office in Media, Pennsylvania, and stole papers that they later leaked to the press. To this day, the identities of the members of the Citizens Committee to Investigate the FBI are unknown, but among the more than 1,000 documents they stole was evidence of a counterintelligence program (COINTELPRO) that frequently operated outside the law. Over the next few years, similar revelations came out about other government agencies, and in the wake of the Watergate scandal, popular distrust of the government soared. Ultimately, the United States Senate moved to uncover the truth by establishing the Select Committee to Study Governmental Operations with Respect to Intelligence Activities, more popularly known as the Church Committee, named for its chairman, Frank Church of Idaho. The findings of the committee are notable for both the scale of the questionable activities in which intelligence agencies were engaged and the justification for such programs as necessary in fighting the "enemies of freedom."

SOURCE: U.S. Senate Select Committee to Study Governmental Operations with Respect to Intelligence Activities, *Final Reports,* 94th Cong., 2d Sess., 1976 (Book 2).

Book II

Final report of the select committee to study governmental operations

With respect to intelligence activities united states senate together with additional, supplemental, and separate views

APRIL 26 (legislative day, April 14), 1976

I. Introduction and Summary

The resolution creating this Committee placed greatest emphasis on whether intelligence activities threaten the "rights of American citizens."

The critical question before the Committee was to determine how the fundamental liberties of the people can be maintained in the course of the Government's effort to protect their security. The delicate balance between these basic goals of our system of government is often difficult to strike, but it can, and must, be achieved. We reject the view that the traditional American principles of justice and fair play have no place in our struggle against the enemies of freedom. Moreover, our investigation has established that the targets of intelligence activity have ranged far beyond persons who could properly be characterized as enemies of freedom and have extended to a wide array of citizens engaging in lawful activity.

Americans have rightfully been concerned since before World War II about the dangers of hostile foreign agents likely to commit acts of espionage. Similarly, the violent acts of political terrorists can seriously endanger the rights of Americans. Carefully focused intelligence investigations can help prevent such acts. But too often intelligence has lost this focus and domestic intelligence activities have invaded individual privacy and violated the rights of lawful assembly and political expression. Unless new and tighter controls are established by legislation, domestic intelligence activities threaten to undermine our democratic society and fundamentally alter its nature.

We have examined three types of "intelligence" activities affecting the rights of American citizens. The first is intelligence collection—such as infiltrating groups with informants, wiretapping, or opening letters. The second is dissemination of material which has been collected. The third is covert action designed to disrupt and discredit the activities of groups and individuals deemed a threat to the social order. These three types of "intelligence" activity are closely related in the practical world. Information which is disseminated by the intelligence community or used in disruptive programs has usually been obtained through surveillance. Nevertheless, a division between collection, dissemination and covert action is analytically useful both in understanding why excesses have occurred in the past and in devising remedies to prevent those excesses from recurring.

A. Intelligence Activity: A New Form of Governmental Power to Impair Citizens' Rights

A tension between order and liberty is inevitable in any society. A Government must protect its citizens from those bent on engaging in violence and criminal behavior, or in espionage and other hostile foreign intelligence activity. Many of the intelligence programs reviewed in this report were established for those purposes. Intelligence work has, at times, successfully prevented dangerous and abhorrent acts, such as bombings and foreign spying, and aided in the prosecution of those responsible for such acts.

But, intelligence activity in the past decades has, all too often, exceeded the restraints on the exercise of governmental power which are imposed by our country's Constitution, laws, and traditions.

Excesses in the name of protecting security are not a recent development in our nation's history. In 1798, for example, shortly after the Bill of Rights was added to the Constitution, the Allen and Sedition Acts were passed. These Acts, passed in response to fear of proFrench "subversion," made it a crime to criticize the Government. During the Civil War, President Abraham Lincoln suspended the writ of habeas corpus. Hundreds of American citizens were prosecuted for anti-war statements during World War I, and thousands of "radical" aliens were seized for deportation during the 1920 Palmer Raids. During the Second World War, over the opposition of J. Edgar Hoover and military intelligence, 120,000 Japanese-Americans were apprehended and incarcerated in detention camps.

Those actions, however, were fundamentally different from the intelligence activities examined by this Committee. They were generally executed overtly under the authority of a statute or a public executive order. The victims knew what was being done to them and could challenge the Government in the courts and other forums. Intelligence activity, on the other hand, is generally covert. It is concealed from its victims and is seldom described in statutes or explicit executive orders. The victim may never suspect that his misfortunes are the intended result of activities undertaken by his government, and accordingly may have no opportunity to challenge the actions taken against him.

It is, of course, proper in many circumstances—such as developing a criminal prosecution—for the Government to gather information about a citizen and use it to achieve legitimate ends, some of which might be detrimental to the citizen. But in criminal prosecutions, the courts have struck a balance between protecting the rights of the accused citizen and protecting the society which suffers the consequences of crime. Essential to the balancing process are the rules of criminal law which circumscribe the techniques for gathering evidence the kinds of evidence that may be collected, and the uses to which that evidence may be put. In addition, the criminal defendant is given an opportunity to discover and then challenge the legality of how the Government collected information about him and the use which the Government intends to make of that information.

This Committee has examined a realm of governmental information collection which has not been governed by restraints comparable to those in criminal proceedings. We have examined the collection of intelligence about the political advocacy and actions and the private lives of American citizens. That information has been used covertly to discredit the ideas advocated and to "neutralize" the actions of their proponents. As Attorney General Harlan Fiske Stone warned in 1924, when he sought to keep federal agencies from investigating "political or other opinions" as opposed to "conduct . . . forbidden by the laws":

When a police system passes beyond these limits, it is dangerous to the proper administration of justice and to human liberty, which it should be our first concern to cherish.

. . . There is always a possibility that a secret police may become a menace to free government and free institutions because it carries with it the possibility of abuses of power which are not always quickly apprehended or understood.

Our investigation has confirmed that warning. We have seen segments of our Government, in their attitudes and action, adopt tactics unworthy of a democracy, and occasionally reminiscent of the tactics of totalitarian regimes. We have seen a consistent pattern in which programs initiated with limited goals, such as preventing criminal violence or identifying foreign spies, were expanded to what witnesses characterized as "vacuum cleaners," sweeping in information about lawful activities of American citizens.

The tendency of intelligence activities to expand beyond their initial scope is a theme which runs through every aspect of our investigative findings. Intelligence collection programs naturally generate ever-increasing demands for new data. And once intelligence has been collected, there are strong pressures to use it against the target.

The pattern of intelligence agencies expanding the scope of their activities was well described by one witness, who in 1970 had coordinated an effort by most of the intelligence community to obtain authority to undertake more illegal domestic activity:

The risk was that you would get people who would be susceptible to political considerations as opposed to national security considerations, or would construe political considerations to be national security considerations, to move from the, kid with a bomb to the kid with a picket sign, and from the kid with the picket sign to the kid with the bumper sticker of the opposing candidate. And you just keep going down the line.

In 1940, Attorney General Robert Jackson saw the same risk. He recognized that using broad labels like "national security" or "subversion" to invoke the vast power of the government is dangerous because there are "no definite standards to determine what constitutes a 'subversive activity, such as we have for murder or larceny." Jackson added:

Activities which seem benevolent or helpful to wage earners, persons on relief, or those who are disadvantaged in the struggle for existence may be regarded as "subversive" by those whose property interests might be burdened thereby. Those who are in office are apt to regard as "subversive" the activities of any of those who would bring about a change of administration. Some of our soundest constitutional doctrines were once punished as subversive. We must not forget that it was not so long ago that both the term "Republican" and the term "Democrat" were epithets with sinister meaning to denote persons of radical tendencies that were "subversive" of the order of things then dominant.

This wise warning was not heeded in the conduct of intelligence activity, where the "eternal vigilance" which is the "price of liberty" has been forgotten. . . .

Summary of the Main Problems

. . . . Too many people have been spied upon by too many Government agencies and to much information has been collected. The Government has often undertaken the secret surveillance of citizens on the basis of their political beliefs, even when those beliefs posed no threat of violence or illegal acts on behalf of a hostile foreign power. The Government, operating primarily through secret informants, but also using other intrusive techniques such as wiretaps, microphone "bugs" surreptitious mail opening, and break-ins, has swept in vast amounts of information about the personal lives, views, and associations of American citizens. Investigations of groups deemed potentially dangerous—and even of groups suspected of associating with potentially dangerous organizations—have continued for decades, despite the fact that those groups did not engage in unlawful activity. Groups and individuals have been harassed and disrupted because of their political views and their lifestyles. Investigations have been based upon vague standards whose breadth made excessive collection inevitable. Unsavory and vicious tactics have been employed—including anonymous attempts to break up marriages, disrupt meetings, ostracize persons from their professions, and provoke target groups into rivalries that might result in deaths. Intelligence agencies have served the political and personal objectives of presidents and other high officials. While the agencies often committed excesses in response to pressure from high officials in the Executive branch and Congress, they also occasionally initiated improper activities and then concealed them from officials whom they had a duty to inform.

Governmental officials—including those whose principal duty is to enforce the law—have violated or ignored the law over long periods of time and have advocated and defended their right to break the law.

The Constitutional system of checks and balances has not adequately controlled intelligence activities. Until recently the Executive branch has neither delineated the scope of permissible activities nor established procedures for supervising intelligence agencies. Congress has failed to exercise sufficient oversight, seldom questioning the use to which its apropriations were being put. Most domestic intelligence issues have not reached the courts, and in those cases when they have reached the courts, the judiciary has been reluctant to grapple with them.

Each of these points is briefly illustrated below, and covered in substantially greater detail in the following sections of the report.

1. The Number of People Affected by Domestic Intelligence Activity

United States intelligence agencies have investigated a vast number of American citizens and domestic organizations. FBI headquarters alone has developed over 500,000 domestic intelligence files, 11 and these have been augmented by additional files at FBI Field Offices. The FBI opened 65,000 of these domestic intelligence files in 1972 alone. In fact, substantially more individuals and groups are subject to intelligence scrutiny than the number of files would appear to indicate, since typically, each domestic intelligence file contains information on more than one individual or group, and this information is readily retrievable through the FBI General Name Index.

The number of Americans and domestic groups caught in the domestic intelligence net is further illustrated by the following statistics:

- Nearly a quarter of a million first class letters were opened and photographed in the United States by the CIA between 1953–1973, producing a CIA computerized index of nearly one and one-half million names.
- At least 130,000 first class letters were opened and photographed by the FBI between 1940–1966 in eight U.S. cities.
- Some 300,000 individuals were indexed in a CIA computer system and separate files were created on approximately 7,200 Americans and over 100 domestic groups during the course of CIA's Operation CHAOS (1967–1973).
- Millions of private telegrams sent from, to, or through the United States were obtained by the National Security Agency from 1947 to 1975 under a secret arrangement with three United States telegraph companies.
- An estimated 100,000 Americans were the subjects of United States Army intelligence files created between the mid 1960's and 1971.
- Intelligence files on more than 11,000 individuals and groups were created by the Internal Revenue Service between 1969 and 1973 and tax investigations were started on the basis of political rather than tax criteria.
- At least 26,000 individuals were at one point catalogued on an FBI list of persons to be rounded up in the event of a "national emergency."

2. Too Much Information Is Collected For Too Long

Intelligence agencies have collected vast amounts of information about the intimate details of citizens' lives and about their participation in legal and peaceful political activities. The targets of intelligence activity have included political adherents of the right and the left, ranging from activitist to casual supporters. Investigations have been directed against proponents of racial causes and women's rights, outspoken apostles of nonviolence and racial harmony; establishment politicians; religious groups; and advocates of new life styles. The widespread targeting of citizens and domestic groups, and the excessive scope of the collection of information, is illustrated by the following examples:

(a) The "Women's Liberation Movement" was infiltrated by informants who collected material about the movement's policies, leaders, and individual members. One report included the name of every woman who attended meetings, and another stated that each woman at a meeting bad described "how she felt oppressed, sexually or otherwise." Another report concluded that the movement's purpose was to "free women from the humdrum existence of being only a wife and mother", but still recommended that the intelligence investigation should be continued.

(b) A prominent civil rights leader and advisor to Dr. Martin Luther ing, Jr., was investigated on the suspicion that he might be a Communist "sympathizer." The FBI field office concluded he was not. Bureau headquarters directed that the investigation continue using a theory of "guilty until proven innocent: . . ."

(c) FBI sources reported on the formation of the Conservative American Christian Action Council in 1971. In the 1950's, the Bureau collected information about the John Birch Society and passed it to the White House because of the Society's "scurillous attack" on President Eisenhower and other high Government officials.

(d) Some investigations of the lawful activities of peaceful groups have continued for decades. For example, the NAACP was investigated to determine whether it "had connections with" the Communist Party. The investigation lasted for over twenty-five years, although nothing was found to rebut a report during the first year of the investigation that the NAACP had a "strong tendency" to "steer clear of Communist activities." Similarly, the FBI has admitted that the Socialist Workers Party has committed no criminal acts. Yet the Bureau has investigated the Socialist Workers Party for more than three decades on the basis of its revolutionary rhetoric-which the FBI concedes falls short of incitement to violence-and its claimed international links. The Bureau is currently using its informants to collect information about SWP members' political views, including those on "U.S. involvement in Angola," "food prices," "racial matters," the "Vietnam War," and about any of their efforts to support non-SWP candidates for political office.

(e) National political leaders fell within the broad reach of intelligence investigations. For example, Army Intelligence nee maintained files on Senator Adlai Stevenson and Congressman Abner Mikva because of their participation in peaceful political meetings under surveillance by Army agents. A letter to Richard Nixon, while he was a candidate for President in 1968, was intercepted under CIA's mail opening program. In the 1960's President Johnson asked the FBI to compare various Senators' statements on Vietnam with the Communist Party line and to conduct name checks on leading antiwar Senators.

(f) As part of their effort to collect information which "related even remotely" to people or groups "active" in communities which had "the potential" for civil disorder, Army intelligence agencies took such steps as: sending agents to a Halloween party for elementary school children in Washington, D.C., because they suspected a local "dissident" might be present; monitoring protests of welfare mothers' organizations in Milwaukee; infiltrating a coalition of church youth groups in Colorado; and sending agents to a priests' conference in Washington, D.C., held to discuss birth control measures.

(g) In the, late 1960's and early 1970s, student groups were subjected to intense scrutiny. In 1970 the FBI ordered investigations of every member of the Students for a Democratic Society and of "every Black Student Union and similar group regardless of their past or present involvement in disorders." Files were opened on thousands of young men and women so that, as the former head of FBI intelligence explained, the information could be used if they ever applied for a government job . . .

(h) The FBI Intelligence Division commonly investigated any indication that "subversive" groups already under investigation were seeking to influence or control other groups. One example of the extreme breadth of this "infiltration" theory was an FBI instruction in the mid-1960's to all Field Offices to investigate every "free university" because some of them had come under "subversive influence."

(i) Each administration from Franklin D. Roosevelt's to Richard Nixon's permitted, and sometimes encouraged, government agencies to handle essentially political intelligence. For example:

- President Roosevelt asked the FBI to put in its files the names of citizens sending telegrams to the White House opposing his "national defense" policy and supporting Col. Charles Lindbergh.
- President Truman received inside information on a former Roosevelt aide's efforts to influence his appointments, labor union negotiating plans, and the publishing plans of journalists.
- President Eisenhower received reports on purely political and social contacts with foreign officials by Bernard Baruch, Mrs. Eleanor Roosevelt, and Supreme Court Justice William O. Douglas.
- The Kennedy Administration had the FBI wiretap a Congressional staff member, three executive officials, a lobbyist, and a, Washington law firm. Attorney General Robert F. Kennedy received the fruits of a FBI "tap" on Martin Luther King, Jr. and a "bug" on a Congressman both of which yielded information of a political nature.
- President Johnson asked the FBI to conduct "name checks" of his critics and of members of the staff of his 1964 opponent, Senator Barry Goldwater. He also requested purely political intelligence on his critics in the Senate, and received extensive intelligence reports on political activity at the 1964 Democratic Convention from FBI electronic surveillance.
- President Nixon authorized a program of wiretaps which produced for the White House purely political or personal information unrelated to national security, including information about a Supreme Court justice.

3. Covert Action and the Use of Illegal or Improper Means

(a) Covert Action.—Apart from uncovering excesses in the collection of intelligence, our investigation has disclosed covert actions directed against Americans, and the use of illegal and improper surveillance techniques to gather information. For example:

(i) The FBI's COINTELPRO—counterintelligence program—was designed to "disrupt" groups and "neutralize" individuals deemed to be threats to domestic security. The FBI resorted to counterintelligence tactics in part because its chief officials believed that the existing law could not control the activities of certain dissident groups, and that court decisions had tied the hands of the intelligence community.

Whatever opinion one holds about the policies of the targeted groups, many of the tactics employed by the FBI were indisputably degrading to a free society. COINTELPRO tactics included:

- Anonymously attacking the political beliefs of targets in order to induce their employers to fire them;
- Anonymously mailing letters to the spouses of intelligence targets for the purpose of destroying their marriages;
- Obtaining from IRS the tax returns of a target and then attempting to provoke an IRS investigation for the express purpose of deterring a protest leader from attending the Democratic National Convention;
- Falsely and anonymously labeling as Government informants members of groups known to be violent, thereby exposing the falsely labelled member to expulsion or physical attack;
- Pursuant to instructions to use "misinformation" to disrupt demonstrations, employing such means as broadcasting fake orders on the same citizens band radio frequency used by demonstration marshalls to attempt to control demonstrations, and duplicating and falsely filling out forms soliciting housing for persons coming to a demonstration, thereby causing "long and useless journeys to locate these addresses";
- Sending an anonymous letter to the leader of a Chicago street gang (described as "violence-prone") stating that the Black Panthers were supposed to have "a hit out for you." The letter was suggested because it "may intensify . . . animosity" and cause the street gang leader to "take retaliatory action."

(ii) From "late 1963" until his death in 1968, Martin Luther King, Jr., was the target of an intensive campaign by the Federal Bureau of Investigation to "neutralize" him as an effective civil rights leader. In the words of the man in charge of the FBI's "war" against Dr. King, "No holds were barred."

The FBI gathered information about Dr. King's plans and activities through an extensive surveillance program, employing nearly every intelligence-gathering technique at the Bureau's disposal in order to obtain information about the "private activities of Dr. King and his advisors" to use to "completely discredit" them.

The program to destroy Dr. King as the leader of the civil rights movement included efforts to discredit him with Executive branch officials, Congressional leaders, foreign heads of state, American ambassadors, churches. universities, and the press.

The FBI mailed Dr. King a tape recording made from microphones hidden in his hotel rooms which one agent testified was an attempt to destroy Dr. King's marriage. The tape recording was accompanied by a note which Dr. King and his advisors interpreted as threatening to release the tape recording unless Dr. King committed suicide.

The extraordinary nature of the campaign to discredit Dr. King is evident from two documents:

- At the August 1963 March on Washington, Dr. King told the country of his "dream" that:

  all of God's children, black men and white men, Jews and Gentiles, Protestants and Catholics, will be able to join hands and sing in the words of the old Negro spiritual, "Free at last, free at last, thank God Almighty, I'm free at last."

The Bureau's Domestic Intelligence Division concluded that this "demagogic speech" established Dr. King as the "most dangerous and effective Negro leader in the country." Shortly afterwards, and within days after Dr. King was named "Man of the Year" by Time magazine, the FBI decided to "take him off his pedestal," reduce him completely in influence," and select and promote its own candidate to "assume the role of the leadership of the Negro people."

- In early 1968, Bureau headquarters explained to the field that Dr. King must be destroyed because he was seen as a potential "messiah" who could "unify and electrify" the "black nationalist movement". Indeed, to the FBI he was a potential threat because he might "abandon his supposed 'obedience' to white liberal doctrines (non-violence)." In short, a non-violent man was to be secretly attacked and destroyed as insurance against his abandoning non-violence.

(b) Illegal or Improper Means.—The surveillance which we investigated was not only vastly excessive in breadth and a basis for degrading counter-intelligence actions, but was also often conducted by illegal or improper means. For example:

(1) For approximately 20 years the CIA carried out a program of indiscriminately opening citizens' first class mail. The Bureau also had a mail opening program, but cancelled it in 1966. The Bureau continued, however, to receive the illegal fruits of CIA's program. In 1970, the heads of both agencies signed a document for President Nixon, which correctly stated that mail opening was illegal, falsely stated that it had been discontinued, and proposed that the illegal opening of mail should be resumed because it would provide useful results. The President approved the program, but withdrew his approval five days later. The illegal opening continued nonetheless. Throughout this period CIA officials knew that mail opening was illegal, but expressed concern about the "flap potential" of exposure, not about the illegality of their activity.

(2) From 1947 until May 1975, NSA received from international cable companies millions of cables which had been sent by American citizens in the reasonable expectation that they would be kept private.

(3) Since the early 1930's, intelligence agencies have frequently wiretapped and bugged American citizens without the benefit of judicial warrant. Recent court decisions have curtailed the use of these techniques against domestic targets. But past subjects of these surveillances have included a United States Congressman, a Congressional staff member, journalists and newsmen, and numerous individuals and groups who engaged in no criminal activity and who posed no

genuine threat to the national security, such as two White House domestic affairs advisers and an anti Vietnam War protest group. While the prior written approval of the Attorney General has been required for all warrantless wiretaps since 1940, the record is replete with instances where this requirement was ignored and the Attorney General gave only after-the-fact authorization.

Until 1965, microphone surveillance by intelligence agencies was wholly un-regulated in certain classes of cases. Within weeks after a 1954 Supreme Court decision denouncing the FBI's installation of a microphone in a defendant's bed-room, the Attorney General informed the Bureau that he did not believe the de-cision applied to national security cases and permitted the FBI to continue to install microphones subject only to its own "intelligent restraint."

(4) In several cases, purely political information (such as the reaction of Con-gress to an Administration's legislative proposal) and purely personal information (such as coverage of the extra-marital social activities of a high-level Executive official under surveillance) was obtained from electronic surveillance and dis-seminated to the highest levels of the federal government.

(5) Warrantless break-ins have been conducted by intelligence agencies since World War II. During the 1960's alone, the FBI and CIA conducted hundreds of break-ins, many against American citizens and domestic organizations. In some cases, these break-ins were to install microphones; in other cases, they were to steal such items as membership lists from organizations considered "subversive" by the Bureau.

(6) The most pervasive surveillance technique has been the informant. In a random sample of domestic intelligence cases, 83% involved informants and 5% involved electronic surveillance. Informants have been used against peaceful, law-abiding groups; they have collected information about personal and political views and activities. To maintain their credentials in violence-prone groups, in-formants have involved themselves in violent activity. . . .

4. Ignoring the Law

Officials of the intelligence agencies occasionally recognized that certain ac-tivities were illegal, but expressed concern only for "flap Potential." Even more disturbing was the frequent testimony that the law, and the Constitution were simply ignored. For example, the author of the so-called Huston plan testified:

Question. Was there any person who stated that the activity recommended, which you have previously identified as being illegal opening of the mail and breaking and entry or burglary—was there any single person who stated that such activity should not be done because it was unconstitutional?

Answer. No.

. . . . Similarly, the man who for ten years headed FBI's Intelligence Division tes-tified that:

> never once did I hear anybody, including myself, raise the question: "Is this course of action which we have agreed upon lawful, is it legal, is it ethical

or moral." We never gave any thought to this line of reasoning, because we were just naturally pragmatic.

Although the statutory law and the Constitution were often not "[given] a thought," there was a general attitude that intelligence needs were responsive to a higher law. Thus, as one witness testified in justifying the FBI's mail opening program:

> It was my assumption that what we were doing was justified by what we had to do . . . the greater good, the national security.

6. The Adverse Impact of Improper Intelligence Activity

Many of the illegal or improper disruptive efforts directed against American citizens and domestic organizations succeeded in injuring their targets. Although it is sometimes difficult to prove that a target's misfortunes were caused by a counter-intelligence program directed against him, the possibility that an arm of the United States Government intended to cause the harm and might have been responsible is itself abhorrent.

The Committee has observed numerous examples of the impact of intelligence operations. Sometimes the harm was readily apparent—destruction of marriages, loss of friends or jobs. Sometimes the attitudes of the public and of Government officials responsible for formulating policy and resolving vital issues were influenced by distorted intelligence. But the most basic harm was to the values of privacy and freedom which our Constitution seeks to protect and which intelligence activity infringed on a broad scale.

(a) General Efforts to Discredit.—Several efforts against individuals and groups appear to have achieved their stated aims. For example:

- A Bureau Field Office reported that the anonymous letter it had sent to an activist's husband accusing his wife of infidelity "contributed very strongly" to the subsequent breakup of the marriage.
- Another Field Office reported that a draft counsellor deliberately, and falsely, accused of being an FBI informant was "ostracized" by his friends and associates.
- Two instructors were reportedly put on probation after the Bureau sent an anonymous letter to a university administrator about their funding of an anti-administration student newspaper.
- The Bureau evaluated its attempts to "put a stop" to a contribution to the Southern Christian Leadership Conference as "quite successful."
- An FBI document boasted that a "pretext" phone call to Stokeley Carmichael's mother telling her that members of the Black Panther Party intended to kill her son left her "shocked." The memorandum intimated that the Bureau believed it had been responsible for Carmichael's flight to Africa the following day.

(b) Media Manipulation.—The FBI has attempted covertly to influence the public's perception of persons and organizations by disseminating derogatory information to the press, either anonymously or through "friendly" news contacts. The impact of those articles is generally difficult to measure, although in some cases there are fairly direct connections to injury to the target. The Bureau also attempted to influence media reporting which would have any impact on the public image of the FBI. Examples include:

- Planting a series of derogatory articles about Martin Luther King, Jr., and the Poor People's Campaign . . .
- Soliciting information from Field Offices "on a continuing basis" for "prompt . . . dissemination to the news media . . . to discredit the New Left movement and its adherents." The Headquarters directive requested, among other things, that:

   specific data should be furnished depicting the scurrilous and depraved nature, of many of the characters, activities, habits, and living conditions representative of New Left adherents.

Field Offices were to be exhorted that: "Every avenue of possible embarrassment must be vigorously and enthusiastically explored."

- Ordering Field Offices to gather information which would disprove allegations by the "liberal press, the bleeding hearts, and the forces on the left" that the Chicago police used undue force in dealing with demonstrators at the 1968 Democratic Convention . . .

(d) "Chilling" First Amendment Rights.—The First Amendment protects the Rights of American citizens to engage in free and open discussions, and to associate with persons of their choosing. Intelligence agencies have, on occasion, expressly attempted to interfere with those rights. For example, one internal FBI memorandum called for "more interviews" with New Left subjects "to enhance the paranoia endemic in these circles" and "get the point across there is an FBI agent behind every mailbox."

More importantly, the government's surveillance activities in the aggregate—whether or not expressly intended to do so—tends, as the Committee concludes at p. 290 to deter the exercise of First Amendment Rights by American citizens who become aware of the government's domestic intelligence program.

(e) Preventing the Free Exchange of Ideas.—Speakers, teachers, writers, and publications themselves were targets of the FBI's counterintelligence program. The FBI's efforts to interfere with the free exchange of ideas included:

- Anonymously attempting to prevent an alleged "Communist-front" group from holding a forum on a midwest campus, and then investigating the judge who ordered that the meeting be allowed to proceed.

- Using another "confidential source" in a foundation which contributed to a local college to apply pressure on the school to fire an activist professor.
- Anonymously contacting a university official to urge him to "persuade" two professors to stop funding a student newspaper, in order to "eliminate what voice the New Left has" in the area.
- Targeting the New Mexico Free University for teaching "confrontation politics" and "draft counseling training."

7. Cost and Value

Domestic intelligence is expensive. We have already indicated the cost of illegal and improper intelligence activities in terms of the harm to victims, the injury to constitutional values, and the damage to the democratic process itself. The cost in dollars is also significant. For example, the FBI has budgeted for fiscal year 1976 over $7 million for its domestic security informant program, more than twice the amount it spends on informants against organized crime. The aggregate budget for FBI domestic security intelligence and foreign counterintelligence is at least $80 million. In the late 1960s and early 1970s, when the Bureau was joined by the CIA, the military, and NSA in collecting information about the anti-war movement and black activists, the cost was substantially greater.

Apart from the excesses described above, the usefulness of many domestic intelligence activities in serving the legitimate goal of protecting society has been questionable. Properly directed intelligence investigations concentrating upon hostile foreign agents and violent terrorists can produce valuable results. The Committee has examined cases where the FBI uncovered "illegal" agents of a foreign power engaged in clandestine intelligence activities in violation of federal law. Information leading to the prevention of serious violence has been acquired by the FBI through its informant penetration of terrorist groups and through the inclusion in Bureau files of the names of persons actively involved with such groups. Nevertheless, the most sweeping domestic intelligence surveillance programs have produced surprisingly few useful returns in view of their extent. For example:

- Between 1960 and 1974, the FBI conducted over 500,000 separate investigations of persons and groups under the "subversive" category, predicated on the possibility that they might be likely to overthrow the government of the United States. Yet not a single individual or group has been prosecuted since 1957 under the laws which prohibit planning or advocating action to overthrow the government and which are the main alleged statutory basis for such FBI investigations.
- A recent study by the General Accounting Office has estimated that of some 17,528 FBI domestic intelligence investigations of individuals in 1974, only 1.3 percent resulted in prosecution and conviction, and in only "about 2 percent" of the cases was advance knowledge of any activity—legal or illegal—obtained.
- One of the main reasons advanced for expanded collection of intelligence about urban unrest and anti-war protest was to help responsible officials cope with possible violence. However, a former White House official with

major duties in this area under the Johnson administration has concluded, in retrospect, that "in none of these situations . . . would advance intelligence about dissident groups [have] been of much help," that what was needed was "physical intelligence" about the geography of major cities, and that the attempt to "predict violence" was not a "successful undertaking . . ."

In considering its recommendations, the Committee undertook an evaluation of the FBI's claims that domestic intelligence was necessary to combat terrorism, civil disorders, "subversion," and hostile foreign intelligence activity. The Committee reviewed voluminous materials bearing on this issue and questioned Bureau officials, local police officials, and present and former federal executive officials.

We have found that we are in fundamental agreement with the wisdom of Attorney General Stone's initial warning that intelligence agencies must not be "concerned with political or other opinions of individuals" and must be limited to investigating essentially only "such conduct as is forbidden by the laws of the United States." The Committee's record demonstrates that domestic intelligence which departs from this standard raises grave risks of undermining the democratic process and harming the interests of individual citizens. This danger weighs heavily against the speculative or negligible benefits of the ill-defined and overbroad investigations authorized in the past. Thus, the basic purpose of the recommendations contained in Part IV of this report is to limit the FBI to investigating conduct rather than ideas or associations.

The excesses of the past do not, however, justify depriving the United States of a clearly defined and effectively controlled domestic intelligence capability. The intelligence services of this nation's international adversaries continue to attempt to conduct clandestine espionage operations within the United States. Our recommendations provide for intelligence investigations of hostile foreign intelligence activity.

Moreover, terrorists have engaged in serious acts of violence which have brought death and injury to Americans and threaten further such acts. These acts, not the politics or beliefs of those who would commit them, are the proper focus for investigations to anticipate terrorist violence. Accordingly, the Committee would permit properly controlled intelligence investigations in those narrow circumstances.

Concentration on imminent violence can avoid the wasteful dispersion of resources which has characterized the sweeping (and fruitless) domestic intelligence investigations of the past. But the most important reason for the fundamental change in the domestic intelligence operations which our Recommendations propose is the need to protect the constitutional Rights of Americans.

In light of the record of abuse revealed by our inquiry, the Committee is not satisfied with the position that mere exposure of what has occurred in the past will prevent its recurrence. Clear legal standards and effective oversight and controls are necessary to ensure that domestic intelligence activity does not itself undermine the democratic system it is intended to protect.

120. Committee on the Present Danger, "Common Sense and the Common Danger"

(1976)

Against the backdrop of defeat in Vietnam, declining public confidence in government after Watergate, and a weakened economy, some Americans feared that the Soviets would press their advantage. In 1976, a number of Cold Warriors—mostly Republicans, but including Democrats and labor leaders—formed the Committee on the Present Danger to remind their fellow citizens of the continuing threat posed by Soviet expansionism. In particular, they worried that with decreased military spending by the United States, the Soviets might become emboldened in supporting revolutions around the world. Later in the decade, when the Sandinistas overthrew dictator Anastasio Somoza in Nicaragua, and the Soviets invaded Afghanistan, the committee saw these events as evidence that its analysis was correct.

SOURCE: Charles Tyroler III, ed., *Alerting America* (Washington, D.C.: Pergamon-Brassey's Publishers, 1984), 3–5.

I

Our country is in a period of danger, and the danger is increasing. Unless decisive steps are taken to alert the nation, and to change the course of its policy, our economic and military capacity will become inadequate to assure peace with security.

The threats we face are more subtle and indirect than was once the case. As a result, awareness of danger has diminished in the United States, in the democratic countries with which we are naturally and necessarily allied, and in the developing world.

There is still time for effective action to ensure the security and prosperity of the nation in peace, through peaceful deterrence and concerted alliance diplomacy. A conscious effort of political will is needed to restore the strength and coherence of our foreign policy; to revive the solidarity of our alliances; to build constructive relations of cooperation with other nations whose interests parallel our own—and on that sound basis to seek reliable conditions of peace with the Soviet Union, rather than an illusory detente. . . .

II

The principal threat to our nation, to world peace, and to the cause of human freedom is the Soviet drive for dominance based upon an unparalleled military buildup. . . .

For more than a decade, the Soviet Union has been enlarging and improving both its strategic and its conventional military forces far more rapidly than the United States and its allies. Soviet military power and its rate of growth cannot be explained or justified by considerations of self-defense. The Soviet Union is consciously seeking what its spokesmen call "visible preponderance" for the Soviet sphere. Such preponderance, they explain, will permit the Soviet Union "to transform the conditions of world politics" and determine the direction of its development.

The process of Soviet expansion and the worldwide deployment of its military power threaten our interest in the political independence of our friends and allies, their and our fair access to raw materials, the freedom of the seas, and in avoiding a preponderance of adversary power.

These interests can be threatened not only by direct attack, but also by envelopment and in direct aggression. The defense of the Middle East, for example, is vital to the defense of Western Europe and Japan. In the Middle East the Soviet Union opposes those just settlements between Israel and its Arab neighbors which are critical to the future of the area. Similarly, we and much of the rest of the world are threatened by renewed coercion through a second round of Soviet-encouraged oil embargoes.

III

Soviet expansionism threatens to destroy the world balance of forces on which the survival of freedom depends. If we see the world as it is, and restore our will, our strength and our self-confidence, we shall find resources and friends enough to counter that threat. There is a crucial moral difference between the two superpowers in their character and objectives. The United States—imperfect as it is—is essential to the hopes of those countries which desire to develop their societies in their own ways, free of coercion.

To sustain an effective foreign policy, economic strength, military strength, and a commitment to leadership are essential. We must restore an allied defense posture capable of deterrence at each significant level and in those theaters vital to our interests. The goal of our strategic forces should be to prevent the use of, or the credible threat to use, strategic weapons in world politics; that of our conventional forces, to prevent other forms of aggression directed against our interests. Without a stable balance of forces in the world and policies of collective defense based upon it, no other objective of our foreign policy is attainable.

As a percentage of Gross National Product, U.S. defense spending is lower than at any time in twenty-five years. For the United States to be free, secure and influential, higher levels of spending are now required for our ready land, sea, and air forces, our strategic deterrent, and, above all, the continuing modernization of those forces through research and development. The increased level of spending required is well within our means so long as we insist on all feasible efficiency in our defense spending. We must also expect our allies to bear their fair share of the burden of defense.

From a strong foundation, we can pursue a positive and confident diplomacy, addressed to the full array of our economic, political and social interests in world politics. It is only on this basis that we can expect successfully to negotiate hard-headed and verifiable agreements to control and reduce armaments.

If we continue to drift, we shall become second best to the Soviet Union in overall military strength; our alliances will weaken; our promising rapprochement with China could be reversed. Then we could find ourselves isolated in a hostile world, facing the unremitting pressures of Soviet policy backed by an overwhelming preponderance of power. Our national survival itself would be in peril, and we should face, one after another, bitter choices between war and acquiescence under pressure.

121. Linda Alband and Steve Rees, "Women and the Volunteer Armed Forces: First Report on a Rocky Romance"

(1977)

The end of the draft and the introduction of the All-Volunteer Force in 1973 came as the women's movement sparked wholesale changes in American culture. In this essay, Linda Alband and Steve Rees describe how these historic phenomena intersected and the transformation of the military that resulted for enlisted women and for the wives of enlisted men. In addition, it captures how, thanks to the gay rights movement, the circumstances of lesbians in the military—and, more generally, homosexuals in the armed forces—emerged as a political issue in the late 1970s. The article appeared in *Radical America*, a bimonthly magazine that grew out of the New Left in the late 1960s largely driven by the energy of a handful of devoted former SDSers, including historians Paul and Mary Jo Buhle. The magazine often featured articles on the GI and Vietnam veterans movement, as well as numerous pieces on feminism. In this essay, the authors confront their largely feminist and antimilitarist readership by showing that pursuing equal rights for women in the military presented a conundrum to some on the left.

SOURCE: *Radical America*, January–February 1977, pp. 19–32.

Former Army Secretary Howard Callaway announced in 1975, with all due authority and a straight lip, the Army's latest scientific discovery: "a woman could do about anything a man could." Young women recruits are now trained in rifle marksmanship and defense combat tactics, and trudge on night marches evading simulated rifle fire and real tear-gas cannisters. WAC First Lieutenant Andrea Kopolka boasts that "The Army's where it's happening for women." Her enthusiasm is shared by her 18-year-old trainee Jean Mehorczyk, who testified at her basic-training graduation, "It's the greatest thing that's ever happened to me." Female non-commissioned officers now exercise immediate authority over hundreds of enlisted men. Of the few dissenting female voices within the ranks, most belong to lesbians who are battling, not to leave the institution, but to stay in.

Are these changes to be celebrated as the gains of the women's movement, dreaded as dangerous signs of the military's new-found legitimacy, or dismissed as token concessions but nothing more? Let's not be too hasty in choosing. Our intent here is not to prove once again beyond the shadow of a doubt that despite these reforms the military remains a bastion of anti-feminism. Nor are we intent on proving that these internal reforms, or any other reforms for that matter, do not alter the basic function of the institution. While believing that both assertions are true, we're not interested in reducing these or any other of the left's commonly-held ideas about the military to a catechism. Rather, we intend to test those ideas against the reality of a military which is breaking with many of its anachronistic traditions. If the left refuses to examine these changes, its understanding of the U.S. military, not to mention its attempts to change it, will become equally outmoded.

The Context

After being defeated in Indochina and humiliated at home, the military had to either adapt or die. The Nixon doctrine of Vietnamization on a global scale made a change in the military's function possible. The Indochinese Revolution and the antiwar movement made it necessary. The all-volunteer-force concept soon followed. What resulted was an overhaul from top to bottom: an end to the draft, a 40% reduction in force, and hundreds of internal reforms, not the least of which was the attempt to make soldiering a job just like anyother. In fact, the relation between GIs and the command soon came to resemble that between labor and management. For motivation, patriotism was replaced by a paycheck. . . .

This trend toward a more modern, streamlined armed forces made it easier for the Department of Defense (DoD) to bring its attitudes and treatment of women more up-to-date. But it was the women's movement that set the standard against which the military's progress would be measured. Not only did the women's movement begin to influence masses of working-class women, but it also spread from one generation to the next. Ten years ago, teenage girls were considered daring if they dreamt of the independent life of an actress or stewardess. Today, many of those teenage girls shudder at the thought of marriage and kids, a dull job, or living with parents, and strike out on their own by turning to soldiering. Ten years ago, women shouting insults at gentlemanly military officers would have been considered unseemly and unfeminine. Today, the women's movement has helped remove these obstacles to action. Enlisted men's wives have, in the last three years, shouted, picketed, petitioned, and press-conferenced their way into many a confrontation with the command. The battered post-war military is in no position to do battle with a trend as compelling as this. Unable to lick 'em, the military has, in a sense, joined 'em. The military has been changed in the process, but not without turning some aspects of the women's movement to its own advantage.

Enlisted Women

In the midst of this flurry of reform activity characteristic of an enormous bu-reaucracy scrambling for its survival, one factor more than any other determined the military's new turn toward women: the demand for labor. Stripped in mid-1973 of its power to conscript, the military was forced to compete on the open market for the recruits it needed. In addition, it had to improve the quality of military life to encourage its career soldiers to stay. Even after the unemploy-ment and inflation percentages climbed into double digits, the military still had profound "manpower recruitment" difficulties. It faced the unprecedented task of recruiting one out of every three available and qualified non-college males. And all this even after a 40% reduction in the number of DoD employees in uni-form, and the civilianization of many jobs traditionally held by soldiers. As re-cruiters fell further behind their quotas (even in the first year of the volunteer armed forces), and as the enticing enlistment bonuses and benefits became too expensive to maintain, the DoD began to realize how important women could be in fulfilling its "manpower" requirements. . . .

Even after the economic slump enabled recruiters to meet their quotas, and reenlistment officers to halt the mass exodus of experienced career personnel, several branches still faced personnel shortages. The Army was still short in the combat arms: artillery, infantry, and armor. The Navy lacked boiler techs, ma-chinist mates, and nuclear engineers. If women could be recruited and trained for many of the noncritical slots, more men could be channeled into the critical specialties. Furthermore, the more far-sighted of the military's manpower man-agers knew that an economic upturn and a decline in the number of available male recruits due to the decline in the birth rate could eventually push the mili-tary's recruiting capabilities to their limits. The prestigious Defense Manpower Commission, it its April 1976 report, recommended that the military prepare to tap the pool of available female GIs-in-waiting as one of the least disruptive re-sponses to this dilemma.

The military's need for women recruits is only half the story. Why do these women need the military? Every survey reveals the same collection of motiva-tions: the desire for education, travel, and training, and the lack of other oppor-tunities. Recruiting ads echo these sentiments: "Who says men don't listen when a woman talks?" "A new life and a new world of travel." "Making her own way." "You can find yourself." Women from poor families, from racial and ethnic mi-norities in the U.S., or from smaller, rural towns have even fewer economic op-tions than do their male peers. Unlike men their age, they are not encouraged to strike out on their own. The military offers a package deal within an authoritar-ian structure that leaves little risk of having to make choices about one's life. Some of the recruitment propaganda plays up to this family-substitute angle, stressing "something different, but not so really different" and "It's more like what you're used to."

In an article in *Ms.* several years ago, B. J. Phillips assembled a composite of the typical WAC she met during her week at Ft. McClellan. "She had been out of high school for a year, and in a recession economy, found jobs nonexistent or dull and low-paid. Unable, for financial reasons, to go on to college or into some type of vocational training program, she chose the army because it offered her both job training and GI Bill benefits for further education after she leaves." In a word, these young women, like their male counterparts, enlist because they lack options elsewhere.

Ultimately, the desires of these recruits and the requirements of the military in time of war will clash. . . . But so long as the defense of the nation requires no extraordinary sacrifices by those in the ranks, that clash may be postponed.

Although the impact of these women on the military has been significant, this is not mainly because of their numbers. Enlisted women make up only slightly more than 5% of the total DoD active-duty force. But even that modest figure is a threefold increase over its 1971 level. And when measured as a percentage of new recruits, women figure more prominently: 9.2% for the Army, 11.4% for the Air Force, and an average of 7.7% for the entire DoD. By 1978, women are supposed to make up over 6% of the DoD active-duty force.

These enlisted women have insisted that the military no longer restrict them to "women's work." The military's need for women was so critical that it had to accommodate the demands that women were making both inside and outside its ranks. In the last two years, the military has announced new plans to provide women with equal opportunity, and has authorized the following changes:

- Rules banning mothers from military service were lifted. The military had reserved the right to judge whether a woman could adequately perform her duties and cope with motherhood, but this reservation was dropped as of July 1975.
- Women can adopt children.
- Women can get married after enlistment, and still stay in.
- Married women can enlist both in the regular service and in the reserves.
- Women are now eligible for the same family benefits as men.
- Women are now full-fledged members of promotion boards, no longer confined to evaluating women only.
- Pay is the same for men and women of the same pay grade.
- Job restrictions have been lifted. Women were previously restricted to 39% of the Army's job categories, but are now eligible for 94%—all but the combat arms.
- College ROTC programs are open to women. One school commandant remarked, "We are finding that competition between the sexes is a good motivator."
- Military academies, such as West Point with its 173-year all-male tradition, are opening their doors to female cadets.
- Policy has changed to permit women to command men, except in the combat units. Several WAC officers have been selected for colonel-level commands.
- All enlisted women in the Army are now required to take defensive weapons training. . . .

• Separate detachments for women are being gradually eliminated, with the result that women are now assigned to duty wherever job vacancies exist. And, in mid-September of 1976 the WAC (Women's Army Corps) was eliminated—now both women and men enlist in the Army.

Two items from this list of reforms are worth examining in more detail: basic training and the opening of non-traditional jobs to women. These are the two most troublesome changes for the Pentagon, and the most fascinating for the young women who join.

Beginning in basic, the Army vacillates between training its women recruits to be soldiers and training them to be ladies. True, fatigue-clad, booted women recruits march, jump, climb, and hurdle their way through an "unladylike" and rigorous physical-training program—a program not always equal in intensity to that of the men, but demanding nonetheless. They drill in formation, dig fox-holes, bivouac, and range-fire the M-16 rifle. The content of the 13-week basic-training program has remained essentially what it was during the Vietnam era; physical-fitness training, marching, warfare-technique classes, and instruction in the use of hand grenades, the M-60 machine gun, and the M-16.

There are, however, two major differences in the training programs for men and for women. One of the two is in the area of tactical-weapons training. Men receive 143 hours of rifle marksmanship and defensive tactics, while women receive 72 hours. The other difference is in the "feminine" arts. Women sit through mandatory classroom instruction in hair care, skin care, weight control, rape prevention, and "family planning" (birth control). The closest equivalent on the male side of the balance sheet is venereal-disease prevention—in itself an interesting comment on the Army's notion of who's responsible for what.

Despite these differences, and despite the Army's admittedly inadequate preparation of these women trainees for combat situations, the camaraderie of a shared ordeal and the pride of discovering previously untapped abilities is the core of basic training for women. They don't leave basic any more patriotic, war-hungry, or infatuated with the military than when they went in. Doctrinal training, or motivational training, is not stressed.

Equal opportunity in the military, as elsewhere, has its limits. Admiral Holloway, Chief of Naval Operations, explained the Navy's limitations in an interview in *U.S. News and World Report:* "ship billets must by law be filled with men, and secondly, we must preserve some billets for those men at sea to rotate to. Otherwise, we would be putting our men on openended sea duty." In the Army, women are still unable to join combat-arms specialties. The Air Force prohibits women from flying. And these are only the more visible limits.

More to the point is to ask what happened when the Army suddenly opened up 415 of its 451 occupational fields to women? According to the Defense Manpower Commission, not much. Their report claims, "Women entering the services are opting for the more traditional female jobs. Many have not had the background or exposure to nontraditional areas. Two-thirds of the military women still work in the traditional medical and administrative fields, with no significant concentration in any of the mechanical or electronic career fields."

This picture should come as no surprise. Recruits have to qualify for the job they request by passing a battery of tests. Even if everyone has an equal opportunity to take the same tests, everyone is not equally prepared to take them. Like other equal-opportunity employers, the military can do no more than reproduce the same division of labor which is already present in this society.

Since the institution of the All-Volunteer Military, lesbians have been one of the most coherent forces which have put pressure on the Pentagon to make good its claims of being an equal-opportunity employer. Some of these lesbian enlisted women are the victims of witch-hunt-like sweeps of the women's barracks by military-intelligence officers who grill women on the details of their barracks-mates' private lives. The military conducts these witch hunts to purge itself of its "undesirable elements." They usually begin when the authorities select one woman they suspect—or say they suspect—of being a lesbian. They threaten her with a less-than-honorable discharge. Then they offer to either let her out with a better discharge, or let her stay in if she gives them the names of other lesbians. This tactic is repeated with subsequent victims, so that the investigation might grow to include dozens or even hundreds of women. Interestingly enough, one lesbian ex-WAVE told us that it is more often the case that straight women get busted in these purges. She went on to say that most lesbians knew how to "cover their ass" and were real good at projecting the "proper military image." Another lesbian WAVE who knew that she was going to be called before a Naval Intelligence Service (NIS) investigation board, prepared herself in this way: "I went into the ladies' room, took off my butch watch with the wide strap, put on my lipstick and mascara, and I was ready for 'em."

Still other enlisted women openly defy the military by announcing their lesbian preference. In the past, both men and women have admitted to being homosexual to get out of the military, whether or not they actually were. But today, the armed-forces code is being challenged from within by individuals who have stood up and declared themselves to be gay and have demanded that the military change its treatment of homosexuals.

The military's response in both cases is invariably to initiate discharge proceedings. The soldiers who are targeted for this treatment range from model soldiers-of-the-month to feminists and the disaffected. Of the many who fight to stay in, not all do so out of any love for the military. As Army Reserve Sergeant Miriam Ben Shalom remarked, "I am defending my basic constitutional rights to work, to privacy, and to the freedom of my lifestyle." Whatever their reasons, the consequences of their actions are questioning the line between the citizen and the soldier. They are challenging the military's determination of what they do after work. Having taken to heart the military's own message that it's a job like any other, they are now setting about to make it just that.

It is not as if the handful of lesbians who are now fighting the military for the right to stay in, or even those 2,000 others booted out every year in semi-secret shame, constitute the entire homosexual population in the military. Two Kinsey

Institute scholars estimated in 1971 that the percentage of homosexuals in the military hardly differed from their percentage in civilian society—10%. The various defense lawyers and experts in the current cases use this standard estimate of 10%. Others believe this is an extremely conservative estimate, and point to the massive network of bars, clubs, and newspapers which make up the ghettoized gay military.

While the movement of lesbians in uniform has been a reflection of the larger movement for equal rights for homosexuals, it may soon become its test case. The ACLU lawyer who defended two gay WACs at Ft. Devens last year speculated, "Sooner or later, one of these cases will produce a court decision declaring discrimination against homosexuals unconstitutional. The military is the key institution. Just as the racial integration of the military in the late 40's set the stage for a national social policy of integration, the critical sexual battles are going to be fought here."

Enlisted Men's Wives

The recent leap into the twentieth-century of the military's treatment of enlisted women has only underlined the medieval status of those nearly one million women whose husbands are soldiers. The Army has an orientation pamphlet for the "Army Wife" (Does the woman marry her husband or the Army?) which best articulates the contrast. "Although no serviceman's career was ever made by his wife, many have been hindered or helped by the social skills of their wives, their flexibility, and their loyalty toward the Army and its customs. . . . As an Army wife, never forget that you are the 'silent member' of the team, but a key 'man.' . . . A wife should try to keep her husband from feeling bitter about the system. If she feels the system isn't too bad, he'll probably agree. . . . Your whole scheme of life revolves around your husband, your children, and a happy home." Captured here is the tension between the military's genuine dependence on its "military wives" and its simultaneous denial of the wives' existence independent of their husbands. When, for instance, an enlisted man's wife steps out of line, the woman's husband is reprimanded by his commanding officer. In fact, the wife is formally outside the jurisdiction of military law. Furthermore, the contribution of the "silent member of the team" is rewarded, not in the form of wages to the woman, but as a dependent's allowance attached to the husband's paycheck.

The young working women who settle with their husbands in the trailer parks and stucco apartments of stateside base towns face a tougher ordeal than most non-military wives. These women experience divorce, alcoholism, and stress at rates far above the national average. With most of their husbands working irregular shifts and logging fifty or sixty hours a week, more and more of the work at home falls to them by default. Women whose husbands are ship-stationed have to reckon with six-month cruises when their husbands are on sea duty, and week-long sea trials and irregular, often very long duty shifts even when their husbands' ships are in port. If a woman's husband is assigned to an overseas base, the military will help her move and cover the moving expenses only if her husband's rank is sergeant (E-5) or up. If not, she can come along only if she can afford the move on her own. A skimming of the conservative bi-weekly women's supplement to the *Army Times* reveals more trials and tribulations than we have room to list here: an entire issue on rape—one of the fastest-growing crimes in the military community; boredom and its remedies—service clubs, volunteer work for the Red Cross, and wives' clubs; how to cope with waiting; and base-town crime.

Any institution which, in the 1970's, produces this quality of life and then insists on a woman's total identification with her husband and his job is asking for trouble. In the last three years, the military's found plenty of it! Not uncommon is the following letter from a Norfolk, Virginia woman whose husband was in the Navy: "A free test of a good marriage is about the only benefit enlisted people are given during their struggle to get by. Up to this point I've tried with difficulty to accept the way things are and the fact that the Navy and the system will always run my life for me. I really don't think it's selfish to say I'd like some control over the situation." . . .

In at least two recent instances, this sentiment has been translated into collective action. In San Diego, enlisted men and their wives organized a group to contest the Navy's illegal nonpayment of reenlistment bonuses. (See the May/June issue of *Radical America*.) For almost two years, the group—VRB/OUT (meaning, give us our variable reenlistment bonuses or let us out)—fought the Navy in the courts and in the papers. The enlisted men in the group, though, were often at sea, leaving the bulk of the responsibility for the organization with their women. The women leafleted the bases, planned legal strategy, and picketed recruiting stations—actions which tarnished the Navy's public image and hurt recruiting. Their public statements were confined to the issue, but off the record the women explained that much more was at stake than the loss of a several-thousand-dollar bonus; forced six-month separations, notoriously inadequate onbase medical care, flimsy finding for family services. . . .

Conclusion

Having described these relatively new trends toward reform, we can venture an interpretation of our own, and a brief critique of mainstream feminist and pacifist views about women in the military. What makes any interpretation difficult, however, is the momentary coincidence of interests between the volunteer military's insatiable demand for qualified labor, and the women's movement's demand for equal access to, and equal rights within, public and private institutions. This convergence has meant that the reforms in the military related to equal rights and access for women were established at the top, without much agitation or direct action by women in the ranks below. The challenges to which the military responded took place, for the most part, outside the military itself. One cannot simply argue, then, that these reforms in the military were merely cooptive measures designed to head off rabble rousing in the ranks, or alternatively that the reforms were concessions squeezed from a weak bureaucracy through the dynamics of class struggle. Like all half-truths, both observations accurately describe two parts of a much more complex totality.

Some radicals, especially within the anti-imperialist and pacifist trends, have decried the recent influx of large numbers of women into the armed forces, and their integration into a more accommodating and up-to-date institution, as signs of the militarization of women. Ultimately, they argue, no one, man or woman, should submit to or volunteer for the profession of soldiering. In the short run, their political activity is geared toward discouraging women from enlisting at all. So reforms which make military life more attractive to potential recruits can only serve to make these radicals' tasks more difficult to realize. In fact, the more just the reform, the more they dread it. These radicals resemble those who believed that the way to abolish capitalism was to dissuade people from working. Those who worked were considered bourgeoisified, and reforms which improved the lot of those who worked were considered sops, crumbs, which could only make the ultimate revolutionary act more remote. During times of revolutionary upsurge, they may have commanded some following. But in times of relative stability, they can do little more than soapbox to uninterested passersby. Our disagreement with these radical soapboxers today is not that we would encourage young working-class women to join up, but that it is through their joining that the stability of the all-volunteer, peacetime military might be undermined. The pacifist perspective is more suited to wartime anti-military work with soldiers, and does not grapple with the possibilities of the present period. Furthermore, they consider the military's women-related reforms statically, fixed in their present scope and form, and ignore the opportunity to drive these reforms beyond their intended limits.

At another extreme, the National Organization for Women (NOW) pose sexual equality as an absolute principle which determines their relationship to the military. Consider these remarks of Pat Leeper, a lobbyist for NOW and a coordinator of their Committee for Women in the Military, offered to the Department of the Army in the first months of 1976: "Should women go into combat? To us the question is completely irrelevant. We only need to know that there are capable women who want jobs." Her recommendations included accelerated entry programs and assertiveness training for women, lifting quotas which limit the number of women recruits, and the use of physical (not gender) standards for every job. If NOW holds any position critical of the military's mission, it is not apparent from Pat Leeper's policy paper.

NOW and the Pentagon's more radical critics certainly have conflicting concerns. NOW's advocates are cheering on the waves of female recruits who appear to them to be successfully assaulting one of the last great bastions of male power: soldiering. And the radicals who fear the imminent militarization of women do what they can to head it off. But neither group's perspective focuses on women in the ranks. Our balance sheet, drawn up after a three-year accounting of the all-volunteer, peacetime force experiment, finds the new situation something to be welcomed, not dreaded.

1. At least in the area of women's rights and sexual equality, the military has been compelled to get in step with the rest of society. This goes directly against the grain of traditional military thinking which insists upon the institution's separateness from the rest of society. The old-time military moguls argue that separated courts, laws, prisons, hospitals, schools, and codes of conduct are made necessary by the military mission. They justify distinct social relations within the institution on the same grounds: laws against fraternization between enlisted men and women; separate quarters, dining halls, and bathrooms for officers; saluting and "yes, sir"-ing; grooming and appearance regulations; an enlistment agreement between the GI and the government that saddles the soldier with the obligations of an indentured servant and gives him or her none of the protections of a contractual agreement. Even during wartime, these habits, rules, and regulations are questionable. But during peacetime, they seem even less justifiable to the enlisted men and women who are degraded by these customs daily. So when the ways of the civilian world begin to intrude on the military's erstwhile separate society, it is often to the advantage of the soldier in the ranks, and rarely to the advantage of the command. If one distinction between the civilian and military worlds can be dispensed with, why not the rest? (This is as true in the area of soldier's First Amendment rights as it is in the area of sex discrimination.) The military's recent opposition to formal sex discrimination, however limited, is one step away from an army of professional legionnaires, and one step toward an army of citizen-soldiers. If there are to be any soldiers at all, better that they march in step with the hesitating syncopation of popular music than the goose-stepping four-four time of John Phillip Sousa.

2. These reforms in the military may have a ripple effect, encouraging similar reforms in institutions outside the military. It's still too early to point to any proof, but there is a strong historical precedent. The military's desegregation program after World War II, and its insistence since 1967 on open-occupancy housing agreements from civilian landlords, contributed to the attack on segregation in some of the regions and institutions most resistant to change. The military has at times been not just a reflection of social movements, but also their dynamo.

3. As young women recruits are called upon to do the work of soldiers, their conception of their own capabilities can only expand and improve. And hopefully, after having discovered the social restrictions on the development of their abilities up till then, they will be even quicker to challenge those restrictions next time they encounter them, and not mistake them for natural ones. In addition, the demand for equal rights and access is on the face of it a just demand, although by no means a revolutionary one at this present time and place.

4. As long as these women continue to question the remaining obstacles to equality, the reforms which initially encouraged their questioning can have a destabilizing effect, creating new tensions even while resolving old ones. First, once the catechism of female equality is officially attacked, even ridiculed, then why restrict the percentage of women in the military to 6% or even 10%, as

Pentagon planners do? Why shouldn't women have 50% representation? Second, if equal rights implies equal obligations, shouldn't women be assigned to the combat specialties if they meet the physical requirements? Military planners are not opposed to this in principle, but oppose its implementation on the grounds that the country isn't ready for it yet. Third, the institutionalization of all these reforms concerning enlisted women has only made "dependent" status less excusable than before. In fact, a recent article in *Army Times,* headlined "Professor Expects Surge of Feminism by Service Wives," summarized the findings of a Mills College sociologist, Dr. Lynne Dobrofsky, who predicted that military wives will become radicalized as they realize that they have no status or identity other than their husbands'. Enlisted men's wives have already shown signs of independence in two significant campaigns—the movement to stop deployment of the attack carrier USS Coral Sea over health and safety hazards in November-December 1974, and the variable-reenlistment-bonus suits—and will probably continue to be a thorn in the Pentagon's side.

122. Dead Kennedys, "Kill the Poor"

(1980)

In "Kill the Poor," hardcore punk band Dead Kennedys envisions a scenario in which the latest in nuclear technology is used not in war but to literally wipe out a whole class of Americans. In the late 1970s, the question of the neutron bomb's development dominated national defense discussions. Designed to detonate in the air above a battlefield, the neutron bomb was supposed to kill an advancing Soviet army but leave the buildings in cities and towns largely undamaged. Protests over the neutron bomb's development led President Jimmy Carter to suspend its production (though Ronald Reagan later resumed production of a small number of W-70 neutron warheads). In 1980, Dead Kennedys was one of the most popular hardcore bands in the United States, combining an almost chaotic punk drive with a surf guitar sound. Notable especially for lead singer Jello Biafra's irreverent lyrics—attacking Democratic governor Jerry Brown in "California Uber Alles," pretentious liberals in "Holiday in Cambodia," and slumlords in "Let's Lynch the Landlord"—the band built a reputation for satirizing the political establishment as arrogant and violent. With "Kill the Poor," Biafra mocked the champagne-sipping rich he thought might secretly wish for a final solution to social problems.

SOURCE: Cherry Red, UK / DKS 4, 1980.

> Efficiency and progress is ours once more
> Now that we have the neutron bomb
> Its nice and quick and clean and gets things done
> Away with excess enemy
> But no less value to property
> No sense in war but perfect sense at home . . .
>
> The sun beams down on a brand new day
> No more welfare tax to pay
> Unsightly slums gone up in flashing light
>   Jobless millions whisked away

At last we have more room to play
All systems go to kill the poor tonight

Gonna
Kill Kill Kill Kill
Kill the poor
Kill Kill Kill Kill
Kill the poor
Kill Kill Kill Kill
Kill the poor. . . . Tonight

Behold the sparkle of champagne
The crime rate's gone, feel free again
O life's a dream with you, Miss Lily White
Jane Fonda on the screen today
Convinced the liberals it's okay
So let's get dressed and dance away the night

While they
Kill Kill Kill Kill
Kill the poor
Kill Kill Kill Kill
Kill the poor
Kill Kill Kill Kill
Kill the poor. . . . Tonight

123. Charlie Daniels Band, "In America"

(1980)

By 1980, the cumulative effects of the defeat in Vietnam, the Watergate scandal, the oil crisis and economic recession, and the protracted Iran hostage situation led President Jimmy Carter to bemoan the "crisis of confidence" experienced by so many Americans. But for country music star Charlie Daniels, the Iranian hostage crisis rallied Americans back to the flag. His ode to that patriotic sentiment, "In America," spoke to millions of Americans who likewise sought something to feel good about. The song effectively predicted the campaign style of Ronald Reagan, who recognized that Americans want their president to be a cheerleader. Born in Wilmington, North Carolina, Daniels (1936–) grew up playing guitar, fiddle, and mandolin. Primarily a session musician through the 1960s, Daniels broke through with his band in the 1970s. At first, he struck an independent stand with songs such as "Long Haired Country Boy" and "Uneasy Rider," but by the late 1970s, he had become more identified with the boosterism associated with "In America." Coming on the heels of his number one hit, "The Devil Went Down to Georgia," "In America" made a big splash on mainstream radio—evidence of how much it resonated with a public hungry to feel good about its country's standing in the world. The line about the Pittsburgh Steeler fan reflected Daniels's appreciation for hard-working, unsung people (whose team had just won an unprecedented fourth Super Bowl).

SOURCE: Charlie Daniels Band, *Full Moon* (Epic 36571, 1980).

> We'll the eagle's been flying slow,
> and the flag's been flying low,
> and a lot of people's saying that America's fixing to fall.
> But speaking just for me
> and some people from Tennessee,
> we got a thing or two to tell you all.
> This lady may have stumbled

but she ain't never fell.
And if the Russians don't believe that
they can all go straight to hell.
We're gonna put her feet back on the path
of the righteousness and then
God bless America again.

And you never did think that it ever would happen again
In America, did you?
You never did think that we'd ever get together again.
Well we damn sure fooled you.
We're walking real proud and we're talking real loud again
in America.
You never did think that it ever would happen again.

From the sound up in Long Island
out to San Francisco Bay,
and ev'ry thing that's in between them is our home.
And we may have done a little bit of fighting amongst ourselves,
but you outside people best leave us alone.
Cause we'll all stick together
and you can take that to the bank.
That's the cowboys and the hippies
and the rebels and the yanks.
You just go and lay your hand
on a Pittsburgh Steelers fan
and I think you're gonna finally understand.

And you never did think that it ever would happen again
In America, did you?
You never did think that we'd ever get together again.
Well we damn sure fooled you.
We're walking real proud and we're talking real loud again
in America.
You never did think that it ever would happen again.

124. Elizabeth McAlister, "For Love of the Children"

(1984)

In "For Love of the Children," Elizabeth McAlister explains her motives in joining with six others to enter Griffiss Air Force Base on Thanksgiving 1983 to pour their own blood on a B-52 and hammer the plane's bomb bay doors. A former nun, McAlister (1939–) and her husband, Philip Berrigan, founded Jonah House, a Catholic community of nonviolence and resistance, in Baltimore in 1973. Along with others acting in the Catholic Worker tradition, McAlister and Berrigan were instrumental in starting the Plowshares movement, in which nonviolent protesters sought to follow the biblical passage from the book of Isaiah, "They shall beat swords into plowshares and their spears into pruning hooks." The first such action took place in September 1980 when eight activists entered the General Electric Nuclear Missile Re-entry Division in King of Prussia, Pennsylvania, and hammered on two nuclear warhead nose cones and poured blood on blueprints and other documents. By 1983, with the Reagan administration's commitment to expanding the nation's nuclear arsenal, and with the public shocked by the made-for-television nuclear war film *The Day After*, the Plowshares actions took on greater urgency and earned widespread publicity. In this piece, McAlister personalizes the Plowshares actions, work she does for the love of her three children and out of obedience to a higher authority. For the Griffiss action, each participant received a prison sentence of two to three years.

SOURCE: Reprinted in Arthur J. Laffin and Anne Montgomery, eds., *Swords into Plowshares: Nonviolent Direct Action for Disarmament . . . Peace . . . Social Justice* (Marion, S.D.: Fortkamp Publishing, 1996), 98–102.

As I was sitting in the Syracuse Public Safety Building (a euphemism for jail in these quarters), some of the reality of what I and my friends had done began to well up in me. It was accompanied, as reality usually is, by terror. Probably one of the hardest things for us human creatures is facing reality. Like so many others, I don't like to think about things like death—my own death or the death of people

454

close to me. I certainly don't like to think about war and that kind of death and, above all, I don't like to think about nuclear war and the death of all we have known.

But I found myself thinking about all of these things while in jail. Once in jail, life becomes radically stripped down; so many of the distractions are gone. It becomes a little bit harder to run away from oneself and from reality and terror. Parenthetically, this is one of the reasons I think jail is an important experience for me—and probably would also be for a lot of people who have never thought about jail in relation to themselves.

I thought about jail in relation to myself only once while growing up. While I was a postulant in a religious community in 1959, I read of the life of St. Bernard of Clairvaux. I read of Bernard as a warrior who experienced his conversion to Christ through a long period in jail, and I thought then that I would need such a jail experience for me to become "holy." But it seemed utter fantasy that such would be my lot. Reality being stranger than fantasy, I have seen the insides of a goodly number of jails, but without the experience of becoming holy.

I was in the Public Safety Building this time because I and six friends had entered Griffiss Air Force Base in Rome, New York, on Thanksgiving 1983. We went inside the building that housed, among other things, a B-52 bomber that was being outfitted to carry a full complement of cruise missiles. Some of us hammered on the bomb bay doors of that B-52, poured our own blood on the fuselage, spray-painted the phrases "320 Hiroshimas" and "Thou Shalt Not Kill" and "If I Had a Hammer" on it, and taped to it photos of our children, and a "people's indictment" of Griffiss Air Force Base that we had drawn up. The other half of the group did similar work in a nearby storage area for B-52 engines. They painted "Omnicide" and "Stop Cruise" in strategic locations.

The government responded to our acts by indicting us for sabotage, for destruction of government property, and for conspiracy. And so I was sitting in jail looking at the possibility of spending twenty-five years there. That much reality can be frightening, especially when the one facing it has three young children aged nine, eight, and two whom she loves deeply.

Into this atmosphere and these ruminations, a friend sent a cartoon. It depicted two children talking. The first asked if the second had seen "The Day After" on TV. The second child responded, "No! My parents wouldn't let me. They thought it would be too scary! Did you see it?" "Yes," responded the first. "Did you find it scary?" "Not as scary as my parents did," said the first. "Oh!" said the second. "What did they find the scariest part?" "The very end," said the first, "when I asked them what they were going to do to stop it."

I sent the cartoon to my older children, Frida and Jerome, along with the letter I was writing them that day. The Day After was televised on November 20; our action was on November 24. Their Dad and I had watched the film with them (as well as with other members of the Jonah House community) and we had talked with them afterward about the meaning of the film. We talked too about the action I was about to undertake (though not the specifics because children don't need that kind of information; they don't need to be responsible for it). We told them that I had been preparing with several others to engage in a disarmament or "Plowshares" action in the coming week. It would mean that I would probably be in jail for some time and be apart from them. Our children have grown up with these realities as part of the air they breathe; they have seen many people in the community in which we live, including their mom and dad, imprisoned for resistance to nuclear annihilation. But to have mom do something like this and to face her possible absence from their day-to-day lives for an indefinite amount of time—this was a large step.

Both of the older children said that they understood, in a new way, why this resistance was so necessary. They were willing to accept the personal sacrifice of my absence as their part in trying to stop a nuclear war from happening, as their part in trying to avoid the suffering that the movie displayed in an understated but nonetheless very clear way. They committed themselves to assume more responsibility around the house and especially to be helpful in dealing with the questions and fears of their little sister who was not able to understand as they were. It was a moment of extreme closeness for the four of us, a moment of accepting together whatever might come, and we concluded our conversation with prayer and big, big hugs.

We all back down from moments like that. The children remain(ed) querulous, somewhat selfish, lazy; they remain(ed), in short, young children. But we don't back down completely. Something of the clarity of a moment like that stays with us, enlightening a dark time. While the children fear prolonged separation, they are proud of their mom and of themselves for offering something, for sharing something of the suffering of children in less privileged environments. They are, as we are wont to tell them, First World children but they have some consciousness of Third World children, which, we hope, will affect their lives and the choices they make in them.

Little Katie is another story. Not because she's our child do I say it; she's a beautiful little person. She is as full of life and joy and love and curiosity as any two-year-old (maybe a little more than many—but that gets too subjective). And watching her grow is watching a miracle unfold. It is hard to think about missing all that. And, for her part, I have to agonize over the potential damage to her spirit. At the same time as she is a deterrent to this kind of risk, she is a spur to it. Nursing her as I did for almost two years—she showed no inclination to be weaned—I heard the persistent question welling up within me: "Will this child be able to grow up?"

To nurture such innocent life and know, as I do, the threat to her life, to know, as many have sought to tell us, the threat to all life on this planet means to make some choices. The options are few and clear: first, I could choose to hide somewhere, anywhere, with my children, to remain protective of them, isolated. But I know there is nowhere we can go. I guess I also know that it would not be possible for me for very long—to choose a "security" for my children that cannot be an option for other or for all parents.

Second, I could pretend that the threat is not there at all; I could live without seeing or hearing or thinking about it. That is all too possible to do. But that would mean making my own body and soul and those of our children part of the problem—part of the numbness, indifference, and resultant selfishness that enables the machinery of war to mushroom out of all control it would also mean surrendering the few clues I have arrived at throughout my life about what it means to be a decent, responsible, caring human being.

Or third, I can ask how I can best love my children and I can answer by working to provide for them and the millions like them a hope for the future. I cannot say that I hope for a future for them without, at the same time, being willing to do something to make that hope become a reality.

The action we took at Griffiss Air Force Base was the sixth such Plowshares action. These actions sprang from our prayerful reflection on the biblical mandate out of Isaiah and Micah to "beat swords into plowshares, and spears into pruning hooks." They sprang from our shared realization that even as the arms race has been built weapon by weapon, decision by decision, disarmament needs to occur weapon by weapon, decision by decision, or as one person expressed it, "dent by dent." Our hope in doing these Plowshares actions is not so much that we will successfully destroy a particular weapon.

Our hope is that in our effort to be obedient to the Spirit, to life, the Spirit might become more present in our world, empowering more and more people to act in whatever ways they can to say a clear "no" to such destructive weaponry, to say a clear "no" to policies that call for the use of such weaponry.

The first Plowshares action took place at the GE facility in King of Prussia, Pennsylvania, in September, 1980. The group of eight participants included my husband, Phil Berrigan, his brother Daniel, two other members of the Jonah House community, and four friends. One of the women who acted at King of Prussia is the mother of six children. The AVCO Plowshares included four grandmothers; they had collectively 37 children and 24 grandchildren. Many of the men and women who have participated in these actions have done so as parents. Each would articulate it differently, but all acted so that the children might have some hope of a future. It would be a great service if these parents' voices could be heard more in our days.

It is so clear how torn-up people are today. If we try to look squarely at what is happening in our world, we become so full of despair, of hopelessness, that we cannot live. And so we withdraw into numbness. I read a lot of Robert Lifton in the Public Safety Building and could identify with so much of what he writes. Then Dan Berrigan sent me a book called *Bringing Forth In Hope* by Denise Priestley (New York: Paulist, 1983). I devoured the book, feeling that it said things for me that I had not been able to say for myself. She writes at one point: "It is very difficult for me and for others to get a handle on how to stop this evil, and that is part of its destructiveness. Everything is presented as so interdependent that there are no longer any limits or boundaries, and the whole system becomes overwhelming. . . . There is no more powerful or destructive weapon than the creation of this kind of confusion in and among people. . . . We begin to believe that this is the only reality that exists, and the possibility and hope for a new way of being is pushed further and further out of our consciousness."

Against this ennui, the seven of us at Griffiss (as well as others who have acted for justice and peace before and since our action) felt hope as an urgent imperative calling us to enunciate (albeit in fear and in trembling) a testimony to life. We sought above all, to enunciate hope, to announce that while this is a time when death appears to reign supreme, it is also a time of hope. The promise of new life is at hand for our world if people reach out and grasp for it, if people in solidarity with one another reach out and dismantle the weapons that block our access to life.

Editors' Note: Adapted from an article that originally appeared in Daniel Berrigan, ed., *For Swords into Plowshares, The Hammer Has to Fall* (Highland Park, N.J.: Plowshares Press, 1984).

125. Andrew Kopkind, "Rambo: Metamachismo Carries the Day"

(1985)

In this essay, journalist Andrew Kopkind extrapolates a post-Vietnam militarism message from one of the most popular films of the 1980s. Kopkind (1935–94) grew up in Connecticut and graduated from Cornell. Through the 1960s and 1970s, he worked for *Time*, the *New Republic*, the *New Statesman*, and *Ramparts*, and from 1982 until his death in 1994, he wrote for the *Nation*. The sardonic commentary on *Rambo* reflects the growing Reagan-era sense that the Vietnam War had been a noble cause, botched by political leaders and undermined by protest at home. In the new muscular Cold War, Kopkind sees that history gets twisted and foreign policy simplified. The promise of the times was a new version of "never again"—never again, Reagan said, would Americans "be sent to fight and die unless we are prepared to let them win." *Rambo* and other top-grossing films such as *Top Gun* (1986) reflected a new chest-thumping patriotism designed, it seemed, to will the national mind into believing again in American military invincibility.

SOURCE: *Nation*, June 22, 1985.

Vietnam has suffered invasions, interventions and expeditions by every great power in this century; it has endured the visits of foe and friend, from Robert McNamara to Jane Fonda; it has survived almost half a century of bombing, mining, corruption, incineration and defoliation. All that, and now this: along comes Rambo, the ultimate weapon in humanoid form, winning with biceps and pecs the war that the mightiest nation in history lost with mere B-52s and Agent Orange. At last, William Westmoreland's dishonorable defeat has been avenged by Sly Stallone.

Rambo: First Blood Part II is at once hilarious and disgusting. It's hard not to howl at Stallone's apish ambition, the blind egomania of a lowland gorilla who looks at his reflection in a jungle pool and sees a limpid Narcissus. It is to laugh when Stallone slaughters whole battalions of Vietnamese and Soviet soldiers

459

("damn Russian bastards!") with crossbow, bazooka and bare hands; steals a helicopter and destroys native villages (the ones the US army missed); rescues American POWs from the Vietcong tiger cages where they have been languishing since *The Deer Hunter*. It is even worth a chuckle when Stallone finally manages to grunt out a complete prepositional clause ("for our country to love us as much as we love it") in the closing thirty seconds, even though we may have to wait for Part III for a whole sentence, with subject and predicate like they have in those European films. When Brando mumbled through *Julius Caesar*, it was tolerated as sheer Method madness; with Stallone, mumbles are the very best he can do.

But even Stallone's camp followers will have a hard time swallowing the twisted history, the racist images and the political line of Rocky's latest horror show. Its premise is that certain villains—bureaucrats, politicians, CIA operatives—sold America down the river in Vietnam and afterwards, thus losing the war and preventing the return of uncounted MIAs. The lowly grunts would have won if left to their own devices, and when they were sent home the society that surrendered despised them precisely because their presence was a constant reproach. *First Blood*, which introduced Rambo, glorified the bitter and violent veteran in his struggle against cowardly authority and a complacent citizenry. In that effort, Rambo turned his wrath against small-town rednecks in the Pacific Northwest and against wave after wave of the national guard. For the damage done, he was sentenced to a season on the prison rock pile.

Post-imperial frustration is a familiar theme in twentieth-century history: cf., Hitler after Versailles, the Tory right after Suez, the China Lobby after Mao's march. The syndrome has several phases. First blood is always drawn internally, from those at home held responsible for the unaccountable defeat. Then come the overseas revenge fantasies, sometimes enacted in terrifying reality. No doubt there are worse scenarios in store for America than the one Stallone and James (*The Terminator*) Cameron created for Rambo, but until the real thing comes along, we are asked to sublimate our death wishes in the Hollywood version.

Rambo is sprung by his old special forces colonel (Richard Crenna) and sent back to Nam. "Do we get to win this time?" he asks in a moment of foreshadowing which epitomizes the subtlety of the plot to follow. The Green Beret replies that it's all up to Rambo, but in fact the same wimps and sell-outs in Congress and the CIA who collapsed after Tet are setting Rambo up for failure. They want him to find no live Americans in-country so that they can continue their dirty diplomatic games of appeasement and accommodation.

Aided only by Co, the Vietnamese girl *contra* (apparently no authentic ethnic actress has succeeded France Nguyen as the all-purpose Pan-Asian heroine, so the part is played by the round-eyed Julia Nickson), Rambo has to do battle with Charlie, Ivan, a band of river pirates, assorted leeches and snakes, the CIA mission commander, the legacy of Henry Kissinger and the ghost of the anti-war movement. It's no contest. Metamachismo carries the day. Rambo sheds only a tear when Co takes an Aka burst in the back (those damn Russian bastards always shoot you as you're running). When, dying, she implores, "Don't forget me," he merely grunts, "Uh-uh." War love is never having to say anything, and these big guys really love making war. Stallone is a Bill Broyles with muscles, but his passion for carnage is no big secret. "You're of Indian-German descent," the CIA man notes approvingly as he reads Rambo's dossier. "It's a hell of a combination." I'll say!

June 22, 1985, THE NATION

126. Shockabilly, "Nicaragua"

(1984)

In "Nicaragua," lyricist Ed Sanders, playing with avant-garde rock band Shockabilly, critiques the Reagan administration's policies in Central America. Born
in Kansas City, Missouri, Sanders (1939–) graduated from New York University
with a degree in classics. A prominent New York poet, writer, and activist in the
1960s, Sanders also co-founded the irreverent folk-rock band The Fugs and
wrote a number of satirical songs, such as "Kill for Peace," about the Vietnam
War. Twenty years later, he found kindred spirits in Shockabilly. Like Sanders,
the band's guitarist/vocalist, Eugene Chadbourne, wrote songs that were critical
of American foreign policy. In "Nicaragua," Sanders and Shockabilly merge
lyrical critique with blistering guitar and the percussion and flutes of Central
America. By 1984, the Reagan administration's blind support for the Salvadoran government's assault on Marxist guerrillas was well established. When, for
example, 794 unarmed civilians were massacred by a government death squad
at El Mozote in 1981, the Reagan administration at first claimed it had been an
attack against leftists. Perhaps prompted by revelations in 1984 that the CIA
had mined Nicaraguan harbors, the song also predicts the coming Iran-Contra
scandal.

SOURCE: Shockabilly, *Vietnam* (Fundamental 08-023162-2 LP, 1984).

> There's a War Caste
> with secret sway
> that wants a permanent war
> with only a season of rest
>
> You can see it in
> the shape of the U.S. advisor's
> squinting eye
> like the tail of a wasp. . . .

Why does my country
so often stand
on the side
of the mean
and the cruel?

The CIA surrounds Nicaragua
And Reagan
says yes to the death squads
of El Salvador

Heraclitus said
"You've got to
put out hubris
more than a raging fire"

Why does my country
so often stand
on the side
of the mean
and the cruel?

The CIA surrounds Nicaragua
And Reagan
says yes to the death squads
of El Salvador

There's a mean streak
in America
it may take 500 years to solve

127. Stacey Lynn Merkt, "The Conspiracy of Sanctuary"

(1985)

In this essay, Stacey Lynn Merkt describes how she came to work in the sanctuary movement on behalf of political refugees fleeing El Salvador and Guatemala for the United States. Merkt (1955–) grew up Methodist in Northern California, graduated from the University of California at Davis, and, after college, lived in a Colorado Springs religious and antinuclear community. There she first encountered Guatemalan and Salvadoran refugees and heard their stories of massacres and torture at the hands of U.S.-trained death squads. In February 1984, she moved to Brownsville, Texas, to work at Casa Oscar Romero, a Catholic shelter for refugees. The two arrests she mentions in this piece occurred shortly after her arrival. At the time, hundreds of churches across the country were openly hosting Central American refugees in defiance of U.S. law. Merkt's two trials and convictions seemed like an opening salvo in a possible government crackdown on the churches. In June 1985, an appellate court judge overturned Merkt's conviction from the first trial. When she later began a six-month sentence for the second conviction, Amnesty International named her the first U.S. Prisoner of Conscience since the Vietnam War.

SOURCE: Reprinted in Arthur J. Laffin and Anne Montgomery, eds., *Swords into Plowshares: Nonviolent Direct Action for Disarmament . . . Peace . . . Social Justice* (Marion, S.D.: Fortkamp Publishing, 1996), 227–32.

Editors' Note: This article was written in early 1985 shortly before Stacey Lynn Merkt was sentenced for conspiring to transport undocumented Salvadoran refugees.

What speaks to us today as we live our lives in the face of hunger and plenty, the homeless and the mansions, the welcomed and the unwelcomed? To whom or to what do we listen to make decisions about how to live responsibly? I cannot begin to list here the biblical passages that try to teach of the sanctity, the gift of life. I cannot begin to list the passages that exhort us to rout out injustice. It's our task to affirm life and in so doing denounce injustice.

Sanctuary offers protection to the refugee in our midst and publicly speaks out against our U.S. policies in El Salvador that have helped create a war there and thus refugees. More important, sanctuary is a faith response of God's people to injustice and those in need. Let's begin with a glimpse of why there is such a need for sanctuary.

El Salvador is a country the size of Massachusetts with a population of approximately five million. A small elite of 14 families, along with the military, dominate land ownership, banking, commerce, and industry. That leaves 70 percent of the population living in poverty with malnutrition, disease, illiteracy, early death, and no recourse. Throughout the last 50 years, numerous peoples' organizations have called for an end to these social injustices and the establishment of a true democracy. But these attempts to bring about change have been thwarted by the oligarchy and military. Seeing armed struggle as the last option available to bring about social reform, some of the major opposition groups banded together over the last eight years to form the Farabundo Marti Liberation Front/Democratic Revolutionary Front (FMLN/FDR). The armed conflict between the Salvadoran government and the FMLN/FDR continues to intensify.

In an attempt to crush all domestic opposition, the Salvadoran government has recently escalated its war against the FMLN/FDR and has repressed all popular dissent. It has labeled as subversives not only those directly affiliated with the FMLN/FDR, but also any group or individual advocating human rights and social change. This includes leaders and members of unions, teachers, students, doctors, nurses, clergy, religious, and those who help the poor. To be labeled subversive in El Salvador means to be labeled "communist," making you free game for the death squads. The death squads, known to be connected to the military, have carried out countless assassinations and are responsible for the disappearances of thousands. Those who "disappear" later turn up dead with obvious signs of torture.

The war against these "subversives" extends to the campesinos, the civilians. Women are seen as factories that produce guerrillas and therefore need to be eliminated. Children are seen as seeds of the guerrillas and therefore need to be eliminated. Currently, the increased bombings of the countryside are killing these civilians.

This is why people are fleeing El Salvador. Men, women, and children are risking the journey through Mexico every day. Already there are 500,000 refugees from El Salvador in the United States. What happens to the refugees once they are in the United States? If they are picked up by the border patrol (the police branch of the Immigration and Naturalization Service), their deportation process begins. The vast majority are indeed deported and face possible death. Why? One reason is that they no longer have their cedula, their I.D. The border patrol keeps it. Without a cedula, a person cannot prove that he or she is not a guerrilla and is thus killed by government forces.

Political asylum is supposed to be an option for the refugee who flees a country and is unable to return because of a well-founded fear of persecution for reasons of race, religion, nationality, or membership in a particular social or political group. Unfortunately, political asylum is not available for Salvadorans and Guatemalans. Less than 3 percent of the Salvadorans who apply for it are granted it. Extended voluntary departure (a stay on deportations while investigations in El Salvador would take place) has been pending in Congress for a year and a half. This status has been granted to nationals from 11 other countries in the past and is now in effect for nationals leaving Poland, Afghanistan, and Ethiopia. But it's not available to Salvadorans. That is because it does not coincide with our foreign policy. The United States has chosen to support the current, repressive government and thus does not support the thousands who flee that government.

I began working at Casa Romero, a hospitality house for Central American refugees, located in San Benito, Texas, in 1984. During the first 27 months after the house opened, more than 2,800 refugees passed through. Comparatively speaking, this is a small number of refugees. But what this small number does for me is put names and faces on what we read as statistics. I have seen the hungry, the homeless, the stranger. And I have seen Christ. "Lord, when did we see you hungry and feed you; or thirsty and give you drink? When did we see you a stranger and make you welcome, naked and clothe you; sick or in prison and go to see you?" And the King will answer, "I tell you solemnly, in so far as you did this to one of the least of these brothers [and sisters] of mine, you did it to me." (Mt. 25:38-40 *JB*)

My response to the refugees comes out of a deep-down spot inside of me that sometimes seems pretty foolish and simplistic. I believe in a God of love, a God of justice. The Greatest Commandment tells me that I am to "love the Lord my God with all my heart, soul, and mind and to love my neighbor as myself." Love is an active choice, not some weak, pansy feeling. Love must be visible in my life. So when I see my sister or my brother in need, I cannot turn my face. My sister of El Salvador or of the Soviet Union. My brother who lives next door. We are one community.

Sanctuary is a faith response to these sisters and brothers in need. It has Old Testament roots. In Exodus, Moses was chosen by God to lead the Israelites out of slavery and exploitation into the promised land. This was no easy task! As they entered into Canaan, God commanded them to set aside six cities of refuge. (Nb. 35) It was God's order to protect from further violence persons who accidently killed. It was a way of saying, "Stop! The violence stops here." The sanctuary is where the authority of God, the Giver of Life, is recognized as ultimate.

Today the need for sanctuary once again exists. Recognizing that the people fleeing El Salvador and Guatemala are fleeing for their lives, realizing that the U.S. policy of sending rifles, bombs, planes, advisers, and training creates the refugees, we, the church as a body without borders, must take a stand. Sanctuary's goals are twofold: to offer protection to the fleeing refugees and to offer a platform from which the voiceless can speak, so that the truth will be told and U.S. policy and involvement will be challenged. Currently over 200 churches of various denominations have made public declarations of sanctuary, officially stating their intention to directly assist refugees and to publicly speak out against the causes of the war in El Salvador.

What is the administration's response to people trying to assist refugees? Indictments. I've come through two trials. In the first trial in March 1984 I was convicted of conspiracy to transport and of transporting Mauricio Valle and Brenda Sanchez Gallan. Their crime? Fleeing for their lives to seek refuge in the United States. In the second trial I was found innocent of transporting two refugees to the bus station, but guilty of conspiring to commit that "crime." In this same trial Jack Elder, the director of Casa Romero, was convicted on six counts of charges ranging from conspiracy to bringing in, landing, and transporting refugees. In January 1985 he was acquitted by a Corpus Christi jury of transporting three refugees to a bus station.

What do we have in common? We are called "church workers." We are regular people who have heard of the atrocities in El Salvador. We have heard too much, seen too much. And we can't keep quiet when our God reminds us that "when an alien resides with you in your land, do not molest him [or her]. You shall treat the alien who resides with you no differently than the natives born among you; have the same love for them as for yourself; for you too were once aliens in the land of Egypt. I, the Lord, am your God." (Lv. 19:33-34 *NAB*)

Living faithfully is becoming subversive. I think people of faith in the United States have a unique opportunity. We are being asked to love by standing with the oppressed and confronting the oppressor, all the while realizing those fine lines within ourselves. The violence of war, the violence of the underlying causes of war, the injustices of hunger, disease, the few having all while the majority have none, we of the United States have the luxury of addressing these violences without dying. The costs for us are courtrooms (and their injustices) and prison time. I do not take either of those things lightly. But the cost of doing nothing, sitting idly by is too high. If I examined Scripture in light of today's realities in Central America and the United States and do not act in some small way, I would not sleep at night. My hope lies in the ripples that come from one small insignificant person seeing her task and doing it. The hope has already been born, killed, resurrected. We are witness to that.

The following was my reflection as I awaited my probation hearing on March 26, 1985, and my sentencing on March 27, 1985:

"He has nothing on!" cries the little boy as the Emperor swaggers down the road in the parade. It's a children's story (an adult's parable) by Hans Christian Andersen, "The Emperor's New Clothes." It's the story of two weavers (liars) who come to the Emperor offering to weave the finest cloth ever seen, so fine that the only ones who couldn't see it were either stupid or didn't know their job. The rules are set. It is mandatory for everyone to see these nonexistent clothes. And so though no one sees the clothes, everyone lives within the set rules, too afraid to question or speak out. Everyone sees the clothes—until the boy's cry. The cry turns into a murmur. The crowd turns it into a shout.

So many parallels jump out of this story for me. The people held on to their lies. They were afraid. The rules were set. Their decision to see clothes when there were none was based on the fear of not conforming, of not being able to speak out for the truth.

What does this have to do with refugees? The fine cloth we are given by this administration is nonexistent. We are told that the Salvadoran government does not make war on its people; it only quells a few Communists. Our role in this war is minimal: we send economic rather than military aid. And the refugees that continue keeping Casa Romero overflowing are economic refugees, not people fleeing war. Political asylum continues to be a fruitless recourse, but the only one offered.

The days between conviction and sentencing have been full ones for me. Full ones inside me. I think I have felt every feeling known to exist but anger, fear, hurt, and depression are my top four. In a nutshell, anger comes from the lies and injustices; fear factors down to being afraid of the unknown; hurt stems from being continually attacked by the U.S. government; and depression occurs because of the sameness of the situation. When will it change? For me it has become a time of letting go, of relaxing and accepting. It is a time for loosening my grip on what we've called our security. In letting go, I return. What I seek to return to is the faithful loving God that I have known for years, the God of Hosea who woos his straying people time and time again to say: "I will break bow, sword and battle in the country and make her sleep secure. I will betroth you to myself forever, betroth you with integrity and justice, with tenderness and love; I will betroth you to myself with faithfulness and you will come to know Yahweh. . . . I will love the Unloved. I will say to No-People-of-Mine, 'You are my people,' and they will answer, 'You are my God.'" (Hos. 2:18-23 *JB*)

We take a stand, risk, and face consequences not so that our commitment or faithfulness to God can be seen, but so God's faithfulness and commitment to us can be seen. I've come full circle. We love because God first loved us. There is hope . . . the hope that sustains me. I remember the God who is faithful to God's people. I act in community with the thousands of people who, propelled by faith, give assistance to the refugees. I and all of us here do not act alone. Our community begins with our brothers and sisters of El Salvador and Guatemala. If I go to prison, I do not go alone. . . .

128. Todd Lencz, "Ollie? Golly!—Public Reaction to Oliver L. North's Testimony"

(1987)

This article from the conservative magazine *National Review* describes the popularity of Lieutenant Colonel Oliver North, the central figure in the Iran-Contra scandal. In August 1987, North, a high-ranking official on the National Security Council staff, testified about his role in redirecting proceeds from illegal arms sales to Iran to the Contras, anticommunist guerrillas in Nicaragua. In a series of legislative amendments, Congress had expressly prohibited any U.S. support at all, "directly or indirectly," to the Contras. Yet this is exactly what North and the National Security Council did. When the scandal broke in the fall of 1986, it became immediately clear that it would jeopardize Reagan's presidency. If it could be proven that the president directed the diversion of funding to the Contras, he likely would have been impeached. North's testimony with immunity before a Senate panel in July 1987 captivated the nation. He acknowledged breaking the law, but remained defiant that assisting the Contras—"freedom fighters," he called them—was the right thing to do. As this article indicates, many Americans agreed with him.

SOURCE: *National Review*, August 14, 1987, p. 40.

Ollie? Golly!

CONSERVATIVE LEADERS report mixed response to Oliver North's testimony before Congress, but among the rank and file the vote is unanimous: Lieutenant Colone North is an American hero. Ollie buttons are selling out; barbers in Washington, D.C. are reported besieged by kids wanting "Ollie cuts."

North's supporters send praise of him everyplace they can think of: to congressional offices, Marine Corps recruiting stations, conservative institutions, and Republican organizations. Steve Baldwin, executive director of YAF, says he has received hundreds of phone calls from people wanting to donate to North and to the Contras. "It's not your typical conservative donor," Baldwin reports; "a whole new type is being drawn out of the woodwork." "We've gotten innumerable calls from people wanting to know how they can donate," agrees David Hirschmann of the College Republican National Committee. "Even from people who say, 'Don't put me on your mailing list. I'm a Democrat, but I love Ollie.'"

An aide to Congressman Jim Courter (R., N.J.) described the volume of calls and letters to Courter's office as "unprecedented." "Ninety-five per cent of those letters praise Colonel North," said Dennis Teti. "The other 5 per cent attack Congressman Courter for merely being on such an evil and misguided committee." Senator Inouye's office has maintained that telegrams to his office are running fifty-fifty. "That's a lie," says Teti. "If that's so, I'll eat those telegrams."

Before North's testimony, many conservatives didn't know what to make of the man Administration officials had called a "rogue colonel." A few days before North took the stand, Conservative Caucus chairman Howard Phillips appeared on a panel with Dole campaign advisor David Keene, Kemp advisor Ed Rollins, and Bush campaign manager Lee Atwater. Of the four, says Phillips, only he expressed unqualified admiration for North. "I have always been an admirer of Ollie," says Phillips. "He has renewed the hope for anti-Communists and given Reagan a new opportunity to campaign for more Contra aid."

But Ed Rollins says North's dramatic testimony hasn't changed his views. "He's earned the title 'hero' from his Vietnam experience," says Rollins. "But there needs to be checks and balances in the White House. Lying to Congress and conducting covert actions out of the basement—or third floor—of the White House is wrong."

David Keene concurs. "North has performed heroically before the committee," said Kenne, "but even if you're a good man with good motives, it doesn't mean you can't mess things up." North's actions, Keene asserts, "have damaged our ability to aid the Contras and crippled the President."

Others dispute Keene's pessimistic assessment of North's effect on Contra aid. Teti believes the political situation hasn't changed that much since last June, when Congress voted aid to the Contras. House Minority Whip Trent Lott maintains North has given pro-Contra forces "some potential votes for Contra aid we haven't gotten in the past." Citing polls showing that a majority of Americans disapprove of Contra aid, House Democratic Whip Tony Coelho claims North's testimony has had no impact on Congress. "The American people agree with Ollie North that he's telling the truth, but they don't agree with what he's espousing," says Coelho. That, at least, is the Democratic leadership's hope when Contra aid comes up for a vote this fall.

129. Jefferson Morley, "The Paradox of North's Popularity"

(1987)

This piece, from the *Nation*, offers an analysis of public opinion polls in the wake of Oliver North's congressional testimony. Although there were significant divisions among the American public, it is clear from the evidence that most saw Iran-Contra (whether they knew it or not) in the context of the Vietnam War. The author alludes to the fact that the scandal broke in the midst of President Reagan's patient campaign to recast the Vietnam War as "a noble cause," lost only thanks to a lack of national will. North, a decorated Vietnam veteran, therefore became a poster boy for the reinvigorated national project of both promoting freedom and containing communism around the world. In this way, North and Reagan most closely resembled the idealists of the Kennedy administration as they committed advisors and millions of dollars to fighting a proxy war in Nicaragua (as Kennedy had in Vietnam).

SOURCE: *Nation,* August 15, 1987, pp. 122–25.

Oliver North is the latest in a string of pop-culture icons representing the legacy of the Vietnam war in American life. Like the black walls of Washington's Vietnam Memorial, the populist patriotism of Bruce Springsteen and the schematic moralizing of *Platoon.* North is a symbol for a country still struggling to figure out why it was humiliated at war.

North is indeed a "folk hero," though not quite in the sense that the media proclaimed. The general consensus of the media was that North embodied the American character with his patriotism, his straight shooting and, above all, his "good intentions." The folk themselves seemed to view North more ambivalently.

A July 9 *Time* poll found that 77 percent of Americans regarded North as a "scapegoat," more than twice as many as described him as a "national hero." Another poll, by ABC and *The Washington Post,* gave respondents the choice of describing North as a "hero," "victim" or "villain"; 64 percent chose "victim," more than three times as many as chose "hero." North is honored by his supposed enemies in the press, pitied by his supposed admirers in the public.

In the fantasies of the right-wing elite in Washington, North is a hero for escaping the clutches of Congressional Democrats and liberal journalists. But as the adulation of North demonstrates. Congress and the media were disarmed by the lieutenant colonel. North was not the victim of any perfidious leftist cabal.

More plausible than the paranoia of the right is the attitude of the majority of Americans. In the public view, North attracts sympathy for his predicament not for his ideology. As Bill Schneider, a pollster at the American Enterprise Institute, noted, the public regards North as "a good soldier for a bad policy." North is not held ultimately responsible for the Iran / *contra* fiasco; his superiors in Congress and the White House are.

North's appeal is thus populist without necessarily being demagogic or right wing, regardless of his penchant for right-wing demagogy. Americans can identify with the eager recruit who hurls himself into illegalities at the behest of his superiors—and then is called on the carpet by those same superiors. The Congressional mannequins who questioned North and the Presidential actor who fired him are seen as avoiding their rightful responsibilities. North's celebrity comes at Reagan's expense.

The ambiguity of North's appeal can be understood only against the background of public opinion on Central America. In 1983 President Reagan made a nationally televised appeal for support of his policy of sending military aid to prop up the government of El Salvador; an ABC/*Washington Post* poll found seven of every ten people opposed. That same year Reagan initiated large-scale military maneuvers in Central America, falsely claiming that they were "the kind we've been holding regularly for years." A Harris poll found 2-to-1 opposition to such maneuvers in both 1983 and 1985. But as with military aid to El Salvador, Congress acquiesced to the Reagan wishes. An unprecedented 21,000 U.S. regular and reserve troops will engage in military exercises in the region in 1987.

The debate over aid to the *contras* exhibits the same dichotomy: popular hesitation and elite support (albeit grudging). The *Los Angeles Times* took the first poll on aid to the *contras* in April 1983. It found the public opposed by a 6-to-1 margin to C.I.A. support for overthrowing the Sandinistas. Four years later, on the eve of North's appearance before the Congressional select committees, opposition to aid to the *contras* was running, according to a Harris poll, at a record high: 74 percent of those asked were against it. In the interim, though, Congress had approved $100 million in *contra* aid.

North has launched the Central America debate into its next phase by dramatically appealing to public opinion and by seeming to succeed. He rallied about one-third of the public to the *contra* cause. His testimony before the Iran/*contra* committees transformed the 2-to-1 public opposition to Reagan's policy to an even split. But the right-wing and liberal pundits who went gaga over this upsurge in support overlooked the fact that Reagan himself had achieved it before. An ABC/*Washington Post* poll had found a similar and temporary level of public approval for the President's Nicaragua policy in June 1986.

As memories of North's television appearances fade, the level of *contra* support also seems to recede. A CBS/*New York Times* poll, taken a week after his appearance, showed 51 percent opposed to supporting the *contras* and 35 percent for it. North's telegenic personality, so similar to Reagan's, had pushed *contra* support to the same high-water mark that the President reached in June 1986—but no higher.

Ironically, North's popularity makes it much harder for *contra* supporters to overlook public opposition to Reagan's policies. That opposition is sometimes dismissed as a regretable side effect of the Vietnam syndrome. If so, the public shows no sign of getting over this malady, or even of wanting to. The percentage of people who disapprove of U.S. intervention in Central America, pre- and post-North, is similar to the percentage of people who say, in retrospect, that we should have stayed out of Vietnam altogether. This impulse, moreover, is not merely isolationist; it is also anti-interventionist.

In May 1985 a CBS/*New York Times* poll found that 34 percent of the public agreed with Reagan's assertion that Vietnam was a "noble cause." Another 13 percent said the war was "wrong but not immoral." But the largest group, 38 percent, said that the Vietnam war was both "wrong and immoral"—the fundamental premise of the 1960s antiwar movement. Not surprisingly, the same poll found 53 percent opposed to the idea that the United States should help overthrow the Sandinistas. On both Vietnam and Central America, the anti-interventionists are more in the American mainstream than are Ronald Reagan or Oliver North.

There are also those who discount public opinion by pointing out that the American people are ignorant about Central America. As late as March 1985, for example, 23 percent of the public thought Reagan supported the Sandinistas. But part of the public's ignorance may be willful. Reagan, after all, has repeatedly tried to teach the public his point of view on Central America. The students simply don't believe the teacher. An ABC/*Washington Post* poll in March 1985 found 72 percent of respondents opposed to supporting the overthrow of the Sandinistas and only 16 percent favoring that course; it also found a 2-to-1 majority convinced that Reagan wanted to do precisely that. If people assume that the President will disregard their views, they may decide to save themselves time and trouble by remaining ignorant of Central America. Ignorance is merely one aspect of a pervasive distrust. That same ABC/*Washington Post* poll found that almost half the public does not believe national leaders when the leaders claim national security is in danger.

This distrust extends to all expressions of the United States' "good intentions" in Central America. The Roosevelt Center, a nonpartisan think tank in Washington, D.C., conducted a series of "focus groups" on Central America in June and July 1986, hoping to probe complex attitudes not captured by the answers to simple poll questions. Among their conclusions: "People care about the deprivation and oppression that plague so many of the inhabitants of Central America, yet they are unprepared to commit U.S. resources for purely altruistic purposes."

Here again North embodies the ambivalence of the American public. Who is more altruistic than North? North was not a smash because he was a stout cold warrior defending the United States from its ruthless adversaries. North, of course, did invoke the Soviet threat, but Reagan had done that twice in nationally televised speeches with no discernible effect on public opinion. North was a smash because he presented himself as a kind of militant liberal, an idealist, a tenderhearted soldier, an apostle of "freedom," the man who was going to do good no matter what an uncaring world thought. The irony of North's celebrity is that he appealed to the waning spirit of American "good intentions."

This in no way implies approval of North's or of Reagan's policies. Quite the contrary. Clearly, the Administration sincerely believed it had only the best of intentions in waging a covert war, breaking the law and deceiving the Congress and the public. If Administration officials hadn't been so sincere, they probably wouldn't have been so brazen. The legitimacy of the Administration's good intentions has now become the heart of the debate about Central America and about U.S. foreign policy in general.

On the one side is the view (sometimes mistakenly labeled "conservative") that places enormous faith in good intentions, at least in those of the Republican President and a group of mostly unelected officials in the national security bureaucracy. Partisans of this position claim that those officials uniquely embody American goodness and that this goodness is the essence of American national will. The task of U.S. foreign policy (it is said) is to Insure that this goodness will prevail over any Soviet-backed adversaries.

At home, this energetic elite believes that its own good intentions justify excluding from any influence over foreign policy those Americans who disagree with them. They are the ones who regard the Vietnam Memorial as a "wall of shame" because it does not celebrate our good intentions in Southeast Asia. Oliver North is their new hero.

On the other side are those who came away from the humiliation of Vietnam with a little humility. This mood (and it is still only a mood) does not yet have a champion of North's verve. Those who share the mood are suspicious of U.S. military involvement overseas, not merely because it costs money and may cost American lives but because they suspect that the supposedly selfless ambition to do good can be used to justify policies that are morally dubious and politically self-destructive.

This silent majority may well have a certain measure of sympathy for idealistic appeals like North's but it knows better than to succumb to sincere and ambitious plans to "save" a fallen world. As Congress and the President stumble into war, scandal and disgrace while pursuing such unwanted policies, the public may feel a certain vindication. They may come to view themselves as they view Oliver North: as victims and scapegoats of the Washington elite.

The paradox of North's popularity is that it embodies a deep split in American society and therefore suggests that the American people will never support his favorite cause.

CHAPTER TWELVE

The Bush Wars, Part I: From the Gulf War to 9/11

130. George H.W. Bush, "Address to U.S. Armed Forces Stationed in the Persian Gulf"

(1991)

In this radio address, President George H.W. Bush congratulates American forces stationed in the Persian Gulf region for their swift and decisive victory over Saddam Hussein's Iraq. The son of a United States senator, Bush (1924–) was born in Massachusetts and graduated from Phillips Andover Academy before joining the navy during World War II; He flew fifty-eight combat missions and was awarded the Distinguished Flying Cross. After the war, he graduated from Yale University and entered the oil business in Texas. Beginning in the late 1960s, Bush entered public service, first as a congressman (1967–1971), then as ambassador to the United Nations (1971–1972) and director of the Central Intelligence Agency (1976–1977). In 1980, he lost the Republican nomination for president to Ronald Reagan, who then chose Bush as his running mate. In 1988, Vice President Bush defeated Michael Dukakis, the Democratic nominee, to become president. This speech came at the end of the forty-two-day war in the Persian Gulf, a conflict marked by overwhelming use of U.S. forces, high-tech weaponry, and twenty-four-hour news coverage. The speech conveys the sense of psychological victory as much as military victory. Earlier in the day, in a speech to state legislators, the president exulted, "By God, we've kicked the Vietnam syndrome once and for all!"

SOURCE: Public Papers of the President: http://bushlibrary.tamu.edu/research/ public_papers.php?id=2758&year=1991&month=3.

1991-03-02

Never have I been more proud of our troops, or more proud to be your Commander in Chief. For today, amid prayers of thanks and hope, the Kuwaiti flag once again flies high above Kuwait City. And it's there because you and your coalition allies put it there.

Kuwait is liberated. And soon hometowns across America will be welcoming back home the finest combat force ever assembled—Army, Navy, Coast Guard, Marines, Air Force—the brave men and women of the United States of America.

Saddam Hussein's dreams of dominating the Middle East by the terror of a nuclear arsenal and an army of a million men threatened the future of our children and the entire world. And the world was faced with a simple choice: If international law and sanctions could not remove Saddam Hussein from Kuwait, then we had to free Kuwait from Saddam Hussein.

And that's exactly what you did. Throughout 7 long and arduous months, the troops of 28 nations stood with you, shoulder to shoulder in an unprecedented partnership for peace. Today we thank you, for the victory in Kuwait was born in your courage and resolve. The stunning success of our troops was the result of superb training, superb planning, superb execution, and incredible acts of bravery.

The Iraqi Army was defeated. Forty-two divisions were put out of action. They lost 3,000 tanks, almost 2,000 armored vehicles, more than 2,000 artillery pieces. And over half a million Iraqi soldiers were captured, defeated, or disarmed. You were as good as advertised; you were, indeed, "Good to go."

This is a war we did not seek and did not want. But Saddam Hussein turned a deaf ear to the voices of peace and reason. And when he began burning Kuwait to the ground and intensifying the murder of its people, the coalition faced a moral imperative to put a stop to the atrocities in Kuwait once and for all. Boldly, bravely, you did just that. And when the rubber met the road, you did it in just 6 weeks and 100 decisive hours.

The evil Saddam has done can never be forgotten. But his power to attack his neighbors and threaten the peace of the region is today grievously reduced. He has been stripped of his capacity to project offensive military power. His regime is totally discredited, and as a threat to peace, the day of this dictator is over. And the bottom line is this: Kuwait's night of terror has ended.

Thomas Jefferson said that the price of freedom is eternal vigilance. We must remain vigilant to make absolutely sure the Iraqi dictator is never, ever allowed to stoke the ashes of defeat into the burning embers of aggression. The sacrifice you've already made demands nothing less. The sacrifice of those who gave their lives will never be forgotten.

Saddam made many mistakes. But one of the biggest was to underestimate the determination of the American people and the daring of our troops. We saw in the desert what Americans have learned through 215 years of history about the difference between democracy and dictatorship. Soldiers who fight for freedom are more committed than soldiers who fight because they are enslaved.

Americans today are confident of our country, confident of our future, and most of all, confident about you. We promised you'd be given the means to fight. We promised not to look over your shoulder. We promised this would not be another Vietnam. And we kept that promise. The specter of Vietnam has been buried forever in the desert sands of the Arabian Peninsula.

Today, the promise of spring is almost upon us, the promise of regrowth and renewal: renewed life in Kuwait, renewed prospects for real peace throughout the Middle East, and a renewed sense of pride and confidence here at home. And we are committed to seeing every American soldier and every allied POW home soon—home to the thanks and the respect and the love of a grateful nation and a very grateful President.

Yes, there remain vital and difficult tests ahead, both here and abroad, but nothing the American people can't handle. America has always accepted the challenge, paid the price, and passed the test. On this day, our spirits are high as our flag, and our future is as bright as Liberty's torch. Tomorrow we dedicate ourselves anew, as Americans always have and as Americans always will.

The first test of the new world order has been passed. The hard work of freedom awaits. Thank you. Congratulations. And God bless the United States of America.

Note: The President recorded this address at 9:15 a.m., March 1, in his private study at the White House. In his address, he referred to President Saddam Hussein of Iraq. The address was broadcast at noon, March 2, over the Armed Forces Radio Network.

131. Lee Greenwood, "God Bless the USA"

(1984)

Although contemporary country-pop artist Lee Greenwood first recorded this song in 1984, it got the greatest radio air play during and after the first Iraq War. Raised in Sacramento, California, Greenwood (1942–) first played saxophone and worked in numerous bands as a young man. During the Vietnam War, Greenwood's draft board awarded him a 3-A hardship deferment because, by the time he reached draft age, he was already married and had children. In the 1970s, he worked as a lounge singer and blackjack dealer in Las Vegas before getting his big break and a chance to record in Nashville. Sounding a lot like Kenny Rogers, his first hit, "It Turns Me Inside Out," went to the top of the country charts. But his biggest hit by far remains "God Bless the USA," which won the Country Music Association's song of the year in 1985, and was widely featured in Reagan-Bush campaign films and events in 1984. When, in the winter of 1990–91, it became clear that the United States would go to war with Iraq, the song (and Greenwood) could be heard everywhere. In 1992, Greenwood tried to capitalize on all of the attention the song had brought him by recording an entire album of patriotic songs, *American Patriot,* but it found few consumers. Even critics at *People* magazine—not known for trenchant analysis—complained that "Old Lee really outjingoes even himself on this album."

SOURCE: MCA 52386, 1984.

> If tomorrow all the things were gone
> I'd worked for all my life,
> And I had to start again
> with just my children and my wife,
> I'd thank my lucky stars
> to be living here today,
> 'Cause the flag still stands for freedom
> and they can't take that away.

And I'm proud to be an American
where at least I know I'm free,
And I won't forget the men who died
who gave that right to me,
And I gladly stand up next to you
and defend her still today,
'Cause there ain't no doubt I love this land
God Bless the U.S.A.

From the lakes of Minnesota
to the hills of Tennessee,
Across the plains of Texas
from sea to shining sea.
From Detroit down to Houston
and New York to L.A.,
well there's pride in every American heart
and it's time we stand and say:

that I'm proud to be an American
where at least I know I'm free,
And I won't forget the men who died
who gave that right to me,
And I gladly stand up next to you
and defend her still today,
'Cause there ain't no doubt I love this land
God Bless the U.S.A.

And I'm proud to be an American
where at least I know I'm free,
And I won't forget the men who died
who gave that right to me,
And I gladly stand up next to you
and defend her still today,
'Cause there ain't no doubt I love this land
God Bless the U.S.A.

132. Sydney Schanberg, "Censoring for Political Security"

(1991)

In this article, journalist Sydney Schanberg criticizes the Bush administration for muzzling the American media during the 1991 Persian Gulf war. Born in Clinton, Massachusetts, Schanberg graduated from Harvard in 1955 with a degree in government. He worked his way up from copy boy to foreign correspondent at the *New York Times*; in the late 1970s he won a Pulitzer Prize for his reporting from Cambodia, work that eventually led to the making of the film *The Killing Fields* (1984). In 1986, he moved from the *Times* to *New York Newsday*. As Schanberg indicates in this essay, the Bush administration's decision to severely restrict media access to the field of battle grew out of the military's experience during the Vietnam War, when reporters were essentially free to roam South Vietnam in search of their own sources. Schanberg mentions a lawsuit brought by a number of news outlets and several writers; the case *The Nation Magazine v. Department of Defense* never resulted in a definitive judicial ruling, and the press pools were eliminated in March 1991.

SOURCE: *Washington Journalism Review,* March 1991, pp. 23–26.

"THIS WILL not be another Vietnam." That oft-repeated pledge by President Bush is his maxim for the war in the Persian Gulf. He and his men leave no doubt as to what it means, for they quickly explain that this time our troops will not have "their hands tied behind their backs." But there's an addendum to that promise which, though clear from the administration's acts, has not been spoken: "This time, the hands of the press will be tied."

So far it would appear from polls and general reaction that a lot of Americans are not displeased by the government's handcuffing of the press. We journalists are not a very popular bunch. Some people see us as whiny and self-important, and some even see us as unpatriotic because we take it upon ourselves to challenge and question the government in difficult times like these. I can't say we haven't invited some of this disapproval through occasional lapses from professionalism.

But I don't think this suggests we should hunker down timidly now and wait for our ratings to rise. We are required to be responsible, not popular.

Let's look at what the administration has done to control and manipulate press coverage of this war and why it has done it.

First, the why. This is easy. The answer is Vietnam. Many politicians and senior military men cling tenaciously to the myth that the press, through pessimistic reporting, tipped public opinion and cost us the war in Vietnam. There's no factual support for this theory, but scapegoats are useful when the historical evidence is painful. And that evidence suggests that a misguided and ill-conceived policy got America bogged down in a foreign war where the national interest was not fundamentally at stake. Eventually the public grew disheartened over the gap between the promises of success the White House kept making and the actuality of failure. Our losses, human and material, were what tipped public opinion.

This time around the White House isn't taking any chances. All reporters in the American portion of the Gulf war zone have to operate under a system of controls that goes far beyond anything imposed in any other modern war—unless you include Grenada and Panama, where reporters were essentially kept away from the action. Those were the dress rehearsals for the press muzzling in the Gulf—test runs, so to speak, to see if either the public or major news organizations would raise much of an outcry (they didn't).

The new controls go like this. To begin with, there is a list of security guidelines laying down the categories of sensitive military information (details of future operations, specifics on troop units, etc.) that the press cannot report because it might jeopardize American or Allied lives. No reporter has any objection to these restrictions. They are essentially the same ground rules the press abided by in World War II, Korea and Vietnam.

It's what has been added to these traditional ground rules, however, that constitutes the muzzle. First, the only way a reporter can visit a front-line unit is by qualifying for the "pool" system, whereby a handful of reporters represents the entire press corps and shares the story with everybody. Only a fraction of the reporters, mostly those from the largest news organizations, can qualify for the pools. The rest are permitted to forage on their own, doing rear-echelon stories, but the rules forbid them to go to the forward areas and warn that if they make the attempt they will be "excluded"—taken into custody and shipped back. (By February 12, as this article went to press, at least two dozen journalists had been detained in this fashion. In some cases their credentials were lifted, though returned later. One reporter, Chris Hedges of *The New York Times*, was grabbed and decredentialized by the American military for conducting what it termed "unauthorized" interviews without an escort. He had been interviewing Saudi shopkeepers along a road 50 miles from the Kuwaiti border.)

It gets worse. Though the pool reporters are allowed at the front, their visits are anything but spontaneous. The pools get taken only where the military decides to take them. They are accompanied at all times by an escort officer, even when interviewing troops, which means that truth and candor on the part of the interviewees often become instant casualties. When a pool gets back from its guided visit, all stories and footage must be submitted to a "security review"—a euphemism for censorship.

Of the two controls—the pool system and the review of stories for possible security violations—it is the former that is the more odious, for this is tantamount to prior restraint. If reporters can go only where their babysitters decide to take them and can stay only a short time, they have already been subjected to the ultimate censorship. Since they've been allowed to see nothing, what possible "secrets" can they be carrying? The system has worked all too well. The press has been crippled, rendered unable to provide the public with a credible picture of what war is like in all its guises. What has been delivered to the public instead are superficial brush strokes across the sanitized surface of war. Bombs fall remotely and perfectly, and no one seems to be bleeding.

The "security review" at the end of the pool process merely applies the final, harassing, delaying, cosmeticizing touches on the information and completes the subjugation of the press corps and, by extension, the public. In a typical incident, one of the censors had a problem with the word "giddy," the use of which he decided was a breach of military security. Fred Bruni of the *Detroit Free Press* had used the word to describe some young Stealth bomber pilots who were buoyant as they returned from their first combat mission. Without consulting Bruni, the censor changed "giddy" to "proud." No reality, please, not even when it's innocuous. When Bruni noticed the change, he protested and got the censor to accept "pumped up." Then the military, giving no reason, held the story for two days before sending it to the Detroit paper.

As anyone can see, the security issue is almost entirely a red herring. With very rare exceptions, the press has never breached any of the security rules—not in World War II, not in Korea and not in Vietnam. Barry Zorthian, who was the official spokesman for the United States Mission in Saigon from 1964 to 1968, said recently that though roughly 2,000 correspondents were accredited to cover Vietnam in those years and hundreds of thousands of stories were filed, only five or six violations of the security guidelines occurred. He recalled most of these as accidental or based on misunderstanding. To his knowledge, he said, none of them actually jeopardized any military operations or the lives of personnel.

Henry Kissinger, who has certainly shown no tolerance for press criticism, was asked on television the other day whether he could recall even one journalist breaching security in Vietnam. He replied: "I can think of some reporting that jeopardized national security, but none in the field." The reports he referred to were leaks out of Washington.

So it's all too clear that the current restrictions have nothing to do with military security and everything to do with political security. Political security requires that the government do as complete a job as possible at blacking out stories that might lead to embarrassment or criticism of the government or to questions from ordinary Americans about the war policy. The press controls in the Gulf are preemptive strikes against the possibility of such stories coming from the front.

But the control and manipulation of information has done something else, too. It has debased the press.

Privately, some government officials have tried to justify the restraints as a necessary counter-tactic against Saddam Hussein's strategy—i.e., his presumed belief that a prolonged war with steady casualties will erode public support of the president. But a president who is seen to be withholding information is also likely to lose public support over time. It may sound corny, but our democracy relies on openness for its strength. It's a messy system, often inefficient and clumsy, but it functions because the public is included, not kept in the dark. It's worth reminding ourselves that the most supremely efficient systems in the world are dictatorships where the press is completely controlled.

When George Bush decided he wasn't going to let the press have a front-row seat for this war, he was deciding against the public—even though at this point many Americans not only seem unaware they're being deprived of anything important to their lives but have even applauded the president's quarantining of the press. Again, the press can't sit around chewing its nails over its popularity ratings. For better or worse, with all of our fallibilities, we are the only professional independent witnesses who have an established role in our system. And we can't abdicate that role, even if the public at some given moment in time doesn't want to hear what we have witnessed.

As I write, more than 800 journalists have been accredited by the military in Saudi Arabia, roughly eighty percent of them Americans or working for American news organizations. Only about 125 have been allowed into the pools. The rest can do other reporting but are officially banned from the front lines. The press guidelines say: "News media personnel who are not members of the official CENTCOM media pools will not be permitted into forward areas. . . . U.S. commanders will maintain extremely tight security throughout the operational areas and will exclude from the area of operation all unauthorized individuals."

When a reporter at a Pentagon briefing asked if this meant that commanders had received an "operational order to detain reporters who show up unescorted out in the battlefield and remove them to the rear," the Pentagon spokesman, Pete Williams, replied: "There is a general order right now."

Contrast this with World War II, when General Dwight Eisenhower issued a quite different order, directing all unit commanders of the Allied Expeditionary Force to give correspondents "the greatest possible latitude in the gathering of legitimate news." The order went on: "They should be allowed to talk freely with officers and enlisted personnel and to see the machinery of war in operation in order to visualize and transmit to the public the conditions under which the men from their countries are waging war against the enemy."

Eisenhower's order went out on May 11, 1944, just before D-day. This makes the comparison with World War II even more appropriate, because President Bush and his men, in trying to erase the Vietnam image, have called upon Americans to think of the Gulf war as D-day at Normandy. Fine, Mr. President, call this war what you like, but please remember that American journalists were allowed to hit the Normandy beaches alongside the troops. And there were no Pentagon babysitters with them.

Also unlike World War II (and Korea and Vietnam), reporters are not being assigned to units and permitted to stay with them for extended periods. They're not even being allowed to fly on bombing missions in those planes where there is room. One such plane is the eight-engine B-52 Stratofortress. It flies in formations of three, each carrying roughly thirty tons of bombs. Such bombloads inflict a tremendous pounding over a wide area, and are usually directed at troop concentrations rather than buildings and installations. Military briefers in Vietnam called it carpet bombing, but the briefers in this war have bridled when reporters have used the phrase. Apparently carpet bombing has a harsh sound and must be deodorized.

In fact, there's a concerted attempt to try to edit out all reminders of Vietnam. It's hard to believe, but the Pentagon has gone so far as prohibiting the filming, or any news coverage at all, of the arrival of war dead at Dover Air Force Base, the main military mortuary. So much for the contention that the press restrictions are necessary for security reasons.

It's not that I don't understand the thinking behind the restrictions. There's hardly a government extant, ours or anyone else's, that wants people not under its control traveling to the front and witnessing a war and then telling everybody else about it—especially telling and showing the terribleness of war. Because the government fears that the terrible images might shape people's opinions.

This doesn't mean our politicians and generals are telling us a pack of lies. Not at all. They're just not telling us anything approaching a complete story. That's not their job as they perceive it. But it is the job of an independent press.

Which brings us, finally, to the issue of what the press has been doing for itself to try to reverse the new restraints. Darned little, sadly.

The break with this country's tradition of relatively open access to military operations began in Grenada in October 1983, when the Reagan White House kept the press out until the fighting was over. The major news organizations complained. To quiet us, the White House and Pentagon threw us a bone—the odious pool system. Oddly, we took it with barely a whimper. Then, on the first test of the system—the 1989 Panama invasion—pool reporters were barred from observing the military engagement all through the first and decisive day of fighting. The rest of the press corps, 500 strong, was virtually interned on a military base, even during the aftermath of the combat. As a result, we still have only the sketchiest picture of what took place and how many civilians and soldiers were killed.

And now we have our sanitized coverage of the war with Iraq. When the consequences of the press controls became obvious during the troop buildup prior to the war, a lawsuit was filed on January 10 in federal court in New York to overturn the restrictions on constitutional grounds. It was prepared by the Center for Constitutional Rights, an established civil liberties group, on behalf of 11 news organizations and five writers. The news organizations are for the most part small, liberal, alternative publications—*The Nation, In These Times, Mother Jones, L.A. Weekly, The Progressive, Texas Observer, The Guardian* and *The Village Voice*—plus

Harper's, Pacifica Radio, Pacific News Service and writers E.L. Doctorow, William Styron, Michael Klare, Scott Armstrong and myself. Agence France-Presse, the French news agency, having been excluded from the press pool, has filed a companion suit.

All the major media organizations were aware of the lawsuit before it was filed, yet as I write, not one has joined it. The suit is about prior restraint of information, a constitutional issue that normally sets the television networks and leading newspapers into instant legal motion. I truly hope they will find their voices soon.

How to explain their inaction now? It's my belief that the press is still living with its own scars from Vietnam. And Watergate. We were accused, mostly by ideologues, of being less than patriotic, of bringing down a presidency, of therefore not being on the American team. And as a professional community we grew timid, worried about offending the political establishment. And that establishment, sensing we had gone under the blankets, moved in to tame us in a big and permanent way. These new press controls are, for me, a reflection of that move.

In late January CBS asked me to appear on "America Tonight" for a program on the press controls. Pete Williams, the Pentagon spokesman, agreed to appear opposite me, which created the potential for a good debate. Then the program's producer called. He said they had to disinvite me because Williams had called back to say the Pentagon's chief counsel had ruled that no Pentagon official could appear with anyone associated with the lawsuit.

The producer explained: "Our feeling was, after much deliberation and discussion, that we felt there was greater value in getting the Pentagon spokesman on and confronting him and pressing him on the air than it was to get you on without the Pentagon. You can understand our position, can't you?"

I said yes, I understood it intellectually, but had he thought about the example, or even precedent, that CBS was setting? Here was CBS, arranging a program about press controls, and what does the network do? It agrees to accept government control over the selection of the other guest.

I asked the producer if he would open the program with an explanation to the viewers about how the participants got selected (Morley Safer was going on in my stead). The producer said he would raise the issue at the network. Then, a couple of hours later, he called to say they had cancelled the whole show and were instead going to use the time slot to do a straight news program on the Gulf war.

Some of you may wonder why you haven't heard more about the lawsuit before this. It's because, shamefully, Big Media have not only ducked the lawsuit, they have, by and large, failed to report it. For example, *The New York Times*, at this writing, has mentioned it only once, in two paragraphs at the end of a long piece out of Riyadh. Coverage in the rest of the major media has been almost as sparse. I hope this doesn't mean what it looks like.

That *Times* story, incidentally, said the press was chafing under the controls and that the military had been making vague promises about relaxing them. But the piece ended by saying that despite such talk, "there was no sign of change here."

How do the large news organizations explain their failure to do more than have meetings with, and send letters to, the Pentagon asking that the rules be softened—especially since the constant response is that the government isn't budging?

Floyd Abrams, a leading First Amendment lawyer who has become an unofficial legal spokesman for the establishment media, told the *New York Law Journal* that the leading news companies may have been reluctant to join the lawsuit because "there is a difficulty in prevailing in a facial challenge to the rules in the early days of the war." Does this mean they'll find their courage only if the war drags on and public opposition grows and then the media will run less risk of being called unpatriotic?

In the same *Law Journal* article, an in-house attorney at *The Times*, George Freeman, said: "We prefer to deal directly with the Pentagon during time of war rather than by what is a more protracted and adversarial way." That sentence speaks volumes about the independence of the press.

The lawsuit, boiled down, says the government's press controls are violative of the Constitution as regards freedom of the press and equal protection of the law. The relief it asks for is a return to the press ground rules of Vietnam, meaning voluntary observance of security rules and freedom of movement and access. The suit is not an anti-war document. Nor do I see it as a hostile act against our political and military leaders.

I see it, instead, as a necessary instrument of leverage which seeks to persuade the government that the suppression of information, for reasons other than national security or protecting the safety of our troops, is a departure from our traditions that will in the end corrode and weaken the public trust that presidents crucially need to govern.

This is no time for the press to cover a desert war by putting its head in the sand.

133. Daniel Hallin, "TV's Clean Little War"

(1991)

Daniel Hallin's article follows Sydney Schanberg's in focusing, in particular, on the television news coverage of the first Iraq War. Hallin, who holds a Ph.D. in political science from the University of California at Berkeley, made a major contribution to the historiography of the Vietnam War with his 1986 book, *The Uncensored War: The Media and Vietnam.* Hallin's research showed that, especially early in the Vietnam War, the media presented the administration's version of events largely uncritically. Only late in the war, as the public became more disillusioned, did the White House and the Pentagon lose the ability to manage the media coverage. In this essay, Hallin shows how the Bush administration learned these lessons from Vietnam and how the television media once again reverted to the role of cheerleader.

SOURCE: *Bulletin of the Atomic Scientists,* May 1991, pp. 17–19.

In the introduction to *Living-Room War,* a book about television coverage of the Vietnam War, Michael Arlen wrote: "I can't say I completely agree with people who think that when battle scenes are brought into the living room the hazards of war are necessarily made 'real' to the civilian audience. It seems to me that by the same process they are also made less 'real'—diminished, in part, by the physical size of the television screen, which, for all the industry's advances, still shows one picture of men three inches tall shooting at other men three inches tall, and trivialized, or at least tamed, by the enveloping cozy alarums of the household."

But Arlen knew that what diminished and prettified television's portrayal of Vietnam was more than the size of the television screen and its location in the domestic space of the home. The nature of television journalism and its relation to its audience, its military sources, and the wider American culture also pushed strongly in this direction. Americans went into Vietnam with a romantic view of war derived largely from the representation of World War II in popular culture.

489

For readers of the *New York Times* and the *Washington Post* the war may have been above all a political policy, part of the global struggle between East and West; television accepted the political rationale, but its focus was different. On television, war was an arena of individual action, a place where men—there was no room for women—could show courage and mastery in a way that was rarely possible in everyday life.

Eventually Vietnam forced a more sober view of war into American culture. *Combat* gave way to *M*A*S*H*, and *The Green Berets* to *Full Metal Jacket*. Older images lived on in such films as *Rambo* but they no longer dominated the culture. But television coverage of the war in the Persian Gulf has brought back much of the guts and glory tradition. And this may prove one of the second living-room war's greatest costs: that it restored war to a place of pride in American culture.

Five interconnected images dominated television coverage of the Gulf War:

- **Technology.** Surely the most powerful images of this war were of triumphant technology: smart-bomb videos, tanks rolling across the desert, cruise missiles flaming into the sky in a graceful arc, the homely but lovable A-10 Warthog. "Deadly streaks of fire in the night sky," ABC's Sam Donaldson reported on January 21. "A Scud missile is headed for Dhahran in eastern Saudi Arabia. And rising to intercept it, a U.S. Patriot missile. Bull's eye! No more Scud!"

The pictures were compelling: it is hard to imagine better video than the explosion of a mine-clearing line charge. And the technical accomplishments were stunning enough to impress journalists, as when CNN anchor David French was "honored" by the air force with a ride on an F-15E Strike Eagle and gushed about its high-tech effectiveness.

The pictures would be different if the cameras were on the ground, where the bombs landed. But in a technological war, especially one in which most of the dying is on one side, this is rarely possible. Even if Iraq had granted the media full freedom to cover the war from its side, journalists would not be interested in experiencing a B-52 attack first-hand. So technological war appears "clean" most of the time, more so when both sides exercise military restrictions on coverage.

Network coverage of the aftermath of the Gulf War, when journalists finally could see its human results, often seemed tamer than print coverage, which was full of references to charred and dismembered bodies. In Vietnam, self-censorship was also significant. Network policies limited the use of the most graphic footage, particularly of American casualties.

- **Experts.** These appeared in two guises. First there were the military briefers, standing calm and assured before the clamoring throng of reporters. Their role was much more important in the Gulf War than in Vietnam, where the daily press briefing in Saigon was grist for wire stories but rarely shown on television. It is not hard to see why—military control of the media in the Gulf, especially restrictions on movement, gave journalists there few other channels of information. In Vietnam, journalists were free to visit any unit that would have them and to travel without an official escort. In the Gulf, until the last days of the war when the pool arrangement broke down, small numbers of reporters were shepherded around under carefully controlled conditions. The military managed the media much as a modern presidential campaign does, releasing carefully controlled doses of information, setting up carefully planned photo opportunities, and minimizing reporters' access to any other source of information.

It is interesting that despite complaints and finally evasion by reporters in the field, major news organizations declined to join in legal challenges to the rules. The networks may well have been so wary of appearing adversarial that they were happy to be able to put on the screen, "Cleared by the U.S. Military."

The tightness of these restrictions was by no means purely a matter of protecting military security. According to a number of reviews of the press in Vietnam, including studies by the Twentieth Century Fund and the army's Office of Military History, the looser rules that prevailed in Vietnam worked well for that purpose. Journalists in Vietnam accepted guidelines for restricting sensitive information as a condition of accreditation to accompany troops in the field. But they neither had to submit their copy for censorship nor travel in pools organized and supervised by the military.

The networks also had their own experts, retired military and Defense Department officials for the most part, whose function was to put the war "into context." This meant that the war was seen from the strategist's point of view, in essentially technical terms sanitized from reference to violence or death. "We have the initiative in the air," reported ABC consultant Tony Cordesman on January 21. Cordesman is a military specialist who has also served as an aide to Republican Sen. John McCain of Arizona. "We can use our aircraft as long as we think we can keep finding valuable targets and killing them before we commit the land forces." (Killing targets is different from killing people.) "We're going to wait . . . as we let air power take what is an inevitable toll and we can undermine and almost destroy the cohesiveness of Iraq's forces." Cordesman stumbled for a moment before saying "destroy," as though he were uncomfortable with a word that connoted violence.

Journalists quickly picked up the language. "From the air, sea, and with artillery they pounded Iraqi troops and armor concentrations in southern Kuwait for three hours," NBC's Tom Brokaw said on February 12. "It was the real thing, yet it was also a useful test of the complexities of mounting an all-out attack with so many forces from many different nations." Again there is the parallel with coverage of presidential elections, the focus on candidates' "game plans" which keeps journalists clear of divisive questions of ideology and policy. The parallel to sports reporting is also clear: one of the most prominent visuals of the Gulf War was the computerized "chalkboard," used to diagram military strategy as it is used to diagram football plays.

• **The fighting men and women**. On August 23 Dan Rather opened the CBS Evening News broadcast with a report on the First Tactical Air Wing of the

U.S. Air Force: "These are the warplanes and these are the fighting men and women who are the heart of the massive U.S. military buildup in the area. We'll show it to you up close and from the inside on tonight's broadcast." The central characters in television's drama of war, in the Gulf as in Vietnam, were the American soldiers, and their moods set the tone of the reporting.

Troops went into Vietnam with high morale, and the gung-ho attitude pervaded the living-room war in the early years. Later, as the troops began to sour on the war, television's image of the war became more negative. In the Gulf crisis the reverse was true. During the troop buildup, soldiers in the Gulf would often be heard expressing doubts about the prospect of war. Once policymakers decided to go to war, however, the troops put aside doubts and focused on doing their job. "Can't wait to do it," said one marine in a typical report on the impending ground war (CBS, January 28). "This is what we have been training for—myself for 13 years." Television reflected and celebrated their enthusiasm, and the war came to be identified with them.

War brings out "valor and grit," in the melodramatic phrase Rather invoked repeatedly the night President Bush announced a cease-fire. But it also brings out hatred—more intensely in a war like Vietnam which had substantial casualties on both sides—and cold indifference to human life. But television cannot speak of this other side of the war culture, because it would show disrespect to the fighting men and women.

A gunner on the battleship Wisconsin said with a big laugh to CBS correspondent Eric Engberg on February 9: "The 16-inch is of course a great counter to the other guy's firepower weapon. It's an anti-materiel weapon. And we prefer shooting at their artillery, their structures. Don't waste the 16-inch on people; you can do that with other things!" But his attitude had to be assimilated to the image of skill and bravery, and its moral implications passed over.

There is an important connection between the images of the fighting men and women and technology. The troops took pride in their mastery of technology, and their skill was an important theme in news coverage. But mastering technology generally means accepting its logic, and the soldiers often added to the chorus of sanitized, technological language.

• **The enemy.** War reporting usually turns the enemy into the incarnation of absolute evil, and one of the reasons the Gulf War played so well in the media is that Saddam Hussein's regime fit the image better than most. Nevertheless, the tendency to portray war as good versus evil distorted Gulf coverage in important ways.

The enemy is considered to practice a kind of evil we could never practice; his actions and ours belong to different moral orders. Reporting on the release of oil into the Gulf, Alan Pizzey of CBS said on January 28: "This is the first time in history that nature has been a direct target." He forgot that the United States defoliated nearly five million acres of forest during the Vietnam War, spraying almost half of South Vietnam's forest area at least once.

Although the presence of television cameras in Iraq added a new dimension to this second living-room war, the effect on public opinion in the West was probably minimal. Images of dead and grieving Iraqis filled the television screens for a few brief but powerful minutes in the aftermath of the bombing of the shelter in Baghdad in which many civilians died. But those images were sandwiched between, and overwhelmed in volume of coverage by, other images: the experts, assuring us that we, unlike the enemy, care about human life; and the fighting men and women, expressing gratitude that planes, not they, were doing the fighting.

If the war had dragged on, Iraq might have taken on a human face different from that of its hated leader. Television has the power to do that, and more so as it becomes a more global institution whose presence is accepted across political lines. American TV never had the kind of access to North Vietnam that CNN had to Iraq.

• **The flag.** The flag never figured prominently in television coverage of Vietnam, in an era when patriotism—or nationalism—was taken for granted. Those who questioned the war were excoriated, but only very late in the war did part of the public feel the need to, literally, wave the flag.

For television, the flag is as sacred as the fighting men and women. These symbols are close to the hearts of ordinary Americans, to whose sentiments television is closely tuned. The flag must be celebrated and is above politics. The patriotism stories were often found at the end of the news and treated with a heavy dose of symbolic visuals, even becoming part of the network's signature. NBC sent a reporter to Mount Rushmore on Presidents Day to interview people about the war, closing the evening news with their unanimous expressions of support for it and for the president, and a lingering shot of the "American shrine."

Producers of network news shows were no doubt sincerely caught up, like most of the nation, in the wave of community feeling, closely connected to solidarity with the troops, which was labeled patriotism. But the flag was also a convenient political protection from charges that the networks were helping the enemy by reporting from Baghdad.

And the flag provided an upbeat closing to the news, something apparently of concern to advertisers. Despite the increase in viewing during the war, advertisers were reluctant to sponsor war news. The New York Times reported on February 7: "CBS executives had even offered advertisers assurances that . . . war specials could be tailored to provide better lead-ins to commercials. One way would be to insert the commercials after segments that were specially produced with upbeat images like patriotic views from the home front." Advertisers, according to the Times, were not impressed. But the networks' preoccupation with this problem may partly explain the flag's prominence in coverage.

NBC adopted as its logo a picture of a fighter/bomber superimposed on the American flag with the words, "America at War." This is a good summary of the Gulf War on television: the good feelings and sacred aura of the flag have been attached once again to war. There has been much commentary about the

Gulf War "exorcising the ghosts of Vietnam," as ABC's Jeff Greenfield put it the day after the cease-fire, and this is assumed to be a good thing. But the nation learned a good deal of value from Vietnam, and if exorcising the ghosts means forgetting that war is not a parade, this is a dangerous turn for American culture.

134. Terry Southern, "The Dogs Bark but the Bandwagon Moves On"

(1991)

Terry Southern's critique of the national mood, published in July 1991, characterizes the American triumph over the Vietnam syndrome in the Gulf as analogous to a title fight between a former champion and an amateur. Southern (1924–95) grew up in Dallas and served in the Army from 1943 to 1945; after graduating from Northwestern University in 1948, he spent two years at the Sorbonne in Paris. A novelist and screenwriter, he was best known for co-writing the satirical Cold War film *Dr. Strangelove: Or How I Learned to Stop Worrying and Love the Bomb* (1964) and the countercultural landmark *Easy Rider* (1969). In addition to writing a number of other screenplays and novels, Southern wrote for *Saturday Night Live* and taught screenwriting at New York University. In this article, Southern juxtaposes the ebullient national reaction to the Gulf War and the American triumph with reports of atrocities and criticisms of moral bankruptcy in finding pride in "defeating the second-rate army of a Third World country."

SOURCE: *Nation,* July 8, 1991, pp. 56–58.

Back last August, when the Bandwagon first loaded up and headed out, it was a grand, indeed one may safely say, *glorious* affair. Flag-bedecked and festooned with yellow bows and ribbons as bright as the sun, the Bandwagon rolled out to the sound of toe-tapping church hymns and high-stepping march tunes. It was irresistible; everyone clambered aboard. Not just Johnny Six-pack and the Missus but plenty of soft-spoken egghead types as well; and lots of lovable old Will Rogers types, and gentle womenfolk of every ilk. It was like being at the cast party for a production of *Our Town*. Only your eccentric, reclusive, misfit, wet-blanket, Ralph Nader/Ramsey Clark types were not represented. But everyone said, "No problem. Good riddance." Things were too perfect to entertain any negative thoughts; the *togetherness* of it all was simply overwhelming; the Bandwagon started picking up steam.

The actual "war" was no hindrance to the Bandwagon; if anything, it was vaguely pleasant and comforting—somewhat like a small-town picnic on a lazy Sunday afternoon, where the fireworks are rather second-rate but still engaging enough not to switch channels, because after all, it was *live* and, theoretically at least, something unpredicted *could* occur at any moment. Who could say, maybe another Scud would get through and something far-out and dramatic would happen. So with sustained fanfare, the Bandwagon rolled on. But inside the war itself, a curious unraveling began:

"Ah may be crazy as a dang coot," a Georgia pilot drawled during an interview with an obscure small-town paper, "but them ops today reminded me of shootin' jackrabbit back home. After a while, me an' Leroy Davis started makin' bets. I don't think ole Leroy had ever been on a jack-shoot, an' he missed a few. 'Hot damn,' he kept sayin', 'them little uns are *fast*!' So I showed 'im how you had to give them little uns about a six-foot lead. He caught on quick an' we raised the bet. Then when we come across a T.C. full of 'em, we didn't jest zap the vehicle with a cannon like we usually would've done, we switched our M.G.s into the single-shot mode an' started plinkin' 'em right outta that truck, one at a time, like empty beer cans. Hot damn!

"An' I'll tell you somethin' else," he concluded. "Ole Leroy turned out to be a pretty damn good shot after all. Yeah, he took me for about three K . . . before he started to throw up."

There was another momentary glitch when some of the so-called Alternative Press began to act up. One magazine reprinted the interview with the Georgia pilot, while another featured a story headlined:

'Too Much Like Shooting Fish in a Barrel,' Complains Marine Col. of Gulf War

But such attempts to denigrate the war effort received short shrift. "If they act up again," commented the President "we'll start kicking butt. Hell, we'll put the I.R.S. on their tail; they'll wish they'd never been born." So the Bandwagon rolled on, as jaunty as could be, and with everyone just as pleased as Punch.

One reason everyone was "pleased as Punch" was because many of the briefings about the "war" were delivered by the commander of the forces himself—a rotund personage whom people looked upon as "joviality incarnate" due to his marked resemblance to one of those colorful bottle-stoppers made in caricature of a happy, slightly demented, peasant innkeeper, sold in the tourist shops of Scandinavia and Luxembourg. It was generally felt that nothing could go wrong while this jolly fellow was in charge, despite the occasional tedious déjà vu images of homeless weeping women and children that somehow leaked into the coverage. No big deal; it was announced that an estimated 150,000 Iraqis had been killed in the saturation bombing.

Then, on a day like any other day, or so it seemed, came the momentous occasion when the President declared that the war was over. "Victory" was proclaimed, and the Bandwagon picked up steam. The Alternative Press, no strangers to buffoonery, and again at the expense of common decency, attempted to downplay the historic moment with garish headlines:

Will a Cakewalk in the Sand Cool Out the Blood'N'Guts Yen of the Old El Wimpo?

Will a Goliath-Kicks-David's-Butt Syndrome Fly in This Man's Hacienda? 'No Way, José,' Says Top Aide, 'We're Looking for Bear.'

Such comments were dismissed in quick order as "sour grapes by the sanction freaks" and had no discernible effect on the momentum of the Bandwagon.

And then came the Big Symposium—held at one of the swanky schools on the East Coast—by a group that the Administration described as "notorious egghead/bleeding hearts," who tried their best to cheapen the image of the Bandwagon and its triumphant journey. "Has American life become so bankrupt," asked one, a professor of sociology, "so empty and wholly devoid of meaning and value . . . that we must look for self-esteem in defeating the second-rate army of a Third World country?"

Also on the panel was a retired Army general, much decorated and formerly known for his gung-ho heroics. "It is true," he said, "that the battlefield is the cradle and fountainhead of self-esteem, but I do not believe any rational man can attain it by inflicting death from miles above, nor by shooting people who are running away." He shook his head, rather sadly it seemed. "That is not the stuff, sir, of which heroes are made."

It was the famous psychologist, however, whose opinion may have been the most vexing. "There are megabucks in war," he said, "and there are megabucks in victory celebrations. By continuing to extol the 'victory' that we know is hollow and absurd, we are using the methods of the cynical politicians of Mississippi who extol and appeal to the 'whiteness' of the voters, equating it with 'Americanism' and whipping up a frenzy of self-righteousness and eager donations."

That did not go over well with practically anyone at all, but he kept at it like a dog with a bone: "The Bandwagon represents an illusion of victory over some dark and nameless adversary. The energy generated in celebrating such a victory is important to the powers-that-be because they can channel it toward whatever end they wish, which includes, of course, setting up the next hit of the New World Order—North Korea? Libya? Cuba?—each replete with its victory celebration."

Despite the acknowledged pre-eminence of its participants, the symposium received scant coverage by the media. It was as though it didn't happen. Even CNN stayed clear of it, which surprised a lot of people. Others were glad, however. "At least it proves," they said, "that Turner isn't as much under Jane Fonda's thumb as we thought." And everyone cheered crazily as the Bandwagon rolled on.

135. Chris Britt, "I Wish I Could Have Marched in the Gay Rights Parade"

(1993)

Chris Britt's editorial cartoon mocks President Bill Clinton's "Don't ask—don't tell" policy on gays in the military. Britt (1959–) grew up in Arizona, and earned a visual arts degree at the University of Illinois at Springfield. Over the course of the 1980s, he worked as a cartoonist at the Sacramento *Union*, the *Houston Post*, the *News Tribune* (Tacoma, Washington), and the *Seattle Times* before settling in at the Springfield (Illinois) *State Journal Register*. Since 1991, his cartoons have been syndicated through the Copley News Service. In the 1992 presidential campaign, Bill Clinton promised that, if elected, he would wipe out by executive order the military prohibition against gays serving in the armed forces. In the transition period between the election and Clinton's inauguration, no issue surpassed gays in the military for controversy. Eventually, Clinton backed away from his promise and negotiated a compromise with the Pentagon in which the armed forces acknowledged that gays in the military would have to stay in the closet: the military would not ask about the sexual orientation of its personnel, and the personnel would not volunteer information.

SOURCE: Copley News Service, April 1993.

136. Kathy Kelly, "Banning Child Sacrifice: A Difficult Choice?"

(1998)

In this report, Kathy Kelly of Voices in the Wilderness reports on one of her many trips to Iraq in the years between the two U.S. ground wars there and critiques America's role in world affairs under the Clinton administration. Kelly (1953–) grew up in a devout Catholic family on the South Side of Chicago. She graduated from Loyola and earned an M.A. in religious education at Chicago Theological Seminary. She has been active in the Catholic Worker movement since the 1970s, and became a war tax resister—she stopped paying federal income taxes around 1980. In 1988, she served nine months of a one-year sentence in federal prison for planting corn on a nuclear missile silo. Kelly founded Voices in the Wilderness to campaign against American-led United Nations sanctions against Iraq in 1996. Between 1996 and 2003, Voices in the Wilderness led more than seventy delegations to Iraq, and for bringing medicine and toys to Iraqi children, Kelly and Voices were threatened with twelve years in prison and fined $20,000 (which they refused to pay). Kelly wrote this article in 1998 as part of a long and largely frustrating campaign to heighten public awareness of Iraqi suffering under the sanctions that limited the flow of food and medicine into the country. For Kelly and Voices, the Iraq War of 1991 never ended; sanctions were another form of war. For this work and her continued work for peace in Iraq, she has been nominated for the Nobel Peace Prize three times.

SOURCE: March 9,1998, courtesy of Kathy Kelly.

Just one month ago, US/ UK bombardment of Iraq seemed almost inevitable. Even though the most comprehensive economic sanctions ever inflicted in modern history have already crippled Iraq, slaughtering over 1/2 million children under age 5, the US and the UK were poised for further assault. Today, the US still threatens air attacks upon Iraq, massive strikes that would heap more agony on civilians who've endured a seven year state of siege.

On February 9, our small delegation of eight, two from the United Kingdom and six from the US, representing thousands of supporters, traveled to Iraq carrying 110,000 dollars of medicines. We were the 11th Voices in the Wilderness delegation to deliberately violate the sanctions as part of a nonviolent campaign to end the US led economic warfare against Iraq.

From previous trips, we knew exactly where to find overwhelming evidence of a weapon of mass destruction. Inspectors have only to enter the wards of any hospital in Iraq to see that the sanctions themselves are a lethal weapon, destroying the lives of Iraq's most vulnerable people. In children's wards, tiny victims writhe in pain, on blood-stained mats, bereft of anesthetics and antibiotics. Thousands of children, poisoned by contaminated water, die from dysentery, cholera, and diarrhea. Others succumb to respiratory infections that become fatal full body infections. Five thousand children, under age five, perish each month. 960,000 children who are severely malnourished will bear lifelong consequences of stunted growth, brain deficiencies, disablement. At the hands of UN/US policy makers, childhood in Iraq has, for thousands, become a living hell.

Repeatedly, the US media describes Iraq's plight as "hardship." Video footage and still photographs show professors selling their valuable books. Teenage students hawking jewelry in the market are interviewed about why they aren't in school. These are sad stories, but they distract us from the major crisis in Iraq today, the story still shrouded in secrecy. This is the story of extreme cruelty, a story of medicines being withheld from dying children. It is a story of child abuse, of child sacrifice, and it merits day to day coverage.

A Reuters TV crew accompanied our delegation to Al Mansour children's hospital. On the general ward, the day before, I had met a mother crouching over an infant, named Zayna. The child was so emaciated by nutritional marasmus that, at 7 months of age, her frail body seemed comparable to that of a 7 month premature fetus. We felt awkward about returning with a TV crew, but the camera person, a kindly man, was clearly moved by all that he'd seen in the previous wards. He made eye contact with the mother. No words were spoken, yet she gestured to me to sit on a chair next to the bed, then wrapped Zayna in a worn, damp and stained covering. Gently, she raised the dying child and put her in my arms. Was the mother trying to say, as she nodded to me, that if the world could witness what had been done to tiny Zayna, she might not die in vain? Inwardly crumpling, I turned to the camera, stammering, "This child, denied food and denied medicine, is the embargo's victim."

I felt ashamed of my own health and well-being, ashamed to be so comfortably adjusted to the privileged life of a culture that, however unwittingly, practices child sacrifice. Many of us westerners can live well, continue "having it all," if we only agree to avert our gaze, to look the other way, to politely not notice that in order to maintain our overconsumptive lifestyles, our political leaders tolerate child sacrifice. "It's a difficult choice to make," said Madeleine Albright when she was asked about the fact that more children had died in Iraq than in Hiroshima and Nagasaki combined, "but," she continued, "we think the price is worth it." Iraqi oil must be kept off the markets, at all costs, even if sanctions cost the lives of hundreds of thousands of children. The camera man had moved on.

"I'm sorry, Zayna, "I whispered helplessly to the mother and child. "I'm so sorry."

Camera crews accompanied us to hospitals in Baghdad, Basra and Fallujah. They filmed the horrid conditions inside grim wards. They filmed a cardiac surgeon near tears telling how it feels to decide which of three patients will get the one available ampule of heart medicine "Yesterday," said Dr. Faisal, a cardiac surgeon at the Fallujah General Hospital, "I shouted at my nurse. I said, 'I told you to give that ampule to this patient. The other two will have to die.' " A camera crew followed us into the general ward of a children's hospital when a mother began to sob convulsively because her baby had just suffered a cardiac arrest. Dr. Qusay, the chief of staff, rushed to resuscitate the child, then whispered to the mother that they had no oxygen, that the baby was gasping her dying breaths. All of the mothers, cradling their desperately ill infants, began to weep. The ward was a death row for infants.

Associated Press, Reuters and other news companies' footage from hospital visits was broadcast in the Netherlands, in Britain, in Spain and in France. But people in the US never glimpsed those hospital wards.

I asked a cameraman from a major US news network why he came to the entrance of a hospital to film us, but opted not to enter the hospital. "Please," I begged, "we didn't ask you to film us as talking heads. The story is inside the hospital." He shrugged. "Both sides use the children suffering," he explained, "and we've already done hospitals." I might have added that they'd already "done" F 16's lifting off of runways, they'd "done" white UN vehicles driving off to inspect possible weapon sites, they'd "done" innumerable commercials for US weapon displays.

While political games are played, the children are dying and we have seen them die. If people across the US could see what we've seen, if they witnessed, daily, the crisis of child sacrifice and child slaughter, we believe hearts would be touched. Sanctions would not withstand the light of day.

I felt sad and shattered as we left Iraq. A peaceful resolution to the weapons inspection crisis was reached, at least temporarily, but Iraqi friends were intensely skeptical. "They are going to hit us. This is sure," said Samir, a young computer engineer. "Anyway, look what happens to us every day." Feeling helpless to notify anyone, we had left the scene of an ongoing crime.

Upon return to the US, customs agents turned my passport over to the state department, perhaps as evidence that according to US law I've committed a criminal act by traveling to Iraq. I know that our efforts to be voices in the wilderness aren't criminal. We're governed by compassion, not by laws that pitilessly murder innocent children. What's more, Iraqi children might benefit if we could bring their story into a courtroom, before a jury of our peers.

We may be tempted to feel pessimistic, but Iraq's children can ill afford our despair. They need us to build on last month's resistance to military strikes. During the Gulf War, I wasn't in the US (I was with the Gulf Peace Team, camped on the border between Saudi Arabia and Iraq and later evacuated to Baghdad). I didn't witness, firsthand, the war fever and war hysteria. But people told me, when I returned to the US, that the war had often seemed like a sporting event. Some people went to bars, raised mugs of beer and cheered when "smart bombs" exploded on their targets. "Rock Iraq! Slam Saddam! Say Hello to Allah!" they shouted.

I think of Umm Reyda when I hear those accounts, a mother who lost nine of her family members when, on February 12, 1991, two astonishingly smart bombs blasted the Ameriyah community center. Families in the Ameriyah neighborhood had gathered to commemorate the end of Ramadan. They had invited many refugees to join them and had made extra room in the overnight basement shelter so that all could huddle together for a relatively safe night's sleep. The smart bombs penetrated the "achilles heel" of the building, the spot where ventilation shafts had been installed. The first bomb exploded and forced 17 bodies out of the building. The second bomb followed immediately after the first, and when it exploded the exits were sealed off. The temperature inside rose to 500 degrees centigrade and the pipes overhead burst with boiling water which cascaded down on the innocents who slept. Hundreds of people were melted. Umm Reyda greets each of our delegations, just as she greeted me when I first met her in March, 1991. "We know that you are not your government," she says, "and that your people would never choose to do this to us." I've always felt relief that she never saw television coverage of US people in bars, cheering her children's death.

Last month, on February 18, 1998, a vastly different cry was shouted by college students. They didn't cheer the bombers, and in Columbus, OH they may well have prevented them from deadly missions. "One two three four, we don't want your racist war." The lines confronted Ms. Albright, crackled across Baghdad. People on the streets smiled at me, an obvious westerner, and counted, "one, two three four . . ."

A week later, UN Secretary General Kofi Annan, at the conclusion of his remarks introducing a peaceful resolution to the weapon inspection crisis, urged young people around the world to recognize that we are all part of one another, to see the world not from the narrow perspective of their own locale but rather from a clear awareness of our fundamental interdependence. What a contrast between his vision of a new generation that wants to share this planet's resources and serve one another's best interests, globally, and the vision that Ms. Albright offers: "If we have to use force, it is because we are America. We are the indispensable nation. We stand tall. We see further into the future."

Ms. Albright's reference to "use of force" is the stuff of nightmares, given the ominous comments some US military officials have made about preparedness to use even nuclear force.

I doubt that other nations will accept that the US "stands tall." It's more likely that international consensus will conclude that the US lacks the moral standing to be prosecutor, judge, and jury in the dispute over Iraq's policies. Most people in the Arab world believe that the US favors Israel and is unwilling to criticize its actions, even when they violate international agreements or United Nations resolutions. People throughout the world point to the hypocrisy of the government of the US in other aspects of international relations. The US is over $1 billion in arrears in payments to the United Nations; it has ignored judgments by the World Court and overwhelming votes in the UN General Assembly whenever they conflict with its desires; and despite its rhetoric about human rights, the US record of support for ruthless regimes is shameful.

Is it outlandish to think that courage, wisdom and love could inform the formation of foreign and domestic policies? Is it overly optimistic to think that we could choose to ban the sale of weapons of mass destruction? Is it too much to ask that economic sanctions against Iraq be lifted and never again used as a form of child sacrifice? For the sake of all children, everywhere, lets continue sounding a wake up call to US officials. They must stop punishing and murdering Iraqi children. The agreement negotiated by UN Secretary General Kofi Annan offers a basis for continued weapon inspections and the earliest possible end to the deadly embargo of trade with Iraq. The deeds of one leader, or even of an entire government, cannot be used to justify an unprecedented violation of human rights. Umm Reyda, through seven years of mourning, still forgives US people. It's time that we respond with remorse and regret for the suffering we've caused and a commitment to end this racist war.

Kathy Kelly
Voices in the Wilderness

137. Phyllis and Orlando Rodriguez, "Not in Our Son's Name"

(2001)

In this letter, first published only four days after the September 11, 2001, terrorist attacks, and widely distributed on the Internet, Phyllis and Orlando Rodriguez, parents of one of the victims, appeal to the government to seek not revenge, but peace. Phyllis (1943–) grew up in Long Island City and the Bronx. She earned her B.A. from City College and her M.S.Ed. in literacy and reading from Fordham University, and she has worked as a teacher, painter, and community activist. Orlando (1942–) was born in Havana, Cuba, and moved with his family to New York in 1955. He earned his B.A. at City College and his Ph.D. at Columbia University. A professor of sociology at Fordham University, he has expertise in criminology, mental health, and Hispanic immigrant life. The Rodriguezes' thirty-one-year-old son, Greg, died in the attack on New York. At a time when a *New York Times* poll found 75 percent of Americans favoring war against Al-Queda, even if civilians would be hurt, the Rodriguezes' reaction seemed uncommon. Rather than seek to punish the perpetrators through war, they argued for a criminal investigation that would bring those responsible to justice. In short order, their letter attracted the interest of many other like-minded people who lost family members in the attacks; together, they formed September Eleventh Families for Peaceful Tomorrows, an organization dedicated to finding peaceful alternatives to war.

SOURCE: Phyllis and Orlando Rodriguez, letter, September 15, 2001, http:// www.peacefultomorrows.org/article.php?id=80.

Our son Greg is among the many missing from the World Trade Center attack. Since we first heard the news, we have shared moments of grief, comfort, hope, despair, fond memories with his wife, the two families, our friends and neighbors, his loving colleagues at Cantor Fitzgerald/ESpeed, and all the grieving families that daily meet at the Pierre Hotel.

We see our hurt and anger reflected among everybody we meet. We cannot pay attention to the daily flow of news about this disaster. But we read enough of the news to sense that our government is heading in the direction of violent revenge, with the prospect of sons, daughters, parents, friends in distant lands, dying, suffering, and nursing further grievances against us. It is not the way to go. It will not avenge our son's death. Not in our son's name.

Our son died a victim of an inhuman ideology. Our actions should not serve the same purpose. Let us grieve. Let us reflect and pray. Let us think about a rational response that brings real peace and justice to our world. But let us not as a nation add to the inhumanity of our times.

138. Robert O'Harrow Jr., "Six Weeks in Autumn"

(2002)

In this article, published in the *Washington Post Magazine*, journalist Robert O'Harrow Jr. chronicles the battle in the nation's capital over what eventually became the USA Patriot Act. O'Harrow is an investigative and financial reporter for the *Post* and a specialist in data privacy. He was a Pulitzer Prize finalist in 2000, and in 2003, he won the Carnegie Mellon Cybersecurity Reporting Award. O'Harrow shows how, in the days and weeks after the September 11 terrorist attacks, Justice Department officials and others in the Bush administration moved to sweep away restraints placed on investigative agencies in the wake of the 1970s COINTELPRO investigations. In response, members of Congress and civil libertarians concerned about ceding too much power to the executive branch fought to remove the most sweeping provisions and to give the act an expiration date. In early 2006, however, the president signed into law the Congress's reauthorization of the act, largely unchanged.

SOURCE: *Washington Post Magazine*, October 27, 2002.

Assistant Attorney General Viet Dinh took his seat in La Colline restaurant on Capitol Hill and signaled for a cup of coffee. It was one of those standard Washington breakfasts, where politicos mix schmoozing and big ideas to start their days.

An intense foot soldier for Attorney General John Ashcroft, Dinh had been in his job for only a few months. He wanted to make a good impression on others at the session and craved the caffeine to keep his edge. As he sipped his fourth cup and listened to the patter of White House and Hill staffers, a young man darted up to the table. "A plane has crashed," he said. "It hit the World Trade Center."

Dinh and the rest of the voluble group went silent. Then their beepers began chirping in unison. At another time, it might have seemed funny. A Type-A Washington moment. Now they looked at one another and rushed out of the restaurant.

It was about 9:30 on September 11, 2001.

Dinh hurried back to the Justice Department, where the building was being evacuated. Like countless other Americans, he was already consumed with a desire to strike back. Unlike most, however, he had an inkling of how: by doing whatever was necessary to strengthen the government's legal hand against terrorists.

Jim Dempsey was sifting through e-mails at his office at the Center for Democracy and Technology on Farragut Square when his boss, Jerry Berman, rushed in.

"Turn on the TV," Berman urged. Dempsey reached for the zapper, and images came rushing at him. Crisp sunshine. Lower Manhattan glinting in the brilliance. A jetliner cutting through the scene.

Dempsey is a lanky and slow-speaking former Hill staffer who combines a meticulous attention to detail with an awshucks demeanor. Since the early 1990s, he has been one of the leading watchdogs of FBI surveillance initiatives, a reasoned and respected civil liberties advocate routinely summoned to the Hill by both political parties to advise lawmakers about technology and privacy issues.

As he watched the smoke and flames engulf the World Trade Center, he knew it was the work of terrorists, and the FBI was foremost in his mind. "They have screwed up so bad," he said to himself. "With all the powers and resources that they have, they should have caught these guys."

At the same moment, it dawned on him that his work—and the work of many civil liberties activists over the years to check the increasingly aggressive use of technology by law enforcement officials—was about to be undone. "We all knew well enough what it meant," Dempsey says now.

The car arrived at Sen. Patrick Leahy's house in Northern Virginia shortly after 9 a.m. The Vermont Democrat took his place in the front seat and, as the car coursed toward the Potomac, he read through some notes about the pending nomination of a new drug czar and thought about a meeting that morning at the Supreme Court.

Half-listening to the radio, Leahy heard something about an explosion and the World Trade Center. He asked the driver to turn it up, then called some friends in New York. They told him what they were seeing on television. It sounded ominous. The car continued toward the Supreme Court and a conference he was to attend with Chief Justice William Rehnquist and circuit court judges from around the country.

Leahy headed to the court's conference room, with its thickly carpeted floors and oak-paneled walls lined with portraits of the first eight chief justices. When Rehnquist arrived, Leahy leaned toward him and whispered, "Bill, before we start, I believe we have a terrorist attack."

As if on cue, a muffled boom echoed through the room. Smoke began rising across the Potomac.

Leahy's country was under attack. And soon enough, the five-term senator realized, he would be as well.

Leahy chaired the Senate Judiciary Committee, putting him at the center of an inevitable debate about how to fight back—a struggle that would subject him to some of the most intense political pressures of his career.

Leahy was more than a Senate leader; he was one of Congress's most liberal members, a longtime proponent of civil liberties who had always worked to keep the government from trampling individual rights. But Leahy was also a former prosecutor, a pragmatist who understood what investigators were up against in trying to identify and bring down terrorists.

He knew that conservatives were going to press him relentlessly for more police powers while civil libertarians would look to him as their standardbearer. Everyone would be watching him: party leaders, Senate colleagues, White House officials, editorial writers and cable commentators, his Vermont constituents.

Leahy wanted to strike the right balance. But after watching an F-16 roar over the Mall that afternoon, he also resolved to do whatever he could, as a patriot and a Democrat, to give law enforcement officials more tools to stop future attacks. "I was just thinking how angry I was," he recalls.

The attacks on the World Trade Center and Pentagon didn't just set off a national wave of mourning and ire. They reignited and reshaped a smoldering debate over the proper use of government power to peer into the lives of ordinary people.

The argument boiled down to this: In an age of high-tech terror, what is the proper balance between national security and the privacy of millions of Americans, whose personal information is already more widely available than ever before? Telephone records, e-mails, oceans of detail about individuals' lives—the government wanted access to all of it to hunt down terrorists before they struck.

For six weeks last fall, behind a veneer of national solidarity and bipartisanship, Washington leaders engaged in pitched, closed-door arguments over how much new power the government should have in the name of national security. They were grappling not only with the specter of more terrorist attacks but also with the chilling memories of Cold War redbaiting, J. Edgar Hoover's smear campaigns, and Watergate-era wiretaps.

At the core of the dispute was a body of little-known laws and rules that, over the last half a century, defined and limited the government's ability to snoop:

Title III of the Omnibus Crime Control and Safe Streets Act governed electronic eavesdropping. The "pen register, trap and trace" rules covered the use of devices to track the origin and destination of telephone calls. The Foreign Intelligence Surveillance Act, or FISA, regulated the power to spy domestically when seeking foreign intelligence information.

The White House, the Justice Department and their allies in Congress wanted to ease those restraints, and they wanted to do it as quickly as possible. Though put into place to protect individuals and political groups from past abuses by the FBI, CIA and others, the restrictions were partly to blame for the intelligence gaps on September 11, the government said.

The administration also wanted new authority to secretly detain individuals suspected of terrorism and to enlist banks and other financial services companies in the search for terrorist financing. What's more, law enforcement sought broad access to business databases filled with information about the lives of ordinary citizens. All this detail could help investigators search for links among plotters.

Dempsey and other civil libertarians agreed that the existing laws were outdated, but for precisely the opposite reason—because they already gave the government access to mountains of information unavailable a decade ago. Handing investigators even more power, they warned, would lead to privacy invasions and abuses.

By the time the debate ended—one year ago, with overwhelming approval of the USA Patriot Act by Congress, and its signing on October 26 by President Bush—the government had powers that went far beyond what even the most ardent law enforcement supporters had considered politically possible before the attacks.

How this happened—through backroom negotiations, political maneuvering and public pressure by Bush administration officials—is a largely untold tale with consequences that will reverberate for years to come.

They stared at a television in the bright sunroom of Dinh's Chevy Chase home, a handful of policy specialists from the Justice Department who wondered what to do next.

Only hours before, they had fled their offices, cringing as fighter jets patrolled Washington's skies. Now, as news programs replayed the destruction, they talked about their friend Barbara Olson, conservative commentator and wife of U.S. Solicitor General Ted Olson. She was aboard American Airlines Flight 77 when it crashed into the Pentagon.

Dinh couldn't believe Barbara was gone. He'd just had dinner at the Olsons' house two nights before, and she had been in rare form. Her humor was irrepressible. Dinh passed around a book of photography she had signed and given to him and the other dinner guests, *Washington, D.C.: Then and Now*.

It was hard to process so much death amid so much sunshine. Dinh and his colleagues tried to focus on the work a head. They agreed they faced a monumental, even historic task: a long overdue reworking of anti-terrorism laws to prevent something like this from happening again on American soil.

Their marching orders came the next morning, as they reconvened in a conference room in Dinh's suite of offices on the fourth floor of Justice. Ashcroft wasn't there—he was in hiding along with other senior government officials. Just before the meeting, Dinh had spoken to Adam Ciongoli, Ashcroft's counselor, who conveyed the attorney general's desires.

"Beginning immediately," Dinh told the half a dozen policy advisers and lawyers, "we will work on a package of authorities"—sweeping, dramatic and based on practical recommendations from FBI agents and Justice Department lawyers in the field. "The charge [from Ashcroft] was very, very clear: 'all that is necessary for law enforcement, within the bounds of the Constitution, to discharge the obligation to fight this war against terror,' " he said.

Dinh's enthusiasm for the task was evident. At 34, he seems perpetually jazzed up, smiles often and speaks quickly, as though his words, inflected with the accent of his native Vietnam, can't quite keep up with his ideas. A graduate of Harvard Law School, he learned his way around Washington as an associate special counsel to the Senate Whitewater committee, and as a special counsel to Sen. Pete Domenici (R-N.M.) during the Clinton impeachment trial.

"What are the problems?" Dinh asked the group around the table.

For the next several hours—indeed, over the next several days—Dinh's colleagues catalogued gripes about the legal restraints on detective and intelligence work. Some of the complaints had been bouncing around the FBI and Justice Department for years.

Because of the law's peculiarities, it was unclear if investigators were allowed to track the destination and origin of e-mail the same way they could phone calls. They could obtain search warrants more easily for a telephone tape machine than for commercial voice mail services. And the amount of information that intelligence agents and criminal investigators were permitted to share was limited, making it much harder to target and jail terrorists.

All of this, the lawyers agreed, had to change. Now.

Dempsey was swamped. Reporters, other activists, congressional staffers—everyone wanted his take on how far the Justice Department and Congress would go in reaction to the attacks. "We were getting 50 calls a day," he recalls.

Like many attuned to the rhythms of Washington, Dempsey knew Congress would not have the will to resist granting dramatic new powers to law enforcement immediately. It was a classic dynamic. Something terrible happens. Legislators rush to respond. They don't have time to investigate the policy implications thoroughly, so they reach for what's available and push it through.

That was a nightmare for Dempsey. Looking for signs of hope that the legislative process could be slowed, even if it could not be stopped, he made his own calls around town.

He didn't find much support, even among longtime allies. "If you could get their attention," Dempsey says, "some members of the House and Senate were, 'Don't bother me with the details.'"

"A crisis mentality emerges, and there was clearly a crisis . . . The push for action, the appearance of action, becomes so great."

Within days of the attack, a handful of lawmakers took to the Senate floor with legislation that had been proposed and shot down in recent years because of civil liberties concerns. Many of the proposals had originally had nothing to do with terrorism.

One bill, called the Combating Terrorism Act, proposed expanding the government's authority to trace telephone calls to include e-mail. It was a legacy of FBI efforts to expand surveillance powers during the Clinton administration, which had supported a variety of technology-oriented proposals opposed by civil libertarians. Now it was hauled out and approved in minutes.

One of the few voices advocating calm deliberation, Dempsey says, was Leahy. But it was not clear what he would be able to do in such a highly charged atmosphere.

Across the city and across the country, other civil libertarians braced themselves for the fallout from the attacks.

Among them was Morton Halperin, former head of the Washington office of the American Civil Liberties Union and a former national security official in three administrations. Halperin, a senior fellow at the Council on Foreign Relations, is personally familiar with government surveillance.

While working as a National Security Council staffer in the Nixon administration, Halperin was suspected of leaking information about the secret U.S. bombing of Cambodia. To this day, Halperin has not addressed the allegations, but his house was wiretapped by the FBI, and the taps continued for months after he left the government.

Now, 24 hours after the attacks, he read an e-mail from a member of an online group that had been formed to fight a Clinton administration plan to make publishing classified materials a crime. The writer warned the plan would now be reprised.

Halperin had been anticipating this moment for years. More than a decade ago, he wrote an essay predicting that terrorism would replace communism as the main justification for domestic surveillance. "I sat and stared at that e-mail for a few minutes and decided that I could not do my regular job, that I had to deal with this," he says.

Halperin banged out a call to arms on his computer. "There can be no doubt that we will hear calls in the next few days for Congress to enact sweeping legislation to deal with terrorism," he wrote in the e-mail to more than two dozen civil libertarians on September 12. "This will include not only the secrecy provision, but also broad authority to conduct electronic and other surveillance and to investigate political groups . . . We should not wait."

Within hours, Dempsey, Marc Rotenberg from the Electronic Privacy Information Center and others had offered their support. Their plan: to build on Halperin's call for legislative restraint, while striking a sympathetic note about the victims of the attacks. They started putting together a meeting to sign off on a civil liberties manifesto: "In Defense of Freedom at a Time of Crisis."

Underlying the discussion about how to respond to the terror attacks was the mid-1970s investigation, led by Sen. Frank Church (D-Idaho), into the government's sordid history of domestic spying. Through hundreds of interviews and the examination of tens of thousands of documents, the Church committee found that the FBI, CIA and other government agencies had engaged in pervasive surveillance of politicians, religious organizations, women's rights advocates, antiwar groups and civil liberties activists.

At FBI headquarters in Washington, for example, agents had developed more than half a million domestic intelligence files in the previous two decades. The CIA had secretly opened and photographed almost a quarter-million letters in the United States from 1953 to 1973.

One of the most egregious intelligence abuses was an FBI counterintelligence program known as COINTELPRO. It was, the Church report said, "designed to 'disrupt' groups and 'neutralize' individuals deemed to be threats to domestic security." Among other things, COINTELPRO operations included undermining the jobs of political activists, sending anonymous letters to "spouses of intelligence targets for the purposes of destroying their marriages," and a systematic campaign to undermine the Rev. Martin Luther King Jr.'s civil rights efforts through leaked information about his personal life.

"Too many people have been spied upon by too many government agencies and too much information has been collected" through secret informants, wiretaps, bugs, surreptitious mail-opening and break-ins, the Church report warned.

Congress responded with a series of laws aimed at curbing government abuses. One was the Foreign Intelligence Surveillance Act of 1978, which gave broad powers for counterintelligence officials to monitor the agents of foreign countries.

Under FISA, authorities had to demonstrate, to the super-secret Foreign Intelligence Surveillance Court, that the principal purpose for their surveillance was foreign intelligence. But the law also restricted the use of those powers for domestic criminal investigations and prosecutions.

For all the secrecy surrounding FISA—and despite the fact the FISA court has never denied an application for electronic surveillance—civil libertarians consider the law one of the key safeguards against domestic spying.

But some conservatives have long contended that the law created unnecessary, even absurd, barriers between criminal and intelligence investigators. The Bush administration believed those barriers were getting in the way of uncovering terrorist cells operating here and abroad.

Law enforcement authorities also chafed at internal guidelines imposed by the Justice Department in response to the Church committee revelations. Agents weren't allowed to monitor religious services without evidence of a crime, for instance, which made it hard to investigate mosques that might be harboring terrorists. Ashcroft claimed that the rules even prohibited investigators from surfing the Web for information about suspects.

When Dinh and his team began taking stock of needed legal changes, the legacy of the Church committee loomed large. They saw a chance to turn back the clock. Standing in their way were people like Dempsey and Halperin.

Scores of people streamed into the ACLU's white stucco townhouse on Capitol Hill on the Friday after the attacks, responding to Halperin's e-mail and calls from ACLU lobbyists.

As with so many privacy battles, there were some strikingly strange bedfellows in attendance: Liberal immigration rights groups. Libertarians from the conservative Free Congress Foundation and Eagle Forum. Technology-savvy activists from the Electronic Privacy Information Center and the Center for Democracy and Technology.

They filled the main conference room downstairs, overflowing through French doors into a garden, and up the stairway to the ACLU's offices. The ACLU's headquarters, recently relocated downtown, has been the site of countless strategy meetings over the years on abortion rights, civil rights, freedom of speech and religious freedom.

Even so, "I had never seen that kind of turnout in 25 years," says Laura Murphy, director of the ACLU's national office. "I mean, people were worried. They just knew this was a recipe for government overreaching."

They also grasped the difficulty of their position. Here they were, trying to persuade Americans to hold fast to concerns about individual freedom and privacy, while the vast majority of people were terrified. Polls later showed that most people were more than willing to trade off civil liberties and privacy protections for more security.

Murphy and others also had reached out to Congress in an effort to head off any instant legislation. They found that normally privacy-minded lawmakers, including Sens. Dianne Feinstein (D-Calif.) and Charles Schumer (D-N.Y.), had no intention of questioning efforts to push a bill through quickly.

Even Rep. Bob Barr (R-Ga.), a conservative and dedicated privacy advocate, couldn't offer much hope. Barr and Murphy had worked closely together in recent years, though they come from different ends of the political spectrum. When she called him after the attacks, he confessed there was probably little he could do to temper the anti-terrorism fervor gripping Washington.

"You could sort of hear the clutch in his voice: 'I don't know how we're going to do this,'" she recalls.

Murphy stood at the front of the room with Halperin, trying to win consensus from those assembled on language they would use to voice their concerns. Dempsey, who arrived late, was off to one side, a sinking feeling in his stomach. For all the numbers, the normally raucous group was subdued. Some in attendance owned up to their own fears about new attacks. Everyone "was a little overwhelmed by the magnitude of the task," Dempsey says.

After debate over how to express clear sympathy for the victims of the attack, the group worked out a 10-point statement. "We must have faith in our democratic system and our Constitution, and in our ability to protect at the same time both the freedom and the security of all Americans," read point No. 10.

The document was signed by representatives of more than 150 groups, including religious organizations, gun owners, police and conservative activists. A few days later, they released it at a press conference and posted it on a Web site.

What kind of impact did it have? Apparently not much. A year later, several key officials from the White House and Justice Department say they have never even heard of the appeal.

To say it was a trying time for Leahy is an understatement. He would later describe those days as among the most challenging and emotional of his 28 years in the Senate: "What made this the most intense were not just the issues, but the great sorrows I felt."

The senator was saddled with the responsibility of crafting the Senate proposal for anti-terrorism legislation. He didn't want to ram a bad law through Congress, but he also didn't want to be seen as an obstructionist. So he offered to negotiate a bill directly with the White House, avoiding the time-consuming committee-approval process. Now he had to come up with a way of maintaining meaningful privacy protections while expanding the government's surveillance powers.

As he worked to reconcile those competing interests, he took long walks around the Capitol and down to the Mall. Everywhere he went the mood was grim. "I saw the same faces as I did when I was a law school student [in the District] and President Kennedy had been killed," Leahy says. "I saw the same shock, and I wanted to make sure our shock didn't turn into panic."

It was crucial, Leahy thought, to take enough time with the legislation to get it right. Or as he put it to senior aide Beryl Howell, a former federal prosecutor. "Let's not do a knee-jerk reaction."

Leahy thought he could serve as a bridge between privacy advocates and the government. He was trusted by civil libertarians, but had a cordial enough relationship with Ashcroft, who was a former Senate colleague. Though Ashcroft was an ardent conservative loathed by many liberals, the two had worked together in Congress on encryption legislation. Even after Leahy voted against Ashcroft's confirmation as attorney general, he called Ashcroft afterward to pledge his cooperation. Since then they'd gotten along fine. In the weeks before September 11, they'd been consulting frequently on a major overhaul of the FBI, which was under fire for bungling a series of high-profile cases.

But the terrorist attacks quickly strained their amicable relations. Within days, Ashcroft held a press conference and called on Congress to approve the Justice Department's legislative plan in a week's time. Leahy was surprised—and irritated. The implication, Leahy says, was "we were going to have another attack if we did not agree to this immediately."

But if he balked, Leahy risked getting hammered as soft on terrorism—or so he and other Democrats feared. Leahy, backed by other Democrats, had begun working on his own anti-terrorism bill, a 165-page tome called the Uniting and Strengthening America Act.

On September 19, congressional, White House and Justice leaders gathered in an ornate room in the Capitol to exchange proposals.

Along with Leahy, Orrin Hatch (R-Utah), Richard Shelby (R-Ala.) and others were there from the Senate. House Majority Leader Richard Armey (R-Tex.), John Conyers Jr. (D-Mich.) and others represented the House. From the White House came counsel Alberto Gonzales. Ashcroft, Dinh and their entourage arrived from Justice.

As the meeting got started, Dinh made a beeline for a seat near the head of the conference table. Leahy and his colleagues raised their eyebrows and shook their heads. Only members of Congress were supposed to sit at the table, one of the senators told Dinh, asking him to sit with the rest of the staff.

Dinh wasn't too troubled by his faux pas. He and his staff were too focused on the 40-page proposal they'd brought with them, the fruit of several all-nighters at Justice. During the crash drafting effort, Dinh had slept on a black leather couch, beneath an American flag, not far from a worn paperback copy of the Federalist Papers.

He handed out copies of his proposal. Leahy did the same with his draft, stressing that he thought the group should move forward deliberately.

It turned out the proposals were similar in some key respects. Both bills called for updates to the pen register and trap and trace laws, clarifying how they applied to e-mail and the Internet. Both included provisions bolstering money-laundering and wiretap laws. They also proposed making it easier for authorities to get approval for wiretaps in spying and counterintelligence cases.

The administration proposal, however, went much farther. It called for indefinite detention of any noncitizen the attorney general "has reason to believe may further or facilitate acts of terrorism," as well as the unrestricted sharing of grand jury and eavesdropping data throughout the government. It permitted Internet service providers or employers to voluntarily allow the FBI to tap e-mail. And it made a small but important modification to the FISA law, changing the legal language so foreign intelligence had to be only "a" purpose of an investigation, rather than "the" purpose, to secure surveillance authority.

Leahy and some of the other lawmakers murmured about those last provisions. Giving criminal investigators unchecked access to FISA powers could break down constitutional safeguards against unreasonable searches and seizures, leading to abuses against U.S. citizens.

Armey, one of the most conservative members in Congress, also expressed concern. It was Armey, in fact, who was already discussing a "sunset" provision to the new law, placing time limits on how long parts of it would remain in effect. A sunset provision would guarantee that some of the most troubling new powers would be revisited by Congress, giving lawmakers an important check on executive authority.

"There were a lot of people in the room, both Republican and Democrat," Leahy says, "who were not about to give the unfettered power the attorney general wanted."

Armey also warned that it might take a few weeks to adopt a bill. In effect, he was urging Ashcroft to back away from his public pressure to approve a law in the next few days.

When the group emerged from the meeting, Ashcroft changed his tone slightly, telling reporters that he wanted to pass a bill as quickly as possible. Leahy likewise struck a conciliatory note.

"We're trying to find a middle ground, and I think we can," he said that day. "We probably agree on more than we disagree on."

But Leahy also made it clear he would not be rushed into approving a bill. "We do not want the terrorists to win by having basic protections taken away from us," he said. It was a boilerplate rendering of a quotation from Benjamin Franklin that Leahy invoked repeatedly: "Those who would give up essential liberty to purchase a little temporary safety deserve neither liberty nor safety."

The truce between Leahy and Ashcroft didn't last long. Despite Ashcroft's shift in tone, the pressure to move quickly on legislation intensified. For Dempsey, it was depressing.

One afternoon in late September, he was invited by Howell, Leahy's adviser, to a legislative briefing. Howell wanted Justice Department officials and civil libertarians to describe to Senate staffers their thoughts about expanding law enforcement authority. The point was to give everyone involved more ideas.

Dempsey was eager to attend. "My hope was there could actually be some sort of debate," he says.

Then the Justice Department folks arrived. Howell hadn't told them they would be discussing their proposals with civil libertarians. "They were livid," Dempsey says. "They explicitly said, 'We don't think outsiders should be here, and we won't talk unless they leave the room.'"

Howell quickly brokered a deal. Dempsey and the other civil liberties advocates could stay to hear Justice's presentation, but there would be no back-and-forth discussion. As soon as the Justice delegation finished speaking about their proposals, "they got up and left," Dempsey says. "I was just in despair. I just thought we are never going to be able to work this out."

At the end of September, Leahy's staff and administration officials spent hours together thrashing out questions about civil liberties, the new police and intelligence powers, and oversight by courts and Congress.

In a push to come to some agreement on the bill's wording, Howell met with White House Deputy Counsel Timothy Flanigan in the Senate Judiciary Committee hearing room. Flanigan was representing the president as well as the attorney general in the negotiations.

Howell and he tangled over whether the law would allow American prosecutors to use evidence from abroad that was obtained through methods illegal in the United States. They also differed over whether a court should serve as a check on the sharing of grand jury, wiretap and other criminal investigative information.

Eventually, Flanigan made some concessions. He agreed that the government would not use evidence about U.S. citizens obtained abroad in an illegal manner under U.S. law, and that a court would review information before it could be shared among intelligence and law enforcement agencies within the United States.

On October 1, Leahy thought he had a final agreement in hand. He was so confident that he stopped by Senate Majority Leader Tom Daschle's office to assure him: "We have it all worked out."

Leahy left the Capitol that evening feeling satisfied. He'd done what he could to protect civil liberties by providing oversight for surveillance and domestic intelligence. But he had also moved quickly to bolster law enforcement and counterintelligence operations. No one could accuse the Democrats of coddling terrorists.

The next morning Leahy sat in his office across a polished wood conference table from Ashcroft, Hatch, Michael Chertoff, chief of the Justice Department's criminal division, and Gonzales, the White House counsel. They'd come together to sign off on the deal. But Ashcroft was having second thoughts about some of Flanigan's concessions. The agreement, he told Leahy, no longer held.

Leahy felt blindsided. He'd invested his prestige in these negotiations, and now it looked like he didn't count. "I said, 'John, when I make an agreement, I make an agreement. I can't believe you're going back on your commitment.'"

Ashcroft's support was critical to the bill's approval. The Senate and Bush administration had agreed to deliver a proposal together, and the process could not go forward without Ashcroft's imprimatur.

Flanigan downplays the dispute, saying it was only one of many disagreements in a tough series of talks that ebbed and flowed.

"There were several points in the negotiations at which they recognized that they had given up too much, and there were other times that we realized we hadn't asked for enough," Flanigan says. "It's understandable. It's the pace of the negotiations.

"You know, there'd be groans around the table and nobody was pleased to see an issue reopened. But I think it all was conducted in a spirit [of] we're all trying to get to a result here."

In any case, there was no hiding the growing animosity between Leahy and the administration. Ashcroft didn't even try. Not long after leaving Leahy's office, Ashcroft held a press conference with Hatch at his side.

"I think it is time for us to be productive on behalf of the American people," said the attorney general. "Talk won't prevent terrorism," Ashcroft said, adding that he was "deeply concerned about the rather slow pace" of the legislation.

"It's a very dangerous thing," Hatch agreed. "It's time to get off our duffs and do what's right."

Leahy was deeply distressed by the collapse of the deal. He felt the administration was intent on steamrolling over him. But there was frustratingly little he could do about it. He didn't even have the political leverage in the Senate to push for the same sunset provision being championed by Armey in the Republican-controlled House. Leahy knew he would have to rely on the House to fight that battle with the administration. He would have to do the same on securing court oversight of the government's new surveillance powers.

Court oversight would be especially important in light of a critical but unheralded portion of the new legislation: Section 215.

For many years, FISA gave investigators access to the commercial records of people under investigation in national security cases, but only from a small range of businesses, including hotels, storage facilities and car rental companies.

Section 215 of the bill would greatly expand that, allowing investigators to obtain records from Internet service providers, grocery stores, libraries, bookstores—just about any business. More importantly, it would remove the requirement that the target of the records search be an agent of a foreign power."

Those changes were significant because of the data-collection revolution of the 1990s. Cheaper computing power and an ever-expanding Internet have enabled businesses to watch what was once unwatchable and glean meaning and profit from the ephemera of daily life. Never before has so much information been collected and parsed about so many of us—often in the name of giving us conveniences, discounts and other benefits.

Someone is likely monitoring us at work, recording what we buy, noting our whereabouts while we use our cell phones, scrutinizing our drug prescriptions. Marketers know our names, addresses, estimated incomes, the size of a family's house, the type of car we drive, the magazines we read, the beer we drink.

Libraries use computers to keep track of what we read. Hotels keep electronic records of when we come and go. Bookstores know what we buy. Many toll roads can say precisely when we have driven by.

The implications of giving the government access to so much personal information unnerved Dempsey and other civil libertarians, who were disappointed that Leahy and his allies couldn't do more to stand up to the administration. While Dempsey understood the political pressures on the senators, he worried that they didn't completely understand some of the compromises they were making.

Leahy was also rueful about the outcome. His bill, introduced in the Senate two days after his acrimonious meeting with Ashcroft, gave Justice much more power than he had originally intended. But he was prepared to swallow hard and support it. To do anything else was politically impossible.

Late on October 11, the Senate assembled to vote. Leahy and Daschle knew every Republican would support the bill. They wanted Democrats to do the same. But Sen. Russell Feingold was refusing to go along.

A liberal who routinely bucks pressure from his own party, the Wisconsin Democrat had deep reservations about the bill hurtling through the Senate. He considered the provisions "some of the most radical changes to law enforcement in a generation" and was particularly worried that Section 215 gave the government way too much power to sift through people's lives. He wanted the Senate to vote on a series of amendments that would do more to protect privacy.

Feingold's stance annoyed Daschle, who cornered him in the back of the Senate floor shortly before the vote. "The bill will only get worse if we open it up to debate," he told Feingold.

Leahy also chimed in, telling Feingold that while he agreed with almost everything Feingold was proposing, the votes simply weren't there. Leahy warned that if Feingold offered amendments, their conservative colleagues would try to give investigators even more extensive powers.

Feingold wouldn't budge.

"There is no doubt," he declared on the Senate floor that evening, "that if we lived in a police state, it would be easier to catch terrorists. If we lived in a country where the police were allowed to search your home at any time for any reason; if we lived in a country where the government was entitled to open your mail, eavesdrop on your phone conversations, or intercept your e-mail communications . . . the government would probably discover and arrest more terrorists, or would-be terrorists . . . But that would not be a country in which we would want to live."

Feingold offered his amendments, and they were rejected. One month after the attacks, the bill passed the Senate, 96-1.

Lawmakers and legislative aides were lining up for nasal swabs and Cipro. Yellow police tape encircled the Hart Senate Office Building. The House had shut down for the first time in memory.

On October 17, the capital was confronting a new threat: anthrax. It was contained in a letter mailed to Daschle, and no one knew how many people might have been exposed. Were there more letters? Were anthrax spores floating through the Capitol's ventilation system? Suddenly, it became more urgent than ever to get the Patriot Act to the president's desk.

Amid the panic, Leahy, Daschle, Flanigan, Dinh and others gathered in House Speaker Dennis Hastert's office to smooth out the differences between the Senate and House versions of the bill. The House bill, which passed in the early morning hours of October 12, included sunset and court-oversight provisions Leahy had been unable to get in the Senate.

There was no longer any question that the Patriot Act would include some court oversight, though not as much as Leahy and Armey wanted. The key issue remaining for those in Hastert's office was how long the new law should be in effect. Leahy and Armey pressed for a four-year "sunset," which would force the White House to win congressional approval of the most controversial provisions of the law all over again in 2005. The administration wanted no time limit on its effect.

"We're feeling very strongly about the sunsetting," Flanigan told the lawmakers. "This is not a war of a fixed duration. And it will not change the culture of law enforcement and national security if we basically make this a short-term fix."

Daschle, who knew how badly Bush wanted to avoid any delay in signing the legislation, turned to the lawyer and smiled. "Mr. Flanigan, does this mean the president will veto the bill?" he asked.

"And then of course," Flanigan acknowledges now, "I had to say no."

They agreed on four years.

In the year since the Patriot Act was approved, the government has moved quickly to take full advantage of new and existing powers.

More than a thousand noncitizens were detained without being charged last fall, and their identities were kept secret. Hundreds of Muslim men—citizens and noncitizens—were placed under surveillance by federal investigators across the country. Their movements, telephone calls, e-mail, Internet use and credit-card charges are being scrutinized around the clock—a campaign that has resulted in criminal charges against 18 suspected al Qaeda operatives near Seattle, Detroit, Buffalo, N.Y., and Portland, Ore.

"We've neutralized a suspected terrorist cell within our borders," Ashcroft announced earlier this month at press conference about the indictments of six in Portland charged with conspiring to aid al Qaeda and the Taliban regime in Afghanistan. He called the indictments "a defining day in America's war against terrorism."

And it's clear that the war is just getting underway. The FBI is still building a data-mining system that will draw in huge amounts of commercial and governmental information and parse it for signs of terrorism. The Transportation Security Administration has begun work on a passenger-profiling system that some officials say would be the largest domestic surveillance system in the nation's history.

All of this makes Viet Dinh smile as he eats curry at a restaurant across from the Justice Department. The Patriot Act, he declares proudly, is making Americans safer, just as intended.

He dismisses criticism that Justice is using a heavy hand in its investigations, and that civil liberties are being compromised. While the government can peer into the lives of Americans as never before, he says, the Constitution is always there as a safeguard.

"It was very clear that we did not tell the American people just simply, trust us, trust law enforcement not to overstep their bounds. Rather we say, trust the law," Dinh says. "The attorney general said very clearly, 'Think outside the box, but not outside the Constitution.'"

Yet at least one federal judge, Gladys Kessler of the U.S. District Court for the District of Columbia, has already accused the government of overstepping its constitutional bounds by refusing to name more than 1,200 people detained since September 11. In response to a lawsuit by civil libertarians, Kessler ordered the Justice Department to release the names, saying that without the information it was impossible to know whether the government is "operating within the bounds of the law."

Kessler's ruling is being appealed by the government, which argues that the secrecy is necessary to avoid compromising its investigation into September 11 and future terror plots. The Justice Department is also challenging an extraordinary decision by the FISA court not to grant criminal investigators the authority to use FISA primarily for criminal prosecutions. The FISA court said earlier this year that, long before September 11, the government had misused the law and misled the court dozens of times in its requests for search warrants and wiretaps. Those warrants and wiretaps might not have been granted in criminal courts, which, unlike FISA, require evidence of probable cause. And if the FISA court won't let criminal investigators make wide use of FISA powers, the Patriot Act won't provide as much investigative muscle as the administration wants.

That would be just fine with Dempsey, who argues that the government already had all the power and information it needed to thwart terrorist attacks before September 11 and failed to make effective use of them.

Now, he says, "we are facing the risk of a fundamental redefinition of the role of government and the freedom of individuals . . . Look at this ocean of information that's available."

In his downtown office, he clacks away at the computer, drafting a legal brief in support of the FISA court's position on limiting the flow of information between intelligence and criminal investigators. The federal courts are the next battleground, Dempsey and other civil libertarians believe, in the clash between national security and privacy rights.

For Leahy, however, the battleground remains the Senate Judiciary Committee, where he and other panel members will be responsible for monitoring how the Justice Department uses its new powers. That won't be easy, given the secrecy involved in terrorism investigations and the administration's reluctance to share sensitive information with Congress. Even so, Leahy and his allies in the House and Senate have no intention of giving Justice a free ride on the Patriot Act. The potential for abuse is too great, they say, and the need for congressional oversight and scrutiny too strong. They'll be watching.

139. John Ashcroft, "Testimony before the Senate Judiciary Committee"

(2001)

In a scene reminiscent of J. Edgar Hoover's appearances before Cold War-era congressional committees, United States Attorney General John Ashcroft here updates the Senate Judiciary Committee on the continuing threat of terrorism following the September 11, 2001, attacks on New York and Washington. Raised in Springfield, Missouri, Ashcroft (1942–) graduated from Yale University and the University of Chicago School of Law. In Missouri, he served as state auditor, attorney general, and governor before being elected to the United States Senate in 1994. In 2000, he lost his bid for reelection even though his opponent, Governor Mel Carnahan, died in a plane crash two weeks before the election. Six weeks later, President-elect George W. Bush chose Ashcroft as his attorney general. This testimony before the Senate Judiciary Committee is notable for Ashcroft's characterization of the terrorist enemy as well as his defense of Justice Department methods in seeking out terrorists. In particular, the attorney general brands critics of the USA PATRIOT Act, which gave sweeping investigative powers to the executive branch, as aiding the terrorists.

SOURCE: Testimony of Attorney General John Ashcroft: Senate Committee on the Judiciary, December 6, 2001, http://www.usdoj.gov/archive/ag/testimony/2001/1206transcriptsenatejudiciarycommittee.htm.

Mr. Chairman, Senator Hatch, members of the Judiciary Committee, thank you for this opportunity to testify today. It is a pleasure to be back in the United States Senate.

On the morning of September 11, as the United States came under attack, I was in an airplane with several members of the Justice Department en route to Milwaukee, in the skies over the Great Lakes. By the time we could return to Washington, thousands of people had been murdered at the World Trade Center. 189 were dead at the Pentagon. Forty-four had crashed to the ground in Pennsylvania. From that moment, at the command of the President of the United

States, I began to mobilize the resources of the Department of Justice toward one single, over-arching and over-riding objective: to save innocent lives from further acts of terrorism.

America's campaign to save innocent lives from terrorists is now 87 days old. It has brought me back to this committee to report to you in accordance with Congress's oversight role. I welcome this opportunity to clarify for you and the American people how the Justice Department is working to protect American lives while preserving American liberties.

Since those first terrible hours of September 11, America has faced a choice that is as stark as the images that linger of that morning. One option is to call September 11 a fluke, to believe it could never happen again, and to live in a dream world that requires us to do nothing differently. The other option is to fight back, to summon all our strength and all our resources and devote ourselves to better ways to identify, disrupt and dismantle terrorist networks.

Under the leadership of President Bush, America has made the choice to fight terrorism—not just for ourselves but for all civilized people. Since September 11, through dozens of warnings to law enforcement, a deliberate campaign of terrorist disruption, tighter security around potential targets, and a preventative campaign of arrest and detention of lawbreakers, America has grown stronger—and safer—in the face of terrorism.

Thanks to the vigilance of law enforcement and the patience of the American people, we have not suffered another major terrorist attack. Still, we cannot—we must not—allow ourselves to grow complacent. The reasons are apparent to me each morning. My day begins with a review of the threats to Americans and American interests that were received in the previous 24 hours. If ever there were proof of the existence of evil in the world, it is in the pages of these reports. They are a chilling daily chronicle of hatred of America by fanatics who seek to extinguish freedom, enslave women, corrupt education and to kill Americans wherever and whenever they can.

The terrorist enemy that threatens civilization today is unlike any we have ever known. It slaughters thousands of innocents—a crime of war and a crime against humanity. It seeks weapons of mass destruction and threatens their use against America. No one should doubt the intent, nor the depth, of its consuming, destructive hatred.

Terrorist operatives infiltrate our communities—plotting, planning and waiting to kill again. They enjoy the benefits of our free society even as they commit themselves to our destruction. They exploit our openness—not randomly or haphazardly—but by deliberate, premeditated design.

This is a seized al Qaeda training manual—a "how-to" guide for terrorists—that instructs enemy operatives in the art of killing in a free society. Prosecutors first made this manual public in the trial of the al Qaeda terrorists who bombed U.S. embassies in Africa. We are posting several al Qaeda lessons from this manual on our website today so Americans can know our enemy.

In this manual, al Qaeda terrorists are told how to use America's freedom as a weapon against us. They are instructed to use the benefits of a free press—newspapers, magazines and broadcasts—to stalk and kill their victims. They are instructed to exploit our judicial process for the success of their operations. Captured terrorists are taught to anticipate a series of questions from authorities and, in each response, to lie—to lie about who they are, to lie about what they are doing and to lie about who they know in order for the operation to achieve its objective. Imprisoned terrorists are instructed to concoct stories of torture and mistreatment at the hands of our officials. They are directed to take advantage of any contact with the outside world to, quote, "communicate with brothers outside prison and exchange information that may be helpful to them in their work. The importance of mastering the art of hiding messages is self-evident here."

Mr. Chairman and members of the committee, we are at war with an enemy who abuses individual rights as it abuses jet airliners: as weapons with which to kill Americans. We have responded by redefining the mission of the Department of Justice. Defending our nation and its citizens against terrorist attacks is now our first and overriding priority.

We have launched the largest, most comprehensive criminal investigation in world history to identify the killers of September 11 and to prevent further terrorist attacks. Four thousand FBI agents are engaged with their international counterparts in an unprecedented worldwide effort to detect, disrupt and dismantle terrorist organizations.

We have created a national task force at the FBI to centralize control and information sharing in our investigation. This task force has investigated hundreds of thousands of leads, conducted over 500 searches, interviewed thousands of witnesses and obtained numerous court-authorized surveillance orders. Our prosecutors and agents have collected information and evidence from countries throughout Europe and the Middle East.

Immediately following the September 11 attacks, the Bureau of Prisons acted swiftly to intensify security precautions in connection with all al Qaeda and other terrorist inmates, increasing perimeter security at a number of key facilities.

We have sought and received additional tools from Congress. Already, we have begun to utilize many of these tools. Within hours of passage of the USA PATRIOT Act, we made use of its provisions to begin enhanced information sharing between the law-enforcement and intelligence communities. We have used the provisions allowing nationwide search warrants for e-mail and subpoenas for payment information. And we have used the Act to place those who access the Internet through cable companies on the same footing as everyone else.

Just yesterday, at my request, the State Department designated 39 entities as terrorist organizations pursuant to the USA PATRIOT Act.

We have waged a deliberate campaign of arrest and detention to remove suspected terrorists who violate the law from our streets. Currently, we have brought criminal charges against 110 individuals, of whom 60 are in federal custody. The INS has detained 563 individuals on immigration violations.

We have investigated more than 250 incidents of retaliatory violence and threats against Arab Americans, Muslim Americans, Sikh Americans and South Asian Americans.

Since September 11, the Customs Service and Border Patrol have been at their highest state of alert. All vehicles and persons entering the country are subjected to the highest level of scrutiny. Working with the State Department, we have imposed new screening requirements on certain applicants for non-immigrant visas. At the direction of the President, we have created a Foreign Terrorist Tracking Task Force to ensure that we do everything we can to prevent terrorists from entering the country, and to locate and remove those who already have.

We have prosecuted to the fullest extent of the law individuals who waste precious law enforcement resources through anthrax hoaxes.

We have offered non-citizens willing to come forward with valuable information a chance to live in this country and one day become citizens.

We have forged new cooperative agreements with Canada to protect our common borders and the economic prosperity they sustain.

We have embarked on a wartime reorganization of the Department of Justice. We are transferring resources and personnel to the field offices where citizens are served and protected. The INS is being restructured to better perform its service and border security responsibilities. Under Director Bob Mueller, the FBI is undergoing an historic reorganization to put the prevention of terrorism at the center of its law enforcement and national security efforts.

Outside Washington, we are forging new relationships of cooperation with state and local law enforcement.

We have created 93 Anti-Terrorism Task Forces—one in each U.S. Attorney's district—to integrate the communications and activities of local, state and federal law enforcement.

In all these ways and more, the Department of Justice has sought to prevent terrorism with reason, careful balance and excruciating attention to detail. Some of our critics, I regret to say, have shown less affection for detail. Their bold declarations of so-called fact have quickly dissolved, upon inspection, into vague conjecture. Charges of "kangaroo courts" and "shredding the Constitution" give new meaning to the term, "the fog of war."

Since lives and liberties depend upon clarity, not obfuscation, and reason, not hyperbole, let me take this opportunity today to be clear: Each action taken by the Department of Justice, as well as the war crimes commissions considered by the President and the Department of Defense, is carefully drawn to target a narrow class of individuals—terrorists. Our legal powers are targeted at terrorists. Our investigation is focused on terrorists. Our prevention strategy targets the terrorist threat.

Since 1983, the United States government has defined terrorists as those who perpetrate premeditated, politically motivated violence against noncombatant targets. My message to America this morning, then, is this: If you fit this definition of a terrorist, fear the United States, for you will lose your liberty.

We need honest, reasoned debate; not fearmongering. To those who pit Americans against immigrants, and citizens against non-citizens; to those who scare peace-loving people with phantoms of lost liberty; my message is this: Your tactics only aid terrorists—for they erode our national unity and diminish our resolve. They give ammunition to America's enemies, and pause to America's friends. They encourage people of good will to remain silent in the face of evil.

Our efforts have been carefully crafted to avoid infringing on constitutional rights while saving American lives. We have engaged in a deliberate campaign of arrest and detention of law breakers. All persons being detained have the right to contact their lawyers and their families. Out of respect for their privacy, and concern for saving lives, we will not publicize the names of those detained.

We have the authority to monitor the conversations of 16 of the 158,000 federal inmates and their attorneys because we suspect that these communications are facilitating acts of terrorism. Each prisoner has been told in advance his conversations will be monitored. None of the information that is protected by attorney-client privilege may be used for prosecution. Information will only be used to stop impending terrorist acts and save American lives.

We have asked a very limited number of individuals—visitors to our country holding passports from countries with active Al Qaeda operations—to speak voluntarily to law enforcement. We are forcing them to do nothing. We are merely asking them to do the right thing: to willingly disclose information they may have of terrorist threats to the lives and safety of all people in the United States.

Throughout all our activities since September 11, we have kept Congress informed of our continuing efforts to protect the American people. Beginning with a classified briefing by Director Mueller and me on the very evening of September 11, the Justice Department has briefed members of the House, the Senate and their staffs on more than 100 occasions.

We have worked with Congress in the belief and recognition that no single branch of government alone can stop terrorism. We have consulted with members out of respect for the separation of powers that is the basis of our system of government. However, Congress' power of oversight is not without limits. The Constitution specifically delegates to the President the authority to "take care that the laws are faithfully executed." And perhaps most importantly, the Constitution vests the President with the extraordinary and sole authority as Commander-in-Chief to lead our nation in times of war.

Mr. Chairman and members of the committee, not long ago I had the privilege of sitting where you now sit. I have the greatest reverence and respect for the constitutional responsibilities you shoulder. I will continue to consult with Congress so that you may fulfill your constitutional responsibilities. In some areas, however, I cannot and will not consult you.

The advice I give to the President, whether in his role as Commander-in-Chief or in any other capacity, is privileged and confidential. I cannot and will not divulge the contents, the context, or even the existence of such advice to anyone—including Congress—unless the President instructs me to do so. I cannot and will not divulge information, nor do I believe that anyone here would wish me to divulge information, that will damage the national security of the United States, the safety of its citizens or our efforts to ensure the same in an on-going investigation.

As Attorney General, it is my responsibility—at the direction of the President—to exercise those core executive powers the Constitution so designates. The law enforcement initiatives undertaken by the Department of Justice, those individuals we arrest, detain or seek to interview, fall under these core executive powers. In addition, the President's authority to establish war-crimes commissions arises out of his power as Commander in Chief. For centuries, Congress has recognized this authority and the Supreme Court has never held that any Congress may limit it.

In accordance with over two hundred years of historical and legal precedent, the executive branch is now exercising its core Constitutional powers in the interest of saving the lives of Americans. I trust that Congress will respect the proper limits of Executive Branch consultation that I am duty-bound to uphold. I trust, as well, that Congress will respect this President's authority to wage war on terrorism and defend our nation and its citizens with all the power vested in him by the Constitution and entrusted to him by the American people.

Thank you.

140. Tom Ridge, "Homeland Security Advisory System Announcement"

(2002)

In this speech, Tom Ridge, the first secretary of the newly formed Department of Homeland Security, announces the unveiling of a national advisory system designed to monitor the terrorist threat level and key it to preventive measures. Ridge (1945–) grew up in Erie, Pennsylvania, and graduated from Harvard University before being drafted into the army. In Vietnam, he was awarded a Bronze Star for valor. He returned from Vietnam to earn his law degree at the Dickinson School of Law and was elected to Congress seven times before being elected governor of Pennsylvania; he served two terms from 1995 to 2001. In October 2001, President Bush chose him to lead the Department of Homeland Security, the motto of which is "Preserving our freedoms, Protecting America." In this speech, reminiscent of Cold War civil defense announcements, Ridge introduces the public to a system of alerts maintained by the department. The idea was to create a common vocabulary of threat conditions and an understanding of the corresponding protective measures likely to be taken by the federal government. Critics charged that the system helped maintain a climate of fear.

SOURCE: "Remarks by Governor Ridge Announcing Homeland Security Advisory System," Department of Homeland Security press release, March 12, 2002, http://www.whitehouse.gov/news/releases/2002/03/20020312–14.html.

Sixty years ago, this building, Constitution Hall, was used by the American Red Cross to help the war effort. It was a time when the civilized world fought enemies bent on our destruction, when civilization itself hung in the balance, when Americans united to support the war effort and took new measures to guard ourselves from attack here at home. In short, a time very much like our own.

We, too, must take new measures to protect our cities, our resources and people from the threat we face today, the threat of terrorism. That is why today we announce the Homeland Security Advisory System. The Homeland Security Advisory System is designed to measure and evaluate terrorist threats and communicate them to the public in a timely manner. It is a national framework; yet it is flexible to apply to threats made against a city, a state, a sector, or an industry. It provides a common vocabulary, so officials from all levels of government can communicate easily with one another and to the public. It provides clear, easy to understand factors which help measure threat.

And most importantly, it empowers government and citizens to take actions to address the threat. For every level of threat, there will be a level of preparedness. It is a system that is equal to the threat.

Here's how it works. The advisory system is based on five threat conditions or five different alerts: low, guarded, elevated, high and severe. They're going to be represented by five colors: green, blue, yellow, orange and red—as you can see by the screen and the graphic to my right and to my left.

Now, the decision to name a threat condition will rest with the Attorney General, after consulting with members of the Homeland Security Council, after consulting with me. He will be responsible for communicating the threat to law enforcement, state and local officials, and the public.

Now, a number of factors will be used to analyze the threat information: Is it credible? Is it a credible source? Have we been able to corroborate this threat? Is it specific as to time or place or method of attack? What are the consequences if the attack is carried out? Can the attack be deterred? Many factors go into the value judgment; many factors go into the assessment of the intelligence.

Now, the American people want to know what is behind these alerts and, to them, perhaps even more importantly, what shall we do in response to them. I believe this system, when in full force and effect, will provide those answers. For the first time, threat conditions will be coupled with protective measures.

Now, for the moment, for the time being, as we are developing this system with our state and local partners, these protective measures will apply solely to the federal government. In time, they will apply to all levels of government, every community, and hopefully, with buy-in from the private sector, the companies in the private sector, as well.

Now, for example, under a guarded or blue condition—that's a general risk of terrorist attack—federal agencies may review and update their emergency response procedures. We want them to test their emergency communication systems. They may also share with the public any information that would strengthen our response.

The next threat condition is yellow or elevated, a significant risk of terrorist attacks. Agencies under yellow condition may increase their surveillance of critical locations, and implement contingency plans where appropriate. Again, we have a level of threat, a level of preparedness, and the recommendation that we give with regard to preparedness is a floor, it's not the ceiling. And this is the same procedure and the same process and engagement that we want the state and local communities to deal with. Take a look at a level of threat, and then assess where your level of preparedness should be. Now, obviously, we're going to be working with the state and local communities in that assessment and in that effort, as well.

Now, presently, the nation currently stands in the yellow condition, in elevated risk. Chances are we will not be able to lower the condition to green until, as the President said yesterday, the terror networks of global reach have been defeated and dismantled. And we are far from being able to predict that day.

And again, this is an information-based system. Based on the information we know—there may be some information and some things going on in the world or in this country that we will know about. But when we get information, and it is credible information, and corroborated, this system will kick into effect.

The fourth is the orange condition, which indicates a very high, high risk of attack. And finally, the red condition, the highest or most severe risk of attack. Under red you might see actions similar to the ones taken on 9/11, when we basically grounded most or all of air traffic for an extended period of time.

We anticipate and hope that businesses and hospitals and schools, even individuals working with their community leaders to develop the local plan, will develop their own protective measures for each threat condition. This system is designed to encourage them to do just that.

The Homeland Security Advisory System also allows us to designate a threat condition for the entire nation or a portion of this country. If we received a credible threat at one of our national monuments, obviously, the Secretary would be very interested in that—it could be designated orange, while the rest of the country remained at yellow. But that would simply mean that the Department of Interior, based on that assessment and the elevation of the risk, would have to elevate or extend the conditions that she had prepared in advance, in response to the higher risk. Again, level of risk, level of preparedness.

Because the threat varies, our system must be versatile and flexible enough to meet it. Now, many states have told us that they are eager to go ahead with their own threat advisory system. States encouraged us to act. And now they have a template to guide their actions. Now, we will not mandate—the federal government cannot mandate the use of this system. As the name implies, it is advisory.

If, for example, governors or mayors choose not to take extra protective measures in face of a credible and specific threat—or conversely, take added measures for a threat that has passed—that is their right. But we are hopeful that with a 45-day review period, when they can take a look at this advisory system and apply it to their communities and to their states, and begin working on the measures that they'll take to protect their communities and states, we will have a national system.

Finally, I think it is very important to underscore—I think the Mayor did it and Jay Stevens did it, and others will—the system will not eliminate risk; no system can. We face an enemy as ruthless and as cunning and as unpredictable as any we have ever faced. Our intelligence may not pick up every threat. And unlike natural disasters, as hurricanes, terrorists can change their patterns and their plans based on our response, based on what they see that we're doing. But the President has certainly pledged to bring every possible human and technological resource to the task of implementing this advisory system.

The Homeland Security Advisory System is designed to encourage partnerships. And this can't be emphasized and reiterated enough. The system is designed to encourage partnerships between the public and the private sectors, between all levels of law enforcement and public safety officials, and between—and among all levels of government.

Our emerging national homeland security strategy will rely on the anti-terrorism plans of all 50 states and the territories. But there are 3,300 counties and parishes, and there are about 18,000 cities. So we all need to work together to coordinate and collaborate our effort to be prepared. Working together is the only way this system will work. It's the only way we can have a national system.

The system is the end result of countless conversations with first responders, local and state officials, business leaders and concerned citizens. And I certainly express our appreciation for their input and their participation. And for the next 45 days, we're going to ask all Americans to comment on this system.

With a Homeland Security Advisory System, we hope to make America safer and more aware. But we also hope to make America better and stronger. Attorney General Ashcroft has said that information is the best friend of prevention. But not just prevention of terrorism, information is also the best friend of crime prevention, fire prevention and disease prevention. It often starts with one doctor, one police officer, one eyewitness. They are America's eyes and ears. And we must work to get that information from the grass roots to government in as quick a time as possible.

Six months after September 11th, our resolve is stronger than ever. Our fight against terrorism is making real progress on both fronts, thanks to the leadership of our President, the strong bipartisan support of these initiatives in Congress, and the extraordinary work that our military has done overseas.

However, we should not expect a V-T day, a victory over terrorism day anytime soon. But that does not mean Americans are powerless against the threat. On the contrary, ladies and gentlemen, we are more powerful than the terrorists. We can fight them not just with conventional arms, but with information and expertise and common sense; with freedom and openness and truth; with partnerships born from our cooperation. If we do, then like the men and women who fought Nazism and Fascism 60 years ago, our outcome will be equally certain: victory for America, and safety for Americans.

141. U.S. Department of Justice, Office of Legal Counsel, "Memorandum for Alberto R. Gonzales, Counsel to the President"

(2002)

This excerpt is the introduction to a fifty-page memorandum, most often referred to as the "torture memo." Generated by the Office of Legal Counsel (OLC), and generally credited to John Yoo and Jay Bybee, the memo was used ostensibly to provide legal cover for interrogation techniques being used on detainees held at Guantanamo Bay, Cuba, and elsewhere. Yoo graduated from Harvard in 1989 and from Yale Law School in 1992 before becoming a law professor at the University of California at Berkeley in 1993. He also clerked for Supreme Court Justice Clarence Thomas and served for one year as general counsel to the Senate Judiciary Committee before being named deputy assistant attorney general in the Office of Legal Counsel in 2001. Yoo's boss, Assistant Attorney General Bybee, graduated from Brigham Young University and its law school, and later took faculty posts at the Louisiana State University and University of Nevada, Las Vegas law schools. He served in the Office of Legal Counsel from 2001 until his confirmation as a federal judge on the United States Court of Appeals for the Ninth Circuit in 2003. Never before this memo was written had the executive branch defined torture so narrowly, nor had it asserted that Congress had no place in regulating interrogation tactics. In June 2004, the OLC, under new leadership, withdrew the torture memo but was careful to state that interrogators had not been committing illegal acts. In 2005, faced with the passage of the Detainee Treatment Act prohibiting "cruel, inhuman, and degrading treatment or punishment," the OLC issued new memoranda which again authorized tactics such as waterboarding as legal; only conduct that "shocks the conscience" could be regarded as unconstitutional, it said.

SOURCE: Reprinted in Karen J. Greenberg and Joshua L. Dratel, *The Torture Papers: The Road to Abu Ghraib* (New York: Cambridge University Press, 2005), 172–217.

RE: *Standards of Conduct for Interrogation under 18 U.S.C. §§2340–2340A*

You have asked for our Office's views regarding the standards of conduct under the Convention Against Torture and Other Cruel, Inhuman and Degrading Treatment or Punishment as implemented by Sections 2340–2340A of title 18 of the United States Code. As we understand it, this question has arisen in the context of the conduct of interrogations outside of the United States. We conclude below that Section 2340A proscribes acts inflicting, and that are specifically intended to inflict, severe pain or suffering, whether mental or physical. Those acts must be of an extreme nature to rise to the level of torture within the meaning of Section 2340A and the Convention. We further conclude that certain acts may be cruel, inhuman, or degrading, but still not produce pain and suffering of the requisite intensity to fall within Section 2340A's proscription against torture. We conclude by examining possible defenses that would negate any claim that certain interrogation methods violate the statute.

In Part I, we examine the criminal statute's text and history. We conclude that for an act to constitute torture as defined in Section 2340, it must inflict pain that is difficult to endure. Physical pain amounting to torture must be equivalent in intensity to the pain accompanying serious physical injury, such as organ failure, impairment of bodily function, or even death. For purely mental pain or suffering to amount to torture under Section 2340, it must result in significant psychological harm of significant duration, e.g., lasting for months or even years. We conclude that the mental harm also must result from one of the predicate acts listed in the statute, namely: threats of imminent death; threats of infliction of the kind of pain that would amount to physical torture; infliction of such physical pain as a means of psychological torture; use of drugs or other procedures designed to deeply disrupt the senses, or fundamentally alter an individual's personality; or threatening to do any of these things to a third party. The legislative history simply reveals that Congress intended for the statute's definition to track the Convention's definition of torture and the reservations, understandings, and declarations that the United States submitted with its ratification. We conclude that the statute, taken as a whole, makes plain that it prohibits only extreme acts.

In Part II, we examine the text, ratification history, and negotiating history of the Torture Convention. We conclude that the treaty's text prohibits only the most extreme acts by reserving criminal penalties solely for torture and declining to require such penalties for "cruel, inhuman, or degrading treatment or punishment." This confirms our view that the criminal statute penalizes only the most egregious conduct. Executive branch interpretations and representations to the Senate at the time of ratification further confirm that the treaty was intended to reach only the most extreme conduct.

In Part III, we analyze the jurisprudence of the Torture Victims Protection Act, 28 U.S.C. § 1350 note (2000), which provides civil remedies for torture victims, to predict the standards that courts might follow in determining what actions reach the threshold of torture in the criminal context. We conclude from these cases that courts are likely to take a totality-of-the-circumstances approach, and will look to an entire course of conduct, to determine whether certain acts will violate Section 2340A. Moreover, these cases demonstrate that most often torture involves cruel and extreme physical pain. In Part IV, we examine international decisions regarding the use of sensory deprivation techniques. These cases make clear that while many of these techniques may amount to cruel, inhuman or degrading treatment, they do not produce pain or suffering of the necessary intensity to meet the definition of torture. From these decisions, we conclude that there is a wide range of such techniques that will not rise to the level of torture.

In Part V, we discuss whether Section 2340A may be unconstitutional if applied to interrogations undertaken of enemy combatants pursuant to the President's Commander-in-Chief powers. We find that in the circumstances of the current war against al Qaeda and its allies, prosecution under Section 2340A may be barred because enforcement of the statute would represent an unconstitutional infringement of the President's authority to conduct war. In Part VI, we discuss defenses to an allegation that an interrogation method might violate the statute. We conclude that, under the current circumstances, necessity or self-defense may justify interrogation methods that might violate Section 2340A.

142. Deborah Caldwell, "How Islam-Bashing Got Cool"

(2002)

This article by Deborah Caldwell reveals how some Americans moved from blaming the terrorists for the 9/11 attacks to blaming Islam. Caldwell is a senior editor at Beliefnet, a "multifaith source for religion, spirituality, and inspiration" on the Internet. Formerly, she held the post of senior writer at the *Dallas Morning News*, and she has written for the *New York Times, Slate,* and other publications. This article won first place for opinion writing in the American Academy of Religion's In-Depth Reporting Awards. Only one year after the terrorist attacks, Caldwell reports on the surge in anti-Islamic sentiment not only among evangelical Christian leaders, but also among many other Americans; for President Bush, who discouraged such sentiment in the weeks after the attacks, the change in climate presented a difficult political dilemma.

SOURCE: Beliefnet, http://www.beliefnet.com/story/110/story_11074_1.html.

In the last six weeks, a major Protestant leader has described the Prophet Muhammad as "demon-possessed pedophile;" a well-known conservative columnist suggested that Muslims get "some sort of hobby other than slaughtering infidels;" the head of a conservative activist group suggested American Muslims should leave the country; and evangelist Franklin Graham described Islam as inherently violent.

Meanwhile, the University of North Carolina is being sued by the Family Policy Network, a conservative group, for asking incoming freshmen to read a book called "Approaching the Qur'an: The Early Revelations," an assignment Fox News Network's Bill O'Reilly compared to teaching Hitler's "Mein Kampf" in 1941. On Wednesday, a North Carolina state legislator told a local radio station his view: "I don't want the students in the university system required to study this evil."

Islam-bashing, it appears, is suddenly not just acceptable, but almost fashionable among conservatives. This isn't a matter of commentators criticizing Muslim extremists. These are remarks that attack Islam, Muslims, the Qur'an, and the Prophet Muhammad as pervasively and inherently bad.

President Bush's repeated attempts since Sept. 11 to describe Islam as a "religion of peace" initially helped quell anti-Muslim rhetoric. But now, conservatives seem to be increasingly ignoring Bush's approach. "The White House has lost control of the issue," says John Green, an expert on religion and politics at University of Akron. "Islam bashing has become more public, and it seems to be more accepted."

And there is a limit, Green notes, to how vehemently Bush is likely to disagree with these conservatives and Christians, since they make up his political base.

The latest round began in June, when the Rev. Jerry Vines, the former president of the Southern Baptist Convention—the nation's largest Protestant denomination, with 15 million members—described Islam's founder as a "demon possessed pedophile." Vines, pastor of the 25,000-member First Baptist Church in Jacksonville, Fla., added that "Allah is not Jehovah either. Jehovah's not going to turn you into a terrorist that'll try to bomb people and take the lives of thousands and thousands of people." Days later, the SBC's current president, the Rev. Jack Graham, pastor of the 20,000-member Prestonwood Baptist Church in Plano, Texas, agreed with Vines.

Ari Fleischer, the President's spokesman, was compelled to differ with the SBC leaders, even though in remarks to the convention a day after Vines' comment, Bush praised Baptists for being "among the earliest champions of religious tolerance." Of the Muhammad comment, Fleischer said: "It's something that the president definitely disagrees with. Islam is a religion of peace, that's what the president believes."

A week after Fleischer's remarks, the hugely popular televangelist Benny Hinn said during an appearance at a Dallas arena: "This is not a war between Arabs and Jews. It's a war between God and the devil."

Evangelical Christians have always believed that Islam is a wrong religion, and refuse to accept Allah as the same as the Christian God. Conservative Christians actively proselytize among Muslims in this country and abroad. But lately, many Christian commentators are pushing these views in broader, secular formats.

Shortly after the attacks, Franklin Graham was forced to apologize for describing Islam as a "Wicked, violent religion." But in his new book, "The Name," released Monday, he writes: "Islam—unlike Christianity—has among its basic teachings a deep intolerance for those who follow other faiths." On Fox News Network's "Hannity & Colmes" program this week, Graham said: "I think it's [terrorism] more mainstream. And it's not just a handful of extremists. If you buy the Qur'an, read it for yourself, and it's in there. The violence that it preaches is there."

Hannity responded: "But this then raises a question. If this is not, Reverend, the extremist fanatical interpretation of the Quran, then we do have a big

problem." Graham replied: "Big problem." This week, in an interview with Beliefnet he reiterated his opinion, saying, "I believe the Qur'an teaches violence,
not peace."

At the Christian Booksellers' Association meeting in Anaheim last month, re-
tailers sold an array of books and tapes describing Islam as a violent religion—
and many of these books will be marketed not just in Christian bookstores, but
also in malls nationwide. For instance, Hal Lindsey author of the 1970s best-
seller, "The Late Great Planet Earth," has come out with a new book called "The
Everlasting Hatred: The Roots of Jihad." Titles by other authors include "Religion
of Peace, or Refuge of Terror," "War on Terror: Unfolding Bible Prophecy," and
"Islam and Terrorism." Among the tapes available was "Terrorism: The New War
on Freedom."

But it's not just Christians. Soon after Vines' comments, a new cascade of
public anti-Muslim comments poured forth.

In a late June interview with NBC's Katie Couric, columnist Ann Coulter said
of Muslims: "I think it might be a good idea to get them on some sort of hobby
other than slaughtering infidels." That comment followed Coulter's comments
about Muslims last September: "We should invade their countries, kill their
leaders, and convert them to Christianity."

Last month, William Lind of the Free Congress Foundation suggested that "Islam is, quite simply, a religion of war," and that American Muslims "should be
encouraged to leave. They are a fifth column in this country."

Also in July, a Secret Service agent admitted scrawling "Islam is Evil" and
"Christ is King" on a Muslim prayer calendar while searching the Michigan home
of a man charged with smuggling bogus checks into the United States. The agent
was put on leave pending the investigation, and officials said he could be fired and
face criminal charges. Around the same time, Peter Kirsanow of the U.S. Civil
Rights Commission suggested that another terrorist attack on U.S. soil could stir
public support for ethnicity-based internments as during World War II. "If there's
another terrorist attack and if it's from a certain ethnic community . . . that the
terrorists are from, you can forget about civil rights."

Says Salam Al-Marayati, executive director of the Muslim Public Affairs
Council, a lobbying group: "It is the fad now to bash Islam and Muslims."

As these events unfolded, representatives from the American Muslim Political
Coordinating Council wrote a letter to the President, begging for a meeting with
the Administration. AMPCC, which includes both Democrats and Republicans,
is comprised of representatives of the Muslim Public Affairs Council, the American
Muslim Council, the Council on American-Islamic Relations, and the American Muslim Alliance. Last week, the President's scheduler responded—Bush said
he was too busy to meet, according to Al-Marayati.

"Either there's negligence or deliberate exclusion," says Al-Marayati, a Democratic insider and moderate Muslim. "There needs to be unequivocal denuncia-
tion of these statements. The President needs to make a decision to clear himself
of this kind of vitriol, or basically say he agrees, because I don't think there's any
room for having it two ways on this issue."

Of course, whenever an Administration loses control of an issue, it's not good news for a President. But usually, "losing control of an issue" means an Administration is losing traction as a President moves ahead with policies, or has lost control of a legislative agenda.

The problem for this Administration is that Islam is a much bigger issue. "It is really a different thing because the President can't control the agenda the same way," Green says. "What the President wanted to do after Sept. 11 was persuade Americans, particularly conservatives, to behave themselves and be civil and restrained about Islam because our domestic and foreign policy is very delicate right now. Here we are making war on Afghanistan and talking about making war on Iraq, so it's important to make a distinction between terrorists who happen to be Muslims, and Islam," Green says. "Having a positive rhetoric on Islam is pretty important."

American Muslims say they're feeling the change in Americans' attitude toward their faith in the last year. After Sept. 11, most Americans swallowed hard and—with President Bush leading the way—decided that anti-Muslim bigotry was wrong. During the fall, he repeatedly called Islam a "peaceful religion," hosted a Ramadan dinner at the White House, and described the Muslim scripture as the "holy" Qur'an.

"That helped to tone down a lot of the animosity," says Hodan Hassan, communications coordinator for the Council on American-Islamic Relations, a Washington lobbying group. "But now, when you have the ratcheting-up of anti-Islam rhetoric and a continuing state of alert and continual warnings from the FBI about Muslim terrorists—that combination is worrying for us. When you dehumanize a whole sector of society, it's a lot easier to lash out."

Until recently, CAIR members handled the backlash with letter-writing campaigns or by asking media outlets or commentators to retract comments Muslims perceived as unfair. Now, Hassan says, the anti-Islam fervor is too widespread to deal with.

"It seems to have gone beyond the evangelical sector and to some of the political commentators," she says. "We routinely get emails from Muslims around the country complaining about their local talk radio basically demonizing Islam. That's been worrying. What's new is the viciousness of it and the fact that it's spreading to relatively well-established leaders."

Asma Gull Hasan, author of "American Muslims: The New Generation," says she's noticing an uptick in hate mail at her website these days. Some are from evangelical Christians, but many are what she calls "live free or die" Americans— secular conservatives who believe all Muslims are inherently anti-American.

"There's really no convincing any of these people," says Hasan, who appears frequently on cable and radio talk shows. "It's pretty nasty email. There's definitely a movement happening."

Hasan traces the upsurge in anti-Islam rhetoric to the escalation of the war in Israel.

"From the beginning, the evangelicals didn't like the things Bush said about Islam, and talk show conservatives didn't either. But when the Middle East violence happened, they felt they could connect it all together," she says. "It made it very easy for people to make a neat parallel that we were attacked by suicide bombers, and Israel was, too."

Hasan says she has appeared numerous times recently on talk radio shows where the interviewer says the purpose is to teach the audience about Islam. "Then I get on and it's a blood bath," she says. And the rhetoric has ratcheted up in recent weeks, Hasan says.

Last week on a Denver radio show, for instance, the interviewer asked Hasan if she is a Muslim first or an American first, and she said she is both. Soon after, a caller said he is Catholic first and that being American is a distant second. Hasan said she then asked the caller to give an example of ways his religion conflicts with being American. His response was that he wants to be able to protest peacefully at abortion clinics; the host asked if he would blow up a clinic. And the caller said yes, if he thought it would do more good than harm.

"Can you imagine if a Muslim said such a thing?" Hasan wonders.

The problem, say Muslims like Hasan, is that moderate voices like hers aren't heard enough. That seems to be the viewpoint of the Bush Administration, even if the White House isn't meeting with American Muslim leaders. Richard Land, a prominent Southern Baptist with close ties to the Administration, says "one of our basic strategies should be to damage the radical [Muslim] voices and support the moderate voices. . . . My perspective is that the President did what he probably had to do in the wake of Sept. 11. He grew up coming to understand what happened to Japanese-Americans after Pearl Harbor and not wanting that to happen again."

Land says he doesn't disapprove so far of Bush's stance toward Muslims.

"He's supposed to be President of all the people," Land says. "As far as I'm concerned, what he's done to date has not been a problem. But I'm afraid that his comment that Islam is a religion of peace is more a wish than a fact. I don't think evangelicals are very happy about it, but there are so many other things they are happy about. Now, if he started showing up at worship services at mosques that would be another thing."

Green says Bush remains in a tricky political position with conservatives for the foreseeable future.

"To the extent that this grousing becomes common, this presents a problem for the President with the war on terrorism," Green says. "It's important for him to maintain this distinction between Islam and terrorism. If a very important part of his political base equates them, that makes the President's job very difficult."

And Bush can't exactly repudiate conservatives, because he needs them politically.

"It may have been that these people were held in check by the President's request that they behave themselves [early on]. I suppose you could fault Bush to some extent" for not keeping the lid on the dissent, Green says.

And here, he repeats what most Americans, at heart, believe: Sure, there are legitimate religious differences between various faiths, but the genius of the

United States is that we tolerate each other. And so, Green says, if we're going to deal with terrorism and threats to our freedom, people who hate each other's beliefs in this country are simply going to have to make an effort to understand each other.

And in the end, that means they're going to have to put up with Islam, and with American Muslims—whether they like it or not.

143. Sleater-Kinney, "Combat Rock"

(2002)

In "Combat Rock," Portland, Oregon–based indie-rock band Sleater-Kinney criticizes the climate of war without end and the stifling of dissent. Formed by Carrie Brownstein and Corin Tucker in Olympia, Washington, in 1994, Sleater-Kinney came out of the Pacific Northwest's riot grrrl tradition and garnered attention for its passionate politics and intense sound. The band's third album, *Dig Me Out* (1997), recorded with new drummer Janet Weiss, established Sleater-Kinney as one of the most influential indie-rock bands. "Combat Rock" appears on *One Beat*, an album especially influenced by the political climate of late 2001. The song critiques the wartime emphasis on unity with almost every verse and, among other points, mocks the patriotic prescription of shopping as a way to support one's country.

SOURCE: Sleater-Kinney, *One Beat* (Kill Rock Stars 387, 2002).

> They tell us there are only two sides to be on
> If you are on our side you're right if not you're wrong
> But are we innocent, paragons of good?
> Is our guilt eased by the pain that we've endured?
>
> Hey look it's time to pledge allegiance
> Oh god I love my dirty Uncle Sam
> Our country's marching to the beat now
> And we must learn to step in time
>
> Where is the questioning where is the protest song?
> Since when is skepticism un-American?
> Dissent's not treason but they act like it's the same
> Those who disagree are afraid to show their face
>
> Let's break out our old machines now
> It sure is good to see them run again

Oh gentlemen start your engines
And we know where we get the oil from

Are you feeling alright now
Paint myself all red white blue
Are you singing let's fight now
Innocent people die, uh oh
There are reasons to unite
Is this why we unite?
If you hate this time
Remember we are the time!

Show you love your country go out and spend some cash
Red white blue hot pants doing it for Uncle Sam
Flex our muscles show them we're stronger than the rest
Raise your hands up baby are you sure that we're the best?

We'll come out with our fists raised
The good old boys are back on top again
And if we let them lead us blindly
The past becomes the future once again

CHAPTER THIRTEEN

The Bush Wars, Part II: Protest and Sacrifice

144. Leslie Cagan, "United for Peace and Justice Statement on the Iraq War"

(2003)

In this statement, the United for Peace and Justice (UFPJ) co-chair, Leslie Cagan, critiques President George W. Bush on the eve of the second Iraq War. A child of activists, Cagan (1947–) grew up in New York City, earned a degree in art history from New York University, and immediately began a forty-year career in activism. In October 2002, as the Bush administration laid out its plans for an invasion of Iraq, Cagan became co-chair of United for Peace and Justice, then a coalition of more than seventy antiwar groups (in time it grew to more than 1,400 organizations). On February 15, 2003, UFPJ helped coordinate the protests of millions of people in more than 750 locations worldwide. On March 22, 2003, in response to this call, some 300,000 marched in New York City.

SOURCE: "Statement by Leslie Cagan, Co-chair—United for Peace and Justice," March 18, 2003, http://www.unitedforpeace.org/article.php?id=1404.

Last night President George Bush spoke to the people of this country and the world. With no shame, with no regret, with no hesitation he announced his plans to wage war against Iraq. George Bush said that Saddam Hussein and his sons must leave their country by Wednesday night, or else the full weight of the U.S. military would reign down on the people of Iraq.

Of course, the president did not explain what unleashing the most powerful and deadly armed force in human history will mean to the children of Iraq. He did not speak of the hundreds of thousands of innocent people the UN estimates will die in this attack. He did not speak of the ways the Iraqi people will suffer, or the potential dangers to the young U.S. servicemen and women already in the region. He did not mention the devastation and horror of war or its impact on our own lives here at home.

Instead the president lied. He claimed that every measure has been taken to avoid war (a blatant lie), spoke of the broad coalition he has gathered (a joke), and asserted this war is to defend us from imminent danger (completely fabricated).

The people of this nation do not want war, as has been expressed by the millions who have marched in the streets, passed resolutions in their city councils and trade unions, lobbied their elected officials and in countless other ways have cried out for peace. And on this Saturday, March 22nd, the people of New York City will again gather in large numbers as we march through the heart of Manhattan demanding an end to the war the Bush administration will most likely have begun.

We will not be intimidated by their repressive homeland security nor by their fighter planes flying in the skies above. We will not be silenced by their claims that this war is being fought to free the Iraqi people. We will not be fooled by their assertions that all they seek is the disarming of weapons of mass destruction when we know full well the issue is access to and control of oil and the expansion of empire.

We fully support the dismantling of all weapons of mass destruction, in Iraq, in the region and throughout the world—including those stockpiled right here at home. As New Yorkers we know all too well the horror of terrorism, and are committed to ensuring that our tax dollars are not used in our names to kill Iraqi civilians.

Bush, Cheney, Rumsfeld, Powell, Ashcroft and the rest of the president's gang will only be stopped by the force of a non-violent global movement.

President Bush's announcement of war does not deter us but rather reinforces our commitment to use every creative ounce of energy to stop this war.

Last month the New York City Police Department, the Mayor and the federal courts told us we did not have a right to march peacefully in the streets of our city. They did everything they could to undermine our protest and create confusion. But on February 15th 500,000 people, in one clear voice, said no to war.

Today, in response to President Bush, we again prepare to gather in large numbers and demand an end to war against Iraq. We have re-won our right to march in the streets and will exercise that right on Saturday, March 22.

At 12 noon we will gather between 36th Street and 42nd Street, and between Sixth and Seventh Avenues for a march down Broadway, past Union Square, ending at Washington Square Park. In all of our diversity and with all of our strength we will tell the world we truly are a peaceful people.

Thank you.

145. Al Gore, "Freedom and Security: Speech to Moveon.org"

(2003)

In this speech, former vice president Al Gore lays out a detailed critique of the Bush administration's PATRIOT Act–era practices, challenging the notion that in wartime, Americans must be prepared to sacrifice some of their freedoms. The son of Albert Gore Sr., Gore (1948–) was raised in Carthage, Tennessee, and earned a degree in government at Harvard before serving as an army journalist in Vietnam. Following a few years as a journalist in Nashville, Gore served as a U.S. congressman from 1977 to 1985 and as a U.S. senator from 1986 to 1993, when he assumed the office of vice president under President Bill Clinton. In 2000, Gore ran for president and won the popular vote but lost a contested recount in Florida that gave George W. Bush enough electoral votes to win the election. As the Bush administration prepared for war with Iraq, Gore spoke out against the war; in the six months after Bush declared an end to major combat operations in Iraq, Gore grew increasingly pointed in his criticisms of the war and its impact at home. This speech before the antiwar group Moveon.org takes particular aim at both the administration's claim of sweeping executive power in wartime and its propensity for secrecy.

SOURCE: Al Gore, "Freedom and Security: Speech to MoveOn.org," November 9, 2003, DAR Constitution Hall, Washington, D.C. (Widely available on the Internet. See, for example, http://www.commondreams.org/archive/2003/11/10/4488/.)

. . . it seems to me that the logical place to start the discussion is with an accounting of exactly what has happened to civil liberties and security since the vicious attacks against America of September 11, 2001—and it's important to note at the outset that the Administration and the Congress have brought about many beneficial and needed improvements to make law enforcement and intelligence community efforts more effective against potential terrorists.

But a lot of other changes have taken place that a lot of people don't know about and that come as unwelcome surprises. For example, for the first time in our history, American citizens have been seized by the executive branch of government and put in prison without being charged with a crime, without having the right to a trial, without being able to see a lawyer, and without even being able to contact their families.

President Bush is claiming the unilateral right to do that to any American citizen he believes is an "enemy combatant." Those are the magic words. If the President alone decides that those two words accurately describe someone, then that person can be immediately locked up and held incommunicado for as long as the President wants, with no court having the right to determine whether the facts actually justify his imprisonment.

Now if the President makes a mistake, or is given faulty information by somebody working for him, and locks up the wrong person, then it's almost impossible for that person to prove his innocence—because he can't talk to a lawyer or his family or anyone else and he doesn't even have the right to know what specific crime he is accused of committing. So a constitutional right to liberty and the pursuit of happiness that we used to think of in an old-fashioned way as "inalienable" can now be instantly stripped from any American by the President with no meaningful review by any other branch of government.

How do we feel about that? Is that OK?

Here's another recent change in our civil liberties: Now, if it wants to, the federal government has the right to monitor every website you go to on the internet, keep a list of everyone you send email to or receive email from and everyone who you call on the telephone or who calls you—and they don't even have to show probable cause that you've done anything wrong. Nor do they ever have to report to any court on what they're doing with the information. Moreover, there are precious few safeguards to keep them from reading the content of all your email.

Everybody fine with that?

If so, what about this next change?

For America's first 212 years, it used to be that if the police wanted to search your house, they had to be able to convince an independent judge to give them a search warrant and then (with rare exceptions) they had to go bang on your door and yell, "Open up!" Then, if you didn't quickly open up, they could knock the door down. Also, if they seized anything, they had to leave a list explaining what they had taken. That way, if it was all a terrible mistake (as it sometimes is) you could go and get your stuff back.

But that's all changed now. Starting two years ago, federal agents were given broad new statutory authority by the Patriot Act to "sneak and peak" in nonterrorism cases. They can secretly enter your home with no warning—whether you are there or not—and they can wait for months before telling you they were there. And it doesn't have to have any relationship to terrorism whatsoever. It applies to any garden-variety crime. And the new law makes it very easy to get around the need for a traditional warrant—simply by saying that searching your house might have some connection (even a remote one) to the investigation of some agent of a foreign power. Then they can go to another court, a secret court, that more or less has to give them a warrant whenever they ask.

Three weeks ago, in a speech at FBI Headquarters, President Bush went even further and formally proposed that the Attorney General be allowed to authorize subpoenas by administrative order, without the need for a warrant from any court.

What about the right to consult a lawyer if you're arrested? Is that important?

Attorney General Ashcroft has issued regulations authorizing the secret monitoring of attorney-client conversations on his say-so alone; bypassing procedures for obtaining prior judicial review for such monitoring in the rare instances when it was permitted in the past. Now, whoever is in custody has to assume that the government is always listening to consultations between them and their lawyers.

Does it matter if the government listens in on everything you say to your lawyer? Is that Ok?

Or, to take another change—and thanks to the librarians, more people know about this one—the FBI now has the right to go into any library and ask for the records of everybody who has used the library and get a list of who is reading what. Similarly, the FBI can demand all the records of banks, colleges, hotels, hospitals, credit-card companies, and many more kinds of companies. And these changes are only the beginning. Just last week, Attorney General Ashcroft issued brand new guidelines permitting FBI agents to run credit checks and background checks and gather other information about anyone who is "of investigatory interest,"—meaning anyone the agent thinks is suspicious—without any evidence of criminal behavior.

So, is that fine with everyone?

Listen to the way Israel's highest court dealt with a similar question when, in 1999, it was asked to balance due process rights against dire threats to the security of its people:

"This is the destiny of democracy, as not all means are acceptable to it, and not all practices employed by its enemies are open before it. Although a democracy must often fight with one hand tied behind its back, it nonetheless has the upper hand. Preserving the Rule of Law and recognition of an individual's liberty constitutes an important component in its understanding of security. At the end of the day they (add to) its strength."

I want to challenge the Bush Administration's implicit assumption that we have to give up many of our traditional freedoms in order to be safe from terrorists.

Because it is simply not true.

In fact, in my opinion, it makes no more sense to launch an assault on our civil liberties as the best way to get at terrorists than it did to launch an invasion of Iraq as the best way to get at Osama Bin Laden.

In both cases, the Administration has attacked the wrong target.

In both cases they have recklessly put our country in grave and unnecessary danger, while avoiding and neglecting obvious and much more important challenges that would actually help to protect the country.

In both cases, the administration has fostered false impressions and misled the nation with superficial, emotional and manipulative presentations that are not worthy of American Democracy.

In both cases they have exploited public fears for partisan political gain and postured themselves as bold defenders of our country while actually weakening not strengthening America.

In both cases, they have used unprecedented secrecy and deception in order to avoid accountability to the Congress, the Courts, the press and the people.

Indeed, this Administration has turned the fundamental presumption of our democracy on its head. A government of and for the people is supposed to be generally open to public scrutiny by the people—while the private information of the people themselves should be routinely protected from government intrusion.

But instead, this Administration is seeking to conduct its work in secret even as it demands broad unfettered access to personal information about American citizens. Under the rubric of protecting national security, they have obtained new powers to gather information from citizens and to keep it secret. Yet at the same time they themselves refuse to disclose information that is highly relevant to the war against terrorism.

They are even arrogantly refusing to provide information about 9/11 that is in their possession to the 9/11 Commission—the lawful investigative body charged with examining not only the performance of the Bush Administration, but also the actions of the prior Administration in which I served. The whole point is to learn all we can about preventing future terrorist attacks,

Two days ago, the Commission was forced to issue a subpoena to the Pentagon, which has—disgracefully—put Secretary Rumsfeld's desire to avoid embarrassment ahead of the nation's need to learn how we can best avoid future terrorist attacks. The Commission also served notice that it will issue a subpoena to the White House if the President continues to withhold information essential to the investigation.

And the White House is also refusing to respond to repeated bipartisan Congressional requests for information about 9/11—even though the Congress is simply exercising its Constitutional oversight authority. In the words of Senator McCain, "Excessive administration secrecy on issues related to the September 11 attacks feeds conspiracy theories and reduces the public's confidence in government."

In a revealing move, just three days ago, the White House asked the Republican leadership of the Senate to shut down the Intelligence Committee's investigation of 9/11 based on a trivial political dispute. Apparently the President is anxious to keep the Congress from seeing what are said to have been clear, strong and explicit warnings directly to him a few weeks before 9/11 that terrorists were planning to hijack commercial airliners and use them to attack us.

Astonishingly, the Republican Senate leadership quickly complied with the President's request. Such obedience and complicity in what looks like a cover-up from the majority party in a separate and supposedly co-equal branch of government makes it seem like a very long time ago when a Republican Attorney General and his deputy resigned rather than comply with an order to fire the special prosecutor investigating Richard Nixon.

In an even more brazen move, more than two years after they rounded up over 1,200 individuals of Arab descent, they still refuse to release the names of the individuals they detained, even though virtually every one of those arrested has been "cleared" by the FBI of any connection to terrorism and there is absolutely no national security justification for keeping the names secret. Yet at the same time, White House officials themselves leaked the name of a CIA operative serving the country, in clear violation of the law, in an effort to get at her husband, who had angered them by disclosing that the President had relied on forged evidence in his state of the union address as part of his effort to convince the country that Saddam Hussein was on the verge of building nuclear weapons.

And even as they claim the right to see the private bank records of every American, they are adopting a new policy on the Freedom of Information Act that actively encourages federal agencies to fully consider all potential reasons for non-disclosure regardless of whether the disclosure would be harmful. In other words, the federal government will now actively resist complying with ANY request for information.

Moreover, they have established a new exemption that enables them to refuse the release to the press and the public of important health, safety and environmental information submitted to the government by businesses—merely by calling it "critical infrastructure."

By closely guarding information about their own behavior, they are dismantling a fundamental element of our system of checks and balances. Because so long as the government's actions are secret, they cannot be held accountable. A government for the people and by the people must be transparent to the people.

The administration is justifying the collection of all this information by saying in effect that it will make us safer to have it. But it is not the kind of information that would have been of much help in preventing 9/11. However, there was in fact a great deal of specific information that WAS available prior to 9/11 that probably could have been used to prevent the tragedy. A recent analysis by the Merkle foundation, (working with data from a software company that received venture capital from a CIA-sponsored firm) demonstrates this point in a startling way:

- In late August 2001, Nawaq Alhamzi and Khalid Al-Midhar bought tickets to fly on American Airlines Flight 77 (which was flown into the Pentagon). They bought the tickets using their real names. Both names were then on a State Department/INS watch list called TIPOFF. Both men were sought by the FBI and CIA as suspected terrorists, in part because they had been observed at a terrorist meeting in Malaysia.
- These two passenger names would have been exact matches when checked against the TIPOFF list. But that would only have been the first step. Further data checks could then have begun.
- Checking for common addresses (address information is widely available, including on the internet), analysts would have discovered that Salem Al-Hazmi (who also bought a seat on American 77) used the same address

as Nawaq Alhazmi. More importantly, they could have discovered that Mohamed Atta (American 11, North Tower of the World Trade Center) and Marwan Al-Shehhi (United 175, South Tower of the World Trade Center) used the same address as Khalid Al-Midhar.

- Checking for identical frequent flier numbers, analysts would have discovered that Majed Moqed (American 77) used the same number as Al-Midhar.
- With Mohamed Atta now also identified as a possible associate of the wanted terrorist, Al-Midhar, analysts could have added Atta's phone numbers (also publicly available information) to their checklist. By doing so they would have identified five other hijackers (Fayez Ahmed, Mohand Al-shehri, Wail Alsheri, and Abdulaziz Alomari).
- Closer to September 11, a further check of passenger lists against a more innocuous INS watch list (for expired visas) would have identified Ahmed Alghandi. Through him, the same sort of relatively simple correlations could have led to identifying the remaining hijackers, who boarded United 93 (which crashed in Pennsylvania).

In addition, Al-Midhar and Nawaf Alhamzi, the two who were on the terrorist watch list, rented an apartment in San Diego under their own names and were listed, again under their own names, in the San Diego phone book while the FBI was searching for them.

Not to put too fine a point on it, but what is needed is better and more timely analysis. Simply piling up more raw data that is almost entirely irrelevant is not only not going to help. It may actually hurt the cause. As one FBI agent said privately of Ashcroft: "We're looking for a needle in a haystack here and he (Ashcroft) is just piling on more hay."

In other words, the mass collecting of personal data on hundreds of millions of people actually makes it more difficult to protect the nation against terrorists, so they ought to cut most of it out.

And meanwhile, the real story is that while the administration manages to convey the impression that it is doing everything possible to protect America, in reality it has seriously neglected most of the measures that it could have taken to really make our country safer.

For example, there is still no serious strategy for domestic security that protects critical infrastructure such as electric power lines, gas pipelines, nuclear facilities, ports, chemical plants and the like.

They're still not checking incoming cargo carriers for radiation. They're still skimping on protection of certain nuclear weapons storage facilities. They're still not hardening critical facilities that must never be soft targets for terrorists. They're still not investing in the translators and analysts we need to counter the growing terror threat.

The administration is still not investing in local government training and infrastructures where they could make the biggest difference. The first responder community is still being shortchanged. In many cases, fire and police still don't have the communications equipment to talk to each other. The CDC and local hospitals are still nowhere close to being ready for a biological weapons attack.

The administration has still failed to address the fundamental disorganization and rivalries of our law enforcement, intelligence and investigative agencies. In particular, the critical FBI-CIA coordination, while finally improved at the top, still remains dysfunctional in the trenches.

The constant violations of civil liberties promote the false impression that these violations are necessary in order to take every precaution against another terrorist attack. But the simple truth is that the vast majority of the violations have not benefited our security at all; to the contrary, they hurt our security.

And the treatment of immigrants was probably the worst example. This mass mistreatment actually hurt our security in a number of important ways.

But first, let's be clear about what happened: this was little more than a cheap and cruel political stunt by John Ashcroft. More than 99% of the mostly Arab-background men who were rounded up had merely overstayed their visas or committed some other minor offense as they tried to pursue the American dream just like most immigrants. But they were used as extras in the Administration's effort to give the impression that they had caught a large number of bad guys. And many of them were treated horribly and abusively.

Consider this example reported in depth by Anthony Lewis:

"Anser Mehmood, a Pakistani who had overstayed his visa, was arrested in New York on October 3, 2001. The next day he was briefly questioned by FBI agents, who said they had no further interest in him. Then he was shackled in handcuffs, leg irons, and a belly chain and taken to the Metropolitan Detention Center in Brooklyn. Guards there put two more sets of handcuffs on him and another set of leg irons. One threw Mehmood against a wall. The guards forced him to run down a long ramp, the irons cutting into his wrists and ankles. The physical abuse was mixed with verbal taunts.

"After two weeks Mehmood was allowed to make a telephone call to his wife. She was not at home and Mehmood was told that he would have to wait six weeks to try again. He first saw her, on a visit, three months after his arrest. All that time he was kept in a windowless cell, in solitary confinement, with two overhead fluorescent lights on all the time. In the end he was charged with using an invalid Social Security card. He was deported in May 2002, nearly eight months after his arrest.

The faith tradition I share with Ashcroft includes this teaching from Jesus: "whatsoever you do unto the least of these, you do unto me."

And make no mistake: the disgraceful treatment suffered by many of these vulnerable immigrants at the hands of the administration has created deep resentments and hurt the cooperation desperately needed from immigrant communities in the U.S. and from the Security Services of other countries.

Second, these gross violations of their rights have seriously damaged U.S. moral authority and goodwill around the world, and delegitimized U.S. efforts to continue promoting Human Rights around the world. As one analyst put it, "We used to set the standard; now we have lowered the bar." And our moral authority is, after all, our greatest source of enduring strength in the world.

And the handling of prisoners at Guantanomo has been particularly harmful to America's image. Even England and Australia have criticized our departure from international law and the Geneva Convention. Sec. Rumsfeld's handling of the captives there has been about as thoughtful as his "postwar" plan for Iraq.

So the mass violations of civil liberties have hurt rather than helped. But there is yet another reason for urgency in stopping what this administration is doing. Where Civil Liberties are concerned, they have taken us much farther down the road toward an intrusive, "Big Brother"-style government—toward the dangers prophesized by George Orwell in his book "1984"—than anyone ever thought would be possible in the United States of America.

And they have done it primarily by heightening and exploiting public anxieties and apprehensions. Rather than leading with a call to courage, this Administration has chosen to lead us by inciting fear.

Almost eighty years ago, Justice Louis Brandeis wrote "Those who won our independence by revolution were not cowards. . . . They did not exalt order at the cost of liberty." Those who won our independence, Brandeis asserted, understood that "courage [is] the secret of liberty" and "fear [only] breeds repression."

Rather than defending our freedoms, this Administration has sought to abandon them. Rather than accepting our traditions of openness and accountability, this Administration has opted to rule by secrecy and unquestioned authority. Instead, its assaults on our core democratic principles have only left us less free and less secure.

Throughout American history, what we now call Civil Liberties have often been abused and limited during times of war and perceived threats to security. The best known instances include the Alien and Sedition Acts of 1798–1800, the brief suspension of habeas corpus during the Civil War, the extreme abuses during World War I and the notorious Red Scare and Palmer Raids immediately after the war, the shameful internment of Japanese-Americans during World War II, and the excesses of the FBI and CIA during the Vietnam War and social turmoil of the late 1960s and early 1970s.

But in each of these cases, the nation has recovered its equilibrium when the war ended and absorbed the lessons learned in a recurring cycle of excess and regret.

There are reasons for concern this time around that what we are experiencing may no longer be the first half of a recurring cycle but rather, the beginning of something new. For one thing, this war is predicted by the administration to "last for the rest of our lives." Others have expressed the view that over time it will begin to resemble the "war" against drugs—that is, that it will become a more or less permanent struggle that occupies a significant part of our law enforcement and security agenda from now on. If that is the case, then when—if ever—does this encroachment on our freedoms die a natural death?

It is important to remember that throughout history, the loss of civil liberties by individuals and the aggregation of too much unchecked power in the executive go hand in hand. They are two sides of the same coin.

A second reason to worry that what we are witnessing is a discontinuity and not another turn of the recurring cycle is that the new technologies of surveillance—long anticipated by novelists like Orwell and other prophets of the "Police State"—are now more widespread than they have ever been.

And they do have the potential for shifting the balance of power between the apparatus of the state and the freedom of the individual in ways both subtle and profound.

Moreover, these technologies are being widely used not only by the government but also by corporations and other private entities. And that is relevant to an assessment of the new requirements in the Patriot Act for so many corporations—especially in the finance industries—to prepare millions of reports annually for the government on suspicious activities by their customers. It is also relevant to the new flexibility corporations have been given to share information with one another about their customers.

The third reason for concern is that the threat of more terror strikes is all too real. And the potential use of weapons of mass destruction by terrorist groups does create a new practical imperative for the speedy exercise of discretionary power by the executive branch—just as the emergence of nuclear weapons and ICBMs created a new practical imperative in the Cold War that altered the balance of war-making responsibility between Congress and the President.

But President Bush has stretched this new practical imperative beyond what is healthy for our democracy. Indeed, one of the ways he has tried to maximize his power within the American system has been by constantly emphasizing his role as Commander-in-Chief, far more than any previous President—assuming it as often and as visibly as he can, and bringing it into the domestic arena and conflating it with his other roles: as head of government and head of state—and especially with his political role as head of the Republican Party.

Indeed, the most worrisome new factor, in my view, is the aggressive ideological approach of the current administration, which seems determined to use fear as a political tool to consolidate its power and to escape any accountability for its use. Just as unilateralism and dominance are the guiding principles of their disastrous approach to international relations, they are also the guiding impulses of the administration's approach to domestic politics. They are impatient with any constraints on the exercise of power overseas—whether from our allies, the UN, or international law. And in the same way, they are impatient with any obstacles to their use of power at home—whether from Congress, the Courts, the press, or the rule of law.

Ashcroft has also authorized FBI agents to attend church meetings, rallies, political meetings and any other citizen activity open to the public simply on the agents' own initiative, reversing a decades old policy that required justification to supervisors that such infiltrations has a provable connection to a legitimate investigation;

They have even taken steps that seem to be clearly aimed at stifling dissent. The Bush Justice Department has recently begun a highly disturbing criminal prosecution of the environmental group Greenpeace because of a non-violent direct action protest against what Greenpeace claimed was the illegal importation of endangered mahogany from the Amazon. Independent legal experts and historians have said that the prosecution—under an obscure and bizarre 1872 law against "sailor-mongering"—appears to be aimed at inhibiting Greenpeace's First Amendment activities.

And at the same time they are breaking new ground by prosecuting Greenpeace, the Bush Administration announced just a few days ago that it is dropping the investigations of 50 power plants for violating the Clean Air Act—a move that Sen. Chuck Schumer said, "basically announced to the power industry that it can now pollute with impunity."

The politicization of law enforcement in this administration is part of their larger agenda to roll back the changes in government policy brought about by the New Deal and the Progressive Movement. Toward that end, they are cutting back on Civil Rights enforcement, Women's Rights, progressive taxation, the estate tax, access to the courts, Medicare, and much more. And they approach every issue as a partisan fight to the finish, even in the areas of national security and terror.

Instead of trying to make the "War on Terrorism" a bipartisan cause, the Bush White House has consistently tried to exploit it for partisan advantage. The President goes to war verbally against terrorists in virtually every campaign speech and fundraising dinner for his political party. It is his main political theme. Democratic candidates like Max Cleland in Georgia were labeled unpatriotic for voting differently from the White House on obscure amendments to the Homeland Security Bill. . . .

The White House timing for its big push for a vote in Congress on going to war with Iraq also happened to coincide exactly with the start of the fall election campaign in September a year ago. The President's chief of staff said the timing was chosen because "from a marketing point of view, you don't introduce new products in August."

White House political advisor Karl Rove advised Republican candidates that their best political strategy was to "run on the war." And as soon as the troops began to mobilize, the Republican National Committee distributed yard signs throughout America saying, "I support President Bush and the troops"—as if they were one and the same.

This persistent effort to politicize the war in Iraq and the war against terrorism for partisan advantage is obviously harmful to the prospects for bipartisan support of the nation's security policies. By sharp contrast, consider the different approach that was taken by Prime Minister Winston Churchill during the terrible days of October 1943 when in the midst of World War II, he faced a controversy with the potential to divide his bipartisan coalition. He said, "What holds us together is the prosecution of the war. No . . . man has been asked to give up his convictions. That would be indecent and improper. We are held together by something outside, which rivets our attention. The principle that we work on is, 'Everything for the war, whether controversial or not, and nothing controversial that is not bona fide for the war.' That is our position. We must also be careful that a pretext is not made of war needs to introduce far-reaching social or political changes by a side wind."

Yet that is exactly what the Bush Administration is attempting to do—to use the war against terrorism for partisan advantage and to introduce far reaching controversial changes in social policy by a "side wind," in an effort to consolidate its political power.

It is an approach that is deeply antithetical to the American spirit. Respect for our President is important. But so is respect for our people. Our founders knew—and our history has proven—that freedom is best guaranteed by a separation of powers into co-equal branches of government within a system of checks and balances—to prevent the unhealthy concentration of too much power in the hands of any one person or group.

Our framers were also keenly aware that the history of the world proves that Republics are fragile. The very hour of America's birth in Philadelphia, when Benjamin Franklin was asked, "What have we got? A Republic or a Monarchy?" he cautiously replied, "A Republic, if you can keep it."

And even in the midst of our greatest testing, Lincoln knew that our fate was tied to the larger question of whether ANY nation so conceived could long endure.

This Administration simply does not seem to agree that the challenge of preserving democratic freedom cannot be met by surrendering core American values. Incredibly, this Administration has attempted to compromise the most precious rights that America has stood for all over the world for more than 200 years: due process, equal treatment under the law, the dignity of the individual, freedom from unreasonable search and seizure, freedom from promiscuous government surveillance. And in the name of security, this Administration has attempted to relegate the Congress and the Courts to the sidelines and replace our democratic system of checks and balances with an unaccountable Executive. And all the while, it has constantly angled for new ways to exploit the sense of crisis for partisan gain and political dominance. How dare they!

Years ago, during World War II, one of our most eloquent Supreme Court Justices, Robert Jackson, wrote that the President should be given the "widest latitude" in wartime, but he warned against the "loose and irresponsible invocation of war as an excuse for discharging the Executive Branch from the rules of law that govern our Republic in times of peace. No penance would ever expiate the sin against free government," Jackson said, "of holding that a President can escape control of executive powers by law through assuming his military role. Our government has ample authority under the Constitution to take those steps which are genuinely necessary for our security. At the same time, our system demands that government act only on the basis of measures that have been the subject of open and thoughtful debate in Congress and among the American people, and that invasions of the liberty or equal dignity of any individual are subject to review by courts which are open to those affected and independent of the government which is curtailing their freedom."

So what should be done? Well, to begin with, our country ought to find a way to immediately stop its policy of indefinitely detaining American citizens without charges and without a judicial determination that their detention is proper.

Such a course of conduct is incompatible with American traditions and values, with sacred principles of due process of law and separation of powers.

It is no accident that our Constitution requires in criminal prosecutions a "speedy and public trial." The principles of liberty and the accountability of government, at the heart of what makes America unique, require no less. The Bush Administration's treatment of American citizens it calls "enemy combatants" is nothing short of un-American.

Second, foreign citizens held in Guantanamo should be given hearings to determine their status provided for under Article V of the Geneva Convention, a hearing that the United States has given those captured in every war until this one, including Vietnam and the Gulf War.

If we don't provide this, how can we expect American soldiers captured overseas to be treated with equal respect? We owe this to our sons and daughters who fight to defend freedom in Iraq, in Afghanistan and elsewhere in the world.

Third, the President should seek congressional authorization for the military commissions he says he intends to use instead of civilian courts to try some of those who are charged with violating the laws of war. Military commissions are exceptional in American law and they present unique dangers. The prosecutor and the judge both work for the same man, the President of the United States. Such commissions may be appropriate in time of war, but they must be authorized by Congress, as they were in World War II, and Congress must delineate the scope of their authority. Review of their decisions must be available in a civilian court, at least the Supreme Court, as it was in World War II.

Next, our nation's greatness is measured by how we treat those who are the most vulnerable. Noncitizens who the government seeks to detain should be entitled to some basic rights. The administration must stop abusing the material witness statute. That statute was designed to hold witnesses briefly before they are called to testify before a grand jury. It has been misused by this administration as a pretext for indefinite detention without charge. That is simply not right.

Finally, I have studied the Patriot Act and have found that along with its many excesses, it contains a few needed changes in the law. And it is certainly true that many of the worst abuses of due process and civil liberties that are now occurring are taking place under the color of laws and executive orders other than the Patriot Act.

Nevertheless, I believe the Patriot Act has turned out to be, on balance, a terrible mistake, and that it became a kind of Tonkin Gulf Resolution conferring Congress' blessing for this President's assault on civil liberties. Therefore, I believe strongly that the few good features of this law should be passed again in a new, smaller law—but that the Patriot Act must be repealed.

As John Adams wrote in 1780, ours is a government of laws and not of men. What is at stake today is that defining principle of our nation, and thus the very nature of America. As the Supreme Court has written, "Our Constitution is a covenant running from the first generation of Americans to us and then to future generations." The Constitution includes no wartime exception, though its Framers knew well the reality of war. And, as Justice Holmes reminded us shortly after World War I, the Constitution's principles only have value if we apply them in the difficult times as well as those where it matters less.

The question before us could be of no greater moment: will we continue to live as a people under the rule of law as embodied in our Constitution? Or will we fail future generations, by leaving them a Constitution far diminished from the charter of liberty we have inherited from our forebears? Our choice is clear.

146. Center for Public Integrity, "Outsourcing the Pentagon: Who Benefits from the Politics and Economics of National Security?"

(2004)

This is the introduction to the Center for Public Integrity's report on Pentagon contracts arising from the Iraq War. Founded in 1990, the Center for Public Integrity is a nonprofit, nonpartisan organization engaged investigative journalism in the public interest. The center, based in Washington, D.C., specializes in publishing accessible investigative reports on issues relating to institutional power, including corruption and influence-peddling. In 2004, when this report appeared, the center won the prestigious George Polk Award for Windfalls of War, its series of reports on government contracts in Iraq and Afghanistan. In this report, from the center's Outsourcing the Pentagon series, Larry Makinson analyzes six years of Defense Department contracts and focuses especially on the biggest contractors.

SOURCE: September 29, 2004, http://www.publicintegrity.org/pns/report.aspx ?aid=385.

THE CENTER FOR PUBLIC INTEGRITY

The Center for Public Integrity www.publicintegrity.org

WASHINGTON, September 29, 2004—The war in Iraq, with its urgent agenda of getting the job done and getting it done quickly, relied to an unprecedented degree not only on the soldiers, sailors, airmen and marines who are expected to fight America's wars, but on a second American army: tens of thousands of civilian contractors hired on for the duration. This new, and often dangerous, role for civilians on the battlefield has raised a host of new questions about the role of private contractors in the nation's defense.

One of the biggest contracts awarded in the war in Iraq went to Kellogg Brown & Root, a key subsidiary of Halliburton Co., the firm Vice President Dick

Cheney ran as CEO before he stepped into the White House and became one of the prime movers urging the president to invade Iraq. Of the $4.3 billion in defense contracts Halliburton won in fiscal 2003 only about half were awarded based on competitive bidding. Another $1.9 billion in contract dollars was awarded on the basis of "urgency" without bidding and without going to any other contractors.

The connection between Halliburton and the Vice President has led to no end of speculation about how that particular firm was chosen. While this report does not address that issue specifically, it does examine the practice of awarding no-bid contracts to well-connected defense contractors. Indeed, one might pose a new question on the role of contractors in the American military: Was the war in Iraq an example of the Pentagon's new way of doing business, or was it an outgrowth of a way of doing business that has been much longer in duration, albeit conducted off the field of battle without a worldwide—or even any—audience?

To find the answers, the Center began in early 2004 to investigate the patterns of Defense Department contracting. Our prime source was the Pentagon's own procurement databases—public information that had been posted for years on an obscure Defense Department Web site.

The Center examined more than 2.2 million contract actions totaling $900 billion in authorized expenditures over the six-year period from fiscal year 1998 through fiscal 2003 (Oct. 1, 1997–Sept. 30, 2003). Most of the research was focused on the biggest contractors, those that won at least $100 million in prime contracts over the period studied. Some 737 prime contractors, mainly but not exclusively for-profit corporations, fit that criteria, along with several thousand of their subsidiaries and affiliates.

After nine months of research, the Center has found:

• Half of all the Defense Department's budget goes out the door of the Pentagon to private contractors. This percentage has stayed virtually constant over the past six years; as the Pentagon's budget has expanded with the wars in Iraq and Afghanistan, so have the dollars going to contractors.

• Only 40 percent of Pentagon contracts were conducted under what it terms "full and open competition." (That percentage drops to 36 percent if you deduct those "full and open" contracts that attracted only a single bidder). Some 44 percent of contracts were given under "other than full and open competition"— usually as sole source contracts. Another seven percent fell under other categories (most often as small business set-asides), and eight percent gave no competition information at all.

• The Pentagon's contracting force is top-heavy, and growing more so. Out of a total universe numbering tens of thousands of contractors, the biggest 737 collected nearly 80 percent of the Defense Department's procurement dollars. The 50 biggest contractors got more than half of all the money; the top 10 got 38 percent.

• Topping the list was Lockheed Martin, with $94 billion in defense contracts over the six-year period. Boeing was second with almost $82 billion. Well behind those leaders were Raytheon (just under $40 billion), and Northrop Grumman and General Dynamics, with nearly $34 billion apiece. Those five companies tower over all other defense contractors. It's worth noting that they collect additional billions, not included in the figures cited, through joint ventures with other companies.

• Most of the contracts awarded to the very biggest defense contractors were won without what the Pentagon calls "full and open" competition. Of the 10 biggest contractors, only one—Science Applications International Corp. (SAIC)—won more than half its dollars through an open bidding process. Three of the top 10—United Technologies, General Electric and Newport News Shipbuilding (now owned by Northrop Grumman)—collected less than 10 percent of their contract dollars through open bidding.

• Larger contractors were also more likely to win favorable terms on their contracts. One-third of the dollars awarded to the top 737 contractors came in cost-plus contracts that offer little incentive for keeping costs under control. Among smaller companies, only 11 percent of the award dollars were for cost-plus contracts.

• Industry consolidation was another major factor in creating a top-heavy group of Pentagon contractors. Over the six-year period of this study, more than 60 contractors were acquired or merged with even larger contractors. This was true both among companies whose main business is defense, and those in other sectors, particularly energy and telecommunications.

• The list of top contractors includes 43 joint ventures, in which major defense firms partnered together forming new companies to manage specific contracts or weapons systems. Four of these joint ventures collected $1 billion or more in contracts over the six-year period and together they accounted for nearly $19 billion in revenues to their partner companies. Lockheed and Boeing again led all others in revenues from joint ventures; Lockheed collected $2.3 billion from six different joint ventures, Boeing earned almost $2.1 billion from five.

• While most of the top 737 Pentagon contractors were American corporations, nearly 100 were foreign-owned. Included on the list were the governments of Canada, Germany and Japan, as well as the Italian Post, Telephone & Telegraph Ministry. The leading foreign corporations were British-based BAE Systems, BP and Rolls-Royce; and Maersk Inc., a Danish shipping giant.

• Political influence, as measured through lobbying expenses and campaign contributions, was a major undertaking by many of the largest Pentagon contractors. But a surprising number of companies on the top contractor list gave little or nothing to political candidates and parties, and chose not to invest in Capitol Bill lobbyists. Indeed, those contractors that spent the most on contributions and lobbying were from business sectors other than defense. The three leaders in political contributions between 1998 and 2003 were AT&T ($9.9 million), SBC Communications ($9.2 million) and FedEx ($8.0 million). Only two of the 10 biggest political contributors among the group were primarily defense companies—Lockheed Martin and Boeing. Nearly a quarter of the top Pentagon contractors made no political contributions whatsoever during the six-year period, and only 202 of the 737 gave $100,000 or more in contributions, either through PACs, soft money, or individual donations from their executives, employees and families. Overall, the top contractors gave nearly $214 million in campaign contributions, two-thirds to Republicans.

• The story was much the same in lobbying expenditures, though the dollar amounts were far higher. Just under half the leading defense contractors reported spending money on Washington lobbyists, but those that did spent a total of $1.9 billion in the effort. Again, the biggest spenders were not primarily defense companies, though the biggest of the Pentagon's contractors did rank near the top. Leading the list was Altria Group (the former Philip Morris), with just under $94 million in lobby expenditures. General Electric was second, with $88.4 million. AT&T was third ($71.6 million), followed by Lockheed Martin ($71.5 million), Boeing ($64.4 million) and Northrop Grumman ($61.2 million).

• President George W. Bush received more than $4.5 million in campaign contributions from the 737 leading defense contractors during the six-year period of this study; his Democratic challenger Sen. John Kerry collected just $332,000. In 2004, however, the proportions switched dramatically. Kerry collected twice as much as Bush between Jan. 1, 2004 and the end of July—$1.6 million versus $824,000 for the president. Including that late money, Bush received nearly $5.4 million from the leading defense contractors; Kerry drew just under $2.0 million.

• Small business contractors are given special preference at the Defense Department, as they are in other federal agencies, since Congress set informal quotas encouraging the government to do more business with smaller companies. Surprisingly, however, the list of "small businesses" includes many dozens of companies with more than $100 million in defense contracts over the past six years. Some 189 of the leading contractors had at least half their contract dollars designated as going to small businesses. For 127 companies, at least 90 percent of their money was classified that way. Leading them all was Chugach Alaska Corp., whose status as an Alaska Native corporation classifies it as a small, disadvantaged business eligible not only for preferences in bidding but for small business set-aside contracts. Taking full advantage of its status, Chugach Alaska won $1.4 billion in defense contracts between fiscal 1998 and 2003. The biggest non-minority small business contractor was GTSI Corp., which retained its small business status despite having long since grown out of it. The company collected nearly $1.2 billion in small business contracts over the past six years—72 percent of their overall total.

• A lucrative loophole in the small business rules has enabled contractors to retain their small business status through the life of each contract—even if they've grown or been acquired by a much larger company. Titan Corp., a San Diego-based defense electronics firm, with a long string of acquisitions over the past six years (and nearly $2.4 billion in defense contracts), won nearly $550 million of contracts under the small business classification. Other companies have done the same, prompting calls that the small business status be reviewed on a much more frequent basis than it has been. Regulations to require that, at least on a limited scale, are due to take effect later this year.

• The Pentagon's shopping list has undergone a gradual, and largely unnoticed, transformation in the past two decades. In 1984, almost two-thirds of its contracting budget went for products rather than services. By the early 1990s, the ratio between the two had evened out. By fiscal 2003, 56 percent of Defense Department contracts paid for services rather than goods. Many of these were for routine jobs—like KP duty or building maintenance—that used to be done by low-ranking military personnel. But the Pentagon also contracts for services that are highly sophisticated, strategic in nature, and closely approaching core functions that for good reason the government used to do on its own. The Pentagon has even hired contractors to advise it on hiring contractors.

• The accuracy of the Defense Department's records—particularly regarding the corporate ownership of its largest contractors—leaves much to be desired. The Center found more than $35 billion in contracts where the ultimate corporate parent was misidentified. In some cases this led to major discrepancies between the amount of contracts actually won by major corporations and the totals reported publicly by the Pentagon.

More details on these findings can be found in the sections that follow. In addition, the report includes detailed statistical contracting profiles for each of the 737 largest prime contractors—the companies that won $100 million or more in defense contracts over the past six years. The profiles include breakdowns of each company's total contract dollars, the types of contracts they won, the competition they faced, a list of their key subsidiaries, breakdowns of their lobbying and campaign contributions, and a list of the chief products and services they sold to the Pentagon.

After nine months of research, however, this report may raise more questions than it answers. It brings to the surface for the first time the patterns of the Pentagon's contracting practices and many details of the $900 billion in taxpayer money the Defense Department paid out to its private suppliers. Both this report and the detailed profiles are designed to provide an important new body of research materials for a new wave of informed reporting about the evermore-expensive, and profitable, business of defending America.

147. Public Enemy, "MKLVFKWR"

(2004)

In this song, rap group Public Enemy pounds home a message of peace. Public Enemy burst on the hip-hop scene in the late 1980s, driven by a revolutionary sound and the revolutionary lyrics of Chuck D (1960–). The son of activists, Chuck D attended Adelphi University on Long Island, where he later formed Public Enemy with Flavor Flav, Terminator X, Professor Griff, and Hank Shocklee. Between 1987 and 1991, the band released four albums that effectively established Chuck D as one of the most politically radical artists in the music industry. MKLVFKWR comes out of the tradition Public Enemy established at the start of its career. A collaboration with New York techno artist Moby, the song was recorded for the 2004 Olympics in Athens (it appeared on the official Olympics compact disc) and is equal parts a call to political engagement and a critique of those in power. According to Mr. Chuck, "the song is a request that being a citizen of the world should transcend nationality in the name of peace."

SOURCE: Public Enemy, *Unity: The Official Athens 2004 Olympic Games Album* (Capitol Records, 2004).

MOBY PEMOBY PEMOBY PEMOBY PE

Chuck:
just gonna drop this on one of them moby beats
here we go

CMON
PUT YOUR HANDS IN THE AIR
ALLRIGHT / YALL

CMON
PUT YOUR HANDS IN THE AIR
ALLRIGHT / NOW

CMON
PUT YOUR HANDS IN THE AIR
ALLRIGHT/ YALL

CMON
PUT YOUR HANDS IN THE AIR
ALLRIGHT / NOW

FINGERS IN THE AIR
LIKE YOU REALLY GIVE A DAMN
PEACE SIGN UP
LEMME HEAR YOU SAY YEAH

POWER TO THE PEOPLE
PUT YOUR HANDS IN THE AIR
PEACE SIGN HIGH
LIKE YOU REALLY DO CARE

FINGERS IN THE AIR
LIKE YOU REALLY GIVE A DAMN
PEACE SIGN UP
LEMME HEAR YOU SAY YEAH

POWER TO THE PEOPLE
PUT YOUR HANDS IN THE AIR
PEACE SIGN HIGH
LIKE YOU REALLY DO CARE

cmon
CMON
PUT YOUR HANDS IN THE AIR
ALLRIGHT / YALL

CMON
PUT YOUR HANDS IN THE AIR
ALLRIGHT / NOW

RATHER BE SITTIN JUST A GETTIN IT
POWER TO THE PEOPLE NOT THE GOVERNMENTS
CAPITALISTS, COMMUNISTS, TERRORISTS
SWEAR TO GOD I DONT KNOW THE DIFFERENCE
MAKIN NEW SLAVES OUTTA IMMIGRANTS
WANNA KNOW WHERE ALL THAT MONEY WENT
ANOTHER TRILLION SPENT BY THE GOVERMENT
HERE THE BOMB GO. SENT BY THE PRESIDENT

POWER TO THE PEOPLE
CAUSE THE PEOPLE WANT PEACE
POWER TO THE PEOPLE

CAUSE THE PEOPLE WANT PEACE
POWER TO THE PEOPLE
CAUSE THE PEOPLE WANT PEACE
POWER TO THE PEOPLE
CAUSE THE PEOPLE WANT PEACE

CMON
PUT YOUR HANDS IN THE AIR
ALLRIGHT / YALL

CMON
PUT YOUR HANDS IN THE AIR
ALLRIGHT / NOW

TELL THE LEADERS
THEY GOTTA FEED US
GRAND THEFT OIL
GONNA BLEED US
NEW WHIRL ODOR
DOESNT NEED US
CALL FOR PEACE
BETTER HEED US
DICTATORS
HUMAN HATERS
HAND ON THE BOMB, MASS DEBATORS
FINGER ON THE BUTTON INFILTRATORS
MKLVFKWR
PEACE WILL SAVE US

CMON

PUT YOUR HANDS IN THE AIR
ALLRIGHT / YALL

CMON
PUT YOUR HANDS IN THE AIR
ALLRIGHT / NOW

CMON
PUT YOUR HANDS IN THE AIR
ALLRIGHT / YALL

CMON
PUT YOUR HANDS IN THE AIR
ALLRIGHT / NOW

FLAV;
check one two we want everybody to put this sign up in the air
and at the count of three

everybody tell me what this sign means
peace

CMON
PUT YOUR HANDS IN THE AIR
ALLRIGHT / YALL

CMON
PUT YOUR HANDS IN THE AIR
ALLRIGHT NOW/

CMON
PUT YOUR HANDS IN THE AIR
ALLRIGHT / YALL

CMON
PUT YOUR HANDS IN THE AIR
ALLRIGHT NOW/

POWER TO THE PEOPLE
CAUSE THE PEOPLE WANT PEACE
POWER TO THE PEOPLE
CAUSE THE PEOPLE WANT PEACE
POWER TO THE PEOPLE
CAUSE THE PEOPLE WANT PEACE
POWER TO THE PEOPLE
CAUSE THE PEOPLE WANT PEACE

MKLVFKWR
MKLVFKWR (R. Hall, C. Ridenhour, W. Drayton); Mixed by Disco D for MCT management at The Booty Barn, Brooklyn, USA; Published by Little Idiot Music/ Warner Tamerlane (BMI) and Terrordome Music Publishing, LLC. (BMI), administered by Reach Global, Inc.

148. Mark Benjamin, "The Invisible Wounded"

(2005)

In this investigative report, journalist Mark Benjamin analyzes the Pentagon's policy of bringing Iraq War wounded home to the United States only under cover of darkness. Formerly the investigations editor at United Press International, and now national correspondent for Salon.com, Benjamin has garnered high praise from the left and the right for his work. In 2004, he won the American Legion's highest journalism award for his coverage of the sick and injured soldiers at Ft. Stewart, Georgia. As the next several documents show, 2005 marked a turn in the war at home. Even with the dead and wounded hidden from sight, as casualties climbed, the experiences of their families came more sharply into focus in the national media. This article, published in March 2005, came out a year after a Freedom of Information Act request succeeded in getting photos of flag-draped caskets at Dover Air Force Base released. The Pentagon later said the release of the photos was a mistake, and the Senate voted 54–39 to defeat a measure that would have instructed the Defense Department to allow photographs of caskets. As Benjamin points out here, no discussion occurred regarding the visibility of the wounded.

SOURCE: *Salon.com*, March 8, 2005, http://dir.salon.com/story/news/feature/2005/03/08/night_flights/.

Injured Soldiers Evacuated to the U.S. Never Arrive in the Light of Day— and the Pentagon Has Yet to Offer a Satisfactory Explanation Why.

In January 2000, then Joint Chiefs of Staff chairman Gen. Henry Shelton told an audience at Harvard that before committing troops, politicians should make sure a war can pass what he called the "Dover test," so named for the Air Force base in Delaware where fallen soldiers' coffins return. Shelton said politicians must weigh military actions against whether the public is "prepared for the sight of our most precious resource coming home in flag-draped caskets."

It's widely known that on the eve of the Iraq invasion in 2003, the Bush administration moved to defy the math and enforced a ban on photographs of the caskets arriving at Dover, or at any other military bases. But few realize that it seems to be pursuing the same strategy with the wounded, who are far more numerous. Since 9/11, the Pentagon's Transportation Command has medevaced 24,772 patients from battlefields, mostly from Iraq. But two years after the invasion of Iraq, images of wounded troops arriving in the United States are almost as hard to find as pictures of caskets from Dover. That's because all the transport is done literally in the dark, and in most cases, photos are banned.

Ralph Begleiter, a journalism professor at the University of Delaware and a former CNN world affairs correspondent who has filed a suit to force the Pentagon to release photographs and video of the caskets arriving at Dover, said news images of wounded American soldiers have been "extremely scarce." Wounded soldiers, like caskets, mostly show up in the news only after they arrive back in their hometowns. Begleiter said the Pentagon has tried to minimize public access to images and information that might drain Americans' tolerance for the war. "I think the Pentagon is taking steps to minimize the exposure of the costs of war," said Begleiter. "Of course they are."

A Salon investigation has found that flights carrying the wounded arrive in the United States only at night. And the military is hard-pressed to explain why. In a series of interviews, officials at the Pentagon's Air Mobility Command, which manages all the evacuations, refused to talk on the record to explain the nighttime flights, or to clarify discrepancies in their off-the-record explanations of why the flights arrive when they do. In a written statement, the command said that "operational restrictions" at a runway near the military's main hospital in Germany, where wounded from Iraq are brought first, affect the timing of flights. The command also attempted to explain the flight schedule by saying doctors in Germany need plenty of time to stabilize patients before they fly to the United States.

From Germany, the military flies the wounded into Andrews Air Force Base in Maryland. Troops with some of the worst injuries are delivered from there to the military's top hospitals nearby, Walter Reed Army Medical Center in Washington and National Naval Medical Center in Bethesda, Md. But both hospitals bar the press from seeing or photographing incoming patients, ostensibly to protect their privacy. Other patients flown from Germany are held at a medical staging facility at Andrews until they are transported to other military hospitals.

Paul Rieckhoff, founder and executive director of *Operation Truth*, an advocacy group for veterans from Iraq and Afghanistan, said the nighttime-only arrivals of wounded, along with the restrictions on coffin photos and other P.R. tactics, are designed to hide from the public the daily flow of wounded and dead. "They do it so nobody sees [the wounded]," Rieckhoff said. "In their mind-set, this is going to demoralize the American people. The overall cost of this war has been continuously hidden throughout. As the costs get higher, their efforts to conceal those costs also increase."

But the Pentagon says it's not trying to hide the wounded from anyone. (Pentagon officials have also denied that banning photographs of coffins at Dover was a P.R. decision.) Capt. Herbert McConnell, a spokesman for Andrews Air Force Base, said that while it's true the flights of wounded arrive only at night, the schedule is not designed to minimize images of wounded soldiers. "There is no conspiracy, I can tell you that. I am absolutely sure there is no effort to bring them in under the darkness of night," McConnell said. "There is nothing shady going on here."

From Andrews, some of the most seriously wounded are driven to Walter Reed or Bethesda Naval Medical Center in buses, ambulances or unmarked black vans. Photos of the arrivals at the hospitals are prohibited. (Salon obtained the images of wounded arriving at Walter Reed at night despite the ban. The images do not show the identities of the patients.)

Nearly 4,000 soldiers hurt in Iraq have been bused from Andrews Air Force Base to Walter Reed, according to the hospital. Because the planes come in late at Andrews, patients arrive at Walter Reed after dark and after the hospital's clinics are closed. The wounded are unloaded into hallways empty of the patients, families and media who typically are present during the day. They are not unloaded into the common entrance closest to the emergency room.

On one recent night at Walter Reed, about 10 hospital medical officials wearing green camouflage lined up gurneys in the empty hospital lobby just before 10. At around 9:45 p.m., someone announced that the "buses are here," and staff began putting on light blue rubber gloves. White school buses converted into ambulances and marked "Walter Reed" pulled up. Two unmarked black vans did too. The convoy did not go through the main circular drive to a covered entrance close to the emergency room and pharmacy, where most patients go in and out. The vehicles instead pulled into a raised drive above that entrance and unloaded the wounded under the open, dark sky.

The medical officials slowly unloaded the wounded who were on stretchers. Others entered in wheelchairs, hobbled in on crutches or walked. Two soldiers brought in on wheeled gurneys were swollen-looking, appeared unconscious and were fully intubated with large ventilators strapped across their beds. A bag of what could have been bloody urine hung off the side of one gurney.

The walking wounded were handed white bags from the Red Cross off a cart outside. A handful of civilians came in at the same time and walked solemnly through the empty hallways to the hospital's Family Assistance Center with suitcases in tow. I witnessed two other arrivals like that on cold winter nights. Soldiers I know at Walter Reed have seen many more.

Walter Reed bars any media coverage of incoming wounded, ostensibly to protect their privacy. But the photos obtained by Salon prove how easy it is to photograph the arrival of patients at Walter Reed without violating privacy rights.

Nothing I uncovered in my reporting ever suggested that troops with serious physical wounds—amputees or gunshot victims—were getting anything less than the care and attention they deserve. Indeed, the Pentagon and Walter Reed have allowed reporters and photographers to cover amputees recuperating at Walter Reed and Army doctors pulling out all the stops to save critically wounded troops on the sandy battlefields of Iraq. By all accounts, these are the things the Army does well. They represent "good news" stories for the Pentagon, showing the great lengths the military goes to care for downed soldiers.

But reporting on the size, scope or mounting cost of the war—like pictures of incoming caskets or the seemingly endless stream of stretchers arriving at Walter Reed—is almost impossible because of Pentagon restrictions.

In a strange twist, Andrews Air Force Base last month did let me videotape a plane of wounded being unloaded in the dark. Andrews officials said the press can watch the wounded arriving, but few reporters ever ask to visit the acres of flat asphalt on the "flight line" there. McConnell, the Andrews spokesman, said that allowing me to videotape the wounded from a distance would let me "see there is no conspiracy going on here."

With my military public affairs escort, I walked around half a mile away from the passenger terminal at Andrews down the flight line. While flight times seem to vary from evening until late at night, the giant gray C-141 Starlifter from Germany that I saw landed just before 6 p.m. (an early arrival, according to my Army sources). Two white buses marked "Walter Reed" backed up to the rear ramp of the plane, followed later by two green buses marked with a red cross.

There was still some daylight when the Starlifter's wheels hit the ground, but it was dark when soldiers carrying stretchers began to descend from the plane. One by one, about 10 stretchers were slowly carried down the ramp and loaded into racks in the buses. It was hard to see the condition of the wounded. A soldier in a wheelchair followed. Then came the walking wounded.

It's easy to imagine any number of reasons for taking off from Germany late in the day, which, in turn, would result in evacuations arriving in the United States at night. The flight from Germany in a C-141 can take up to 10 hours, and there is a six-hour time difference with the United States. The Air Mobility Command's off-the-record explanation did not, however, account for the consistent arrivals of nighttime flights. And its written response was vague: "Missions are scheduled to depart [Germany] in compliance with airfield operational restrictions, allowing patients a restful night before the long trans-Atlantic flight, and giving medical personnel sufficient processing time for those patients who may require special handling/treatment."

John Pike, the director of GlobalSecurity.org, a defense information Web site, has spent a great deal of time trying to tease out the difference between facts and Pentagon spin. He said it is odd that the Pentagon hasn't done a good job of explaining the late-night flights. "It is puzzling because there are perfectly sensible explanations for this, but those are not the explanations being offered," Pike said. "And the explanation being offered makes no sense. It makes no sense."

Pike and veterans' advocate Rieckhoff both said the Pentagon has employed a raft of techniques to manage domestic perceptions of the war. The Department of Defense Dictionary of Military and Associated Terms defines "perception management" as "actions to convey and/or deny selected information and indicators" to influence "emotions, motives, and objective reasoning." Although the dictionary describes such techniques only as they apply to foreign audiences, the

Pentagon has come under fire for employing some pretty aggressive techniques at home, too.

President Bush himself has garnered some criticism for deciding not to attend the funerals of fallen soldiers, opting for private meetings with their families instead.

Some critics, including the American Legion, have blamed the Pentagon for tinkering with even the most basic data on the war. Pentagon "casualty reports," for example, only reflect troops hurt by the bullets and bombs of the enemy—excluding over 20,432 troops evacuated from Iraq and Afghanistan for injuries or illnesses the Pentagon deems not caused directly by combat, like Humvee accidents or mental trauma.

The Pentagon in 2002 closed its Office of Strategic Influence after harsh criticism followed reports that the office intended to plant fake news stories in the foreign press. Some press reports, however, assert that the mission of the Office of Strategic Influence lives on somewhere else in the Pentagon.

Last fall, military commanders in Iraq combined the public affairs and psychological warfare offices there, according to the Los Angeles Times. One office is supposed to get accurate information to the public, the other to bedevil the enemy by using information as a weapon. The decision to combine them prompted Gen. Richard Myers, chairman of the Joint Chiefs of Staff, to warn the joint chiefs in a memo that "such organizational constructs have the potential to compromise the commander's credibility with the media and the public." And in an obvious effort to control some of the news, the Pentagon now has its own news channel. The Dish Network will soon carry the *Pentagon Channel*, beaming its version of the truth to 11 million viewers worldwide.

But the Pentagon's critics say it is not doing the American public any favors by restricting and controlling images of war as it has. Begleiter, the University of Delaware journalism professor, said the American people deserve to get a clear picture of war, even when that picture might be disturbing. "The American people have a right to see what the military is doing in their name," he said.

149. George Packer, "The Home Front"

(2005)

In this article for the *New Yorker*, veteran war correspondent George Packer takes the measure of wartime America through the lens of a grieving father. Raised in the San Francisco Bay area, Packer (1960–) graduated from Yale and served in the Peace Corps. He has taught writing at a number of colleges and universities, including Harvard and Columbia, and has published two novels and three works of nonfiction, including *Blood of the Liberals*, which won the 2001 Robert F. Kennedy Book Award. In 2005, he published *The Assassin's Gate: America in Iraq*. This article is more about Iraq in America and American households, as Packer builds outward from a chronicle of one family's quest for understanding to examine what the public and the politicians knew and understood about the Iraq War and when they knew it. At the center of the essay is a meditation on public support for war and how it erodes.

SOURCE: *New Yorker*, July 25, 2005, pp. 48–59.

A Soldier's Father Wrestles with the Ambiguities of Iraq

On November 8, 2003, at around 7:40 P.M., a convoy of two Humvees drove out of the front gate of the American base at Al Rashid Military Camp, in southeast Baghdad. The mission was to pick up a sergeant who was attending a meeting at the combat-support hospital inside the Green Zone, the secure area where the American-led occupation authority was situated. The convoy belonged to the scout platoon of Headquarters Company, 2-6 Infantry, First Armored Division. In the rear left seat of the lead vehicle sat a twenty-two-year-old private named Kurt Frosheiser.

Frosheiser was from Des Moines, Iowa. The son of divorced parents, he had a twin brother, Joel, and a married older sister, Erin. During high school, he had been a rebellious, indifferent student, and by the age of twenty-one he had become a community-college dropout, living with his sister and her family, delivering pizza, and partying heavily. He had a brash, boyish smile and his father's full mouth and thick-lidded eyes; he liked Lynyrd Skynyrd and the Chicago Cubs; and one day in January, 2003, he flew through the door with the news that he had just enlisted in the Army.

His father, Chris, who also lived in Des Moines, wasn't thrilled to hear it. The Frosheisers were not a military family; Chris, fifty-eight, a salesman's son from Chicago with a flat Midwestern accent, had joined the Army reserve in 1969, mainly to avoid going to Vietnam. But he wasn't the kind of father to impose his views on his children—he never pushed Kurt to share his own interest in history and politics—and he didn't try very hard to talk Kurt out of joining up. Their relationship was what mattered, and his son needed his support. A few weeks later, Kurt dropped by his father's apartment around two in the morning, after a night out drinking, and said, "I want to be part of something bigger than myself."

Kurt watched the invasion of Iraq on TV, looking, according to his sister, more serious than she had ever seen him. He had an option to get out of serving, but he left home on April 16th for basic training at Fort Knox, Kentucky. In June, the family drove down to see him on Family Day, and Chris was stunned by the transformation: his son stood at perfect attention on Pershing Field for forty-five minutes in his dress uniform. It was the same in August, when they attended graduation: Private Frosheiser, marching, singing with his classmates, "Pick up your wounded, pick up your dead." Chris found the words chilling, but the music, the sharpness of the formation, the bearing of his son, filled him with pride. After the ceremony, Kurt told his father, "You weren't hard-core enough for me." Chris always lingered in the gray areas, asking questions; Kurt wanted the clear light of an oath and an order.

They all drove back to Des Moines for their last two weeks together before Kurt would join the First Armored Division, based in Baumholder, Germany. He partied every night, but the departure hung over everyone, and on the last night, when Erin dropped him off at one final party and turned to look at him, he said, "I know," and ran off.

Late that night, Kurt told his father, "Well, old man, I'm probably not going to see you for two years." They both started to cry, and Chris ran his hand through his son's crew cut. "I know I'm going to be in some deep shit," Kurt said. "But you know me, I'm a survivor." Chris knew that the words were meant only to comfort him. His son said, "Live your life, old man."

In Germany, Kurt was bored and eager to join the rest of the division, which was already in Iraq. Once, on the phone with his father, he noted that weapons of mass destruction might not be found. "We're fucked, aren't we?" he said. His father responded that there might be other reasons for the war, such as democracy in the Middle East. (Condoleezza Rice, the national-security adviser, had offered this rationale in a speech that Chris, a devoted viewer of C-SPAN, had seen.) Chris told him that the W.M.D. threat might just have been the easiest rationale to sell to the public. Kurt wasn't really interested in the politics of the war anyway. He was more concerned about confronting guerrilla warfare. His officers at

Baumholder had warned the soldiers not to pick up trash bags, and not to take packages that kids would rush up to give them.

Suddenly, Kurt was on a transport plane to Kuwait, where he awaited deployment for a few days. By the end of October, he was in Baghdad. On November 6th, he managed to get online and e-mailed his sister:

> Our secter that we patrol is a good one we don't get shot at that much nor do we find IEDs (improvised explosive devices) thats their main way of attacking us. They usually put them in bags but now their putting them in dead animals or in concrete blocks to hide them better. It's kinda scary knowing their out there but like I said our secter is pretty secure so Ill be allright.

Writing to his father about his first mission in Baghdad, an uneventful night operation, Kurt was more explicit:

> I found myself thinking that Im in a country where a lot of soldiers lost their lives but where we at it was so quiet except all friggin dogs barking the Iraqis hate dogs so they're all wild probubly never had a bath their whole lives this country is a shit hole they dont have plumbing so they dig little canels and let all the shit and piss run into the streets . . . theyre places that smell so bad you almost throw up from what I see its goin to take alot longer then Rumsfeld and G.W are saying to get this shit hole up and running.

He spoke to his father once, briefly, on the phone. "I.E.D.s, old man, I.E.D.s," he said.

On the evening of November 8th, Kurt was sitting on his bunk, sorting and counting his ammunition, when word came of a mission to the combat-support hospital. He was training for his license as a Humvee driver, and he was eager to experience driving through Baghdad by night. In his short time with the battalion, he had earned a reputation as a hard worker who was quick to volunteer. He and his best friend in the unit, Private Matt Plumley, a Tennesseean, raced each other to the vehicle. Because the right rear door was hard to open, they both headed for the left. Kurt got there first.

The convoy left the base and began cruising north, toward downtown Baghdad. Five minutes later, on the left shoulder of the dark highway, thirty feet ahead of the convoy, two 130-mm. artillery shells packed with Russian C-4 explosives detonated, in a flash of light, black smoke, flying dirt. Hot chunks of shrapnel tore through the legs of the lead Humvee's driver, Private First Class Matt Van Buren, but he accelerated a few hundred yards along the highway, thinking that he would try to make it to the hospital. Then Staff Sergeant Darrell Clay, who was sitting next to him, told him to stop.

In the back of the Humvee, Kurt was slumped in his seat. Plumley checked Kurt's pulse, and found none. Kurt had been looking out the window, which had no glass. His head was turned to the left, and a small piece of metal had penetrated the right side of his skull just below his Kevlar helmet, breaching his brain. Private Kurt Frosheiser was taken by helicopter to the combat-support hospital in the Green Zone, where he was pronounced dead, at 8:17 P.M.

At six-thirty the next morning, a Sunday, the phone rang in Chris Frosheiser's cramped apartment, where he had been living since his divorce. The caller was a lieutenant colonel in the Iowa National Guard; he was two blocks away and trying to find the address. "I have a message from the Army," he said tersely. The previous week, Chris Frosheiser had asked an officer what to expect if something happened to Kurt; the officer had said that he would receive a phone call if Kurt was wounded, a visit if he had been killed. Frosheiser met the lieutenant colonel outside the building and invited him in, hoping it was all a mistake, and they briefly made small talk in the living room. Frosheiser went to the kitchen for a cup of coffee. When he returned, the lieutenant colonel suddenly stood at attention: "I regret to inform you that your son Kurt was killed as a result of action in Baghdad."

On November 11th, Veterans Day, Kurt's battalion gathered in formation at the base in southeast Baghdad for a memorial service. A captain, Robert Swope, later wrote an account of the ceremony:

> At 1430 the ceremony is supposed to begin, but it doesn't start until 1448 because we have to wait for a couple generals to arrive. The memorial ceremony begins with an invocation by the chaplain, and then the battalion commander and the company commander both speak. Two privates who knew the soldier follow them. One of the privates chokes and starts tearing up while giving his tribute. I look around me out into a sea of sad faces and in the very back of the battalion formation I see that one of the female soldiers attached to our unit is crying.
>
> A bagpiper plays a crappy version of "Amazing Grace" and halfway through it doesn't even sound much like the song anymore. . . . The chaplain reads a few verses from the Bible, and then gives a memorial message and prayer. It's followed by a moment of silence.
>
> Then, the acting First Sergeant for the company does roll call, yelling out the names of various soldiers in the unit. They all answer, one after another, that they are present. When he comes to the private who died, everything is quiet.
>
> He calls out again his name, and still there is no answer. He does it a final time, using his full name and rank:
> "Private First Class Kurt Russell Frosheiser!"
> Silence.
>
> And then the mournful melody of "Taps" begins. Midway through the bugler begins slowly walking away, letting the music softly fade out in the distance. Seven soldiers with seven rifles fire off three series of blanks, giving Private Frosheiser a twenty-one-gun salute.
>
> When they're finished the battalion commander walks up to the memorial, which is an M-16 with a bayonet attached and driven into a wooden stand. Resting on top of the butt stock is a helmet and hanging down are a

pair of dog tags with Kurt's name, social security number, blood type, and religion on them. Directly in front of the M-16 and in the center of the memorial stand sit a pair of tan combat boots. To the left and to the right are a bronze star and purple heart ensconced in their silk and velvet cases.

This is the second time I've had to go to a ceremony like this so far this year, and I don't feel comfortable doing it. I walk up to the memorial the way I did last April for the other soldier in my company. I don't lower my head and pray or whisper anything, as so many others do before me. I don't lean over and touch the tip of his boots like the sergeant major ahead of me just did. I just salute and then turn and walk away.

Chris Frosheiser initially wanted to escort his son's body back from Baghdad, or at least meet it at Dover Air Force Base, in Delaware. In the end, it was enough to receive the coffin at the Des Moines airport with thirty family members and friends and see Kurt's face one more time. At the wake, Frosheiser tried to say that his son's courage filled him with awe, but he wasn't able to express himself well. Kurt received a military funeral after a Catholic service, and was buried nearby, in Glendale Cemetery.

A few days before the funeral, Kurt's mother, Jeanie Hudson, had told the local paper, "He loved this land and its principles. He loved Iowa. It's an honor to give my son to preserve our way of life." She had become an evangelical Christian, and she said that Kurt had volunteered to fight the forces of evil. For Chris Frosheiser, this was too apocalyptic, suggesting some kind of religious war; he was a Catholic, but he thought that mixing politics and religion—whether Islam or Christianity—was dangerous. Anyway, Kurt had not spoken of the war this way. On the night after Kurt's death, Iowa's governor, Tom Vilsack, had called to offer condolences and said that he hoped the country's policies were as good as its people. Frosheiser was troubled by the thought that it might not be so. In January, 2004, one of Kurt's friends from Fort Knox wrote him in an e-mail, "I don't suppose he was in an up-armored HMMV, was he? Probably not, Uncle Sam wouldn't give us Joe's the good stuff." Frosheiser didn't know the answer, but thinking about it only deepened his grief.

Frosheiser dreamed that he was in the Army with Kurt. It was unclear whether they were father and son or friends; both of them were sitting on the right side of the Humvee and, when the explosion came, they fell out together and everything was O.K. He was nagged by the thought that he hadn't had time to send Kurt a book he had requested, Tolkien's "The Return of the King." On his wrist he wore Kurt's watch, still set to Baghdad time, with an alarm that went off at 6:30 A.M.—9:30 P.M. in Des Moines.

Frosheiser was a lifelong Democrat. In 1968, as a student at Drake University, he had supported Robert Kennedy for President. He couldn't identify with the antiwar movement, though; he thought that Vietnam was a terrible waste but not a reason to hate your country. Even the Eugene McCarthy campaign struck him as too élite, too unconventional, and when McCarthy said that Kennedy was "running best among the less intelligent and less educated people" it touched the resentful nerve of a lower-middle-class college kid. The Tom Haydens of the world were going to make it no matter how they spent their youth; the Chris Frosheisers had to be more careful.

He didn't join the backlash that elected Nixon and Reagan, however; he remained a liberal, mostly on economic grounds. For many years, he worked in the insurance business without enthusiasm; in 1993, he started a new career, as the Salvation Army's director of social services in Des Moines. "I wanted to do something more meaningful—kind of like Kurt," Frosheiser said. Meanwhile, he had grown increasingly unhappy with the "weakness" of Democratic leaders and the anti-military views of much of the Party's base. After Kurt's enlistment and then his death, the feeling deepened into estrangement. Frosheiser venerated those who put on a uniform and served. He was uneasy with friends who called Iraq "another Vietnam," and he couldn't tolerate hearing that Kurt's life had been wasted. When a local Catholic peace group got in touch to offer condolences and let him know that Kurt's picture, along with those of other fallen Iowans, would be on display at a weekly candlelight vigil, Frosheiser told the group not to use Kurt's photograph. But when he bought a long-life candle at a Christian bookshop and told the cashier that it was for his son's grave, and she said, "Thank you for your sacrifice," that, too, sounded wrong.

That winter, in the Iowa caucuses, Frosheiser supported Senator John Edwards; he had misgivings about John Kerry. When a friend called Kerry's vote against the eighty-seven-billion-dollar war appropriation a "protest vote," Frosheiser said, "Kind of a serious issue to be casting protest votes on." He wondered if Kerry could hold steadfast in Iraq under pressure from the Party's dissenting base. If not, what would Kurt's death mean then? When President Bush said in a speech, "We will hold this hard-won ground," he found the language inspiring. Kerry's rhetoric did not inspire him. Frosheiser kept remembering Lincoln's 1862 Message to Congress: "As our case is new, so we must think anew, and act anew. We must disenthrall ourselves, and then we shall save our country." He longed to hear words like these from a wartime leader; politics required the art of explanation. But Bush, who had made so many mistakes, was unable to admit or see his errors, even as the war was getting worse; he had the best education money could buy, but he seemed to know little about the world. Frosheiser admired men who seemed driven more by patriotism than by ideology, such as Thomas Kean and Lee Hamilton, of the 9/11 Commission, and Senators Joe Lieberman and John McCain. Iraq was too important to be left to the partisans.

Not long after Kurt's death, Chris Frosheiser read a piece I wrote for this magazine about Kurt's battalion. Frosheiser was looking for some way to comprehend Kurt's short life and his death in Iraq. After I got back from Iraq, we began a correspondence by e-mail. Frosheiser's letters were full of the restless questions, the constant return to the same inconclusive themes, of a man who has suffered a trauma and is determined to feel every contour of it:

APRIL 1, 2004: Democrats need a foreign policy and a national security strategy to back it up. . . . Now, I have gone on too long and not answered your questions very well. It shows my ambivalence and the difficulty in talking beyond the personal. Sorry. May I write more later? I can't go on now. . . . I have reread Truman's "Truman Doctrine" speech and Marshall's Harvard Commencement speech of June 1947. I admired them and those policies. I must avoid bitterness. In honor of Kurt and the other soldiers, bitterness seems inappropriate.

MAY 15, 2004: Sometimes I think about Kurt being in Baghdad, Iraq, as part of something called "Operation Iraqi Freedom." Kurt said he wanted to be a part of something larger than himself. He was in the middle of something so huge it nearly defies understanding. There is more to be said about this, I just don't know what it is. My son died for something. And there is honor in simply enlisting, let alone serving in Iraq.

AUGUST 28, 2004: Next Tuesday, George Bush will be campaigning near Des Moines, in a farm community called Alleman, Iowa. Apparently, the campaign invited us as Kurt's family to be there. Joel and I talked about it and Erin too. And we will attend. It is a tribute to Kurt, I think. It may or may not be construed as support for Bush. But, you know, I will put my Democratic loyalty up against anyone's. As a tribute to Kurt I am entitled to shake hands with the President. Besides, it is still a bit odd I think that very little was said to me, a loyal Democrat, by leading Democrats, about Kurt's service. I know a guy who was the state party chair and who was an early Edwards supporter. I had expressed an interest in talking to Edwards about Kurt's service. It was never arranged. I thought someone like Edwards should speak to someone who lost a child in combat. Is there a larger issue exposed here? About Democrats and the soldiers? Sometimes it feels like I don't have a party. John Kerry did send a card to both Jeanie and me, but I really think there is an ill-at-ease sense among activist Democrats about the "warriors" because of opposition to the war.

SEPTEMBER 5, 2004: In follow-up to my previous e-mail about meeting Dubya, it didn't happen. Out of a sense of obligation to honor Kurt, to receive his Commander in Chief's offer of tribute and condolences I went. We were just part of the crowd. . . . We did get to hear the "stump speech," a longer version of which he gave to the Convention. He speaks of the "war against terror" as if it includes Iraq, no distinguishing between them. . . . I will be happy when the election is over. I can't take much more of the hyperbolic bullshit!

SEPTEMBER 11, 2004: Grandson Colin spent the night last night. We ate popcorn, visited Borders, watched Star Wars, and this morning took a dip in the pool (a bit cool). Life goes on, ready or not. I have to say that Kurt is never out of my thoughts. Ever. That may not be healthy but it is the way it is. I am 57 years old, George, I may never fully recover from this. And maybe I shouldn't.

OCTOBER 4, 2004: A better Iraq? Is it possible? Why did we go into Iraq? What justifies our remaining? American lives have been lost, precious lives, for what? Can something be achieved that is worthy of the sacrifice? Are there things not known to anyone other than the President and his advisers? No one in the Senate or any of the "attentive" and "informed" organizations? That would justify the sacrifice? And how much more sacrifice can be justified? For us to turn Iraq over to civil war would be hard to take. I don't have the right to advocate continued involvement because of my sacrifice—that would lead to more, many more. What is best for America and Iraq? What is reality on the ground in Iraq? What is possible to achieve? Can Kerry and a team of his choosing do it? It is a great leap of faith.

And most of the time none of this matters to me. I want my son. My son.

The home front of the first two years of the Iraq war was not like that of the Second World War, and it was not like that of Vietnam. It didn't unite Americans across party lines against an existential threat. (September 11th did that, but not Iraq.) There were no war bonds, no collection drives, no universal call-up, no national mobilization, no dollar-a-year men. Nor did the war tear the country apart. Almost as soon as it began, the American antiwar movement quietly capitulated. On the first and second anniversaries of the invasion, there were large demonstrations in Europe and parts of the Middle East and Asia, but in this country organized opposition was muted by the imperative to support the troops. Candlelight vigils like the one in Des Moines, which displayed the photographs of fallen Iowans, strived for a tone of respectful dissent.

In the media, Iraq generated words as bitter as any event in modern American history. But most Americans didn't turn against other citizens, any more than they joined together in a common cause. Iraq was a strangely distant war. It was always hard to picture the place; the war didn't enter the popular imagination in songs that everyone soon knew by heart, in the manner of previous wars. The one slender American novel that the war has inspired so far, "Checkpoint," by Nicholson Baker—a dialogue over lunch in a Washington hotel room between two old friends, one of whom is preparing to assassinate President Bush—has nothing to do with Iraq and everything to do with the ugliness of politics in this country. Michael Moore, the left's answer to Rush Limbaugh, made a hugely successful movie, "Fahrenheit 9/11," in which Saddam's Iraq was portrayed in a crudely fantastical light—a happy place where children flew kites. Iraq provided a blank screen onto which Americans projected anything they wanted, in part because so few Americans had anything directly at stake there. The war's proponents and detractors spoke of the conflict largely in theoretical terms: imperialism, democracy, unilateralism, weapons of mass destruction, preëmption, terrorism, totalitarianism, neoconservatism, appeasement. The exceptions were the soldiers and their families, who carried almost the entire weight of the war.

Whereas the street fights of the late nineteen-sixties were the consequence of Vietnam, the word fights of this decade were not the consequence of Iraq—if anything, it was the other way around. It was the first blogged war, and the characteristic features of the form—instant response, ad-hominem attack, remoteness from life, the echo chamber of friends and enemies—helped define the tone of the debate about Iraq. One of the leading bloggers, Andrew Sullivan, responded to the news of Saddam's capture, in December, 2003, by writing, "It was a day of joy. Nothing remains to be said right now. Joy." He had just handed out eleven mock awards to leftists who expressed insufficient happiness or open unhappiness at the news. In response to an Iraqi blogger's declaration of heartfelt thanks to the coalition forces, Sullivan, sitting at his computer in Washington, wrote, "You're welcome. . . . The men and women in our armed forces did the hardest work. They deserve our immeasurable thanks. But we all played our part." Sullivan's joy was, in fact, vindictive and narcissistic glee. (He has since had second thoughts about the Administration's conduct of the war.) Similarly, as the insurgency sent Iraq into tumult most antiwar pundits and politicians, in spite of the enormous stakes and the awful alternatives, showed no interest in helping Iraq become a stable democracy. When Iraqis risked their lives to vote, Arianna Huffington dismissed the elections as a "Kodak moment." It was Bush's war, and, if it failed, it would be Bush's failure.

Iraq was too complicated for the simple answers each political side offered. The American invasion brought death, chaos, and occupation to Iraq; it also ended a terrible tyranny and ushered in the possibility of hope. American forces achieved local successes in rebuilding infrastructure and setting up new institutions of government; they also lost ground every day in the estimation of Iraqis. The war had something to do with national security, something to do with oil, and something to do with democracy. Few Iraqis I met felt compelled to rifle through the contradictions and settle on one story line; many of them acknowledged that America, while ridding them of Saddam, had acted out of its own self-interest. But in America there were comparatively few people who could handle the kind of cognitive dissonance with which Iraqis lived every day.

Some journalists visited Iraq simply to reinforce their preconceptions. In the summer of 2003, Christopher Hitchens, who had just published a book with the premature title "A Long Short War: The Postponed Liberation of Iraq," flew in with the entourage of Paul Wolfowitz, the Deputy Secretary of Defense, spent several days in Wolfowitz's wake, and came back to tell Fox News that the postwar reconstruction was succeeding splendidly, with the Americans busy rebuilding the place, gathering intelligence, apprehending Baathists, and making friends with the people—none of which was appearing in press coverage. "I felt a sense of annoyance that I had to go there myself to find any of that out," Hitchens told the Fox interviewer. The following March, with the long short war showing signs of turning into a short long war, Fred Barnes, the executive editor of the strenuously pro-war *Weekly Standard*, parachuted into the Green Zone and discovered that the only thing wrong with Operation Iraqi Freedom was Iraqis. "They need an attitude adjustment," Barnes wrote. "Americans I talked to in ten days here agree Iraqis are difficult to deal with. They're sullen and suspicious and conspiracy-minded." Before the invasion, hawks like Barnes had described

Iraqis as heroic figures, but now something had to explain all the bumps in the road. A successful democracy would emerge in Iraq, Barnes said, only after "an outbreak of gratitude for the greatest act of benevolence one country has ever done for another." Naomi Klein, a columnist for the bitterly antiwar *Nation*, visited Baghdad at the same time as Barnes and found that the insurgency was mushrooming because the occupation authority was "further opening up Iraq's economy to foreign ownership"—in other words, because Iraqis shared her own anti-globalization views.

America had become too politically partisan, divided, and small-minded to manage something as vast and difficult as Iraq. Condoleezza Rice and other leading officials liked to compare Iraq with postwar Germany. But there was a great gulf between the tremendously thoughtful effort of the best minds that had gone into defeating Fascism and rebuilding Germany and Japan, and the peevish, self-serving attention paid to Iraq. One produced the Army's four-hundred-page manual on the occupation of Germany; the other produced talking points.

In the aftermath of September 11th, President Bush was granted what few Presidents ever get: national unity and the good will of both parties. In the days that followed the terror attacks, something like a popular self-mobilization emerged. Yet President Bush did nothing to harness the surge of civic energy, or to frame the new war against Islamist radicalism as a national struggle. The war on terror should have been the job not only of experts in the intelligence agencies and Special Forces but also of ordinary American citizens. And the war demanded more than a military campaign—it required intellectual, diplomatic, economic, political, and cultural efforts as well. "The Bush Administration has chosen to prosecute this war in a way that the average citizen won't feel the burden," Andrew Bacevich, a professor of international relations at Boston University and a retired Army officer, told me. "The global war on terrorism, a task that's supposed to be equal to that of the greatest generation, is being fought by 0.5 per cent of the citizenry—predominantly people who don't exercise a lot of clout in our domestic politics." Bacevich, in his recent book "The New American Militarism," proposes reviving the role of the citizen-soldier by, for example, tying college scholarships to national military service. "The political leadership of the country needs to expend political capital to make clear that support for the global war on terrorism must come from all sectors of society," he said. "Then they need to put their money where their mouth is and encourage their children to join. If this is such a great cause, let us see one of the Bush daughters in uniform. That would send a powerful message. But it's considered in bad taste even to suggest such a thing."

Bush's rhetoric sometimes soared, but his actions showed that he had a narrow strategy for fighting the war, which amounted to finding and killing terrorists and their supporters. His other political agendas, such as tax cuts and energy policy, stirred bitter fights and disrupted the clarity and unity of September 11th. Whatever national cohesion that remained by mid-2002 came undone in the buildup to the invasion of Iraq. The White House forced a congressional vote on a war resolution one month before the 2002 midterm elections, in an atmosphere of partisan invective; Republicans on the floor of the House and Senate accused their dissenting Democratic colleagues of Chamberlain-like appeasement of Saddam. Meanwhile, Senator Joseph Biden, the Democratic chairman of the Senate Foreign Relations Committee, working with his Republican colleague Richard Lugar, drafted a war resolution that stood a better chance of getting bipartisan support; it placed a few constraints on the Administration's ability to act, making it slightly less likely that America would go to war without international participation. The White House maneuvered to block the Biden-Lugar bill and got its own passed, on a more partisan vote. The strategy of Bush's political adviser Karl Rove paid off in November, when the Republicans regained the Senate and added to their majority in the House. But the Administration left behind an embittered Democratic minority and an increasingly divided electorate, just as it was preparing to take the country into a major land war.

In the fall of 2002, it still might have been possible for President Bush to construct an Iraq policy that united both parties and America's democratic allies in defeating tyranny in Iraq. Such a policy, however, would have required the Administration to operate with flexibility and openness. The evidence on unconventional weapons would have had to be laid out without exaggeration or deception. The work of U.N. inspectors in Iraq would have had to be supported rather than undermined. Testimony to Congress would have had to be candid, not slippery. Administration officials who offered dissenting views or pessimistic forecasts would have had to be heard rather than silenced or fired. American citizens would have had to be treated as grownups, and not, as Bush's chief of staff, Andrew Card, once suggested, as ten-year-olds.

After the invasion, European allies would have had to be coaxed into joining an effort that desperately needed their help. French, German, and Canadian companies would have had to be invited to bid on reconstruction contracts, not barred by an order signed by Paul Wolfowitz (who once wrote that American leadership required "demonstrating that your friends will be protected and taken care of, that your enemies will be punished and that those who refuse to support you will live to regret having done so"). American contractors close to the Pentagon would have had to be subjected to extraordinary scrutiny, to avoid even the appearance of corruption. The U.N. would have had to be brought into Iraq as an equal partner, not as a tool of American convenience. The top American civilian in Iraq might even have had to be a Democrat, or a moderate Republican such as the retired general Anthony Zinni, whom a senior Administration official privately described as the best-qualified person for the job. ("You've got to rise above politics," the official told me. You've got to pick the best team. You've got to be like Franklin Roosevelt.") The occupation authority would have had to favor hiring not political appointees but competent, non-partisan experts. It would have had to put the interests of Iraqi society ahead of the White House agenda.

And when no weapons of mass destruction were found in Iraq the Administration would have had to admit it. The President would have had to scratch evasive formulations like "weapons of mass destruction-related program activities" from his State of the Union address. Officials and generals who were responsible for scandal and failure would have had to be fired, not praised or promoted. When reporters asked the President to name one mistake he had made in Iraq, he would have had to name five, while assuring the country that they were being corrected. He would have had to summon all his rhetorical skill to explain to the country why, in spite of the failure to find weapons, ending tyranny in Iraq and helping it to become a pioneering democracy in the Middle East was morally correct, important for American security, and worthy of a generational effort. In fact, he would have had to explain this *before* the war, when the inspectors were turning up no sign of weapons, and thus allow the country to have a real debate about the real reason for the war, so that when the war came it would not come amid rampant suspicions and surprises, and America would not be alone in Iraq.

The Administration's early insistence on Iraq's imminent threat to national security later made it difficult for many Americans to accept broader arguments about democracy. "What would be worth it?" Chris Frosheiser asked. "W.M.D. imminence? Yeah. Linked to Al Qaeda? Yeah. After that? We're concerned about humanitarianism in Iraq, and the Kurds and all. But democracy in Iraq?" He wasn't so easily convinced.

What prevented open and serious debate about the reasons for war was, above all, the character of the President. Bush's war, like his Administration, was run with an absence of curiosity and self-criticism, and with a projection of absolute confidence. He always conveyed the impression that Iraq was a personal test. Every time a suicide bomber detonated himself, he was trying to shake George W. Bush's will. If Bush remained steadfast, how could America fail? He liked to call himself a wartime President, and he kept a bust of his hero Winston Churchill in the Oval Office. But Churchill led a government of national unity and offered his countrymen nothing but blood, toil, tears, and sweat. Bush relentlessly pursued a partisan Republican agenda while fighting the war, and what he offered was optimistic forecasts, permanent tax cuts, and his own stirring resolve.

I asked Richard Perle, the former chairman of the Defense Policy Board and a leading war proponent, whether top Administration officials ever suffered doubts about the Iraq War. "We all have doubts all the time," Perle said. "We don't express them, certainly not in a public debate. That would be fatal." Expressing doubts in public would empower opponents. In public, Perle himself essentially said, "I told you so." Soon after the invasion, he told a French documentary filmmaker, "Most people thought there would be tens of thousands of people killed, and it would be a long and very bloody war. I thought it would be over in three weeks, with very few people killed. Now, who was right?" As the war became longer and bloodier, Perle was still right, but in a different way: If only ten thousand Iraqi National Congress members had gone in with the Americans as he had wanted, if only Ahmad Chalabi had been installed at the head of an interim government at the start, all these problems could have been avoided. None of the war's architects publicly uttered a syllable of self-scrutiny.

Leslie Gelb worked in the Pentagon during the last years of the Johnson Presidency, and he directed the writing of the Pentagon Papers, the secret history of the Vietnam War which had been commissioned by Robert McNamara, the

Defense Secretary, before leaving office. I expressed my doubts to Gelb that Donald Rumsfeld, Bush's Defense Secretary, had commissioned a secret history of the Iraq war. "You can bet your bippy," Gelb said, laughing. "It's not accidental that President Bush, during the campaign, couldn't answer the question whether he ever made a mistake. I've never seen those folks say they were wrong. Vietnam was a liberals' war. This is not." Comparing Bush to his own boss, Gelb went on, "Johnson was a tragic figure. He was driven by the imperative not to lose the war. He knew he couldn't win. Bush is Johnson squared, because he thinks he can win. Bush is the one true believer, a man essentially cut off from all information except the official line."

Chris Frosheiser once told me, "I don't expect to hear Bush say he made a mistake, but I want to hear something that shows he knows what the hell he's doing. And I still don't hear that from him. That gets back to the soldier's oath." He was referring to the oath of personal obedience that Kurt had sworn to the Commander-in-Chief. "It implied that the President must be very wise and knowledgeable and have foresight before deploying men, because he's going to be responsible for them."

The strategy of projecting confidence served the President well in domestic politics. Steadfastness in wartime is an essential quality, and after the 2004 election no one could reasonably doubt his ability as a politician. For him, the result also proved his critics wrong. "We had an accountability moment, and that's called the 2004 election," Bush said. But in Iraq, which had a reality of its own, the approach didn't work as well.

When Bush spoke—as he did in his acceptance speech at the Republican Convention in September, 2004, and again in his inaugural address in January, 2005—about the power of freedom to change the world, he sounded deep notes in the American psyche. But Iraq itself, which was visibly deteriorating, looked nothing like the President's exalted vision. Bush's assertions that the war was succeeding forced the entire government to fall in line or risk the White House's wrath. So agencies sometimes issued prettified reconstruction reports—even when Iraq's electricity grid remained in terrible shape. War is less tolerant of untruth than domestic politics is. Bush's imperviousness to unpleasant facts actually made defeat in Iraq more likely.

Sir Jeremy Greenstock, Britain's envoy in Baghdad, watched governments in Washington and London try to bend Iraq to their own political needs and concluded that the Coalition Provisional Authority was hampered by its creators. "You have to make decisions judged against the criteria within and about Iraq, not within and about any other political context," Greenstock told me. "If you want the American and British publics to be happy about the results in Iraq, you don't say, 'What do they want next?' You look at Iraq, and you produce the substance that will make them happy. You don't produce the presentation that might make them happy tomorrow."

When Bush's first chief of the postwar operation, the retired general Jay Garner, was replaced by L. Paul Bremer III and recalled from Iraq, in May, 2003, he was taken by Rumsfeld to the White House for a farewell meeting with the President. The conversation lasted forty-five minutes, he told me, with Vice-President Dick Cheney and Rice sitting in for the second half, and yet the President did not take the chance to ask Garner what it was really like in Iraq, to find out what problems lay ahead. When Garner had come back from northern Iraq in 1991, after leading the effort to save Kurdish refugees following the Gulf War, he had answered questions for four or five days.

Bush thanked Garner for his excellent service. Garner told Bush, "You made a great choice in Bremer." Garner's end-of-duty report had assured the President that most services in Iraq would be restored within a few weeks. Anyone listening to the conversation could only conclude that Operation Iraqi Freedom was a triumph.

"You want to do Iran for the next one?" the President joshed as the meeting came to an end.

"No, sir, me and the boys are holding out for Cuba," Garner said.

Bush laughed and promised Garner and the boys Cuba.

Garner shook hands with the President, then with the Vice-President, who had said nothing the whole time. He told me that he caught Cheney's "wicked little smile" on his way out, adding, "I think the President only knows what Cheney lets in there."

On the day before the 2004 election, the senior Administration official told me that Bush "was enshrouded by yes-men and yes-women. George Tenet"—the former director of the C.I.A.—"is at the top of the list: people who can smell the political angle and furnish the information that will give the President what the political angle is. No one ever walks into the Oval Office and tells them they've got no clothes on—and persists." He went on, "I think it's dangerous that we have an environment where our principal leader cannot be well informed."

When a transport helicopter was shot down near Falluja in November, 2003, killing fifteen soldiers who were flying out on leave, the public waited for the President to make a statement about the single worst combat incident of the war. Bush said nothing for two days, until, when pressed by reporters while he was touring wildfire damage in California, he put his hand over his heart and said, "I am saddened any time that there's a loss of life. I'm saddened. Because I know a family hurts. And there's a deep pain in somebody's heart. But I do want to remind the loved ones that their sons and daughters—or the sons, in this case— died for a cause greater than themselves, and a noble cause, which is the security of the United States." The President seemed not to know that two of the soldiers in the helicopter were women. Ronald Reagan or Bill Clinton would never have missed such a detail. It wasn't indifference on Bush's part. It was a deliberate strategy of not being told too much, not getting bogged down in the day-to-day problems of the war, not waiting up past midnight for the casualty figures to come in, like Lyndon Johnson in the Situation Room. Not knowing kept the President from appearing distracted and discouraged. And, politically, it worked. Bush never seemed to be a President under siege.

To downplay the mounting death count in Iraq, the Administration enforced a ban on the filming or photographing of coffins arriving at Dover Air Force

Base. The decision achieved a political success by keeping the death toll an unreality for those Americans who were not personally linked to a soldier. It played its part in making Iraq a remote war.

I asked Chris Frosheiser what he thought about the policy. He said, "We need to see the coffins, the flag-draped coffins. The hawks need to see it. They need to know there's a big price to pay. If they don't have skin in the game, they need to see it. And the doves need to see the dignity of the sacrifice. They don't always see that." He wanted to collect Kurt's posthumous medals, his folded funeral flag, his autopsy report, and a photo of the head wound, and take them on the road, making fifteen-minute presentations around the country. He would tell those who supported the war, "Suit up and show up." He would tell war opponents about the nobility of a soldier's duty. Or he wouldn't say anything at all. He simply wanted people to see.

The idea of diminishing the threat from the Middle East by spreading democracy, beginning with Iraq, had occurred to the Bush Administration before W.M.D.s turned out not to exist. Some officials had been promoting the notion for years, and the President had made the argument in a speech before the American Enterprise Institute a month before the invasion. But this was hardly the casus belli that the Administration had presented to the American people. When the Administration changed its rationale later on, without ever admitting to the shift, it had every appearance of a bait-and-switch.

Nevertheless, the idea deserved to be taken seriously by the political opposition at home and by America's allies. A few Democrats, like Biden and Ambassador Richard Holbrooke, took up the idea without diluting their criticism of the Administration's conduct in Iraq. This was a difficult mental balancing act, but it was also important, because what Iraqis and democracy needed most was a thoughtful opposition that could hold the Bush Administration to its own promises. Yet most of the war's critics, including leaders of the Democratic Party, refused to engage in debate. They turned the subject back to the missing weapons, or they scoffed at the Administration's sincerity, or they muttered about the dangers of utopianism, or they said nothing. As a result, the Administration never felt concerted pressure from the left to insure that Iraq emerged from the war with a viable democracy.

The lack of dialogue between the Republicans and the Democrats brought out the destructive instincts of each party, and Iraq got the worst of it. Abdication also left the Democratic Party in a bad position, both morally and politically. The Party's fortunes during the election year came to depend on Iraq's turning into a disaster. When a journalist pointed this out to the antiwar candidate Howard Dean, he said, "I'm hoping against it, but there's no indication that I should be expecting anything else." An informed argument that the American presence in Iraq could only make matters worse deserved a hearing, and some Democrats believed that heavy civilian casualties were reason enough for ending the war. But most critics offered a detached and complacent negativism. The election year proved to be the year in which Iraq did turn into a disaster, yet the Democrats failed to benefit, in part because they had nothing to offer instead. Chris

Frosheiser ended up voting for Kerry by a hair, more out of party loyalty than anything else, but, between Bush's attempts at Lincolnian rhetoric and Kerry's unconvincing multi-point plans, a slender majority of American voters went for jury-rigged hope. And yet month after month the war grew less popular.

The cynicism on both sides was bound to reach the troops in Iraq. For many enlisted men and women, the mission became harder to understand and justify. Last summer, at the American base outside Mahmudiya, an insurgent strong-hold in an area south of Baghdad which soldiers had nicknamed the Triangle of Death, I talked with several of Kurt Frosheiser's platoon buddies, including Matt Plumley, who had been next to him in the Humvee the night he was killed. We sat in a stifling trailer. They were privates, all but one of them in their early twenties, and they expressed a tender and fatalistic affection for the young man they called Fro.

"That incident woke me up," Marcus Murphy, a blond, soft-spoken Indianan, said. "These people are trying to kill us."

"It's amazing," Plumley said. "We're here trying to help."

Latrael Brigham, a black soldier from Texas, took Kurt's death as a failure of leadership. "I was pissed off, because we're riding around here with messed-up equipment. If you send men to war, you have to prepare them and equip them so they can fight. And have a vision of the aftermath of the war, have a plan about how you're going to finish it. And not just jump into it. And not put the whole burden on us Americans.

"We got ourselves into something," Brigham went on. "I wish I could have some real answers to why we're here, but I don't think I'll ever have them. Not any time soon."

Plumley, Kurt's best friend in the unit, had a shy manner, and his voice had a Southern twang. He was less ready than Brigham to write the whole thing off. "If everyone here hated us, there'd be I.E.D.s every five inches," he said.

Brigham said, "I don't see us changing hundreds of years of religion, and I don't see us bringing democracy to the region. We might be here ten years—depends on the casualties, the body bags coming home."

Murphy said, "What this country needs is a big civil war. There's so many religions—we need to leave and let them work it out themselves."

"I think we might have did it too fast," Plumley said.

"I love our democracy, but we can't impose it," Brigham said.

"I would hate if we did pull out," Plumley told him. "That would be very self-ish for our country. We done messed it up."

Brigham said, "I don't think we're going to be here long enough. The insur-gency's going to get worse. We can't stop it. There's always going to be more of them."

I asked the soldiers about the meaning of Kurt's death. Plumley said that there was a reason that he was alive instead of Kurt, but he didn't know what it was.

Brigham remembered Kurt arriving at basic training, out of shape, and beat-ing him by two minutes in the two-mile run. But Kurt had worked hard to be-come a soldier.

"I never seen him in a bad mood," Plumley said.

"I think about Fro every day," Brigham said.

Plumley was smiling, remembering his friend. He had been the speaker at the Veterans Day memorial who couldn't hold back his tears, and for the first few days he had felt depressed. "Then I thought, How would Fro want me to be if he could see me? Every time I don't want to do something or think it's stupid, I say to myself, 'Would Fro think that? No.' So he gives me a lot of drive."

They were all quiet. Then they asked how Kurt's family was doing.

For Chris Frosheiser, Iraq posed an unanswered question about his son and his country. He didn't need to be proved right; he needed to find out what was right, in order to honor Kurt and the other soldiers who had died in Iraq. The war that had taken his son became an essential connection to his son, and he wanted to feel a connection, also, to the soldiers with whom Kurt had served and to the country where he had died. Nothing irritated Frosheiser more than when someone urged him to get on with his life. He searched obsessively, even frantically, through poems, song fragments, magazines (he read not just the New Republic but the left-wing In These Times and the right-wing American Enterprise), Army documents, e-mails, the First Armored Division Web site, American history books, tomes on the theory of a just war, Kurt's belongings, and his own memories. "What was my son involved in? Was it right?" he asked. "I'm looking for an account of it that can sit well in my mind and in my heart. I'm proud of Kurt's service. But the whole thing—were these guys misused? And for what?" He never made it easy for himself.

Frosheiser wrote to me not just as a father but as a citizen as well. Our e-mail exchange, however, didn't prepare me for the raw grief I encountered when I went to see him last year in Des Moines, over Memorial Day weekend. Within minutes of picking me up at the airport, Frosheiser was in tears; he was in tears when I left his apartment, two days later. His narrow blue eyes were always redrimmed behind glasses, his fair skin raw with faint lines etched into his cheeks, his nose stuffed up. His sentences were often interrupted by a nervous laugh that broke into a sob before he regained control.

The Sunday before Memorial Day, we drove a few miles northeast of Des Moines to the new development of Altoona, where Erin, his daughter, lives. Neighbors were having a cookout in their driveway. (They had continued bringing over food and taking out Erin's trash months after Kurt's funeral.) Erin smiled kindly at her father when she saw that he was upset. "Not already, Dad." After dinner, we went to Erin's house and sat around the dining-room table, where, spread out, were photos of Kurt in his youth; his graduation portrait from Fort Knox, in which he was standing in front of a Bradley armored fighting vehicle; his combat patches; his "Killed in Action" banner, framed in red; his Purple Heart and Bronze Star; and his tricornered funeral flag, in a wooden frame.

Erin, a woman in her early thirties with a direct gaze, was having difficulty explaining things to her small children. Her five-year-old son, Colin, kept asking,

"Why didn't he shoot them? Why are they there? Her three-year-old, Madelyn, wouldn't remember Kurt when she grew up.

Erin had been trying hard to picture Iraq: the lives of Iraqi mothers, the dangers they lived with. "I have trouble imagining anyone's life but mine," she said. "Does that sound selfish? Sometimes I fear it's going to keep going until we blow up the world. And I wish we had a better plan." When she first saw the photos from Abu Ghraib, she said, "I thought, They blew up my brother—more power to them. Then more rational thoughts came up: We're trying to win them over, and this humiliation isn't helping our cause." She supported the war, but on a bad day in April, 2004, when twelve Americans were killed, she said to herself, "We've got to get out. I don't want other families to go through what we went through. But what do you accomplish? Because we lost Kurt for nothing, then."

For her father, the great challenge was simply to keep going. "This one-day-at-a-time thing works for me," he said. "I get in trouble when I start thinking, How am I going to get through these days and weeks and seasons?"

"Most days, I just pretend like it didn't happen," Erin said.

"Me, too. Sometimes I think it didn't happen—just for a minute. Then I know it did."

The alarm on Kurt's watch went off.

Frosheiser and I drove back to Des Moines. His apartment felt smaller than it was, because it lacked natural light and had become the cluttered repository for many of Kurt's things—his clothes and sports gear, his CDs stacked next to his father's old records and books, his memorial spurs, plaques, medals, flags. Frosheiser had been sleeping on the livingroom couch, as if keeping a vigil, since the day Kurt left for basic training. I slept in Kurt's room. A dust-covered black U.S. Army shaving kit was on the toilet tank; in the closet, desert and jungle fatigues hung above desert combat boots, winter-weather boots, and a guitar. It was a long time before I fell asleep.

The grave was a patch of dark earth and green grass, surrounded by the graves of veterans of earlier wars; little Memorial Day flags were planted it each of them and fluttered in the breeze of a beautiful Midwestern spring morning. Frosheiser, in nylon blue sweats, saluted. "Hey, buddy," he said, kneeling to run his hand over the stone marker, which was engraved with a cross and the words

> Kurt Russell Frosheiser
> PV2 US Army
> Iraq
> Jul 10 1981 Nov 8 2003
> Purple Heart

"It was hard to keep the snow off it because it kind of built up all winter," he said. "When the dirt was soft, you could press it and leave your handprints. That was a good thing." He was talking to the grave now. "It's less painful trying to forget it, but you have to keep remembering. Random thing, just a random thing. Kurt said, 'Live your life, old man,' and that could mean I'd be a bitter son of a gun, and I don't want that. That could very easily happen." He was adjusting the long-life candle under blue glass. "We know that people live on in our hearts, but do they live on in another way? We just don't know the answer to that." He slowly got to his feet, and we walked back to the car. "What does it all mean? It means nothing. How we respond is what it means."

A Memorial Day ceremony was taking place in a park next to the state capitol, and was attended by a small crowd, including a number of old men in veterans' caps. A woman from the committee that had organized the event recognized Frosheiser and escorted him over to a row of folding chairs, where he exchanged awkward greetings with his ex-wife. Jeanie was wearing a jacket bearing an image of the American flag and the words "These Colors Don't Run," but her face was crumpled with grief. A politician gave a short speech, and then the names of the Iowans who had been killed in Iraq—fourteen of them—were read. Frosheiser stood in line to place a rose beneath an M-16 that had been stuck, bayonet first, into the ground with a helmet perched on top, as had been done at the service in Baghdad.

After the ceremony, we drove across the state, toward the Illinois border, to the high-school graduation party of his ex-wife's niece. (Frosheiser wanted to keep family relationships as strong as possible, especially now.) We passed grain silos, seed factories, and fields of early corn and baled hay speckled with the shadows of fleecy white clouds racing across a blue sky. The pleasures of the road seemed to free Frosheiser's thoughts from the morning's burdens. "I wonder what Bush in private thinks about being against nation-building and now being waist-deep in it," he said. "What is that—paradox, or irony?" Since America was extending itself so deeply into other countries, Frosheiser said, the country needed to create a whole cadre of citizens who had been educated in the humanities and were capable of working overseas. "I was thinking of that song the other day, 'Ain't Gonna Study War No More.' Maybe we should study it. Otherwise, we're going to screw it up. Because it's going to be our kids and grandkids doing it." He had heard the new Bush foreign policy described as Wilsonian, an inspiring term. "There's this phrase, 'America the great and the just.' Reagan used to talk about 'the city on the hill.' The first time I heard Condi Rice talking about democracy in Iraq, I got chills up my back. But then you ask, 'How do you do it? Is it necessary?' " Frosheiser drove in silence for a while, and when he spoke again his voice was quieter. "That's where I kind of run up against a wall with regard to Kurt."

I asked him what he meant.

"Kurt's life—was he worth that? I'd say no. He was more important than that. So I pull back."

That night, back at his apartment in Des Moines, we were watching CNN—thirteen Memorial Day-weekend deaths in Iraq—when the phone rang. It was Matt Van Buren, the driver of Kurt's Humvee, calling from Germany, where he was still recovering from his shrapnel wounds. Frosheiser muted the sound and sat up in his rocking chair. The stress of the day had left him with a headache. "I'm not sure what I can ask you," he said to Van Buren. "Let me know if I go too far." On the other end, Van Buren was describing that night. Frosheiser said, "He got whacked on the head pretty good. He never had much of a chance—I understand that. He got hit in the wrong place."

I was watching the muted television: terror attacks in Saudi Arabia, gun battles outside Najaf, Special Forces operations in Afghanistan, Memorial Day ceremonies in America. Without sound, these felt like scenes from a war that had already receded into history.

"He wasn't able to talk after he was hit, was he?" Frosheiser asked. Listening, he broke into a sob. "But he was trying? Yeah, that sounds like him. I believe it. Yeah, I believe it."

150. Christopher Hitchens, "Don't 'Son' Me: End This Silly Talk About Sacrificing Children"

(2005)

Christopher Hitchens responds here to George Packer's *New Yorker* essay on the Froheiser family (document 149). Born in Portsmouth, England, Hitchens (1949–) graduated from Oxford with a degree in philosophy, politics, and economics. In the 1970s, he worked as a journalist for a number of British papers including the *New Statesmen*. In the United States, Hitchens wrote a weekly column for the *Nation* from 1982 to 2002, when he left the magazine because of philosophical disagreement over its role as a vehicle for the antiwar movement— "the voice and the echo chamber of those who truly believe that John Ashcroft is a greater menace than Osama bin Laden." Although he was formerly a socialist, by the 21st century, his politics were difficult to peg (he has written devastating critiques of public figures ranging from Bill Clinton to Henry Kissinger to Mother Theresa), though he has became an outspoken critic of "fascism with an Islamic face." In this essay, Hitchens, with his characteristic acerbic wit, mocks the idea of families "sending" their children to die in wars. A brief reply from Packer follows.

SOURCE: *Slate*, June 28, 2005.

Oh, Jesus, another barrage of emotional tripe about sons. From every quarter, one hears that the willingness to donate a male child is the only test of integrity. It's as if some primitive Spartan or Roman ritual had been reconstituted, though this time without the patriotism or the physical bravery. Worse, it has a gruesome echo of the human sacrifice that underpins Christian fundamentalism. . . .

The fathering of a grown male child does not entitle you to exclude from the argument anybody who is not thus favored. A childless person is not prevented from speaking in time of war. Nor is a person whose children are too young to serve. Nor are those of enlistment age, who are unlikely to have sons of their own. Nor is a person who has disabled children. One could easily extend the list of citizens who have exactly the same right to opine on their country's right to fight—or not to fight.

Recent events in Fallujah mean that we shall have to add "or daughter" to the above hypotheses. And why not? Women have argued for many decades that they should have the right to a more equal participation in the U.S. armed forces, and the preceding struggle to desegregate the armed services was a precursor to the wider desegregation of society. Come to think of it, what happened to the loud and widespread demand that gays be allowed to serve in uniform? Surely that was not just a Clinton-era campaign to be dropped in favor of gay marriage at just the time when the country needed troops in Afghanistan (generally agreed) and in Iraq (much disputed)?

I don't intend a taunt in the above sentence (it's more of a tease, really, as well as a serious question to which I have heard no answer), but I resent the taunt that is latent in the anti-war stress on supposedly uneven sacrifice. Did I send my children to rescue the victims of the collapsing towers of the World Trade Center? No, I expected the police and fire departments to accept the risk of gruesome death on my behalf. All of them were volunteers (many of them needlessly thrown away, as we now know, because of poor communications), and one knew that their depleted ranks would soon be filled by equally tough and heroic citizens who would volunteer in their turn. We would certainly face a grave societal crisis if that expectation turned out to be false.

But when it comes to the confrontation in Iraq, the whole notion of grown-ups volunteering is dismissed or lampooned. Instead, it's people's children getting "sent." Recall Michael Moore asking congressmen whether they would "send" one of their offspring, as if they had the power to do so, or the right? (John Ashcroft's son was in the Gulf, but I doubt that his father dispatched him there, and in any case it would take a lot more than this to reconcile me to Ashcroft, as Moore implies that it should.) Nobody has to join the armed forces, and those who do are old enough to vote, get married, and do almost everything legal except buy themselves a drink. Why infantilize young people who are entitled to every presumption of adulthood?

A new offender in this overwrought style is George Packer of *The New Yorker*, whose work on Iraq has hitherto generally been enviable. In an essay too-glibly titled "The Home Front," he tries to register the pain of the Frosheiser family, whose son was killed in Iraq in late 2003. Or rather, he attempts to register the anguish of Kurt Frosheiser's father. This is because the father was cooperative, voluble, and also very "conflicted" about the war and able to argue it from all points of view. Kurt's mother was more monochrome. "He loved this land and its principles," she said of her fallen son. "He loved Iowa. It's an honor to give my son to preserve our way of life." And that's mostly that, from this embarrassing woman who not only sounds like a Gold Star Mother from World War II but has also become (oh, dear) "an evangelical Christian." Yet isn't the point of such essays supposed to be that they illustrate the grief and emotion of the parents? Packer says that the bereft woman's son "had not spoken of the war this way."

Well, what's that got to do with it? He was a free man, and he joined up. By definition, he doesn't have to agree with his mother. (A hint to George Packer: A journalist does not acquire the grave and majestic qualities of a brave and tormented family merely by writing about them.)

Further on in the same portentous article, we encounter one Andrew Bacevich, a "professor of international relations at Boston University and a retired Army officer." What could be more impressive? This expert delivers himself of the opinion that, "If this is such a great cause, let us see one of the Bush daughters in uniform." Let me do a brief thought experiment here. Do I know a single anti-war person who would be more persuaded if one of the Bush girls joined up? Do you? Can you imagine what would be said about such a cheap emotional stunt? Stalin's son was taken prisoner by the Nazi invaders (and never exchanged), and Mao's son was killed in the war that established the present state of North Korea. I am not sure how encouraging such precedents are supposed to be, but they have nothing at all to do with the definition of a just war.

Much more important than this, however, is the implied assault on civilian control of the military. In this republic, elected civilians give crisp orders to soldiers and expect these orders to be obeyed. No back chat can even be imagined, let alone allowed. Do liberals really want the Joint Chiefs to say: "Mr. President, I'll respect that order when you have a son or daughter in uniform"? It was a great day when President Lincoln fired Gen. George B. McClellan. It was a great day when President Truman fired Gen. Douglas MacArthur. No presidential brat needed to be on the front line for this point to be understood.

The wars in Afghanistan and Iraq are either worthwhile or they are not (and I see that nobody as yet requires an "exit strategy" from Afghanistan). The worst exploitation of a hero by our military has certainly been the crass lying by the Pentagon about the "friendly fire" death of Pat Tillman, who was looking to risk his life against the Taliban. However, the majority of American dead have still been civilians living in America, and those who prattle on about the sacrifice of children seem not to have read about Beslan, or thought about it, or broken with the lazy old American habit that supposes that war is always "over there."

Remarks from the Fray

George Packer Responds:
Slate readers will have to get a copy of *The New Yorker* to know how badly Christopher Hitchens has twisted what I wrote, because unfortunately my piece isn't online. I didn't say that people who don't put on a uniform have no moral standing to an opinion about the Iraq War. Hitchens is welcome to continue having his, and sometimes I'll agree with them. I didn't say that the father in the piece "sent" his son to war and thereby earned atavistic authority for his "sacrifice"; the son enlisted against his father's wishes. (What I did say was that the opinionmaking press has been far more intent on winning arguments about Iraq than grappling with the realities of the war.) I am surprised, though, at how ca-

sually Hitchens dismissed or overlooked several facts that threaten the war effort he supports: first, that the armed forces are stretched desperately thin; second, that the unequal burden of the war—a matter of political choice, not wartime inevitability—is breeding cynicism among those who carry it and detachment among those who don't; third, that, partly because of this inequality, the public's commitment to the war is fading; and fourth, that the Bush administration, with its partisanship and mendacity, has polarized the country over Iraq when the war requires as much unity as possible. If the thoughts of the father I wrote about don't mean anything to Hitchens simply because the man's son was killed in combat, they should matter because he's a citizen whose support the administration and the war once had and are losing.

151. Matt Taibbi, "Bush vs. the Mother"

(2005)

In this article, Matt Taibbi chronicles Gold Star mother Cindy Sheehan's encampment on president Bush's Texas doorstep. Sometimes referred to as the "next Hunter S. Thompson," Taibbi (1970–) went to Bard College, worked in the former Soviet Union for ten years, and wrote for alternative media sources, such as the *New York Press*. He wrote a book about the 2004 presidential election campaigns, *Spanking the Donkey: Dispatches from the Dumb Season*, before becoming a contributing editor at *Rolling Stone*. In this essay, Taibbi not only reports on the start of a significant turn in the antiwar movement—privileging the voices of Sheehan and other military families— but also takes an irreverent measure of the president's supporters as well as his opponents.

SOURCE: *Rolling Stone*, September 8, 2005, pp. 60–62.

On the President's Doorstep—A Dead Soldier, an Aggrieved Housewife and the Start of Something Big

CRAWFORD, THE HOME OF PRESIDENT GEORGE W. Bush, is a sun-scorched hole of a backwater Texas town—a single dreary railroad crossing surrounded on all sides by roasted earth the color of dried dog shit. There are scattered clumps of trees and brush, but all the foliage seems bent from the sun's rays and ready at any moment to burst into flames. The moaning cattle along the lonely roads sound like they're begging for their lives. The down-town streets are empty. Just as the earth is home to natural bridges, this place is a natural dead end—the perfect place to drink a bottle of Lysol, wind up in a bad marriage, have your neck ripped out by a vulture.

It is a very unlikely place for a peace movement to be born. But that's exactly what happened a few weeks ago, when an aggrieved war mom named Cindy Sheehan set up camp along the road to the president's ranch and demanded a meeting with the commander in chief.

Sheehan's vigil began on Saturday, August 6th, and was originally a solitary affair. Her twenty-four-year-old son, Casey Sheehan, was killed way back in April 2004, when he was one of eight Marines struck down in an ambush in Baghdad's Sadr City.

Sheehan's demand was that Bush meet with her and explain to her what, exactly, her son had died for. The demand, and the accompanying solitary vigil, began as a simple, powerful, unequivocal political statement—the unarguably genuine protest of a single grieving individual. It was a quest that began on a moral territory almost beyond argument: How could anyone quibble with a mother who'd lost her son?

But Sheehan quickly became more than just the Next Big Media Thing, a successor to Kobe, Laci and Michael. Her campsite became the epicenter of a national anti-war movement that until recently had been largely forgotten. And by the end of a full week of media insanity, it seemed fit to ask if anything was left of that original simple message—or if something else had taken its place.

I arrived in Crawford early in the afternoon on Thursday, August 11th, the sixth day of Sheehan's vigil. The campsite, dubbed "Camp Casey," was a small row of tents lining the side of a road cutting through a bleak stretch of singed ranch land, some three miles from the president's compound. There were about a hundred people there when I showed up, a large chunk of them reporters—whose presence, clearly, the protesters had already adjusted to. Along one row of tents, a small group of sunbathing young activists was trying out a new cheer for KCEN, the local NBC affiliate:

"C! I! N-D-Y! She deserves a reason why!"

On the other side of the camp was Sheehan herself, a tall, deliberate, sad-looking woman with sun-lightened hair and a face red from the afternoon heat. I didn't get within ten feet of her before I was intercepted by a pair of young women from the feminist anti-war organization Code Pink. Alicia and Tiffany had apparently assumed the role of press secretaries; Sheehan was already operating on a rigid media schedule.

Throughout my stay in Texas I would run into a steady stream of young volunteers who seemed to consider it a great honor to be able to announce that "Cindy is too busy to talk with you right now." A solemn code of Cindy-reverence quickly became a leitmotif of the scene; preserving the sanctity of Sheehan's naps, meals and Internet time became a principle that the whole compound worked together to uphold.

On my first night at the camp, a protester parked too close to a gully, and her car slipped into a ditch. While a bunch of us tried to extricate it, pushing the car as its wheels spun, one protester leaned over to another.

"Blame George fucking Bush!" he said, pushing.

"I blame George fucking Bush for everything!" was the answer.

They were kidding, but we still didn't get the car out of the ditch that night.

If the pre-Sheehan anti-war movement had a problem, it was stuff like this. The movement likes to think of itself as open and inclusive, but in practice it often comes off like a bunch of nerds whose favored recreation is coming up with clever passwords for their secret treehouse. The ostensible political purpose may be ending the war, but the immediate occupation for a sizable percentage of these people always seemed to be a kind of rolling adult tourist attraction called Hating George Bush. Marches become Hate Bush Cruises; vigils, Hate Bush Resorts. Hence the astonishingly wide variety of anti-Bush tees (Camp Casey featured a rare film-fantasy matched set, home at various times to BUSH IS SAURON and DARTH INVADER); the unstoppable flow of Bush-themed folk songs. If you spend any amount of time involved with peace protests, as I have, you very quickly start to notice that Hating the President just seems like a little too much of a fun thing for too many of your brothers-in-arms.

Then again, here as in the rest of America, there's no shortage of folks who spend too much time sick with the opposite disease, Loving the President. In downtown Crawford, the two groups are separated by a Mason-Dixon line. While the anti-Bush protesters congregate at a Zonker Harris-style commune called the Crawford Peace House, the pro-Bush crowd has a meeting place in a giant gift shop called the Yellow Rose.

It's a striking visual scene: On one side of the railroad tracks running through town there's a creaky old house, bedecked with peace signs, that looks like the home of the Partridge family. A few hundred yards away, across the tracks, is the Yellow Rose—a patriotic storefront drenched in red, white and blue whose entrance is obscured by a Liberty Bell, flanked by two huge stone tablets bearing the Ten Commandments. Together, the two places look like a pair of rides in a *Cross-fire* theme park.

Early on my third day I was browsing in the hat section of the Yellow Rose when a clerk approached me.

"Excuse me," I said, holding up two Old Glory mesh hats. "Which of these do you think looks more American?"

She smiled and walked away. A friendly feeling welled up inside me. Within five minutes I was talking to store owner Bill Johnson, a fanatical Bush devotee with a striking resemblance to frozen-sausage king Jimmy Dean. I introduced myself as a Fox TV booker named Larry Weinblatt and told Bill I wanted to bring Sean Hannity down to do a whole show with Sean standing between the Ten Commandments tablets. Bill was all over the idea.

"We want to have that kind of godlike effect," I said.

"Right," Bill said, nodding.

"Secondly, Sean, when he travels," I said, "he brings his own Nautilus equipment. He pumps iron before he goes on."

"Does he really?"

"Yeah," I said. "We get a lot of demonstrators when Sean does his show, and so what he likes to do, when he finishes the broadcast, he takes his shirt off and flexes his muscles for the crowd. You know, *rrrr* . . ."

"Is he really built like that?"

"Oh, man, he's huge," I said.

We went on like this for a while. Fifteen minutes later, we wrapped up the negotiations.

"Again," I said, "we'd like to use the bell, the Ten Commandments, that backdrop, some horses, and if you have those good-looking Christian girls, we'll take them, too."

"Whatever you want, we'll do it," Bill said.

We shook hands. From there, I went to the inevitable conservative counter-demonstration, which was organized by Dallas right-wing talk-show reptile Darrell Ankarlo. Sheehan's transformation in the right-wing media from anonymous war mom to the great horned pinko Satan was unusually rapid, even by their standards.

The chief talking points were established within four days after her vigil started: Sheehan was a fame-seeking narcissist, an anti-American traitor who dishonored her dead son (Bill O'Reilly questioned her motives and suggested people might see her actions as treasonous) and a stooge for Michael Moore. This Dallas jock Ankarlo chipped in with a claim that he'd received a series of death threats, some of which, he implied, had come from Sheehan's peaceniks.

There are times when American politics seems like little more than two groups in a fever to prevent each other from trespassing upon their respective soothing versions of unreality. At one point at Camp Casey, an informal poll taken around a campfire revealed that six out of a group of ten protesters selected at random, believed that the United States government was directly involved in planning the 9/11 bombings. Flabbergasted, I tried to press the issue.

"Do you know how many people would have to be involved in that conspiracy?" I said. "I mean, start with the pilots. . . ."

"The planes were flown by remote control," a girl sitting across from me snapped.

But things were no better at Ankarlo's counterdemonstration. Aaron Martin, 31, had never heard the administration say that Iraq had nothing to do with 9/11, but Martin did remember one thing about Iraq that he said he'd heard "prior to 9/11."

"They had a fuselage," he said. "It was like a 747 fuselage that they use for training purposes for terrorism."

Was there any other reason he believed Iraq was connected to 9/11?

"It's just a general feeling," he said.

Another group I spoke with asked me why I believed Iraq wasn't connected to 9/11. I answered that Saddam Hussein's secular government was a political enemy of the Islamic fundamentalists.

"Well," said Raymond Smith, 42, "the enemy of my enemy is my friend."

He laughed, and the group nodded at me triumphantly.

It was like a scene from *Spinal Tap*. Three seconds passed.

"But," I said finally, "that doesn't make any sense, does it?"

Everyone shrugged impatiently. Who gives a fuck? We believe what we believe—and fuck you if you don't like it. The Iraq war is like the sun: No one wants to stare at it too long.

BY THE TIME I FINALLY SAT DOWN with Sheehan, I was deeply frustrated with all of this, and I was ready to blame her for what had become, in my mind, a noisome exercise in blind chest-puffing on both sides. By the eighth day of her vigil, practically every anti-Bush movement under the sun had wiggled into Crawford to get a piece of the action, and it seemed to me that all had been lost and that Sheehan had allowed the illogic of a media hurricane—noise for noise's sake—to take over her protest. Particularly irritating was the sight of a giant school bus bearing the inscription "Free the Cuban Five" parked in front of the Peace House. Jesus, I thought. The Mumia people can't be far behind.

"What's the Cuban Five?" Sheehan asked when we finally sat down, alone.

"They're on the front lawn here. . . ."

She shook her head helplessly. She had no idea who they were.

We met in a trailer parked outside the Peace House that someone had volunteered for her use. The trailer-sanctuary added to the movie-star vibe that followed Sheehan around everywhere in Crawford; I half expected to see a director's chair marked MS. SHEEHAN parked out front.

But for all this, Sheehan seemed a very lonely woman. Tall, lanky and clunkily built, with the most common and therefore most tragic of faces—the forgotten housewife whom life, with all its best joys, has long ago passed by— Sheehan had begun to move around the compound with a preternatural slowness, like a ghost. She floated, rather than walked, into the trailer. After a week of media madness, she was like a superhero unable to return home after falling into a vat of disfiguring acid. Her past—the middleclass family life in Vacaville, California, with her four kids and the yellow station wagon they nicknamed the Banana-Mobile—all that was gone.

She had been through so much in the past week. In still more proof that red-blue politics often comes before family in this country, her in-laws had released a statement cruelly denouncing her. Her estranged husband, perhaps a coward and perhaps unable to handle the stress, filed for divorce. Revelations about her personal life were spilling into print, and all around the country, heartless creeps like Drudge and Ankarlo were casting themselves as friends and protectors of her fallen son and criticizing her for dishonoring him.

In return for all that, what Sheehan got was this: her own trailer, a couple of weeks' worth of airtime and a bunch of people who called themselves her friends but were really just humping the latest cause. They would probably be moving on soon, and Sheehan would be left with nothing. And meeting her now, I was struck by one more thing: At the end, when it was all over, her son would still be gone.

I felt very sorry for her.

"I never knew," she said, sighing. "Not only that I would become the face of the anti-war movement but also that I would become the sacrificial lamb of the anti-war movement."

I asked her if she was referring to all the personal attacks. She nodded.

"But I'd still do it again," she said. "Because it's so important."

Sheehan's political sincerity has been questioned, and in almost every case the charges against her have proved monstrous, calculating and untrue. An example of the kind of thing that's been pinned to her: Matt Drudge blasted her for being a flip-flopper after digging up seemingly pro-Bush Sheehan quotes from a California newspaper after she and other war parents met with the president.

Among those were "That was the gift the president gave us, the gift of happiness, of being together." Drudge implied that Sheehan was referring to the meeting with the president. In fact, what Sheehan was saying was that the real gift Bush gave the families was the opportunity to meet each other, not the president.

Things like this are what Sheehan's detractors are using to describe what they call "Cindy's Political Agenda," but I didn't observe any agenda from Sheehan, just a very tired woman. Like everyone else in anti-war circles, Sheehan does sometimes speak in the clubby language of Camp Bush Hater—but when she does this, she sounds like a follower, not a leader. In the end, the movement might overtake her, but while she is still at its center she seems genuinely to be trying to do the right thing.

"This thing," she said, "it's bigger than me now."

Sheehan believes that no matter what happens, one thing she accomplished was the returning of the Iraq war to its rightful place at the forefront of the national consciousness. She describes an experience earlier in the week when a TV producer offhandedly mentioned to her that her timing was perfect, that Sheehan had been lucky to hold her vigil on what was otherwise a slow news week.

"And I said to her, 'A slow news week? Didn't thirty soldiers die in the war this month?'" She shook her head. "It's crazy. Iraq should be the lead story every day."

LATE THAT NIGHT, a car pulled up at the campsite. There was a woman at the wheel, and she was crying.

She was a Bush supporter who lives in the area, but her son was about to be shipped off to Iraq. She had made a special trip out here to complain about the long row of white crosses the protesters had planted along the side of the road—each cross bearing the name of a fallen soldier. "Y'all are breaking my heart!" she cried. "My son hasn't gone yet, and I have to see those crosses every morning." She collected herself, wailed, and cried again, "You've broken one woman's heart!"

She drove off.

In the Sixties, the anti-war movement was part of a cultural revolution: If you opposed Vietnam, you were also rejecting the whole rigid worldview that said life meant going to war, fighting the Commies, then coming back to work for the man, buying two cars and dying with plenty of insurance. That life blueprint was the inflexible expectation of the time, and so ending the war of that era required a visionary movement.

Iraq isn't like that. Iraq is an insane blunder committed by a bunch of criminal incompetents who have managed so far to avoid the lash and the rack only because the machinery for avoiding reality is so advanced in this country. We don't watch the fighting, we don't see the bodies come home and we don't hear anyone screaming when a house in Baghdad burns down or a child steps on a mine.

The only movement we're going to need to end this fiasco is a more regular exposure to consequence. It needs to feel its own pain. Cindy Sheehan didn't bring us folk songs, but she did put pain on the front pages. And along a lonely Texas road late at night, I saw it spread.

152. David Rees, Get Your War On

(2005)

In this cartoon, David Rees plumbs a familiar theme: examining the American home front through characters not touched directly by the war. Rees (1973–), a graduate of Oberlin, worked as a temp—a fact checker—at *Maxim* magazine in New York until shortly after the September 11 terrorist attacks. He started the strip *Get Your War On* in October 2001, as the United States prepared to attack Afghanistan, writing ironic and often profane dialogue over public domain clip-art images (downloaded from the Internet) of office workers speaking to each other over the phone, from their cubicles, or on lunch break. Within weeks, the strip became an Internet sensation. "The whole point is to show the perpetual state of anxiety and change," he said in 2002. Soon, it led to the publication of two books (Rees gave all the proceeds to an organization that clears land mines in Afghanistan because he did not want to profit from the war) and weekly publication of the strip in *Rolling Stone*. The targets of Rees's satire in this strip are pretty self-evident.

SOURCE: *Rolling Stone*, September 8, 2005.

"The Bush administration is **SIGNIFICANTLY LOWERING EXPECTATIONS** of what can be achieved in Iraq, recognizing that the United States will have to settle for far less progress than originally envisioned. . . . The United States no longer expects to see a model new democracy, a self-supporting oil industry or a society in which the majority of people are free from serious security or economic challenges. . . ." (The *Washington Post*, 8/14/05).

153. John Mueller, "The Iraq Syndrome"

(2005)

In this essay, political scientist John Mueller examines the dynamic of declining public support for the Iraq War and the White House reaction to the decline. Mueller (1938–) was born in Minnesota, graduated from the University of Chicago in 1960, and earned his Ph.D. in political science at UCLA in 1965. The recipient of numerous awards, he has taught at the University of Rochester and at Ohio State University, where he holds the Woody Hayes Chair of National Security Studies. He established himself as an expert on public opinion in wartime with his 1973 book on the Korean and Vietnam War eras, *War, Presidents, and Public Opinion*. This essay extends his expertise to the phenomenon of the rapidly plunging public confidence regarding the Iraq War in late 2005. He notes the administration's strategy to lower expectations (see document 152) in the face of this "Iraq syndrome."

SOURCE: *Foreign Affairs* 84, no. 6 (November/December 2005), 44–54.

The War and the Public

American troops have been sent into harm's way many times since 1945, but in only three cases—Korea, Vietnam, and Iraq—have they been drawn into sustained ground combat and suffered more than 300 deaths in action. American public opinion became a key factor in all three wars, and in each one there has been a simple association: as casualties mount, support decreases. Broad enthusiasm at the outset invariably erodes.

The only thing remarkable about the current war in Iraq is how precipitously American public support has dropped off. Casualty for casualty, support has declined far more quickly than it did during either the Korean War or the Vietnam War. And if history is any indication, there is little the Bush administration can do to reverse this decline.

More important, the impact of deteriorating support will not end when the war does. In the wake of the wars in Korea and Vietnam, the American public developed a strong aversion to embarking on such ventures again. A similar sentiment—an "Iraq syndrome"—seems to be developing now, and it will have important consequences for U.S. foreign policy for years after the last American battalion leaves Iraqi soil.

Drowning by Numbers

The public gave substantial support to the military ventures in Korea, Vietnam, and Iraq as the troops were sent in. In all cases, support decreased as casualties—whether of draftees, volunteers, or reservists—mounted. In each case, the increase in the number of people who considered the venture to be a mistake was steep during the war's early stages, as reluctant supporters were rather quickly alienated; the erosion slowed as approval was reduced to the harder core. (The dramatic early drop in support for the war in Korea reflected the large number of casualties suffered in the opening phase of that war.)

The most striking thing about the comparison among the three wars is how much more quickly support has eroded in the case of Iraq. By early 2005, when combat deaths were around 1,500, the percentage of respondents who considered the Iraq war a mistake—over half—was about the same as the percentage who considered the war in Vietnam a mistake at the time of the 1968 Tet offensive, when nearly 20,000 soldiers had already died.

This lower tolerance for casualties is largely due to the fact that the American public places far less value on the stakes in Iraq than it did on those in Korea and Vietnam. The main threats Iraq was thought to present to the United States when troops went in—weapons of mass destruction and support for international terrorism—have been, to say the least, discounted. With those justifications gone, the Iraq war is left as something of a humanitarian venture, and, as Francis Fukuyama has put it, a request to spend "several hundred billion dollars and several thousand American lives in order to bring democracy to . . . Iraq" would "have been laughed out of court." Given the evaporation of the main reasons for going to war and the unexpectedly high level of American casualties, support for the war in Iraq is, if anything, higher than one might expect—a reflection of the fact that many people still connect the effort there to the "war" on terrorism, an enterprise that continues to enjoy huge support. In addition, the toppling of Saddam Hussein remains a singular accomplishment—something the American people had wanted since the 1991 Persian Gulf War.

When one shifts from questions about whether the war was a "mistake" or "worth it" to ones about whether the United States should get out, much the same pattern holds for Korea, Vietnam, and Iraq: relatively steep declines in support for continuing the war in the early stages, slower erosion later. However, it is close to impossible to judge how many people want to get out or stay the course at any given time because so much depends on how the question is worded. For example, there is far more support for "gradual withdrawal" or "beginning to withdraw" than for "withdrawing" or "immediate withdrawal." Thus in August 2005, The Washington Post found that 54 percent of respondents favored staying and 44 percent favored withdrawing when the options were posed this way: "Do you think the United States should keep its military forces in Iraq until civil order is restored there, even if that means continued U.S. military casualties, or, do you think the United States should withdraw its military forces from Iraq in order to avoid further U.S. military casualties, even if that means civil order is not restored there?" But in the same month, a Harris poll tallied only 36 percent in support of staying and 61 percent in support of withdrawing when it asked, "Do you favor keeping a large number of U.S. troops in Iraq until there is a stable government there or bringing most of our troops home in the next year?" Still, no matter how the questions are phrased, all the polls have logged increases in pro-withdrawal sentiment over the course of the war.

Many analysts have tried to link declining support to factors other than accumulating combat deaths. For example, the notion that public opinion sours as casualties increase has somehow turned into "support drops when they start seeing the body bags"—a vivid expression that some in the Bush administration have apparently taken literally. As a result, the military has worked enterprisingly to keep Americans from seeing pictures of body bags or flag-draped coffins in the hope that this will somehow arrest the decline in enthusiasm for the war effort. But such pictures are not necessary to drive home the basic reality of mounting casualties.

Growing opposition to the war effort also has little to do with whether or not there is an active antiwar movement at home. There has not been much of one in the case of the Iraq war, nor was there one during the war in Korea. Nonetheless, support for those ventures eroded as it did during the Vietnam War, when antiwar protest was frequent and visible. In fact, since the Vietnam protest movement became so strongly associated with anti-American values and activities, it may ultimately have been somewhat counterproductive.

Moreover, support for the war declines whether or not war opponents are able to come up with specific policy alternatives. Dwight Eisenhower never seemed to have much of a plan for getting out of the Korean War—although he did say that, if elected, he would visit the place—but discontent with the war still worked well for him in the 1952 election; Richard Nixon's proposals for fixing the Vietnam mess were distinctly unspecific, although he did from time to time mutter that he had a "secret plan." Wars hurt the war-initiating political party not because the opposition comes up with a coherent clashing vision—George McGovern tried that, with little success, against Nixon in 1972—but because discontent over the war translates into vague distrust of the capacities of the people running the country.

The impact of war discontent on congressional races is less clear. Democrats attempted to capitalize on the widespread outrage over Nixon's invasion of Cambodia in 1970 but were unable to change things much. And subsequent developments, including campaign reform legislation, have made incumbents increasingly less vulnerable.

Damage Control

President George W. Bush, like Lyndon Johnson before him, has made countless speeches explaining what the effort in Iraq is about, urging patience, and asserting that progress is being made. But as was also evident during Woodrow Wilson's campaign to sell the League of Nations to the American public, the efficacy of the bully pulpit is much overrated. The prospects for reversing the erosion of support for the war in Iraq are thus limited. The run-ups to the two wars in Iraq are also instructive in this regard: even though both Presidents Bush labored mightily to sell the war effort, the only thing that succeeded in raising the level of enthusiasm was the sight of troops actually heading into action, which triggered a predictable "rally round the flag" effect.

Although the impact of official rhetoric is limited, favorable occurrences in the war itself can boost support from time to time. In the case of the war in Iraq, for example, there were notable upward shifts in many polls after Saddam was captured and elections were held. These increases, however, proved to be temporary, more bumps on the road than permanent changes in direction. Support soon fell back to where it had been before and then continued its generally downward course. The same is true of negative occurrences: a drop in support after the disclosure of abuses at Abu Ghraib in 2004 was in time mostly reversed.

Some scholars have argued that support for war is determined by the prospects for success rather than casualties. Americans are "defeat-phobic" rather than "casualty-phobic," the argument goes; they do not really care how many casualties are suffered so long as their side comes out the winner. For example, the political scientists Peter Feaver and Christopher Gelpi have calculated, rather remarkably, that Americans would on average be entirely willing to see 6,861 soldiers die in order to bring democracy to Congo.

There never were periods of continuous good news in the wars in Korea or Vietnam, so there is no clear precedent here. But should good news start coming in from Iraq—including, in particular, a decline in American casualty rates—it would more likely cause the erosion in public support to slow or even cease rather than trigger a large upsurge in support. For support to rise notably, many of those now disaffected by the war would need to reverse their position, and that seems rather unlikely: polls that seek to tap intensity of feeling find that more than 80 percent of those opposed to the war "strongly" feel that way. If you purchase a car for twice what it is worth, you will still consider the deal to have been a mistake even if you come to like the car.

Also relevant is the fact that despite the comparatively mild-mannered behavior of Democratic leaders in the run-up to the Iraq war, partisan differences regarding this war, and this president, are incredibly deep. Gary Jacobson, a political scientist at the University of California, San Diego, has documented that the partisan divide over the war in Iraq is considerably greater than for any military action over the last half century and that the partisan split on presidential approval ratings, despite a major narrowing after the attacks of September 11, 2001, is greater than for any president over that period—greater than for Clinton,

Reagan, or Nixon. This means that Bush cannot look for increased Republican support because he already has practically all of it; meanwhile, Democrats are unlikely to budge much. There may be some hope for him among independents, but their war-support patterns more nearly track those of the almost completely disaffected Democrats than those of the steadfast Republicans.

Moreover, it is difficult to see what a spate of good news would look like at this point. A clear-cut victory, like the one scored by George H.W. Bush in the Gulf in 1991, is hugely unlikely—and the glow even of that one faded quickly as Saddam continued to hold forth in Iraq. From the start of the current Iraq war, the invading forces were too small to establish order, and some of the early administrative policies proved fatally misguided. In effect, the United States created an instant failed state, and clambering out of that condition would be difficult in the best of circumstances. If the worst violence diminishes, and Iraq thereby ceases to be quite so much of a bloody mess, the war will attract less attention. But there is still likely to be plenty of official and unofficial corruption, sporadic vigilantism, police misconduct, militia feuding, political backstabbing, economic travail, regional separatism, government incompetence, rampant criminality, religious conflict, and posturing by political entrepreneurs spouting anti-American and anti-Israeli rhetoric. Under such conditions, the American venture in Iraq is unlikely to be seen as a great victory by those now in opposition, over half of whom profess to be not merely dissatisfied with the war, but angry over it.

In all of this, what chiefly matters for American public opinion is American losses, not those of the people defended. By some estimates, the number of Iraqis who have died as a result of the invasion has reached six figures—vastly more than have been killed by all international terrorists in all of history. Sanctions on Iraq probably were a necessary cause of death for an even greater number of Iraqis, most of them children. Yet the only cumulative body count that truly matters in the realm of American public opinion, and the only one that is routinely reported, is the American one. There is nothing new about this: although there was considerable support for the wars in Korea and Vietnam, polls made clear that people backed the wars because they saw them as vital to confronting the communist threat; defending the South Koreans or the South Vietnamese per se was never thought of as an important goal.

The Politics of Debacle

In Iraq, as they did in Vietnam, U.S. troops face an armed opposition that is dedicated, resourceful, capable of replenishing its ranks, and seemingly determined to fight as long as necessary. In Vietnam, the hope was that after suffering enough punishment, the enemy would reach its "breaking point" and then either fade away or seek accommodation. Great punishment was inflicted, but the enemy never broke; instead, it was the United States that faded away after signing a face-saving agreement. Whether the insurgents in Iraq have the same determination and fortitude is yet to be seen. The signs thus far, however, are not very encouraging: the insurgency does not appear to be weakening.

Many people, including President Bush, argue that the United States must slog on because a precipitous exit from Iraq would energize Islamist militants, who would see it as an even greater victory than the expulsion of the Soviet Union from Afghanistan. A quick exit would confirm, the thinking goes, Osama bin Laden's basic theory: that terrorists can defeat the United States by continuously inflicting on it casualties that are small in number but still draining. A venture designed and sold as a blow against international terrorists would end up emboldening and energizing them.

The problem is that almost any exit from Iraq will have this effect. Bin Laden, as well as huge majorities in Muslim countries and in parts of Europe, believe that the United States invaded Iraq as part of its plan to control oil supplies in the Middle East. Although Washington has no intention of doing that, at least not in the direct sense that bin Laden and others mean, U.S. forces will inevitably leave Iraq without having accomplished what many consider to be Washington's real goals there—and the terrorist insurgents will claim credit for forcing the United States out before it fulfilled these key objectives. Iraq has also, of course, become something of a terrorist training—and inspiration—zone.

When the United States was preparing to withdraw from Vietnam, many Americans feared that there would be a bloodbath if the country fell to the North Vietnamese. And indeed, on taking control, the Communists executed tens of thousands of people, sent hundreds of thousands to "reeducation camps" for long periods, and so mismanaged the economy that hundreds of thousands fled the country out of desperation, often in barely floating boats. (What happened in neighboring Cambodia when the Khmer Rouge took over makes even the word "bloodbath" seem an understatement.)

There is a similar concern this time around: Iraq could devolve into a civil war after the Americans leave. Thus, U.S. officials have updated "Vietnamization" and applied it to Iraq. They are making strenuous efforts to fabricate a reasonably viable local government, police, and military that can take over the fight, allowing U.S. forces to withdraw judiciously. In Vietnam, of course, communist forces took over less than two years after the United States installed a sympathetic government. Although the consequences of a U.S. withdrawal from Iraq are likely to be messy, they may be less dire. The insurgency in Iraq, albeit deadly and dedicated, represents a much smaller, less popular, and less organized force than the Vietcong did, and it does not have the same kind of international backing. Moreover, many of the insurgents are fighting simply to get U.S. troops out of the country and can be expected to stop when the Americans leave. The insurgency will likely become more manageable without the U.S. presence, even if there is a determined effort by at least some of the rebels to go after a government that, in their eyes, consists of quislings and collaborators. It is also impressive that efforts by the insurgents to stoke a civil war between the Shiites and the Sunnis have not been very successful thus far; most Shiites have refused to see the insurgents as truly representative of the Sunni population.

Even if Iraq does turn out to be a foreign policy debacle—by declining into a hopeless quagmire or collapsing into civil chaos—history suggests that withdrawing need not be politically devastating (unless, perhaps, failure in Iraq leads directly to terrorism in the United States). As it happens, the American people have proved quite capable of taking debacle in stride; they do not seem to be terribly "defeat-phobic." They supported the decision to withdraw U.S. troops from Lebanon in 1984 after a terrorist bomb killed 241 Americans in the civil war there; the man who presided over that debacle, Ronald Reagan, readily won reelection a few months later. Something similar happened to Bill Clinton when he withdrew troops from Somalia in 1994: by the time the next election rolled around, people had largely forgotten the whole episode.

The most remarkable, and relevant, precedent is the utter collapse of the U.S. position in Vietnam in 1975. The man who presided over that debacle, Gerald Ford, actually tried to use it to his advantage in his reelection campaign the next year. As he pointed out, when he came into office the United States was "still deeply involved in the problems of Vietnam, [but now] we are at peace. Not a single young American is fighting or dying on any foreign soil tonight." His challenger, Jimmy Carter, apparently did not think it good politics to point out the essential absurdity of Ford's declaration.

Moreover, even if disaster follows a U.S. withdrawal—as it did in Vietnam, Lebanon, and Somalia—the people dying will be Iraqis, not Americans. And the deaths of foreigners, as noted earlier, are not what move the public.

Indispensable Nation?

After the war in Vietnam, there was a strong desire among Americans never to do "that" again. And, in fact, there never was "another Vietnam" during the Cold War. Due to this "Vietnam syndrome," Congress hampered the White House's ability to pursue even rather modest anticommunist ventures in Africa and, to a lesser extent, Latin America (though there was bipartisan support for aiding the anti-Soviet jihad in Afghanistan). Meanwhile, the genocide in Cambodia was studiously ignored in part because of fears that paying attention might lead to the conclusion that American troops should be sent over to rectify the disaster; over most of the course of the genocide, the three major networks devoted a total of 29 minutes of their newscasts to a cataclysm in which millions died.

No matter how the war in Iraq turns out, an Iraq syndrome seems likely. A poll in relatively war-approving Alabama earlier this year, for example, asked whether the United States should be prepared to send troops back to Iraq to establish order there in the event a full-scale civil war erupted after a U.S. withdrawal. Only a third of the respondents favored doing so.

Among the casualties of the Iraq syndrome could be the Bush doctrine, unilateralism, preemption, preventive war, and indispensable-nationhood. Indeed, these once-fashionable (and sometimes self-infatuated) concepts are already picking up a patina of quaintness. Specifically, there will likely be growing skepticism about various key notions: that the United States should take unilateral military action to correct situations or overthrow regimes it considers reprehensible but that present no immediate threat to it, that it can and should forcibly bring democracy to other nations not now so blessed, that it has the duty to rid the world of evil, that having by far the largest defense budget in the world is necessary and broadly beneficial, that international cooperation is of only very limited value, and that Europeans and other well-meaning foreigners are naive and decadent wimps. The United States may also become more inclined to seek international cooperation, sometimes even showing signs of humility.

In part because of the military and financial overextension in Iraq (and Afghanistan), the likelihood of any coherent application of military power or even of a focused military threat against the remaining entities on the Bush administration's once-extensive hit list has substantially diminished. In the meantime, any country that suspects it may be on the list has the strongest incentive to make the American experience in Iraq as miserable as possible. Some may also come to consider that deterring the world's last remaining superpower can be accomplished by preemptively and prominently recruiting and training a few thousand of their citizens to fight and die in dedicated irregular warfare against foreign occupiers.

Evidence of the Iraq syndrome is emerging. Already, Bush has toned down his language. When North Korea abruptly declared in February that it actually possessed nuclear weapons, the announcement was officially characterized as "unfortunate" and as "rhetoric we've heard before." Iran has already become defiant, and its newly elected president has actually had the temerity to suggest—surely the unkindest cut—that he does not consider the United States to be the least bit indispensable. Ultimately, the chief beneficiaries of the war in Iraq may be Iraq's fellow members of the "axis of evil."

154. Matthew Rothschild, "Handcuffed at the Border—Akif Rahman"

(2007)

In this excerpt from his book *You Have No Rights*, Matthew Rothschild tells the story of American-born Akif Rahman in the Homeland Security age. A Harvard graduate, Rothschild started at the *Progressive* as an associate editor in 1983 and worked there in a number of different editorial roles; since 1994, he has been the magazine's editor. He also hosts a weekly half-hour radio show, *The Progressive Radio Show*, and writes a web column, *McCarthyism Watch*, that chronicles incidents of repression in post-9/11 America. *You Have No Rights* includes eighty accounts of ordinary people who, because of intensified national security policies, have found their civil rights violated. This is one example.

SOURCE: Matthew Rothschild, *You Have No Rights: Stories of America in an Age of Repression* (New York: The New Press, 2007), 113–15.

Akif Rahman was born in Springfield, Illinois. Like a lot of young entrepreneurs, he went into the computer business, establishing his own consulting firm. With employees not only in the United States but also in Pakistan and India, Rahman travels a lot. And he gets hassled a lot.

Four times within a fourteen-month period, U.S. Customs and Border Protection yanked him out of lines at airports and held him for questioning. "The first time I was detained was in March 2004," he says. "I was flying back from a business trip into L.A. from Hong Kong and Pakistan. While I was picking up my bags I was asked to come to the secondary screening area." Customs agents started to drill him, asking questions like: "Why were you traveling? Who did you meet? Why were you in Pakistan? Why are you returning to L.A. and not Chicago?"

Rahman says he felt "absolutely alarmed. I didn't know what this was all about." After a couple hours, they let him go.

Five months later Rahman was returning again from a business trip to Pakistan. This time, he flew into O'Hare.

"I was met on the jetway," he says. Once again, they took him to a screening room and ran him through a similar battery of questions. "At first they were hostile, and somewhere in the middle they'd get a little kinder," he recalls. When he asked them why they were doing this to him again they said, "Just standard procedure." Rahman asked to speak to a supervisor, who told him he could fill out a Freedom of Information Act request. Rahman took the paperwork.

The very next month Rahman went to Montreal with his parents. On the way back, at the airport in Montreal, U.S. Customs officials delayed him for more than three hours. "I went through the whole drill again," he says. As a result he ended up missing his flight and a business meeting. At that point Rahman decided he better find out what was going on, so he filled out the FOIA request. "In April of '05 I got a response saying I was misidentified," he says. But that didn't prevent Customs from misidentifying him again one month later. "I was visiting my in-laws in Canada with my wife and two little kids, who were four and two at the time. We drove back across the Detroit-Windsor tunnel. Basically, I pulled up to the booth, handed them our passports, and then was told to turn off the engine and hand over the keys to the car."

Immediately, they asked him whether he had a weapon, which he didn't.

"I was walked into the border office, with two agents standing right behind me," he says. "When I went into the office I was put against the wall, with my hands up in the air. My body was searched, one of the agents kicked my feet apart, and then they handcuffed me behind my back and cuffed me to a chair."

The handcuffs hurt. "I asked the agent whether they were necessary," Rahman says. "They said this is part of the normal procedures." But this time they didn't ask him the same old questions. "I was interviewed by an un-uniformed agent from Immigration and Customs Enforcement. He asked me whether I knew someone who was funding terrorist activities or whether I knew any of the 9/11 hijackers. I felt like a suspect, like a criminal. They were asking me a bunch of questions I have no knowledge of." After more than five hours, they finally released Rahman to his wife and kids. The little ones were crying.

Rahman had had enough. "You're scared, you're frustrated, you're humiliated, you're confused, you're concerned about why it's happening and whether it will happen again. I've never been handcuffed before in my life, and who knows what's going to happen next time?"

A day or two after getting back from Canada, Rahman contacted the ACLU of Illinois. On June 28, 2005, he filed suit against the government for violating his Fourth and Fifth Amendment rights. And on June 19, 2006, he joined a lawsuit the ACLU of Illinois was filing on behalf of eight others, including his wife.

"I can't comment on the specific suit," says Bill Anthony, senior spokesman for Customs and Border Protection at the Department of Homeland Security, "but we will not let anyone in the country until we know who they say they are and that they are not here to do harm to our citizens or violate our laws."

155. Witness Against Torture, "Letter to Office of Foreign Assets Control"

(2006)

In December 2005, two dozen American activists violated federal law banning travel to Cuba to visit prisoners being detained and tortured at the U.S. naval base at Guantanamo Bay. Activists coming primarily from the Catholic Worker movement and the tradition of Dorothy Day, the group marched fifty miles from Santiago de Cuba to Guantanamo from December 6 to December 12. At the same time, vigils were held in solidarity with the marchers around the United States. When the group arrived at Guantanamo and the authorities would not allow access to the prison (the marchers hoped to perform the Christian work of mercy of visiting the incarcerated, as called for in the Gospel of Matthew 25:36), they fasted and held prayer vigils and camped outside the Cuban side of the gates. This letter was written in reply to the Treasury Department's requirement to furnish information on the trip. As this book goes to press, no one in the group has been charged with a crime.

SOURCE: Witness Against Torture, "Letter to U.S. Department of the Treasury, Office of Foreign Assets Control," January 24, 2006, courtesy of Frida Berrigan.

January 24th, 2006

U. S. Department of the Treasury
Office of Foreign Assets Control (OFAC)
Attn: Diana Reyes
1500 Pennsylvania Avenue, N.W. (Annex)
Washington, D.C. 20220

Re: Amanda W. Daloisio (CT-258629) et al (see attached list)

Dear Ms. Reyes:
　　This letter is in response to your "Requirement to Furnish Information."
We are a group of North American people of faith in the nonviolent

tradition of Dorothy Day and the Catholic Worker Movement. After much prayer and reflection, we decided to accept President Bush's June 20th, 2005 invitation that those concerned about conditions at Guantanamo are "welcome to go down there . . . and take a look at the conditions."

From December 5th to 16th, we took part in an attempt to visit the prisoners at the US Naval Base in Guantanamo Bay, an attempt to perform a work of mercy integral to our faith.

The following report shall serve as a response to your inquiry and should cover the relevant information for OFAC to consider.

"We made this camp for people who would be here forever. You should never think of going home. You'll be here for all your life . . . Don't worry. We'll keep you alive so you can suffer more."

—A US interrogator speaking to a juvenile prisoner named Mohamed in Guantánamo

The detention center at the United States (US) Naval Base at Guantánamo Bay was made for the purposes secrecy, unaccountability and impunity. The few reports that do reach us tell of prisoners—men who are fathers, sons and brothers—without contact with their families, with very little or no contact with attorneys, of interminable detention without legal charge, of rendition, of kidnapping and the sale of prisoners to US authorities, of the desecration of the Qur'an, and of unconscionable prisoner humiliation and abuse.

Inspired by the nonviolent tradition of Dorothy Day and the Catholic Worker, we, people of faith from the US, marched solemnly to the US Naval Base in order to state without compromise our rejection of torture and abuse and loudly proclaim our stance in defense of human dignity. Recognizing that it degrades not only the humanity of its victims but also that of its perpetrators, we appeal to the soldiers at Guantánamo, our brothers and sisters, to end the torture. We approached the base to inform the world at large and the prisoners held within that their treatment is not countenanced by people of goodwill.

We went with a simple request coming from the mandate to Christians to perform the Works of Mercy: we went to visit the prisoners. As people of faith, we believe our own dignity and humanity are bound up undeniably with the dignity and humanity of all other people. We are driven by faith and conscience to respond to this humanity. We hear the cry of the prisoners when we read of hunger strikes and are compelled to do what little we can, to answer: you are not forgotten.

We went so far to visit the prisoners, to do a Work of Mercy, because the very existence of the detention camps at Guantánamo Bay defies a coherent ethical explanation. Putting detention camps at Guantánamo Bay Naval Base is an effort to hide both the prisoners and the inhuman and illegal practices allowed and enforced from ordinary Americans like ourselves. This secrecy, this silence, cannot go on.

Ordinary citizens have been asked by government and military leaders to tolerate, indeed to fund, the continued violence as we go on with our lives. Mohamed, the prisoner mentioned above, has said, "Before I came to Guantánamo, I had hope. After this, I lost all hope." We cannot go on with our lives if it means we must tolerate what is happening; while few are guilty of torture, we are all responsible. We do, and we must, believe that we can do better than this.

We hold the treatment of prisoners, especially those, like Mohamed, at Guantánamo Bay, as a mirror to our societal soul—as long as some of us are degraded, all of us are; as long as some of us are chained, none of us are free.

We have been open and honest about our trip to visit the prisoners in Guantánamo Bay. We did not intend to violate OFAC regulations, and we will not give up our rights under the First and Fifth Amendments to the Constitution of the United States.

Below is a list including the names and addresses of those who went to visit the prisoners.

Sincerely,

Jackie Allen, Hartford, CT
Gary Ashbeck, Baltimore, MD
Frida Berrigan, Brooklyn, NY
Anna Brown, Jersey City, NJ
Dana M. Brown, Ithaca, NY
Daniel Burns, Ithaca, NY
Mark Colville, New Haven, CT
Susan Crane, Baltimore, MD
Matthew Daloisio, New York, NY
Amanda Daloisio, New York, NY
Thomas J. Feagley, Malden, MA
Clare Grady, Ithaca, NY
Teresa Grady, Ithaca, NY
Steve Kelly, SJ, Oakland, CA
Art Laffin, Washington, DC
Scott Langley, Raleigh, NC
Anne Montgomery, RSCJ, New York, NY
Grace Ritter, Ithaca, NY
Patricia Santoro, Jersey City, NJ
William Streit, Louisa, VA
Sheila Stumph, Raleigh, NC
Carmen Trotta, New York, NY
Tanya Theriault, New York, NY
Matthew Vogel, New York, NY

156. Kevin Tillman, "After Pat's Birthday"

(2006)

In 2002, Kevin Tillman, along with his brother Pat Tillman, a star defensive back for the Arizona Cardinals professional football team, enlisted in the army. The Tillmans grew up in San Jose, California, and were star athletes. Pat (1976–2004) played football for Arizona State University, from which he graduated summa cum laude with a degree in marketing; in 1996 and 1997, he was an Academic All-American. In 1998, he was drafted by the Cardinals, for whom he later broke the single-season tackles record. In the offseason, Pat Tillman pursued a master's degree in history. Following the terrorist attacks in New York and Washington, Pat made a decision with his brother—himself a star baseball player, drafted by the Anaheim Angels—to join the Army Rangers. Pat passed on a $3.6 million contract offer and put his football career on hold to serve his country. On April 22, 2004, he was killed in Afghanistan in what the Pentagon at first characterized as an ambush. Later, it came out that the army covered up the circumstances of Tillman's death by friendly fire in order to exploit his sacrifice as a model of American heroism in the war on terror. The anger expressed here by Kevin Tillman fueled his request for a congressional investigation into the Bush administration's role in politicizing his brother's death. At the time this book went to press, that investigation was ongoing.

SOURCE: Truthdig.com, October 19, 2006, http://www.truthdig.com/report/item/200601019_after_pats_birthday/.

It is Pat's birthday on November 6, and elections are the day after. It gets me thinking about a conversation I had with Pat before we joined the military. He spoke about the risks with signing the papers. How once we committed, we were at the mercy of the American leadership and the American people. How we could be thrown in a direction not of our volition. How fighting as a soldier would leave us without a voice . . . until we got out.

Much has happened since we handed over our voice:

Somehow we were sent to invade a nation because it was a direct threat to the American people, or to the world, or harbored terrorists, or was involved in the September 11 attacks, or received weapons-grade uranium from Niger, or had mobile weapons labs, or WMD, or had a need to be liberated, or we needed to establish a democracy, or stop an insurgency, or stop a civil war we created that can't be called a civil war even though it is. Something like that.

Somehow our elected leaders were subverting international law and humanity by setting up secret prisons around the world, secretly kidnapping people, secretly holding them indefinitely, secretly not charging them with anything, secretly torturing them. Somehow that overt policy of torture became the fault of a few "bad apples" in the military.

Somehow back at home, support for the soldiers meant having a five-year-old kindergartener scribble a picture with crayons and send it overseas, or slapping stickers on cars, or lobbying Congress for an extra pad in a helmet. It's interesting that a soldier on his third or fourth tour should care about a drawing from a five-year-old; or a faded sticker on a car as his friends die around him; or an extra pad in a helmet, as if it will protect him when an IED throws his vehicle 50 feet into the air as his body comes apart and his skin melts to the seat.

Somehow the more soldiers that die, the more legitimate the illegal invasion becomes.

Somehow American leadership, whose only credit is lying to its people and illegally invading a nation, has been allowed to steal the courage, virtue and honor of its soldiers on the ground.

Somehow those afraid to fight an illegal invasion decades ago are allowed to send soldiers to die for an illegal invasion they started.

Somehow faking character, virtue and strength is tolerated.

Somehow profiting from tragedy and horror is tolerated.

Somehow the death of tens, if not hundreds, of thousands of people is tolerated.

Somehow subversion of the Bill of Rights and The Constitution is tolerated.

Somehow suspension of Habeas Corpus is supposed to keep this country safe.

Somehow torture is tolerated.

Somehow lying is tolerated.

Somehow reason is being discarded for faith, dogma, and nonsense.

Somehow American leadership managed to create a more dangerous world.

Somehow a narrative is more important than reality.

Somehow America has become a country that projects everything that it is not and condemns everything that it is.

Somehow the most reasonable, trusted and respected country in the world has become one of the most irrational, belligerent, feared, and distrusted countries in the world.

Somehow being politically informed, diligent, and skeptical has been replaced by apathy through active ignorance.

Somehow the same incompetent, narcissistic, virtueless, vacuous, malicious criminals are still in charge of this country.

Somehow this is tolerated.

Somehow nobody is accountable for this.

In a democracy, the policy of the leaders is the policy of the people. So don't be shocked when our grandkids bury much of this generation as traitors to the nation, to the world and to humanity. Most likely, they will come to know that "somehow" was nurtured by fear, insecurity and indifference, leaving the country vulnerable to unchecked, unchallenged parasites.

Luckily this country is still a democracy. People still have a voice. People still can take action. It can start after Pat's birthday.

Brother and Friend of Pat Tillman,
Kevin Tillman

157. Gathering of Eagles,
"Our Mission Statement"

(2007)

In this mission statement put out by the prowar group Gathering of Eagles, the authors take issue with the sentiment expressed by the antiwar movement that one could oppose the war but still support the troops. Mobilized in 2007 to stage a counterprotest at an antiwar rally held near the Vietnam War Memorial in Washington, D.C., Gathering of Eagles is made up primarily of veterans and other self-styled patriots. With chapters all over the country, and national and state web sites to coordinate efforts, the Eagles gather wherever they can find antiwar protests or antiwar sentiment. The group has boycotted movies that it thinks show the military or the current war effort in a poor light, and frequently shows up with flags and banners to disrupt protest demonstrations. At one Shut Down Guantanamo demonstration in New York's Times Square, the Eagles came armed with signs calling the detention camps "Club Gitmo: Terrorism's 5 Star Resort."

SOURCE: http://gatheringofeagles.org/our-mission-statement/.

1. Gathering of Eagles is non-partisan. While each member has his or her own political beliefs, our common love and respect for America and her heroes is what brings us together.

2. We are a non-violent, non-confrontational group. We look to defend, not attack. Our focus is guarding our memorials and their grounds.

3. We believe that the war memorials are sacred ground; as such, we will not allow them to be desecrated, used as props for political statements, or treated with anything less than the solemn and heartfelt respect they—and the heroes they honor—deserve.

4. We are wholly and forever committed to our brothers and sisters in uniform. As veterans, we understand their incredible and noble sacrifices, made of their own accord for a nation they love more than life itself. As family members, we stand by them, and as Americans, we thank God for them.

5. We believe in and would give our lives for the precious freedoms found in

our Constitution. We believe that our freedom of speech is one of the greatest things our country espouses, and we absolutely hold that any American citizen has the right to express his or her approval or disapproval with any policy, law, or action of our nation and her government in a peaceful manner as afforded by the laws of our land.

6. However, we are adamantly opposed to the use of violence, vandalism, physical or verbal assaults on our veterans, and the destruction or desecration of our memorials. By defending and honoring these sacred places, we defend and honor those whose blood gave all of us the right to speak as freely as our minds think.

7. We vehemently oppose the notion that it is possible to "support the troops but not the war." We are opposed to those groups who would claim support for the troops yet engage in behavior that is demeaning and abusive to the men and women who wear our nation's uniform.

8. We believe in freedom at all costs, including our own lives. We served to protect the freedoms Americans enjoy, and we agree with Thomas Jefferson's assertion that "From time to time, the tree of liberty must be watered with the blood of patriots and tyrants."

9. We will accept nothing less than total, unqualified victory in the current conflict. Surrender is not an option, nor is defeat.

10. We stand to challenge any group that seeks the destruction of our nation, its founding precepts of liberty and freedom, or those who have given of themselves to secure those things for another generation. We will be silent no more.

158. Andrew J. Bacevich, "A Father's Responsibility"

(2007)

Andrew Bacevich's article on the death of his son in Iraq and critics' charges that his father was at least partly to blame captured the tenor of American political discourse four years into the war. Bacevich (1947–) was born in Illinois and graduated from the U.S. Military Academy at West Point. He served in the army in Vietnam and in time advanced to the rank of colonel before retiring in the early 1990s. He holds a Ph.D. in diplomatic history from Princeton and has taught military history and international relations at West Point, Johns Hopkins, and Boston University. Among other books, in 2005 he published *The New American Militarism: How Americans Are Seduced by War*. His son, a first lieutenant, died in Iraq on May 13, 2007, the victim of a suicide bombing in Salah-al Din province. As in his other work, in this article Bacevich wrestles with questions of political power and the public's role in supporting and contesting wars.

SOURCE: Originally published as "I Lost My Son to a War I Oppose. We Were Both Doing Our Duty," *Washington Post*, May 27, 2007.

Parents who lose children, whether through accident or illness, inevitably wonder what they could have done to prevent their loss. When my son was killed in Iraq earlier this month at age 27, I found myself pondering my responsibility for his death.

Among the hundreds of messages that my wife and I have received, two bore directly on this question. Both held me personally culpable, insisting that my public opposition to the war had provided aid and comfort to the enemy. Each said that my son's death came as a direct result of my antiwar writings.

This may seem a vile accusation to lay against a grieving father. But in fact, it has become a staple of American political discourse, repeated endlessly by those keen to allow President Bush a free hand in waging his war. By encouraging "the terrorists," opponents of the Iraq conflict increase the risk to U.S. troops. Although the First Amendment protects antiwar critics from being tried for treason, it provides no protection for the hardly less serious charge of failing to support the troops—today's civic equivalent of dereliction of duty.

What exactly is a father's duty when his son is sent into harm's way?

Among the many ways to answer that question, mine was this one: As my son was doing his utmost to be a good soldier, I strove to be a good citizen.

As a citizen, I have tried since Sept. 11, 2001, to promote a critical understanding of U.S. foreign policy. I know that even now, people of good will find much to admire in Bush's response to that awful day. They applaud his doctrine of preventive war. They endorse his crusade to spread democracy across the Muslim world and to eliminate tyranny from the face of the Earth. They insist not only that his decision to invade Iraq in 2003 was correct but that the war there can still be won. Some—the members of the "the-surge-is-already-working" school of thought—even profess to see victory just over the horizon.

I believe that such notions are dead wrong and doomed to fail. In books, articles and op-ed pieces, in talks to audiences large and small, I have said as much. "The long war is an unwinnable one," I wrote in this section of *The Washington Post* in August 2005. "The United States needs to liquidate its presence in Iraq, placing the onus on Iraqis to decide their fate and creating the space for other regional powers to assist in brokering a political settlement. We've done all that we can do."

Not for a second did I expect my own efforts to make a difference. But I did nurse the hope that my voice might combine with those of others—teachers, writers, activists and ordinary folks—to educate the public about the folly of the course on which the nation has embarked. I hoped that those efforts might produce a political climate conducive to change. I genuinely believed that if the people spoke, our leaders in Washington would listen and respond.

This, I can now see, was an illusion.

The people have spoken, and nothing of substance has changed. The November 2006 midterm elections signified an unambiguous repudiation of the policies that landed us in our present predicament. But half a year later, the war continues, with no end in sight. Indeed, by sending more troops to Iraq (and by extending the tours of those, like my son, who were already there), Bush has signaled his complete disregard for what was once quaintly referred to as "the will of the people."

To be fair, responsibility for the war's continuation now rests no less with the Democrats who control Congress than with the president and his party. After my son's death, my state's senators, Edward M. Kennedy and John F. Kerry, telephoned to express their condolences. Stephen F. Lynch, our congressman, attended my son's wake. Kerry was present for the funeral Mass. My family and I greatly appreciated such gestures. But when I suggested to each of them the necessity of ending the war, I got the brushoff. More accurately, after ever so briefly pretending to listen, each treated me to a convoluted explanation that said in essence: Don't blame me.

To whom do Kennedy, Kerry and Lynch listen? We know the answer: to the same people who have the ear of George W. Bush and Karl Rove—namely, wealthy individuals and institutions.

Money buys access and influence. Money greases the process that will yield us a new president in 2008. When it comes to Iraq, money ensures that the concerns of big business, big oil, bellicose evangelicals and Middle East allies gain a hearing. By comparison, the lives of U.S. soldiers figure as an afterthought.

Memorial Day orators will say that a G.I.'s life is priceless. Don't believe it. I know what value the U.S. government assigns to a soldier's life: I've been handed the check. It's roughly what the Yankees will pay Roger Clemens per inning once he starts pitching next month.

Money maintains the Republican/Democratic duopoly of trivialized politics. It confines the debate over U.S. policy to well-hewn channels. It preserves intact the cliches of 1933–45 about isolationism, appeasement and the nation's call to "global leadership." It inhibits any serious accounting of exactly how much our misadventure in Iraq is costing. It ignores completely the question of who actually pays. It negates democracy, rendering free speech little more than a means of recording dissent.

This is not some great conspiracy. It's the way our system works.

In joining the Army, my son was following in his father's footsteps: Before he was born, I had served in Vietnam. As military officers, we shared an ironic kinship of sorts, each of us demonstrating a peculiar knack for picking the wrong war at the wrong time. Yet he was the better soldier—brave and steadfast and irrepressible.

I know that my son did his best to serve our country. Through my own opposition to a profoundly misguided war, I thought I was doing the same. In fact, while he was giving his all, I was doing nothing. In this way, I failed him.

159. Charles Simic, "Driving Home"

(2007)

The final document in this collection comes from the fifteenth poet laureate of the United States, Charles Simic. Born in Yugoslavia, Simic (1938–) moved to Paris at age fifteen and then to the United States at age sixteen. He attended the University of Chicago until the army drafted him in 1961. Following two years in the service, he completed his bachelor's degree at New York University, and he later taught at the University of New Hampshire for thirty-four years. By 2007, he had published eighteen books of poetry. He has received many honors for his work, including a MacArthur Fellowship in 1984, and the Pulitzer Prize for poetry in 1990 for his book of poems *The World Doesn't End*. In "Driving Home," first published in the *New Yorker*, Simic's characteristic minimalism is on display as he frames his narrator's drive down a lonely road in wartime America.

SOURCE: *New Yorker*, August 20, 2007.

> Minister of our coming doom, preaching
> On the car radio, how right
> Your Hell and damnation sound to me
> As I travel these small, bleak roads
> Thinking of the mailman's son
> The Army sent back in a sealed coffin.
>
> His house is around the next turn.
> A forlorn mutt sits in the yard
> Waiting for someone to come home.
> I can see the TV is on in the living room,
> Canned laughter in the empty house
> Like the sound of beer cans tied to a hearse.
> —Charles Simic

Permissions

We are grateful for permission to reproduce the following copyrighted material (in cases where copyrighted information is omitted for works not in the public domain, every effort has been made to contact the copyright holders; any omissions will be corrected in subsequent printings):

"A Devout Meditation in Memory of Adolf Eichmann," by Thomas Merton, from *Raids on the Unspeakable*. Copyright © 1966 by The Abbey of Gethsemani, Inc. Reprinted by permission of New Directions Publishing Corp.

"A Father's Responsibility," by Andrew Bacevich. Copyright © 2007. Reprinted by permission of the author.

"A Poem at Christmas, 1972 during the Terror-Bombing of North Vietnam," by Denise Levertov, from *The Freeing of the Dust*. Copyright © 1975 by Denise Levertov. Reprinted by permission of New Directions Publishing Corp.

"A Woman's Declaration of Liberation from Military Domination," by Women Strike for Peace. Copyright © 1970. Reprinted by permission of the Swarthmore College Peace Collection.

"America's Window to the World: Her Race Problem," by John Hope Franklin. Copyright © 1956. Reprinted by permission of John Hope Franklin.

"Banning Child Sacrifice: A Difficult Choice?" by Kathy Kelly. Copyright © 1998. Reprinted by permission of the author.

"Beyond Vietnam: Address Delivered to the Clergy and Laymen Concerned about Vietnam," by Martin Luther King Jr. Copyright © 1967. Dr. Martin Luther King Jr.; copyright renewed 1991 Coretta Scott King. Reprinted by arrangement with the heirs to the Estate of Martin Luther King Jr., c/o Writers House as agent for the proprietor New York, NY.

"Bush vs. the Mother," by Matt Taibbi, from *Rolling Stone*, September 8, 2005. Copyright © *Rolling Stone* LLC 2005. All rights reserved. Reprinted by permission.